Choice & Change

APRIL O'CONNELL
Santa Fe Community College
JACQUELINE WHITMORE
Santa Fe Community College
VINCENT O'CONNELL

Choice & Change: the Psychology of Adjustment, Growth, & Creativity

SECOND EDITION

PRENTICE-HALL, INC., Englewood Cliffs, New Jersey 07632

Library of Congress Cataloging in Publication Data

O'CONNELL, APRIL.
  Choice & change.

  Bibliography: p.
  Includes index.
  1. Personality.   2. Maturation (Psychology)
I. Whitmore, Jacqueline.   II. Title.   III. Title:
Choice and change.
BF698.027   1985   155.2'5   84-18150
ISBN 0-13-133042-X

Editorial/production supervision and interior design: *Edith Riker*
Manufacturing buyer: *Barbara Kittle*
Cover design: *Lundgren Graphics, Ltd.*
Cover photograph: *Geoff Grove, The Image Bank*
Photo credits: *see page vi*

Printed in the United States of America

10 9 8 7 6 5 4 3 2 1

ISBN 0-13-133042-X   01

Prentice-Hall International, Inc., *London*
Prentice-Hall of Australia Pty. Limited, *Syndey*
Editora Prentice-Hall do Brasil, Ltda., *Rio de Janeiro*
Prentice-Hall Canada Inc., *Toronto*
Prentice-Hall Hispanoamerica, S. A., *Mexico*
Prentice-Hall of India Private Limited, *New Delhi*
Prentice-Hall of Japan, Inc., *Tokyo*
Prentice-Hall of Southeast Asia Pte. Ltd., *Singapore*
Whitehall Books Limited, *Wellington, New Zealand*

To
Alan Robertson
our college president
and
to all our colleagues
who have participated with us
in the process.

Photo Credits

Contents in Brief

PREFACE, xvii

One   *Knowing Ourselves: A Look at the Process of Conscious Choice and Creative Change*

   1   PSYCHOLOGY: THE STUDY OF ALL HUMANKIND AND THE STUDY OF ONESELF, 1

   2   LIFE-SPAN: THE CYCLES OF OUR LIVES, 37

   3   DISCOVERING OUR INDIVIDUAL DIFFERENCES, 94

Two   *The Bodymind/Mindbody: As an Ecological System*

   4   WHEN THE SYSTEM IS OVERLOADED: PERSONS UNDER STRESS, 143

   5   WHEN THE BODYMIND IS ON OVERLOAD: PHYSICAL AND EMOTIONAL BREAKDOWN, 177

   6   THE PHYSICAL APPROACHES TO PERSONALITY INTEGRATION, 203

   7   OUR ONE AND MANY SELVES: THE SEARCH FOR INTEGRATION, 234

Three *The Emotional Self: And the Personal and Impersonal Forces of Society*

  8   PEOPLE LIVING TOGETHER: LOVE, SEX, MARRIAGE, AND PARENTING, 268

  9   PEOPLE WORKING TOGETHER: VOCATIONAL CHOICE AND CAREER DEVELOPMENT, 306

Four *Becoming More Conscious: Processing Toward Transcendence*

  10   CENTERING OURSELVES: TRANSCENDING PERSONAL CRISES, 336

  11   ALTERED STATES OF CONSCIOUSNESS, 365

  12   THE CHOICE IS ALWAYS OURS: TOWARD HIGHER LEVELS OF PERSONALITY INTEGRATION, 413

       NOTES, 445

       BIBLIOGRAPHY, 447

       GLOSSARY, 461

       INDEX, 481

Contents

PREFACE, ix

One *Knowing Ourselves: A Look at the Process of Conscious Choice and Creative Change*

1 **PSYCHOLOGY: THE STUDY OF ALL HUMANKIND AND THE STUDY OF OURSELVES,** 1

The Macro-Micro Approaches to the Study of Human Nature, 3
Psychology: The Timeless Quest for Conscious Awareness, 5
Historical Models of Human Nature, 6

Historical World Views, 7   The Consequences of Models, World Views, and Assumptions in Our Personal Lives, 9   The Limitations of Historical Models, World Views, and Basic Assumptions, 10

The Ever-New Science, 11

Assumptions versus Theories, 11   The Limitations of Psychological Theory, 11 Dealing with the Complexity of Human Behavior and Human Existence, 11 The Many Levels of Human Functioning, 13

The Tenets (Assumptions) of Growth Psychology, 15

1. Growth Psychology Emphasizes the *Situational* Aspects of a Person's Experience, 17   2. It is Sometimes Appropriate to be "Stressed" or "Unadjusted" or "Maladjusted" or "Unhappy" or even "Irrational," 18   3. Growth Psychology Affirms the Validity and Primacy of the Individual, 20   4. Growth Psychologists are

Humanistic, 21   5. Growth Psychologists Emphasize the Unique Differences Among Us, 21   6. Growth Psychologists Emphasize the *Process* of Living: The *Means* Rather than the *Ends,* 22   7. Growth Psychologists Affirm Conscious Choice and Creative Change, 22

Self-Actualizing: Persons in Process, 23

The Mechanistic Model, 23   The Emergence of the Humanistic Model, 24

Applications and Coping Techniques, 28

2   LIFE SPAN: THE CYCLES OF OUR LIVES, 37

The Social and Emotional Changes in Our Lives, 39

Sigmund Freud: The Psychosexual Development of the Child, 40   Carl Jung: The Second Half of Life, 49   Arnold vanGennep: The Rites of Passage, 51   Erik Erikson: The Psychosocial Development of the Person, 52   Daniel Levinson (and Gail Sheehy): Seasons and Passages of Our lives, 61

The Cognitive Development of the Person, 68

Piaget: Four Stages of Cognitive Development, 69   A Final Synopsis of Cognitive Development, 77

The Moral Evolution of the Child: Also a Developmental Process, 78

Sigmund Freud, 79   The Hartshorne and May Studies, 79   Piaget: The Moral Reasoning of the Child, 80   Lawrence Kholberg: Further Studies of the Moral Development of the Individual, 84

Applications and Coping Techniques, 86

3   DISCOVERING AND OWNING OUR INDIVIDUAL DIFFERENCES, 94

Learning to Value Our Individual Differences, 96

Commonalities versus Individual Differences, 96   The Search for General Principles of Human Functioning: Freud, 98   The Search for Individual Differences: Breaking off from Freud, 99

Alfred Adler: The Individuality of One's Life Style, 99

Constructive and Destructive Life Styles, 99   Superiority-Inferiority Complex, 100 Compensation and Overcompensation, 101   Some Neurotic Life-Style Patternings, 102   Positive Life-Style Patterning: Social Feeling and Character, 103

Carl Jung: Type Psychology, 105

Individual Differences as Innate and Inborn, 106   Introversion versus Extroversion, 106   Jung's Four Functions: Sensing/Intuiting/Thinking/Feeling, 108   Using Type Psychology to Understand Ourselves and Others, 110   Creative Living, 111

Eduard Spranger: *Types of Men,* 112

Aesthetic/Political/Economic/Religious/Social/Theoretical, 112   Allport's Use of
Spranger's Work: The Study of Values, 120   We Are All Mixtures, Most Likely, 121

William Sheldon: Somatotypes, 122

Is There a Correlation between Physical and Personality Characteristics?, 122
Mesomorphs, Endomorphs, and Ectomorphs, 123   Basic Biological
Differences, 124

Research Evidence: The Child is Father to the Man, 124

Early Infancy/Childhood Differences . . ., 125   . . . That Seem to Be Long
Lasting, 125   Personality Traits Seem to Cluster, 125   The Result of the *Twin
Studies,* 128   The University of Minnesota Twin Study, 129

Daniel Freedman: The Surprising Differences in Neonates, 130

Left-Brain/Right-Brain Individuals?, 131

Applications and Coping Techniques, 135

Two   *The Bodymind/Mindbody: As an Ecological System*

4   WHEN THE SYSTEM IS OVERLOADED: PERSONS UNDER STRESS, 143

The Need for a Defense System . . ., 145

The Origins of Our Defense Mechanisms, 147

. . . But Defense Mechanisms Are Also Barriers to Growth, 153

Our Conditioning Makes Us Robotlike, 153   How Can We Know When We Are
Defending Ourselves?, 155

The Defense Mechanisms, 156

Defending by Attack, 156   Defending by Withdrawal, 156   Defending by
Physiological Anesthesia: Alcohol, Narcotics, "Pill Popping", 158   Defending by
Psychological Anesthesia: Repression, Amnesia, 160   Defending by
Rationalization, 161   Defending by Insulation, 162   Defending by Manipulative
Behaviors, 163   Defending by Distortion, 165   Some Healthier Defenses, 166   Is
There Any Right Way to Be?, 169

Applications and Coping Techniques, 169

5 WHEN THE BODYMIND IS ON OVERLOAD: PHYSICAL AND EMOTIONAL BREAKDOWN, 177

The Bodymind and the Mindbody, 179

Primitive Beliefs about Disease, 179   The Doctrine of Specific Etiology, 181

The Beginnings of the Psychosomatic Approach to Disease, 181

Hysterical Conversion, 182   Perceptual Defense, 183   Accident Proneness, 184
Disease of the Respiratory System, 185

What Actually Happens to Our Bodies Under Stress?, 186

The Flight-or-Fight Syndrome, 186   The General Adaptation Syndrome, 187   The
Effects of Life Change and Life Crises on Health, 189

Helplessness and Loss: Recent Findings, 191

When the Pressure Is On . . ., 191   When We Experience Loss and
Loneliness, and When We Are Frightened to Death, 192

Applications and Coping Techniques, 196

6 THE PHYSICAL APPROACHES TO PERSONALITY INTEGRATION, 203

Contributing to a Sound Bodymind/Mindbody Through the Body, 205

The Physiological Needs: Maslow's Hierarchy, 206

The Basic Physiological (Bodily) Needs, 206

Body-Energizing Approaches for Bodymind/Mindbody Integration, 211

Gurdjieff: Breaking Through Our Conditioned Responses, 211   Wilhelm Reich:
Breaking Through Our Bodily Armor, 212   Alexander Lowen: The Bioenergetic
Approach, 215

Body-Relaxing Approaches for Bodymind/Mindbody Integration, 216

Edmund Jacobson: Progressive Relaxation, 216   Massage, 217   Yoga, 218

The Relevance of any Physical Activity to Bodymind/Mindbody Integration,
220

Wolpe: Deconditioning-Reconditioning Approach, 221

Mind/Spirit Approaches for Bodymind/Mindbody Integration, 223

Meditation, 223   Biofeedback Techniques, 225

Applications and Coping Techniques, 226

7 OUR ONE AND MANY SELVES: THE SEARCH FOR INTEGRATION, 234

The More Debilitating Forms of Emotional Patterning, 236

The Passive-Dependent Personality, 236   The Obsessive-Compulsive Personality, 236   Extreme Phobic Reactions, 238   The Severe Depressive Reaction, 238   Suicidal Depression, 239   The Hysteric Personality, 239   The Manic-Depressive Reaction, 240   The Schizophrenic Personality, 240   The Schizoid Personality, 241   Multiple Personality, 242   Psychopathic and Sociopathic Personalities, 242

The Development of the Dialogic Insight Approach to Growth, 244

A Very Brief History of Therapeutic Treatment, 244   The Use of Hypnosis, 245 Freud: The Development of Psychoanalysis, 246   Sullivan: The Interpersonal Approach, 246   Rogers: The Client-Centered Approach, 247   Group Therapy, 247   Summary: A Shift in Paradigms, 251   Berne and Harris: Transactional Analysis, 251   Perls: Gestalt Therapy, 253

Three Therapies Directed Specifically Toward Behavioral Change, 256

Stamfl, Implosive Therapy: 257   A Modified Implosive Approach, 257   Ellis: Rational-Emotive Therapy, 258   Glasser: Reality Therapy, 260

Other Therapies, 261

Applications and Coping Techniques, 261

Three *The Emotional Self: The Personal and Impersonal Forces of Society*

8 PEOPLE LIVING TOGETHER: LOVE, SEX, MARRIAGE, AND PARENTING, 268

Why Is It So Hard to Live with the People We Love?, 270

An Historical Overview of Sexual Arrangements and Family Structures, 270 The Wide Variations of Living Together Today, 275

Some Fallacies and Realities of the Loving Relationship, 275

The Fallacies of the Loving Relationship, 276   The Realities of Mate Selection, 279   Styles of Parenting: Authoritarian, Permissive, Authoritative, 289   The Wide Variation of Living Arrangements: Types of Marriages and Alternative Life Styles, 291   Some Dimensions of the Loving Relationship, 293

Applications and Coping Techniques, 298

9 PEOPLE WORKING TOGETHER: VOCATIONAL CHOICE, CAREER DEVELOPMENT, AND INTERPERSONAL PROCESSING, 306

Work and Career as Personality Development, 308

Work as Basic to Self-Esteem, 308   Work as Basic to Family Stability, 308   Work as Basic to a Person's Emotional and Physical Health, 309   Work as Basic to Our Identity, 309

The Social Stratification of Work in America, 310

Blue-Collar Workers, 310   White-Collar Workers, 311   The Double-Income Couple: A Change in the Family Scene, 311

Factors Involved in Vocational Choice, 313

Our Environmental Background: Our Limited Social Mobility, 313   Our Personality Type, 314   The College Experience as Moratorium and Exploration, 314

Career Success: Enjoying What One Does, 318

The Working Class: Working to Live, 318   The Professional Class: Living to Work, 319

Communication Skills as a Requisite for Career Success and Interpersonal Processing, 319

The Scientific Study of Language: General Semantics, 320   Learning to Listen, 320   Understanding Our Paralanguage, 325

Applications and Coping Techniques, 329

Four Becoming More Conscious: Processing Toward Transcendence

10 CENTERING OURSELVES: TRANSCENDING PERSONAL CRISES, 336

The Light and the Dark, 338

Jung and the Great Archetypal Themes, 338   Are We a Death-Denying Society? 340

The Acceptance of Death: Elisabeth Kübler-Ross, 341

For the Critically Ill Patient and the Family: Some Practical Suggestions, 344

Unexpected Death: Suicide, 348

Learning to Process Crises: Death and Divorce, 351

The Stages of Grief and Recovery, 354   Divorce as a Kind of Dying, 356
Reintegrating Oneself into Society after Death and Divorce, 356   Differences in
Status Between the Formerly Married Woman and the Formerly Married
Man, 356   Divorce and Children, 357   Changes for a Successful Remarriage, 358

Applications and Coping Techniques, 359

11   **ALTERED STATES OF CONSCIOUSNESS,** 365

Defining Altered States of Consciousness, 367

Perceptual Defense, 367   Cognitive Dissonance, 368

ASC-Producing Drugs: Their Effects on Our Neurobiology, 369

Input: Sensory Neurons, 369   Output: Motor Neurons, 369   Central Processing
Neurons: The Brain and Spinal Cord, 370   Stimulants, 371   Depressors, 372
Pain-killers: Anesthetics and Analgesics, 372   Hallucinogens, 373
Marijuana, 375   Alcohol, 376

The Altered States of Meditation, 377

What is Meditation?, 378

The Altered State of Consciousness We Call Hypnosis, 380

Some Theories About Hypnosis, 381   Uses of Hypnotism, 383

The Altered State of Consciousness We Call Dreams, 387

A Brief History of Dream Interpretation, 387   Freud's Contribution to the Study of
Dreaming: The Royal Road to the Unconscious, 390   Basic Elements of Freud's
Theory of Dreams, 391   Jung and the Discovery of the Symbolic Self in Dreams,
394   Our Need for Restful Sleep and Cathartic Dreaming: Scientific Advances, 401

Applications and Coping Techniques: "To Sleep! Perchance to Dream!", 404

12   **THE CHOICE IS ALWAYS OURS: TOWARD HIGHER
LEVELS OF PERSONALITY INTEGRATION,** 413

The Memorable Originals: Persons "Ever in Process," 415

Insights of the Personality Theorists, 419

The Continual Development of One's Intellectual or Cognitive Function: The
Rational Use of Reason, 419   The Steady Unfolding and Enriching of One's
Emotional Repertory: The Self and the Interpersonal Dimension, 423   The Striving to
Direct One's Destiny: Self-Fulfillment and Self-Realization, 428   Transcending Self:
The Spiritual Dimension, 431

Integration Techniques, 436

NOTES, 445

BIBLIOGRAPHY, 447

GLOSSARY, 461

INDEX, 481

Preface

We are much gratified by the continuing warm response to *Choice and Change*. For those of you joining us for the first time we would like to call your attention to the major themes that provide the underlying threads of continuity in our highly diversified art and science of [growth] psychology.

We have a process world view that holds human existence, human behavior, human endeavor (whatever you choose to call it) as a complex of multitudinous and diverse biological, social/emotional, and cognitive adaptations and interactions. Personality integration then is the overall process of an individual's adapting and responding to myriad internal and external needs, challenges, crises, and changes. The process point of view has multidimensional correlates.

We all are persons-in-process. Carl Rogers describes us as persons-in-process, from infancy to old age. We are ever in the process of experiencing, learning, and growing. Maslow and Piaget viewed us as being involved in a constant evolution of higher cognitions and motivations. Gordon Allport suggested that we replace the name for our life-form from *human being* to *human becoming*. Agreeing with his process perspective we have added the term *humanity becoming*—humanity evolving, as it were, to ever higher self-awareness and self-realization.

We value our individual differences in process patterning. Because of our genetic inheritance, the circumstances of our birth, and our distinct life experiences, the way each of us processes his or her life events is highly individual. How each of us assimilates, accommodates, adapts, and responds to life's experiences reflects our individual differences. We hope that our readers come to appreciate their own unique process style, and as Carl Jung describes, their own personality type.

We value the individual differences (in the process patterning) of others. Just as we hope our readers come to appreciate their own unique process patterning we hope they come to appreciate the process style of others with whom they live and work. Indeed, our individual differences make life far more complex, surely more perplexing, yet much more interesting.

Our individual differences reflect the multidimensional parameters of human possibility. Each of us has an individual path, an individual interpretation of reality, an individual character and an individual processing-in-the-world.

Personality integration is a never-ending, ever-new process. Living is not a [homeo]static state but is a dynamic flow of psycho-physical events. Self-knowledge then is not an achievement that happens at this time or that time in our life. Self-knowledge is a continual process of self-discovering and self-realizing. It was Maslow who emphasized this point: That every experience we have, every new competence we gain, every struggle we live through [and process in our own unique way] has the potential for increasing our personality integration and developing our personal creativity. We wholeheartedly agree.

We view all experiences, no matter how difficult or painful, as grist for further human evolution.

We experience ourselves as life-forms capable of conscious choice and transcending change.

The format of this edition follows the previous (revised) edition with the following changes and additions. *Chapter 1* (on psychology as a study of humankind) is still an introduction to the field of personal growth and creativity. However, the focus has been enlarged to include the historical and cultural determinants of the human psyche. *Chapter 2* (on the cycles of our lives) is new. It is an enlargement of the life span approach to human growth and development. In addition to the material on vanGennep, Freud, Erikson, and Levinson there are expanded sections on Piaget, Kohlberg, Spranger, and Jung. *Chapter 3* (on individual differences) has been enlarged and updated to include Alfred Adler, Carl Jung, left/right brain research, and research on ethnic differences. *Chapters 4, 5, and 6* (on stress, breakdown, and holistic health including psychosomatic research) are expanded and updated. Slowly the reseach is beginning to systematically clarify the many paratypical techniques. *Chapter 7* (on dialogic therapy) is an expanded section on hypno-therapy including an actual transcript of a hypno-therapy session. *Chapter 8* (on family and relationship bonding) has been greatly revised and expanded to include the major psychological and sociological research on the changing American family relationship styles. *Chapter 9* (on vocational/career development) is new. We believe it to be useful since work and careers are viewed as process situations. *Chapter 10* (on crises such as death, divorce, and reintegration) has been updated. *Chapter 11* (on altered states of consciousness) was previously the dream-and-sleep chapter. Expansion includes the altered states of consciousness: drugs, meditation, relaxation, yoga, and hypnosis. *Chapter 12* (on transcending change through personality integration) was previously Chapter 13 (on the highly self-actualizing, highly integrated person). There are additional contributions from Erich Fromm, Rollo May, and Viktor Frankl.

We would like to acknowledge our colleagues, friends, and students who have been of inestimable value in helping us to understand the process of living, loving, and working together. With especial recognition of Judith Block, our chairperson, who has supported our book in every way; Tal Mullis who has supported our efforts since the book's inception; Robert Myer, a most facilitative administrator; Robert Wheeles with whom we have dialoged on the process; and Heija Wheeler who ever emphasizes quality. We also thank our very especial colleagues: Henry Gooch, Norma Jensen, Stan Lynch, Marilyn Peyton, Stephan Sussman, Jane Wedemeyer, and Marcia Wehr.

We want to express our appreciation to J. Raymond Entenman, Hillsborough Community College for his review of the second edition.

We welcome you to *Choice and Change*. While you are reading, pondering, questioning, should you like to interact with us—do so! We invite you to write to us with your questions, your suggestions, your examples and requests and we will do our best to answer your letters.

April O'Connell
Jacqueline Whitmore
Vincent O'Connell
October 1984

The inner process is the inner reality. Reality is not a state of being but is always in the process of becoming. Thus reality is process and process is an evolvement of change. The inner reality or process is the core of all change, the center of every becoming. . . . It is not only the center process but represents the whole process.

Jung Yung Lee, *Patterns of Inner Process*.

Life itself is a process of growth that starts with the growth of the body and its organs, moves through the development of motor skills, the acquisition of knowledge, the extension of relationships, and ends in the summation of experience that we call wisdom. These aspects of growth overlap, since life and growth take place in a natural, cultural and social environment. And though the growth process is continuous, it is never even. There are periods of leveling off when the assimilation of experience occurs, preparing the organism for a new ascent. Each ascent leads to a new high or summit and creates what we call a peak experience. Each peak experience, in turn, must be integrated into the personality for new growth to occur and for the individual to end in a state of wisdom.

Alexander Lowen, *Bioenergetics*. 1975.

What I am really interested in is the new kind of education which we must develop which moves toward fostering the new kind of human being that we need, the process person, the creative person, the improvising person, the self-trusting, courageous person, the autonomous person.

Abraham H. Maslow, *The Farther Reaches of Human Nature*. 1971.

Clients seem to move toward more openly being a process, a fluidity, a changing. They are not disturbed to find that they are not the same from day to day, that they do not always hold the same feelings toward a given experience or person, that they are not always consistent. They are in flux, and seem more content to continue in this flowing current. The striving for conclusions and end states seems to diminish. . . . They begin to appreciate [themselves] as a fluid process.

Carl R. Rogers, *On Becoming a Person*. 1961.

1

Psychology: The Study of All Humankind and the Study of Ourselves

THE MACRO-MICRO APPROACHES TO THE STUDY OF HUMAN
    NATURE

PSYCHOLOGY: THE TIMELESS QUEST FOR CONSCIOUS AWARENESS

HISTORICAL MODELS OF HUMAN NATURE
    Historical World Views
    The Consequences of Models, World Views, and Assumptions in Our
        Personal Lives

THE EVER-NEW SCIENCE
    Assumptions versus Theories
    The Limitations of Psychological Theory
    Dealing with the Complexity of Human Behavior and Human
        Existence
    The Many Levels of Human Functioning

THE TENETS (ASSUMPTIONS) OF GROWTH PSYCHOLOGY
    1. Growth Psychology Emphasizes the *Situational* Aspects of a
       Person's Experience
    2. It Is Sometimes Appropriate to Be "Stressed" or "Unadjusted" or
       "Maladjusted" or "Unhappy" or even "Irrational"
    3. Growth Psychology Affirms the Validity and Primacy of the
       Individual
    4. Growth Psychologists Are Humanistic
    5. Growth Psychologists Emphasize the Unique Differences Among Us
    6. Growth Psychologists Emphasize the *Process* of Living: The *Means*
       Rather Than the Ends
    7. Growth Psychologists Affirm Conscious Choice and Creative
       Change

SELF-ACTUALIZING: PERSONS IN PROCESS
    The Mechanistic Model
    The Emergence of the Humanistic Model

APPLICATIONS AND COPING TECHNIQUES

THE MACRO-MICRO APPROACHES
TO THE STUDY OF HUMAN NATURE

Psychology is the scientific study of how we are born into this world such frail and unconscious beings that we must be taken care of and nourished far longer than any other terrestrial life form—or we shall die—and yet how we grow—physically, emotionally, mentally—to become the most variable, the most complex, the most adaptable, the most powerful, and the most remarkable life form on this planet.

In its most comprehensive sense, psychology is the study of the broad **commonalities** that identify us as a species—how we share a common biological base, how we develop our human response adaptations, and how we erect societal superstructures that govern our moral/ethical interactions. This is the **macro approach** to the study of *Homo sapiens*.

But psychology is also, in its most personal sense, the study of how we differ from the moment of our conception, and how we have different life experiences that result in our becoming uniquely creative individuals. This is the **micro approach** to the study of *Homo sapiens*.

These two approaches, macro (large and general) and micro (small and specific), are but the two ends of a vast scientific continuum that reaches into every area of our human existence and human endeavor.

Psychology is a complex science and a hybrid science extending over many areas and disciplines. As a psychoneurological science, psychology is the study of how we "take in" information from our environment through our senses and how we transmit and organize these billions of fleeting sensory impressions into unitary perceptions of the external world within dimensions of time, space, and motion.

As a behavioral science, psychology is the study of how we learn to be who and what we are through our lifetime experiences, i.e., how we are *conditioned* to act as we do from the moment of birth, perhaps from the moment of conception, until the end of our days upon this earth.

As a genetic science, psychology is the study of how we are *predisposed* to be as we are as the result of our inherited characteristics—all the physical and mental and emotional traits that have been passed on to us through the cast of the genetic dice.

As a social science, psychology is the study of how we relate with each other in various types of groups: first in one-to-one relationships within our families, later in the larger groups of friends and peers, associates and colleagues, and finally, in our wider ethnic and cultural subgroups—even responding to an overall structure of a global, international society of humankind.

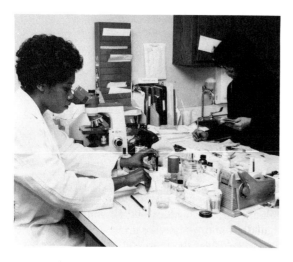

As a science, psychology is the study of how we are born into this world such frail and unconscious beings that we must be taken care of and nourished far longer than any other terrestrial life-form: and how we grow physically—to become the most adaptable, the most variable, the most powerful life-form on this planet.

As a developmental science, psychology is the study of how we grow, how we learn to love and mate and bear children, how we grow old, and even how we die.

As an intrapersonal science, psychology is the study of how we "experience" our world with its many joys and pleasures, its heartaches and sufferings, its twists and turnings, and its unexpected and surprising challenges.

As an educational/vocational science, psychology is the study of how we learn the tasks and skills needed to become contributing adults in our society, to support ourselves financially, to work with others—finding a place for ourselves "under the sun."

As a cultural science, psychology is the study of how we create the art and artifacts of our generation, to leave our "mark" behind us, and to pass on a civilization as a result of our collective consciousness for the next generation to inherit.

In the final sense, psychology is the study of how we are attempting to understand one another, not as citizens of hostile nations or as alien beings but as (all races, all religions, all ethnic groups) belonging to the one, overall grouping—"the family of humankind."

PSYCHOLOGY: THE TIMELESS QUEST FOR CONSCIOUS AWARENESS

We psychologists are wont to say that the scientific study of human behavior began in the last quarter of the nineteenth century[1] and by that reckoning, we are a fairly new science when compared to the study of medicine or chemistry or physics or astronomy, all of which go back for hundreds and even thousands of years.[2] But that is only part of the story. In a larger sense, human beings have always speculated on our place in creation, where we came from, and how we can live tomorrow better than we live today. From that long-ago moment when we became aware of ourselves as beings who are born and live and die, we were no longer content merely to exist but driven, also, to understand existence itself. It was a quantum leap of consciousness when our species began to ponder the question of causation and possibility: Who are we? What are we? Where are we going? How should life be lived? What is the good, the true, and the beautiful?

This quest for self-understanding and self-awareness has been the reason that poets have sought to express our joys and our pain in lyric poetry, to record our deeds in saga and epic, and to compose hymns of praise and songs of suffering. It is the reason painters and sculptors have sought to express what they see in great works of art. It is the reason that adventurers have sought to explore the surface of the earth, the floors of the ocean, and now the farther edges of our universe—the skies above us and even the stars beyond. All this is part and parcel of our human motivation for knowledge about ourselves and the universe in which we live and of which we are a part. Through our electromicroscopes we peer into

Thou hast made him a little lower than the angels. (Psalms 8 : 5)

Man is the measure of all things. (Protagoras: in *Diogenes Laetius Protagoras* IX, li)

What a piece of work is man! (Shakespeare: *Hamlet* II, ii)

Man is by nature a political animal. (Aristotle: *Politics* I)

There are many wonderful things in nature, but the most wonderful of all is man. (Sophocles: *Antigone*)

Man is a reasoning animal. (Seneca: *Ad Lucilium* XLI)

Man is but a reed, the most flexible thing in nature, but he is a thinking reed. The entire universe need not arm itself to crush him. A vapor, a drop of water suffices to kill him. But if the universe were to crush him man would still be more noble than that which killed him, because he knows that he dies . . . . (Pascal: *Pensées*)

Man is the only animal that laughs and weeps; for he is the only animal that is struck with the difference between what things are, and what they ought to be. (William Hazlett: *Lectures on the English Comic Writers* I)

The greatest enemy to man is man, who, by the devil's instigation, is a wolf, a devil to himself and others. (Robert Burton: *Anatomy of Melancholy* I.1.1)

Man is the only animal that blushes. Or needs to. (Mark Twain: *Pudd'nhead Wilson's New Calendar*)

Man is intelligence in servitude to his organs. (Aldous Huxley: *Themes and Variations*)

the cellular structure of life itself. Through the enormous lenses of our giant telescopes we catch glimpses of far-off galaxies. We reconstruct the past. We attempt to predict the future. We discuss the many possible meanings of life. And we wonder endlessly about ourselves.

What is man that thou art mindful of him? (Psalms 4:4). So sang the Hebrew psalmist thousands of years ago. So have we asked ourselves again and again in one way or another through the ages and in many languages. In these many languages, out of these many cultures, we have ventured many answers, have formulated diverse interpretations of the reality of life on earth. (See box 1.1.)

HISTORICAL MODELS OF HUMAN NATURE

Our conclusions have of necessity been various and contradictory, representing as they do such widely varying societies. For some we are not much more than brute savage, enslaved by our animal passions. For others we are noble, even heroic. Some have said we are born in sin and devilishly motivated. Still others have preferred to describe us as beings of great sensibility and compassion. Some have seen us as comic figures in a giant *comedia del arte*. Others have seen us as tragic figures in the human drama. One model of humankind asserts that we are nothing more than "naked apes" who live in "human zoos" (Morris 1967, 1970). But whatever our conclusions, we are the only life form (so far as we know) that considers the question of its own existence and seems unable not to—driven by some universal compulsion.

Historical World Views

In the course of human history each society and civilization develops its own image of the world, a kind of **world view** about things as they are and as they should be. These world views have varied widely. For example, to many primitive peoples the universe was experienced as a quixotic mystery of terrifying and unpredictable events. Fire, flood, drought, and disease were understood not as natural phenomena but as the work of nature gods or evil spirits. Our early ancestors lived in daily terror within a world of unexpected and inexplicable events. Homer tells us that the lives of the Greeks were not within their control (fate) but lay outside themselves. To Homer, as to all the Greeks of his time, mortals were created as pawns for the gods and goddesses, the chess pieces whereby the Olympians played out their deadly games of love, jealousy, and war (Jaynes 1967).

To the medieval European life was a brief moment of physical suffering and mental torment. The only hope for happiness lay in a promise of life after death—if one could escape the ever-present yawning jaws of hell! To the New England Puritan, on the other hand, earthly existence was an opportunity to manifest God's beneficence. By hard work and earnest endeavor God would grant material success. In fact, worldly wealth was an index to one's "puritan" life of righteous thinking and healthy industry.

So it has gone. Every culture has developed its own unique world view concerning the parameters of existence and the nature of human life.

Box 1.2	SOME HISTORICAL WORLD-VIEWS

A Primitive World View

The world I live in is frightening, unpredictable, and dangerous. The demons of the sky thunder at us and send lightning to warn us of their anger. The river demons overwhelm our crops and drown our tribal members. The sun god sends blights to dry up the soil and makes our animals die of thirst. I do not know what to do, but the shaman says that if we sacrifice to the demons and the gods, their anger may be placated. Tonight I will pray to the spirits of my dead ancestors to help our tribe ward off the evil all around us. Perhaps the evil is caused by our enemies on the other side of the mountain. They are said to make incantations against us. I think our chief will lead a hunting party to kill them all, and then we can return to our families and live in peace and survive.

An Athenian World View

There has been no civilization in history like that of our Athenian democracy. We are free and thinking men who know there is nothing in the universe that cannot be understood. The universe is orderly and knowable. The good life is the freedom to pursue the liberal arts: mathematics, the humanities, physical sports, music, politics, rhetoric, and—the queen of all the disciplines—philosophy. We like nothing better than to congregate with other free and thinking persons in the Acropolis each day under our brilliant sun and blue sky discoursing on "the good, the true, and the beautiful." Or perhaps we may spend a few days at the Games or the drama festivals. We are fortunate that we have time for these elevating studies. That is because we have slaves to perform the menial labors of farming and manufacturing. We leave the women at home to take care of household management, which is what they are fit for—oh, yes, and for child bearing. Menial labor is illiberal and demeans the mind and soul of man, which should be uplifted and concerned with higher things.

A Medieval World View

This world is a vale of tears. We are endlessly engaged in battles and wars. Last year the Plague came through and decimated our fiefdom. The lords exact more and more taxes from townsfolk and serfs alike. Life is short and suffering is constant. The priests tell us that there is a paradise in heaven that is ours if we follow the teachings of the Church. But although the spirit is willing, the flesh is weak. I scourge myself with whips and make confession for my sins to the priests. But still I am tempted to and do engage in sin. I yearn for the peace and happiness of heaven, but I falter at every step, and even death is not welcome, for I fear the flames of hell. At night I have erotic dreams and the wife of my brother tempted me in my sleep. I think she must be a witch and the devil's handmaiden. Tomorrow I will tell the priest how she torments my soul. Perhaps she will be put to the stake, and then I will be tempted no more.*

A Renaissance World View

What a delight to be alive! The world is resplendent with beauty and excitement. Everywhere I look artisans and craftsmen produce a feast for my eyes. Musicians create arias to stir the soul. We are graced by the

---

*Aldous Huxley has suggested in his classic treatise on witchcraft, *The Devils of Loudon*, that perhaps a million women were tortured, put to the stake, or otherwise mutilated because of such accusations made of them by men unaware of their own inner erotic desires (Huxley 1979b).

presence of our lovely and gracious ladies. Perhaps I will write a poem tonight to win the mistress of my heart. Tomorrow I will make a visit to Machiavelli to learn the secrets of governing my state. And next year, perhaps, I will join our soldiers of fortune who bring back riches from the East and the New World. Ah, yes, I am not concerned with what comes after death, but just in case the priests are right, I must not forget to drop a few gold coins in the hands of that fat bishop of ours. It's just as well to play both sides of the street.

A Puritan World View

We accept no priest or government official as a mediator between ourselves and God. We read the Scriptures for ourselves. We govern ourselves and make our own laws. We pray directly to God and do not need a priest to tell us what we can or cannot do. We are persons of principle. We have made our way to the New World where there is land for all or for any who wish to work hard to get it. I know that I am leading a good life because I am prospering. I labor from morning to night because I know that idleness is the devil's workshop. The devil is everywhere at work. When I am in church on the Sabbath, I sometimes am askance at the altogether unbecoming behavior of the younger, unmarried men and women I see there. The young men are dressing too colorfully, and the women are revealing too much of their bodies. We shall have to deal sternly with them, so they do not go astray. If they remain stubborn and opinionated in their views, perhaps a good dunking or flogging in the town square will straighten them out.

The Consequences of Models, World Views, and Assumptions in our Personal Lives

The kinds of world views a people develops will permeate everything they think and do: their religion, their literature, their art, their politics and economics, and their practial everyday existence. These world views, in other words, are belief systems and generate unquestioned assumptions about how life must (or should) be lived. Since primitive tribes believed they were at the mercy of whimsical and bestial gods, the best that could be hoped for was to placate the gods with human offerings and, if need be, human sacrifice. As primitive and superstitious as these assumptions are, they represent the first attempts to find explanations for the natural phenomena of wind, storm, lightning, thunder, the seasons, and so on.

To the heroes of the *Odyssey* and the *Iliad* the assumption was that one's fate was determined by the gods and goddesses of Olympus. One could not then escape one's fate—it was *written in the wind.*

Since one could not escape one's fate, one's only choice lay in *how* one met one's fate: with cowardice and ignobly or with courage and heroism. The Gothic cathedrals of the medieval era, with their flying buttresses and pointed arches, seemed to urge humankind to lift its gaze above earthly existence toward a more heavenly (and the assumption of a) happier afterlife. Renaissance men and women, on the other hand, were delighted with the world of sensual enjoyment and cultural pleasures. Their assumption was that the world was for their enjoyment. As their talents and money could afford, they filled their lives with music, literature, and art. They dallied as well in politics, in commerce, and in romance and the sheer pleasure of the intrigue. By contrast, the New England Puritans were suspicious of sensual pleasures. With their somber dress and their devotion to hard work, they bequeathed to later generations of Americans the famous **work ethic** for which we (Americans) are still so well known. The assumption here was that hard work leads to success and happiness. (In fact, this is an assumption that many of us still accept.) With our bequeathed assumption that hard work leads to happiness, we have developed an intolerance for those who prefer to take a leisurely approach to human existence.

The Limitations of Historical Models, World Views, and Basic Assumptions

One problem about these assumptions is that they tend to be *simplistic*. Simplistic explanations often lead us astray because they do not explain things so much as explain them away. Human events are reduced to either-or explanations, and the myriad possibilities in between and beyond are ignored.

"Man is evil." "Man is good." "Man is a little lower than the angels." "Man is little better than the brute." "Man is noble." "Man is an animal." These all-or-nothing statements do not take into account the breadth and complexity of human functioning. However, we are satisfying our human compulsion to seek answers to our questions. For example, some of us have wondered why human beings kill each other and rape and steal and plunder from others of our kind! If we hold to the assumption that human nature is "sinful" or little better than savage, then such actions do not seem all that strange to us. They follow as the natural consequence of a "sinful" or "savage" nature.

But human beings have demonstrated also extraordinary and altruistic "good Samaritanism." They have performed great acts of sacrifice, even to laying down their lives for others. Such acts cannot be the manifestation of a totally corrupt and "sinful" nature. Furthermore, human society has developed civilizations that bespeak something more than brute intelligence, civilizations of rational thought, of heroic action, of compassionate legislation and peaceful government. We are not *just* this or *just* that. Such thinking is two-dimensional, and human nature is more than that. Two-dimensional thinking focuses on only one facet of the many-faceted expressions of human **personality**. We are not "unidetermined" but multidetermined. *We are, in fact, multifaceted, multidimensional, and multidetermined.*

THE EVER-NEW SCIENCE

Assumptions versus Theories

To call man sinful or noble or corrupt is to make essentially simplistic **assumptions** about human nature. We could have called these models and assumptions *theories of human nature,* a more sophisticated term. In fact, some textbooks have called them that. But **theories** are derived from **empirical data**; that is, *from some kind of demonstrable and/or experimental facts that can be recorded by anyone who wishes to replicate (repeat) that demonstration and/or experiment.*[3] Theories, too, are generalizations. But they are generalizations abstracted from many actual observed and recorded individual events. These many individual observations of actual events have been organized into larger, more comprehensive statements.[4] Some theories are so comprehensive that they seem to unify great quantities of empirical data (facts). These theories are referred to as "unified field theories."

The Limitations of Psychological Theory

Some social scientists have made broad theories about human nature. Some have been brilliant; some have been patently wrong; some elegant; some simplistic. We will discuss a number of these theories as we go along. But in general, psychology as yet has no such overall field theory to explain human nature. Because human nature is composed of many levels of functioning, and our understanding is still so limited, we are far, indeed, from any real field theory of human behavior. We are more like Lilliputian researchers all at work examining the different aspects of the giant *Homo sapiens.*[5] In truth and in point of fact, at this time we are still unable to explain or predict any solitary act of human nature with any great degree of certainty (even though we may explain or predict what a certain group of persons may do). Let us illustrate.

Dealing with the Complexity of Human Behavior and Human Existence

Suppose we hear that a man has shot and killed another man. Suppose we know that these two men had been fighting in the street before the shot rang out. We might leap to the conclusion that the argument arose from some personal *emotional* conflict. Suppose, then, that we learn that the two men were from two distinct *ethnic* groups. We might then suppose that the reason for the killing was *sociological:* interracial conflict. But suppose we find out, still later, that the man who fired the shot had been in and out of mental institutions most of his life and that he did not even know the other man before he shot him. Then we might say that the reason was "psychiatric" ("He was crazy")—that there was a distortion of

At present, psychologists are like Lilliputians swarming over Gulliver, the giant *Homo sapiens,* trying to examine him piecemeal and not yet getting an image of the whole person.

his *thinking processes* ("He was in a dazed and confused state and mistook the murdered man for someone else"). But what if the murderer were suddenly to have a heart attack and die. And suppose further that he is given an autopsy and is found to have a tumor in that part of his brain that has to do with aggressive acts (and there is such a place!). We would then have to revise all our previous conclusions and assume that the "cause" was *neurological,* that is, at the level of the central nervous system.

Such is the dilemma in making theories about human nature. Any behavior we exhibit may arise from any of these many levels of human functioning. Sometimes we psychologists forget that. We get so involved in our own research that we squeeze a "fact" into our pet theory—we limit our perspective and are blind to wider parameters. Sometimes we get ourselves so entrenched in one particular school or camp that we emphasize one level of human functioning over another.

And we quarrel constantly among ourselves. But that is nothing to be ashamed of. For it is out of argument and debate (and *not* agreement) that new concepts are born and old concepts are refined. It is out of opposing ideas and arguments (and *not* from unanimity) that more creative ideas take shape. It is out of diversity of opinion (and not out of consensus) that we make those quantum leaps in our understanding and our scientific theory making.

In a sense, psychology is still in a very adolescent stage of growth as a science. We tend, like adolescents, to be very enthusiastic and eager about our interpretations of reality. And like adolescents, we tend sometimes to think we know more than we do.

Nevertheless we have made a lot of inroads in our science in the last one hundred years. Although we still may not be able to know and predict what any *single* person will or will not do in certain situations, we *can* make broad general predictions about what *groups* of people will do (according to these circumstances and under these conditions). But we need always to remember that we human beings have *many* levels of functioning, from that of the most elemental biological neuronal network to the highest level of ethical valuing. It is well at this point to take stock of these many levels of human functioning.

The Many Levels of Human Functioning

WE ARE BIOLOGICAL ORGANISMS. Basic to our human functioning is our biological self. We have certain physiological needs that must be met in order for us to manage survival in our external environment. Psychologists, neurologists, medical researchers, ophthalmologists, audiologists, and many other scientists engage themselves in the questions of how human beings function at this level, how they function most optimally, and what causes them to be "sick" or limited physically, with problems of vision or hearing or handicapped in other ways.

We are coming also to understand that our diet, our degree of physical activity (or inactivity), our weight, and what we smoke, drink, or otherwise ingest (even medicines), can have consequences on our emotional and cognitive levels of functioning. To understand ourselves, we need to be aware of our health (or lack of it). We need to be aware how our body responds to the stresses in our lives, to the emotions we experience, to our attitudes and life style. Our psychology is not independent of our physical body. *Our body and mind are an ecological unit*. A sound mind is more possible in a sound body. To approach it from another perspective, a sound body is more possible with a mind that is joyful and alert than with one that is depressed and despairing. What affects one part of our ecological bodymind/mindbody must affect all of us.

WE ARE EMOTIONAL BEINGS. We are also very emotional creatures. Of all the animate kingdom, human beings have the richest and most varied repertory of emotions. One theorist believes that it is our emotional functioning that gives meaning to the events of our lives and punctuates our existence with memorable events. Ergo, we have memory (MacLean 1973). The possibilities for a rich emotional life are not a "given" but the end result of many interactions: our congenital "predispositions," our early environment, the circumstances of our station in life, even our intelligence. Too, twentieth-century researchers are helping us to understand how we are being influenced even before birth—in the womb, the prenatal ocean in which we are all formed. Great scientists and theorists like Ivan Pavlov, Sigmund Freud, and B. F. Skinner have helped us understand that our emotions do not *just happen*. They are oftentimes a response to our early experiences and our **conditioning**.

Our possibilities for growth do not stop there. As we grow through life, we are given still further opportunities to experience and develop a broad spectrum of emotional responses.

WE ARE THINKING CREATURES. At another level of our humanness, we are **cognitive** creatures; that is to say, we "think." We do not just live in the here-and-now world of animal existence. We are creatures who remember our past, and because we remember our past we can envision a future different from what has been. Because we have a memory we have a continuity of experience that tells us where we have come from, where we are so far, and where we may be heading. Thus we are able to plan for the future as similar and different from what has been. We imagine what might be—we are able to "see ahead" and reach for something for tomorrow better than what we believe we have today. Not just for ourselves but for our children and our children's children. This is one of the truly remarkable characteristics of the human species. We are capable of transcending our present consciousness.

AS A PEOPLE WE ARE MEMBERS OF OUR CULTURE AND OUR SOCIETY. As the great humanistic psychologist Abraham Maslow put it, we are *encultured* by our society (Maslow 1976), by our *subcultural* ethnic roots, and by our world view. Whether we are American, Russian, or French; whether we are Catholic, Protestant, Jewish, or Moslem; whether we are from a large metropolis, a small rural area, or the highest mountain regions, we share the cultural, philosophic, religious, and artistic traditions and artifacts of *our homeland* and *our people*. At this level not only have we been *socialized* by our society, we have also been *stratified* by the circumstances of our birth. Our thinking and emotional response have been influenced by whether we were born into the upper class, the lower class, or the great middle class. Whether we are children of a banker or lawyer or farmer, whether we are male or female—all the **demographic variables** interact to influence how we behave in our various **social roles** (Kluckhohn 1949).

WE ARE DEVELOPMENTAL LIFE FORMS. More than any other species, human beings are changed by the simple (additive) number of years that we live upon this earth. Once an animal, say a dog, reaches maturity, in two or three years, it changes very little. It lives out the rest of its life without much more change or growth. In that respect, it is much the same at ten or fifteen years of age as at five, only older.

Human beings, on the other hand, are often quite wiser creatures at fifty than they were at forty, thirty, or twenty years. We continue to develop and change in our understandings, in our emotional-social interests, in our attitudes, in our values, in our life styles.

Some psychologists attribute our continued capacity to grow, to learn, and to change to an extended **neotony**, i.e., humankind's long infancy and childhood during which we must be taken care of, protected, and nourished for a far longer time than any other life form. But our extended neotony also means that we have a much more plastic nervous system, which continues all our healthy lives to form more and complex associational pathways and connections. Thus each moment we have the potential to continue to learn and to develop new possibilities. In other words, we have more degrees of freedom to adapt to our environment and in our behavior than any other earth species.

Consequently, as we develop from birth into our adulthood and beyond, mate and bond with others of our kind, we continue to experience new needs and find new satisfactions and possibilities coming ever to the fore. Living (at its most creative moment) is *not* a steady energy state; it is rather a continual and dynamic process of self-expression, of change, and of growth.

THE TENETS (ASSUMPTIONS) OF GROWTH PSYCHOLOGY

We have noted that every age and epoch develops assumptions about humankind. Now when we develop assumptions about humankind, we are actually talking about personality functioning—what it is and what it is supposed to be. But we noted that many historical assumptions tended to be simplistic and to ignore the complexity of our human nature. Furthermore, these assumptions tend to limit our potentiality for action. *Growth psychology differs significantly in that it allows for the continuing growth of the individual and the continual evolution of the species.* We have discussed the many levels of human functioning that make it possible for us to predict what *large groups* of people will *tend to* do and have emphasized how difficult it is to predict the responses of any *single* human being. Now we add another dimension that complicates any statement we make about human personality: the *tenor of our times*. Today we are living through tremendous technological and sociological changes. We are already experiencing, in many ways, the "future shock" Alvin Toffler (1970) saw and predicted. It is here: today! now! Not only in our society but in many societies throughout the world. Even if we had not changed an iota ourselves, the world around us has been changing at such a swift rate that what was true for many groups and many individuals only a few decades ago no longer accurately describes or predicts what they may do now.

As a result, theories and generalizations about the way human beings are "supposed to be" and are "supposed to act" are no longer so rigidly defined—rather they are changing, noticeably, even within our own lifetime. The possibilities for human personality functioning are open for consideration and discussion—open for individual choice. No longer are we prescribing a set of presumptions for a "happy" life or a "normal" existence; our attention now is focused on each person's own *conscious* decision-making process, how he or she can make sense of living today—as a contributing member of society. Any definition of creative personality functioning, in our times, then, must remain open-ended, so to speak, and calls upon each person to discover what is truly growthful for him or her. These are the two basic assumptions of growth psychology:

1. We are life forms who are capable of *conscious choice.*
2. We are life forms capable of *creative change.*

Joy, sadness, anger, indifference, depression—even occasional maladjustment—are all part of the growth process.

1. Growth Psychology Emphasizes the *Situational* Aspects of a Person's Experience

Growth psychology has been called by many names: *humanistic psychology, existential psychology*, the *psychology of individual differences*, the *psychology of human potentiality*. Whatever it is called, growth psychology is a point of view that minimizes such labels as "mental illness" or "abnormal behavior" or "neurotic personality" (Szasz 1974; Frank 1964; Lang 1967; Menninger 1968). Growth psychologists believe it to be misleading and theoretically invalid to put people into simplistic *either-or* categories with such labels as "healthy" or "unhealthy," "sane" or "insane." Growth psychologists prefer to look at the **situational** aspects of the person's life experience; i.e., the environmental stresses of his or her world and the person's ability (or inability) to deal with such pressure.

Because we are living in a time of complexity and ever-increasing change in our high-technology society, we are *all* experiencing a vast amount of life *stress* (Selye 1956). If (at times) we feel bewildered and unsure of ourselves; if (at times) we feel swept up in a vortex of current events and not in control of our lives; if (at times) we even *break down* or fall into *lethargy* and *depression*—it is small wonder. It is natural to experience the entire spectrum of emotions in the course of our daily existence. If from time to time one or another of us reaches that *trigger point* of desperation so that we may behave in ways that seem *out of step* (even *bizarre* to our family or friends and to society in general), it behooves us to remember that *all of us have a trigger point, even the most normal of us.* We are *all* subject to moments of such desperation and despair that we may do and say things which later, at more "rational" moments, make us wonder how we could ever have been so foolhardy or confused or "irrational." These moments of irrationality may have more to do with the complexity of our life space and the increasing demands on our life space than they have to do with being "neurotic" or being "abnormal" or whatever.

THE MYTH OF "MENTAL ILLNESS": THOMAS SZASZ. Thomas Szasz, a psychiatrist of our times, has always been in the forefront of "protestant" thinking (i.e., protesting the fallacies of his time). He objected to the diagnostic attitude that makes people think of themselves as *patients* and to the way his colleagues labeled people as *sick*. Szasz nailed his "ninety-five theses" to the walls[6] of the medical society. He declared: "There is no such thing as *mental illness*. We invented it! The majority of the people who are called mentally ill are mostly those who are too poor or too ignorant to defend themselves from such accusations." Furthermore, he insisted that they have been hindered, not helped, by our treatment of them (Szasz 1961).

THE MYTH OF "MENTAL HEALTH". In like manner we have invented a myth of *mental health*, a myth that seems to imply a state of perfect emotional/mental homeostasis.[7] Since we invented this term, *mental health*, we have a tendency to identify with it and to believe that this ideal state is possible for most of us for at least part of our lives. Sometimes the concept of mental health is discussed in social-science literature as if it were something one achieves (like a diploma) or is awarded (like a medal). We are beginning to realize that, at best, the concept of mental health is a fantasy-ideal of our perceptions of personality integration within the confines of our particular culture and time in history. It is another model of human nature that changes with different epochs and different world views.

As a concept, mental health is similar to another fantasy-ideal, *success*, which William James, the pioneering American psychologist, once called the "bitch goddess" (James 1890). James characterized her (success) as an eternal seductress who never delivers: No matter how close you get to her she always recedes farther and farther into the distance. She is only a mirage after all, a fantasy-dream that we make up. Like success, mental health is also a "bitch goddess," a "false god," a mirage that does not last. Trying to reach that mirage is a "losing game," for it is an ideal that no one can actually achieve—at least for any length of time.

2. It Is Sometimes Appropriate to Be "Stressed" or "Unadjusted" or "Maladjusted" or "Unhappy" or Even "Irrational"

Living, when it comes right down to it, is not easy, especially in this day and age. In the words of one philosopher, "Life is problematic" (Marcuse 1974). Moreover, as our society becomes increasingly complex and totters on the edge of worldwide disasters (pollution, lack of fossil fuels, the threat of global nuclear warfare), we are finding it ever more difficult to *process* what is happening "inside" of us because of what is going on "out there."

The small personal anxieties that have been a part of our everyday affairs are now compounded by "global anxiety." Global anxiety pertains to our despair, our doubt that we may even survive as a species on this planet—if we persevere on the path we are now following. Global anxiety hangs like a shadow over all our everyday affairs so that our personal anxieties become ever more magnified. (See box 1.3.)

Living in today's world is intense. It is appropriate, we believe, to have moments of sadness as well as elation, to be depressed as well as joyous, to feel "giddy" as well as being "rational." *We are all* going through the experiences of pain and sorrow, moments of failure, feelings of inadequacy and inferiority, and even a sense of overwhelming helplessness from time to time.

In fact, all of these emotions are part of the growing process. Growing persons have not achieved a magic formula for happiness that makes them invulnerable to pain or injustice. On the contrary, growing persons do suffer humiliation, misfortune, hurt, fear, and anxiety. And it is even appropriate to feel as if one is dying. (See box 1.4.) Throughout this book we shall emphasize that any person, from time to time, can experience feelings of depression, contemplate suicide, suffer from anxiety, use "defense mechanisms," or engage in behaviors that can be labeled "neurotic," just as most of us also can be "unadjusted" to new situations or can experience transient states of unreality. We would prefer not to label someone "emotionally sick" since those very human experiences can happen to any one of us from time to time. Sometimes the appropriate response to a situation *is* to be

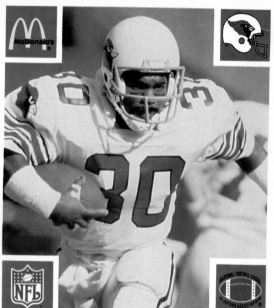

#30 Stump Mitchell RB

TEAR HERE

RUB OFF FOR NFL GAME, DATE AND McDONALD'S COUPON OFFER

...OF SOCIAL AND GLOBAL ANXIETY

...uccessful.
...ieve and to climb the social and vocational ladder.
...well informed and concerned.
...young, slim, and beautiful.
...ld War III.
...ncern with cold wars, territorial disputes, nuclear
...e inability to maintain peace.
...ational terrorism.
...h the "American dream."
...light of our cities, dollar devaluation, increasing taxation,
...eficit spending.
...f the poor, the ghettos, the underprivileged; inequities in
...r legislative system; lack of equal rights for all; and
...y level of our court and penal systems.
...concern with violence: political assassinations, increased
...nized crime, and white-color crime.
...our economic self-confidence.
...e planet: guilt and fear of survival.
...how we have poisoned the soil we farm, the air we
...es and seas we fish.
...he pollution of our world may be irreversible.
...earch to find new energy sources as our fossil fuels run

...ation of modern life.
...e of life.
...ess" as 20 percent of Americans move every year.
  c. The size of our country, in which families live at great distances and lose
     contact with each other.
6. *The "organizational person" complex in the coprorate and megacorporate*
   structure.
   a. The "plastic" society and our separation from woods, countryside, and
      bodies of water.
   b. The "assembly worker" cog-in-the-wheel experience.
   c. The lack of status and control of their lives for blue-collar workers.

Box 1.4 | **TO PART IS TO DIE A LITTLE. . .**

Partir c'est mourir un peu
 mourir á
Mourir à ce qu'on aime.

On laisse un peu de soi-meme
En tout heure; en tout lieu.

To part from someone is to die a
 little within,
To die to something that one
 loves.

One leaves a little of oneself
In every moment and every place
 one has been.

Source: Edmond Haraucourt from Choix de poésies (1891) *Rondel de l-Adieu,* trans. A.
O'Connell

anxious, depressed—even "maladjusted." The point is not that one is labeled *this* or *that* but what this anxiousness or depression or "maladjustment" says about one's current living situation, and what one can do for oneself to get through that stressful situation and its crisis and reach through to a "new plateau" of balance. The welcome result of such conflicts and crises is a new perspective, a heightened self-awareness, and a more profound understanding of human experience.

BUT WHAT ABOUT THOSE WHO ARE NOT FUNCTIONING WELL IN OUR SOCIETY? Of course there are persons who have been so tormented, so "out of their minds," so twisted by the events of their lives, or so enfeebled physically that they are unable to live with others, either permanently or temporarily, in the framework of a free and unstructured society. For these persons, we provide havens of more rigid structure whereby they are less in danger of running amuck or being victimized by others. We call these places by various names: mental institutions, prisons, correctional detention centers, old-age homes, hospitals, hospices, halfway houses, runaway shelters, and spouse-abuse homes. They are asylums, actually (to revert to a more archaic word), that are supposed to protect and harbor these fragile "souls" as well as protect the rest of the society—but so often do not! Asylum for these unfortunates is all well and good, but we need to come to a recognition that persons are not to be consigned there for life, put out of the way, so to speak, so that we do not have to contend with them ever again. These maladapted persons may be a symptom of our high-tension technocracy that indicates all is not well. Their problems in living instruct us as to what is going wrong in a culture that has stood out among all others in the world as having "the best standard of living," and of "being the most advanced." To the extent that we can enable these persons to return to the mainstream of our society we have come to recognize what is wrong within our society and have become willing and able to do something about it.

3. Growth Psychology Affirms the Validity and Primacy of the Individual

We do not want to "adjust" you to your society. We do not want to bend, fold, or otherwise mutilate you—in any way. We do not want to give you a set of rules: dos and donts for "adjusted living." We do not want to prescribe this or that way of being, for what is proper, right, and just for you may be improper, invalid, and plain unjust for someone else. We live in a (relatively) free society, and it behooves us all to understand and appreciate that freedom involves *choice* and the right to make appropriate *changes* in our living as we see fit to do so and as circumstances so dictate. *Adjusting* the person to society is no longer a valid goal for either the person or for our present society. *The growth approach puts the person first* before the job, before the institution, even before any particular psychological theory. The growth approach works toward the "farthest reaches" of what human personality is and what it can become (Rogers 1971, Maslow 1976).

4. Growth Psychologists Are *Humanistic*

Growth psychologists are interested in the clinical research findings of those who study "sick" individuals, but we also seek to study creative and "gifted" people—and all those "in between." We study, also, the experimental findings of animal research but are inclined to be very cautious about applying these findings to human beings without further corroborative evidence.

Even as so-called humanists, growth psychologists welcome statistical data on normative behavior, and we recognize and accept also that the "creative" individual cannot be enclosed in the same set of psychological **paradigms** with the "average" person. In fact, growth psychologists agree that the "average" person is a statistical abstraction that does not really exist. We say now that the breathing living, sensing, loving, multifaceted human being is more than a statistical average and certainly more than a laboratory rat. And we welcome that *more* of our humanness even though this complicates our research and investigations immensely.

5. Growth Psychologists Emphasize the Unique Differences Among Us

There was a time when we, as a society, tried to enforce a standard of behavior that was predicated on a denial of who and what we are in reality. In a country made up of myriad ethnic groups, we decided on a standard of physical beauty and normative behavior that was based on a narrow sample of statistical data—namely, white, Anglo-Saxon, Protestant (the WASP culture), and middle class. That was the fantasy-ideal. Unfortunately, we urged our immigrants to become "Americanized," our black citizens to become more "white," and our working class to model itself after the great, and perhaps nonexistent, middle class. Fortunately, we are beginning to value not only our common heritage but also our cultural differences. We are even coming to prize those differences among us. We no longer want to "homogenize" our various ethnic groups. "Black is beautiful," and so is brown, red, yellow, and white. Acceptance of the variations of physical and facial structure has given us a more global range of artistic vision. Longer hair is acceptable, or shorter hair—or even no hair. Women have forged for themselves more avenues of their true worth and self-expression. Now we can feel worthy whether we are plain or thin or fat or intellectual. We have much in common with each other, but it is our heterogeneity and our willingness to express our racial and ethnic and individual differences that make us a truly creative nation. It is the person who dares to be himself or herself, who decides to follow his or her particular "star," using his or her special talents and unique gifts, who becomes one of the "shining lights" of our society (be it in the world of business and finance, the world of scholastics and science, the world of adventure, art, music, and literature, or whatever). As a people, we are coming of age. As a society, we are coming to recognize ourselves as a "mix" of many colors and cultures—and recognize that we are in a continuing evolution as a nation. As social scientists we are more willing to emphasize and appreciate our individual differences.

6. Growth Psychologists Emphasize the *Process* of Living: The *Means* Rather than the *Ends*

Growth psychologists, by and large, don't tell you what your life objectives or life goals should be. Those decisions are yours, we say. We say, also, that if you look only to the *ends*, you will miss the essential aspect of living—the *process*. We have been mentioning the process aspect of life from time to time, and it is about time that we define this concept more succinctly. Carl Rogers puts it this way:

> The good life is a *process*, not a state of being. It is a direction, not a destination. The direction which constitutes the good life is that which is selected by the total organism, when there is psychological freedom to move in *any* direction. [Rogers 1971, p. 187]

Like the term *mental health*, the word *process* is an abstraction, but it is one that is rooted in concrete events going on within us and around us this moment. Living consists of many processes. There are the biological processes of breathing, digesting, metabolizing, eliminating, and the like. There are the developmental processes of learning how to crawl, to grasp, to speak, to walk—to become a physically competent human being. There are, also, the cognitive (intellectual) processes of thinking, perceiving, discriminating, and so on. There are the emotional processes of loving, caring, feeling joy and sadness, and reaching all the way through sufferings and resentments to forgiveness and (again) loving. All these processes are part of what has sometimes been called *personality integration.*[8]

The way each person processes (lives) his or her life events is unique. And that is as it should be. Again and again throughout this book we will stress our individual differences, as a constant reminder that although psychologists and other social scientists tend to make large generalizations about persons, what is generally true about most people may not be accurate for you or another individual. You (and only you) can decide if these generalizations are valid for you at this time and place in your life space. If the generalizations hold true for you at the moment, well and good. If they do not accurately describe your process at the present time, put the concept or theory on the shelf for reconsideration at some later date. Sometime in the future this information may apply to you or to someone you know and may be helpful in recognizing a particular pattern of the process.

7. Growth Psychologists Affirm Conscious Choice and Creative Change

Some persons seem to process their life events in odd and confusing ways. They seem to react at primitive levels of their anger and/or their helpless irrationality. Other persons seem more involved in their process of personality integration than the rest of us. In a sense, they have reached what we might call a highly integrated level of personality functioning. These persons have reached a level of being-in-the-world[9] that allows them to view life as a joyful adventure—despite the setbacks and despite the discouragements to which we are all subject. They maintain their sense of excitement, hope, love and compassion. It is important that you understand that these persons differ from the rest of us only in degree, not in kind. But by their willingness to be *all* that they are, they are more *conscious* of their process. By becoming more conscious (and therefore less at the mercy of their *unconscious* motivations), they have developed the ability to bounce back after setbacks and tragedies, a characteristic psychologists call *ego strength*.

The extent to which we become aware of our process (and remember our processing) is the extent to which we become ever more conscious beings who can perceive and comprehend what is happening in our lives from moment to moment. Being aware, we can then choose alternative routes of action. As conscious, aware beings we are less driven by impulse and/or conditioned ways of being. We are less dominated by past traumatic and feared memories. We are less intimidated by specters of "what if . . . " possibilities. We are less burdened by guilt and remorse and shame. We do not waste time being depressed by what we may have done or may not have done (or what we think has been done to us). We are thus more able to use these experiences as information to help us understand our past, assess our present situation, and plan for the future.

SELF-ACTUALIZING: PERSONS IN PROCESS

The Mechanistic Model

Before the advent of the growth approach, psychology had developed a model of human functioning as a kind of biological gyrosystem. This *mechanistic* approach to personality perceived the human person as similar to any other living entity and as having certain bodily needs (air, food, water, sex). According to that theory, when our bodies lack enough of one of these basic elements we suffer a **tension** (or **need**) that results in a **drive** to restore the body to its proper state of **homeostasis** (a state of bodily biochemical balance [Cannon 1929]). To put it more simply: When we are hungry, we seek for food; when we are cold, we look for shelter or other ways to warm ourselves. In satisfying (or not satisfying) our built-in homeostatic biochemical gyromechanisms, humankind happened upon better ways of doing things: building houses instead of living in caves, raising animals instead of hunting them, and weaving and sewing clothes instead of donning animal hides. According to this mechanistic model of personality, once a person has achieved a homeostatic state of balance, he or she is no longer motivated to want to engage in goal-seeking behavior. According to this model, more bodily tension is needed to initiate some further activity or behavior (Hall 1943). This is the approach of Desmond Morris, the scientist who proposed that our species, *Homo sapiens*, is not much more than "a naked ape" in clothing and who views our present society as a kind of "civilized zoo" (Morris 1967).

One model of humankind asserts that we are nothing more than "naked apes" who live in human zoos.

The Emergence of the Humanistic Model

We know now that there is more to human life than the mere response to bodily needs or the reduction of drive states. Many famous men and women were independently wealthy and could have had lives of luxury and ease (all their bodily needs satisfied), but they lived for something more than the satisfaction of their appetites. In fact they were often willing to undergo much sensory deprivation (lack of food, luxury, shelter) in order to pursue knowledge, explore unknown continents, or produce great works of art (White 1963).

GORDON ALLPORT: HUMAN BECOMINGS. Gordon Allport, one of America's most distinguished theoretical psychologists, was one of the first to challenge the mechanistic model of personality theory. He believed one must perceive people in terms of their **propriate strivings**—motives of a higher order than those of **tension reduction** or **self-preservation** (Allport 1955). These higher order motivations, Allport stated, lead people to accomplish things hitherto unknown.

Allport compared the *systematic approach* of mature persons to the life style of the "mental patient"—who seems unable to maintain long-term goals and has difficulty maintaining a life style that involves expectation, planning, problem solving, and intention. Allport's theme is that humanity's greatest achievements stem from our *propriate strivings* to reach for new heights of achievement and levels of awareness. Human beings, he said, have an *instinct* for *evolution*. He said to think of ourselves not as human beings but as **human becomings**. Or to put it another way, we are all humans becoming.

ABRAHAM MASLOW: A HIERARCHY OF NEEDS. The "higher" levels of human personality functioning have been called by various names. Among these terms are *individuation* (Jung 1955), *self-realization,* (Horney 1942), *fully functioning* (Rogers 1951), and *mature* (Allport 1955). Maslow directed the attention of American psychologists toward another dimension, toward those persons he designated as **self-actualizing**. Maslow described these persons as having a clear idea of their life goals, and as being able to mobilize their energies for their life goals in relatively efficient ways. They are not ruthless personalities, however. They are, in point of fact, very sensitive to the needs of others. Not only do self-actualizing persons evolve their own consciousness, they also enable others in their society to evolve. Maslow called them the "shining lights" of civilization. We discuss the self-actualizing person more completely in chapter 12. We turn our attention now to another aspect of Maslow's studies; his hierarchy of needs. Maslow concluded that for a person to become self-actualizing, he or she must have fulfilled a specific set of more basic motivations. He agreed with the mechanistic theorists that human beings have certain need-drive states that must be satisfied. But he (like Allport) insisted that once we have fulfilled these biological needs, other needs, higher and more human, arise. True, we need food. True, we need water, air, and shelter. There is no denying these basic needs that we share with other life forms. But once these needs are satisfied, human beings have higher needs, not shared by other primates. Human beings have needs, as well, for companionship, for love, for self-respect, for esteem, and for the expansion of consciousness.

These higher needs and values, then, are peculiarly human; they distinguish us from other life forms. We describe this Hierarchy of Needs in box 1.5, but we ask the reader to remember that these needs are not as discrete as shown in the diagram but continually overlap, ebb, and flow with different intensities throughout our lives. Before people can lift their gaze to the stars, their bodily and other earthly needs must first be met. Similarly, if one of our more basic needs is depleted by illness, by losing a job, by emotional stress, we may very well plummet (however temporarily) to a more primitive need level.

Box 1.5 **MASLOW'S HIERARCHY OF NEEDS**

Physiological Needs

The first needs that must be taken care of have to do with survival—or what social and biological scientists have called the instinct for self-preservation. These are the basic biomechanisms that maintain the body in homeostatic balance: general and specific hungers, sex, water, air, and seeking of shelter. The person who is deprived of these levels of being will seek to satisfy these needs by any possible means, including working for slave wages, begging, stealing, or accepting charity or welfare. We are mistaken if we think the hobo or the panhandler suffers unduly from pride when he begs for a quarter for a "cup of coffee." What he values is the food or the drink he will buy with that quarter. His need is to satisfy his hunger whether for food or for alcohol.

Safety Needs

To grow we need to feel safe. We need to feel secure in our jobs and to have a certain stability in our lives. We need to feel some structure and order in our everyday living so that we are not overwhelmed by chaos. We need to have a safe place to rest our heads and calm our hearts, a "territorial" place that is ours. All this codifying may sound obvious but many of you may not often go home to a place that is peaceful and free from anxiety. Many persons have found themselves living in tension because the people they live with make it so! Each person must find his or her own place, no matter how small or how humble, that can offer us sanctuary where we may replenish body and soul.

Belonging and Love Needs

Many of our belonging and love needs have been satisfied by a close and caring family, if we have had one, or by our friends, and by those others we love and care for and hold dear. But these needs emerge over and over again in our lives in varying ways. The need for love and a sense of belonging becomes particularly important during our adolescence when this need cannot be satisfied by our nuclear family. We need, then, an "extended" family—a "peer family," a different kind of loving and belonging.

Sometimes young people come to college not yet having found a group with which to identify and to which they can belong. Intellectually advanced and emotionally sensitive high school students sometimes find themselves out of step with the currently popular personality type. For these kinds of students college provides a welcome harbor: It is here that such students can find others like themselves and can begin to belong to a group with real conviction and identify.

In increasing numbers older people are coming back to college. They feel somewhat awkward and out of place in a classroom full of younger persons, particularly at first, even though elsewhere they have their needs of belonging well satisfied. Eventually, however, they too will find they are accepted and belong.

Esteem Needs

If all we had to do was to feel safe, have enough to eat and clothes on our body, and people who love and accept us, then we might be as happy as South Sea islanders are purported to be. Most human beings need to feel not just loved but also *needed* by others. We need to feel that we contribute something unique and worthwhile and that we are esteemed for what we contribute. We need to feel that our daily existence and our day-to-day activities make sense and make a difference to someone else. We like to know that our offering to society, however great or small, is valuable. For some this will come through great achievement as a natural leader, as an artist, or as a writer. For others it may come about through significant scientific discovery. Others may find those needs satisfied by caring for our planet and making it a better place to live.

Needs for Self-Actualizing

Finally, there is the highest of all needs (as Maslow saw it): the need for self-actualizing. Maslow described this as *the need to be and to express the highest potential that one is capable of achieving.* When we have achieved all the other basic needs, there remains still the human urge to explore our highest individual differences and to actualize our own talents and gifts. In a word, we want and need and desire to become that which we truly are: our most expressive creative, dynamic selves, with freedom to master our fate and to go beyond our current conditioned states of being. This need takes many forms, from a sense of freedom to be utterly oneself to that overwhelming and mystical sense of being in perfect harmony and at one with the universe.

NEED FOR SELF-ACTUALIZATION

Self-mastery, desire to help others, ability to direct one's own life, rich emotional experiences, a sense of meaning to one's life.

ESTEEM NEEDS

Self-esteem, esteem of others, achievement, recognition, dignity, appreciation, self-confidence, mastery of oneself and one's environment.

BELONGINGNESS AND LOVE NEEDS

Love, affection, belongingness need for family, friends, group, clan, territorial imperative; community.

SAFETY NEEDS

Security, stability, dependency, protection; freedom from fear, anxiety, chaos; need for structure, order, limits, etc.

PHYSIOLOGICAL NEEDS

Homeostasis; specific hungers sex, food, water; air, shelter, and general survival.

SOURCE: Adapted from Abraham Maslow, *Motivation and Personality* (New York: Harper & Row, 1954).

To recap here, for a moment: Where once psychologists talked mainly of homeostatic needs and drive reduction, we now speak also of those other motivations that we sense and, so far, cannot always name. It is the "human yearning to go beyond the known" and to understand something now only dimly perceived. To achieve a new level of consciousness for oneself or even for humankind seems to be an "innate" characteristic of us all. From the dawn of our history, humankind seems to have striven constantly to become more than we have been so far, to evolve toward higher levels of consciousness and personality integration. This transcending consciousness represents the most basic tenet of growth psychology.

APPLICATIONS AND COPING TECHNIQUES

1. Consider Life as a Constant Process of Discovery

The main theme of this chapter has been that our human experience is *not* just a steady homeostatic state. It is a process. This process changes according to our age, era, and **life segment** on earth. The life process has been likened to a river's journey, beginning at a source, fed by tributaries, and flowing out, sometimes in several directions, sometimes meandering, sometimes rushing. Like rivers, our lives will have twists and turns, rapids and narrow places, and outflow and overflow into greater waters. No place on our journey is ever like another, and we cannot know what lies ahead until we get there. *From birth to death, we are ever in process.* This understanding will help us to better sustain the difficulties of the journey.

2. Think of Yourself as a "Human Becoming"

Let us recall Gordon Allport, who proposed the concept of "human becoming," i.e., the notion that the healthy, creative person is always in a state of *becoming*—evolving, as it were, into something beyond what he or she has been. We have frequently heard college students express the desire to know who they "really are." It is, perhaps, something you yourself have said. This yearning is part of the need to discover and realize our fullest potential. But such a yearning rests on a mistaken notion; it implies that knowing who we "really are" is a permanent state of knowing.

Knowing who we really are is a life-long process of self-discovery. We are not the same person at twenty that we were at ten, and we are not the same person at thirty that we become at forty. We are becoming something more . . . and more . . . and more. Everything we learn, everything we master, every experience we endure adds a little bit more to us in terms of human personality and functioning. Let us continue to remember that the process never ends—at least, not until our life ends. Let us take to heart the essence of Allport's model of human personality as *always becoming that which one truly is.* Here is an example of someone we know who understands just that.

She was orphaned at an early age and lived with relatives who both rejected and abused her. She said, "I was a freaky, gawky teenager who stuttered terribly and didn't know how to get along with others." Our acquaintance did, however, manage to go on to college, graduate with a degree in speech pathology, and eventually win some notice for her work in that area. A childhood acquaintance of hers looked her up after many years and was amazed by the changes in her: Our friend now was poised, spoke easily, was liked by her students and colleagues, and seemed very different from how her acquaintance remembered her. Our friend listened to these comments and smiled. "You remember a person I hardly know any more," she said to her childhood acquaintance. "In fact, you know her much better than I do. It is true that this person (whom we both know) has my name, and we look something alike (although I am much older now than she is), and we share many of the same memories. Besides these things, we do not have much in common now. I do hope you are willing to get acquainted with me as I am now."

So it is for all of us. We are persons ever in process.

3. Accept Yourself as the Best that You Are Able to Be at this Moment

You have survived. You have grown to your present place of development. And you are striving for still more awareness and further growth. Don't expect more of yourself than that, we say. You are a person with limitations, yes, but so are we all. You also have your individual strengths and abilities, and you share with the rest of us the capacity, the ability, the potential to transcend your present stage of development. You will see in chapter 12 how highly integrated and creative people accept every aspect of themselves, even their shortcomings, weaknesses, and defense mechanisms.

Now one of the problems that comes as we grow, learn, and become wiser is that we often have a tendency to wish we could have lived our lives otherwise than we have. Or to wish we had not made a certain choice for ourselves earlier. We may experience what some persons call mistakes, but which we do not. "Oh, to have had at twenty the wisdom I have now" (at thirty, forty, or fifty years of age). The only way we acquired the wisdom we have now is through having made those earlier choices—some of which some people call mistakes, but which growth psychology does not. For no matter how we may have stumbled or slid and belly flopped, we *learned something from those choices.* We learned what happens when we make *that* kind of decision in *that* kind of situation. We have become wiser.

As a matter of fact, it would be useful to eliminate such concepts and labels as "failure," "mistake," "stupidity," "idiocy." We probably learn more from these kinds of experiences than from our more "successful" ones. Push these concepts right out of your vocabulary and thinking. Or better still, reprogram your thinking to regard these experiences as information—information that tells you that that particular choice is no longer viable, or this particular value doesn't accord with where you are now.

There is a wonderful story about Thomas Edison, who seems to have been a rather redoubtable and self-determining individual. Edison and his associates struggled through many months of research trying to find a filament for his electric light bulb—to no avail. After many years, one of Edison's associates finally voiced his discouragement. "Damn, Tom," the man said, "We've tried two thousand things that don't work! We're right back where we started from." "Not at all," said Edison (or so the story goes). "We know two thousand things that don't work."

We don't know if this story is apocryphal or factual. Nevertheless, it is a useful story. It illustrates a principle we are trying to get across, namely, that all experiences, *all* of your experiences, are grist for the process of personality integration. Without experiences, and that includes *all* kinds of experiences, there would be no opportunity for learning. True enough, sometimes we seem to have to learn the same lesson over and over again. But many of us eventually do learn and change—especially when we finally get hit with the proverbial "two-by-four."

4. Be Prepared to Question Terms Such as "Normal" or "Perfect" or "Rational" or "Just" or "Loving" or Any of the Other Wonderful and Admirable Standards You Will Come Across

Karen Horney said that one of the most debilitating neuroses of our time is the desire to be perfect. Psychoanalyst Horney described that particular trap as the "tyranny of the should," and it involves the attempt to be perfect. This person, she said, is caught in a self-defeating trap, believing that he must always exhibit:

> the utmost of honesty, justice, dignity, courage, unselfishness. He should be the perfect lover, husband, teacher. He should be able to endure everything, should like everybody, should love his parents, his wife, his country; or he should not be attached to anything or anybody, nothing should matter to him, he should never feel hurt, and should always be serene and unruffled. He should enjoy life; or he should be above pleasure and enjoyment. He should be spontaneous; he should always control his feelings. He should know, understand, and foresee everything. He should be able to solve every problem of his own, or of others, in no time. He should be able to overcome every difficulty of his as soon as he sees it. He should always be able to find a job. He should be able to do things in one hour which can only be done in two or three hours. [Horney 1942]

The lesson to be learned from Horney's clinical wisdom is simply this: We all have moments when everything we do seems to go wrong, when our attempts to improve things seem like one step forward and two steps backward. And in this sense, we all make mistakes. We all, at times, have to give up. We all have suffered moments of depression and lethargy. We all, at times, lose our joy and competence. We all suffer pain and despondency. And we sometimes can get so irritated with ourselves that we could "just kick" ourselves. We want to stress *this* point: It is all right to cry, to want to shout, to be immature, to be silly, to be just plain stupid from time to time.

Many persons in this generation are eager to raise their consciousness, to become more spiritual, and to achieve certain life goals. Certainly it is good to have goals, but it is all right, too, just to mope around, to run away, or to waffle back and forth while moving toward a new level of growth. When things go wrong or we discover we have made a mess of things, we simply go back to the drawing board and start again.

5. Be Sensitive to the Ever-Emerging Values and Goals that Will Surface During the Course of Your Lifetime

We tend to believe that if we accomplish this or that life task, *then* we'll be satisfied and can "take life easy, ever after." If we take Maslow's hierarchy of needs with any seriousness at all, such thinking is erroneous. When we accomplish our basic survival and physiological goals, then other motivations come to the surface. Satisfying one level of needs only makes it possible for us to attend to higher and more transcending needs. The new needs may be surprising to us, but they are what motivate us to new levels of consciousness and experiencing. In fact, for some theorists it is only the *process itself* that counts: the living of life, not the achievement of goals; the quest, not the victory; the ever *going on*, not the end-in-sight (Fromm 1956; Frankl 1962; Rogers 1970; May 1973b).

6. Recognize the Many Levels of the Process

We have said that persons who have developed higher levels of personality integration and functioning regard living not as a static state but as a flowing and ever-changing process (Rogers 1951; Maslow 1954(b); Allport 1955). They understand that the only constant in the world is the process; thus they are more willing to experience the changes the process brings within themselves. Such willingness to change may involve actual *destructuring* and *restructuring* of their life space, if need be, in that they discard what is stagnant and seek what is more growthful to them (Adler 1931; Levinson 1978).

We are willing to be cognizant of ourselves as physical beings who do attend to our physical needs: to enjoy ourselves, for example, as sexual beings (Maslow 1954); and to be able to share our sexuality in open, joyful and loving ways (Masters and Johnson 1970).

We are willing to explore our "unconscious processes" no matter how anxiety provoking it may be at times. For example, we are willing to understand and confront our defense mechanisms and dream-selves (Jung 1961; Freud 1965; Maslow 1976). We are willing to discover just what is going on within us when we make "slips of the tongue" and "slips of the pen." We are willing to be conscious of our fantasies (Jung 1964) and our daydreams (Singer 1975) and to discover the meaning of our "flights of fiction." We are no longer embarrassed by our fantasies and by our daydreams and our made-up "flights of fiction." We understand that the great novels and great dramas are the hard-won creative products of just such "other realities."

We are willing to become more introspective about our conscious processes and to become more "intelligent" in our decision making.

7. Don't Let Anyone Dare to Tell You Who You Are or What You Are Becoming

Be wary of anyone who attempts to tell you what is right for you. You are attaining adulthood in your own way. Remember, too, we are living in a time when the progression of world events is undergoing enormous changes in all areas of human existence: political, economic, scientific, social, and philosophic. We are venturing into a future that is still unknown. What may be truly right for us as a people or individually *now, today,* may not be right for us tomorrow. Personality theory—what we are and what we can become—is now understood to be more self-determined than ever before in history. We urge you again to become actively involved in the continuous selection of what you believe to be appropriate for your circumstances and for your unique complex of experiences, talents, strengths, limitations, aspirations, goals, and overall personality type.

The human experience of living is always and ever a dynamic flow of changing events within which we observe, partake, learn and grow—and in that process we strive to be ever more conscious of:

Living fluidly with the awareness of ourselves as *persons in process.*

Participating in this process by utilizing our opportunities for conscious choice and intentional change.

Ever expressing the *more* that we are: humanity becoming.

SUMMARY: POINTS TO REMEMBER

1. Every age and every society has developed its own model of human nature and world view about what it means to be part of life on earth—to be born, live our lives, and die. Prescientific and nonscientific approaches to personality theory are limited because they tend to rest on oversimplified assumptions regarding human nature and to ignore the full complexity and the multidimensional level of human functioning.

2. The complexity of human functioning demands recognition of the many levels of human nature: the biological, the emotional, the cognitive and the social-cultural determinants of personality. In addition, we are also a delicate balance of our genetic inheritance and our environ-

mental experiences. Finally, we are developmental persons with changing needs and values from infancy to old age. Because of these many determinants of human personality, each of us is a truly unique being. In its present state of the art and science, psychology can make generalizations and predictions about groups of people, but we cannot, with any certainty, predict how any one individual will develop or do under varying circumstances.

3. Growth psychology emphasizes the transcending aspects of human consciousness. Fundamental to this transcending aspect are two basic tenets of growth psychology: (1) the ability of the person to become consciously aware of choice (the

alternative courses of action in one's life) and (2) the ability of the person to make creative change (constructive modification within one's psychology and in one's life space). Other tenets include: (3) the avoidance of labeling persons as "neurotic" and "sick" and the emphasis, instead, on the situational aspects of living that cause anxiety and stress; (4) the recognition that such terms as *mental health* and *success* and *normal* are only hypothetical constructs or abstractions that have little to do with the reality of day-to-day living; (5) the understanding that it is perfectly appropriate to be "unadjusted" from time to time and to experience fear, anxiety, depression—even irrationality; (6) the person is valued rather than the state, the corporation, or blind conformity to any set of rules and prescriptions (even those in this text); (7) the focus on healthy, creative, highly integrated and self-actualizing persons. While growth psychologists maintain an interest in experimental research on animals, statistical data of the "average" person, and clinical studies of emotionally dysfunctioning persons, we do not forget that we are primarily a *human* science seeking ways for functioning persons to live even more effectively and creatively in their many environments; (8) the uniqueness of every individual. We differ significantly because of our sex, our race and ethnic affiliation, our cultural background, and our educational and socioeconomic status. We no longer subscribe to a single WASP model of physical beauty or emotional/social behavior. Instead, we value the diversity of our heterogeneous population and affirm the person's individuality; (9) emphasis on the *process* aspect of living. The good life is less a set of goals to be achieved as a series of experiences to be understood and integrated. It is by living through and processing our life experiences that we become truly self-actualizing and individuated persons. Biological life is a complex of many subprocesses from basic physiological functions to the higher human

processes of cognitive awareness, emotional responding, ethical valuing, and so on. Personality integration is the sum total of these various levels and subprocesses as we seek to make sense of our daily interactions and the world we inhabit. Living, then, is not a homeostatic state but a constant and fluid responding to the various environments in which we find ourselves. Each person's process is uniquely his or her own as the result of his or her personality structure and life experiences.

4. Gordon Allport emphasized the process aspect of personality integration when he called us "human becomings" (to which we have added "humans becoming"). That is to say, we are ever in the process of personality integration. Allport believed that we cannot understand truly creative individuals if we insist on viewing their motivation as mere physiological-need reduction or self-preservation. He believed that humanity becoming have motivations that are specifically unique and which he called *propriate* strivings.

5. Abraham Maslow developed a hierarchy of needs and human valuing ranging from the most basic physiological needs necessary to survival to the highest order of needs which he called self-actualizing. Maslow was one of the first to study those he believed to be at the level of self-actualizing—truly creative and integrated persons.

6. The reader is urged to adopt a *process perspective of life*. By appreciating that living is a matter of ebb and flow, expansion and contraction, equilibrium and disequilibrium, we are better able to process the darker events and to enjoy the brighter moments also. We start always with self-acceptance (our special strengths, gifts, abilities, as well as our limitations), knowing ourselves, understanding that we are the best we are capable of being at the present moment. We do not mourn "what might have been" nor scourge ourselves for so-called past mistakes. We understand wisdom comes

only with age and experience, and we learn as much from our mistakes as we do from our success. We avoid the American desire to be "perfect" and recognize that perfection is not a *human* attribute.

Rather do we recognize that every experience, painful as well as joyful, is an opportunity for learning—learning to become wiser and to grow in grace.

SIGNIFICANT TERMS AND CONCEPTS

abstraction
anxiety: personal, societal, global
assumption
average (statistical)
choices and alternatives
conditioning
consciousness
conscious change
cognition
commonalities
culture
defense mechanisms
developmental process
demographic variables
dichotomy
ego strength
empirical data
fallacy
flights of fiction

future shock
genetics
growth psychology
heterogeneity
homeostasis
hierarchy of needs
human becomings
individual differences
introspection
liberty versus license
macro-micro approaches
mechanistic models
model
myth of mental illness/ mental health
need/drive state
neotony
neurosis
paradigm
personality

personality integration
personality theory
process
process perspective of living
propriate strivings
self-actualizing
self-preservation
subculture
situational aspects of life experience
social roles
socialization process
success
tension reduction
tyranny of the should
transcending models of human nature
theory
unconscious processes
world view
work ethic

FILL IN THE BLANKS WITH SIGNIFICANT TERMS AND CONCEPTS

1. There are two basic approaches to the study of humankind. The macro approach, which looks for c _____ or principles and can be applied to all or most persons, and the micro approach, which studies i _____ d _____ s.

2. How we are as persons is the result of many factors: our g _____ or inherited characteristics; our c _____ g as a result of our environmental experiences; our racial or e _____ subculture, etc.

3. Only human beings, of all life forms on earth, seek self-understanding and self-awareness. Every culture develops a w _____ view about the meaning of life and a m _____ about human nature.

4. Primitive world views considered the universe as quixotic and terrifying. The Greeks, on the other hand, viewed the world as rational, logical, and understandable. Medieval man was instructed to avoid the temptations of the flesh for fear of hell. Renaissance man enjoyed the physical world and delighted in its beauty. The Puritan point of view valued material success gained through manual labor and so bequeathed us the w _____ e _____ .

5. Most historical models about human nature are limited because they rest on oversimplified a _____ s concerning personality functioning.

6. To appreciate the complexity of human

nature we must recognize the many levels of human functioning. These levels include our basic functioning; our c _____ process or capacity to think; our emotional responding; and the fact that we are enculturated by our racial and ethnic affiliations and socialized by our immediate family, friends, and peers.

7. We need also to remember that, unlike other life forms, we have a long n _____, which is to say we have an extended childhood.

   Because we are a d _____ life form we have different wants and needs from infancy to old age.

8. Growth psychology differs from mechanistic models because the latter are based on need-drive states and t_____-r_____. While the former maintain two basic tenets; namely, that we are capable of c _____ (we are *not* completely determined) and that we can make changes in our life space.

9. Thomas Szasz wrote a book in which he declared the fallacy of m _____ i _____. We declare m _____ h _____ to be a fallacy as well.

10. Rather than labeling persons as neurotic or sick, growth psychologists prefer to direct their attention to the s _____ aspects of emotional distress. Furthermore, we are living at a time of great anxiety: personal, social and g _____.

11. For many decades Americans subscribed to a WASPish model of beauty and behavior. Now we are coming to recognize the broad heterogeneity of our population and to value our i _____ d _____.

12. We also recognize that certain words like success and m _____ h _____ are merely abstractions, which have little to do with reality. Growth psychologists recognize that no one is perfect, that we all experience many emotions. Growth psychologists emphasize the p _____ aspect of living rather than end goals or achievement.

13. The sum total of our sensing/perceiving/responding to our inner drives and external realities (making sense of our world) is called p _____ i _____.

14. The ability to maintain psychological equilibrium despite problems and setbacks is called e _____ s _____ .

15. The optimal bodily internal physiological balance is called h _____.

RECOMMENDED BOOKS FOR FURTHER READING

Allport, Gordon. *Becoming: Basic Considerations for a Psychology of Personality*. (New Haven: Yale University Press, 1955.) This small book, written by an outstanding American personality theorist, presents a dynamic (process) model of human nature in contrast to the fatalistic determinism of the mechanistic and Freudian theorists. He presents a transcending and positive view of human functioning.

Jaynes, Julian. *The Origin of Consciousness and the Breakdown of the Bicameral Mind*. (Boston: Houghton Mifflin, 1977.) This is a highly readable book on human consciousness and its evolution. Drawing on his classical knowledge of literature of antiquity and also from the recent scientific research on split-brains, Jaynes has evolved a highly original theory of human nature.

Maslow, Abraham. *Motivation and Personality*. (New York: Harper & Row, 1954). Anyone who wants an in depth understanding of humanistic psychology should read Maslow's original work. Although a fairly large book, it is not only highly readable, it has a reading level within the comprehension of first-year college students. The student who wishes to know more about the self-actualizing person will get much more information on this subject.

Morris, Desmond. *The Naked Ape*. New York: McGraw-Hill, 1967. It presents very clearly the "approach from below" to human personality; i.e. human beings are not much more than "naked apes" who live in "human zoos." This book and *The Human Zoo* (New York: Dell Publishing Company, 1970) are an interesting contrast to Allport's *Becoming: Basic Considerations for a Psychology of Personality*.

Rogers, Carl. *On Becoming a Person*. (Boston: Houghton Mifflin, 1977). Along with Abraham Maslow, Carl Rogers brought the humanistic point of view to the American consciousness. Almost single handedly he transformed the therapeutic situation from a medical model to a non-medical model with *Client-Centered Therapy* (see references). It is in this book that the student can experience Rogers' own struggling for personhood even as he is receiving accolades for his professional insights and research.

Szasz, Thomas. *The Myth of Mental Illness: Foundations of a Theory of Personal Conduct*, rev. ed. (New York: Harper & Row, 1970). More than anyone else, Szasz has been willing to explode a hypothetical construct that mental health workers have been talking about for over a century: namely, mental illness. Although readers may not agree with Szasz they cannot help but get astonishing insights into the mega-corporate structure of our mental hospitals and prison systems. Very few of the rich, says Szasz, are to be found there. Is that because they are mentally healthier? No, answers Szasz, only that they have enough money to keep out of these places while the poor and the ignorant do not.

2

Life Span: The Cycles of Our Lives

THE SOCIAL AND EMOTIONAL CHANGES IN OUR LIVES
Sigmund Freud: The Psychosexual Development of the Child
Carl Jung: The Second Half of Life
Arnold vanGennep: The Rites of Passage
Erik Erikson: The Psychosocial Development of the Person
Daniel Levinson (and Gail Sheehy): Seasons and Passages of Our Lives

THE COGNITIVE DEVELOPMENT OF THE PERSON
Piaget: Four Stages of Cognitive Development
A Final Synopsis of Cognitive Development

THE MORAL EVOLUTION OF THE CHILD: ALSO A DEVELOPMENTAL
PROCESS
Sigmund Freud
The Hartshorne and May studies
Piaget: The Moral Reasoning of the Child
Lawrence Kholberg: Further Studies of the Moral Development of the
Individual

APPLICATIONS AND COPING TECHNIQUES

THE SOCIAL AND EMOTIONAL CHANGES IN OUR LIVES

One of the truly significant developments in psychology has happened in the last twenty to thirty years, namely, the development of the **life-span approach.** Now it may seem rather strange to the reader that we call this approach a significant and recent event. After all, we psychologists have been studying people from cradle to grave for many decades. In point of fact that is so, but our emphasis has been concentrated on the *quantitative* changes brought about as a person grows and develops and gets older. We have measured people's height, weighed them, and produced statistics on their blood pressure, respiration, and brain activity from infancy to old age. We have done longitudinal studies on their intellectual growth via academic achievement scores and IQ tests. What, then, is so new about the life-span approach?

Just this: We are beginning now to focus on the *qualitative* changes that come about in a person as he or she transits from infancy to childhood to adolescence to adulthood and beyond. Of course, that brings up a question: What do we mean by *qualitative* changes?

To put it simply, it means that *as we go through our life span our needs and wants and interests are significantly different in later years from what they were*

Personality integration is the means by which we integrate our biological, emotional, social, and intellectual experiences toward purposeful action and further growth.

earlier. What motivates us and makes us feel nourished changes from one life stage to another. We all remember that the toys and goodies we thought were so wonderful as children seemed "childish" to us as we grew up. Now we are coming to realize that what we deem important to our lives in our twenties may no longer hold our interest or nourish us in our thirties, and what we thought so important to us in our thirties may undergo profound disintegration through that segment of our life span called the mid-life. Every age-stage, the research suggests, has a *quality* of its own, emotionally and cognitively different from the one that preceded it.

To put it in more sophisticated language, the qualitative changes that come about alter our **phenomenology,** that is, how we *experience* the world with its multitude of events and possibilities. In chapter 1 we described how whole societies and civilizations develop different world views and how these various world views affect the consciousness of members of those societies and civilizations. In an analogous manner, the qualitative changes that come about as the result of the age stage in which we find ourselves alter our very perceptions and feelings and *thinking*. In fact, we have different *world views* at different times in our lives.

We have said that this understanding of the changes that occur during our life span has come about in the last two or three decades. But its root-beginnings can be found much earlier in the history of psychology. No idea or revolution in thought is ever born like Athena, who fully mature and clothed, sprang from the head of Zeus. As we look back, we can find references to these changes in our consciousness throughout the centuries in the writings of many of the great writer-philosopher-psychologists. One of the first to explore scientifically the qualitative changes in our fundamental process was Sigmund Freud, who outlined a **psychosexual theory of development** of the child-to-adult.

It has been said that four persons changed the course of twentieth-century thinking. Charles Darwin changed our understanding of our *biological* inheritance; Albert Einstein changed our understanding of the *physical universe;* Karl Marx influenced our understanding of *politics* and *economics* (how the *wealth* and *power* of the earth may be distributed among humankind); and Sigmund Freud transformed our beliefs about *human psychology*. It is appropriate to begin with Freud's work, not only because of his profound insights into human personality but because he was a pioneer in **developmental psychology.**

We are going to spend considerable space in presenting Freud's work. It is not that we believe that Freud was correct *in toto*, for he was not. But he *was* a giant of a thinker; and if we are going to disagree with him, at least we ought to know what it is we are disagreeing with.

Sigmund Freud: The Psychosexual Development of the Child

When Sigmund Freud proposed his revolutionary theories of depth psychology, nothing (probably) was quite as shocking to the society of his times as his insistence that the infant is born a highly sexual being. Moreover, he insisted that this sexual drive was a necessary part of the child's psychic development. If the sexual drive (which he called the *libidinal instinct* or **libido**) was overly restricted or **repressed,** the child could become psychologically warped, resulting in neurosis or even psychosis. The reader must remember that Freud was speaking to the Victorian society of his time, a time when, for example, childhood masturbation was threatened with dire consequences: "If you don't leave your 'Peter' alone, I will cut it off!" (Freud 1935). Freud viewed the person as a maelstrom of instinctual and often opposing drives. One such instinctual drive is that of **self-preservaton.** The sexual instinct (the libidinal drive) is almost as powerful and energetic as the instinct for self-preservation. The sexual instinct, however, had become so complicated by commandments, rules, excessive modesty, guilt, shame, denial, and so on, that pent-up libidinal energy was doing psychic damage to members of Western society. Yet, Freud said, some taming of this powerful and aggressive force by society is necessary to transform the basically savage, primitive, lusting, incestuous, narcissistic infant into a civilized adult. In this process of **taming** and **socializing,** the basic raw instinctual drives would be sublimated into other forms of expression such as work, art, poetry, and scientific achievement (Freud 1949).

The socializing process of the child results, according to Freud, in two separate but interrelated psychosexual developments. The first centers on the child's sexual development; the second deals with the child's psychic development (Freud 1962).

HUMAN SEXUAL DEVELOPMENT: PSYCHOSEXUAL STAGES. As posited by Freud, the child goes through several developmental phases before reaching full adult sexuality. The first two stages Freud called the **oral stage** and the **anal stage** of infant sexuality.

The oral stage. In the first year of life, the energy of the libidinal drive is organized around the pleasurable activities of the mouth. The breast is not only life giving, it also is a source of sexual excitation, sensation, and pleasure. Eventually, anything that is associated with the mouth, such as the thumb, pacifier, or any inanimate object, becomes a source of sexual pleasure. The infant, at this stage of development, is passive and *autoerotic*, that is, sexual pleasure is centered on the child's own body. If the adult continued to gratify his or her sexual instincts through oral means, Freud considered it perverse. But even in the fully heterosexual adult, traces of the oral stage can be discerned in nail biting, pencil chewing, smoking, and drinking to excess.

Today we are much more able to accept the idea of infant sexuality. We witness the infant's delight in finding things to put into its mouth, for this is one of the ways the infant discovers the world, namely, that *this* thing is edible and *that* thing is not; that *this* thing is soft and chewy and good to eat while *that* thing tastes terrible (Piaget 1973; Kagan 1978). Later we observe the child hugging a blanket and sucking on it. In fact, the idea of a "security blanket" has passed into popular language.

The anal stage. With the development of teeth, the child leaves the *passive oral* stage and shifts to an *active* orientation to the environment. The child can now chew its own food. This also is the beginning of toilet training. Not only is the control of bladder and bowels a source of parental love and approval (or con-

Box 2.1 FREUD'S STAGES OF PSYCHOSEXUAL DEVELOPMENT

AGE SPAN	LIBIDINAL (SEXUAL) DEVELOPMENT	PSYCHOLOGICAL DEVELOPMENT	LEVEL OF CONSCIOUSNESS
Birth to about 2 years	Oral stage	Libidinal drive focused on mouth area. Passive-dependence on world for needs	Child is born an id, ruled by "pleasure principle."	Baby is an "unconscious" being, unaware of being a separate entity from mother or mother's breast—the source of "all good."
About 2 to 3 years	Anal stage	Libidinal drive diverted to toilet training activities. Active-aggressive development.	Superego develops as the result of toilet training and other prohibitions. Beginning of socialization period.	Freud equated the superego with conscience. The superego is more accessible than the "unconscious" id and thus is "pre-conscious material."
About 3 to 4 or 5 years.	Phallic stage	Sexual curiosity; discovery of masturbation. Oedipus (Electra) complex comes to the fore. Libidinal drive now focused on parent of the opposite sex.	Ego is developing and *reality* principles now guide the child. Parent of same sex is seen as a rival.	Child becomes a conscious being aware of self and others.
Between 4 and 6 years			Child becoming aware of its own sexual identity.
Between 6 and 11 years	Latency stage	Libidinal drive dormant as a "developmental phase" or repressed as a part of *socialization* and the *reality* principle.	Child gives up attachment to parent of opposite sex and becomes identified with parent of the same sex.	Child is identifying with its own psychosexual role.
At puberty	Full genital stage	Libidinal drive is now fully phallic.	Person is able to engage in sexual activity with full physiological responses.	Person experiences self as a fully (hetero-) sexual being.

versely, parental anger and disapproval if the child should not control them), but the child also discovers the pleasure associated with control of bodily functions. Urination and defecation have a decidedly pleasurable aspect, and Freud considered this pleasure as having a strong sexual element. The libidinal instinct now is centered at the anal orifice (where it formerly had been focused on the oral orifice).

If the child overlearns the control of bladder and sphincter, remaining **fixated** at this level of sexual development, he or she is in danger of becoming what Freud called an **anal personality:** one who cannot "let go" of the feces easily and who holds on to the point of constipation. A constipated (anal) personality overvalues money (symbolic of feces), hangs on to it for dear life (is a miser), is excessively clean and tidy (harboring a secret fear of being dirty and overcompensating for it), and displays great obstinacy (refusal to let go or give in).

The phallic stage. By the fourth year of the child's life, a new phase of libidinal development is reached, in which his or her genital organs begin to play a more dominant role. The child discovers that manipulation of the genitals is a source of pleasurable sensations. But parental disapproval puts an end to this activity (or it becomes more secretive).

The latency stage. At this point, Freud said, the child enters the **latency** period, from about age six to the onset of puberty. This is the stage at which sexual activity in the child becomes less dominant. Freud assumed that the libidinal drive had become somewhat dormant, but he also believed that parental disapproval of childhood masturbation was part of this seemingly *quiescent* period of the sexual drive. At any rate, the sexual drive reemerges at puberty with greater force than ever before.

The full genital stage. With the onset of puberty, the adolescent is ready to enter into adult sexuality, which Freud identified as full genital coitus with a person of the opposite sex. But before the young man can become a fully genital person, he must give up his attachment to his mother, which Freud called the **Oedipus complex.** Similarly, the young girl must give up her attachment to her father, which Freud called the **Electra complex**.

During his research into the meaning of dreams, Freud believed he had discovered a basic theme in the deep attachment of sons to their mothers and of daughters to their fathers. As he studied how these attachments developed in the psychosexual evolution of the child, Freud began to notice that certain themes in the family's interpersonal relations already had been discussed in the world's great myths. Freud noticed particularly how the ancient Greek story of Oedipus described what he saw happening in the family life in his own time. Oedipus was the Theban king who had (unknowingly) violated the most sacred taboos of society, that of killing his father (patricide) and having intercourse with his mother (incest). (See box 2.2.)

Freud believed that the story of Oedipus did indeed represent aspects of human relationships that are often hidden from conscious awareness. He surmised that other abiding truths about the history of civilization and human psychosexual development might be revealed in other mythological tales. With regard to the

Box 2.2	**THE STORY OF OEDIPUS**

Before the birth of Oedipus, a certain King Laius of Thebes received a message from the gods that he would sire a son who ultimately would kill his father (Laius) and marry his mother (Laius' wife, Jocasta). That possibility was just as horrifying to a king in ancient Greece as it is to us today. So to prevent such an eventuality, as well as to save his own life, Laius gave the infant to a shepherd with orders to leave the child outside so that it would die from exposure or starvation or be killed by wild beasts.

The shepherd, however, took pity on the baby and, instead of leaving the child to die, carried him to the neighboring city-state of Corinth, where the child was adopted by King Polybus and brought up as a prince. When Oedipus learned he was not the true son of Polybus, he went to Delphi to consult the priestess of the god Apollo. The message he received was cryptic (as oracles tended to be): Oedipus was simply told not to return to his own land, for if he did, he was fated to kill his own father and to marry his mother. He therefore set out for Thebes, completely unaware that he was doing exactly what the oracle had warned him not to do!

On the road to Thebes, he met an older man who rudely told him to give way so that he might pass on the narrow road. Oedipus had been reared as a prince and was not used to such treatment. In the ensuing fight over the right of way, the older man was killed. But what Oedipus did not know is that the man he killed was Laius, King of Thebes—his own father!

When Oedipus arrived at the outskirts of Thebes, he learned that the city was being devastated by the Sphinx, a lionness with the head of a woman. The Sphinx killed anyone who could not anwer her riddle: "What has one voice and yet becomes four-footed, two-footed, and three-footed?" Oedipus correctly answered "Man, for he crawls on all fours as a baby, walks upright on two legs in adulthood, and needs the use of a cane in old age to walk, which makes him three-footed." The Sphinx thus was outwitted and destroyed, and Oedipus entered Thebes as a hero.

In the meantime, news had come to Thebes that the king had been killed by persons unknown. There was grieving for the death of Laius, but the citizens of Thebes were too overjoyed at the death of the Sphinx to mourn for long, or even to determine how the king died. Instead, they turned tp Oedipus, their hero, and asked him to become the new king of Thebes by marrying Queen Jocasta. The couple lived happily together and produced four children.

All went well for Thebes until the children of Oedipus and Jocasta approached adulthood, when a great plague descended on the city. An oracle again was consulted and a cryptic message again was delivered: the plague would cease only when the murderer of Laius was discovered and was driven from the city! When Oedipus began to investigate the killing, he discovered that he, himself, was the murderer of his own father, Laius, and that he had married his own mother! In his grief and guilt, Oedipus blinded himself and, chased by winged furies, went into exile. Jocasta hanged herself. Their two sons killed each other in their fight for the throne, and their two daughters died in terrible ways. The violation of a societal taboo is suffering and death.

Oedipus myth, he said that when a boy is born into a family the mother and the child develop a natural, close attachment. This attachment or bond is cemented in the love, caring, fondling, nursing, and comforting the mother gives the child. A child who receives that kind of attention from his mother in babyhood grows up psychically strong and stable.

Freud believed that the young boy would like to get rid of his father, as did Oedipus in the legend, for then he could keep his mother all to himself—she would be his alone. Before you dismiss this idea out of hand, we ask you to remember how children very easily play "kill" with their playmates. Children have a somewhat different concept of death than do adults. In their fantasy play, children very often kill each other ("Bang-bang—you're dead"), and they see their playmates fall and "die," and then everyone gets up to play some more. Death as a finality has little meaning for children until some real death of a friend or relative hits home.

Moreover, anyone who has been around family life long enough has witnessed a little boy saying to his mother (or a girl to her father), "I'm going to marry you when I grow up." But when the little boy begins to show a preference for his mother and makes demands on her time and attention, he soon begins to realize that the giant (his father) receives the mother's first attention when he is around. Furthermore, if the child interrupts at certain times, he can be spanked or pushed away and soon learns that he should keep such power demands to himself.

We do not intend to overlook girls, here, for the girl soon enough begins to show a preference for her father. In turn she is his pet, his darling, his love-in-miniature. Freud called this relationship the Electra complex, after another Greek legend. (For a modern version of that myth, you might want to read or see the play by the American playwright Eugene O'Neill *Mourning Becomes Electra*.) Freud observed that the Oedipus theme is revealed throughout the literature and mythology of Western culture—for example, in Henrik Ibsen's *Rosmersholm* and in William Shakespeare's *Hamlet*. Hamlet, as you will recall, killed his stepfather and simultaneously loved and hated his mother. Freud believed the play reflected Hamlet's own confused Oedipal feelings toward his mother. For example, the fact that Hamlet killed his stepfather (also his uncle) instead of his father is simply the psyche's way of making the truth of patricide more palatable.

We have outlined very briefly Freud's theory on the sexual stage of the psychosexual development of the child. It needs to be understood that this part of the process invokes primarily the *physiological* thrust of the libidinal drive. But that is only half the story. Each of the sexual stages is accompanied, according to Freud, with specific *psychological* developments. It is because of these two aspects, the physiological and the psychological, that Freud called it *psychosexual* development. We address ourselves now to the psychological aspects of this process and which has been called Freud's **topography** of human personality functioning.

FREUD'S TOPOLOGY OF HUMAN PERSONALITY: THE ID, THE SUPEREGO, AND THE EGO. Early in Freud's career he posited two aspects of human mentality: a **conscious** and an **unconscious** part of the mind. The idea of an unconscious mind was not totally new; for a hundred years and more, philosophers had been discussing the possibility of an unconscious mind. (Whyte, 1979.) But it took Freud's research into *hypnosis* and **free association** to give substance to this hypothesis. Freud found that a person under hypnosis was able to remember events long forgotten, or "repressed." Later, he discovered that **repressed material** could be elicited under the conditions of **free association,** the technique of encouraging the patient to say whatever came into his or her mind without fear of being considered "bad," "naughty," or "sick." Freud's further work on the unconscious led him to formulate three aspects of human personality: the *id*, the *ego*, and the *superego*.

The id. A newborn baby has no sense of "I." Since the infant still lacks a sense of separateness from the environment, it is largely an "unconscious" being. Freud called this baby-unconsciousness an *id* (the Latin word for "it"). The id can be thought of as an organism of undifferentiated energy, which strives only for its growth and pleasure. Far from possessing anything that approaches the rationality of adulthood, the infant, according to Freud, is a cauldron of primitive emotions and instincts. Thus, by its very nature the *id* is impulsive, blind, irrational, and pleasure-seeking. Very simply, the baby cries when frustrated and responds with delight to pleasure. The *id* stage of personality is essentially self-centered, oriented only toward its own pleasure and the avoidance of pain. That baby *id* is dominated and controlled by this **pleasure/pain principle**.

The superego. This life of having every wish indulged cannot continue forever, since eventually children must realize that there are other persons in the world. For example, as they crawl around they discover that they are not allowed to touch certain objects unless they want their hands slapped. They are taught also, when the time comes, that they may not urinate or defecate whenever and wherever they feel the need to do so. They discover also, sometimes to their surprise and displeasure, that they may not hit their little brother or sister without running the risk of getting hit in return. In other words, they are initiated into the **socialization** process. More often than not, they rail against the limitations imposed on them. They sulk, pout, whine, and engage in any kind of maneuver that will enable them to continue to get their own way.

According to Freud, these early confrontations or encounters with the "outside world" (the parents and other members of the family) result in the development of the superego. (*Superego* is Latin for "over I.") In other words, *the superego emerges as the result of socialization*. Children learn that *this* is the right thing to do and that *that* is the wrong thing to do. According to Freud, *the superego is the basis of our conscience* and is one of the enduring aspects of personality.

The ego. At the level of the "blind," instinctual *id* we simply say, "I will do what I want to do," while the *superego* is the power of parents and society, which

According to Freud, the ego is a battleground between the *id* and the *superego*.

says, "You may do this; you may *not* do that." It is from compromising between the directives from the id ("I will . . .") and the superego ("You may not . . .") that children's sense of self eventually comes into being. It is through these experiences that children begin to understand and to acknowledge that they are an I, an individual entity who is indeed separate from their mothers and their physical surroundings. This beginning sense of self Freud called the **ego** (Latin for I). *The ego is therefore the conscious level of personality*, that part of ourselves of which we are aware and which we identify as the seat of reason, intelligence, self-knowledge, and so forth.

FIXATION OR NEUROSIS. *Freud saw the ego as a kind of battlefield between the id and the superego*, which could be caught in the conflicts between the two. Freud called these conflicts **fixations** or **neuroses.** A fixation or neurosis is what happens when a child does not pass successfully from one libidinal stage to another but gets "hung-up" at an earlier (more primitive) psychosexual stage and thus does not achieve fully genital, adult sexuality.

If the socialization process in the family is essentially a real caring of the child and if it is relatively consistent, the ego of the child becomes relatively healthy and aware of reality, and the person learns how to function according to the **reality principle** rather than the pleasure/pain principle. The reality principle is the recognition by the infant that it may not do everything it wants to (have its own way in all things) because of the restrictions set by the environment. If children, however, are not cared for, if they are neglected or treated inconsistently in these early years (indulged too often, frustrated too often, or both at various times), their "egos" can then become fixated at certain "crisis" points. These crisis points, according to Freud, may occur during the oral and anal developmental stages. If a personality is fixated at the *oral level,* even as an adult the person will lack those societal standards by which one recognizes that other people also have feelings, rights, and needs. Such persons remain passive-dependent personalities who wish to be taken care of all of their lives and find spouses who will *mother them,* clean up after them, and allow them to avoid responsibility.

If children have been overdisciplined (instead of overindulged), then they may grow up constantly concerned about not doing the "right" thing. The danger of overdisciplining occurs at the anal stage, when children learn to "do their duty" in the "potty" instead of in their pants. It is also during this stage that one is asked to give up the pleasure principle—not to hit one's sister when one wants to, not to throw food on the floor, and so forth. A certain amount of discipline develops character; too much instills endless guilt, remorse, and feelings of inferiority—in other words, the "neurotic anxieties" of our times. The person overly toilet trained may very well be overly concerned about rules, or what is "supposed" to be done or not done. Such a person may be so scrupulous about keeping things orderly that he or she makes others uncomfortable—the excessive neatness, the cleaning, the endless absorptions in the minutest details can be disturbing.

An example of fixation. People may be able to operate in many (even most) areas of everyday life in an integrated manner, yet "have **fixations**" in other areas in which they function less well because of conflicts and unfinished situations stemming from early life. We recognize a fixated behavior *by its highly repetitive nature* (Maier 1949). Fixated people respond in essentially the same manner to a given stimulus every time. They seem to lack a wide repertory of emotional responses to a certain category of situations. They just keep doing or saying the same kinds of things over and over again. Their behavior is simply uncreative, monotonous, and predictable. An example will illustrate this.

A man we know is highly creative in his work and job, gets along well with his associates, has an apparently satisfying relationship with his wife and children, yet he has an unreasoning, irrational, and highly prejudicial emotional reaction to police officers, lawyers, judges, administrators—anyone distinctly representative of authority. His behavior toward them (and he often talks about the Establishment) is highly stereotyped; he always reacts to them in more or less the same way, with fear, hatred, resentment, and feelings of persecution. Any mention of the law or the police provokes in him verbal abuse, harangues about corruption or the government—just as if someone had pushed his button. At these moments, his coworkers, friends, and relatives brace themselves for a sermon (which they have heard many times before) or quietly excuse themselves.

Carl Jung: The Second Half of Life

Freud's work on the psychosexual development of the child was monumental, but he said very little about development past the stage of puberty. It was as if all the determinants of human behavior happened to us very early in life, and whatever people did for the rest of their lives was the result of the first three to six years of their existence. When pressed to discuss what were the characteristics of the healthy adult, Freud answered very succinctly: "Leiber und Arbeiter," "To love and to work." In other words the adult was able to perform two acts: *to work* and *to love* (i.e. to engage in complete and satisfying heterosexual activity). But we must remember who Freud's patients were. They were men and women so emotionally warped and psychologically crippled that they were unable to carry out their daily tasks. They were often confined to their beds, could not sleep at night, and remained in their rooms while the rest of the family enjoyed each other's company.

Jung viewed the life span in four great eras. The second half of life (after forty) is significantly different from the first half.

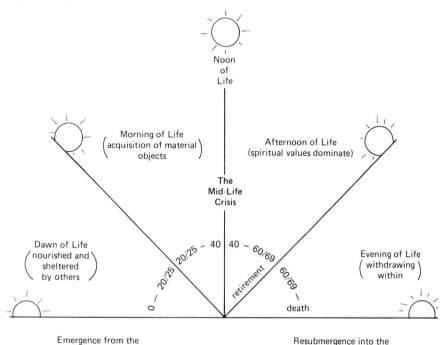

It took Carl Jung, one of Freud's students, to call attention to the whole life span. In contrast to Freud, Jung saw many persons who were not neurotically disabled but who were out in the world and often world famous personalities. They were not emotionally crippled, but instead, quite intelligent, vital, energetic persons who sought Jung's help only at particularly critical times in their lives (Jung 1955). If Freud gave us an insight into our childhood, Jung gave us an insight into the second half of life. From his work with people in their maturity, Jung concluded that the second half of adult life was a vastly different experience from the first half of life, and that this latter segment of our "three score years and ten" had its own special characteristics and quality.

JUNG'S FOUR DEVELOPMENTAL STAGES. Jung divided the person's life into four developmental stages: childhood, youth, maturity, and old age. *Childhood* is roughly that stage from birth to puberty and the early twenties. It is a time, said Jung, of learning how to make meaning out of the chaotic state of internal and external experience. The second stage is *youth*, which extends from the early twenties into the middle of life, somewhere between the thirty-fifth and fortieth year. We might think this rather old to be entitled *youth*, but Jung saw these years as having two specific tasks: *to develop an ego complex* and *to accumulate various possessions* (education, job, status, spouse, family, house, material comforts, and fame). The third stage, *maturity*, begins where youth leaves off, in the years around thirty-five to forty. At this age, people become aware of how one-sided their lives have been. They have stressed all the material aspects of existence and have neglected the other side, which Jung called the *spiritual* aspect (Carl Jung 1955).

Suddenly all the attainments of youth—achievement, money, success— seem to have less value, and people go in pursuit of something else. The object of that pursuit Jung calls the soul, the other side of oneself. Aware of how one-sided their lives have been, people frequently become quite different in the second half of their lives. If he has been a chaste husband, he may now become a *roué*. If she has been docile and domestic, she may now become quite aggressive and pursue a career. Finally, there is *old age*, whose crisis is to recognize that life is not mounting and unfolding any more but that "an inexorable inner process forces the contraction of life." It is the task of old age to focus on itself, to attain an illumination of its own. If the *morning of life*, said Jung, is significant in terms of a person's achievement in the outer world, the *afternoon of life* must focus on the facts of one's death and one's relationship with things of the spirit. The old person becomes *submerged* once again in unconscious psychic happenings, a reversal of the task of childhood in which the child *emerges* from the unconscious state (Freud would have called it the *id* state) into (self-) consciousness (Jung 1955). We cannot help but reflect how similar Jung's stages of life are to the four stages of life as laid down by the Indian philosophy of Yoga developed over two thousand years ago. (See box 2.3.) Europeans tend to have a comprehensive view of life. At least that is how it seems to us when we compare their writings with those of the "youth culture" of the United States. At any rate, their writings reflect a better understanding of the life process from birth to death. For more of this broader view of life we now look at the work of two men, native to northern Europe: Arnold vanGennep

THE FOUR STAGES OF YOGIC LIFE

1. *brahmachari*, the celibate student life;
2. *grihastha*, the householder with worldly responsibilites;
3. *vanaorastha*, the hermit who seeks spiritual truth;
4. *sannyasi*, the forest dweller or wanderer, free from all earthly considerations and concerns.

SOURCE: Paramahansa Yogananda, *Autobiography of a Yogi* (Los Angeles: Self-Realization Fellowship, 1972), p. 288.

of Belgium and Erik Erikson, who was born in Denmark but emigrated to the United States fairly early in his professional life.

Arnold vanGennep: The Rites of Passage

Les Rites de Passage by Arnold vanGennep was published in 1908. We mention this fact to underscore his far-reaching vision. He was not a sociologist, an anthropologist, or even a "social scientist." He simply thought deeply about life, and his meditations led him to study how societies throughout the world and throughout time have responded to life, marriage, growing up, parenthood, and other changes of status. vanGennep noted that in both tribal and civilized life these transits and passages are marked by what he called *rites of passage*, which allow the person to celebrate this transit and enable others in the person's environment to adjust to the person's new status. These stages of life are charcterized by designated behaviors by the individual concerned and celebrated by the whole community with festivities, feasts, and holidays. Thus we have the rites of baptism and

VANGENNEP: RITES OF PASSAGE

The life of an individual in any society is a series of passages from one age to another and from one occupation to another. . . . Transitions from group to group and from one social situation to the next are looked on as implicit in the very fact of existence, so that a man's life comes to be made up of a succession of stages with similar ends and beginnings; birth, social puberty, marriage, fatherhood, advancement to a higher class, occupational specialization, and death. . . . In this respect, man's life resembles nature, from which neither the individual nor the society stands independent. The universe itself is governed by a periodicity which has repercussions on human life, with stages and transitions, movements forward, and periods of relative inactivity.

Arnold vanGennep, *The Rites of Passage*
(Chicago: University of Chicago Press, 1960).

circumcision, and the rites of first communion (marking the transition from infancy to childhood), the rites of puberty, and the rites marking the end of childhood (confirmation in Protestant and Catholic churches and bar and bat mitzvah in the Jewish synagogues); and every society, no matter how primitive, has a public rite of passage from the single to the married state. (See box 2.5.)

Especially important are the evolved funeral rites of each group or society, for those rites are meant to accomplish several purposes. First, the funeral rite helps the deceased reach the other side; second, the rite ensures that the deceased does not remain as a malevolent ghost; third, it enables the tribe to demonstrate their grief by weeping, wailing, and decking themselves out in sackcloth and ashes; and finally, the rite allows the members to resume group life, thus mending the gap left by the departed person.

There also is the rite that marks the transit from the *profane* life to the *sacred* life: the initiation of the person into holy orders. We are somewhat familiar with these rites through the Catholic and Protestant rites of priesthood and the rites connected with monastic life. But all societies across cultures and over time have celebrated publicly the transformation of the person from a mundane to a holy state, including the anointment with oil of the ancient Hebrew priests or the attainment of knighthood in the feudal era (Renault 1958). VanGennep's work was not published in England until 1961, but his work had tremendous influence on European thinking and on European psychologists. One of these psychologists was a man who called himself Erik Erikson.[1] He extended vanGennep's stage theory.

Erik Erikson: The Psychosocial Development of the Person

Erik Erikson started his professional career as somewhat of a neo-Freudian; that is to say, he adhered principally to Freud's libidinal theory of human personality functioning and the primacy of early experience as the twin determinants of adult personality. But as he became more and more engaged with the struggles of modern personalities within the context of our highly socialized, highly industrialized society, he began to envision the life journey as a continual process of struggle for self-discovery and self-mastery. In that respect, his theoretical framework is not unlike Carl Jung's, but Jung envisioned four great stages in human life. Erikson envisions eight great stages from infancy to old age. Each stage has its particular **crisis** to be met and **life task** to be accomplished. If the person accomplishes the life task successfully, growth to the next stage is easy. If the life task is not successfully accomplished at any point along this journey, then the person remains emotionally and socially crippled. Furthermore, like vanGennep, Erikson does not place all the importance of the person's personality development upon the successful resolution of the libidinal drive. He adds the *social context of the environment* and the culture or society the person finds himself or herself within, in proceding from one stage to the next. Thus Erikson calls his theory the **psychosocial** theory of human development, as distinct from Freud's *psychosexual* theory of human development. We now take a close-up look at Erikson's eight life-stages.

Box 2.5 OVERVIEW OF SOME RITES OF PASSAGE

AGE/STAGE	TRADITIONAL SOCIETIES	HEBREW/JUDAIC TRADITION	CATHOLIC/PROTESTANT CHURCHES	FEDUAL PERIOD	CONTEMPORARY SECULAR SOCIETY
Birth	Sometimes circucision Gift giving	Circumcision	Baptism		Baby showers Passing out cigars Sending out birth announcements
Childhood	Colonial days: the "breeching ceremony"	Beginning the study of the Torah	First communion	Beginning initiation as a page	First day of school
Adolescence	Sometimes circumcision	Bar or bat mitzvah	Confirmation	Initiation as a squire	First date Enters high school
Adulthood and Marriage			Marriage rites through most societies	Become a knight	
Death			Funeral rites through most societies		
Recognition of "Sacredness"	Becomes a shaman, witch doctor, medicine man, vestal virgin, oracle, sybil	Ordained as a rabbi	Ordained as a priest or minister; take vows as monk or nun	Takes vows of tertiary orders (as in Knights Templar)	Takes an oath as a physician, attorney, government official, marriage vows

BOX 2.6 IMPLICATIONS OF ERIK ERIKSON'S EIGHT LIFE STAGES

STAGE	AGE	TASK	SUCCESSFUL ASPECTS OF TASK	UNSUCCESSFUL ASPECTS OF TASK	SUCCESSFUL OUTCOME
I	Infancy: 0–1 year	Basic trust versus basic mistrust	Physical and emotional "mothering." A sense of order and stability in the events experienced; feelings of being wanted, loved, and cared for.	Life remains chaotic, unconnected. Child is sickly, physically and psychologically disabled. High infant mortality; childhood autism; academic retardation.	Drive and hope
II	Toddler: 1–3 years	Autonomy versus shame and doubt	Learns to stand on own two feet; feed self, etc. Controls bodily functions. Makes basic needs known through language. Discovers choices: learns to say *no* and yes. Accepts *no* as well as yes. Learns the rules of society: "may do" and "may not do."	Lack of autonomy produces passive dependence on others; unable to assert own will; results in *overobedience*: unable to accept "no," results in personality constantly in rebellion; perhaps "delinquent."	Self-control and will power
III	Preschool: 4–5 years	Initiative versus guilt	Learns geography and time, can go and come back, can think in terms of future, has developed memory, learns beginning adult roles. More loving, cooperative, secure in family. Good chance of becoming a "moral" person.	Wants always "to be in control." Sense of competition drives person to be "overcompetitive." May always be outside the law.	Direction and purpose
IV	School: 6–12 years	Industry versus inferiority	Learns the "how tos" of society; in Western society masters 3 Rs; begins to understand matrices of society. Learns to feel worthy and competent.	If person fails to learn industry, begins to feel inferior compared to others. If overlearns industry, may become too "task oriented" and overconform to society.	Method and competence

V	Adolescence: 12–late teens or early adulthood	Identity versus role confusion	Sexual maturation and sexual identity. Discovers *role* in life; ponders question "who am I?" as distinct from family. Develops social friendships; rejects family.	May not achieve a personal identity separate from family. May not become socially adult or sexually stable.	Devotion and fidelity
VI	Early adulthood	Intimacy versus isolation	Learns to share passions, interests, problems with another individual. Learns to think of "we," "our," "us," instead of "I," "me," "mine." Affiliates with others: family, place of work, community. Achieves stability.	Inability to be intimate with others. Becomes fixated at adolescent level of sensation seeking and self-pleasure. Avoids responsibility. Lacks "roots" and stability.	Affiliation and love
VII	Middle adulthood	Generativity versus stagnation	Transition to transpersonal values. Fosters creativity and growth in others younger than self; provides leadership; seeks to contribute to community, next generation, world. May be most creative period of life.	Becomes "cog-in-wheel," automated. Growth limited; remains rooted in past. May experience breakdown of zest for life. Feels life is passing him or her by.	Production and care
VIII	Old age	Ego identity versus despair	Recognizes and accepts diminished faculties; realizes one's mortality. Feeling of having lived good life and paved the way for future generations. Luminosity of truly "wise" person.	Reaps bitter fruits of what one has or has not sown earlier. Fears death. An old age of misery, anxiety, and despair.	Renunciation and wisdom

SOURCE: Adapted from Erik H. Erikson, *Childhood and Society*

STAGE I: BASIC TRUST VERSUS BASIC MISTRUST. The task to be accomplished in infancy, said Erikson, is *trust*. The infant is virtually helpless. The baby is completely dependent on others to take care of it: feed it, bathe it, protect it from the elements and give it that kind of physical and emotional mothering which will give it the will to live and to accept the world as a kind and loving place. If by some chance, the infant is neglected, abused, or rejected by a mothering figure, it may never learn to trust the world sufficiently to grow in grace—physically or emotionally strong. We know from innumerable studies of children who have not had this kind of mothering that (if they survive at all) they are physically, intellectually, and emotionally stunted. Research has piled up evidence that babies left too long in day-care centers, orphanages, or hospitals tend to be more sickly, more neurotic in their behavior, and academically retarded in school and may even suffer mental illness then or later on in life (Provence and Lipton 1963; Bowlby 1957). Because they were thrown into a world not sufficiently loving, kind, and supportive, they fail to achieve stability out of the "blooming, booming confusion of sights and sounds" that William James called the infant consciousness (James 1950). A sense of order or stability constitutes what is called a strong *ego structure*, and through it we make sense out of the thousands of stimuli received every moment. Without this thread of continuity, a person lives in a torment of confused, unconnected, and meaningless events. Throughout life the world seems to go on doing things to one without rhyme or reason. In extreme cases the lack of ego structure is so extreme that there is little logical continuity in moment-to-moment awareness, and one's waking life is a continuous nightmare, which we call *schizophrenia*. The identity being learned is human-ness: the *drive* to live and the *hope* that sustains human life.

STAGE II: AUTONOMY VERSUS DOUBT AND SHAME. Erikson described this stage as that time when we begin to stand on our own two feet, to do things "by ourselves" and "for ourselves." As infants, all had to be done *for* us, all was done *to* us; we had no choices at this age. But then somewhere between seven months and two years, we begin to move around under our own locomotion, to feed ourselves, to get control of our bodily functions, and to have some control over our life. With the beginning of language we can let the world know our needs and even our desires. "Cookie" or "bye-bye baby" may get us something to eat or lifted into the air. We can say no now, so we have choices available to us that were not available to us in infancy. All of these events, which give us some control over ourselves and our environment, enable us to meet the next life crisis and task, that of *autonomy*.

In addition to learning what they can do for themselves, children also learn what they may *not* do. They may not mess in their pants anymore; they may not hit their baby brothers or throw food on the floor. Thus they learn the "I may dos" and the "I may not dos" that enable them to get along in the world.

If these life tasks are not accomplished, children may remain obedient but passive and dependent on others, on the one hand, or aggressive and rebellious, on the other. If they do not learn that they can say no if they want to, then they will always need permission from someone else to do things and will remain dependent all their lives. (We all know adults who seem to need constant attention from others and who borrow money, clothes, cigarettes from others with no intention of returning them.) On the other hand, if they do not learn that the *world* can say no as well, then they may never get through the egocentric and narcissistic stage of development. They may remain determinedly defiant and self-seeking, forever resisting the conventional rules of society—the kind of adults who always are just a little shady and who gain satisfaction from outwitting the law, suckering other people by winning over them. This is the stage, then, at which children learn the underlying essence of both *yes* and *no*. The *yes* allows children to be spontaneous and self-expressive: the *no* is so they do not always have to test their legal or moral limits, ending up as juvenile delinquents or as adults who remain just outside the law. The identity being learned is self-awareness as a human being. The accomplishments are *self-control* and *will-power*.

STAGE III: INITIATIVE VERSUS GUILT. Somewhere in the age range of three to six, children take another step. They have learned how to take care of their immediate needs; now they learn how to plan ahead, to think in terms of yesterday and tomorrow. They are beginning to have a sense of time, a memory of the past and a concept of the future.

Initiative includes learning how to play with others, how to get two or three friends together and to organize what they will do. They even may plan exactly what they are going to do before they do it. "Let's play house and I'll be the Daddy and you can be the Mommy and Petey can be the baby. And I'll get up and go to work and you'll take care of the baby till I come home . . . and . . . and . . . " This kind of "let's pretend" may go on for a long time; in fact, by the time the children finish planning, they may not play it out at all but go on to jump rope or some other kind of activity. In that case the *planning has been the play itself*. Play enables children to integrate their perceptions of family life into some kind of order.

Children also are not confined to their immediate environment. They are beginning to develop a sense of geography. They learn where their house is and where their friends are, how far they may go and still be able to find their way home. Besides learning the basic elements of geography, they are learning some sense of time. They may not be able to read the clock, but they can sense that it is just about time to go home and turn on a favorite TV program.

They also are getting a sense of themselves. They have learned that there are others in the world and are more willing to share with them, to *cooperate* with the world. If they do not learn to cooperate with others in their society, they tend to be overly competitive, which for an adult takes the form of always "being on the make," wanting to conquer, to take over, or to always be in control. As they learn to initiate and to cooperate, they become the kinds of individuals who are morally responsible and who seek to find niches for themselves in the world, ready to contribute and to do their share for others. If they do not, they remain defiant, not outside the law but constantly sticking their necks out, pitting their physical and mental energies against others, seeking to conquer the opposite sex and to win out over others competitively.

The lasting accomplishments of stage III are those of *self-direction* and *purpose*. The child is now becoming a *moral* human being, one who can successfully adjust his or her (internal) wants and needs with those of the (external) society.

STAGE IV: INDUSTRY VERSUS INFERIORITY.   In primitive societies this passage takes the form of learning the "how tos" of the tribe: if one is an Eskimo, how to catch a seal; if one is a Polynesian, how to spear a fish; if one is an African, how to follow an animal spoor. These tasks prepare children to become industrious members of their society. Through mastering these tasks, children gain a sense of *competence*. If they cannot do what the other members of their tribe can do, they fall prey, Erikson said, to feelings of inferiority.

What are the tasks that children in our society must learn to do to become a functioning member? Erikson said that it is learning the three Rs—how to read and write and manipulate numbers. These skills are necessary to get and keep a job, to take care of household accounts, to pay one's income tax, to keep abreast of the news, to vote, and the like. It is not just the tools of basic literacy that people need. They need the "widest possible basic education" for the greatest number of possible careers.

The identity the person is acquiring in stage IV is that of a *competent* human being, and in fact the child's not only acquiring a sense of competence but is also acquiring a methodology for a competence that he or she does not yet have. Erikson noted how well we Americans enable a person to discover how to do things, via our schools, via our numerous library facilities, via our life-long continuing education, via our mass media with its how-to books, magazines, and TV programs. We are a people who "can" and who "do." If we can't, we know where to go to find out who can help us accomplish what we want. This ability—to make, to design, to build, to engineer, to invent, to improve, to create—has been one of the most conspicuous American characteristics ever since the beginnings of our nation (deTocqueville 1944).

STAGE V: IDENTITY VERSUS ROLE CONFUSION.   The passage through adolescence is another long one, and indeed for some it never ends since those individuals never reach psychological adulthood. They live and die adolescents. We are concerned here, however, with the narrower interpretation of adolescence, which starts somewhere after ten or eleven years of age and continues to early adulthood. The task of the adolescent, according to Erikson, is *identity*. By identity Erikson meant sexual identity, but he also meant our larger identity as well—who one is as a person, what one stands for, and what place one will carve for oneself in society. It is in this adolescent period that the young person begins to ask himself or herself some of those universal questions such as, "Who am I" and "What do I stand for?"

Adolescence is the "big crisis" because it is at the adolescent period that many previous unresolved life crises erupt again in all their demonic and primitive force but now with all the additional thrust and strength of the physically and emotionally powerful adult. It is as if one has the power of the adult but the emotions still of the child. If the process is carried through successfully, however, if parent can weather the "storm and thunder" that accompanies adolescence, one frequently is able to resolve some of the uncompleted tasks of earlier stages.

In the hunt for their own identity adolescents reject their families and frequently all their families' values. But they cannot stand alone, so they cling to their peer groups in groups, adopting each other's styles, clothes, language, walk. In the struggle to find an identity outside the family they try many roles, imitate many persons, and wander through a complex of ideas until they find those that seem best suited to their temperaments and personalities.

Perhaps in no other stage of life can the struggle for identity be so clearly discerned. The specific aspect of the identification process being acquired is that of *self*-identity. With the accomplishment of this task, the two lasting outcomes that follow are *devotion* and *fidelity*. Devotion and fidelity is a course of action, such as a vocational goal.

STAGE VI: INTIMACY VERSUS ISOLATION. Adolescents are concerned with "I," "my," and "me." The world centers on *their* needs, *their* wants, and *their* confusions. It is hard for them to consider the needs of other people. That is the task the young adult needs to accomplish: the ability to think of "we" and "us."

Erikson called the life task associated with this stage *intimacy*, by which he meant not only sexual intimacy and emotional intimacy but also psychological intimacy. One is able to allow other persons within one's world, to think of their needs, desires, hopes, aspirations, and fears, as well as one's own. It is the age at which the individual can say "we" instead of "I," "our" instead of "mine." They share their lives, houses, belongings with others; with a spouse, with children, and with parents if they need their support. Later, the "we" can be extended to one's colleagues, one's community, and one's world.

If adults retreat from this task, they are subject to *isolation*, the inability to be intimate with others. They see others in the world as different from themselves. They develop protective devices to keep others away; they remain disengaged with the world and thus are subject to feelings of loneliness within themselves, prejudice toward others, or alienation from the world.

The type of identification that is being acquired through our young adult years is, according to Erikson, the identification of ourselves as *responsible* human beings. We have gone beyond the self-ness of adolescence and are now willing to extend our caring to others in the world in our personal, professional, or social lives. From this accomplishment comes the ability to genuinely *love* others and to *affiliate* with them.

STAGE VII: GENERATIVITY VERSUS STAGNATION. Middle adulthood is marked by the cessation of those pleasures that brought satisfaction as young adults: the acquisition of possessions, status, home, family, children, recognition, and so forth. At this time the acquisitive motive is no longer dominant. Middle-aged adults have advanced in their jobs as far as they want or will be able to; they have raised their children, who are one by one leaving the nest; they have obtained enough security to satisfy their wants and needs; and they have achieved enough to satisfy their sense of accomplishment.

It is at this point that the individual needs to recognize that another level has been reached. Carl Jung had already noted that it is the time of life when, having taken care of our physical and emotional needs, we must satisfy our spiritual needs. Erikson expressed it differently, but the meaning is similar. He said that at this age, the person needs to know that his or her life is being lived and lived well, not just for himself or herself but in relationship to the whole psychological-social-historical development of humankind. We need to feel that we have contributed to the course of human existence on earth. Sometimes this need is satisfied by parenting.

On a less ordinary level, this need is frequently satisfied by becoming a leader in one's community or organization, one who enables others to take their place in the community or to make that community a better place in which to live. The middle adult learns to generate the growth and creativity of younger persons. Thus Erikson called the life task at this stage **generativity**. Its opposite is **stagnation**.

The identification that is being accomplished here is the identification of oneself as a *transpersonal* human being, one who is aware of the universal themes of life: life and death, the meaning of human existence, and the larger philosophic considerations not of what is useful and pragmatic but of what is enobling and enhancing for one's own heirs or to all the inheritors of life on earth. This transpersonal identity results in the two characteristics of production and care, not for one's own egoistic desires but for others now presently in the world or coming after us.

STAGE VIII. EGO INTEGRITY VERSUS DESPAIR.   The task of old age is the recognition and acceptance of one's diminished faculties, the waning of the life force, and the nearness and reality of death, not with despair, not with bitterness, but with the peace of a life well lived and with a sense of having bequeathed something of significance to other generations.

In this country we do not know very much about this passage. Other, more primitive societies have handled this stage better than we do. Their old people are the keepers of the tribal history, the wise who are the storehouse of the tribal wisdom or the elders to consult when the tribe or a member is in a crisis. Americans, though, reject the idea of age. We send our old people to hospitals or homes for the aged, thus denying them a valid place in our civilization.

In order for us to accomplish the task of old age, we need to have a full, rich, productive, and creative life. The task of old age, like that of infancy, is not achieved in that time span. It needs to have been done before. By old age it is too late. If by that time people have not met all the preceding life crises, and lived and worked through their associated life tasks, then they can only live out their lives with regret or enfeebled in body and mind. The task of old age is, ironically, the reaping of what one has earlier sown. If one has lived life well and with meaning, then one may live out the end peacefully and with the knowledge that one's life has been a significant contribution in the (unfolding of generations).

The identification to be acquired here is that of a (spiritually) *aware* human being, aware that one's own individual life is coming to an end but that life will go on. Erikson calls the outcomes of this awareness *renunciation* and *wisdom*—renunciation of personal desires, which leads to true impersonal wisdom. If the reader thinks that this is a dismal prospect, one can point to the many persons who lived out their old-age with a luminosity and gentleness that made the end of life not a tragic event but as Kübler-Ross has called it, "the final stage of growth." If the reader cannot think of any such persons in his or her own immediate experiences, then we can point to some of the extraordinary historical figures of our Western civilization: Socrates, Diogenes, Plato, Albert Einstein, Eleanor Roosevelt, Albertus Magnus, Blaise Pascal, Benjamin Franklin, Carl Jung, Albert Schweitzer, Jean Piaget, Alfred North Whitehead, Mother Theresa of India—all of whom lived or are living out the end of their lives with a luminosity that has inspired others.

A FINAL NOTE ON ERIKSON'S LIFE STAGES: A FAVORABLE RATIO. Erikson warned us that his developmental stages were somewhat misunderstood by social scientists as *achievement status*; that is, when the person has developed trust in the stage of infancy, that trust is secure for a lifetime. Not at all. "These life tasks," he said, "must not be thought of as "a goodness' " that is "impervious to changing conditions." The life tasks are a continual process of integration as "the personality engages with the hazards of existence," even as we must continue to cope physically with the various processes of metabolism. At every turning point there are moments at which the personality first progresses and then regresses in its struggle to maintain equilibrium.

What Erikson suggested is to think in terms of a **favorable ratio** of (say) basic trust over basic mistrust. Although this task should be accomplished in infancy, there will be times when the person (even at a later stage) may very well lose this favorable ratio and have to learn to integrate that task once more, relative to the new life crisis and life stage. There will be times when all of us suffer from feelings of mistrust, dependence, guilt, shame, or doubt. Furthermore, none of us can or should feel completely autonomous, trusting, industrious, or intimate. We will vary from person to person in our completion of these tasks, as well as from culture to culture. What is important is that enough of these tasks are learned at the critical stage so that when we do suffer setbacks we can draw from the reservoir of that competence to sustain us until the favorable ratio is again accomplished.

Daniel Levinson (and Gail Sheehy): Seasons and Passages of Our Lives

We come now to two other works on our life-cycle development. The first is by a group of researchers at Yale University led by Daniel Levinson (Levinson 1978). Levinson and his associates intensively studied forty men over a period of ten years: their problems, their concerns, their life changes, their aspirations, their disappointments, and their gratifications. What they discovered, it seemed them, was a confirmation of the developmental process throughout a man's life, related *not* to socieconomic level, *not* to profession, *not* even to intelligence, but to age-related factors. These forty men represented widely differing backgrounds, from author to engineer to blue-collar worker. Yet the life crises of these men, although varying with each person, seemed to demonstrate that there is a common, underlying ebb and flow to the fundamental life process.

The second study was done by a journalist, Gail Sheehy (Sheehy 1976), who found herself making significant changes at her own mid-life period and who set out to find if other men and women were experiencing the same kinds of life-shattering crises. Because Sheehy drew so largely from Levinson's work, and because Levinson's work is so much more scientifically precise, we shall devote most of our discussion to the Yale University research results.

THE FOUR GREAT ERAS Like Jung, Levinson divided up the life span into four great eras, which correspond roughly to Jung's great developmental divisions. Levinson compared these eras to the acts of a play or the chapter divisions of a novel in which the writer divides the life of the characters. The sequence of development is defined as follows:

1. Childhood and adolescence: roughly from birth to twenty-two years
2. Early adulthood: roughly from seventeen years to around forty-five years
3. Middle adulthood: roughly from age forty to about sixty-five years (or retirement)
4. Late adulthood: from about sixty years to end of life

The reader will notice that these four great age segments are of twenty to twenty-five years each. Furthermore (and this is of great significance), each age overlaps with the others over a span of four or five years. It is during these overlapping transitional years (late adolescence, age forty to forty-five, and retirement) that the person experiences his or her *major* life changes, and these years are characterized by sweeping destructuring and restructuring of physical, emotional, intellectual, and spiritual existence. Levinson called these great structural changes the **cross-era transitions,** and they are punctuated, so to speak, by what he called marker events: separation from family, marriage, divorce, sickness, and death, rather like vanGennep's "rites of passage." Finally, within each of the great eras there are minor cycles, phases, and transitions. All in all, *Levinson concluded that living is a constant process of structuring, destructuring, and restructuring of life style to meet our changing needs, values, and aspirations.*

In combining all these major eras, cross-era transitions, and other subdivisions, Levinson formulated a developmental model for human life, as seen in box 2.7. Now let us take a closer look at what they entail in terms of life events and developmental tasks.

The early-adult transition. This is, in essence, terminating one's childhood and moving into the early-adult era. Up until this time, the person has been harbored and supported by his or her family. At about seventeen to twenty-two years, the person begins the separation and transformation process necessary to become an adult. The route this separation takes varies according to the individual and his or her socioeconomic background: he or she may leave the home by running away, going to college (or even to a reform school), or entering the armed services. He may even transfer his home to another quasi-home structure with surrogate parents. She may continue living in the parental home until the early twenties or later but still accomplish this developmental task by becoming more socially, economically, and psychologically independent.

This physical separation should lead to the second developmental task, that of gaining a more realistic understanding of the world, the people in it, and of his or her own abilities and values.

The adult era. Having made the painful transition from childhood to adulthood, the person enters the *early-adult period* in which he or she begins the tasks of structuring his or her first *realistic* life choices (many of his or her choices at ages seventeen to twenty-two often are unrealistic and are based more on fantasy than on experience). Most persons now begin to find a vocational niche for themselves, contemplate and enter the marriage and family state, and become independent adults, financially, socially, and psychologically.

The age-thirty transition. Levinson warned that no life structure is ever perfect or permanent. Even if this structure from ages twenty-two to twenty-eight seems, to all intents and purposes, to be successful and "happy," there comes a mid-era transition, at about age thirty, in which the person begins to feel hemmed in by the very successful structure he or she has created. Sheehy called this transition "Catch-30," meaning that the person feels trapped in a tight life structure, the very structure that he or she has spent a decade creating. Some persons may get a divorce at this time; others may decide to find a new job; and still others may go back to school. It is a time of destructure and restructure. Although this particular life crisis is moderate for most persons, some may even hit "rock bottom." How the destructuring process occurs varies with each person. This person may destructure intentionally and thoughtfully, while another person's whole life structure may seem to "come apart at the seams," but both Levinson and Sheehy believed that it will, to some extent, become dismantled.

Age thirty to forty: settling down again. After the age-thirty crisis, most persons seem to settle down into one of their most productive and satisfying new life structures. This age period is associated with career and all its associated values: social status, good salary, esteem as a member of the community, creativity, and a family life that seems to have "quality," that is, to be rewarding and satisfying. Somewhere toward the end of this period (from thirty-five to forty years), most persons are coming into their own at their place of employment; beginning to be accepted as a "voice of authority," and taking on more and more responsibilities at work and in the community.

The mid-life crisis: age forty. Toward the end of the thirties, according to Levinson and Sheehy, there comes another crisis, even more sweeping than the age-thirty transition. Because this transition is such a major one in our society, we shall discuss it more fully. For many years, psychologists and social workers have discussed the "menopausal depression" of women that comes about this time. At this time, many women seem to experience severe depressions that may be tied to hormonal changes or to a feeling that they are losing their youth and sexual attractiveness or that their job as mother and wife seems to be coming to an end with nothing to take its place. Men, too, seem to undergo a psychological crisis, which may take the form of uprooting themselves from family through divorce or psychological separation. They may even change their entire life style and appear to others to have become mentally and emotionally deranged.

Box 2.7 LEVINSON: THE ANATOMY OF THE LIFE CYCLE (RESEARCH ON FORTY MEN IN VARIOUS WALKS OF LIFE)

ERA	MAJOR PERIODS	QUALITY	SOME DEVELOPMENTAL TASKS	SOME ASPECTS OF MAJOR PERIODS
0–22	Early childhood: 0–3 years	Conflicts between self-drive and society.	Distinguishes between the "me" and the "not me." Recognizes validity of other family members.	Center of attention. Harbored and protected by family.
	Transition to middle childhood: 5–6 years	Readjustments necessary to larger world.	Expands awareness of neighborhood, school, peers.	No longer center of attention in family or school.
	Middle childhood: 7–11 years	Period of relative stability.	Becomes disciplined, industrious; learns basic skills.	Has resolved early emotional struggles (family and transition to school, etc.).
	Puberty: 12–13 years	Sweeping physical and emotional changes.	Withdraws emotionally from family attachments.	Conflicts with family.
	Adolescence: 12–17 years		Culminates preadult era.	Beginning of "dreams" about future and self-in-society.
Cross Era	Early adult transition: 17–22 years	Separation from family. Feelings of loss and anxiety about future.	Terminates and moves away from childhood, tests some initial life choices (rarely realistic; much fantasy).	Establishes new home site: college, military, training school, running away. Initial choices involving much movement: job to job, college to college, place to place.
22–50		A "novice adult."	Forms a "life/dream scheme" and makes provisional life structure.	Takes on responsibilities.
	Entrance into adult world: 22–28 years	Creation of first stable, realistic life structure.	Forms mentor relationships. Forming an occupation. Forms love relationships, marriage and family.	Has learned much from unrealistic choices and experiences of 17–22 age period. Establishes home base.
	Age 30 transition: 28–30 years	Some modification of first life structure.	Works out flaws of 22–28-year period; revises life dream/scheme. Creates more satisfactory life structure.	"Marker events" may have changed sense of self, death of one or both parents, love affair, divorce. Begins to think "If I'm to make something of myself, I'd better do it now."

	Period			
	Settling down: 33–40 years	Beginning of new stability. Becoming "one's own person." Voice of authority; may be senior member at work.	Renews commitments to work, family, friends, and community. Redefines dream/scheme as a personal enterprise. Culmination of early adulthood.	Career ladder becomes important. Now a "junior" executive. "Quality of life" becomes important: home, family, friends.
Cross Era	Midlife transition: 40–50 years	Destructuring process and upheavals. Moderate to severe crises.	Reappraises life and goals. Provides a bridge to middle adulthood. Begins to flail against established conventions and structures.	"What have I done with my life?" "What do I really want from my job, family, wife, children, life?" May appear to others as "sick" or "irrational."
40–65	Entrance into middle adulthood: 45–50 years	Beginning of new stability but marked by events that influence life: drastic job change, divorce, love affair, serious illness, death of loved ones.	Violent upheavals of midlife transition cease. Builds a new life structure. Begins tasks of individuation.	Some make viable adjustments to world but not to self so that inner life has no meaning. They resign, decline, and fail to make adequate new life structure.
	Age 50 transition: 50–55 years	Moderate readjustments (similar to age 30 transitions).	Modifies 45–50-year life structure work later in mid-life transition.	May be a crisis time for those who changed too little at midlife transition.
	Culmination of middle adulthood: 50–60 years	Stable period (analogous to "settling down" period of late thirties).	Builds a middle-adult structure; rejuvenates self.	For those who can "individuate" successfully, this period may be beginning of great fulfillment.
Cross Era	Late adult transition: 60–65 years	Major turning point of one's life.	Terminates middle adulthood; creates basis for late adulthood. Must release authority and "center stage." Infirmity increases.	Because no longer "center stage," capable now of illumined wisdom. Increasing frequency of death and serious illness of loved ones, friends, colleagues.

SOURCE: Adapted from Daniel J. Levinson and others, *Seasons of a Man's Life* (New York: Alfred A. Knopf, 1978).

What is happening, said Levinson, is that these persons are beginning to discover how much of their lives are based on illusion (what the Indians call *maya*). They are suffering from disillusionment. Suddenly all the values that they have esteemed seem empty and meaningless. Furthermore, they must solve four *polarities* that now exist in their lives, the kinds of polarities that Carl Jung stressed so often (Jung 1953).

Resolving the mid-life polarities. The first polarity the person must solve is the *young/old polarity*. Although the man, at forty, feels himself to be still young and is not ready to join the "middle-aged" generation, he finds that younger persons are beginning to address him more respectfully and to consider him as one of the older generation. The second polarity pertains to the *destruction-creation polarity*, which seems to include the awareness of his own death. At about age forty he may be experiencing the deaths of one or more of his parents, grandparents, relatives, and close friends, all of which brings his own mortality a little closer. Such awareness makes him suddenly and acutely conscious of what he has done to hurt others (parents, children, spouse, colleagues, friends), and he wonders how to make amends. He becomes aware of love and the richness or lack of it in his own life. He wonders also how to be more creative, to participate in human welfare, and to give of himself to the world. The third polarity is that of *femininity-masculinity*. For much of his life, a man may have denied much of his "feminine" side (his tender, loving, emotional feelings), preferring to put his psychic energies into work and achievement. Now he may begin to allow himself to do more nurturing things or to express the artistic and creative aspects that have heretofore been suppressed. Finally, he resolves the polarity of *attachment-separateness*, which Carl Jung called the search for the soul and things of the spirit. Material and worldly success becomes less of a motivation, and the person seeks to relate to transcendent values. If he has been estranged from relatives and friends, he may now seek a rapprochement. If he has been tyrannized by personal ambition, he now may devote himself to supra-personal concerns and projects, to community projects, to charitable organizations, or to worldwide causes.

The continuing process. Levinson described what happens after the forty-to-forty-five transition. There is again another "settling down" period during the fifties. Then yet another transition, and so on. (See box 2.8.) So it goes throughout our lives, according to Levinson and Sheehy; it is a matter of "changing seasons" and "passages," life cycles and stages. We build what we think is a good, viable, and permanent life structure. But no life structure that we make can ever be either perfect or permanent. We are part of a constant process of examining what is faulty and out of proportion in our current life structure, of destructuring what is no longer valuable or significant, and of exploring ways to restructure our lives so that we can live our next years more creatively. It is not easy. Transitions frequently involve feelings of being uprooted and alienated. Change is never easy, but the alternative is *stagnation*.

Box 2.8 SHEEHY'S PASSAGES OF ADULT LIFE

AGE	STAGE	QUESTIONS	CRISIS	SUCCESSFUL RESOLUTION
Late adolescence (18–22 yrs)	"Pulling Up Roots"	"Who am I?" "How can I establish my own identity distinct from my family?"	The grass is greener elsewhere. (I have to get away from family/hometown to college/ service/ "see the world"/ anywhere but here.)	May have many false starts but begins to feel self-supportive and a person in own right.
Early Adulthood	"The Trying Twenties"	"How do I put my aspirations into effect?"	Faces enormous tasks of mastering life work, getting a family started, and establishing self in community.	If successful, person has sense of stability, putting down roots.
Age 30	"Catch-30"	"What kind of a trap have I gotten myself into?"	A feeling of "rock-barren" and a general tearing down of life choices built in twenties.	Can be a time of new vision, life partnership, aspirations.
34–45	"The Deadline Decade"*	"Why am I doing all this?"	Experience the waning of youth, failure of physical powers, attractiveness.	Person can arrive at a new authenticity of self.
After 45	"Renewal or Resignation"	"What can I do with the rest of my life?"	Parents may have died; children have grown up and left home; job is not "a dream of possibility" but just a job.	New wisdom and understanding. Parents are forgiven their inadequacies, children their selfishnesses, and friends are more important.
After 50	More Critical Learnings	"What have I done with my life?"	Sense of desolation.	More objectivity about life, more willingness to be oneself—"less facade."

*Sheehy believed this deadline came earlier for women (age 35) than for men (40 to 45 yrs).

SOURCE: Adapted from Gail Sheehy. *Passages* (New York: E. P. Dutton & Co., Inc., 1976).

THE COGNITIVE DEVELOPMENT OF THE PERSON

Up to this point in our discussion, we have focused primarily on the emotional and social growth of the individual. But human beings are more than emotional and social organisms. We also think! Psychologists call the process of "thinking" the **cognitive** process, just as they call our emotional experiencing the **affective** process. Philosopher-psychologists down through the ages have been fascinated by the cognitive process of humankind. The fact that we can talk, plan ahead, create a social order with commandments and laws and rules for living together is what truly distinguishes Homo sapiens from other life forms on this earth. But despite the centuries of speculation about how it is that we are able to deal in the highly abstract areas of numbers and linguistic concepts, it is only in recent years that psychologists have gotten a foothold on how this cognitive process develops in humankind. Our emotions are more evident. They are more visible. They can be observed. We can see how people laugh, cry, become depressed, express joy and delight. We can observe how emotions are developed from infancy up to adulthood. People can talk about emotions. Granted we may make some powerfully wrong inferences about what we are observing, but at least there are external manifestations of our emotional functioning.

Thinking is a process that is much more hidden, indirect, and complex. It is so indirect and complicated a process that the medieval Church considered the mind to be "mysterious," "supernatural" and divine: a part of the soul. Since it was part of the divine soul, it was under the aegis of the Church—the Church's province. To try to study the mind scientifically would be to hazard being brought before the dreaded Inquisition for heresy, and if found guilty, one would have been condemned to torture, death, and (a fate far worse than death) eternal damnation (Fancher 1979).

It wasn't until the mid-eighteenth century that scientific headway was made. The locale was Germany, and the German philosopher-scientists who made the first scientific advances did it by investigating how our senses operate: how we see, how we hear, how we taste, feel, experience pain. Since it is through the physical senses that we "take in" information from the world, they reasoned, by learning how to measure our sight, hearing, and gustatory senses, we could begin to understand how we come to know what we know.

But that assumption was naive. As exciting as their discoveries were, it had to be admitted that *measuring our sense perceptions is not the same as knowing how human beings think.* After all, even animals have the same kinds of sensory processes as we do; some, in point of fact, have even more sophisticated senses than human beings. Yet, they do not *think* as we do. It was obvious that if psychology was ever going to make a deeper foray into the "mysterious" territory of the mind and the thought processes that go on therein, it was going to take a giant of a philospher-scientist to lead the way. That giant turned out to be a Swiss psychologist by the name of Jean Piaget.[2] Piaget's method was not to study the sensory or cognitive processes in adults but to study how the cognitive process *develops* in children from birth to adolescence.

Jean Piaget has now become such a famous face and figure to psychologists all over the world that one book devoted to his work has on its cover an abstract design consisting of nothing but a French beret, a meerschaum pipe, horn-rimmed spectacles, and a bicycle! Psychologists the world over easily recognize to whom these appurtenances belong. Well, he is famous now, and highly respected, but it took American psychology many decades before it could award him an honored place in our (apocryphal) Psychology Hall of Fame. As is the fate with so many revolutionary thinkers, his theoretical formulations were for a long time regarded with much skepticism by his colleagues and fellow scientists. For what Piaget was saying was that children are not simply smaller and younger editions of adults in their thinking processes. In fact, they do not think like adults—at all! They have distinctly *qualitative* differences in their mediational processes when compared to those of the adult. They live in worlds phenomenologically different from ours, rather as if they are a different life-form or species with their own distinctly different paralogic.

Piaget explained that from birth to adulthood, the human being goes through four separate organizations of mind, each of which is distinctly and *qualitatively* different from the other, i.e., different in *kind* of information processing, not just in degree. Piaget was a biologist before he became a psychologist, and he dared to present the idea that these four reorganizations of mind are *actually evolutionary quantum leaps of consciousness*. These four evolutions of consciousness must take place, according to Piaget, before a child can begin to think in the logical, rational manner of an adult. Because we are dealing with Piaget's contribution to cognitive growth and its influence on personality function, we will keep our discussion focused on the broad qualitative aspects of a child's psychology. Piaget is difficult to comprehend at first reading. For this reason, we will present his work in its most "psychological" sense for easier first-reading comprehension.

Piaget: Four Stages of Cognitive Development

1. THE SENSORY-MOTOR STAGE (BIRTH TO TWENTY-FOUR MONTHS). The newborn baby, according to Piaget, is really nothing more than a rather unorganized entity that has only very primitive sensory functioning but strong primitive reflexes (the reflexes of sucking, swallowing, and so on). The baby is not at all "conscious," and in that Piaget agrees with most psychologists including Freud, William James, and J. B. Watson. A newborn can see light and dark, focus on moving objects, and feel the pangs of hunger or the press of a nipple in its mouth. But these sensations are not connected; in fact they are very disconnected fleeting sensory impressions that are "happening" somewhere and to someone but not even to "a self." These sensations are being experienced, but they have little meaning except as vague "comfort" or "discomfort" or something light or something moving. But there is no consciousness. There is not even an "external" reality or "internal" reality such as we adults have.

Box 2.9   JEAN PIAGET: STAGES OF COGNITIVE AND MORAL DEVELOPMENT

STAGE (AGE)	COGNITIVE DEVELOPMENT CHARACTERISTICS	MORAL DEVELOPMENT CHARACTERISTICS
1. Sensory-Motor (birth to twenty-four months)	No mediation at birth. No object, shape, size permanence. No external or internal connectedness. Just fleeting sensations. The infant is driven by sensory-motor reflexes. Little by little, objects begin to have meaning, stability, and permanence. Eventually, the child begins to have a sense of space and time (even if limited) and to be able to hold an abstract idea in mind: ergo, child has come to live in a human world and to be able to think and use language.	None.
2. Preoperational (two to about seven-and-one-half years)	The child is able to make *choices* and has a mediated intelligence, even though primitive and characterized by animistic, functional, and egocentric thinking. Able to classify and seriate along one dimension but cannot hold two abstract ideas, and so cannot decentrate as yet.	Stage of moral reality or morality of constraint. The child is aware that there are rules which are not to be disobeyed but not the reasons for the rules. Punishment for disobedience is harsh and rigid and immediate and has little to do with crime. The child is centrated on *effect*; unable to consider motivation or extenuating circumstances.
3. Concrete Operations (seven-and-one-half to about twelve years)	Child is able to hold two abstract ideas in mind at the same time, so can decentrate and understand principles of reversibility and classifications which allows the child to understand concrete operations of simple arithmetic and algebraic operations. Thinking is still *concrete* in that hypothetical thinking is very difficult if not impossible for child.	Stage of moral relativity. The child can now appreciate another person's point-of-view and can consider extenuating circumstances. Justice is tempered somewhat by mercy. The punishment befits the crime. At about 10 years of age, the child becomes fascinated by the "rules of the game," as preparation toward responding to societal laws, rules, and regulations.
4. Formal Operations (about twelve years to adulthood)	Reasoning can be more sophisticated. Child is able to reason inductively as well as deductively. Can approach problem from logical experimental base rather than through trial-and-error. Can make many mental operations necessary for geometry, scientific thinking, and hypothesis making.	With the understanding that rules are made by people, the child becomes more compassionate in world view. Becomes interested in *principles* of human *behavior* just as cognitively he has become interested in *principles* of arithmetic and *geometric operations*. Mental and moral development continue to go hand-in-hand.

Now so far, this sounds like the Aristotelian idea of a wax tablet or the Lockean idea of a blank slate or even the Freudian idea of the unconscious. And to some extent that is so. But all of these theorists and others, too, like Pavlov and B. F. Skinner (who formulated our first concepts of conditioning) place all, or almost all, of our ensuing cognitive growth of associations (concepts and ideas) upon the sensory-emotional stimulation we receive from our external environment. Piaget does not. He insists that there is something *inborn* in animate life that seeks to *organize our sensory data into meaningful perceptions* and *to act upon them.* Even the newborn, almost completely reflex-dominated, is organizing these internal and external sensations into comprehensive units of perception. There could be no association or ideas thrust upon a baby's sensory-perceptive cortex if there weren't something **innate** in the mechanism of our central nervous system that responds to these sensory data and is actually *seeking* them. Sound, no matter how loud it is, makes no impression on deaf ears. This *innate* characteristic of animate life is where Piaget turns the corner from the strict "environmentalists." What he is doing, in fact, is melding the "genetic" camp with the "environmentalist" camp in what has been called an **interactionist** viewpoint.

During the course of the first few months, the moving objects that come within a baby's visual focus become face-objects or bottle-objects or things-that-shine-and-jingle-objects. The fact that the baby begins to recognize these objects brings smiles to his face and he *acts* upon them. Now we are getting to the crux of the first of Piaget's stages. The infant is a *sensory-motor being.* There is no thinking as such. The infant's *organization* of *mind* has no "*mediation.*" His sensory attention is caught by objects or noises or pressure, and he responds to them. *He has no choice* to do otherwise. Put a bunch of shiny keys in front of a four- or five-month-old baby so that her visual attention is riveted upon them, and she will then hold out her hand and try to grab them. If she is successful she will probably try to put them into her mouth. She is like a cat that *must* respond to something moving—by crouching, leaping, and attacking the moving object.

Eventually a baby will begin to attach meanings to the objects or sounds that cross his visual field or penetrate his hearing. We have said that the undifferentiated visual objects are becoming face-objects and bottle-objects and foot-objects. But these differentiated objects still appear and disappear, and when they disappear, they are "gone." They no longer exist. The three-month-old child is in a permanent here-and-now. Sometime later, around six to eight months, objects will begin to have existence whether or not the baby sees them, and psychologists call this *object permanence.* He will continue to hunt for a set of shiny keys when they are hidden in front of him. So now we know there is some *continuity of time* developing, even if it is only a few seconds in duration. He can remember that the *keys were here just a moment ago,* which is the beginning of the evolution of past time, however brief. He is also developing a sense of *space* and will look under a cloth for the keys. Now when we begin to function with the human dimensions of time and space, we are on the verge of our adult human reality. But not quite. Other events must also come to pass; for example, *future* time and the ability to use *symbols* have to be mastered. By eleven months of age, these two aspects of human cognition *are* developing. What Piaget discovered in regard to these phenomena can be illustrated by one of his observations of his own children.

One day his eleven-month-old daughter was watching her mother putting on a hat and suddenly began to cry. That was what was happening on the surface. Underlying these behaviors, Piaget realized, was the fact that the child recognized that the mother was about to leave and was unhappy with this prospect. But Piaget's genius was such that he further recognized an even deeper underlying phenomenon: the process of the mother's putting on her hat had become symbolic to the child. The child recognized in this event that her mother was about to leave. This event, by the way, illustrates something beyond memory and association. The child had now developed a sense of *future time*: Mommy is putting on her hat = she *will be* gone soon. A *symbolic* understanding in *future tense*.

Intelligence as choice. It is this symbolic achievement that marks the *end of the sensory-motor period* at the age of two, according to Piaget, involving, as it does, the ability to *think about a sensory experience instead of being driven to act upon it*. Consider this event. A child of just under two, shall we say, has had a

---

Box 2.10	**SYMBOLS AND THE "MIRACLE OF LANGUAGE"**

With the ability to use symbols comes the ability to use language. For that is what language is—a series of sounds uttered by the various tissues and organs of our mouth, throat, and lungs that are interpreted in the cerebral cortex as a specific object. "Say aaah," says the doctor, probing your throat with his wooden tongue depresser. (There is nothing inherently meaningful in sounds, per se.) Dutifully, you say "aaah." Now say "aaah" again, but this time start the sound with your lips closed, and you will hear the two sounds put together, which will sound like "maaaaaah." If you have accomplished this, repeat the process twice in rapid succession. If you do this demonstration in reasonably distinct fashion, you are now uttering four previously meaningless sounds together, which now comes out as the first word most infants utter. In many languages this word stands for (symbolizes) one particular object: Mama. It is, moreover, the easiest combination of four sounds it is possible to make, since it consists of the mere opening and closing of the lips under the pressure of a voiced exhalation of breath. With that first utterance the child has begun to acquire the human ability to communicate symbolically to others.

The ability to use (symbolic) language was no small accomplishment for early humankind. With that achievement in the dawn of time, the human race went on to develop the ability to count, to categorize, to read and write, to record its past, to engage in trade and commerce, and develop culture. Through these endeavors arose the great civilizations of human history. For that reason this human ability (which so clearly demarcates us from other life forms) has been called "the gift and the miracle of language."

---

sharp and painful experience with a pin-object. At six months of age, the child might still have been compulsively driven by his see-reach-grab-put-in-mouth schema and been pricked or even badly cut. He had no *choice* but to complete that reflex-driven primitive schema. But by two years of age, he can look at the pin-object and hold the symbolic idea in his head: *pin*. Now the child has what psychologists call the ability to **mediate** between his sensory discovery of the pin-object and his motor reaction. The child can now walk away from the pin. Or he can simply think "Pin . . . no-no . . . don't touch." Or he can point to it and call for his mother and say, "Pin, Mommy, pin," and mother quickly picks it up and puts it away. The two-year-old has thus three other possible **adaptations** to the pin-object: At three months of age, he had none, only the compulsion to see-reach-grab-etc. Notice, too, that what Piaget calls adaptations can also be called *alternative actions* or *choices*. It is this ability to symbolize, together with the ability to make choices, that Piaget calls *thinking*. In fact, *Piaget equates choice with intelligence*. The more choices we have, the more adaptive responses any of us have to situations, the more intelligent we are. This concept of choice is one we will return to again and again in the ensuing chapters. The fact that the child can make *intelligent* choices—at least between *this* possible action and *that* possible action—and can consider the consequences of these acts is for Piaget the indication that there is occurring an *evolutionary shift in consciousness* : a whole new organization of mind, to what he called the *preoperational* stage.

2. THE PREOPERATIONAL STAGE (FROM TWO TO ABOUT SEVEN-AND-ONE-HALF YEARS).   It may not be difficult for the reader to understand the sensory-motor functioning of infancy as being *qualitatively* distinct in experience from adult consciousness. After all, we know that babies are babies and can't *think*. But what about older children, say four or five years of age? Our ancestors used to regard them as simply little grownups and dressed them accordingly (Aries 1965). Are children of this age so radically different from us? They walk and converse with us, sometimes quite intelligibly. But their consciousness is childlike. It is, says Piaget, *egocentric, functional*, and *animistic,* much like the world view of primitive humankind (chapter 1, page 7). What Piaget means by these terms needs to be understood.

The egocentric world of childhood. By egocentric Piaget does not intend the connotation of selfishness, as we so often do. What Piaget means is a kind of thinking in which the child views the world from her or his point of view—and no other. Let us give a common Piagetian example. Suppose you place a three-year-old child in front of a table with several objects on it, objects such as a teddy bear, a book, a ball, and a doll. Now suppose you arrange the objects so that the *book is nearest to the child,* and the other objects are scattered elsewhere, with the *teddy bear nearest to you*. If you ask our three-year-old what object is nearest to him, he will correctly say that the book is nearest to him. Now suppose you pick up the doll and hold it on your lap, and ask the child what the doll can see that is nearest to her. The child will still say *it is the book*.

Or have any of you had this experience with a three- or four-year old? She runs in excitedly to show you a picture she has drawn and holds up the blank side of the sheet, with the drawing facing herself. When you say, "Hold it so we can see it," she doesn't turn it around. She merely holds it up higher in the air or comes closer to you, the blank side still *facing you!*

The functional world of childhood. The paralogic of a child's mind extends to his concepts about the phenomena of the universe. All events in nature are interpreted in terms of the child's egocentric point of view. Things exist *for* or *against* him. Why does night come? So he can sleep. Why does snow fall? So he can build a snowman or make snowballs. Why is there sand on the beach? So he can dig. If it rains, somebody or something is being MEAN to him because now he can't go out to play. This need to find reasons for events is part and parcel for his seemingly endless "why" questions at the age of four. He believes every event has a function that is related to him.

The animistic world of childhood. Children live in an animistic world of magical and fairy-tale thinking. What is magical, fairy-tale thinking? It is the belief that things happen to us *without* logic, *without* cause, and *without* reason. It is not the rational world of cause and effect. It is the world view that events happen of their own accord or because something mysteriously makes them happen. If things go wrong, it is because the evil forces in the world (like demons, witches, and malevolent spirits) have cast a spell upon us; if things go well, we are the fortunate recipients of a fairy godmother. It is a world in which good and bad are absolutes. People who oppose our wishes seem to the primitive consciousness to be the forces of evil; those who advance our aims and fulfill our desires are viewed as the forces of good. It is the simplistic thinking and two-dimensional world of early humankind. It is also the kind of thinking that puts the control of our lives (as well as the responsibility for our actions) outside ourselves.

Suppose children are asked why they did something. They cannot answer. They do not know themselves. Something "made" them do it, or somebody told them to; after all, they could not have done it of their own free will! They do not know how it happened. As a matter of fact, some children will deny that they did it. Having said that, it becomes the truth (for them)! It happened "of its own accord"—as in the fairy-tale world in which anything can appear or disappear, inanimate objects talk, and witches put spells on you![3]

Preoperational children, particularly in the two-to-five-year-old period, live in a world in which play and dreams and fantasy and our waking reality have no clearly demarcated lines. Children pass from one of these states of consciousness to another without effort and are not always aware which is which. The three-year-old who wakes up with a nightmare is not at all certain that she has been really dreaming; the monster in her dreams is still very real, as real as her parents, who are now trying to soothe her and telling her no such monster exists. The little boy who is playing "airplane" by himself changes his identity within miliseconds from Tommy to the airplane to the pilot steering to the bombadier ready to let bombs go—and he may even be the bomb itself! WOW! CRASH! Who can say which of these identities at the moment is more "real" and "rational"?

The world will bcome more real and rational in the next stage.

3. THE STAGE OF CONCRETE OPERATIONS (SEVEN-AND-ONE-HALF TO ABOUT TWELVE YEARS). We come now to the next evolution of human consciousness, according to Piaget. *If the stage of preoperations is characterized by the ability to hold one abstract idea or one physical property in the mind, then the outstanding characteristic of the third stage is the ability to hold two concrete ideas or two physical properties in the mind.* What this means is that the child will now understand certain physical relationships he or she was not able to perceive previously.

The eight-year-old child will easily be able to *classify* or *categorize* objects according to *two* relationships. Suppose you ask a child to sort a variety of toy objects that look like fruit, tableware, furniture, and cards, putting everything that has to do with *eating* in one group. The child of four may pick up the objects that look like cookies and bananas and other fruit, but she will not be able to identify the toy spoons, forks, and knives as having to do with eating. The eight-year-old will be able to add these objects to the larger classification of eating. Or suppose you ask a four-year-old and an eight-year-old to sort white and black triangles, circles, and squares into just *white circles*. The eight-year-old will do it without a moment's hesitation. "That's easy!" he will announce with a sense of pride and then wait expectantly for the next problem you give him. The four-year-old may start off with a white circle and maybe even another white circle, but suddenly her attention will be caught by the whiteness (she can't hold the circle property in mind too long), and she may add a white square and a white triangle. (Now she is responding to the white property.) Then noticing she has a line of objects, she may well add anything that comes to mind and say, "See? I made a train."

The four-year-old can count, but the eight-year-old has a concept of numbers that is more than rote memory of a sequence of sounds: She has a comprehension of additive and subtractive properties and their relationship to multiplication (which is really shorthand counting) and division (which is really shorthand subtraction). The four-year-old who cried because her brother got twenty-five "monies" (twenty-five pennies) and she only got one "money" (one quarter) has grown up to be a sturdy eight-year-old. She doesn't mind getting a quarter now, at all, even if her brother gets two dimes and a nickel because she understands these kinds of transformations. Because she has grasped the concept of additive and subtractive properties, she is ready for beginning algebraic functions. Now thus far we have discussed the child's ability to deal with the operations of reversibility and classification. But what has all this to do with the child's phenomenology? Well, for one thing, the child is beginning to understand how something may be perceived by another person. For example, the child now has a sense of fairness and even a sense of justice. The five-year-old may have dim intuitions of equality, particularly if it involves his fair share. "Jeannie got two cookies, so I should get two cookies." But now he can see things from another point of view. He can remember that he got a cookie that morning and Jeannie didn't, so now he can say, "Jeannie should get two and I should get one."

At this stage children now understand that adults have problems, too, and can be unhappy. They can be more sympathetic to a classmate and side with the "underdog." The ability to see things less egocentrically means they can appreciate the problems of others less fortunate, and they can be somewhat compassion-ate toward the poor, the hungry, the sick, and the handicapped. They are willing to try to help, and they will, given the opportunity. What then is lacking in their evolution to adult consciousness? Just this: They are rooted in the pragmatic solu-tions of everyday events. They respond very well to ideas or solutions presented to them by others or that they have read about. But they are not yet capable of formulating new solutions to ideas or inducing a *higher* principle from several facts. That must wait for the stage of formal operations.

4. THE STAGE OF FORMAL OPERATIONS (ABOUT TWELVE YEARS TO ADULT-HOOD). The last stage begins just about at the age of puberty and continues, according to Piaget, for the rest of a person's life. It is only in this stage that the individual is capable of those kinds of cognitive abilities that are associated with what we call analysis, logic, and hypothetical and scientific reasoning. What is the essential element here? Just this: the ability to derive *new* ideas, to think up *new* solutions, to abstract from the available data new approaches to problems. If the child in the stage of concrete operations could consider two ideas or properties, they were ideas or properties rooted in concrete reality, something the child had already experienced. Now the young adolescent is capable of something more. He is capable of deducing and inducing, so to speak, some possibility not yet in his adaptive repertory of behaviors. Let us consider a classic Piagetian example.

A basin of water is presented to the child. She is asked to classify the objects as to whether they will float and to explain the basis of her classification. Then she is encouraged to go ahead with her experiment and when she has sorted them out into two piles, she is asked to state a law or principle that explains the reason that some objects float and some do not float. (We are oversimplifying the example for the sake of clarity.)

The preoperational child will find a specific but **paralogical** answer. Her an-swer may go something as follows:

"I don't know" (with a shrug of confusion).
"Because this one can float and that one can't."
"Because it wants to float?"

At the stage of concrete operations, the child will easily say that these objects are heavy and those objects are not. So far so good. But now the child may be confron-ted with another factor. More objects are placed in the basin of water and some of the large objects do float and some of the small objects don't float. Of course, what is operating here is Archimedes' famous law of floating bodies: An object will float if its specific gravity is less than 1.00—if its density is less than that of water. But the eight-year-old is puzzled. He is confused by the fact that his previous classifi-cation system is not working. He may give up without a reason or he may even regress to the functional level of the preoperational child. If the child is, say, ten or eleven years of age, he may have an intuition that there is a principle involved that he does not know about, and he may even make some vague approach to it.

"Well, it is bigger but it is lighter, I guess." But he is not sure why it is "lighter." He hasn't yet acquired the third principle to add another classification to the law of floating bodies. That would require an inductive process, which he is beginning to sense; but it hasn't been crystallized, even at the end of this stage of cognitive development.

The fifteen- or sixteen-year-old will easily grasp the essential element, *density*. He may have already had it in school in his physics course. But what about the twelve- or thirteen-year-old who has not learned it as a scientific law and who is just entering into the last stage? That is interesting. Here are some of the possible responses.

"The wooden object [the larger one] has holes inside so it is lighter."
"The iron object [the smaller one] is really heavier."
"It needs more lightness inside. The bigger one has air in between."
"The small one is more solid and sinks. The large one isn't as heavy as the water."

Obviously the child is grasping the principle of water displacement or density—even if he cannot name it. He is, as a matter of fact, coming upon a newly formulated consciousness that he has never had before right there on the spot. That is precisely what is involved in formal operations. *He is operating on his operations*—evolving new principles and laws for himself. It is this last evolution of cognition that allows humans not only to make observations about what can be easily seen but to infer what is not so easily observable. This level of pattern recognition is necessary for creative invention.

A Final Synopsis of Cognitive Development

The stage theory of mental development indicates that there is a *readiness* for certain learnings, which according to Piaget, ought not to be pushed but should be allowed to develop in its own time. (We Americans do have a tendency to push our children into more and more sophisticated situations.) One American psychologist says that pushing develops a sense of inferiority (Erikson 1950).

For example, if the stage of formal operations is the first time a child can deal adequately with hypotheses making and inductive reasoning (which happens at about eleven to fourteen years of age, depending on the child), what are we doing to our children when we introduce such situations to our fourth graders, who are nine or ten years of age? It could be that the frustration the average child feels when he only dimly comprehends what the teacher is saying is setting up the child to experience the sense of *inferiority* that Erik Erikson is concerned about. Many American psychologists and educators are, fortunately, sensitive to this question. They have been doing research on *reading readiness* for the major part of the twentieth century. But the lay public is not sensitive to this question. Boards of trustees and legislators all too frequently urge that more and more information (they call it the basics) be administered to children earlier and earlier in order to "keep pace" with the Russians or the Chinese or the whomever. Books on the

Piaget stresses that we allow the child to progress at his own pace and not try to hurry his cognitive/moral development.

market are advertising turning babies into geniuses by starting their education in the crib. Our desire to push our children and speed up their natural Piagetian process, results, says David Elkind, in the syndrome of the "hurried child" (Elkind 1981). While some very bright children are able to be "speeded up," some clinical and child psychologists are particularly disturbed over this phenomenon because of the tragic results that have occasionally been reported.

Finally, Piaget helped us to see that moral development cannot develop before cognitive development. Children's mental perceptions must enlarge before they can become truly ethical persons. And for that understanding we turn now to Piaget's studies in the moral development of children.

THE MORAL EVOLUTION OF THE CHILD: ALSO A DEVELOPMENTAL PROCESS

So we come now to another aspect of human behavior that has perplexed social scientists for over a century; namely, how do we develop a system of morality, or a set of guiding principles, or an ethical system? Call it what you will, the human race has created many kinds of social orders and belief systems by which people have lived together and died together—governed themselves by various kinds of leadership, ranging all the way from despotic dictatorships to the myriad forms of democracy that exist in the world today. It is characteristic of the human race to establish written edicts, ordinances, laws, and commandments to govern the interactions of persons and to erect also a network of *social sanctions* for reasonable, ethical guidelines for delicate interpersonal behaviors. These guidelines are called **mores**. How a person comes to act out what his or her *culture* deems appropriate is called by Abraham Maslow **enculturation** (Maslow 1970). The specific ways that parents, siblings, and teachers implement this enculturation is more usually called by psychologists the **socialization** process.

Sigmund Freud

We have already had some introduction to the process of morality in our previous discussions of Sigmund Freud. But it is well, at this point, to recap briefly. Freud viewed the human being as coming into the world not as an "angel from heaven" (as Victorian literature often described the baby) but as an unconscious being (**id**) driven by the libidinal instinct toward his or her own self-pleasure (the pleasure-pain principle), who rails fiercely at restrictions to his or her immediate self-pleasure. What turns this savage instinctual being into a moral being is the weaning and toilet-training process and the many ways in which the adults lay down admonitions, prohibitions, warnings, and such. Eventually, all these events are **introjected** (*internalized*) into the child's psyche and become the superego, or conscience. From these two oppositional forces in the psychosexual development of the child is formed the *ego* (our consciousness). Freud maintained always that the beleaguered ego is the eternal battlefield upon which these two conflicting pressures (what one would *like* to do and what one has been taught one *should not* do) are played out, and this forms our **character** (Freud 1933).

The Hartshorne and May Studies

One of the first scientific explorations of children's morality was done in the twenties and carried out in New York City public schools from grade 1 to grade 8 (Hartshorne and May 1928–30). The psychologists defined morality by such terms as *honesty, trustworthiness* and *self-control*. What they discovered was that young children will steal (money or candy) or cheat (look at test answers on the teacher's desk) if they have opportunity and if they think they will not get caught—*all* young children. Little by little, over the course of time, as they progress from grade 1 to grade 8, they begin to develop what we call honesty and trustworthiness and self-control. They do it by getting caught and, probably, by the constant admonitions of what will happen if they do get caught. Morality, too, they concluded, is something that develops over time, bit-by-bit.

Moreover, they discovered that *morality seems to be* **situational.** A child might do something "wrong" in a public school that he would not do in Sunday School. Or he might think it wrong to steal from "old Mr. Swenson" at the neighborhood grocery store, but "it's not so bad" to shoplift from the big department store downtown—after all, "they're rich and won't miss it!"

Thus our concept of what is moral and what is not does not necessarily generalize from one situation to another and, in fact, develops piecemeal, so to speak, with gaping spaces in between. Even as adults we may be scrupulous in our personal dealings with people we know, but we may not believe that it is necessarily wrong to evade income taxes or we may be a bit unscrupulous in our business ethics (Hassett 1981).

Piaget: The Moral Reasoning of the Child

Piaget's conclusion to this moral paradox is that cognitive and moral development go hand-in-hand and the development of moral/ethical standards is also an age/stage function.

MORALITY OF REALISM AND RESTRAINT.   Piaget concluded that before the stage of concrete operations—before the child is seven or eight—the child can have no *real* morality, i.e., an *internalized* code of ethical principles. Children as young as three years of age can learn the rules and commandments and laws. But these rules exist simply because they have been told they exist—they have been told that such and such must be, not because they have any knowledge that there are *reasons* for the rules. Why should he not go out into the street? Because he might get hit by a car? Well, he never really believes *that* can happen to him. Not really! If he obeys the injunction not to go into the street, it is mainly because he just better NOT! Why? Because Mama said so! Besides, he might get caught! And that would cause trouble! Obedience, not the reason for obedience, is the first commandment!

When justice is meted out, it must be meted out equally for all. There is no sense yet of extenuating circumstances, special needs and considerations, and relativity—i.e., that what would be right and just for one person may not be right and just for another. No. It is a morality not of relativity but of *realism*. It is equal for all, but it is *uncompromising*.

And it is harsh! If one does trespass, one ought to be punished, and punished severely—a grim Old Testament justice that demands "an eye for an eye and a tooth for a tooth." It took humankind millenia to develop and accept the idea of a merciful and compassionate God, the God of Amos and Micah and the God of the New Testament. It will take the child a few more years to gain that perspective—at about the age of ten morality becomes relative. Ask a five-year-old, what should be done with a poor boy and a rich boy who both steal bread. The young child will say, "They should both go to jail." By the time the child has reached the age of eight, or nine or ten (the stage of concrete operations) he will mediate more mercy to the poor boy, "because he was hungry."

THE RELEVANCE OF FOLKLORE AND FAIRY TALES.   Some psychologists believe that folklore and fairy tales have a very special place in a child's world because they represent, in a very poignant way, the more *primitive consciousness* of a preoperational child's world. In folklore and fairy tales evildoers *must* be punished. The Wicked Witch is thrown into her own oven by Hansel and Gretel. Fairy tales, like the great myths of the world, retell the eternal themes of existence: *good* versus *evil, poor* versus *rich, weak and helpless* versus *strong and mighty,* and ultimately crime and punishment. They deal also with the existential problems of fear, death, injustice, and despair.

There is another reason for their continuing fascination: they hold out the

LONDON: A PRESENT-DAY EXAMPLE OF MORAL REALISM

"Public Hangings Would Cut Crime," British Students Say

Students at a suburban London junior high school believe the crime rate in Britain, where capital punishment was abolished fifteen years ago, would drop if criminals were punished by public hangings, thumb screws, whipping or amputation, a British news agency reported Sunday.

The children, aged eleven and upwards, were asked by their teachers at Charnwood Comprehensive School in the low-income area of Clifton, in the London area, to suggest ways of solving the problems of a violent world, the Press Association of Britain said. It did not say how many children took part in the poll.

According to the agency, some children suggested public punishments including hangings and the televised broadcast of executions.

A choice of electric chair, guillotine or the gas chamber was proposed for serious crime, and for lesser violence, the rack and thumb screws, it said.

The agency quoted the children as saying the thieves should have a hand or two chopped off, juvenile delinquents should be whipped, shoplifting should bring ten years in prison, and the theft of a chocolate bar at least nine months.

It said the children also suggested force-feeding hunger strikers, arming women with knives and guns for their own protection, and closing bars on Christmas Eve.

One of the more lenient children suggested abolishing life sentences and holding prisoners only until the age of seventy or eighty, the agency reported.

It said another child offered this simple remedy for violence: more work and less sex.

Capital punishment was abolished in Britain in 1965.

SOURCE: Gainesville Sun, January 19, 1981; used by permission of The Associated Press.

promise of love, hope, justice, and deliverance, and they teach a kind of morality, primitive as it may be. Evil is eventually punished, the good are eventually rewarded, the poor become rich, the weak and helpless are elevated, the ugly duckling becomes beautiful, the heart's secret longing is fulfilled, and all who deserve it, live "happily ever after."

Finally, say the personality theorists, the fairy tale embodies our familial conflicts, wishes for revenge, adolescent rebellions, and hopes and struggles for self-identity. In fairy tales, said Freud, our parents appear as the kindly king and queen while the child identifies with the prince or princess of the stories. When we are children, our parents seem to us to be wonderful, majestic beings who can do no wrong, the benign rulers of the child's realm. Then comes that shock of awakening when the father and mother no longer appear so benevolent—they punish us or treat us sternly. This is the beginning of our ambivalent feelings toward our parents. The mother is then no longer the "good queen" nor is the father the "good king." In the child's eyes they have been transformed into the "wicked king" and the "wicked queen" or "wicked stepmother." But children are told to love their parents; to hate them is wrong. Thus as children we resolve this conflict by identifying two mothers: a good mother, who is "nice" and does what we want, and a wicked stepmother, who is "mean." In the fairy tale, this resolution appears as a "good queen who died in childbirth" and the "wicked stepmother" whom the good king married in his bereavement. Children are able to hate the wicked stepmother because she is not really related to them. After all, their real mother would never do mean things to them.

Folklore and fairy tales have that grim Old Testament justice we mentioned earlier. They contain none of the gentler messages of Christianity with its gospels of love and compassion but are filled with murder, revenge, mutilated bodies, and witches who poison others and cast spells on the innocent. No turning the other cheek or forgiving the enemy as in the Christian message; no message of caring and loving others and doing unto them as you would have others do unto you; rather the evildoers are punished, their powers are destroyed, and they must suffer for their crimes (Fromm 1957; Bettelheim 1976).

THE STAGE OF MORAL RELATIVITY.   At about ten there arises an intense preoccupation with rules. Rules! Rules! Rules! A preoccupation did we say? Let us rather say that it is an obsession. Watch children of this age at play. They will spend as much time as they do playing—even more time—discussing who played fairly and who did not! They will go back over the rules of the game. They will even change them in midstream. (Especially if that benefits the changer.) They will argue about the rules that were set up the last time they played the game. Piaget tells a wonderfully illustrative story about the time he observed a group of school boys let out for recess in his native Switzerland.

It was winter, and like children over here, the boys were delighted at the snow and made preparations for a snowball fight. But before they got into making the actual snowballs, Piaget noticed that they got into a heated discussion over the "rules of the game": how the teams would be composed, the election of the captain of each team, where they would have the opposing sides, what would be "fair" and "not fair"—and what would be the forfeit if someone broke a rule. So long was this discussion, reports Piaget, that they didn't have much of the recess period left to actually get into the *play* part (Piaget 1973).

But rule making is not just play. When we consider the social fabric of our society, we cannot but observe the number of house rules, of school rules, of federal laws, or club regulations, of community ordinances. Everywhere our society is bounded by what we *must not* do or what we *may* do, what we *ought* to do, and what we *ought not* to do. The more complex a society becomes, the more complex become the rules by which the society lives. The obsession for rules in play may spring from the constant barrage we adults foist upon our growing children. Wherever the obsession for rules comes from, it stands children in good stead. Rules and laws and regulations are the gears by which the whole machinery of our

Box 2.12

FOLKLORE AND FAIRY TALES

Eventually, the human race ceased to believe in deities that performed acts of murder and incest and genocide. Eventually, humankind began to accept a new concept of deity, that of a Father-God, so unlike anything that had been previously conceived, that no graven image could be made to show His Unimaginable Being. The next step in religious evolution was a Son-God, so loving and compassionate that he would give his life for mortal beings, no longer the pawns of whimsical or cruel gods but now recognizing themselves as the "children of God." Mortals now could transcend their original sinful natures. Such a profound reversal of theological meaning and symbol was a radical transformation of human psychology, a transformation of spirit that only the most elevated of men and women could understand. Despite the spread of Christianity throughout the pagan world, most human beings retained deep in their unconscious a belief in malevolent or mischievous entities who still needed to be feared and placated. Although the pagan gods were dethroned by the early Christian missionaries, they were not annihilated. The ancient gods and goddesses may have been stripped of their powers, but they were not dead by any means. They went into the unconscious to emerge as the fairies, witches, elves, and goblins of folklore and fairy tales. But even in this demoted status, they continued to embody the irrational and primitive hopes, fears, and wishes of humankind. Even now, to children, they are very real entities.

Those who have studied folklore and fairy tales tell us that fairy tales differ from myths and sagas, in that fairy tales are not connected with any specific country or locale; nor are they identified with a specific person. Fairy tales happen in an indefinable past ("Once upon a time . . . ") and usually do not involve gods and goddesses. To be sure, the main characters of fairy tales have names, but these names always point to some specific but impersonal characteristic or rank, like the King, the Queen, the Wicked Stepmother, the Prince, the Fairy Godmother, or the Wicked Witch. Sometimes, a character may have a symbolic name, such as Snow White (a person of goodness and beauty) or Sleeping Beauty (indicating both her beauty and the spell she is under), or Prince Charming (referring to both his rank and personality).

The essence of the fairy tale, then, is *plot*, which often is simple, and usually ends with a happy ending. Do not be misled by the innocent beginning: "Once upon a time far away . . . " and the ending " . . . and they all lived happily ever after." For between these two innocuous phrases, the fairy tale deals with the fears and taboos of humankind. Because some persons think that fairy tales are so barbaric many of the fairy tales of the brothers Grimm have been eliminated from children's fairy tale anthologies, and those which are included have been "cleaned up" considerably.

technological society is kept together (just as our rules of etiquette and politeness are the oil that makes the gears function smoothly and with as little friction as possible).

The children are learning to be rule abiding, which prepares them to be law abiding later. They are putting their rules together for the purpose of fair play. Later they are willing to abide by the laws and regulations of the larger society (even if they don't understand the reasons for them), and they will instinctively know they are there for a purpose. Well, most of the time, anyway, in most situations.

Lawrence Kohlberg: Further Studies of the Moral Development of the Individual

We cannot leave this chapter (and our discussion of the moral development of the individual) without mentioning the work of Lawrence Kohlberg (Kohlberg 1964). Kohlberg discovered the work of Jean Piaget early in his university days, at a time when so many American psychologists were skeptical about Piaget's methodologies (the case study approach to human behavior). He determined early on to devote his career to following up on Piaget's work on the moral-cognitive development of children, and that is exactly what he has done. Kohlberg has invented a number of ways to get at not just the *verbal responses* of children to moral-ethical situations but the *reasoning* behind their responses. He presents children with ethical problems and through a series of follow-up questions attempts to get at what lies behind their judgments. A typical ethical situation is as follows: Two boys have accidents. The first boy has an inadvertent accident and breaks fifteen dishes. The other boy breaks one dish, but he has broken it because he was doing something he wasn't supposed to do. After hearing the situation, the child is questioned minutely about his understanding of the situation, about the circumstances, about the effects, and about the causes. He is asked also to respond in an evaluative to both situations and to give his reasoning for what he says (and thinks). Kohlberg extended the age range of his subjects down to three years of age and up to sixteen and older. The result of Kohlberg's work has been a more definitive stage theory—a fine-tuning of Piaget's work (Kohlberg 1964, 1981).

In Kohlberg's analysis there are three overall levels that are age-stage acquired but that can be applied to the general population as well. There is the *preconventional* level, which applies to children from three to ten. The child's reasoning is not based on any real inner judgment but on external control. The child refrains from doing wrong so that he won't be caught or so that he can reap rewards. Kohlberg made note, also, that sociopathic personalities, such as criminals, have the same kind of moral attitude.

The second level is what Kohlberg calls *conventional morality*. This level begins about the age of ten. It is also the morality of most persons in any given society. At this level the person has internalized moral judgments, not necessarily because they are good for the person involved but for the usual reasons given by

Box 2.13

LAWRENCE KOHLBERG: STAGES OF MORAL DEVELOPMENT

Level One: Preconventional Morality

Stage 1: *Obedience-disobedience.* An orientation toward punishment and reward. "Children should not do bad things so that they stay out of trouble and do not get spanked."

Stage 2: *Hedonistic Self Interest.* Being nice to others gets you favors in return. "If I let Johnnie play with my toys, he'll let me play with his."

Level Two: Conventional Morality

Stage 3: *Good child reputation.* Orientation to seek and win love and approval from others. "I want my Mommie and Daddy to be proud of me." "The guys will like me."

Stage 4: *Respect for law, duty, and authority.* Orientation to obedience to law and upholding prevailing social, political, and religious rules, regulations, and laws. "Shouldn't break the law or there would be anarchy."

Level Three: Postconventional Morality

Stage 5: *Social contract.* Orientation to equality and mutual obligation. "We should abide by the rules whenever possible, although sometimes you have to bend them a little to be fair."

Stage 6: *Individual conscience.* Orientation to high ethical principles even if that means taking an unpopular stand or breaking the law in order to protect the individual. "Here stand I. I can do no other." "Civil disobedience."

most people: "We have to have law and order," "I want people to think well of me," "What's fair for one is fair for all."

The third level is the *postconventional morality* level. The standards of right and wrong are no longer limited to societal rules and regulations as they are at the second level. The standards are now the result of some deeply felt convictions of conscience. At this level the person may realize that his own convictions conflict with those of his society, and he is willing to bend, break, or otherwise mutilate the rules and laws of convention. An example of this, of course, would be the Germans in the late thirties who helped Jews to escape from the Nazis and thus avoid the death camps. Another example is portrayed by Mark Twain. When Huckleberry Finn discovers the runaway slave, Joe, he has a monologue with himself. He has been taught by his foster parents, school, and church that slaves are the properties of their masters and that to help one escape is like stealing. But Joe is his friend. He does not want to see him go back and be beaten. The jaws of hell open wide and he considers his dilemma. At last he shrugs. He guesses he will just have to go to hell, and off he runs with runaway Joe. A monologue just as soul-searching as Hamlet's "To be or not to be" speech.

Each of these levels has two more definable stages, making six stages in all. The last stage, which may start about the age of thirteen, is reached by very few people. In fact, Kohlberg posits that perhaps only 10 percent of the adult population ever attain the highest stage (postconventional level). This last, postconventional, stage has been highly criticized by some psychologists and educators as fostering asocial behavior. In recent years Kohlberg has withdrawn this stage, out of deference to the criticism. This saddens us, since it has long been recognized that the greatest thinkers and doers of our society have been at least slightly out of step with their culture—or they could not have been the thinkers that they were. To be highly creative is to be out of norm—to live at a level of consciousness beyond the bounds of the culture. Perhaps research in the future will be able to better explain the phenomenon Kohlberg describes.

APPLICATIONS AND COPING TECHNIQUES

1. ACCEPT THE EBB AND FLOW OF THE LIFE PROCESS. There is a natural ebb and flow to human development. We are age-and-stage influenced from the beginning to the end of life. The forces that push us and pull us will vary from time to time and place to place, and we will discover (sometimes with startling surprise) that what we thought we wanted, what we worked so hard to achieve may, at some later time in our lives, seem to us to be illusionary and unprofitable—in a deeper sense, not worthwhile. We may structure and restructure our living in accord with our newly emerging values and understandings. We may shock others; we may even shock ourselves. We may wonder if we are "coming apart at the seams." Yet if we process these inner and external dynamics with courage, we can discover that the changes and transitions of our lives, painful as they may be, lead us to a more comprehensive understanding of what living is all about. Nor do we have to bemoan the fact that these changes will be coming. What would it be like, really, were we never to experience changes of directions, new goals and objectives, new ways of being and living in the world? If nothing ever changed, the passage of our adult years would consist of the same experiences year after year, decade after decade, with the tedium of more of the same. Our ability to change and grow, to destruct and reconstruct, to find and discard what is stagnant and demeaning and limiting and to desire what is joyful and motivating is what keeps us youthful in spirit and glad to be alive. It is *disequilibration*, said Piaget, that forces us toward more adaptive, higher levels of intelligence. Conflict and Resolution is what makes it possible for us to attain new levels of consciousness.

2. REMEMBER THAT THE MOST DIFFICULT TIMES OF OUR LIVES OCCUR AT THE TIMES OF PASSAGE AND TRANSITION. The human organization is essentially conservative. Change does not come easily to us. The passage from the prenatal existence to an independent one is, in all likelihood, not welcomed by the infant. That momentous rite of passage, the "first day of school," may have been eagerly anticipated by the young child, but it is not without its fearsome aspects, and the first year of school is a process of learning to relate to a world that is unlike the safer harbor of family life. Ultimately, the child's peer group will become more important than the child's parents, but the six-year-old cannot see that now. The transition to school requires a new psychological reorganization and time to integrate the many events that the child is processing.

The big transitions that we make throughout our life generally will be experienced as our most stressful moments. We will, from time to time, wonder if we are able to cope. At these times, we need to remember that it is natural to experience confusion, depression, anxiety, alienation—all of this is part of the growth process and may even be necessary to it, if we are to make the passage to the next stage.

Adults, like children, are fearful of what lies beyond the bend. It is well to remember at these times that if we can successfully process the emotional turmoils and physical destructuring, there is generally a calm flow up ahead and a landscape more creative and richer than the one we have left behind. In our present youth-oriented society we tend to emphasize the joys and values of early life; yet each age has its own harvest of joys and rewards, which we can know fully only when we get there. Parent life with small children is certainly a lovely time, but it has its problems: health concerns and doctors' bills, balancing love with discipline, the increasing expectations of school work and "conferences" when Johnny is not learning or is "acting up." The joys of grandparenthood, on the other hand, can include loving the children, even spoiling them, without the concerns and responsibilities of living with them every day. Thus grandparents can participate in the joys of family life but also be able to retreat to the peaceful privacy of their own lives again.

3. STAYING WITH THE PROCESS REQUIRES LETTING GO OF THE PAST, REMAINING ROOTED IN THE PRESENT, AND WELCOMING THE FUTURE. Some persons remain fixated at some past level of their lives. You may know such persons, for example, the man who "replays" his war experiences over and over again. Somehow that seems to him to have been his "finest hour." Or take the woman who bemoans her current existence with adolescent children and looks back at those happier times when the children were so young and needed her. These people are trapped in their own pasts.

Other persons are fixated not in the past but in the future. They are always planning to do the things they want to do when . . . he or she is out of school, when the children are grown up, or when "we retire." Living in the future prevents us from experiencing what life has to offer here and now. Furthermore, that future that is being planned for, saved for, and toiled for seems somehow never to happen. Their psychological farsightedness prevents them from seeing what is at hand.

We need to learn to let go of the past, to remain rooted in the present, and to welcome the future. The ancient Greeks had a saying: *You can never step in the same river twice.* What is gone is gone, and the future can never be fully foreseen. This is *not* to say that we cut off all our past ties, and it is *not* to say that we do not make goals for the future. On the contrary, friends become more important, not less so, as we get older. Without setting goals for ourselves, we can hardly achieve them. We value the past, for it helps us understand our own history, from where we have come and where we are now. Memory helps to bind all our experiences together and is a vital part of the integrative process. The ability to see ahead (imagination) enables us to plan for a better and more creative future life. What is essential to remember, however, is that we do not *live* primarily in the past nor only for the future, but we live in our moment-by-moment experiencing and awareness of the now—staying with *the process*.

4. LET US ALLOW OUR CHILDREN TIME TO BE CHILDREN. If there is one thing we have learned from Freud and Erikson and Piaget, it is this: Childhood is a different experience from adulthood. We cannot expect adult understandings or adult emotions from children. They are developing at their own rate and in their own time and sequence—an evolution of our human race in one small lifetime. As children, they will understand as children, play as children, and be happy with childish things. We cannot expect otherwise until they are ready for the next level of emotional-social-intellectual development (awareness). As Americans, we have a tendency to push our children, to expect them to perform, to be perfect, to be talented, to be outstanding in some way. There is a gradual unfoldment of their development as in ours. If we push this development, we may well "develop" them, but we may also develop anxiety and dread. Do not expect adult "honesty." Realize that a child in the preoperative stage has a preconventional morality that has more to do with "not getting caught." Higher levels of morality will come later. Do not try to solve all their problems. It is that disequilibration in what she can and cannot quite achieve that will stimulate her intellectual and emotional adaptations. Do not get unduly upset when your toddler exhibits narcissistic tendencies or your preschooler regresses at the birth of a sister or brother. Allow them to process their hurts and pains and confusions just as you are needing to process yours. Tears, laughter, the expression of jealousy or anger are part of their processing, also, just as depression and anxiety and confusion may be part of ours. We cannot protect them all their lives. We need to do our best to facilitate their confrontation with life's experiences and help them experience their reality—as long as it does not become overwhelming. If there is a formula (and we are always skeptical of formulas), it is to let them discover what they can accomplish on their own and to be there to help them over the hurdle if it is just a bit too high.

5. NOT ALL PERSONS WILL REACH THE "HIGHEST LEVELS" OF INTELLECTUAL, EMOTIONAL AND MORAL DEVELOPMENT. ARE YOU A CANDIDATE? You will remember from chapter 1 that Maslow believed only a small portion of the population, perhaps only 10 percent, were ever able to reach the level of self-actualizing. In this chapter we have learned that Kohlberg has made the same estimate for those who reach the highest level of postconventional morality. Who are the persons who will achieve this level? They are, according to Kohlberg and others, those who come from the rising middle class and above, who are college educated, and who have been allowed and encouraged to consider moral and ethical problems. If you are in college now, you are probably a candidate for this highest level of personality functioning (Maslow) and moral-ethical character structure (Piaget/Kohlberg). But not necessarily. It is not an automatic process. Maslow warned that self-actualizing is not to be found easily among college students. His point was that we grow into wisdom over a period of years. That you are in college makes you a candidate for this achievement. The level of self-actualizing depends on your determination to become the best that you can be. Similarly postconventional morality, with its universal theme of understanding and compassion, can be begun in adolescence. But achieving higher ethical levels does not happen in a single, discrete step. It is a gradaul evolution into deeper awareness and higher consciousness. That, too, is a life-long process.

6. WE CAN FOSTER MORAL-ETHICAL CHARACTER IN MORE YOUNG PEOPLE.   We have put a lot of emphasis on the intellectual development of our children. We are much more timid about the character development. It is a touchy problem since our country is predicated upon the *separation of church and state* and thus the separation of ethics/religion and public education. Apart from a few church-related schools, the education of our young is secular. We are afraid to teach moral principles or to get into class discussions concerning ethical issues. We are being unduly sensitive here—and somewhat short-sighted. Class discussion of problems with moral-ethic considerations do not have to involve the teaching of any specific religious-belief system. In fact, the Piagetian-Kohlbergian method is not to teach precise moral-ethical behaviors or attitudes but rather to promote the child's or adolescent's own consideration of various problems and to derive resolutions for himself. The teaching methods advised are question asking, class discussion, open debate, value clarification—mental activities that are in accord with their age-stage level of development. That, after all, is one of the purposes of our democratic education. Most educators and thinkers are in agreement with this point of view. Yet class after class in our schools is more devoted to academic knowledge than to character-building application of knowledge.

At the same time, we sit down with our children to watch television shows or take them with us to movies in which violence of all types is enacted before their eyes. We "enjoy" the action as much as they. Paradoxically, we wonder why acceptance of violence is becoming more and more commonplace in our society. If we do not teach other kinds of ethical behavior, we are at least condoning the violence that is being portrayed in the public media.

In dealing with our children at home, we can set examples for them in our everyday lives. How we are as models will affect their interaction with others. If we are violent with them, they will be violent with others. (If we beat them, they will be aggressive toward others.) If we break laws in front of them, they will learn to disregard those laws in the same way—and they may even generalize to other laws. If we urge them to stand up to others and fight (instead of urging a more rational approach), fighting with others is exactly what they will learn to do.

Finally, when they have done something wrong, it is better to discuss the situation with them than to punish them because they have broken a rule. It is through discussion with them that we find out what their reasons were for what they did, and that will better enable you and them to figure out what compelled their action. Discussion of the reasons can be followed up by a discussion of what they could have done to solve their problem—and what they can do in the future. If they stole something from a store because they wanted it and didn't have any money, they can be encouraged to discover ways to earn the money or to make their wants known—perhaps their birthday is coming up or Christmas, or some financial money matching might be in order.

It does not have to be a surprise. Looking forward to the gift is almost as pleasurable as the receiving of it.

7. THE ATTAINMENT OF THE HIGHEST LEVELS OF ETHICAL-MORAL CONSIDERA-TIONS MAY PUT YOU INTO CONFLICT WITH YOUR SOCIETY.   One of the great truths you will learn is that there exists in our society or in any society what the sociologists call **cultural lag,** which simply means that *our rules and laws and organizational structure* (including values, attitudes, and mores) *lag behind the technical advances of that culture*. We may have scientific information on basic social problems and even on how to solve them, but the population simply lags behind in acceptance, and even the understanding, of new possibilities.

We know, for example, that prisons do not reform people; in fact, they are so antiquated in their brutality and boredom that we create more criminals than we rehabilitate—or habilitate (Guze 1976). We know this. We know, too, some of the kinds of situational factors that do enable a prisoner to achieve a more constructive approach to life. Yet we continue to build the very kinds of institutions that generate more "criminality." The public support is for the traditional methods. Public attitudes and values support the old ways. But of course there is always that edge of new awareness and new understanding on the part of some citizens—and thus those who have reached the highest levels of ethical values turn their efforts toward what they see needs to be done, however unpopular that cause and despite public disapproval. So eventually change does ensue.

Becoming a highly self-actualizing (or highly ethical) person does not mean you will necessarily be the happier for it. It probably means that you will be more aware of the cracks in our intitutions and the rips in our social fabric. You may find yourself bending the rules occasionally or even breaking them in order to respond to a "higher" justice than the one prescribed by laws or regulations. It means that you cannot be a totally "by-the-book" person. You may well agonize over situations that your peers and colleagues would not bother their heads about.

We do not offer you condolences if this be your lot. We do congratulate you and encourage you to live a thought-provoking, challenging, heartfelt life. We wish you courage and stamina. We welcome you to the powerful world of conscious choice and creative change.

SUMMARY: POINTS TO REMEMBER

1. The life-span approach studies both quantitative and qualitative changes in a person's development from infancy to old age.
2. One of the first persons to study the qualitative changes of a person's life was Sigmund Freud who developed the psy-

chosexual theory of personality functioning. Freud believed that the person's driving psychosexual life force or libido passed from the oral stage to the anal stage to the phallic stage before the person achieved full heterosexual maturity. If the child's psychosexual development does not progress properly (as an adult) he will remain fixated at an earlier, more primitive level of functioning. In other words, he has a "neurosis." The id, ego, and superego form Freud's topography of personality. The ego is the conscious self while the id and superego compose unconscious motivations.

3. As Freud began the developmental aspect of personality development, Carl Jung expanded it into adult life. Jung emphasized the second half of life, following the age-forty crisis, which for most persons in Western society is a spiritual one because of our material orientation during the first half of our lives. He divided the life span into four major segments: childhood, youth, maturity, and old age.

4. Arnold vanGennep envisioned the life span as a series of passages or transitions from one state to another and marked by public ceremonies or "rites of passage."

5. Erik Erikson expanded the life-span segments even further into a psychosocial theory of personality development. He identified eight life stages, each having its own life crisis to be understood and life task to be mastered.

6. Daniel Levinson and his Yale University associates studied forty men from four different walks of life and generally confirmed Jung's conclusions. He concluded that *age*, alone, is the single most important factor in our changing needs and values throughout our lifetime. Levinson stressed the process aspect of the life-span approach. Since no life structure can be either perfect or permanent, we are con-stantly structuring, destructuring, and restructuring our lifespace. Although there are several transition periods, the big one, according to Levinson, is the age-forty transition.

7. Another contributor to the stage theory of development was Jean Piaget, who devoted his life to the study of how thinking develops in children. He concluded that children do not think like adults and that they must go through four qualitative organizations of mind before they are capable of achieving rational and scientific adult thought processes. Each of these stages has its special characteristics.

8. The Hartshorne and May studies of the 1930s confirmed that children's morality is developmental and that it is *situational*, i.e, children are more likely to be honest if they think they might get caught.

9. Folklore and fairy tales may represent the optimistic but harsh world of the child's pre-operational phenomenology with their themes of good versus evil, poor versus rich, weak and helpless versus strong and mighty, and ultimate crime-and-punishment.

10. Lawrence Kohlberg's research has generally validated Piaget's work on the moral development of children. In Kohlberg's frame of reference there are three major levels of moral development: pre-conventional morality of children and delinquents, conventional morality of most adults, and finally, post-conventional morality which is a level only a minority of adults reach.

SIGNIFICANT TERMS AND CONCEPTS

adaptation	concrete operations	initiative
affective process	egocentric thinking	intimacy
animistic thinking	ego integrity	fixation
anal personality	Electra complex	functionalism
anal stage	favorable ratio	formal operations
assimilation	identity	generativity
autonomy	industry	latency stage
basic trust	intelligence as choice	libido

life span
life tasks
mid-life crisis
moral realism
moral relativity
neurosis
Oedipal complex
oral personality
oral stage

phallic stage
phenomenology
pleasure-pain principle
psychosexual development
psychosocial development
qualitative changes
quantitative changes
reality principle
repression

rites of passage
rules of the game
second half of life
sensory-motor stage
socialization process
structuring, destructuring,
restructuring
superego

FILL-IN THE BLANKS

1. Sigmund Freud posited three essential parts of the human personality. The baby is born an unconscious id, dominated by the p _____-p _____ principle. Eventually the id is socialized and the l _____ drive is focused at the anal level. As a result of the socialization process the second part of the personality is formed, the superego. Out of the external conflict of the id and superego is born the e _____, or the conscious part of the personality.

2. According to Freud, if the psychosexual development of the child is overly restrictive, the person's development is fixated; i.e., the person has a n _____.

3. At the phallic stage, the boy develops a strong emotional bond with his mother, which Freud called the O _____ c _____. The girl child's attachment to her father is called the E _____ c _____.

4. Freud believed that the adult personality was formed during the first six years of life. Carl Jung, however, called our attention to the s _____ half of life, marked by the mid-life crisis.

5. Arnold vanGennep formulated the life-span as a series of passages marked by cermonies or "r _____ of p _____."

6. Erik Erikson formulated a wide panorama of p _____-s _____ development; consisting of eight stages. Each stage is characterized by a life-c _____ to be confronted and a life-t _____ to be mastered.

7. For example, the baby's first life-task is to develop b _____ trust. He learns to stand on his own two feet and control his bodily functions, which Erikson called developing a sense of a _____. In the fourth stage, the child learns i _____. Adolescence is marked by the need to achieve i _____, etc.

8. Daniel Levinson and his associates at Yale University intensely studied forty men from various walks-of-life. In general, Levinson supported Jung's four great eras. The times of greatest conflict are the years of t _____, but the whole-life span, Levinson concludes, is a continual process of structuring, d _____, and r _____. The greatest unpheaval generally happens at age _____.

9. Jean Piaget studied the intellectual or c _____ development of children. His conclusion was that children do not think like adults at all. Their phenomenology is qualitatively different from ours. For example, from two to seven years, the child is in the pre-operational stage, characterized by a type of thinking that is a _____, e _____, and f _____.

10. "The sun goes down, so I can sleep" is an example of a child's f _____ thinking. The child stumbles over a rock and hurts

her foot, whereupon she kicks it and calls it a "bad rock!" This is an example of a child's a _____ thinking. The child is unable to view the world from the perspective of another person, which Piaget called e _____ thinking.

11. Piaget equated c _____ with intelligence.

12. Piaget believed that moral development and c _____ development go hand-in-hand. A young child's morality is rigid and focused on e _____ and not cause. As the child gets older, he is more able to consider causation. As well, the older child is preoccupied with the r _____ of the game.

13. A child may think it is not okay to steal from the neighborhood grocery store because Mr. Brown, the owner, is a "nice man," but it is okay to steal from the department store downtown because "They're rich and won't notice it." This is an example of s _____ morality.

RECOMMENDED BOOKS FOR FURTHER READING

Bettleheim, Bruno. *The Uses of Enchantment: The Meaning and Importance of Fairy Tales*. (New York: Alfred A. Knopf, 1976.) Bettleheim has won international renown for his work with emotionally disturbed children. Two of his previous books, *The Empty Fortress: Infantile Autism and the Birth of the Self* and *Love Is Not Enough* deal with the diagnosis and treatment of what has been called childhood schizophrenia and autism. In this book, he deals with the psychological significance of folklore and fairy tales and makes a case for bringing this literature back into the experiential world of children so that they can deal with the mythic themes of human existence. Bettleheim writes masterfully of universal themes. It is an excellent book for those going into early childhood education, pediatrics, nursing, or the like.

Erikson, Erik H. *Childhood and Society*. (New York: W. W. Norton, 1964.) Erikson's list of publications is long but this is his major *opus* and deals extensively with his eight life stages. In particular, the reader's attention is drawn to his chapter on adolescence. Erikson believes that we Americans do well in helping our children attain the first four life tasks (particularly *industry*) but that we do not deal very well in the fifth life task of identity.

Jung, Carl. Approaching the Unconscious. In Carl G. Jung et al. eds., *Man and His Symbols*. (Garden City: Doubleday & Company, 1964). We recommend this book as a beginning entree to Jung's works and ideas. It is superbly illustrated (many photographs in color) and is a summary of Jungian concepts including the Persona and Mask; the Archetypes, and the Four Functions. The other chapters, contributed by Jungian practitioners are also magnificently delineated and illustrated.

Levinson, Daniel, et al. *The Seasons of a Man's Life*. (New York: Alfred A. Knopf, 1978.) This book presents in detail Levinson's life-span theory. The student who is interested in understanding his approach need read only the first 80 to 100 pages since the rest of the book is devoted to detailed case histories (of the preceding case histories).

Sheehy, Gail. *Passages*. (New York: E. P. Dutton, 1967.) This book hit the best-seller list and stayed on for many weeks. Evidently it spoke to many persons and enabled them to come to terms with the changes that go on in their lives. We dislike the journalistic style (Sheehy is not a social scientist but a journalist) but students find her style appealing.

3

*Discovering
and Owning
Our Individual
Differences*

LEARNING TO VALUE OUR INDIVIDUAL DIFFERENCES
>   Commonalities versus Individual Differences
>   The Search for General Principles of Human Functioning: Freud
>   The Search for Individual Differences: Breaking off from Freud

ALFRED ADLER: THE INDIVIDUALITY OF ONE'S LIFE STYLE
>   Constructive and Destructive Life Styles
>   Superiority-Inferiority Complex
>   Compensation and Overcompensation
>   Some Neurotic Life-Style Patternings
>   Positive Life-Style Patterning: Social Feeling and Character

CARL JUNG: TYPE PSYCHOLOGY
>   Individual Differences as Innate and Inborn
>   Introversion versus Extroversion
>   Jung's Four Functions: Sensing/Intuiting/Thinking/Feeling
>   Using Type Psychology to Understand Ourselves and Others
>   Creative Living

EDUARD SPRANGER: *TYPES OF MEN*
>   Aesthetic/Political/Economic/Religious/Social/Theoretical
>   Allport's Use of Spranger's Work: The Study of Values
>   We Are All Mixtures, Most Likely

WILLIAM SHELDON: SOMATOTYPES
>   Is There a Correlation between Physical and Personality
>   Characteristics?
>   Mesomorphs, Endomorphs, and Ectomorphs
>   Basic Biological Differences

RESEARCH EVIDENCE: THE CHILD IS FATHER TO THE MAN
>   Early Infancy/Childhood Differences . . .
>   . . . That Seem to Be Long Lasting
>   Personality Traits Seem to Cluster
>   The Result of the *Twin Studies*
>   The University of Minnesota *Twin Study*

DANIEL FREEDMAN: THE SUPRISING DIFFERENCES IN NEONATES
>   Left-Brain/Right-Brain Individuals?

APPLICATIONS

LEARNING TO VALUE OUR INDIVIDUAL DIFFERENCES

The thesis of chapter 1 was simply this: Personality integration is a process that involves every aspect of growth and development—physical, mental, emotional, and spiritual—and by spiritual we are using the meaning given by Jung and Levinson in the sense of coming to terms with our relationship to others and to the whole "family of humankind."

The thesis of chapter 2 was that there is a natural ebb and flow to our lives and as we go from childhood to adolescence, from adolescence to adulthood, from adulthood to beyond the midforty transition, and so on, our needs and wants, our motivations, our joys, our dissatisfactions also have an ebb and flow, a developmental push and pull toward this or that emerging value. Living is never static but a continual and surprising process of changing balance and direction.

The thesis of *this* chapter is that living *well* means being willing to search out what has meaning for us—what it is that gives us energy and what it is that fosters our own particular creativity. For each of us it is different. Why should that not be so? We are born in different circumstances. We grow up differently. We have different talents, abilities, and aspirations. In this chapter we turn our attention to just those differences among us with the hope that each of our readers can come to an appreciation of his or her uniqueness from all others, and to appreciate his or her individual mode of being-in-the-world.

Commonalities versus Individual Differences

By the very virtue of their professions scientists look for laws and principles that apply *generally* to the phenomena of the world. When social scientists study people, they are (for the most part) looking for what applies to *most* people in *most* cases. Thus most general psychology texts take the approach of discussing what is true for *groups* of people and are less inclined to discuss exceptions to the rule or the individual differences among us that make us unique. Time and again, therefore, you will read in social science text books that, as *groups*, people will *tend* to do this and *tend* to do that. You may want to respond something like, "But that isn't (wasn't) the way it is (was) for me!" Good! We recognize the validity of your experience and do not want you to doubt your own perceptions and your own reality. We are not yet sophisticated enough as a developing science to account for *all* the facts *all* the time. That is not to denigrate the "generalist" approach. Not at all. But we can get very confused when we read something that is offered as a *general truth* but somehow does not seem to apply to us in our particular circumstances nor to anyone else we have encountered so far in our lives. Let us give an exam-

We are the most variable,
complex, and individual
species on earth.

ple. A fine scientist, Stanley Schacter, discovered that if they were going to be subjected to pain, most college subjects would prefer to be with others rather than by themselves—probably for the comfort that comes with being with another human being. But not all his subjects chose that situation (Schacter 1959). Some of his subjects would prefer to be by themselves. Some of you will recognize this difference among us if we give an everyday example. When we become sick or have to be subjected to a stay in a hospital, there are some of us (and Schacter's research indicates that probably *most* of us are like this) who take comfort in having people—a lot of people—come to see us. But there are those of you reading this book who react oppositely—sickness or surgery tend to make you shy away from much contact with your friends. You might be glad to see a few very close friends, but you would not be at all comfortable with constant visitors or a roomful of people. You're the type, in fact, who needs to "close in on yourself" and actually be protected from well-meaning visitors.

The Search for General Principles of Human Functioning: Freud

Freud too was a scientist. It is little known that before his career as a psychiatrist, he had been a neurologist and had already produced some papers on neurology. Like other scientists, he looked for broad general principles of adult psychiatry. It was his hope to develop what we might now call a field theory of human behavior. Of course that was doomed to failure because Freud was either unaware of, or chose to ignore, the many **variables** that we now know do influence human functioning—variables such as *culture* and *subculture*, the *stratification* elements that have to do with the social and educational background of our families and ourselves and our world. Too, we have come to appreciate the wide spectrum of human variation as he did not. But of course Freud was dealing with a very homogeneous segment of society, mainly the upper-middle-class society of Vienna, whereas we represent one of the most diverse societies in history and in the world today. For example, he viewed any deviation from a rather strict (and "puritanical") sexual conventionality as a *polymorphous perversity*. Today we have a broader approach to sexual preference and practice. Nevertheless, he returned to the men and women of our day a profound respect for the power, and sustaining motivation, of our sexual needs and drives.

Despite the attacks he endured from the church and other institutions, and despite the rejection of his work by members of his own medical profession (which disappointed him deeply), there were others (physicians and laymen) who were inspired to join him in Vienna, where he lived, to study his new theories of human sexuality. Eventually this group organized themselves into a loosely knit organization, *The Psychoanalytic Congress of Vienna*, with Freud as the official president. But Freud was rather an autocrat and so convinced of the overriding dominance of the libido as the primary motivator of human action, that he seemed little able to tolerate disparate views.

The Search for Individual Differences: Breaking Off from Freud

For a while the group worked amicably together. But as one after another of his colleagues and associates began pointing to other variables of human motivation and their attempts to enlarge his theoretical base came to naught, they had little choice (it seemed to them) but to break off from the Psychoanalytic Congress in order to explore the clues they found valuable in the unravelling of the human psyche (Jones 1961). Two such persons were Carl Jung (whom we met in chapter 2) and Alfred Adler. Alfred Adler was one of the first social scientists to take a stand for the importance of individual differences in human affairs. In fact, he was ultimately to call his thoretical work *Individual Psychology*.

ALFRED ADLER: THE INDIVIDUALITY OF ONE'S LIFE STYLE

The term *life style* has become familiar to us in recent decades and has come to mean our financial status or the way in which we live—whether we live moderately, frugally, or luxuriously. But, as Adler devised this term, life styles had a much larger connotation. It meant the whole flow, pattern, and direction of a person's life. Adler considered our individual life styles as "acts of creation" involving our goals, our values, our aspirations, the sum and substance of what is known as our *personality*, our attitudes, and our achievements. No two styles can ever be alike. Adler wrote that one's entire life style is more than the sum of a person's minute, day-by-day behaviors. To understand a person's life style, one must study the person's whole existence from source to ultimate direction. One must be able to see its flow, harmony, and poetry and to discover the person's great underlying themes and rhythms. Life style is exactly what novelists try to describe in character portrayals (Adler 1930). It is what students mean when they say, "I like psychology because I like to know what makes people tick and why different people do the things they do!"

Constructive and Destructive Life Styles

Although we may not fully comprehend the whys and wherefores of a person's life style, we often are able to discern whether this person seems to have a destructive or constructive life style or whether *this* person seems to have little direction or *that* person seems to be "getting somewhere." Some life styles seem to have purpose, to be active and dynamic, while others seem stagnant and confused. Some seem to be picking their way cautiously toward their life aims while others seem bent toward alcoholic or barbiturate suicide. Some life styles seem to be a frantic circular chase for sensation and excitement, while others may seem limited and dull. Furthermore, one's life style may be in direct contradiction to one's verbalized aspirations and intent. Consider, for example, an acquaintance of ours who has stated many times that his chief goal in life is "to do some serious research and writing—to make a significant contribution to science." His actual behavior, however, belies his expressed intentions. Although he has been married only a few years, one of his chief pastimes seems to be to demonstrate his masculine attractiveness. He wears see-through shirts, rides a powerful motorcycle, has many conferences with his female students, discusses sexual games with his office mates, and generally gives the rest of us the impression that his interest in women has less to do with their charms than with his conquest of them. The destructiveness of this man's life style is not just in what he is doing but in what he is *not* doing. Despite his professed aspirations to make a significant contribution to science, his energies and the time needed for scientific endeavor are going elsewhere. None of us can know what is driving this man to lead the life style that he is creating for himself, for we know only of these external expressions of his life. In point of fact, the man *himself* may not know what drives him to do what he does or live as he lives. In that case, we say that his motivations are largely *unconscious*.

Superiority-Inferiority Complex

It was Adler's conclusion that the life styles of all persons are determined very early in life by feelings of *inferiority*. Children live in a universe of powerful, giantlike adults, who are all *superior* to them in strength, in ability, in power, in language, in just about "everything." This superiority of adults (which is overwhelming and intimidating to a child) leads to a **superiority-inferiority complex** in adulthood. It was Adler who gave us this term, which we use now in everyday parlance. The term seems contradictory to some extent, and in a sense, it is. The child grows up with such overwhelming feelings of inferiority that unless he finds something in which he can excel, life is unsupportable. He endeavors to find some area of expression that allows him to feel himself as somehow superior. The key to this complex is that the more the child/adult experiences an inner inferiority to others, the more desperate are his attempts to act superior. A case in point: Have you ever noticed how some very tall and strong men seem to be very much "at ease" in the way they walk or stand. They don't have to be constantly proving their physical superiority. They sometimes talk very quietly and move very quietly. They know themselves to be superior in height and strength and do not have to throw challenges out to others by their verbal or body language.

By way of contrast, the classic example of an inferiority-superiority complex (and one often used in psychology text books) is the well-known Napoleonic complex. Napoleon was very short, and it has been hypothesized that perhaps his drive to conquer all of Europe was his "unconscious" attempt to compensate for his small stature. We cannot know if this was actually so, but the overall portrayal of such a *personality* would certainly correlate with the characteristics we've discussed as the *superiority-inferiority* complex described by Adler. Interestingly enough, another *personality* that fits this correlation is that of Alexander the Great, also very short and who conquered all the known civilizations of his day. Two examples in explanation of a *possibility* are a beginning basis for exploring a

The child develops an inferiority complex as the result of feeling overwhelmed and impotent in the world of giant and superior adults.

working hypothesis although they are not considered adequate empirical data on which to base a *generalization*. They are, however, grounds for thought that generates research. But on to Adler.

Compensation and Overcompensation

The quest to achieve superiority is set so very early in life that we can actually see it in action by the time the child is two years of age, according to Adler.[1] *This* particular child is aggressive with his playmates and strives to *boss* them. *That* child is already showing jealousy toward one or more of her siblings. These childish actions, Adler says, are not simply *stages* the child goes through but are actually the first evidence of the life style of the person. This life style and how it is carried out is the means by which the child is attempting to *compensate* or *overcompensate* for his or her experiences of inferiority (Adler 1927).

Some Neurotic Life-Style Patternings

By *neurotic* Adler meant that there is some level of distortion of *reality*. Adler provides us with some specific examples of the way the child tries to balance the scales of his or her inferiority by becoming superior in some way to others. Some children may have felt overlooked by a parent in a favor of a sibling. The jealousy felt by the child for the *favored* one may result in a desire to outstrip the favorite in some way or other (perhaps in sports and games or in scholastic achievement or even in being "good"). This desire to outdo the sibling becomes the life style of the individual and in adulthood manifests itself as a powerful competitive drive. For instance, a businessman's desire to "succeed" (his mark of showing up the inferiority of others) may be so powerful as to lead him toward success even when the success excludes a value of good or even a modicum of "ethical business tactics." In a sense, the jealousy the child felt for his sibling is transferred to whatever fellow humans come into his business arena. This adult individual must "show them" who's the most superior in making money or in cornering the market or in some way edging out competitors.

A girl-child who feels she was not loved because the family favored her prettier sister may, as a result, pursue a lifelong goal of proving herself just as attractive—or more attractive—than the prettier sibling. She spends much of her adult life attending to her clothes, her hair, her cosmetics. She engages in flirtations, or "affairs," and may even become that *femme fatale* of French literature.

Adler was particularly concerned for the child who has been overpetted, or overpampered and has not had the opportunity to deal with the challenges of the world. As a consequence, pampered children may feel so very weak and helpless that their life style is that of avoiding responsibility and resisting the ordinary tasks and duties of the everyday world. Those persons manage to get others "to do" for them, to take care of them, and to continue pampering them all of their lives. Unfortunately, this limits their ability to live courageously in the world. They lack self-confidence. Their lives are restricted and constricted. They are prisoners of their own incompetency. According to Adler, they harbor a secret joy of superiority in being so clever that they can manipulate others into feeling sorrow for them, "protecting" them, and making them the "petted darling," so to speak, of everyone's concern and attention. We might say of them that they consider themselves to be "privileged characters," and we all know persons who seem to manifest just that opinion of themselves.

The point is: How do the rest of us cooperate with such a life style? When we wait on a fellow human hand and foot (not counting cases where it is obviously necessary, such as illness), what life-style patterning might we be creating for ourselves? How do we recognize a lifestyle patterning as positive or negative?

Positive Life-Style Patterning: Social Feeling and Character

Essential to Adler's thesis of the superiority-inferiority complex is that the life goal of an individual may hide under a *veil of perfection* or *goodness* or *heroism*. Of course, in such instances the child's life goal has been influenced by an opposing force, which Adler called the **social feeling** that enables a person to live out his or her life style in a constructive way. This development of a *social feeling* was for Adler the mark of the evolved human being and what gives transcending qualities to the human species (Adler 1931).

Unlike Freud, Adler was not at all convinced that humanity was doomed to be forever at the mercy of their libidinal drivings. It was his conviction that the development (evolution) of human consciousness has been the development also of human *relatedness*, the willingness to look out for each other in an ever-widening circle of "brotherly love." He called this developing social feeling *gemeinschaftsgefuhl*, a term he invented. Although we have translated it into English as "a social feeling" or "brotherly love," the German word has much more the connotation of a compassionate understanding of the whole human race despite our foibles, despite our foolishness, despite our childish vindictiveness—even despite our apparent berserk madnesses at times. He saw this trait manifesting in many human beings in their *conjunctive* character traits: a joyous willingness to join with others; an ability to laugh at ourselves with the benefits of the liberating experience of seeing how we appear in our own eyes or in the eyes of others; the ability to be genuinely compassionate, reaching out for others appropriately as they need support. No doubt, he thought, these conjunctive behaviors stem from our need to overcome our essential feelings of isolation and loneliness, but what of that?

"Happiness," he wrote, "is probably the best manifestation of the conquest of difficulties" (Adler 1929). Avarice, envy, jealousy, in fact even ambition, pride—all of the "cardinal vices"—are clues to the inferiority-superiority complex of the individual. If there has been developed a substantial (all the way to "perfect") *social feeling*, it appears as the classic "cardinal virtues" of charity, patience, tolerance, cheerfulness, and so on. Adler was particularly impressed with the quality of cheerfulness as a manifestation of a person's character. (See box 3.1.) Perhaps this level of continuing joy and happiness is one of the keys to the truly integrated person. We know, for example, that delinquent teenagers have a poor self-concept, that abusive parents have a low self-esteem, that "psychotics" live in a private hell, and that the "neurotic person" has only moments free from obsessions, guilts, and fears (Bachman et al. 1971; Walker 1979, 1981; Bourne & Newberger 1979).

BOX 3.1

CHEERFULNESS: AN EXPRESSION OF CHARACTER

We have certainly drawn attention to the fact that we can easily measure anyone's social feeling by learning to what degree he is prepared to serve, to help, and to give pleasure to others. The talent for bringing pleasure to others makes a man more interesting. Happy people approach us more easily and we judge them emotionally as being more sympathetic. It seems that we sense these traits as indicators of a highly developed social feeling, quite instinctively. There are people who appear cheerful, who do not go about forever oppressed and solicitous, who do not unload their worries upon every stranger. They are quite capable, when in the company of others, to radiate this cheerfulness and make life more beautiful and meaningful. One can sense that they are good human beings, not only in their actions, but in the manner in which they approach, in which they speak, in which they pay attention to our interests, as well as in their entire external aspect, their clothes, their gestures, their happy emotional state, and in their laughter. That far-seeing psychologist, Dostoyevsky, has said that "One can recognize a person's character much better by his laughter than by a boring psychological examination." Laughter can make connections as well as break them. We have all heard the aggressive notes of those who laugh at others' misfortunes. There are some people who are absolutely unable to laugh because they stand so far from the innate bond which connects human beings that their ability to give pleasure or to appear happy is absent. That there is another little group of people who are utterly incapable of giving anyone else joy since they are concerned only in embittering life in every situation which they may enter. They walk around as though they wished to extinguish every light. They do not laugh at all, or only when forced to do so, or when they wish to give the semblance of being a joy-giver. The mystery of the emotions of sympathy and antipathy are thus made understandable.

The opposite of the sympathetic type occurs in those who are chronic kill-joys and marplots. They advertise the world as a vale of sorrow and pain. Some individuals go through life as though they were bent by the weight of a great load. Every little difficulty is exploited, the future appears black and depressing, and they do not miss an occasion in which others are happy, to utter doleful Cassandra-like prophecies.* They are pessimistic in every fibre, not only for themselves but for everyone else. If someone is happy in their neighborhood they become restless and attempt to find some gloomy aspect of the event. This they do, not only with their words, but with their disturbing actions, in this way preventing others from living happily and enjoying their fellowship in humanity.

*Cassandra, a Trojan princess, had the gift of prophecy, but there was a catch to it—no one would ever believe her propecies until it was too late.
Source: Adler 1929, 1959, pp. 199–200.

Famous people who have been spoken of as "saints" or "enlightened" are often described in their biographies as having lived joyfully, seeming to emanate an inner glow of happiness despite their problems and quite frequently their sufferings (Underhill 1960). Is it that kind of person who experiences life to the fullest—growing, as it is said, "in wisdom and in grace" throughout their lives? Then perhaps the degree to which we feel what is called happiness and joy is the extent to which we are becoming more and more ourselves, not driven and hounded by doubt and anxiety but following our own path (wherever it may lead), no longer at the mercy of worldly difficulties—free to grow through conscious and intelligent choice.

CARL JUNG: TYPE PSYCHOLOGY

Like Adler, Jung emphasized the individual differences in a person. Like Adler, he too broke with Freud. Like Adler, he believed that human beings were capable of developing deep "spiritual" qualities. But there were also differences between the two men. Adler was convinced that the differences that are so apparent in people (and which are discernible very early, while they are toddlers at play) are *solely the result of their early environment*. In that regard he is squarely in the *environmentalist* camp: We are what we are solely because of our early experiences in life. The environmentalist theory is one that we Americans take very seriously. As a nation, we took to heart the teachings of Freud with his insistence that our personalities are shaped by the time we are six years of age. We were also impressed by the work of Ivan Pavlov in his conditioning of dogs, and later by the work of such *behavioral* psychologists as J. B. Watson (1920) and B. F. Skinner, who both developed a theoretical framework for the conditioning of human behavior (Skinner 1938). As a nation and as a people, we have come to accept (quite wholeheartedly) the assumption that what we are is the result of our environmental differences (and nothing else!). So *internalized* (ingrained) is this assumption that we are willing to put millions (yes, even billions) of dollars into education, into welfare, into medicine, into public housing, and so on, in order to equalize the environmental advantages of those born into less favorable circumstances. There is much to be said for (much evidence to validate) the assumption that the environment into which we are born and in which we grow up has profound effects upon the developing person. In a society such as ours, which values loving nourishment and the material well-being of their children, a child born into an affluent family and to parents who provide loving, nourishing support will certainly have a "better start" than the child who is born into a family that has so many mouths to feed that they can hardly be concerned about the psychological and educational well-being of any one of them. Thus we are affected by our cultural environment based on the cultural assumptions of "equality," "the worth of formal education," "the value of affluence," and "the responsibility to provide," just to list a few of the cultural variables here. However, in addition to the noticeable effects of the environment on the developing person, other psychologists focus on the *naturing* possibilities rather than the *nurturing* possibilities. Jung studied the *nature* of the individual and explained things differently.

Individual Differences as Innate and Inborn

As we come now to discuss Jung's **type** psychology, we discover that he believed our differences are **innate**; namely, that we are born into this world very distinct human personality *types*. Furthermore, he insisted that these personality differences are *biological*—just as being born male or female is not the result of our environment but is biological (Jung 1924). Two of these *types* have become so accepted in our culture that we use them in everyday speech: *introvert* and *extravert*.

Introversion versus Extraversion

Introversion and extraversion are ways of being-in-the-world.[2] Jung emphasized the fact that the introversion-extraversion dimension *scale* is not discrete but is a continuum. Most of us, however, tend to be on one side or the other of the midpoint of this continuum; that is to say, while we all have tendencies in both directions, each of us is predominantly *introverted* or *extraverted*.

Those of us who are **extraverted** are turned out toward the world and find living in the world of people and human relationships easy for us and nourishing. We are at home in social situations, and we enjoy anything that is people related.

Jung believed we are innately different personality types: we are born either introverted or extroverted.

Introverts, on the other hand, are turned inward toward their own thoughts and/or feelings. We may enjoy a brief sojourn into the world of people and society, but we are ever ready to retreat into our own psyche (our own inner thoughts and feelings), to re-establish our sense of well-being and creativity. There is never a "better" between introversion and extraversion. Both orientations have their advantages and disadvantages, which we now discuss more fully.

THE EXTRAVERTED TYPE. Since the consciousness of an extraverted person looks out onto the external world for meaning and value, the extravert is immensely interested in other people who come their way, in the events of their immediate environment, and also in the larger social scene. Generally the orientation of extraverted persons is compatible with societal values, making them rather easy to be around. Extraverted persons seem to accommodate to others relatively easily and manage the interpersonal and social arenas with relative efficiency. At their best, extraverted persons are adaptable and affable, and can get projects and tasks accomplished with relative ease. That is why they make skillful executives—they know how to run meetings and are able to calm an atmosphere when a discussion gets prickly and people are at each other's throats.[3] At their worst, extraverts do not seem to have a sense of themselves, and thus they pursue "popularity" to the extent that they are overconforming and seem to lack self-identity and self-direction.

THE INTROVERTED TYPE. In contrast to the extraverted type the introverted type focuses on his or her internal feelings, thoughts, ideas, and fantasies. Since introverted types are more motivated by their subjective experiences, they are less interested in public opinion or even what others think of them. They are stimulated by new ideas and theories but always by their own reactions to what they come upon. The introvert is less outgoing than is the extravert, more solitary, more independent of thought, and more able to take firm stands on issues regardless of public approbation or disapproval. The introvert is harder to understand and get along with and less able to express emotions. Finally, introverted types do not value status or economic achievement as much as the pursuit and understanding of what they deem important to them. The introvert makes a good scientist, scholar, accountant, or political theorist. All such designations are a matter of degree.

The two types are different even in the psychological disturbances they exhibit. The extraverted type is apt to be oversuggestible and therefore more prone to hysteria and other psychophysical ailments. The introvert's most frequent neurosis is morbid fantasy, a type of depression, and this type person can become a recluse. The extravert suffers from a loss of selfhood; the introvert suffers from agonies of the spirit. It has become axiomatic that Americans have developed an essentially extraverted philosophy and mode of life with their emphasis on participatory democracy, group membership, peer acceptance, and the importance of "popularity," physical attractiveness, and youth. The introvert, by contrast, in our society may be so out of touch with the prevailing mores of his or her society as to become a "born loser." Nevertheless, one can find highly successful introverts in the United States in the universities, in the scientific laboratories, in art studios, and in any place where human endeavor relies more on highly individualistic emotional and intellectual insights than on group cooperation.

Jung's Four Functions: Sensing/Intuiting/Thinking/Feeling

Jung's work on introversion-extraversion was followed by his work on what he called the **four functions** of human personality. Jung concluded that how we evaluate our experiences and act on them can be divided into four distinct functions; **sensing, intuiting, thinking,** and **feeling.**

THE SENSING FUNCTION.   According to Jung, there are two basic ways of receiving information and making sense of the world, by *sensing* or by *intuiting*. Sensing is what we do when we systematically apprehend our surroundings through the physical senses. We observe the size and shape of a room, estimate a person's weight, get a "map" in our head when we walk or drive somewhere, observe how someone is dressed and that person's physical features. Persons who are good *sensors* appreciate neatness and orderliness, are able to remember names and faces, and generally have a grasp for how physical things work and operate. Consequently, they make good engineers, construction foremen, carpenters, accountants, office managers—jobs that require an accurate perception of external details.

THE INTUITIONAL FUNCTION.   The intuitional function is something like a hunch or an "extra sense." It enables us to know not only what is there but what is *not* there. It allows us to imagine possibilities and to grasp the intangible. People who have a strong intuitive sense may not be able to tell you *how* they have come to a conclusion, but they seem to do it quickly. The sensing person will take out a pocket calculator and will be very good with it; the intuitive one prefers to make a hypothetical guess first and then to corroborate it. Although the intuitive person may arrive at some completely wrong guesses, at other times the intuitive person may provide an answer or solution that astonishes colleagues and friends. Highly

---

BOX 3.2

OPPOSITE ENDS OF THE SENSOR-INTUITIVE CONTINUUM

A good example of the difference between a *sensor* and an *intuitive* can be seen in the lives of Thomas Edison and Albert Einstein. Edison had a remarkable genius for grasping a pragmatic problem and for understanding the physical properties of elements. His ability to put things together resulted in hundreds of practical inventions, including the phonograph and the electric light. Einstein, who represents the classic *intuitive,* bequeathed to us nothing of a directly practical nature, but his insights into the relationship of mass and energy enlarged (and fine-tuned) our entire perception of the universe itself.

---

intuitive persons are not as steady and sure-footed in the physical world as are the persons with a strong sensing function. They can be very absent-minded, lose their keys and wallets, not be sure what day it is, or even not realize that a friend has shaved his beard weeks or months ago. But if intuitive persons do not have a good grasp on external reality, they seem to be able to grasp the intangible aspects of everyday situations and interpersonal relationships. When a problem seems to have no logical, rational, easily found solution, the intuitive may be able to cut through the impasse with a new idea or perceive a more direct relationship between the identified variables.

THE THINKING FUNCTION.   We have said that the intuition-sensing polarity is the way by which we *perceive* the events that shape our lives. The other polar function of thinking-feeling pertains to how we *evaluate* this information, how we react to it, and what we conclude about it. We do so, according to Jung, in one of two ways: we *think* it through, step by step, and try to reach an accurate and logical conclusion, or we come to an *emotional* appraisal of the situation. Persons who have a strong thinking function weigh the pros and cons of a situation and the advantages or disadvantages of one of several solutions and make what we would call a rational decision. The person who has a strong thinking function does well in those situations that need objective analysis and precise decision making and for which the necessary raw data can be supplied.

THE FEELING FUNCTION.   The feeling function is another evaluative mode. It is not only whether we like or dislike someone or something but whether that someone or something will have a positive or a negative outcome for us. Not all situations can be properly apprehended in a completely disinterested and logical way, since we do not have all the facts at all times. The person with a strong feeling function can, in a sense, fill in the missing data by picking up the "mood" or "feeling" that does not show up in a set of figures or specifications. For example, the *thinker* can respond to what a person says, but the *feeler* can pick up what another is feeling but is unable to express directly or doesn't want to express. Feeling types make excellent elementary-school teachers, nurses, and counselors because they are able to deal with a person's emotional responses even if the person is unable to verbalize them.

USE OF ALL THE FUNCTIONS.   Each of us uses all four functions even if we rely predominantly on just one or two. When we need to come to logical conclusions using facts and figures or when we need to make a rational analysis of current conditions, that is the time to use our *thinking* function. When we need to decide the value of something to us, or whether this or that course of action would be *better* for us, that is the time to use our *feeling* function. When we need to get around in our physical or social world, that is the time to use our *sensing* function. When we need to break out of our conditioned mind set and make a breakthrough into something new, that is the time to use our *intuition*. To *think*, to *feel*, to *sense*, and to *intuit*: These are the four elements that Jung considered the basic functions of human personality.

Using Type Psychology to Understand Ourselves and Others

When we do not understand other persons, it is probably because their way of functioning in the world differs significantly from ours. Some people *feel* their way around the world and are comfortable with the emotional self: laughter, tears, pain, and joy all are experienced naturally and easily. These people understand their emotions and the emotions of others. *Feelers* may not understand people who seem to *think* everything through, who are cool emotionally, and whose actions are based on a more rational decision-making process. In fact, if you ask a *thinker* what his or her feelings are on a certain situation (or topic), he or she may very well be unable to tell you (and wonders privately what feelings have to do with it). Marriage can be difficult when one partner is predominantly a *feeler* and the other is predominantly a *thinker*. In like manner, the strong *intuitive* type may be irritated by the strong *sensor* type, since the *sensor* seems to stay too close to the surface or to the facts. The *sensor*, on the other hand, may accuse the *intuitive* as not "sticking to the facts."

BOX 3.3	**THE *THINKING* HUSBAND AND THE *FEELING* WIFE**

In our culture, women are more likely to be *feeling* types, and men are more likely to be *thinking* types.

Read the following imaginary conversation between a couple coming home from a party and see if it correlates with any experience you have had.

WIFE:	(happily) That was a lovely party.
HUSBAND:	As parties go.
WIFE:	Well, I enjoyed myself. Didn't you?
HUSBAND:	Met a few interesting characters.
WIFE:	Like that Mr. Bergman.
HUSBAND:	(preoccupied with his driving) Mmmmm.
WIFE:	What did you think about him?
HUSBAND:	Didn't have much to say.
WIFE:	Yes, but didn't you feel something unusual about him?
HUSBAND:	Unusual? Didn't talk much. What's unusual about that?
WIFE:	Well, there was something about him. A kind of hidden quality, as if he doesn't say things but he knows so much.
HUSBAND:	How can you judge a man by what he doesn't say?
WIFE:	Oh, men! Honestly? Didn't you get a feeling about him at all?
HUSBAND:	(a little irritable) Feeling about him? I hardly *know* the man. He had one or two interesting views. Can't make much on that. You women and your feelings.
WIFE:	(a little despondently) Men are so unfeeling.
HUSBAND:	(wryly) Women are so irrational.

Source: Adapted from McCaully, 1977.

SOME NEUROSES AS THE RESULT OF LIVING OPPOSITE TO ONE'S BASIC *TYPE*.
Now Jung emphasized repeatedly that our basic personality functions stem from *biological* differences and that these are basic characteristics the person exhibits immediately at birth. It seemed to Jung that all children display these differences from earliest childhood, even in infancy, despite the similarity of environmental conditions. Children can be forced to act against their basic type by one or the other of their parents, just as children can be forced to switch from using their left hand to using their right hand, (presumably it forces the neurological system to act in reverse). In just such a way, people acting contrary to their basic personality type eventually must become neurotic, according to Jung, falsifying their own basic behavioral type.

Creative Living

Many persons came to Jung perplexed and bewildered. They were discontented and unhappy; yet they seemed to be living rich, full lives. They were successful, yet desolate. They were busy, yet poignantly restless. They were perplexed even about their perplexities. It seemed to Jung that often their basic problem was not that they were *neurotic* in the Freudian sense of being fixated at an infantile level. On the contrary, they were mature and responsible individuals. They had achieved many of their life goals, and for all intents and purposes, they were *successful* in their cultural milieu. What was twisted, or so it seemed to Jung, was that they were living their lives counter to their basic personality *types*.

BOX 3.4

JUNG'S APPLICATION OF PSYCHOLOGICAL TYPES TO HIMSELF AND HIS MENTOR, SIGMUND FREUD

An interesting aspect of Jung's psychological type theory was his observations of himself and Sigmund Freud, his teacher, as representing the two basic types of introvert and extravert. Of all Freud's students, Carl Jung was the youngest and considered by many as the most brilliant. Jung and Freud had developed a sort of father-son relationship, and it was known among the psychoanalytic group that Freud considered Jung as the "crown prince" who would take over the work of the psychoanalytic school of psychiatry. But Freud and Jung had serious disagreements, and eventually Jung broke away to form his own school, which he called analytic psychology.

In his autobiography Jung explained that part of their difference was that Freud was essentially an extravert, while he (Jung) had always been introverted. It was easy, said Jung, for Freud to preside over a group of extremely able, intellectual physicians, thinkers and theoreticians. Jung said that he, himself, was incapable of such a position, and true to his own *type,* he retired to his home in Switzerland and thereafter ventured very little into the social or political world (Jung 1963).

Jung's therapy consisted of having these persons discover their basic personality orientations and realign or reharmonize their life styles more in accord with their types. Jung made an interesting statement about the differences between himself and Freud. He attributed the differences to their different psychological types. (See box 3.4.) A businessman actively engaged in the world of people and competition (a fundamentally extraverted position) may actually be out of harmony with his own basic introverted type. What he may be longing for, in the midst of social engagements and business enterprises, is that quiet and contemplative life space so necessary to the introvert. A woman who is confined to hearth and home and who has rarely engaged in the world of people and events may not be having the opportunity to fulfill her *extraverted* needs. We are beginning now to confront such possibilities. But in Jung's day a man was supposed to deal primarily in the external world while a woman was often imprisoned within her own home. It was Jung's insight to widen the parameters of choice within the sex roles of the culture—no matter our *sex*, our *gender identity*, or any other cultural limitations.

The therapeutic resolution was *not* to adjust the person to a mode of being that was antagonistic to his or her basic personality type but rather to have that person live more in accord with it. It was oftimes a difficult reprocessing of their life space, but the overwhelming relief people described (and demonstrated) in restructuring their lives more in harmony with their basic nature convinced Jung of the validity of personality *types*.

EDUARD SPRANGER: *TYPES OF MEN*

Can there be such things as *personality types*? When Jung first presented his *type* psychology to the public, his ideas were more widely accepted in Europe than in the United States. Europeans have always placed more emphasis on heredity than on environment and so were much more open to "being born" a certain way. Europeans have long been comfortable with the basic assumption that there are certain *types* suited to *this* or *that* profession or *this* or *that* life. One German psychologist-philosopher picked up Jung's thesis and published a work that was to become a classic in Europe but which is very little known here. His name was Eduard Spranger, and the book he wrote is entitled *Types of Men: The Psychology and Ethics of Personality* (1928). Spranger was a psychologist in the same tradition as Erik Erikson, Erich Fromm, our own William James, and (more recently) Daniel Levinson. These men have the ability to grasp the widest scope of human experience and have great powers to organize what they observe in large, comprehensive vistas. Spranger's book is fascinating to read, for he seems to catch the essence of certain motivating forces within human nature.

Aesthetic/Political/Economic/Religious/Social/Theoretical

Like Jung, Spranger was frank to admit that there are few "pure" types of personality, but he was convinced that he had identified six basic life **orientations**: the **aesthetic**, the **political**, the **economic**, the **religious**, the **social**, and the **theoreti-**

cal. While we cannot summarize his work in any really adequate way, we can at least present some of the flavor of his personality "types." We beg the indulgence of our female readers in that we refer only to men, but that was Spranger's focus. Were he living in these times, he would no doubt have included women in his study of orientations.

THE THEORETICAL ORIENTATION. The first orientation discussed in Spranger's book is what he called the theoretical type. This is the person who sets *truth* as the basic meaning of life. He seeks objective knowledge and intellectual understanding for the events of this world. This type is easily identified as the scientist, the scholar, the historian, and certain writers who have a *nose for news* and an unquenchable thirst to discover "the facts." The basic mental processes are logic, reason, and analysis; seeking to objectify what has taken place. He wants to break through the ignorance of superstition and to discover the general principles and laws of the universe.

The theoretical type is not much interested in *doing* anything with this knowledge except to let it be known. He does not necessarily want to change the order of things, and in that respect he is not a political person and is rarely a revolutionary. Personal political leanings *may* be very radical, and he often gets into trouble with the powers that be, but that is generally because of political naiveté (a few of our own scientists have gotten themselves into difficulty with the government). On the other hand, he may very well be totally apolitical and very little concerned with what is going on in society. To know what is happening is enough. All other arenas take second place. He may view religion as superstition, based as it is on *belief* rather than *knowledge*. If inclined toward religion at all, it is toward **metaphysics,** i.e., the "causal" factors of the physical universe as demonstrated by scientific discoveries. If the theoretical type believes in God or a godhead, it is in the aspect of *God is Truth*.

Nor is the theoretical type attracted toward the sensual world. Art is useful only if it represents a truthful interpretation of *what is*. Money is useful only in that it affords a laboratory for use, books to serve as reference, and journeys to archeological digs or other field-research sites. But otherwise, he has little use for the luxuries money can bring. In fact, not only may he disregard the practical economic aspects of life, he may actually be very helpless in coping with everyday financial affairs. In the interpersonal arena, the "pure" theoretical type is basically *asocial*. He may have a few close personal friends, but rewards do not come from the emotional arena of family and interpersonal relationships. Work is valued and his main interpersonal relationships are with colleagues. Because of that, this type may be one of the least prejudiced of persons since he does not value class distinctions: *Who* a person is is not as important as *what* a person does to further knowledge. Thus the theoretical type is the true cosmopolitan.

THE ECONOMIC ORIENTATION. The economic type is motivated by *utility*; that is to say, what is useful and practical and makes for a sound and secure financial base is the ultimate value. The economic type is the one who enjoys the "good life" and the luxuries money can bring. He is not a roustabout, however—not at all. He is, as a matter of fact, a good "family man." He provides for the family's well-being as well as his own and works hard in business or whatever to see that the family is well taken care of. He is therefore politically conservative (or even reactionary), for he profits best from a stable social order. This type has a firm conviction that *business is business* and the signed contract must be honored because he values *what is*. Since he trusts the business and social contract, he supports *law and order*. He does not believe in divorce. He regards marriage as a social contract, at least, and sometimes a business contract. He will honor a written contract because it is the glue that holds our society together.

He may enjoy art and even collect art objects. But the enjoyment of art is in its inherent worth: They are "investments." He may be an ardent church goer. But attendance is valued for the business contacts that can be made rather than for any real religious sentiment. If he is religiously inclined, God is the *Giver of Gifts*, from whom we get "our daily bread." The economic type is very "social" and has many interpersonal contacts. "Public relations is good business." He is, for the most part, gracious, hospitable, charming—a fine host.

His attitude toward truth is pragmatic. What is *useful* and *functional* is true. Will it make money? Is it practical? Is it economically profitable? These are the values by which he is guided. And these values are applied to himself first, then the family, and then to the state.

It is easy to recognize the business person in this short thumbnail sketch, but this orientation can be found in other arenas as well. He may, for example, be found among lawyers and physicians whose motivation into these professions are less guided by a desire to help humanity than to find a profession that leads to economic security. He may be found on "the other side of the law"—the shady character who makes money through illegal means but who is a devout family man, i.e., the "godfather" of a crime syndicate. It is axiomatic that Americans have a high percentage of economic types. So do the West Germans and the Japanese, or any nation that has business *know-how*.

THE POLITICAL ORIENTATION. The political type is not motivated by *money*, as is the economic type, but by *power*. He wants power because, unlike the economic type, the political type wants to *change things*. In fact, change is his raison d'être. He does not operate on *what is* but on *what could be*. He envisions a future that is radically different from the present reality, and because of this, he frequently makes a high type of executive. If his motivations are altruistic, he can make a formidable statesman at the forefront of social change. If personal motivations are self-serving, however, he can become a dictator. If his motivations are extremely radical, he can become a revolutionary. Whatever his motivations, he is sure that he sees what is wrong with the present social scene and is convinced that he has the answer or some of the answers to correct what is wrong.

Since power and change are his basic motivations, all other interests are geared toward those ends. Art and music will be valued mainly as backdrops to political themes by way of political posters, patriotic literature, marching bands, and national anthems. His politics are his religion, although he may align with the institution of the State or Church (or some denomination thereof). He is more often a radical, who believes that *religion is the opiate of the masses* and attempts to replace it with another ideology or even science. His attitude toward truth *tends to be cautious*. Since he is not always sure that the masses are ready for *all the truth*, truth may have to be withheld to avoid chaos and panic. He has a keen interest in the social sciences (especially psychology), for these studies may hold the key to what motivates people, and motivate is what he seeks to do. He prides himself on being a keen student of human nature, and is often charismatic in personality. He is at his best with large groups of people. He has neither the time nor the inclination to develop personal relationships. He is less interested in the individual than in inspiring large groups of people to follow his leadership. He frequently has no *personal* life at all.

In Spranger's analysis of the political orientation, we can easily recognize the revolutionaries: Nicolai Lenin, Simon Bolívar, Tom Paine, and Fidel Castro. But before we regard the political person as the dictators and leaders of armies, we need to remember that they are to be found in other arenas as well. Martin Luther was a politically effective religious reformer, as were John Calvin and Oliver Cromwell. To this list we can add the names of such modern persons as Martin Luther King and Franklin D. Roosevelt, who did much to change the social order. It must be remembered that any one orientation is not, in and of itself, positive or negative. It is how that orientation is manifested in world affairs.

THE SOCIAL ORIENTATION. The basic motivation of the social person is somewhat different than we might expect. He is not the person who enjoys entertaining and the life of wine, women, and song. (That is the economic type.) The social type that Spranger describes might better be called (in American psychology) the *interpersonal* type. But let us stay with Spranger's term: social orientation. What motivates Spranger's social type is *love*: to love and be loved. Feelings, warm and deep feelings shared with others, are what nourish these persons. They are understanding and encouraging to others, and do what they can not only to make them happy but to help them reach their highest potential. Toward that end they can give of themselves, even to the point of seeming self-sacrifice. Of course, it is only others who deem it self-sacrifice. The social person sees giving not as sacrifice but as joyful opportunities to give with love. To give is to love and be loved. Such an orientation sometimes leads to acts beyond the ken of most persons. Social persons may give all their lives to others. Ultimately they may even give their own life. In a sense, perfect love may lead to perfect Christianity ("to do good to those that persecute you") or to perfect communism ("give all you have to others"). In this continuum of Christianity/communism there have developed those religious communes in both the East and West where all life is directed toward the group as a whole and, in particular, to those less fortunate. The social type does not judge the foibles and weakness of others nor ponder the inhumanity of human to human but simply relates to all others, since all of us are "children of God" and worthy of love. For this type *God is Love*.

That is the highest manifestation of the social type, bordering on and mixed with, as it so often is, the religious orientation. Here we can identify the great and loving saints of all religions, who spent their lives doing "unto others as you would have them do unto you." But in less dramatic form, they are to be found elsewhere: the missionary-physician who spends his life in serving the starving of a war-torn Africa; the foster parents who open their homes to waifs who have nowhere else to go; the gentle teachers and counselors and nurses who regard their professions not just as a way to make money but as a way to serve humankind.

Lest the reader think there would be no possible negative aspect to the social type, we present the darker side of this orientation. If the need to love and be loved becomes too self-motivated, then love can go awry and become possessive, jealous, clinging, and deadly. It can even turn to hate and be the motivation for personal retaliation and vindictiveness; even mother love can become *smother love*—or worse. Spranger uses an example from Greek mythology: the horrifying story of Jason and Medea. Medea's love for Jason turned into such hatred that she killed their children out of her desire to revenge his betrayal and abandonment of her.

The other arenas of life have little value to the "pure" social type. Truth may have to be withheld if it will hurt or destroy. Art is not beautiful if it presents humanity in an ignoble light. Knowledge is useful if it serves a humanitarian purpose, and that does not include economics, which is considered selfish and self-seeking.

THE AESTHETIC ORIENTATION. The aesthetic type is perhaps the easiest to identify. We find him in the arts, in the world of music and dance and literature and drama. Today he is frequently found in show business. He may be found, too, in architecture or among those who design ships, cars, and planes and those who know how function and line are related. But we find the aesthetic in other areas, too: the flower breeder or the person who tends his lawn and garden for the sheer beauty it brings.

The central motivation of this person is, of course, beauty. At his most ardent, he wants to create art. In a less ardent form, perhaps, he wants to make his life a work of art—and we call him, sometimes, a dilettante. Also like the theoretical type, the true aesthetic type does not have much regard for money except insofar as what he can buy in order to further his work. Indeed, he may be willing to starve for years in the proverbial artist's garret. Also like the theoretical type, he is not much interested in the political world. He may be vaguely liberal, but his is a lukewarm liberalism. He is seldom to be found in the front lines of a demonstration, for "causes" weary him after a while. Unlike the theoretical type, however, the aesthetic type does not avoid interpersonal experiences and has a passionate engagement with life. As with the social type, feelings dominate, but they arise from a different motivation. The aesthetic type is open to everything life has to offer: suffering as well as joy, pain as well as delight. For the aesthetic type, "Beauty is truth; truth, beauty" (John Keats). There *is* one experience that the aesthetic person cannot abide, and that is boredom. Boredom is to be avoided at any cost. People are valued for the excitement they engender in the aesthetic type. Once the excitement is gone, so is the aesthetic type. It's as if they are saying to the world, "Love me, hate me, make me angry, sad, or elated—but don't *bore* me." This constant desire for continual sensation may lead the aesthetic type to extremes—for example, drug addiction, or into sexual sadomasochism, or into the utter jadedness that comes from satiation of one's worldly appetites. Love, even romantic love, may be not so much a heartfelt emotion (as it is for the social type) as an experience. In the last analysis, he is less interested in an enduring and deep emotional commitment than in what he can learn within an emotional relationship—until there is nothing more to learn. Then he leaves. Emotionally, he is not cold but cool.

THE RELIGIOUS ORIENTATION. The primary motivation of the "pure" religious type is to derive *meaning* from life. Of course, he is not alone in that. We are all, in one way or another, trying to make sense out of the many events that we encounter. We are all trying to make sense of such seemingly *senseless* things as poverty, illness, war, degradation, and other "evils' of life. But where we are content to derive small personal answers, the religious type is not. He is searching for the underlying and universal meaning of existence itself. He is certain there is such meaning, and from time to time he is certain he has had glimpses into the riddle of the world and of the universe and of *why* we are here. The rest of us may be willing to wait for those answers or to never know them at all—simply to take life as it comes. The religious type is not.

The religious type is determined to search out those answers, and spends his life working toward that quest. Sometimes while searching it seems that he has grasped some brilliant insight into the "why" of life, and he describes the moment of insight as being accompanied by experiences of transcendent joy. Other times he feels at one with the universe itself (Bucke 1961). The sense of cosmic consciousness is his keenest desire. The true religious type is a mystic.

It is not easy for us, in this day and age, to comprehend the pure religious type. He is not so fashionable in this era of materialism and scientific skepticism. Too, the mystic does not speak in a voice that others easily understand. Indeed, sometimes what he has tried to tell us may take centuries to be grasped. In his own time and era he was (and oftentimes still is) called a *fool*, a *lunatic*, a *dreamer*. Sometimes he is persecuted or put to the fire or otherwise crucified.

Nevertheless, the religious type continues his search to know God and the purpose of life. As he makes his life journey, he attempts to avoid the ensnarements of worldly passions and spends whatever time he can in prayer, in contemplation, in meditation—or in whatever manner his religious tradition has provided—so that he may hear that "still, small voice" within him. Because of his one-pointedness toward cosmic union, he may regard art as seduction. He pays scant attention to the political network of human society ("Render unto Caesar the things that are Caesar's"). Money is so many "pieces of silver," and power is one of the temptations of the "devil." Even education does not impress, cognizant as he is that all we mortals can know of the universal truth are small fragments of the whole. The understanding that he seeks does not come by education or by academic scholarship or by scientific advances. He is seeking the ultimate religious or mystic experience, and that comes only by way of *revelation*. For him *God is a spirit and must be worshipped in spirit and in truth.*

His attitude toward others is kindly. Like the social type, he will stop to help others less fortunate. He, too, will give what he has to the poor. He, too, will minister to the sick of body and weary of heart, but his acts arise not from personal love but from universal compassion. Human relationships are not his highest value since his *primary relationship is to God* (Buber 1957, 1958, 1970). Toward the possibility of mystic union, he mortifies his flesh and avoids personal human in-

Box 3.5   PERSONALITY TYPES AS IDENTIFIED BY SPRANGER

		THEORETICAL	ECONOMIC	POLITICAL	SOCIAL	AESTHETIC	RELIGIOUS
1.	Motivations	TRUTH Objective knowledge; logic, reason (he analyzes, classifies).	UTILITY Self-preservation; security, the "good life," comfort, luxury	POWER To change world, influence others; be a force in the world.	LOVE Service to others; to nurture, to love and be loved.	BEAUTY To create art; to make of one's life a work of art.	MEANING Ultimate knowledge comes only from God.
2.	Values and Trusts	Progress through knowledge; education, research, and science.	What works and is useful; money and family; written and social contracts.	Self-autonomy; freedom from physical passions; oriented toward future.	Feelings are predominant; encourage the highest potential; warm, sympathetic.	People valued as emotional experiences; open to all experience.	Deals kindly with others; primary relationship is with God.
3.	Highest value	To break through ignorance, to discover.	To enjoy security, comfort, and luxury.	To influence the lives of others; effect social change.	To love and be loved.	To express self and individuality.	To receive spiritual gifts and the "grace of God."
4.	Attitude toward politics	Apolitical or radical.	Conservative or reactionary; "law and order."	Revolutionary.	Pure socialism; perfect Christian communism.	Liberal; not active.	Political indifference.
5.	Attitude toward beauty	Only truth is beautiful.	Art prized for "net worth."	As background for political themes.	People are the ultimate beauty.	Highest good only meaning.	World is not beautiful.
6.	Attitude toward truth	Truth at any price.	What is functional.	Withhold to avoid panic.	A sword that can help or destroy.	Beauty is truth; Truth is beauty.	Truth is divine.
7.	Attitude toward religion	If religious, metaphysical; God is truth.	Church-goer; God is giver of gifts.	God is all-powerful ruler of world.	We are God's children. God is love.	Everything is God; God is everything; God is beauty.	Seeks union with God; God is spirit.

8.	Attitude toward money	May be impractical.	Able to multiply resources; Everyone "has a price."	Useful for political purposes; Own life austere.	To bring health or happiness to others.	Has negative value; art is invaluable.	Little use; brings neither goodness nor happiness.
9.	Attitude toward knowledge	Values education; progress through knowledge.	Values practical knowledge; technology.	Power of knowledge; of motivation of others.	Knowledge applied in service to others.	Experience is knowledge.	Revelation; ultimate knowledge is from God.
10.	Attitude toward social interaction	Asocial; cosmopolitan; work is life; likes quiet life.	Many social relationships; Everyone has a price.	Charismatic leader; may have no personal life.	Compassionate, warm, loving; human life is sacred.	Impersonal; others valued for experience, not in and of themselves.	Kindly with others; primary relationship with God.
11.	Attitude toward emotions	Distrusts feelings; values thinking.	Focused on family comforts; power of caring.	Little, if any, emotional personal life.	Guided by emotions of love, agape.	Passionately emotional; only boredom avoided.	Self-denial of human emotions.
12.	Education	Science, research.	Technological education.	Political science.	Helping professions.	Humanities.	The word of God.
13.	Highest type	Philosopher, scholar, researcher: Plato, Aristotle, Einstein.	Executive businessman: Alexander Hamilton, Andrew Carnegie.	Statesman, diplomat: Thomas Jefferson, Franklin Roosevelt.	Humanitarian, counselors: Tolstoy, Abraham Lincoln.	Artist, director playwright: George Sand, Mozart, Shakespeare.	Saint, "man of the cloth": William Blake, Albert Schweitzer, Francis of Assissi

SOURCE: Adapted from Eduard Spranger, Types of Men: The Psychology and Ethics of Personality (New York: Johnson Reprint Corp., 1928). Note: Some of the names listed for types are Spranger's; others are ours. We would be interested in the readers' nominations for category 13.

volvements. His rewards come when he receives spiritual gifts—what various religions have called the *grace of God, satori, Zen, enlightenment, at-one-ment*, and *divine realization*. But in between these moments of splendid illumination, the religious types may suffer long dry periods when they seem to be unable to have those visions that mean so much to them. At these times, they suffer the doubt and loneliness St. John of the Cross describes as "The Dark Night of the Soul." To point to some of these religious types, we need only mention such Western figures as Francis of Asissi, the Protestant Meister Eckhart, the astonishing Teresa of Avila, or that entity who died on the cross two thousand years ago, Jesus Christ. The East, too, has its religious types: Guatama, Buddha of India, Lao-Tsu of China, Milarepa of Tibet, and Zoroaster of the Middle East. These are the gemstones of the religious type. There are also the darker elements as well, for no one type is without its negative manifestations. There are those who become the *crazy fool* or the *dark magician*, the one who "sells himself to the devil," or becomes a devil worshipper. Simon Magus, in the first century A.D., fell to his death, believing he could fly. Goethe's Faust sold his soul to the devil. Torquemada, of the terrible Inquisition, tortured those he believed to be heretics—to save their souls. In our times, we have witnessed the religious type gone wrong with the Jonestown tragedy.

Allport's Use of Spranger's Work: The Study of Values

We said earlier that Spranger's work had an impact mainly upon European psychology. But it had an impact, also, on this side of the Atlantic. Although it is not generally well known, we did make use of Spranger's orientations in a most interesting way. The American psychologist Gordon Allport (whom we mentioned earlier) used Spranger's work for our first generally accepted vocational interest test. Allport and his associates translated Spranger's theoretical formulations into what they called *The Study of Values Inventory* (Allport, Vernon, & Lindzey 1951). It is a simple paper-and-pencil test, which can be self-administered and self-scored. What it does is present a series of questions such as "If you have a free evening, would you rather go to the theater or attend an organization meeting for a cause you are supporting?" That is not an actual question, but the reader can easily see what such an item is trying to tap—are you more interested in artistic expression (the aesthetic orientation) or in effecting change (the political orientation)? Gordon Allport believed, very firmly, that we are not entirely controlled and dominated by unconscious forces, nor that we are necessarily always at war with our *unconscious strivings*. He believed (as you will remember from chapter 1) that we all have *propriate strivings*, individual to us, which motivate us to the highest achievements of our lives (Allport 1955).

He believed that healthy persons can act at a very rational and conscious level and can be fully aware of those motivations, motivations that are fully as important to the individual as his or her sexual motivations. He believed, moreover, that the healthy personality is one that recognizes these motiviations within the self. The word *propriate* has the connotation of being basic and unique to one's

BOX 3.6

THE PROPRIATE STRIVINGS OF ROALD AMUNDSEN

Allport cites Roald Amundsen as an example of a man who early recognized what he wanted from his life and even at an early age lived his life according to his most *appropriate* and *propriate* motivation.

Early in life, when just an adolescent, Roald Amundsen determined to be an explorer. The young Amundsen was afraid that the world was running out of unexplored territory, so he decided that he would discover the North Pole. He figured that it was so difficult to reach the Pole, it would still be undiscovered by the time he had prepared himself and gathered the funds to organize the dog-sled team and equipment for the journey. For years he trained for the challenge, a challenge that had already cost the lives of several others in tragic attempts. He learned to trek by dog sled in the snow (he was Norwegian, so it was relatively easy to find snow). He put himself on semistarvation diets, learned to eat what we now call K-rations, and did arduous physical training. He often spent months in isolation in preparation for that time when there would be nothing and no one else in his world save gray skies and white, blinding snow. He learned the habits and strengths of his huskies over many weeks and months of wind and fury. There is very little here that seems to show sexual motivation. But there does seem to be a very deep other motivation, which Allport called propriate to Amundsen. But we have told only half the story. Just as he had gotten to that point where he could set off on his across-the-seas journey, the North Pole was discovered by Robert E. Peary. It might have been enough to knock the life winds out of another person's sails. But not Amundsen's! Nothing could keep him from his central goal—not obstacles, disappointments, discouragement, fatigue, hunger, ridicule, or danger. He simply turned his compass sights in the opposite direction and was the first man to reach the South Pole—a journey far more hazardous than the one northward (Allport 1955).

self. Propriate strivings propel us toward a creative future, i.e., a life *appropriate* for our own specific and personal well-being and sense of satisfaction. Fulfilling our propriate strivings enables us to lead the kind of life *we* want to lead, and not what others want us to do. It is from this satisfaction of having done what was important to us that we know we are living (as it is said) a *well-lived life* (Allport 1955).

We Are All Mixtures, Most Likely

There is probably no such animal as a *pure orientation* type according to Spranger's theoretical framework. We are probably all mixtures of two or more components. Thus we may be put off by someone's exterior, not recognizing the person's most basic orientation. But it is probable that one of the orientations prevails in each of us. We give as example the famous and awesome Dr. Albert

Schweitzer. Schweitzer was born to well-educated and well-to-do parents in Germany in the last century. He could have had a life of ease. He was, moreover, a remarkable young man not only because of his intellectual abilities but also because of his musical gifts. When he went to college, he achieved not one, but four, Ph.D. degrees, in music, medicine, philosophy, and religion. He was a gifted interpreter of Bach and could have had a brilliant career as a concert organist, a college professor, a physician, or as a theologian in a very distinguished and wealthy church.

Thus he was a combination of orientations: theoretical, aesthetic, social, and religious. What he did choose to do with his life was to become a medical missionary in Lambaréné, Africa. A famous personality theorist of our acquaintance visited Albert Schweitzer at his world-famous field hospital and found him "cold and distant"—not at all his picture of a compassionate humanitarian—in fact "a phony." Well, hardly that! But that distant quality, which our friend saw in him, indicates that Schweitzer's *social orientation* was not his dominant one. He was devoted to the natives of Africa, but his motivation was not to develop warm, interpersonal relationships with them. It was, not even by his own admission, *to minister to the sick and the poor* but, as a result of his deeply religious orientation, *"to follow in the footsteps of Christ."* He was a wise enough man to understand his motivations, for he could have had any one of the most famous chairs in European universities—in any of his several degrees. He chose what brought him most satisfaction (Schweitzer 1980). And perhaps that is what wisdom is—or part of it: "To know who we are and where we belong" (Heidegger 1969).

WILLIAM SHELDON: SOMATOTYPES

So far we have been looking at the matter from a clinical point of view; that is to say, the *types* have been described by persons who are acutely observant of human nature. But psychologists are never content with clinical data. American psychologists, in particular, endeavor to back up such clinical data with more sophisticated kinds of research. One of the first to tackle the problem of individual *types* was a man by the name of William Sheldon (Sheldon, Stevens, & Tucker 1940). Sheldon was determined to see if there are any genuine correlations between our physical characteristics and our social-emotional-mental dispositions, so to speak.

Is There a Correlation Between Physical and Personality Characteristics?

There is a kind of literary tradition that one's physical characteristics indicate one's emotional temperament. For example, we picture jolly old St. Nick as fat and good natured, but Ebenezer Scrooge, that old skinflint of Dickens's famous story, is portrayed as thin and bony—miserable not only in temperament but in physique. Shakespeare characterized that lover of women and wine, Falstaff, as large and portly but Cassius (the man who plots the assasination of Julius Caesar) as having a "lean and hungry look" and asserted that "such men are dangerous."

That is the literary tradition. Is there, psychologists have wondered from time to time, any truth to this in real life? Is there a correlation between a corpulent frame and a love of *the good life?* Are thin persons misanthropic and discontented? This was a question Sheldon attempted to answer.

Mesomorphs, Endomorphs, and Ectomorphs

These were the kinds of questions Sheldon undertook with his investigations, correlating physical constitution and mental-emotional attributes. He photographed four thousand young college men in the nude; compared their likes, dislikes, interests, hobbies, recreations, and values; and concluded his research by suggesting that there are three basic body types: the *mesomorph*, the *endomorph* and the *ectomorph*, each of which is correlated with three basic temperaments. Sheldon based his three types on embryonic tissue development: *visceral* tissue, *nervous* tissue, and *muscular* tissue. The **mesomorph** is mostly muscle, bone, and connective tissue, giving a person's body a hard, firm, strong, and rectangular shape. These persons, with their concentration of muscle, have athletic, active, temperaments and constantly use their motor apparatus—and are always "on the

Can you identify these persons according to Sheldon's physical classifications?

go." The **endomorph,** by contrast, has proportionately more of his body given over to the visceral organs and to those areas of the body connected with the digestive tract. Such body types tend to be rounder, and physically softer and possess an emotionally *easy temperament*. They prefer spectator sports, like to eat, enjoy the *good things* of life. In general, they are affable in disposition. The **ectomorph,** on the other hand, is thin, poorly muscled, *all skin and nerves*. The ectomorph prefers quiet, intellectual activities and is quite a bit more introverted than the other two types are. Many college professors seem to fit the physical and emotional characteristics of the ectomorph.

Again, one should not get the impression that there is any such thing as a pure type. Most of us will be a combination of types and have mixed characteristics. Sheldon's research has been highly criticized, but we are left with the inescapable fact that Sheldon and his associates did discover that certain physical and emotional characteristics seem to correlate. If that is the case, then even the body type we are born with may influence our personality.

Basic Biological Differences

After Sheldon's work, there developed an interest in the biological differences of human beings. Researchers working in the field of physiology began to note wide variation in our actual physical structure. They began to realize that there are vast differences among us. Some of us have high metabolic rates of functioning; others have slower metabolic rates. Some persons are colorblind. We vary in our visual acuity, in our hearing acuity, even in how acutely we smell and taste and feel pain and pressure. Some of us, for example, have a high threshold for physical pain; some have a lower threshold. It has been noted, for example, that women have a lower pain threshold than men, and women tend also to have better hearing than men—that is to say, they are able to hear more acutely and to hear higher frequencies than men (Grastyn & Molnar 1981). We demonstrate differences in almost every psycho-physical continuum there is—so much so that some biophysiologists and psychologists are convinced that these differences must affect our total psychological organization, which may account for our "natural" interests, motivations, enjoyments, and satisfaction (Anastasi 1965; Williams 1969, 1979; Levine & Shefner 1981). Whether these differences are the result of environment or whether they are the result of some innate quality with which we come into the world is still a very tentative question. But it is the kind of question psychologists and other social scientists like to ponder and research.

RESEARCH EVIDENCE: THE CHILD IS FATHER TO THE MAN

In the 1950s and 1960s a group of researchers, Thomas, Chess, and Birch, (1970) began to study the personalities of infants and neonates. As physicians, they had frequent occasion to interact with families with "problem" children and also with families that did not have such problem children. The families themselves did not seem to be significantly different in background or treatment of their children. As they continued their research, they began to grow impatient with the Freudian (and neo-Freudian) insistence that our basic personality structures are entirely the result of our early childhood. They decided to launch a long-range investigation of a child's behavioral traits and see if they were simply *phases* a child goes through or whether these traits were basic and innate and predictive of adult personality.

Early Infancy/Childhood Differences . . .

Now it is difficult to describe personality traits in a toddler, much less in an infant. So the kinds of characteristics they isolated are a little different from what we may describe as adult personality traits. The kinds of characteristics they were able to isolate were such things as the following. Did the child have a "high activity level" or a "low activity level"? (Did she squirm and move around a lot when eating or crying or sleeping?). Did she demonstrate a high or a low "sensitivity to stimuli"? (Was she easily awakened? Did she respond quickly to touch or to visual objects put in front of her? Was she generally in a good mood and playful or did she cry or often seem irritable and unfriendly?) In fact, they identified nine such characteristics. (See box 3.7.)

. . . That Seem to be Long Lasting

They found, too, that these characteristics tended to be long lasting into childhood, and then as they further followed up these children, they found that these characteristics proved to be long lasting into adolescence and adulthood. For example, one child whose observers reported as high in *activity level* almost from birth continued to demonstrate this activity level very clearly. At six months he was constantly *swimming* in his bath; at twelve months he squirmed so much that his parents had difficultly dressing him; and at fifteen months he was on the go so quickly that his parents spent much time chasing after him. In nursery school his teacher reported that he was so active that he seemed to climb like a monkey and run like an unleashed puppy. His kindergarten teacher reported that he would "hang from the walls and climb on the ceiling." Part of this child's school problems could be attributed to his hyper (but not pathological) activity.

Personality Traits Seem to Cluster

What the researchers discovered also is that certain traits seemed to cluster together. They were described as the *easy child*, the *slow-to-warm-up child*, and the *difficult child*.

THE EASY CHILD. Easy children were generally positive and cheerful in mood, had a low or moderate intensity of reaction, were adaptable, quickly estab-

Box 3.7 MUSSEN AND CONGER: INDIVIDUAL DIFFERENCES

TEMPERAMENT	RATING	6 MONTHS	1 YEAR	5 YEARS	10 YEARS
Activity level	High	Bounces in crib.	Climbs into things.	Always runs.	Sports; can't sit still.
	Low	Plays quietly.	Sleeps easily.	Slow moving.	Chess, reading; eats slowly
Quality of mood	Positive	Plays; smiles.	Laughs loudly.	Laughs easily.	Enjoys new accomplishments.
	Negative	Cries over food.	Cries if left alone.	Cries if frustrated.	Cries when tired; can't do.
Approach/ withdrawal	Positive	Likes new foods.	Approaches strangers.	Glad to go to school.	Glad to go to camp.
	Negative	Plays with new toys.	Sleeps in own bed.	Sad to go to school.	Homesick at camp.
Rhythmicity	Regular	Punctual sleeping.	Naps regularly.	Bedtime is sleeptime.	Sleeps, eats at regular times.
	Irregular	Naps, eating vary.	Naps poorly.	Sleep, food vary.	Sleep, food vary.
Adaptability	Adaptive	Likes new foods.	Not afraid of toys.	Now likes school.	Learns enthusiastically.

	Not adaptive	Fusses and cries.	Rejects new foods.	Hand-led to school	Does not adjust well.
Threshold of responsivity	Low	Refuses foods; hides.	Spits out foods.	Wants foods just so.	Adjusts things to just right.
	High	Eats everything.	Strangers are okay.	Focused attention.	Never complains, even when sick.
Intensity of reaction	Intense	Cries loudly.	Laughs & cries hard.	Rushes to greet dad.	Slams doors; tears up mistakes.
	Mild	Cries rarely.	Fusses rarely.	Laughs rarely.	Corrects mistakes quietly.
Distractibility	Is	Will stop crying.	Makes things a game.	Can be lead toward.	Difficult choosing; silence.
	Is not	Cries until bottle.	Rejects substitutes.	Cries when hurt.	Read, watch TV; same time.
Attention span and persistence	Long	Watches intently.	Plays by self.	Practices intently.	Does homework carefully.
	Short	Sucks tentatively.	Gives up easily.	Fidgets; gives up.	Interrupts own activities.

SOURCE: Adapted from Paul Mussen et al., Psychological Development: A Life-Span Approach (New York: Harper & Row, 1979).

lished regular sleeping and feeding schedules, and later participated easily in school routines. They presented very few problems in child rearing either at home or at school. Easy children comprised about 40 percent of their total sample.

THE SLOW-TO-WARM CHILD. *Slow-to-warm* children had a low activity level, but unlike the *easy* children, they tended to withdraw from new situations and were slow to adapt. They were somewhat negative in mood and needed time to get used to new routines. Once they did so, however, they were able to fit in to what was asked or required of them. They just took longer to adapt. They made up 15 percent of the sample.

THE DIFFICULT CHILD. *Difficult* children were difficult from the beginning, both in their bodily functions and in their psychosocial functions. They had irregular feeding and sleeping routines. They found it hard to adapt to new situations. They tended to cry a great deal, and even their laughter and crying had a certain characteristic, loud quality. They were a trial to their parents and also to their teachers, and they comprised about 10 percent of the sample.

SOME CHILDREN UNDERGO CONTINUAL CHANGE. What about the rest of the sample? Well, some of the children could not be described as belonging to any of the other categories, and many of these children had characteristics that seemed to belong to all three categories, so the researchers decided (very wisely indeed), not to force categories on these children to make a nice fit. One thing they did notice was that some of these children did not show a basic constancy of temperament but in fact seemed to have a remarkable characteristic of manifesting extraordinary change at one or another time in their lives. Although the researchers did not have the opportunity to follow up this observation, they opined that perhaps there are some children (and adults) in whom inconsistency is a basic characteristic.

What can we deduce from this kind of longitudinal research? Well, there are mothers who have been saying exactly that—this child was easy to care for right from birth while her other child was a handful from the moment she got him home. But there is a question that is still not answered. Can such differences in personality be inborn, or are they environmentally developed? The environmentalists would insist on this line of argument: We are not beginning *early* enough in our study of persons. Environment does not begin at birth but in the womb. In fact, the womb may be the most influential and intimate environment there is.

The Results of the *Twin Studies*

How else can we get at this question, then? One way would be to take identical twins and separate them at birth. If the children are identical twins, then we know that their genetic characteristics are the same, and any differences that show up would seem to be the result of their environmental experiences. Now psychologists cannot do that kind of thing no matter how much they might yearn to. However, owing to various tragic circumstances, there have been a remarkable number of such cases: identical twins who have been adopted at birth into different families and raised under different circumstances. These twins have been studied by a number of researchers and, over time, the statistics have been examined and re-examined and the results hotly debated. At the present time, however, the weight of prevailing opinion is as follows: Identical twins raised in different environments tend to show more similarity to each other than to their adoptive parents or to their adoptive siblings! This resemblance shows up in a number of ways, moreover. Their physical traits remain remarkably similar not only in childhood and adulthood but in their sixties and seventies. In tests of intelligence this same similarity was discovered. The kinds of physical diseases they came down with were the same and at the same age period. This similarity in disease vulnerability demonstrated itself even in the area of mental illness. If one twin demonstrated a tendency to schizophrenia, so did the other (Farber 1980, Newman, et al. 1982).

The University of Minnesota Twin Study

One of the most intensive studies of twins raised in different environments is being carried on at the present time at the University of Minnesota (Holden 1984). Although it will be years before all the findings are in and tabulated, some of the early research-in-progress reports have been published in some of our most popular scientific journals—and fascinating reading it is! This study is virtually unprecedented in scope because it involves a wide interdisciplinary team of psychologists, psychiatrists, and physicians, who are studying the twins in every way possible, including psychological case histories, medical histories, physiological tests, testing of personality, tests of special abilities, intelligence testing, vocational interest testing, and personal interviews. What they wear, what they eat, how they walk, talk, gesture—even their idiosyncracies—are being observed and recorded. A few of these twins had never seen their siblings before the study. Yet the resemblances were remarkable.

One example from this study is the English twins, Bridget and Dorothy, who were thirty-nine years old at the time of investigation and had never met before. When they first met, to take part in the study, it was noted that each twin had manicured hands and wore seven (no less—seven!) rings. They had, apparently, an attachment to jewelry, since they each also wore two bracelets on one wrist and one bracelet on the other. The investigators in this study are still spooked by the rings phenomenon.

Thomas Bouchard, the chief investigator, admits that he began his research squarely in the camp of the environmentalists. He has been astounded at some of the similarities in personality and physical appearance. Take, as another example, the Jim twins, as they have come to be known. The two Jims were adopted as infants into working-class Ohio families, and they, too, never knew each other before the study. Yet they both liked math and disliked spelling. They both had law-enforcement training and had worked as deputy sheriffs, part time. They had both vacationed in Florida. Both preferred Chevrolets. Both had the same smoking patterns and liquor patterns. And if that is not enough, they both had a tendency to chew their fingernails right down to the nubs.

One interesting note was tendered by the researchers: Twins who were reared separately may even be more similar than those reared together. The reason for this, they explain, is that twins reared together tend to take polar positions. If one is more aggressive, that twin will tend to be the leader and the other the follower. If one twin does more of the talking, the other will be content to let him or her talk. When twins are reared separately, these exaggerated differences do not seem to show up.

We will leave the twin studies to return to two areas of research that have recently opened up: racial and ethnic differences and the differences that are associated with what is called left-brain/right-brain dominance.

DANIEL FREEDMAN: THE SURPRISING DIFFERENCES IN NEONATES

The study we quoted earlier that focused on long-range personality characteristics from infancy (Thomas, Chess, & Birch 1970) lacked an essential perspective. That personality patternings in infants were likely to be characteristic of the children in later years, even into adolescence and adulthood, there seemed to be no doubt. But these findings were criticized in that the babies were studied a few weeks and months after birth. Could those few weeks and months, with the intervening environmental influences, account for the personality differences?

A psychologist by the name of Daniel Freedman went about the nature/nurture controversy in a most enterprising fashion (Freedman 1974). He decided to investigate the individual differences of whole *ethnic* populations at the very earliest neonatal period possible—in the neonatal nurseries. Now it so happens that Freedman's wife is racially Chinese, while he himself is Caucasian. This happy circumstance would deter accusations of **ethnocentrism,** they thought, so they decided to begin their investigations in a hospital located in and around the Chinatown section of San Francisco. The test they used was a very simple one. On the advice of one of America's most famous pediatricians, Berry Brazelton, they performed the following experiment. They placed a cotton hankerchief on the faces of the neonates very loosely so that there was room underneath for the babies to turn their heads easily. The results were astonishing even for Freedman and his wife. The Chinese babies moved their heads slightly but seemed not to find the handerchiefs intolerable. They made the psychological adjustment very quickly. The Caucasian babies, by contrast, yelled their lungs out. As Freedman writes, they knew they had struck pay dirt! Other experiments with other ethnic groups found similar differences. Navajo babies, for example, hardly murmured. Nor do Navajo babies rail against being swaddled into a cradleboard as do Caucasian babies. That we have known for a long time. But Freedman's data suggest that some of the most cherished beliefs of psychologists are going to have to be demolished. The first belief is that no matter what our genetic inheritance, we are born fundamentally alike. Another is that any difference in how we develop is due

Studies of neonates reveal innate physical and psychological characteristics that have proven to be predictive of adult personality.

to the environmental circumstances of our upbringing. And now Freedman dares to suggest that the Chinese are stoical *by nature!* The popular anthropological viewpoint has been that the Chinese culture, with its emphasis on tradition, its respect for personal privacy, and its avoidance of overt emotional expression has produced the stoic ("inscrutable") Chinese character. Freedman's rather radical idea is that it may be the other way around; that the basic stoicism of the Chinese character may be a primary factor in the formation of the subtleties of the Chinese culture. Something to think about. For example, is it the energetic Caucasian *temperament* that has caused that particular race to cross the seven seas, colonize new lands, and climb the highest mountains just (as the Englishman said), "because it was there"?

Left-Brain/Right-Brain Individuals?

In the middle of the last century some French physicians discovered the *speech center* in our left hemispheric brain. Since that time neurologists have been disturbed by the idea that maybe, just maybe, our left and right cerebral hemispheres were not identical in function. This idea was not easy to accept because, externally, the two halves of our brain seemed to be physiologically symmetrical. But the fact that we are generally right-handed or left-handed indicated that one of our brain hemispheres was dominant over the other. In most of us the left hemisphere is dominant, and since the left hemisphere controls the right side of our body, most of us are thus right-handed. Those of us who are left-handed (anywhere from 4 to 10 percent of the population) have a right-hemisphere dominance. It may seem strange that the left hemisphere controls our right side while the right hemisphere controls our left side. The neurological reason for this is that the ascending and descending nerve tracts cross over (called *decussation*) at the area of our necks. There has been considerable speculation about this crossing over of our nerve tracts. While it is still being debated by the neurologists, some have suggested that this decussation gives us more integration of our central nervous system. We might be very divided organisms indeed if we were completely divided into left halves and right halves from our crown to our toes. In fact, neurologists have suggested that having a *dominant* hemisphere may keep the two halves of our body from fighting each other. Be that as it may, in the last three decades some interesting and exciting research has turned up more evidence that our two hemispheres seem to operate somewhat differently. The two hemispheres are connected by a series of neuron fibers very easily identified visually since they are white in color (contrasting greatly with the *grey matter* of our cerebral cortex). These bundles of white fibers are called the *corpus callosum*, and they transmit *information* received from one side of our brain to the other, presumably so that our bodies can act in a coordinated fashion.

In the 1950s two psychologists, R. W. Sperry and R. E. Meyers, cut the corpus callosum in cats and also their *optic chiasmas* so that no visual information could pass from one hemisphere to the other. What they discovered was that right after splitting their brains in this manner, the cats literally seemed to have two visual brains in their head, and visual information could not pass back and forth between the hemispheres (Sperry 1974, 1975).

The next step in this line of research involved epileptic patients. There are several kinds of epilepsy. One of the most severe is what is called *grand mal* (big sickness), and it is life threatening. Neurologists have discovered that the epileptic attack is a kind of random (inappropriate) and massive firing of neurons in the brain, which seems to start in one hemisphere and spread to the other. When both hemispheres are firing in such disorderly fashion, the patient goes into convulsions and coma and may even die. Neurologists reasoned that if they cut the corpus callosum, the firing could not spread to the other hemisphere, and perhaps the patient's epileptic attacks could be held somewhat under control. The big question was, *What would be the side effects?*

It must take a certain kind of stamina and fortitude to do such exploratory neurological experiments on human beings. But the first experiment was done on an American who had survived a prison camp after being captured in the Korean War. He had been so severely brain damaged as the result of being beaten with a rifle that he was suffering from terrible and frequent epileptic seizures, and death

Box 3.8	TWO BRAINS: TWO COGNITIVE STYLES

Left Hemisphere	Right Hemisphere
Verbal	Nonverbal, visuospatial
Sequential, temporal, digital	Simultaneous, spatial, analogic
Logical, analytic	Gestalt, synthetic
Rational	Intuitive
Western thought	Eastern thought

SOURCE: Sally P. Springer and Georg Deutsch, *Left Brain, Right Brain* (San Francisco: W. H. Freeman and Company, 1981), p. 185.

looked imminent. It is on such patients that radical life-saving explorations are given priority. Surgeons cut his corpus callosum. Immediately after the operation there were some noticeable effects. His speech was slurred, and he did not have coordination of his voluntary muscles, as he did have before. This same lack of coordination was noticed in the cats also, but over time the cats had somehow managed to coordinate their two neurological sides and eventually moved with their usual feline grace. The same recovery was true of the Korean veteran. Over time he gained more coordination of his speech and his actions, and his intelligence seemed not to have suffered any significant drop. All seemed to be going along well—except at certain times. He reported that sometimes his body had a *mind of its own*. The doctors soon discovered that his body did things that were embarrassing to him, like unzipping the fly of his pants. They discovered further that these events "happened" to him when he was in emotional conflict.

The neurologists and psychologists began to suspect that just as the left-dominant hemisphere seemed to be the language and logic hemisphere, it might be that the right hemisphere was the *silent* but *emotion-feeling hemisphere*. Like many new ideas, it was breathtaking. Since this first split-brain operation there have been some two dozen, all of which have been carefully studied. Psychologists began to study the resulting psychological reactions. First of all, the right (minor) hemisphere seems to perceive complex visual patterns better than the left and to remember them more easily. The minor hemisphere also seems to be the hemisphere that initiates our emotional expressions—our smiles, frowns, and grins. It may control the emotional quality of our voice. We seem to have different cognitive styles in the two hemispheres, also. The left (dominant) hemisphere seems to be not only the language-dominant hemisphere but also the more sequential, logical, analytic, and what we call *rational* and *critical* hemisphere, while the right (minor) hemisphere seems to be more involved with more *primary perceptions*, such as the visual and tactile senses, as well as with expressive feelings (*emotional affect*). Other experimental data suggested that our minor hemisphere may be more involved with dreaming and fantasy, with music and with (was this possible?) those elements we call *intuition* and *metaphor* (Springer & Deutsch 1981; Gazzaniga & LeDoux 1978).

Intuition? Metaphor? Music? Dreaming? The scientists were beginning to speculate on the differences between human beings. Was it possible that certain people we call *artists* are more right-brained? Are persons who operate more linguistically and *logically* more left-brained? Several lines of investigation began to open up. One line of experimentation involved the measuring of electrical activity in the brains of lawyers (who are presumably very logical and linguistic) and the electrical activity of artists (who are presumably very visual and emotionally open). Sure enough, the researchers found that while they were at work, there was more activity in the left sides of the lawyers' brains and more activity in the right hemispheres of the brains of the artists (Springer & Deutsch 1981).

Other social scientists began to hypothesize that there have been two modes of operating in the world, represented by Eastern and Western thought. Western thought has tended to emphasize the orderly, rational, and scientific procession of ideas, while Eastern thought has tended to emphasize the intuitive, holistic, subjective, and more *direct* way to primary perception and understanding (Ornstein 1977). Whether or not this is so, it seems useful to think of the minor brain as the less "socialized" brain, that is to say, the dominant hemisphere organizes the "flashes" and "images" we get into what we call rational thoughts, with all of the judgments and societal constraints. The problem is, says Ornstein, that in the West, our need to organize our primary perceptual data may very well lead us to logical but very misleading answers. It is his contention that we should learn to use our right brain more so that we are more in touch with our non-judgmental and spontaneous "primary" perceptions, as a way of developing less rigid and more creative responses to the events we encounter. For example, one artist and writer is convinced that she has developed techniques for developing artistic ability even in "nonartistic" persons. She calls her major work *Drawing from the Right Side of the Brain*, and she illustrates the book with work done by her students before and after her "right-brain" training (Edwards 1979).

Now much of this discussion is simply *conjective*. But this kind of conjective speculation is an important part of the scientific method—the "yeast" that science is made of. If we begin to correlate and synthesize the various speculative ideas, we see that we find validation for the theories of Carl Jung and his personality *types*; namely, that we come into the world as basically different, and that we tend to be *feeling* or *thinking, intuiting* or *sensing, introverted* or *extraverted*. The minor hemisphere seems now to coordinate with Jung's *feeling* and *intuitive types*, for example, and the major hemisphere seems to coordinate with our *thinking* function. What other coordinates can we establish? Only time and further breakthroughs in our understanding will tell us. There are many lines of philosophic speculation possible, and we are only beginning to tap into them. Do you see any emerging preferences for right-brain activities from our culture? Can it be that when we are praying and meditating we are using our minor hemisphere? Is this the area through which we get our *intuitions* and *answers* that seem so primary and seem also to cut through the logic of our major hemisphere? Can it be that the minor hemisphere is our less "socialized" in the Freudian sense (Springer & Deutsch 1981)? Or is it that the minor hemisphere is simply the more *animal* aspect of ourselves, while the major hemisphere is what makes us *human* by organizing these primary perceptions in a logical and linguistic way? (Eccles 1965; Jaynes 1977.) Whatever answers we come to, there seems to be substantial evidence that we may be primarily left-brained or right-brained from the time we are born, and that these two modes are evident in what we choose to do with our lives, the professions we go into, and what gives us enjoyment and sustains our interest through our life span.

APPLICATIONS AND COPING TECHNIQUES

1. THE HUMAN SPECIES IS MARKED BY A GREAT VARIATION OF PERSONALITY EXPERIENCING AND FUNCTIONING. Scientists, in their quest for the great generalities and commonalities of human behavior and human existence, tend to concentrate on how we are similar rather than how we are different from each other. Yet it is these essential differences among each of us that makes us so extraordinarily interesting as a species. It is these slight variations, perhaps, that account also for the reason we are fascinated by some persons and "turned off" by others. It is certainly our basic differences that give us feelings of wholeness and harmony in the realm of art, while others feel more at home in the domain of mathematics and business, and still others are driven to the scientific and academic areas.

2. WE TEND TO ASSUME THAT *OUR* PERSPECTIVE AND *OUR* FRAME OF REFERENCE IS THE ONLY ONE OR AT LEAST THE CORRECT ONE. We are emphasizing this point because of the fact that we so often tend to assume that what *we* feel and what *we* experience must be what *others* feel and what *others* experience. Yet nothing can be further from the truth. We (all of us) live in slightly different phenomenal worlds. We are separated not only by our experiences but by our individual *interpretation* of those experiences. To perceive and acknowledge our differences is to come nearer to understanding how each of us is unique and alone while sharing similar human forms. When we hear people argue heatedly over some subject, it is generally because each person truly believes that he or she has the truth, the whole truth, and nothing but the truth (so help them God!), and that the other person is simply blind or ignorant.

In this respect we are very much like the six blind men from Hindustan who each grabbed a certain part of an elephant. The blind man who held a leg said the elephant was very like a tree trunk. But the one who had hold of the tail insisted that an elephant was more like a rope, while the blind man holding the trunk insisted an elephant was much more like a snake, and so on. Psychologists have called this personal *world vew* many things: *a mental set* (Kohler 1970); *a personal construct about the world* (Kelly 1974); *a vision of reality* (Polanyi 1969); *a perceptual field* (Combs, Richards, & Richards 1976). But whatever, each of us views things differently.

3. SOMETIMES WE GET INSIGHTS INTO OTHER WAYS OF PERCEIVING. A well-known psychologist-philosopher, Joseph Chilton Pearce has described this world view quite charmingly (Pearce 1971). He writes that each of us constructs a theory about the universe based on the way we perceive and experience it. This theory of the universe he says is like a *cosmic egg* that we all carry about with us. We are very limited in our view of the universe, naturally, but we are absolutely convinced that this cosmic egg we are carrying around is accurate. Then one day something happens to us, and this cosmic egg gets a little *cracked*. We are surprised or astounded or even scared out of our wits as we get a glimpse through this crack into what we had not formerly perceived. Now this understanding, this *crack* in our *limitation of perception*, can come about in many ways. It can come about through drugs, and in the sixties and early seventies many young people actually sought it out through use of various substances. But this *crack* can come about also through meditation, through prayer, through sickness and fever, through startling dreams, through therapeutic processing, by allowing ourselves visions of what we have not yet realized. It can come about, and frequently does, for artists in the throes of their artistic passions. Musicians also talk about *getting out of themselves* when they are jamming with other musicians. What we are talking about, of course, are altered states of perception (altered states of consciousness—ASCs). Ordinarily we perceive the world in a certain way, which is our *usual state of consciousness*. Then one of these experiences jolts our preconceptions and our assumptions about the world, and we speak of having been in an *altered state of consciousness* (Tart 1969).

Ideally, accurate awareness of how others function differently from us will lead to appreciation of our differences, for it is difficult to imagine what it would be like to live in a world where all persons were carbon copies of ourselves. Of course, we all have moments of extreme irritation with others when they behave differently than we do but a world of complete sameness would be nothing less than boring, wouldn't it? Let your imagination seek out the possible ramifications of living in a world in which all other persons were exactly like ourselves. Then follow us to the next application.

4. BECOMING AWARE OF OUR DIFFERENCES FROM OTHERS IS ESSENTIAL TO THE PROCESS OF PERSONALITY INTEGRATION. In our infancy, we are taught what we *may* or *may not* do in the circle of our family and home environment. Later in our childhood, much of our schooling is devoted to acquiring the *mores* and *principles* that govern our particular society. In adolescence we are further influenced in how we talk, dress, think, and so on, by the *pressure of our peer groups*. In adulthood we are further molded and *shaped* by the business or profession to which we belong, by the rules and regulations of the social clubs and political groups to which we give allegiance, and finally, by the taboos and values of the society into which we were born and in which we participate, however limiting or far-reaching that societal participation may be.

And in our particular society we have television holding up models of family life that nothing in reality can match; opinion polls publishing weekly the responses of Americans to questions about what they are thinking and what they are doing. It is small wonder that the process of self-discovery is difficult *here*. Multitudinous forces of society are monitoring our behaviors and molding our thought processes continually.

Remember! it is those persons we most admire who have the most influence on our tendency to conform to others, not those toward whom we feel antagonistic.

When we're in disagreement with a person or an organization, we find satisfaction in being different from them. (We call this phenomenon *alienation*.) By way of contrast, we conform most to those we like and who we hope will like and accept us. In our teen years we strove desperately to be acceptable to our adolescent peers. If we have had a good relationship with our parents, we are more likely to conform to their ideas, opinions, and modes of behavior. Therefore one of the most difficult tasks to be confronted is to be willing to see ourselves as different in some respects from those we most like and admire—and even love. That is not to say that we must consider our family members wrong or our peers wrong in their attitudes and behavior. Valuing individual differences in ourselves and others goes beyond the black/white concepts of *wrong* and *right*. We come to understand that what is *right* for others in this particular situation or that particular situation is not necessarily *right* for us. And vice versa. Perhaps one of the reasons that many novelists begin to write by fictionalizing their own autobiographies is that they experienced so acutely their differences from their families or communities.

When we begin the process of self-identification, then, we are on the road to what Carl Jung called **individuation** (Jung 1924). By that he meant the ability to see ourselves as persons in our own right. He was of the opinion that most of us do not begin that process until the midlife crisis. But for those of you who are reading this book and whose whole educational process is involved with your self-determination we believe the process of self-discovery and individuation can begin now, with your college experience.

5. WE OFTEN GIVE UP OUR INDIVIDUALITY AND PERSONAL PREFERENCES FOR THE SAKE OF FRIENDSHIP AND/OR *LOVE*. Besides the *unconscious conditioning* that is being exerted upon each of us from the the moment we are born, we have a tendency to deny ourselves our individuality in order to "make others happy" or to "keep peace" in the family or to keep a balanced cooperation wherever we experience *social interaction*. Alas, such maneuvers may keep peace—for a while—and they may even seem, at times, to make others happy, but in the long run, such giving up of our personal preferences can lead to a level of tedious conformity and mediocrity.

A husband and wife who are fond of each other may give up their individual interests and activities for the sake of being with each other. The husband gives up his fishing because his wife does not share the pleasure of it. The wife, who enjoys being politically active in her community, gives up these associations because they take her away from her husband, who spends his evenings at home. By silent agreement they deny themselves the very recreations and sources of excitement they may need, and they may end up spending most of their leisure hours at home watching television—maybe even television reruns! Let's hope if they reach that point they will become aware of their dull life style and will work their way back into self-expressive activities that are propriate to their growth and change. (So far we have no research that indicates that TV on a regular nightly basis year after year, however "together" it may be experienced, is healthy—i.e., health producing. When we share our reality in such surplus and stagnating activity, the result must be boredom and tedium.) You could take a withheld expression of self and experiment with your choices. If you wish to, identify a limit in your life that does not please you right now and that you believe could reasonably be *lifted* or *extended*. We always wish you luck with your sincere efforts to be yourself—*the best of your possible selves*.

6. AS PARENTS, WE CAN REMEMBER TO REMAIN AWARE OF THE INDIVIDUAL DIFFERENCES IN OUR CHILDREN.   No two children come into the world exactly alike. Even twins vary in some way or other. We shall sidestep the issue of nature versus nurture and state what is now generally known and accepted. Even newborns are very different human beings, and these differences may become more emphasized as the result of their experiences throughout their childhood. Yet we tend to treat our children alike, out of concern not to show *favoritism* and also because of our cultural belief that *what is right for one is right for the others.*

We may then be doing exactly what is the most injurious, since our children, in all probability, are not alike. The little boy who is very active from birth may not require the amount of sleep his older sister requires, and to insist that he take an *equal* afternoon nap may be very unproductive, even destructive. What he may need is plenty of activity to enable him to utilize his energy in constructive ways and to be relaxed enough to rest when he does go to bed in the evening. Rather than treat all our children with the same exact methods of discipline and upbringing, we can become more sensitive to what *works well* for each particular child, each particular time. *This child is emotionally sensitive*, and a few words will suffice to bring her around to a better way of getting what she needs. *That child is less emotionally sensitive* and needs stronger measures, for he seems deaf to mere words. For him the use of behavior modification may be a more appropriate choice.

7. BY RECOGNIZING THE INDIVIDUALITY OF OTHERS, WE CAN BECOME BETTER TEACHERS AND BETTER PARENTS.   We tend to *lockstep* children in school. Try as we may, with all our *individualized instruction* and groupings of academic ability, we still tend to think that all children need to have *all* the educational experiences of a common curriculum. Yet we do much injury in forcing *all* our school children to partake of *all* school offerings at *all* times no matter where the child is in his or her growth pattern, physically, emotionally, and mentally. Some examples: A young boy of our acquaintance has what is called tone-deafness. He cannot distinguish one tone from another, and consequently he sings terribly off key at all times. Yet his teachers believe that by participating in music, he will improve his musical ability. Such a possibility is out of the question. (Yet he surely will have opportunity to develop a poor sense of self with enforced experiences of failure where he is told to succeed!) His tone deafness is not common. It is, as a matter of fact, quite rare, but it *is* tone deafness. He is in misery most of the time because of the looks of other children. He dreads going to school because of it, and a school phobia is very definitely developing. He would be better off if we allowed him to go to the library and read or have another session in the biology lab.

Perhaps that is also one of the characteristics of competent parents: They allow their children to manifest their talents, abilities, and preferences in their own time and in their own way. The less we shape our children's personalities, the more we allow them to unfold according to their personality types and propriate strivings; the more truly competent we are as parents.

SUMMARY: POINTS TO REMEMBER

1. This chapter focuses on the differences among us as opposed to the commonalities. It is in recognizing our unique individual differences that we come to know who and what we are as our "own persons."

2. Freud, being a scientist, was interested in developing a unified theory of human personality. He therefore tended to ignore the variables of human functioning such as our socio-economic stratification, culture, and ethnic roots. Freud's unified theory centered around our libidinal needs, but we have many other needs and motivations that account for our personality differences. Thus, one-by-one, several of his student-colleagues broke away from the Psychoanalytic Congress of Vienna to investigate the individual differences between human beings.

3. Alfred Adler emphasized our individual life-styles, by which he meant the ebb and flow of our life span. When viewed in our moment-by-moment actions, or even our day-to-day actions, our motivations may seem contradictory, but if we understand a person's whole life course, then we can perceive his life style. Life styles can be constructive or destructive, cautious or impulsive, aggressive or timid. Adler also gave us the concept of the inferiority-superiority complex, which is the result of a child's feelings of being overwhelmed and powerless in a world of adults. A classic example is the Napoleonic complex in which a short person overcompensates for the lack of stature by conquering the world. To Adler, the hallmark of the evolved human being was the development of a strong social feeling (*gemeinschaftsgefuhl*), by which he meant brotherly love or compassion for others.

One character trait of an evolved social being is an emanating sense of joy or cheerfulness.

4. Carl Jung, emphasized the differences among us with the formulation of personality "types." His concept of the introversion-extraversion continuum has passed into common parlance. He also formulated two other polarities: the thinking-feeling function and the sensing-intuitional function. Jung believed that we can develop a type neurosis if we live opposite to our basic "type." In contradistinction to Freud and Adler, he believed our basic personalities are not environmentally determined, but genetically determined.

5. Eduard Spranger emphasized different motivations or Orientations. His six Orientations include: the Theoretical (seeker after truth); the Economic (advocate of the financially secure and comfortable life); the Political (agent of change); the Social (love motivated); the Aesthetic (pursuer of beauty); and the Religious (searcher of meaning). These Orientations are known as the basis of the Allport-Vernon-Lindsey Vocational Interest Test.

6. William Sheldon investigated personality "type" and body physique. He concluded that there are three basic bodily types: the mesomorph which is a very muscular physique and correlates with the athletic type; the endomorph which is a rounder physique and correlates with the lover of the good life; and the ectomorph who is all "skin and nerves" and who is of a more introverted and intellectual temperament.

7. A series of research studies, beginning in the 1950s and 1960s indicate that emotional traits of infants are indicative of

adult personality. Nine different traits have been identified.

8. Another approach to the nature/nurture controversy is the study of twins who were separated at birth and raised in different environments. These studies indicate that identical twins, even when reared in extremely different circumstances, show remarkable similarity in many factors including physical health, emotional stability, attitudes and preferences, intelligence, and longevity.

SIGNIFICANT TERMS AND CONCEPTS

aesthetic orientation
alienation
altered states of consciousness
analytic psychology
commonalities or generalities
compensation or
    overcompensation
corpus callosum
dominant hemisphere
"difficult" child
"easy" child
economic orientation
ectomorph
endomorph
environmental versus innate
environmental factors
feeling function
gemeinschaftsgefuhl
heredity factor
individual differences

individuation
inferiority-superiority complex
introversion/extraversion
intuitive function
left-brain/right-brain
    differences
left-brain dominance
libidinal needs
life style
mesomorph
metaphysics
minor hemisphere
motivations
Napoleonic complex
nature/nurture controversy
optic chiasma
overcompensation
Psychoanalytic Congress of
    Vienna
personality "types"

political orientation
polymorphous perversity
religious orientation
right-brain dominance
sensing function
silent hemisphere
"slow to warm" child
social feeling
social orientation
split-brain research
stratification
superiority complex
theoretical orientation
thinking function
twin studies
"type" psychology
unconscious motivation
variables

FILL-IN THE BLANKS WITH SIGNIFICANT TERMS AND CONCEPTS

1. This chapter focuses on i_____ d_____ in contrast to the generalities or c_____ among us.
2. Freud, in his search for a unified t_____ of human motivation, focused on our l_____ needs and chose to ignore the other variables of human functioning. Some of Freud's student-colleagues broke away from the P_____ C_____ of V_____.

3. Alfred Adler emphasized our individual l_____ s_____s, by which he meant the whole course and flow of our total life span. Adler also bequeathed us the concept of the i_____ - s_____ complex. A classic example of which is the N_____ complex. For Adler, the mark of the truly evolved person was the development of the s_____ feeling (gemeinschaftsgefuhl).

4. Carl Jung also emphasized individual differences in his "t_____" psychology, but whereas Adler believed these differences to be the result of our environmental experiences, Jung believed them to be i_____ or inborn. Jung gave us the i_____/e_____ continuum, as well as the four basic functions of personality: th_____; f_____; s_____ and i_____.

5. Eduard Spranger devised a motivational framework involving six basic Orientations: the T_____; E_____, P_____, S_____, A_____ and the R_____. We are probably all of us a mixture, but no doubt we can identify the prevailing motivations within us.

6. William Sheldon correlated bodily physiques and emotional patterns. The e_____ lives the "good life" and has more visceral and fatty tissue; the e_____ is more "skin-and-nerves" and tends to intellectual pursuits; while the m_____ is more muscular and athletically inclined.

7. American researchers have discovered nine emotional traits of infants to be long-lasting into adulthood. These traits cluster in combinations that are called the e_____ child, the d_____ child, and the s_____ child.

8. Another approach to the nature/nurture controversy is the study of identical t_____ raised in separate environments. These studies indicate remarkable similarity in mental, emotional, and physical traits.

9. Daniel Freedman's research on neonates (still in the hospital nursey) demonstrates measurable differences in e_____ populations.

10. Split-brain operations indicate that our l_____-brain is more involved with analytic, sequential thinking, and language, while our r_____-brain is involved with the holistic, visual, and emotional.

11. The recognition of our individual differences and the willingness to express them leads to what Carl Jung called the i_____ of personality.

RECOMMENDED BOOKS FOR FURTHER READING

Adler, Alfred. *The Education of the Individual.* Rpt. of 1958 ed. (Westport, CT: Greenwood Press, 1969.) There are many books by Adler including, *The Diagnosis of a Life Style, Education of Children*, and *The Practice and Theory of Individual Psychology.* We chose this book because of its pragmatic aspect: down-to-earch advice on how Adler believes we can get the most out of our lives by coming to terms with and expressing our individual needs and aspirations. Very readable.

Freedman, Daniel. *Human Infancy: An Evolutionary Perspective.* (New York: Halstead Press, 1974.) Those who were intrigued by the Freedman research on ethnic differences in neonates will enjoy this book. Freedman writes in a popular style and is delightful to read.

Jung, Carl G. *Memories, Dreams and Reflections.* Aniela Jaffe, ed. (New York: Pantheon Books, Inc., 1963.) This is Jung's autobiography written in the last decade of his life. Like the introvert that he describes himself as being, his autobiography deals not with the external "facts" of his life but with his "inner life"—his emotional and intuitive responses to the givens of his culture, and of extreme interest is the description of his relationship with Freud. It is an experience to read and students report being deeply moved by this extraordinary work.

Spranger, Eduard. *Types of Men: The Psychology and Ethics of Personality.* Trans. 5th Ger. ed. (New York: Johnson Reprint Corporation, 1928.) We could not begin to do justice to this social scientist's classic work. We recommend, without reserve, that every serious student of the social sciences add this book to their "must read" list. It is little known that Gordon Allport and his associates derived their well-known vocational inventory test (A Study of Values) from this book.

Springer, Sally P. and Deutsch, Georg. *Left Brain, Right Brain.* (San Francisco: W. H. Freeman and Company, 1981.) There are a variety of books on left brain/right brain explorations and conclusions. This one presents the wide spectrum of scientific research and opinions concerning the data. They write a remarkably objective book even when presenting discussions that differ radically from their own speculations.

Edwards, Betty. *Drawing on the Right Side of the Brain.* (Los Angeles: J. P. Tarcher, Inc., 1979.) For art students, photography students, or for any of the students in the humanitites, this book may be of extreme interest. The author declares that she has been developing, over the years, a technique to help people tap into their right brains (the more visual, artistic, imaginative, creative side). An artist herself, she has illustrated the book very beautifully and included before and after pictures of her students' work.

4

*When the System
Is Overloaded:
Persons under
Stress*

THE NEED FOR A DEFENSE SYSTEM . . .
 The Origins of Our Defense Mechanisms

. . . BUT DEFENSE MECHANISMS ARE ALSO BARRIERS TO GROWTH
 Our Conditioning Makes Us Robotlike
 How Can We Know When We Are Defending Ourselves?

THE DEFENSE MECHANISMS
 Defending by Attack
 Defending by Withdrawal
 Defending by Physiological Anesthesia: Alcohol, Narcotics, "Pill
  Popping"
 Defending by Psychological Anesthesia: Repression, Amnesia
 Defending by Rationalization
 Defending by Insulation
 Defending by Manipulative Behaviors
 Defending by Distortion
 Some Healthier Defenses
 Is There Any Right Way to Be?

APPLICATIONS AND COPING TECHNIQUES

THE NEED FOR A DEFENSE SYSTEM . . .

In the spring of 1981 the scientific community and general public alike heard of a new disease that had strange and sinister undertones to it. The first symptoms seemed innocuous enough. It began like an ordinary flu, as if perhaps the person had been overdoing it in his or her social life and needed a holiday to rest up a bit. The trouble was that, unlike flu or a general feeling of fatigue, the victim didn't seem to get over the symptoms. The whatever-it-was hung on for six, twelve, eighteen months. Then some of the victims began to die. By the spring of 1983 the disease had struck almost a thousand persons, and of these thousand, a third were dead. Even more ominous—of the first few hundreds to contract the disease, only a fourth were still living two years later. The disease was originally thought to be strictly venereal and passed via sexual activity. The early victims were discovered to be active homosexuals. Then other persons began to come down with the disease: Haitians, children, and drug addicts. Now some epidemiologists are concerned that the disease may spread to the general population through blood banks, and at the present time the Center for Disease Control and other national and state health agencies are working round the clock for ways to check the spread of the disease and, if possible, to find a cure. The National Cancer Institute in the U.S. and the Pasteur Institute in France have both announced that they have independently "identified a virus as the probable cause of AIDS." (*Discover* 1984, p. 10.)

One of the significant aspects of this disease is that the persons who have died have not died from it per se. They have died from a host of other diseases: pneumonia, cancers of all types, and respiratory distress, for example, and any number of ailments that the body is ordinarily immune to or can heal if proper medical steps are taken. For this reason the disease came to be known as AIDS, or Acquired Immune Deficiency Syndrome.

We are not trying to add to the general panic but rather to point up the fact that we survive mainly through our body's natural defense system.

In like manner, we have an emotional defense system. If it were not so, we might not survive the "thousand natural shocks that flesh is heir to" or even the stress of everyday life. We emphasize this because in some circles it has become popular to confront someone with the statement "You're being defensive!" That kind of confrontation implies that the speaker himself or herself is free of defenses. Do not let anyone play that game with you. We need our defense mechanisms until we can discover better ways to cope with the world and the problems that confront us. We need not be ashamed, then, of our emotional defense mechanisms, any more than we need be ashamed of our physiological defense mechanisms. They are a part of our nature; they are necessary to our survival and there is

When physical pain overwhelms us, we lose consciousness; when psychological pain threatens to overwhelm us, we escape via our defense mechanisms.

no one who is completely free of them. We do not have to be "defensive" about our defense mechanisms. We all have them. The real question is not whether we have defense mechanisms but how well they are working for us and if we can find better ones. Our defense mechanisms, then, are necessary because they help protect us from *pain*. Each of us can endure just so much pain. When *physical* pain becomes too intense, we lose consciousness and thereby effectively block out further painful stimuli. Physical pain is one such stimulus; anxiety or *mental* pain is another.

Each one of us can stand only just so much anxiety. When that point is reached, a kind of psychological trigger point, we begin to defend ourselves against further painful stimulation. In short, we begin to use our defense mechanisms.

The Origins of Our Defense Mechanisms

Our defending mechanisms have their origins in our early experiences as an infant and child. Human beings have a long **neotony,** which is to say that we are more helpless and vulnerable than all other life forms on this planet for a longer period of time. We need to be taken care of and nourished for many, many years before we can survive on our own. Personality theorists have placed much emphasis on the helplessness of the human infant and young child, who find the world a complex and frightening place to be. That helplessness is so overwhelming at times that many of us, perhaps most of us, never feel completely adequate, even as adults, to confront and manage the vicissitudes of living. When we find ourselves overwhelmed by fear, by anxiety, by shock, by shame, by guilt, or by any of the many painful emotions we can experience, we fall back to any way we can find to deal with the stressful situation. How we come to develop our particular defense mechanisms has been a subject for much speculation and debate, and we present some of these views and theories now to the reader. We do not ask you to accept any of these theories simply because they have been formulated but to consider them in light of your own experiences and intimate observations of children you have watched grow up—and perhaps you'll be able to remember at least some things about your own childhood.

SIGMUND FREUD: BIRTH AND THE BEGINNING OF ANXIETY.   Very early in his writing career Freud postulated that when the baby is thrust from the warm, dark, safe, and paradisical environment of its mother's womb, where all its needs were taken care of, into the confusing, demanding environment of the external world, it has its first frightening experience of anxiety. He believed that the very act of birth, with the contractions and labors that make it possible, form the basis of later adult anxiety (Freud 1962[b]).

OTTO RANK: THE BIRTH TRAUMA.   Otto Rank was one of the early student-colleagues who joined Sigmund Freud in Vienna. He was particularly impressed with Freud's theories concerning the importance of the child's early experiences in the formulation of the adult character and structure. He was much taken with Freud's idea of the anxiety a baby must experience at birth and broadened its importance by suggesting that the *birth trauma* is one of the underlying motivations of human personality development. What Rank said was that the process of birth, with its hours of protracted labor, its intense contractions, and the pressure and force that the emerging baby must experience at some level, is so powerful and brutal (even to the point occasionally of strangulation and death) that the human psyche is forever shaped and marked. (Remember that both Freud and Rank were physicians as well as psychoanalysts and were well acquainted with the biological events of human life.)

Laing: Rebirthing therapy. The birth trauma has not had as much direct and overt acceptance in this country as it has in Europe. Ronald Laing, for example, a British psychiatrist, believes that some of his schizophrenic patients experienced such brutal births and an unwantedness from the mother-host that they never gained the most primary, confident foothold in the world of external reality.

He and other psychiatrists have worked in the area of "rebirthing" schizophrenic persons by enabling them to go through the "conception," "pregnancy," and "birth" process again in symbolic form. This time, however, the patient is welcomed into the world by the therapist and, hopefully, overcomes the original and deep experience of being forced into a hostile and rejecting world (Laing 1976).

Leboyer: Gentle birth. On this side of the Atlantic we are beginning to demonstrate a kind of indirect acceptance of the birth trauma via the introduction of the "gentle birth" of Frederick Leboyer. Leboyer is a modern French physician who took the "natural" or "prepared" childbirth methods to the next logical step. The "natural" or "prepared" childbirth methods are directed at enabling the mother to experience positive feelings toward the birth of her child and to cooperate in the birth procedure by use of breathing and pushing-down movements at the proper time. The underlying theme of these methods is that birth is not to be considered a disease but rather a natural event—indeed a very significant natural phenomenon.

The "natural" childbirth methods were found to be superior for both the mother and child in the vast majority of births. But most of the natural-birth techniques had been focused on the mother's well-being. Now Leboyer was focusing on the baby's well-being. He was opposed to the operating room with its glaring lights, its cold temperatures, and its vicious jabbing at the baby for this or that "healthful" precaution.

Instead Leboyer's babies are ushered into a fairly dark, very warm room where there is little or no noise—an environment as similar as possible to the dark, warm, quiet environment of the womb. The baby is put on the mother's abdomen to rest right after birth (the place as close as possible to where the baby has been for the past nine months) and is held gently by the physician and stroked soothingly. The umbilical cord is not severed until it stops pulsating (about six minutes), and then the baby is lowered into a basin of warm water, not only to clean it but to alleviate the effects of gravity (for the baby has emerged from a watery uterine environment).

Leboyer reasoned that such a gentle, welcoming, "nonviolent" birth must have an effect upon the baby's ability to adapt to the world and to thrive. Follow-up studies on children born in this way are being done, but it is too soon to know for sure whether the Leboyer babies will prove to be as spontaneous and confident as Leboyer expects (Leboyer 1975, 1976).

ALFRED ADLER: THE CHILD'S INFERIORITY. We have already discussed Adler's *inferiority-superiority complex* as his explanation for how we develop the character traits we do. We add here a note to this previous discussion (while explicating the origins of our defense mechanisms) because of Adler's own willingness to speak with extraordinary and candid openness on his own childhood and youth with all his added insight as a mature, competent, and creative psychoanalyst (Adler 1959).

Adler relates that he was always extremely frightened of the prospect of death. Adler's younger brother had died when Adler was only a child. Adler himself almost died of pneumonia in early childhood, and even his family had given

Otto Rank's theory of birth trauma has been taken more seriously in Europe than in the United States. Dr. Leboyer's "gentle birth" is the natural result of this theory.

him up for lost. He never completely lost this childhood fear of death he tells us, and he chose the occupation of physician in order to overcome death, so to speak, or at least to lose his fear of it (Adler 1959). In addition to his close encounters with death, Adler was also a physically frail child, who was for a long time chronically sick with various ailments. He was unable to compete athletically with his older brother or friends, and his brother, jealous of the attention that their parents gave Alfred, goaded him from time to time. Adler confesses that he grew up with a sense of what he called organ inferiority. He was essentially honest enough (nondefensive) to note that his "helplessness" as a child provided some secondary gains: a good deal of sympathy and concern from those around him. Thus, Adler's inferiority of physical weakness and frailty was compensated for by the love and concern of his family members. Adler's candid "confessions" unmask how even "goodness" may be a defense mechanism.

HARRY STACK SULLIVAN: THE COMMUNICATION OF ANXIETY. Harry Stack Sullivan was an American psychiatrist who was intensely devoted to the work of several personality theorists: Freud, Jung, and Piaget, in particular, all of whom we have met in previous chapters. From his work with schizophrenic patients, Sullivan became convinced that much of our anxiety is communicated to us, verbally and nonverbally from others. Since the infant does not differentiate himself or herself from the world, he or she picks up (almost as if by osmosis) the anxiety of the mothering person. As a nursing infant and later as a toddler and child, the emerging personality feels the mother's anxiety as his or her own. An anxious, depressed, confused mother is the source of the child's basic confusion and anxiety. Because it happens at such an early age, Sullivan believed that this anxiety can never be removed or destroyed for the remainder of the person's life. Having been inoculated with its first dose of unmanageable emotion, the human organism remains always ultrasensitive and vulnerable and insecure. Sullivan believed that we continue to experience other people's anxieties as we grow older, and for this reason, Sullivan emphasized the *interpersonal* aspects of our emotional difficulties (Sullivan 1953).

In recent years there has been much corroboration, clinically, that a strong, secure mothering figure will produce a strong, self-confident, and competent child. Studies of mothers who are depressed and anxious during pregnancy and in the early months of infancy reveal that their babies are often "collicky" and as school children are often "immature" and have various school problems. The importance and primacy of a good mothering relationship has even been demonstrated in animals. Monkey babies that have been reared in isolated ways, without the benefit of *touching* contact with their mothers, develop severely "depressed" and unself-confident behaviors. Even more interesting is the fact that later, as adults, these "neurotic" monkeys are unable to adequately care for their own babies, suggesting that inadequate and rejecting mothering may very well continue to later generations (Harlow 1958, 1970). Thus we have been able to add supporting information to the basic studies that shows how human babies need confident mothering—someone with the ability to love and care for them (Bowlby 1960; Ainsworth 1982).

EXPERIMENTALLY CONDITIONED FEAR AND ANXIETY. The work of the early personality theorists depended on their clinical observations of others and also upon their own introspective insights into their own personality dynamics. Their work toward our understanding of human development was admirable. But psychology is a science that seeks to corroborate clinical findings with experimental research. The experimental evidence of the relationship of anxiety and early environment came to us through what has been called the laws and facts of conditioning, and for this evidence, we turn now to the work of such men as Ivan Pavlov (1849-1936), John B. Watson (1878-1958), and B. F. Skinner (1904).

Ivan Pavlov: Conditioned neurosis in dogs. Ivan Pavlov was a Russian physiologist who had done his major work on the digestive system of dogs. In fact, he received the Nobel Prize in science for his work in 1904, at which time he made public his preliminary work on what he called conditioned reflexes and which he summed up later in a book under that title (Pavlov 1927). Pavlov's classical-conditioning experiments demonstrated very clearly that when an adverse or painful stimulus, like shock, is presented with a *neutral stimulus*, such as a bell, the neutral stimulus ultimately produces a reaction similar to that produced by the original shock (Pavlov 1960). In Pavlovian terms, the previously *neutral stimulus* (bell) becomes a *conditioned stimulus* for fear. The fearful behavior now produced in the dog is called a *conditioned response*.

John B. Watson: Conditioning anxiety in an infant. The news of Pavlov's work was electrifying to the psychological world, and an American psychologist, John B. Watson, was quick to see if such conditioning could be reproduced experimentally in an infant. Watson chose an infant named Albert for his experiment. Watson first demonstrated that at nine months Albert (who evidently was a fairly happy and confident baby) showed no signs of fear when a small white rat was placed in his crib. The second part of the experiment took place when Albert was twelve months old. The white rat was placed in the crib with Albert and in baby-fashion Albert leaned over to touch or play with it, as babies are wont to do with novel items given to them. But this time Watson and his associate, Raynor, made a loud noise that frightened Albert so that he began to cry or show other signs of fear. In fact, every time the baby began to play with the white rat, the experimenters made another loud noise, which also frightened Albert. The third part of the experiment was to place the white rat in Albert's crib but not make a loud noise. Albert immediately showed fearful behavior at the very presence of the white rat. The conditioning of fear and anxiety in an infant had been successfully demonstrated through experimental research.

Furthermore, and this was an important feature, little Albert now showed signs of fear at any object that was white and furry, such as a white beard, a white muff—even a white rabbit. Pavlov had called these associated stimuli *generalized stimuli* because they arouse similar *generalized responses*.

As Watson pointed out, this virtual phobia toward anything white and furry had been produced in the infant before the advent of language, and so that when Albert was grown up, he would never be able to discover the source of his phobia. He might even, said Watson, come to fear his wife's white fur coat and be unable to explain it (Watson 1920, 1970).

Conditioning and "unconscious" prejudice. For our present purpose conditioning can be said to be responsible for many of our likes and dislikes and for our fears, phobias, and anxieties as well as for many of our preferences for certain kinds of life situations. They are conditioned (that is, acquired) at an early age.

Like Pavlov's dogs or Albert, contemporary psychologists say, we may have been conditioned to dislike blacks or whites. Consider, for example, a white child growing up in a prejudiced white family. If no one conditions the child, he may éventually begin to walk home from school with a black child with whom he has become friends. The mother in this hypothetical family sees the two walking home, and she is immediately horrified; she calls the child into the house and proceeds to deal with the child in an emotionally fearful way. Behavioral psychologists would say that the parent has given the child his first pairing of the stimulus *black person* (a previously neutral stimulus) with the stimulus *bad/horror/shame/negative/guilt*. As he continues to grow up, the child learns also that his father says "damn" everytime he uses the word "nigger" (in tones of contempt or hatred). Slowly, even without anyone telling him how to think or react to blacks, the child is being conditioned to dislike, distrust, and avoid associating with persons who have black skins.

A similar thing can, of course, happen in black families that carry forward hatred and resentment of whites. The children in those black families grow up similarly to fear and/or hate all whites as the result of conditioning in their early lives. Our prejudices against certain people or groups of people are early learned responses over which we have had, by and large, very little control. In childhood, we can be conditioned *directly* because we do not yet understand the subtlety of *nonverbal language*; that is, "*the sound of the bell or the sight of the white rat equals fear.*" It is hard for any of us to trace where or how we learn prejudice. But if we have grown up in a group of people who harbor fear, dislike, and prejudice toward another group, it would be well-nigh impossible to escape such conditioned responses in ourselves. Thus Arabs and Israelis go on fighting an age-old situation of hate. Thus the Catholics and Protestants of Northern Ireland continue their religious hatred and killing of each other. Thus the Communist-controlled countries and Western-allied countries continue to build up armaments in their suspicion of each other's motivations, preparing for an all-out total conflict.

Generalized stimuli and "first impression." Favorable and unfavorable first impressions of people also may be accounted for as *generalized responses to generalized stimuli*. Suppose your mother (of whom you were very fond) had a preference for blue and wore a certain pleasant perfume. Suppose you meet one day an attractive woman wearing a blue dress and enveloped in an aura of similar perfume. Would it not create in you a most delightful first impression? Of course, since she has created just such a delightful impression on you, you will convey this response to her in verbal and nonverbal ways as you communicate with each other. The fact that you find her so charming, no doubt, works a chemical magic in her, and she responds quite favorably to you . . . and so you fall in love.

B. F. Skinner: Operant conditioning. B. F. Skinner is an American psychologist who demonstrated what he called *operant conditioning*. Operant conditioning revolves more around the *voluntary* behaviors of the organism. In a typical operant conditioning experiment, a rat is put into a *Skinner box*—usually a cage equipped with certain mechanical devices. When first put into the cage, the rat will engage in *exploratory behavior*; it runs around the cage, sniffs, stretches, cleans itself, and runs around again and exhibits various other exploratory behaviors.

There is a bar in the cage which, when pressed, activates a mechanism that drops a food pellet down a chute to the rat. In the course of its exploratory behavior, sooner or later the rat is bound to accidentally touch the bar, whereupon a food pellet is immediately released. The rat eats it and looks around for some more. When it does not find any more food, it may go to the opposite end of the cage, sniff, and wander around aimlessly. Eventually, however, it does manage to hit the bar again and is *reinforced* (rewarded) by another food pellet. This process is repeated over and over, and eventually the rat discovers that a certain action or behavior (pressing the bar) produces a reward—namely, food. The animal's behavior then becomes less random and more purposeful, and it quickly engages in pressing the bar and eating the released food pellets until it has had enough. This method of conditioning relies more on self-learning than does the classical conditioning approach (Skinner 1938, 1970).

Human babies, too, are not just passive organisms. As they grow up, they operate on their environment and experiment with a variety of behaviors. Some of these behaviors are reinforced, and others are punished by the environment. The "baby" of a large family indulges in "cute" behavior at the dinner table, and to its delight discovers that it is the focus of attention and laughter. The child now has been reinforced for acting in such a droll way, tries it again and again, and each time is thrilled with those familiar sensations of laughter and applause. When the child tries out these jokes at school, her classmates also enjoy the antics. The child has discovered a way of eliciting that longed-for applause from her audience, a pattern of reinforcement that could one day result in her becoming a stand-up comic. On the other hand, her conditioned behaviors may make her the "office cut-up" whom people laugh *at*, and not *with*, or the class "clown" whose defense against being scolded by the teacher is to seek the reinforcement of laughter from her classmates by additional pranks or delinquent acts.

. . . BUT DEFENSE MECHANISMS ARE ALSO BARRIERS TO GROWTH

While our defense mechanisms are aimed at helping the organism survive, some defensive operations can become so dominating and self-perpetuating that they block further psychological growth. A certain defensive maneuver may have been a means of coping with frustrating and threatening situations when we were children, but when continued in adulthood it may create difficulties because the behavior is no longer appropriate to adult life. For example, children who have learned how to get their mother's attention by whining or having temper tantrums have found that that pattern of behavior is a fairly successful way to getting attention when they need it. If they continue to rely on whining, they prevent themselves from developing more mature ways of interacting with others. These people will be called immature or childish and will eventually discover that, rather than getting them what they want, this behavior is self-defeating.

Our defense mechanisms impose a barrier to personality integration in that they blur our vision of the world, deafen our ears to what others are saying to us, and generally distort or confuse our perceptions of everyday experiences. Two psychologists, John Dollard and Neal Miller, put it very bluntly. Our defense mechanisms make us "dumb" so that we do not demonstrate our intelligence. (Dollard & Miller 1966).

Our Conditioning Makes Us Robotlike

If we consider how our *defensive* conditioning habits can determine our habits of eating, our habits of sleeping, our habits of talking and just about everything we do, it is easy to understand how we grow up to have defensive and destructive attitudes in our lifestyles without ever realizing it.

Box 4.1

SOME EXAMPLES OF CONDITIONED DEFENSE MECHANISMS

The Case of Sally

Sally, a nine-year-old black child, had come to expect trouble (derision, hitting, name calling) from *all* white children because a *few* white children had treated her in this way. Accordingly, she distrusted the friendly advances of whites. She had a negative, suspicious, hostile attitude toward all whites and kept friendly whites from trying to establish communication with her. In other words, she had not only developed a generalized response to *white* people, she even began to condition them to dislike her and stay away from her.

The Case of Michael

Michael is a youngster who received reinforcement from his environment in sports, so he has a certain amount of self-esteem and confidence on the athletic field. However, he has always been somewhat small in stature, and that continues to be a point of insecurity in his personality development. When he was in the lower elementary grades, Michael was hauled off the recess field several times because of fighting. As we investigated each incident, we discovered a common element in many of his fights: someone had called him a name which made him angry. These names generally referred to his small size: "shorty," "smallfry," "pipsqueak," "shortstop," "peanuts," and the like. Michael's reaction to these stimulus words was to prove to the name caller that he might be short but he was also tough and not someone to provoke too often. Consider now that Michael's behavior was so automatic that any casual reference to his size resulted in the inner command, "Fight!" As long as he had no other response but "Fight!" to the stimulus words, he was not in control of his own behavior. He was conditioned to respond in just one way. As long as anyone could arouse his anger and call forth the fight response in him through the stimulus words, that person was more in control of Michael's behavior than Michael himself was. We have control of our behavior only when we have *at least two* (significantly different) *choices available.* Michael, seemingly (most of the time) had only one choice available, and that was the push-button reaction to fight when called one of these painful names. In his robotlike conditioned defensive responses (fight), Michael is unfree even today. The slightest joke about his height angers him. He may not punch others out, but his feelings of anger and resentment block his positive feelings toward "tall persons," and he's always trying to out wit them, show them up in some way or other.

The Case of Thomas

Many of our values have been conditioned to our own disadvantage. Thomas wants to be a better student. He probably has the capacity to get through college, but he lacks the motivation to study or even take his courses seriously. Thomas comes from a family that placed little value on education. His father used to take him on fishing and hunting trips and encouraged him to go out for the football team, and they had a most gratifying father-son relationship. His father never got past junior high school, however, and Thomas has frequently heard his father condescendingly refer to the university population as "eggheads." Thomas was conditioned early to value the "manly" things his father approved of, such as hunting and fishing, and he was conditioned also to look down on the pursuit of intellectual knowledge. Any stimulus associated with school, books, studying, or learning, simply "turns him off." *He has developed a conditioned defense response patterning against his school anxiety.*

The Case of Edith

Edith was a "sickly" child. She found that even though it was scary to be sick, she was also showered with presents and special things to eat. She could also stay home from school and watch TV and play with her games. As she grew older, she became physically stronger and healthier. But she continued to develop "headaches," "stomach pains" and other ailments that kept her home from school frequently. As an adult, she is unable to keep a job because of her high rate of absenteeism. She is not even a very competent mother since she is often in bed with a migraine or other ailment. Her five-year-old daughter also has developed headaches and stomach pains, which come and go mysteriously and for which the physicians can find no basis.

When we are completely unaware that many of our behavior patterns are indeed conditioned, we may then be considered *determined*—controlled ultimately by our past experiences and therefore "unfree." For example, when we are unaware of the choices available to us at a given moment and behave with *old* conditioned responses to a *new* situation, at that point and to that extent we are more like automatons and machines—that is to say, *predictable* because we repeat old responses over and over like a machine. Our conditioning then can work against us when our own behaviors call forth rejection, ridicule, impatience, irritation, and anger from others. (See box 4.1 for examples of how our conditioned defense mechanisms erect barriers to our daily living, further growth, and creative problem solving.)

How Can We Know When We Are Defending Ourselves?

Now that we understand that our defense mechanisms are a protection from the overwhelming pain of anxiety, we need to determine when they are operating. It is not easy to become aware of our defense mechanisms. With a little detective work, however, we can begin to discover them underneath their camouflage of rational and orderly behavior. The key is to catch ourselves when we are doing or saying something that does not fit the situation or the people involved.

Perhaps you have found yourself doing something not characteristic of your "usual self." Or perhaps you have heard other people make remarks such as: "I was so overwrought I didn't know what I was doing," "I knew I was saying the wrong things, but I just couldn't help myself," or "He didn't seem to be himself." On occasion one does not seem to be oneself: We feel out of sorts or at our wit's end.

This feeling of being out of control, not acting like oneself, not being able to make a decision, or being "tied up in knots" is one of the signals that there are forces at work within us of which we are only partially aware. Any one of a number of things may be happening. We may be experiencing so much anxiety that we feel helpless and confused, our self-esteem may be threatened, or we may simply be unclear about our own feelings. We may be temporarily under so much stress that our usual adaptiveness and energy are at a very low ebb. Finally, the choices confronting us may be conflicting, and we seem unable to make a constructive decision. Again, all of these explanations (anxiety, self-esteem, frustrations, conflicts, stress) are abstract and need to be defined. When we find ourselves in uncomfortable situations and when we sense discomfort and pain, we can be sure that our defense mechanisms are operating.

THE DEFENSE MECHANISMS

Defending by Attack

THE PAIN-ATTACK RESPONSE. Attack is the most physical, most primitive, and most aggressive form of defense—and certainly the most uninhibited form of defense. The need to strike back has been studied under experimental conditions by Nathan Azrin (1967), who described this response as an instinctual reflex in animals. Azrin observed that when animals are shocked by electric current they will immediately attack another animal nearby. If there is no other animal to attack, a shocked animal will bite and attack an inanimate object, such as a ball. Should there be nothing else on which to vent its rage, the animal may even bite itself. Azrin concluded that this pain-attack response is a kind of "push-button" response with the same sequence, shock-pain-attack, following always in rapid order. Furthermore, there seemed to be no lessening of the attack response over time: the animal attacked every time. Many readers will recognize this response if they have ever had an injured dog. When the owner bends down to help, the dog may even bite its owner. Azrin's experiments suggested that any kind of intense pain is a total organismic sensation and that the organism—be it animal or person—tends to react to the intense stressor by striking back at the closest object.

VERBAL AGGRESSION. We generally outgrow the childish or adolescent need to strike out physically at the human object we think is the cause of our pain, or we find other ways to strike back at the person who has frustrated our desires. All of us have shouted, screamed, or said things that we wish later we had not said.

SARCASM, RIDICULE, AND WIT. Verbal aggression in adults is generally more sophisticated and may even become habitual behavior. These persons have become so sensitive to actual or imagined insults that they adopt a kind of acid defense called sarcasm. In some groups, particularly among adolescents, verbal insult is used as a method to relate to others. For the high school student sarcasm may even denote friendship for another person.

People who rely on acid remarks in later life as a way of relating and defending themselves are adopting a life style of verbal aggression. They may continue to feel as though they were winning battles with their associates. Indeed, their associates may adopt behaviors aimed at appeasing them, such as letting them have their own way to avoid the acid comment. They may even "cozy up" to them in the mistaken belief that appeasement is the way to avoid attack. Sarcastic people may seem to have a keen wit and may even consider themselves competent and successful in everyday living. What they do not realize is the extent of their loneliness and their lack of genuine friendship. They may sense that others do not trust them, that others may actually fear and dislike them. Yet they are caught in the vicious cycle of verbal aggression in which wit does not ease but causes uneasiness and distance. So the cycle spirals, culminating in the anecdote of the person who shouts at his or her therapist, "I said, I don't know why I don't have any friends. Why don't you listen, you blockhead!"

VANDALISM. In the larger social context, acting-out behaviors can take the form of riots or vandalism. The adolescent who wants to get even for being picked up as a shoplifter may later come back and throw a brick through the store owner's window. The vandalism and race riots of the ghettos have been attributed to "black rage," the spilling over of frustration and anger at the white establishment (Grier & Cobbs 1961).

Defending by Withdrawal.

Instead of aggressing against another, human beings can withdraw when the pain of anxiety or frustration is too much to bear and when they cannot cope with it assertively. This defense often is seen in children, who may turn away and pout, cry, or fantasize. *Withdrawal* is a kind of defeat in the face of an overwhelming environment.

REGRESSION. **Regression** is reverting to an earlier behavior that relieved anxiety. When the baby is brought home from the hospital, the older sibling may suddenly begin thumb sucking or have "accidents," behaviors that may have been given up months before.

As children get older, they may simply withdraw from situations that elicit feelings of inferiority. The late-maturing adolescent boy may avoid any attempt to enter into sports or athletic competition. The adolescent girl who feels unpopular or ugly may become isolated and not attempt to make friends with others (finding it safer to stay in her shell). We recognize this kind of person in the shy child who hangs back in any social gathering or who prefers watching television to joining after-school clubs. The "milquetoast" personality is a fixture of the office: the one who stays apart and never ventures an opinion at the office or at home with his or her spouse. Watching television seems to have become an American form of escape for the person who finds interpersonal situations too risky. It is not uncommon for a family to eat in front of a television as a way of avoiding dinner conversation. These are the relatively "mild" forms of withdrawal. Other forms are less benign.

FLIGHT INTO FAILURE.   A series of experiments several years ago studied the effects of failure on achievement. They revealed that when we fail in some task or project we tend to lower our goals (Sears, Maccoby, & Levin 1957). These experiments confirm the observations of school psychologists that some students just seem to decide in advance to fail, apparently so they will not be disappointed when they do fail. Thus avoiding success is yet another method of insulating ourselves against the fear of failure. We see this sort of behavior in students who avoid studying for a test. If they pass the test they can congratulate themselves for achieving a passing grade and for knowing that they could have gotten a higher grade if they had studied. If they fail, on the other hand, they can console themselves with the fantasy that they would have passed if they *had* studied.

Frequently truant juvenile delinquents may be really running from the school in which they experience failure and may feel that they do not measure up to others. Rather than make the effort to study, they find a boost to their self-esteem on the street with other, similar adolescents in showing their prowess in looting, shoplifting, getting drunk, and dealing in marijuana and other drugs.

THE BORN LOSER.   The born loser is another example of flight into failure. Somehow this person always seems to miss the mark. This person is the employee who seems always to be passed over for promotion, the student who studied the wrong chapter for the test, the family member who always seems to be left out of things. We may find ourselves feeling sorry for this person, but after trying to help this individual, we begin to discover that the situation is more complex than we had thought. No matter what we do to "help" that person, he or she outwits our attempts, and we find ourselves mired down by the person's life style of helplessness and confusion. At last, we realize that there is a powerful self-sabotage going on.

One of the more subtle, and ultimately destructive, forms of the born loser's flight into failure is to choose a marriage partner, maybe even several in succession, who sees to it that the spouse's goals are never achieved. Some men will deliberately select the kind of wife who will nag, belittle them, compete fiercely with them, and point out their failures. At first marriage of this kind can be blamed on inexperience. But when such a man divorces and then marries a second wife just like his first, we can rightfully suspect that although the choice seems accidental, the goal (failure) is not.

Defending by Physiological Anesthesia: Alcohol, Narcotics, "Pill Popping"

Related to flight into failure are the defenses by which a person blocks out the pain of anxiety by a number of anesthetizing devices. Human beings can be amazingly resourceful and creative and can avoid reality by many routes. One may use alcohol to drown out anxiety to such an extent that one becomes an alcoholic, which ultimately alienates friends, spouse, and children and destroys one's career. One may choose drugs, a common form of flight today, or one may direct tensions and conflicts into psychosomatic illnesses, "psychosomatizing" anxiety into chronic invalidism, thereby closing off and limiting capacities to deal with everyday life. (We will discuss this form of defense also in chapter 5.)

There also are the vast array of analgesics and other nonprescription drugs by which one blocks any symptoms of anxiety—the headache, the upset stomach, or the general case of "nerves." All of these are effective ways to anesthetize by "pill popping" the *symptom* of our distress and anxiety but only prolong our confrontation with the *causal* situations that have aroused them.

THE NEED TO STAY IN TOUCH WITH PAIN SIGNALS. Pain (both psychological and physical) is a warning system: It informs us that all is not well within our internal universe. We have receptors throughout the whole body (inside and out), which can be compared to giant antennae bringing information that things are safe and well or unsafe and not well. Lately we have taken to anesthetizing this early warning system with drugs (aspirin, codeine, tranquilizers, psychedelic drugs). Such readiness to take drugs that are essentially painkillers and tension reducers results, however, not only in diminishing the experience of the pain itself but also in the more pertinent effect of taking our attention away from the causes of the pain. Pain is a signal not to be ignored, any more than the blinking red and yellow traffic lights that say "Stop!" "Slow Down!" "Proceed with caution!" "Yield!" Attention to all levels of our sensory awareness is one of the primary avenues to personality integration—which means that we need to learn to pay attention to our pain signals and to stay with those symptoms of our anxiety. This is a most difficult task, since the impulse to avoid pain is instinctively so fast that we hardly have time to focus on what is causing us pain before we run from it! Yet if we are able to focus in on this pain or that anxiety, the resulting awareness can tell us something about our current living.

BLOCKING THE BODY'S NATURAL ANALGESICS. Anesthetizing our bodies (pill popping and drug addiction) artificially has another consequence: namely, we block our body's natural pain-defense system. Some of the most exciting research of recent years has been the discovery of the body's natural analgesics. These analgesics have many names, including *enkephalin*, *endorphin*, and *opiate peptides*. These naturally produced chemicals that originate in our brain seem to have the effect of reducing physical and psychological pain (Snyder et al. 1974; Snyder 1976). For example, there seems to be a significant increase in a woman's endorphin level just before she gives birth to a child (Gintzler 1980).

We already know that drugs such as morphine block the body's production of enkephalins. Eventually, of course, if the use of morphine is stopped, the body will eventually begin once more to manufacture its own analgesics. But in the meantime, addicts who go "cold turkey" suffer agonizingly. They are cut from the pain reduction of their daily "fix" of morphine or heroin, and they do not have the benefit of the body's enkephalins. No pain-reduction benefits. The slightest physical stimulation becomes excruciating, even painful. The littlest psychological rebuff or put-down has a magnitude that is overwhelming (Barker & Smith 1980). Furthermore, chronic abuse of amphetamines will cause an overproduction of dopamine, which eventually produces a paranoia similar to schizophrenia (Turkington 1983).

Defending by Psychological Anesthesia: Repression, Amnesia

REPRESSION.   Children who are told by their teachers to have a parent sign a failing test paper may actually "forget" about it when they get home. As adults we are well aware that we may "forget" we have a dentist's appointment or that we have to pay a bill. Freud called this forgetting **repression.** He considered it the basic defense mechanism and the goal of his form of therapeutic method, psychoanalysis, was to unlock the unconscious mind and release the repressed material (Freud 1935[b]).

Since Freud, we have obtained other clinical evidence that events in our life may never really be forgotten, particularly the important ones. Wilder Penfield, a

Defense mechanisms are ways of defending ourselves. Unfortunately, we sometimes resort to very primitive defenses.

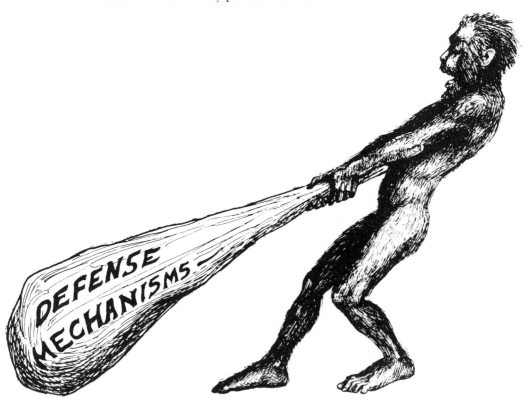

psychoneurologist, published a paper suggesting that under certain conditions, people can remember events long past and forgotten. Penfield's subjects were patients suffering from epilepsy, and the conditions under which Penfield observed these findings were extremely unusual—he was operating on the temporal lobes of their brains. The patients were awake and conscious and could relate their experiences as he pressed a small electrical current against various parts of their brains. Depending on where he pressed the current, the patients reported seeing persons from their past, remembering events from early childhood, hearing melodies, and even smelling certain scents. Penfield concluded that we may never lose complete memory of anything (Penfield & Jasper 1954).

Repression is what occurs, as Freud explained, when there is an event that is so overwhelming and bewildering that we are just not able to face it and need to remove it from our consciousness and awareness. We can turn to repression, denial, amnesia, or "forgetting" as ways of protecting ourselves from unbearable overstimulation. When we use repression to reduce pain or other kinds of stimulation, we block out our awareness and refuse to see what is there. The result is that we are not conscious of the event. Let us consider an example in which a child is injured and dies in its mother's arms. If the mother at that moment cannot face the reality of the situation, she may insist for a time that her child is still alive and then rage at those around her for not doing something to help her child. She is saying, in effect, "I cannot, I will not believe this event is happening. This awful thing cannot be happening to me. I refuse to accept the truth."

AMNESIA. Amnesia is another form of denial, but here the "forgetting" (or repression) is used not just to cloud one's awareness of a specific event but to keep anything associated with it out of consciousness. Soldiers in combat have been known to reach such a peak of fear, anxiety, and exhaustion that they can no longer function and collapse suddenly with "battle fatigue." At such times they can also become amnesic and block out of consciousness the events which led up to their physical breakdown. Likewise, a person who has killed someone may not remember the event, since recognizing himself as a murderer may be more than he can integrate into his conscious awareness of himself. So he "forgets" the killing; that is, he represses the knowledge of the homicide and the events leading up to it.

Defending by Rationalization

Rationalization about ourselves, our acts, or our motivations is another one of the more common defense mechanisms. Compared to other defensive mechanisms, rationalizing is a relatively mild way of protecting our identities from pain. To rationalize (in the sense we are using it here) means to give a logical but false and self-serving explanation for something. For example, students who get a failing grade on an exam and who cannot or will not acknowledge their own responsibility may rationalize it by claiming that they and the teacher have a personality clash and that the teacher failed them out of spite, or that the exam did not cover the course material, or whatever. Rather than face up to their own (real) lack of preparation, they *rationalize*—attribute their failure to some other factor. This defense mechanism always resorts to spurious reasons, explanations, and excuses.

Although rationalization is less self-crippling than other defense mechanisms are, it is still a defensive maneuver that prevents us from seeing something of ourselves. We always need to be suspicious of our excuses, if we are honest in our desire to learn how to integrate our personality. Excuses, excuses, always excuses—this is the key for those who use rationalization as a major defense. Instead of doing a job, they give an excuse for why it has not been done.

SOUR GRAPES AND SWEET LEMONS. The "sour grapes" form of rationalization is found in Aesop's fable about the fox and the grapes. The fox tries unsuccessfully to reach the grapes on the vine. After many attempts, it finally gives up and, as it walks away, mutters to itself, "The grapes were probably sour anyway." A young man who fails to make the football team may rationalize his failure by telling himself that he did not really want to play on the team, that he would probably get injured anyway.

The "sweet lemons" form of rationalization, on the other hand, is when people extract a *positive* result from their frustration and disappointment. The wife whose husband is jealous may tell herself that his behavior is really proof of his love for her. A student who does not get the part she seeks in a play may comfort herself by saying that she now has more time to study. Sweet lemons is not the same as maintaining a cheerful, optimistic attitude toward life. Optimism and cheerfulness prevent one from becoming so cynical that one ignores the good this complex world does have to offer. "Sweet lemons" denies the pain altogether and twists any situation so that it is superficially a positive event. This is in direct contrast to highly integrated people who acknowledge all their feelings, even painful ones.

Defending by Insulation

Another way we defend ourselves against feelings of horror, shame, or guilt is to prevent ourselves from feeling anything at all. We turn off, so to say, the recognition that this event applies to us! We do not deny the experience, and we do not react to it. Instead, we build a zone of unfeeling into our understanding of the experience (Darley & Latane 1967).

Persons who work at predominately intellectual (cognitive) pursuits seem to rely often on that kind of defense if they begin to discover that they are unable to manage the emotional situations and strains of the usual family life. Such a person might rely on insulation to defend against the stresses of being in direct contact with spouse and children; that is, he or she withdraws emotionally from family life. He or she is present physically, but his or her attention and interest are directed somewhere else. For example, this person may spend much time at the office "doing research" or may retreat into his or her study when at home to "get some work done." This person may also spend vast periods of time reading as another means of preventing interpersonal contact.

Defending by Manipulative Behaviors

We come now to the more sophisticated forms of defense. You may all know little boys or girls who try temper tantrums and other kinds of blackmail when they do not get their way. Adults, like children, discover manipulations to make others do what they want. Persons working in psychological and psychiatric clinics have written many books on the subject. Eric Berne, Fritz Perls, and Everett Shostrom are three who have written best sellers on manipulative defense mechanisms. Berne's *Games People Play* describes thirty or so ways that adults can tie each other up with manipulative devices. Shostrom describes eight common manipulative styles that put other persons in defensive positions (see box 4.2). Perls was an expert at unmasking the "power play" of the weak, helpless "underdog." We can sketch only briefly some manipulative defense mechanisms by which people seek to gain their ends. We add, however, that many other kinds of manipulative styles (and ways to avoid them) will appear again and again in the pages of this book.

ERIC BERNE: GAMES PEOPLE PLAY. One of the games that Berne describes he named: "If It Weren't for You!" (Berne 1964). In this game a woman marries a domineering man who is rather authoritarian and prevents her from doing things she is afraid to do anyway. Neither he nor she is aware of what they are really doing. They are both convinced that he is keeping her from getting out into the world, having a career, or whatever. Now the twist of this life game is that she does not want to go out into the cold, cruel world. She married him to be protected and taken care of, but now she complains about how little liberty and freedom she has as compared to other women, "If it weren't for you, I could have. . . . " thereby making her husband feel guilty about his demands on her. In order to salve his conscience, he ends up by giving in to her various "small" demands, like where they will go on vacation, what kind of a house they will live in, and a maid to help her in the house.

FRITZ PERLS: UNDERDOG. Similar to this life game of Berne's is Perls's "underdog." Instead of the more direct, aggressive concept of confronting another individual with anger or irritation, some of us take another tack, which is called underdog. In interpersonal friction one person appears as the underdog, *the one who has been hurt, crushed, or misunderstood by the other party* in the situation. This is a cat-and-mouse game in which the mouse becomes the winner! For if any of us really believes that we have hurt the underdog's feelings in some way, we may suddenly find ourselves apologizing to the underdog. Now *we* are on the defensive, and the underdog has the upper hand (Perls 1969).

What these manipulative mechanisms have in common is their "around behind" approach. The person frequently appears on the surface to be a "nice guy," a "weakling," or a "clinging vine," but these soft, kindly, helpless types seem to be able to get exactly what they want.

Box 4.2

EVERETT SHOSTROM: MANIPULATIVE STYLES

Everett Shostrom classified eight manipulative styles. Although each form of manipulation has a distinct character, Shostrom's description emphasizes the element of power found in each case.

1. The *Dictator* is one who dominates others, or tries to, by giving orders, quoting authorities, or by pulling rank and age. He or she acts as a "Father Superior" or "Mother Superior," or "Junior God." He or she always is the Authority.
2. The *Weakling* seems to be the victim of the Dictator, but he or she has also developed great skill in sabotaging the Dictator's demands. He or she "forgets" to do what he or she is told, does not hear what is said to him or her, and becomes "mentally retarded" when confronted by the Dictator. Some of the role variations of this type are the Worrier, the Stupid-like-a-Fox, the Giver-Upper, and the Confused One.
3. The *Calculator* is the one who tries to use his or her wits to gain control over situations and people. He or she "plays it cool" and will lie, seduce, con, or blackmail others to get what he or she wants.
4. The *Clinging Vine* controls by being dependent on others. This person needs to be "taken care of" and protected. Actually he or she is quite skillful at getting his or her own way (and getting others to do what he or she wants) by being the Parasite, the Crier, the Perpetual Child, the Hypochondriac, the Helpless One, or the Attention Demander.
5. The *Bully* controls and manipulates by aggressing against others with unkindness, cruelty, and sadism. If he or she is not actually cruel, there is nonetheless always a veiled threat in his or her mannerisms. Variations of this manipulative style are the Humiliator, the Hater, the Tough Guy, the Threatener, and in the case of women, the Bitch or the Nagger.
6. The *Nice Guy* controls by killing with kindness, caring, and love. Shostrom said that this is one of the most manipulative types of all and is the hardest to cope with, since it is difficult to fight a Nice Guy. He seems to want to please us, to be nonviolent, to be virtuous, and not to offend us. He is also the Noninvolved One, the Organization Man, and the Never-Ask-For-What-You-Want individual.
7. The *Judge* controls through criticism. He or she is out to make others feel stupid, guilty, or wrong. Variations of this form of manipulation are the Know-It-All, the Blamer, the Deacon, the Resentment Collector, the Vindicator, and the Convictor.
8. The *Protector* controls by being oversympathetic and overprotective. He or she prevents others from caring for themselves, taking care of themselves, or finding out things for themselves. Variations are the Mother Hen, the Defender, the Embarrassed-for-Others, the Fearful-for-Others, the Sufferer-for-Others, and the Unselfish One.

Source: Everett Shostrom, *Man the Manipulator* (New York: Bantam Books, 1968).

Defending by Distortion

We come now to the more virulent defending mechanisms, the kind that can ultimately cause others to be victimized to a terrible degree.

PROJECTION. Projection is one of the more frequent defense mechanisms. It is a powerful way of defending ourselves from insight into our own motivations. In its simplest meaning, projection means attributing the emotions, feelings, and motivations we experience to something else, particularly to other persons.

Projecting our feelings onto others is a natural way to understand other people. Because of this ability, it is possible to identify with another's joys and sorrows and to help that person grow. Because of their ability to project their feelings and insights, the novelist, poet, or playwright can create great works of art. It is only when projection becomes a barrier to growth that it becomes a negative rather than a positive force. An example is the husband who is secretly eager to have affairs with other women and may attribute his own motivations to his wife, even accusing her of seeking or actually having an affair with other men when she is simply being friendly toward them. He is not able to come to grips with his own desires, and thus he projects these impulses onto his wife, who in this instance is blameless. Projection may also explain the behavior of a mother who has not faced up to her own earlier promiscuity and now suspects her adolescent daughter of being promiscuous, when there is no reality in the mother's suspicion.

Projection as a form of defending the self against inadmissible impulses and desires is a powerful defense mechanism. Its power is that we deny that these very impulses and needs are part of our own personality. Yet the impulses and needs are there and may not be repressed with impunity. It is good for us to acknowledge their existence.

SCAPEGOATING. When projection becomes so powerful that it becomes a destructive force to others in the society, we call it scapegoating. The word itself comes from the biblical custom of symbolically heaping the sins of the community onto a goat, which was then killed, thereby relieving the people of the burden of their anxieties. More recently scapegoating has come to mean blaming a particular person or group for the misfortunes of oneself, one's group, or even one's entire nation or race. For example, Adolph Hitler, who had a good understanding of group psychology, directed his own sense of frustration and failure into anti-Semitism. No leader of a nation, whether an authoritarian dictator or a democratic prime minister or president, can carry out a major policy (for long) that the populace does not accept. In Hitler's case he merely channeled and orchestrated the prevailing anti-Semitism.

Scapegoating takes many forms. In the United States, our own particular form has been the scapegoating of the black race by white society. We have attempted to amend this injustice through social legislation. Our move toward remedying former inequities is a measure of our capacity to grow as a nation. We are left with the residues of scapegoating in our language as evidenced by such words as *nigger*, *wop*, *redneck*, *gook*, *kike*, and *spik*. These words prevent us from seeing other persons as human beings because we label or categorize them as stereotypes. Not only do these labels perpetuate in adults the kinds of prejudicial attitudes that keep people from understanding each other, they also foster such attitudes in our children so that our sins are indeed "visited upon the third and fourth generations."

REACTION FORMATION.   In reaction formation we defend ourselves against feelings, thoughts, and wishes by repressing these impulses and then developing opposite or polar behaviors. For example, a child may have feelings of jealousy and hatred for a baby brother because she feels "displaced" by him as the object of the parents' affection. The child might directly express how she feels by fighting with her brother or finding various ways of making him miserable. Suppose, however, that the child begins to be frightened by the depth of her hatred and even wishes (unconsciously) that her brother would die. Let us suppose also that the parents do not realize how she feels, that they do not appreciate this inner conflict, and that they forbid her to hurt her brother. The child can deal with this complex of feelings and needs in many ways, but if she resorts to reaction formation to reduce the anxiety, she may repress her hatred and jealousy and become solicitous (perhaps overly so) of her brother's welfare. Outwardly she no longer feels hatred but a concern for her brother's welfare. To that end, she may watch out for her brother and make sure "nothing bad" happens to him. But oversolicitous behavior is not the same as affection, and it has different results. No matter how "good" the older child is to her little brother (seeming even sometimes to be a second mother), the younger child's life is still a misery. When playing with his big sister, somehow the little boy gets hurt, or he gets lost when going somewhere with his big sister, and "accidents" seem to happen whenever the two children are together. The repressed hatred and jealousy emerge in subtle, almost unrecognizable forms, but emerge they do.

Other examples of reaction formation can be seen in the oversolicitous attention a man gives to his dominating mother in order to make up for his own wishes for her death, or in the seemingly loving care a man may give to an outrageously nagging wife, putting up with her nonsense or even bringing home flowers as a way to convince himself that he does not secretly want to get rid of her. But again, such attention only *resembles* love and affection. Actually, there is not the freedom and spontaneity of real love. There is too much politeness and too much pussy-footing in these relationships. One feels as if one were walking on eggs.

Some Healthier Defenses

Are there any really "healthy" defense mechanisms? In a sense, all defense mechanisms are useful in that they help the person to survive, but in another sense no defense is healthy, since all defenses interfere with our vision and understanding of what is really occurring from moment to moment. But in the sense that they are more benign (less injurious), there are four ways of coping with anxiety that tend to have more positive than negative results: substitution, sublimation, compensation, and fantasy.

SUBSTITUTION.   We are taking a path to the city, and our way is blocked; most of us will simply find another path and get around the obstacle if we can. This is a simple example of the process of substitution. If a young man cannot take one young woman to the movie, he finds another woman who can go. The boy who withdrew from sports may develop, instead, an interest in mechanics, piano, or reading. By substituting one constructive situation for another, we find a more creative way to manage our feelings of pain.

SUBLIMATION.   Frequently this alternative behavior becomes autonomous; that is, it becomes a driving force of our personality, or so it seemed to Freud, as he thought about what makes a writer write, an artist paint, or a musician compose. Freud defined sublimation as the redirection of the *libido*, or sexual energy, into constructive channels. Freud believed that sublimation is one of the main defenses responsible for creative and artistic production, and we continue to accept his definition though we no longer believe that great art comes into being *solely* because of rechanneling so-called neurotic drives and needs.

Sublimation can be important to personality integration: Using this defense people attempt to redirect their frustrated or antisocial impulses into socially acceptable and constructive behaviors. Anna Freud, Sigmund Freud's daughter and an analyst in her own right, called sublimation the "normal" defense (Freud 1967). It is certainly a more creative defense.

You will understand how sublimation functions in your personality if you begin to notice the art forms, leisure activities, or choice of vocations that appeal to you: how you attempt to express certain basic needs through poetry, storytelling, painting, or physical projects of any kind. A childless woman may adopt children or breed animals. A "bossy" individual may find satisfaction in executive management. A young man unrequited in love may turn that experience into a work of art. Sublimation is a "tidy" defense and one that deserves close examination if you want to allow for your dreams and yet are hemmed in with the compromises of reality.

COMPENSATION (OR EVEN OVERCOMPENSATION).   Sometimes people react to inadequacy or inferiority (imaginary or real) by refusing to admit defeat. Overcompensation sometimes can have astonishingly productive results. Demosthenes was one of the greatest orators of ancient Greece, yet it is said that he stammered as a child and even as a young man. How he overcame his infirmity, according to legend, was by practicing every day on the beach, where he would fill his mouth with pebbles and try to shout above the roar of the ocean. In this way, by overcompensating, he learned to speak not only clearly but well. Several speech pathologists of today have gone into their field because of their own early speech problems.

Biographers of great athletes sometimes note a similar kind of compensation. As children, these athletes may not have been well endowed physically—indeed, they may have been relatively puny in stature and musculature, and relatively small for their age. As "handicapped" persons in childhood, they learned to adapt early to their environment, but always with the acknowledged understanding that they had no intention of submitting to their fate. In fact, they reacted against their limitations by developing a degree of physical prowess and endurance that no one expected them to attain. Once weak, they became strong; once apparently incapable, they became models of capability, demonstrating what people can do once they set their mind to the task.

FANTASY.   The last defense mechanism we shall discuss in this chapter is fantasy, the psychological term for daydreaming. It is the substitution of *thinking* about an event instead of *doing* it. The adolescent boy who daydreams that he is an adventurer, the young girl who sees herself as a ballerina, the child who is playing airplane and is at the same time both the pilot and the airplane all are indulging in fantasy. Why do we list it as one of the more creative defense mechanisms? First, daydreaming harms no one else. Second, the person is not denying or distorting his or her secret drives and wishes—he or she is dealing with them if only on a wishful level. In his book *Daydreaming* (1975) Jerome Singer stated that daydreaming may actually be the lode-star of our motivations and ambitions. (See box 4.3.)

One of Singer's favorite daydreams was the desire to become a geat scientist, and he has indeed gone a long way in the area of clinical research. Our daydreams to become a physician may at least point us in the right direction, to one of the health-related areas like pharmacy, perhaps. But even these defenses can become harmful. Daydreaming and fantasy can, if overindulged, become a substitute for action. The person may while away a whole life in wishful dreaming rather than in doing something about it. Like other defenses, daydreaming also has its negative aspects. Daydreaming is destructive when it replaces all action: we daydream rather than act.

Box 4.3 | **DAVID KRECH: THE USES OF FANTASY**

When David Krech, one of America's noted research psychologists, was asked to discuss the relation between fantasy and the birth of an idea, he responded: "There is no question that I do a lot of fantasizing and daydreaming about the research problems that I am working on, and in my fantasies and daydreams, I solve them all. And these solutions, in turn, lead to other and greater achievements! It's a real Walter Mitty routine. But I'm not sure that these fantasies or daydreams provide me with anything more than perhaps motivation or persistence. . . . Once I'm in a Walter Mitty daydream, challenges can be overcome at will. . . . I play with my ideas, I live with them, and fantasize about them. . . . In that way I keep them salient."

Source: Stanley Rosner and Lawrence E. Abt, eds., *The Creative Experience* (New York: Grossman Publishers, 1970), p. 61.

Is There Any Right Way To Be?

We have spent an entire chapter on the forces at work that cause mental and emotional anxiety. We also looked at what anxiety and stress can do to us as well as what we do to defend ourselves from the pain of that anxiety. We saw how we can "break down" psychically and emotionally if the pressure and anxiety become too great. We saw how our pattern of defenses can warp human personality, the twisting and turnings human personality can take, and the "knots" we make of our lives, as Ronald Laing (1972) put it, that prevent our further growth and creative living.

The reader may well wonder if there is any "right" way to grow and how to recognize these "right" ways. The answer, unfortunately, is *no*, there is no model that we can copy to ensure our continued growth and successful living. Human personality changes from epoch to epoch, and what was right for our forefathers can no longer be said to be right for us. Even what may have been right for our parents cannot be said to be right for us. Human personality is in a process of evolution. Today as never before we are witnessing a freedom and exploration of that process. Freedom, said Paul Tillich[1], requires the courage to be (Tillich 1952). Another social psychologist, Erich Fromm, pointed out that humankind "escapes from freedom" (Fromm 1963). In former ages with established traditions of behaviors for the individual, it was easier to know what to do and how to be. Depending on one's sex, status, and stage of life, there were definite and prescribed rules for behavior. Today we are exploring a vast number of possibilities of human life style regardless of sex, status, and stage of life. In that sense each of us is a pioneer on the frontier of personality development, examining what it is and what it can become. It is challenging to be a pioneer; it is also sometimes lonely and a bit frightening. It puts the responsibility and burden of our development squarely on our own shoulders.

COPING TECHNIQUES

1. Learn to Read the Anxiety Symptoms of Your Own Personality Patterning

One of the problems with anxiety is that it is hard to confront straight on. Anxiety is painful. We try to avoid the feelings of anxiety, and as we have learned in this chapter, our defense mechanisms are actually defending us from experiencing this pain of anxiety. One of the first steps, then, in dealing with anxiety is to discover how it is manifesting itself in our psychology and in bodily symptoms. For each of us those signals may be somewhat different. In a sense we all have our own distinctive syndrome of anxiety symptoms. For one person, who tends to be "hyper," anxiety may take the form of being on edge all day and having to be on the run and being unable at night to unwind enough to get to sleep and so suffer from insom-

Headache	Tenseness of body	Desire to run away
Excessive sneezing	muscle cramps	Tic in eye or elsewhere
Sighing (excessive)	Nervous cough	Muscle spasms
Overeating	Stuttering	Prolonged fatigue,
Not being able to eat	Mouth noises (like	weariness, listlessness
Chain smoking	tongue clucking)	Clammy hands
Insomnia	Talking too much	Biting lip
Nightmares	Unable to talk	Feeling cold frequently
Stomach cramps	Talking too fast	Hyperactivity
Diarrhea	Lump in the throat	Sleeping ten to twelve
Constipation	Dependence on	hours a day
Nausea	drugs	Vomiting or frequent
Butterflies in stomach	Excessive perspiration	queasy stomach,
Feeling faint	Blushing	heartburn
Stroking beard or	Fingernail biting	Heart palpitations
mustache	Leg wagging	Specific phobias
Hair twirling, pulling, or	Rocking back and	Clenched fists
tossing	forth	Feelings of choking or
	Gritting teeth	not being able to
		breathe

nia. In another it may show up as a lethargy that makes it difficult to concentrate and causes the individual to sleep more than the average seven or eight hours. In many of us anxiety may be converted into bodily symptoms such as queasy stomach, perspiring hands, a feeling of not being able to breath well, or even a fast heart beat. The symptoms of anxiety are numerous. (See box 4.4.)

2. Discovering the Source of Our Anxiety

The problem with anxiety is that it seems to be nonspecific. We can't seem to focus on just what is "ailing us." All we know is that we seem to be feeling miserable, and we want to take it out on someone or something or simply get away from it. The big next step is to discover just what is the *present* source of our *present* anxiety. To do this we have got to put ourselves in a very introspective state. Every therapist has ways of enabling persons to locate the source of their anxiety, but one concrete step is to try to remember just when the present anxiety first began to manifest. Was it this morning? Yesterday? A week ago? Time is an important and key element. If you keep a journal (and that's often an excellent thing to do for one's growth, and many a creative person has done just that), you might want to review the events that were going on at the time of the onset of the anxiety. If you do not have a journal, then it is a matter of retracing your daily events back to the time when you began to feel anxious or depressed or "hyper" or "sick" or whatever. Something triggered the anxiety. You must be the detective discovering the trigger point and the trigger event.

It may have been something someone said: a warning, a put-down, a threat of some sort. It may have been something that you said and you are sorry for. It may have been something that was done to you that at the time you didn't think much of. Only later do you realize it upset you. Or it may have been something that wasn't done, and now you feel rejected, unappreciated, unloved, whatever. Or it may have been something for which you feel responsible or ashamed or embarrased or guilty.

3. Doing Something About Anxiety-Provoking Situations

A number of research studies in the area of coping (whether they were with students who were having difficulty in their college career or old persons who were having to make adjustments in their living environment or patients who were having to undergo surgery or chemotherapy) have all revealed one outstanding commonality in their findings. The persons who were coping successfully and had a better chance to survive were those who felt they were not completely helpless, that in fact they could do something to help themselves (Pfeiffer 1974; Butler & Lewis 1977; Baum, Singer, & Baum 1981). The students or aged persons or patients who did not survive as well were those who were passively accepting their fate or who felt as if there was nothing they could do to help themselves; they felt as if they had no control over their lives.

What gives us a feeling, then, that we can have some control over what happens to us? For one thing, it is having information about what is causing us anxiety (Egbert et al. 1964). Patients who were given information about their hospital procedures by a supportive hospital staff so that they knew what to expect before, during, and after medical treatment healed better and more quickly than uninformed patients. The students who were having trouble in school but sought the personal and academic help they needed received better grades and had a higher survival rate (White 1976). The aged persons who were allowed to have a part in the decision-making process of *where* they would live and *how* they could manage their living had a better mental and social adjustment in their retirement years. The lesson to be learned from this is obvious but certainly worth putting into words: The more information we have concerning an anxiety-producing event we must go through, the more able we are to cope with it. The more that we take an active part in the situation facing us, the more we are able to deal effectively with the situation. Furthermore, the more determined that we are that we do *not* have to accept a situation but that we can do something about our lives, the less psychic energy is being drained away into anxiety and the more physical energy we have available to us to act rather than worry.

4. Minimizing Anxiety by Avoiding Catastrophic Statements: Staying in the Here-and-Now

We minimize the stress level of anxiety-producing events when we move out of the future and into the present. One of the ways to do this is to understand the mistaken use of the catastrophic statement. A catastrophic statement is a way of enlarging a situation so that it looms like a mushroom cloud simply by our emotional reaction to it. Albert Ellis, who helped us understand catastrophic statements, describes them as rational declarations of events followed by irrational conclusions. Let us give some examples:

> If we have fallen down on the job: "My God! I'm going to get fired!"
> If our loved one gets angry at us: "Oh, he doesn't love me anymore!"
> If we have made a public gaffe: "I'll never be able to hold my head up again!"
> If something has become general gossip: "I'll be ruined!"
> If we have had a disappointment: "Nothing good ever happens to me!"

Notice how the statements predict future catastrophe, as if one's personal world is coming to an end. One way to minimize the catastrophic feeling is to convert your emotional statements into statements that are centered in the *here-and-now* and eliminate the *never, all,* and *nothing* statements. You may rephrase as follows:

> "Right now I'm *feeling* so scared that I'm afraid I'm going to lose my job."
> "I am *afraid* that if he forgot this, he doesn't have as much love for me *as he used to*."
> "At this moment I feel as if I'll never be able to hold my head up *because I am embarrassed*."
> "Right now I'm feeling so ashamed that I don't want to go out in public."
> "*I'm so upset* about this *right now, I feel* as if my career is ruined."
> "Whenever something like this happens to me, *I* tend to *think* that nothing good ever happens to me."

You are now *objectifying* your emotion: Looking at the *way* you are responding to the event and now putting it outside of yourself, so to speak, while you remain at your center.

5. Talk the Problem Over With Someone: A Friend, A Counselor, A Teacher—Someone

When we keep an anxiety-producing situation to ourselves and harbor it as a secret fear, it gnaws away at us. One of the consistent findings of the encounter-growth group is that when we air our problem and our anxiety about it with someone else, the experience of mere *sharing* deintensifies the emotional response that "has" us. Freud called that experience **catharsis.** What we have done is taken the problem and associated anxiety we feel about it out of the shadows and brought it into the sunshine. Furthermore, the person we have shared our anxiety with may have some very helpful ideas as to how we can do something about it. A good friend, the saying goes, is a strong defense. But we have to tell that person that we would like his or her advice about it. Two heads can be better than one. The other person is in a much more rational state of mind than we are at the present time. And it must be emphasized: We need to listen. All the advice in the world on how to rectify a situation is useless if it is falling on deaf ears. (See chapter 9 on *how to listen.*)

6. Plan a Course of Action

The advice our friend (or teacher or whoever) gave us may not be satisfactory for *us*. But at least it may be an idea that we can build on, or it may give us a new perspective from which to consider alternatives. If we have a problem with our job, we may decide to talk to our boss and get her reactions. In the event of angry words from a spouse, we may call him on the telephone and very quickly say we were very angry and did not know how to respond at the moment. We would like an opportunity to discuss it when we are both feeling calm. In the event of a public "disgrace," we may not want to go out in public, and the best thing might be not to! In a few days there'll be other things happening, and gossip on past events becomes as old as yesterday's newspaper. Sometimes the best coping is *not to cope now* but to give yourself *time off*. If you can get a few days away to visit some-one, now might be the time to do it. When you come back, you will feel different since time is a great healer. Other people will feel different. And the gossip tele-phone line has picked up on something else. When you do make your appearance in public, you will face a public that has known about the incident for several days or a week or more, and the event has already become *passé*.

7. Exchange the Word *Failure* for the Word *Learning*

One of the worst catastrophic statements we make about ourselves is calling our-selves a failure. "I have failed as a parent." "I have failed as a wife/husband." "I have failed as a teacher/student/whatever." "I'm a failure!" It is easy to fall into this because we have been *conditioned* all of our lives, from first grade up, to think in terms of passing and failing grades. Of course, that is all just nonsense. No one fails at everything, and it is a pity that our educational system has indoctrinated this pass/fail notion into us. It would be far better if our educational system were to say something like, "This child still needs to learn this." Then we would be influenced to say just, "I still need to learn this" (and eventually, "I am still learning this").

In one sense, there is no such thing as *failure*, there is only *more informa-tion*. The information we are receiving is that this or that has not worked (at least, not to our satisfaction). Now we need to discover what might work, and for that we can enroll in a course, read a book, consult an expert, talk to others in the same predicament, or do any of the multitude of things that can get us more information. The word and concept *failure* is simply not useful.

Think then of "failure" or "setbacks" or "obstacles" as simply information as to what has not worked up to now. Then approach the problem from a new angle—from your new perspective.

SUMMARY POINTS TO REMEMBER

1. We all have defense mechanisms. Without them, we could not survive. Defense mechanisms defend us against the overwhelming pain of anxiety, guilt, shame, remorse, and so on.

2. The origins of our defense system go back to early childhood. They were the ways we coped with stressful situations as children.

3. Sigmund Freud posited the idea of a birth trauma, but it was Otto Rank who developed it into a theory of adult anxiety. Although not accepted in this country to any extent, the theory of birth trauma has found acceptance in Europe: as for example, in the "gentle birth" of Frederick Leboyer.

4. Alfred Adler believed we develop defense mechanisms as a way to cope with the overwhelming inferiority we experience as children in a world of adults.

5. Harry Stack Sullivan became convinced that schizophrenic and rejecting mothers transmitted anxiety to the nursing infant

and toddler; we pick up the confusion and anxieties of our chief caretakers.

6. Harry Harlow, an experimental psychologist, reared baby monkeys in isolation from their mothers. They developed "depressed" and "neurotic" behaviors. As adults, these monkeys were unable to fill normal mothering roles.

7. Ivan Pavlov and his associates conditioned neurosis in dogs by electric shock. The neurosis in this situation is considered as a conditioned response. Later, John Watson conditioned anxiety in the infant, Albert. It may be that many of our attitudes and values are simply conditioned responses.

8. Defense mechanisms enable us to survive but they are also barriers to growth, and can make us function less intelligently.

9. We defend by attack when we physically or verbally aggress on others. Defending by withdrawal is exhibited in such behaviors as alcoholism, nomadism, and fantasizing; even flight into failure. De-

fending by anesthetizing is demonstrated in drug abuse and pill-popping.

10. The use of narcotics has the effect of dysfunctioning of the brain's natural analgesics: the enkephalins, the endorphins, and the opiate peptides.

11. Repression can be seen in amnesia or forgetting a dentist's appointment.

12. Eric Berne believed we all play "games" with each other. Fritz Perls identified the "top dog"/"under-dog" game that people play with each other. Everett Shostrum has identified eight manipulative styles.

13. Some of the more destructive defense mechanisms include projection, scapegoating, and reaction formation.

14. Readers are urged to identify their anxiety patterns and to be patient with themselves as they seek more growthful coping techniques.

SIGNIFICANT TERMS AND CONCEPTS

alcoholism
amnesia
analgesic
anesthetic
anxiety as mental pain
anxiety: personal, social global
birth trauma
born loser
classical conditioning
compensation
conditioned response
conditioned stimulus
coping techniques
defense mechanism
endorphin
enkephalin

fantasy
flight into failure
gentle birth
generalized response
generalized stimuli
Harlow's neurotic monkeys
insulation
natural birth
neutral stimulus
nomadism
operant conditioning
organ inferiority
pain-attack response
peptides
pill-popping
prepared birth

rationalization
reaction formulation
rebirthing
regression
reinforcement
repression
sarcasm
scapegoating
sublimation
superiority-inferiority complex
"sour grapes" defense
substitution
"sweet lemons" defense
trauma
unconditioned response
unconditioned stimulus

FILL IN THE BLANKS WITH SIGNIFICANT TERMS AND CONCEPTS

1. When we are overwhelmed by painful or _____ events and unable to cope with them, we fall back on the use of d____m_____ s.

2. Personality theorists like Freud and Rank believe that the proto-anxiety is the b_____ t_____. Americans have not given much credence to this construct but European psychologists have been very much concerned with it. Dr. Frederic Leboyer, for example, has focused on the baby's experience of coming into this world with his technique of g_____ b_____.

3. Alfred Adler hypothesized that children feel overwhelmed by the superiority of the giant adults in their world of experience and that they seek ways to c_____ for their feelings of inferiority.

4. Harry Stack Sullivan suggested that anxious and schizophrenic mothers transmit their own a_____ to their infants. Harry Harlow has demonstrated that baby monkeys who were reared without adequate physical or psychological mothering developed into n_____ or depressed adults unable to mother their own offspring.

5. Through his c_____ c_____g

methods, Ivan Pavlov induced neurosis in his dogs. Later John Watson conditioned anxiety in the baby infant, Albert. Not only did Albert come to fear white rats, he also came to fear anything white and furry. Albert's response is called a g_____d r_____ to the white and furry objects which are called g_____d s_____.

6. Defense mechanisms enable us to survive t_____ events but they can also be barriers to further growth since they distort our perceptions of the world. In short, we are less free and less intelligent.

7. Defending ourselves by aggression includes all manner of physical violence but it also includes verbal aggression such as ridicule and s_____.

8. Defending ourselves by withdrawal includes pill-popping, alcoholism, and n_____ (frequently changing jobs, changing environment, changing spouses, etc.).

9. Rationalization is another form of defense in which the person denies the reality of the painful experience by constructing a more pleasant result such as "s_____ g_____" and "s_____ l_____."

10. A person who "doth protest too much" might be exhibiting the defense mechanism of r_____ f_____.

11. Ascribing our own thoughts and emotions to outside influences is called p_____.

12. Anna Freud called s_____ the "healthy defense." But we really cannot live without defenses. The issue is whether they are primitive and destructive to our life style or whether they are working well for us. When our behavioral responses enable us to handle our life situations well, we call them c_____ t_____s.

RECOMMENDED BOOKS FOR FURTHER READING

Berne, Eric. 1964. *Games People Play*. New York: Grove Press. This book gives insights into the way people manipulate each other and get caught up in each other's "games." This book is highly readable and entertaining as well as a learning experience.

Hoffer, Eric. 1966. *The True Believer*. New York: Harper & Row. Hoffer is an ex-longshoreman turned philosopher and writer. Although he is not a psychologist, he writes convincingly on the psychology of one of the most malevolent of all neuroses: the True Believer, the fanatic who seeks causes to worship and die for.

Laing, R. D. 1967. *The Politics of the Family and Other Essays*. New York: Balantine Books. The politics of the family can and does breed neurosis on the unfortunate member who does not realize how subtle the forms of defense mechanisms can be. A real shocker and eyeopener!

Leboyer, Frederick. 1975. *Birth Without Violence*. New York: Alfred A. Knopt, Inc. This work is Leboyer's classic first book and he lays out his basic concepts here. But the reader is directed also to his other magnificently illustrated books: *Loving Hands: The Traditional Indian Art of Baby Massaging*. New York: Alfred A. Knopf, Inc., 1976; *Inner Beauty Beauty, Inner Light*. New York: Alfred A. Knopf, Inc., 1978.

Putney, Snell and Putney, Gail J. 1972. *The Adjusted American: Normal Neuroses in the Individual and Society*. New York: Harper & Row Publishers, Inc. The problem with "normal neuroses," they say, is that they are shared by so many Americans it is difficult to become aware of them. Some of the neurotic American personality types they describe are the martyr, the wolf, the "dutiful" family member, the little tin god, and the jealous wife.

Singer, Jerome. 1975. *The Inner World of Daydreaming*. New York: Harper & Row Pubishers, Inc. By exploring his own adolescent and adult d aydreams, Singer helps us come to terms with, and even enjoy, one of our most creative defense mechanisms.

Shostrom, Everett, 1968. *Man the Manipulator*. New York: Bantam Books, Inc. In addition to the manipulative patterns described in this chapter, Shostrom presents some ways for people to actualize themselves instead of manipulating each other.

5

When the Bodymind Is on Overload: Physical and Emotional Breakdown

THE BODYMIND AND THE MINDBODY
    Primitive Beliefs About Disease
    The Doctrine of Specific Etiology

THE BEGINNINGS OF THE PSYCHOSOMATIC APPROACH TO DISEASE
    Hysterical Conversion
    Perceptual Defense
    Accident Proneness
    Diseases of the Respiratory System

WHAT ACTUALLY HAPPENS TO OUR BODIES UNDER STRESS?
    The Flight-or-Fight Syndrome
    The General Adaptation Syndrome
    The Effects of Life Change and Life Crises on Health

HELPLESSNESS AND LOSS: RECENT FINDINGS
    When the Pressure Is On . . .
    When We Experience Loss and Loneliness, and When We Are
        Frightened to Death

APPLICATIONS AND COPING TECHNIQUES

THE BODYMIND AND THE MINDBODY

In the last chapter we discussed the psychological results of anxiety: defense mechanisms and destructive life styles. In reality, however, there is no such thing as a purely "psychological" reaction to stress. As we are coming to understand more and more, the body and the mind are not two separate and independent systems, but an interacting unity of biochemical balance and changes. When the stress of life becomes overwhelming, and the emotional overload is reaching "critical mass," not only do we suffer emotional depression, we also fall victim to a host of physical diseases. More and more, we are coming to understand that disease is actually being *ill at ease* or *dis-eased*. In, perhaps, oversimplified terms, the happier we are, the healthier we are. Conversely, the unhappier we are, the more likely we are to undergo minor ailments and debilitating illnesses. The evidence for the close interrelationship between our emotional and physical well-being (or lack of it) is piling up from many areas of research into health and sickness. The Greeks said "*A sound mind in a sound body.*" And as with so much of their wisdom, we are only now, more than two thousand years later, coming to a full appreciation. Where once we used to speak of "the body" and "the mind" we have now come to recognize that they are so closely intertwined and interacting that it might be better to think of ourselves as a *bodymind* or a *mindbody*.

In order to appreciate the Greeks' insight to emotional and physical health, we need to understand how primitive peoples responded to disease, so we shall backtrack historically just a little to gain a more comprehensive perspective.

Primitive Beliefs About Disease

You will remember from chapter 1 that primitive peoples saw human life as being beyond their own control. They were the helpless pawns of whimsical gods or bestial deities. As part of this world view, they ascribed premature accidents and sickness as being the work of evil spirits, the revenge of their gods, or punishment for sins.

The Old Testament attitude toward disease was that it was sent by Jehovah as a punishment for the wrongdoing of an individual or of a whole nation. One of the ten plagues that God visited on the Egyptian people when the pharaoh refused to release the Hebrews from slavery was disease, and the story is still remembered in the Judaic-Christian tradition as an instance of divine retribution. Another biblical explanation for disease was that it tested a person's faith; such is the message of the Book of Job. (See box 5.1.)

PRIMITIVE BELIEFS ABOUT DISEASE

If thou wilt not observe to do all the words of this law that are written in this book, that thou mayest fear this glorious and fearful name, THE LORD THY GOD;

Then the LORD will make thy plagues wonderful, and the plagues of thy seed, even great plagues, and of long continuance, and sore sicknesses, and of long continuance.

Moreover He will bring upon thee all the diseases of Egypt which thou wast afraid of; and they shall cleave unto thee.

Also every sickness, and every plague, which is not written in the book of this law, then will the LORD bring upon thee, until thou be destroyed. (Deuteronomy 28:58-61)

Moreover, as man puts himself into communication with spirits through their names, so they know him through his name. In Borneo, they will change the name of a sickly child to deceive the evil spirits that have been tormenting it (St. John, *Borneo,* vol. I, p. 197). In South America, among the Abipones and Lenguas, when a man died, his family and neighbours would change their own names (Dobrizhoffer, "The Abipones," E. Tr., London, 1822, vol. ii., p. 273; Southey, "History of Brazil," London, 1819, vol. iii., p. 394) to cheat Death when he should come to look for them. (Edward B. Taylor, *Early History of Mankind.* Chicago: University of Chicago Press, 1964, p. 109.)

Let a Maori chief lose some valued article, or suffer from an attack of illness, and he immediately concludes that he has been bewitched. Who has bewitched him? He fixes, as a matter of course, on the individual whom he conceives to be his enemy, and orders him to be put to death. Or he resorts to some potent witch, and bribes her to exercise her influence to remove the maleficent spell under which he is labouring. (W. D. Adams, *Curiosities of Superstition.* London: J. Masters and Co., 1882, p. 244.)

Primitive societies still tend to believe that sickness comes from evil spirits who are out to do one harm, and frequently animal or human sacrifice is made to appease these spirits. (See box 5.1.) The people of the Middle Ages frequently ascribed disease to the work of the devil or to persons who consorted with the devil.

It was not until the fifteenth century that a few scientists began to suspect that disease was caused not by evil spirits but by tiny, invisible particles of life now called germs. These early researchers called these germs "living seeds of disease" and believed that they could develop out of nothing, a kind of spontaneous generation in the blood streams of humans and animals.

The idea of *contagion*, that disease could be transmitted from one person to another did not occur until the fourteenth century when great waves of bubonic plague swept over Europe. In the seventeenth century bacteria and other minute life forms were first seen under the microscope. But the germ theory of disease was still not fully accepted until the late ninteenth century, with the work of Robert Koch, Louis Pasteur, Robert Lister, and others. These scientists helped to disprove the idea that disease was caused by "evil spirits"; the evil spirits turned out to be living organisms (Zinsser 1935).

The Doctrine of Specific Etiology

These scientists also discovered that each disease has a specific "causal" microorganism. In other words, tuberculosis is caused by the tubercle bacillus, and none other. Furthermore, the tubercle bacillus causes only tuberculosis and not mumps, chicken pox, or scarlet fever. That all seems elementary to us now, but it was a significant understanding in the history of medicine. It was such a breakthrough that it was difficult to see anything amiss with the germ theory of disease.

It is an axiom in science that for a theory to be valid it ought to be *sufficient* to cover all the *necessary* conditions and to account for *all* the facts. When we apply this test to the germ theory, it seems to hold for most facts of disease, but it cannot account for some embarrassing exceptions to the rule. How is it, for example, that if we all are in contact with a disease (such as when the flu runs through a city or place of work), some of us may get it but not *all* of us? Why, if there are flu viruses in an area, do we *all* not contract the disease? To say that some of us are "immune" is not to *explain* these exceptions but only to *explain them away*.

Furthermore, as science began to uncover more of the facts of our biological environment, scientists came to acknowledge that the world is full of germs and microorganisms of all kinds. Indeed, the interior of our bodies is now known to be a virtual "hothouse" for bacteria. In fact, if our digestive tract did not teem with helpful bacteria, we would have a difficult time digesting the food we eat and eliminating what we no longer need.

It was when scientists began to pay attention to these exceptions that researchers began to look for a larger explanation for disease, one which could include the *facts* of germs and also the *exceptions* to those facts.

THE BEGINNINGS OF THE PSYCHOSOMATIC APPROACH TO DISEASE

One of the earliest hints that what we call disease may have a psychological component happened as far back as the mid-nineteenth century. A French physician, J. M. Charcot, was demonstrating the uses of hypnosis to medical students, among whom was a young man by the name of Sigmund Freud. Charcot was demonstrating that persons who were "crippled" or who stuttered could be "healed" instantly by a hypnotic suggestion, but only as long as they were in the hypnotic state (Boring 1950).

We also should mention those other interesting persons who had "cured" people through "mesmerism" (named for Anton Mesmer) and who seemed to restore a person to health by "magnetic powers." An American woman, Mary Baker Eddy, convinced that she had been cured of illness by acquiring the proper mental attitude, began a new religious sect, Christian Science, based on a positive mental health approach to perfect physical health. But these phenomena, as interesting as they are, were not examined under the harsh light of scientific inquiry as were Charcot's hypnotized patients. One explanation for all these cures is that the

When the bodymind is subjected to prolonged anxiety and stress, we can breakdown emotionally and/or physically.

patient was actually suffering from a hysteric symptom or hysterical conversion (Kelsey 1976).

Hysterical Conversion

An hysterical conversion refers to that condition in which the person with severe, free-floating anxiety converts the anxiety to a localized physical problem such as paralysis, blindness, or deafness. We label this *hysterical* paralysis, *hysterical* blindness, or *hysterical* deafness. Freud described a hysterical condition known as *glove anesthesia* in which the person was unable to feel anything from the wrist down, a complete numbness of the hand. The neurological "wiring" of our body is such that our nerves run *lengthwise* from the end of the fingers up the arm to the spinal cord so that a condition in which the person can have sensation to the wrist but not beyond is a neurological impossibility. Therefore, it is said to be "psychological" or "hysterical" numbness or anesthesia. Even **amnesia** can be said to be an hysterical conversion if there is no physiological reason for the amnesia.

When Freud discussed the hysterical conversion symptom, he postulated two patterns of behavior: **suppression** and **repression**. Suppression and repression are often confused, but they do not mean the same thing. Suppression means being aware that one wants to do something, such as hitting someone but not doing it, in other words, *suppressing* the act. Repression, on the other hand, means that the desire to hit someone may produce so much guilt that the person not only suppresses the action, but also the desire and impulse to do it are denied, "forgotten," *repressed*. It is also possible to confuse the word **hysteria** as used by clinicians with the popular usage of the word, in which a person who is called "hysterical" screams, laughs, and displays a generally "overwrought state." It is a pity that there is this confusion because in the psychological diagnosis of hysteria, the person seems to behave exactly the opposite, calm, resigned, even tranquil, *since all anxiety has been converted to the hysterical symptom.*

In Freud's time hysterical reactions were quite common. We believe that was so because the Viennese milieu (the society in which Freud grew up and whose customs he attempted to study) was heavily committed to defending itself against both sexuality and the emancipation of women. It is small wonder, then, that some women in that culture began to express—in symptoms—what the culture was doing to them . . . quite specifically! Part of the sickness of that society was the suppression and repression of sexuality—particularly feminine sexuality or sensuality. Men also experienced hysterical reactions but in more subtle forms. The authors, however, worked with a man who was suffering from what is an almost classic example of a hysterical reaction. (See box 5.2.)

Perceptual Defense

Cases of hysterical blindness or hysterical deafness may seem to us, at first, to be extraordinary situations that do not pertain to most of us. But they can be understood as extreme cases of something that all of us have experienced, which psychologists call **perceptual defense**.

Perceptual defending occurs in several small ways in our daily lives but primarily as "selective (in) attention." Rather than blocking off whole sensory *modalities*,[1] as in hysterical blindness or deafness, we simply screen out the particular items or stimuli we do not wish to see, hear, or feel. For example, a child learns to screen out his mother's nagging if she suggests, for example, that he clean his room or mow the lawn. We all can remember the child who responds with "What?" every time he is asked to do something like that, as if he had some kind of hearing defect. But let the mother mention that a delicious dessert is waiting for him in the refrigerator, and the child then seems able to hear the message very well indeed. By the time we enter school, most of us have become experts in perceptual defense. We hear the complaint among teachers, "He seems to let everything go in one ear and out the other."

Box 5.2

A CASE OF HYSTERICAL PARALYSIS

Mr. Smith, as we shall call him, was a man of "moral" fiber, and his conduct in business was ethical to an extreme. Mr. Smith treated his employees with unusual diplomacy and dignity, and they in turn were loyal to the firm and to him. He had many friends, and he was, as he himself admitted, a friendly and genial person. His home life seemed to him satisfying. He liked his wife, who happened to be intelligent, and his children who were doing well in school. But one day, before he came to see us and to his astonishment, he had awakened paralyzed in his right arm. He had already made the rounds of family physician, internist, and neurologist, all of whom concluded that there was nothing wrong with his arm neurologically or anatomically. They had suggested to him that his trouble might be—"psychological" in nature and that maybe he should consider psychotherapy. The thought that there could be anything wrong with him psychologically obviously seemed somewhat amusing to him as he sat in our office on that first day of our acquaintance, but he was willing to try anything to get cured—even psychotherapy!

After a few therapy sessions, he gradually became aware that all was not as "ideal" in his life as he had supposed, particularly in his relationship with his wife. He began to realize that while he deeply respected his wife—who was intelligent, capable, and a good mother—she also was a source of irritation for him. He began to remember situations in which her nagging had got to him, and as he recalled those instances again, he began to feel and remember the headaches that resulted.

When he returned one week later, he was no longer paralyzed in his right arm.

Mr. Smith was also able to remember what had led to his paralysis. The night before his arm had become paralyzed, his wife had been (in his words) "giving him hell," and he had raised his arm to strike her. At the last moment he realized what he was doing, and he stopped himself and left the house. He had been horrified to realize that he could be capable of such violence. After suffering some moments of guilt and shame (gentlemen do not hit women!), he was able to return to the house, apologize to his wife for his behavior, and go to bed with a headache. The next morning his arm was paralyzed.

"The strange thing," he said with a smile of remembrance, "was that I had forgotten the incident of the previous night—both the disagreement with my wife and my impulsive urge to hit her."

Accident Proneness

By the 1920s, the clinical relationship between certain physical diseases and psychological tensions and strains was becoming more well known. People were talking now about "tension" headaches and "worry" ulcers. Early studies in industrial psychology began to reveal an interesting fact—that certain persons were more "accident prone" than others and that these persons seemed to have certain demographic personality characteristics. They seemed to come from broken homes and from larger families, and they appeared to be more aggressive and maladjusted and to display more acting-out behaviors than those who did not have this kind of accident frequency. There has been some reconsideration of the earlier studies on accident proneness, and the correlations do not tend to be as high. But not only have even more recent investigators sustained the implication that some people are simply more accident prone than others are, there also is evidence now that all of us can be liable to accidents at certain times—those times when the pressures in our life become so intense that we are less aware of ourselves in the physical world. At those times we hit our head on a cabinet, or we underestimate the distance and back our car into a tree, or we jab ourselves with an instrument we have been using for years (Maier 1973).

Some investigators believe that this self-mutilation is actually an expression of hostility and anger toward an uncaring world—only it is turned inward, against the self. At any rate, the evidence seems to suggest that there is more truth than poetry in the saying "There goes an accident looking for a place to happen" when we see an automobile racing far above normal speeds.

Diseases of the Respiratory System

The earliest diseases to be identified with emotional problems per se were asthma and hay fever. By the late twenties and early thirties, clinical psychologists and psychiatrists were beginning to notice the close correspondence of persons suffering with these ailments and certain commonalities in their personality structure and family background, namely, a smothering relationship between the patient and the parents, particularly the mother.

ASTHMA.   Asthma is the psychosomatic response in which the person experiences an extreme degree of difficulty in breathing. In the asthma attack the person feels as if he or she might suffocate at any moment. Sometimes the attack will last for hours, and the wheezing and coughing can continue until the person feels exhausted. An asthma attack frequently ends with convulsive coughing, an experience no one wants to repeat once he or she has experienced it. Asthma attacks are now acknowledged to be intimately related to emotional upset. For example, asthma in children is found mostly in extremely anxious and insecure children who feel rejected or "smothered" by one or both of their parents. If the asthmatic child continues to grow up as an "asthmatic," his or her asthma attacks can become the principal method of expressing anger, hostility, resentment, and general unhappiness. When a person gets into a tight emotional spot with which he or she feels unable to cope, a way to get out of it is by having an asthmatic attack right then and there. This response is calculated to bring on others' concern, guilt feelings, and eventually the physical attention he or she feels necessary to survive (Alexander 1963).

HAY FEVER.   Another respiratory ailment that caught the attention of early psychosomatic clinicians is hay fever. Like asthma, hay fever is an allergy in which certain substances come in contact with the skin or skin receptors causing the mucous membranes of the nose, mouth and eyes to swell and produce a coldlike reaction that lasts for a certain period of time, when the pollen count is high. Over and beyond the person's physical susceptibility to pollen, the case history of people who suffer from hay fever seems to indicate a certain common background, an overprotected childhood and one in which they were told they could not do this or that for fear of . . . and so forth. Under therapeutic treatment both the hay fever patient and asthma patient frequently have long periods (of years) when the vulnerability to this disease is decreased, and in fact the hay fever or asthma does not occur even though the person is in the same environment as when the attacks did occur. They report also that this improvement can be correlated with the fact that their social and family life is at an even keel and that their social life is active.

THE COMMON COLD.   Once the psychosomatic elements of hay fever and asthma were identified, the common cold (another respiratory ailment) also came under suspicion. Clinicians had long noticed a peculiar relationship between the symptoms of the common cold and the external effects of crying. Therapists often have noticed that after some family blowup or an on-the-job "slight," the patient may say that it really did not have much effect but soon after develops a cold. The person does not weep for one reason or another but instead contracts a cold, which has all the physical symptoms of weeping: watery eyes, sniffling, a red face, and puffy eyes. In this way, clinicians say, the body is able to do the weeping it needs to do even when the person denies that he or she feels hurt or wounded and does not permit himself or herself the needed release of weeping or crying (Dunbar 1955).

WHAT ACTUALLY HAPPENS TO OUR BODIES UNDER STRESS?

The Flight-or-Fight Syndrome

At about the same time these early clinical researchers in psychosomatic medicine were working Walter B. Cannon, one of the early and great workers in psychosomatic research, stated his understandings of the body-mind interrelationship, in a book entitled *Wisdom of the Body* (1963). The body, he said, has to maintain a state of homeostasis in order to survive. When the body gets cold, we shiver, thereby warming us up; when we get too hot, we perspire, thereby reducing the temperature of our body. If we are not getting enough air, we may yawn and take in more oxygen. Thus the body has a kind of "inner wisdom" which produces various bodily responses. One of these responses is the *flight-or-fight syndrome*, which is precisely the opposite of the homeostatic state—it is an emergency state in which the body goes through many physiological changes in order to fight the threat in the environment or to flee from it. Suppose, for example, a cat scents a

When confronted with a threat, the organism reacts with the "flight-or-fight" syndrome.

dog in the environment. It immediately freezes, and its body responds with the flight-or-fight syndrome. Rate of respiration, heart rate, and sugar production increase markedly, and thus more energy becomes available so the animal can prepare itself to stand and fight the "enemy" or to take flight if that is more appropriate. The pupils of the eyes also dilate (improving vision), and the blood tends to withdraw from the body surface, thereby protecting the animal against bruising and bleeding of the skin and increasing the supply of blood to the vital organs. Blood-clotting capacity also increases as does the tension in the striated muscles, providing for more rapid behavior response when needed.

These same physiological changes are also produced in us when we experience a threat or emergency in our environment. At these times we may react with superhuman strength. Newspapers often carry stories of persons who have reacted with just this kind of strength in times of crisis. It may be no more than an item describing how John Jones lifted the front end of his sports car to free a loved one pinned underneath or how someone jumped from the second-floor window of a burning building and landed unhurt. In such situations the body reacts to the emergency stress with a kind of total psychophysiological response clearly beyond our usual capacities. How the body and the mind were interrelated was explained further by the formulation of the *general adaptation syndrome*, described by Hans Selye, a physician researcher in the area of psychosomatic research (Selye, 1956).

The General Adaptation Syndrome

This is the term Selye used to describe what happens when animals experience a dangerous amount of stress. Selye began his research with experimental animals.

The beginning of the *stres syndrome* always seemed to involve a primary period he called the *alarm reaction*. With further stress, the *stage of resistance* appeared. If stress at this level continued, the animal's abilities to cope diminished, and the final stage, the *stage of exhaustion*, would appear, and ultimately death would occur.

1. THE ALARM REACTION. When an experimental animal is first subjected to physical or psychological stress (electrical shock, extreme cold, poison), the animal's body reacts by increasing the rate of production of certain hormones and the levels of certain sugars and salts. All of these secretions strengthen the body's defense systems against the oncoming stressors. Such a response is the body's normal method of meeting an emergency since these increased levels of body chemicals (hormones, salts, sugars) increase one's strength and endurance. There is a certain similarity between Selye's alarm reaction and Cannon's flight-or-fight syndrome, but there also is this important difference. Cannon studied dramatic emergency situations. Selye studied less dramatic stressful situations that continue over time, or *prolonged* stress. In the alarm reaction the animal continues to secrete sugars, salts, and hormones (to defend itself against the emergency stressor) for so long that the animal's body functions begin to break down, as Selye's research showed, in the form of a withered thymus, diseased adrenal glands, bleeding ulcers, and the like.

2. STAGE OF RESISTANCE. If the stressor (physical or emotional) is not too severe and the animal does not die, the animal seems to be able to recover from the first-stage alarm-reaction pattern. Its adrenal glands return to normal size, although they continue to function at abnormally high levels of secretion. The ulcerative condition also disappears, and the thymus returns to a normal state. In the *stage of resistance*, the animal's body thus *seems* to be adapting to the stressful condition by maintaining certain physiological defenses—for example, an increased production of white blood cells to defend against noxious germs and viruses. On the surface everything appears to have returned to normal. Indeed, it was sometimes hard for Selye to tell the experimental animals (the animals under stress) from the control animals (the animals not subjected to the stressor). All seemed well . . . for a while.

3. STAGE OF EXHAUSTION. The apparent adaptation of Selye's experimental animals did not last for more than a few weeks. After that the animals got progressively weaker, their internal organs became dangerously diseased again, sugar and chloride production fell again to dangerously low levels, and the animals began to die within a month. In other words, the organism can sustain the supercharged defense rate for only so long. Its defenses or resistances then collapse and life ceases. The *stage of exhaustion* is similar to the initial alarm reaction in that the same sets of responses are present and the same syndrome can be seen.

In the stage of resistance the body's defenses are marshaled only against the original stressor—for example, extreme cold. If the animal survives the alarm-reaction stage and manages to achieve an adequate defense in the stage of resistance, it is a defense against only that one stressor condition. If the experimenters now add another stressor at the same time (say, electrical shock, which is considered an emotional stressor), the animal collapses immediately. *Selye thereby demonstrated conclusively that as the number of stressful conditions in the environment increase, the organism is correspondingly less able to cope (or even survive).*

What does this mean for human existence? Let us take a theoretical application from the life of a young man who is doing his best to earn a living and provide for his wife and baby. He is having problems at his job which cause him some difficulty, but he manages to cope and live through this first stage of alarm. His body gears itself up to working under stressful conditions; as a result he is able to pass through the stage of alarm and is reacting to the stage of resistance. However, just as he thinks he is beginning to get on top of the mess at the job, his mother-in-law comes to visit and makes life hell for him at home as well. This additional stressor may very well be just enough to crack his stage of resistance, and he may then break down as revealed by some physical symptom—maybe a cold in the head or the flu.

Selye made it very clear that *stress* is simply part of the natural "wear and tear" of life on the tissues of organisms. We cannot escape natural stress even if we wanted to, and who would want to lead such a dull life, if that were possible? Selye did point out that an excess of stress or prolonged stress of any kind can do more than the normal wear and tear—it can break down body tissue.

INTOXICATION BY STRESS. Selye concluded that stress is the everyday wear and tear of life; it is the "common feature of biological activities." Stress cannot be avoided, he said, for even excitement and enjoyable recreation produce wear and tear on our bodies. But we need to recognize when we are getting too keyed up (those jittery feelings and tingling sensations), to acknowledge when we are not getting enough rest, and to listen to our bodies when we begin to feel on edge or "all tensed up." Selye believed that a man could become intoxicated by his own hormone production and that it was wise to be aware also of the signs of *overstimulation. Intoxication by stress* is usually insidious simply because it may actually be enjoyable: We can become "addicted" to it. It is not always so easy to turn down the level of stimulation of one's body as it is to turn down the volume of the television. Selye thought we must provide for relaxation in our daily lives. Relaxation does not necessarily mean play, for play can be taken too seriously. We can become overexcited, and we are again trapped in overproduction of hormones.

The Effects of Life Change and Life Crisis on Health

Selye studied the stress syndrome as it appeared in experimental animals and then extrapolated from those findings to the effects of stress on humans. More recently there have been some equally challenging studies of stress as it appears in the form of change. This work was done with humans, and the researchers discoverd that *change alone*—even when it is seen as beneficial or "happy"—can have ill effects upon a person's psychosomatic balance or health. Two researchers, T. H. Holmes, and R. H. Rahe, developed a "life change units scale," which measures how much change an individual has been subjected to over a given period of time. Some of the items in their scale note obviously hurtful and traumatic events—the death of a loved one, being fired from a job, a painful divorce, being flunked out of school, and so forth. What is thought provoking about their research findings is that even agreeable changes in one's situation—marriage, birth of a baby, promo-

Box 5.3

STRESS RATINGS OF VARIOUS LIFE EVENTS

EVENTS	SCALE OF IMPACT
Death of spouse	100
Divorce	73
Marital separation	65
Jail term	63
Death of close family member	63
Personal injury or illness	53
Marriage	50
Fired at work	47
Marital reconciliation	45
Retirement	45
Change in health of family member	44
Pregnancy	40
Sex difficulties	39
Gain of new family member	39
Business readjustment	39
Change in financial state	38
Death of close friend	37
Change to different line of work	36
Change in number of arguments with spouse	35
Mortgage over $10,000	31
Foreclosure of mortgage or loan	30
Change in responsibilities at work	29
Son or daughter leaving home	29
Trouble with in-laws	29
Outstanding personal achievement	28
Wife begins or stops work	26
Begin or end school	26
Change in living conditions	25
Revision of personal habits	24
Trouble with boss	23
Change in work hours or conditions	20
Change in residence	20
Change in schools	20
Change in recreation	19
Change in church activities	19
Change in social activities	18
Mortgage or loan less than $10,000	17
Change in sleeping habits	16
Change in number of family get-togethers	15
Change in eating habits	15
Vacation	13
Christmas	12
Minor violations of the law	11

SOURCE: Adapted from T. S. Holmes & T. H. Holmes, ''Short-term intrusions into life-style routine.'' *Journal of Psychosomatic Research*, 14 (1970), 121–32.

tion, a vacation—are considered emotionally stressful.[2] This was found to be the case not only with American subjects but also with Europeans and Japanese (Holmes & Rahe 1967).

Holmes and Rahe began to see that persons with many life changes—those with high *life crises unit* (LCU) scores—were more likely to suffer from ill health than those with lower LCU scores. Moreover, there seemed to be a definite additive aspect to the scale: The higher the LCU score, the more likely the person was to come down with an abrupt and serious illness.

Of the crises rated by Holmes and Rahe, the death of a spouse is assigned the highest LCU score (100). This makes sense, for the death of a spouse involves not only the sense of personal loss and grief that follow but also severe dislocations in personal habits (such as eating and sleeping) and the continued stress of learning to adapt to social relations as a single person rather than as a couple. But any kind of externally imposed change in accustomed habit patterns can result in an increase in one's LCU score: going away to college, moving to another place, going into the army—all of these can be stressful because of the changes in eating, sleeping, relaxation, and recreation habits, not to mention giving up old friends and the effort in finding new ones.

Holmes and Rahe's early research showed there was a marked correlation—a definite relationship—between a high LCU score and an abrupt and serious change in a person's health. *Within eighteen months* of registering such a score, persons came down with major illnesses: tuberculosis, mononucleosis, cancer, leukemia, and so on. Their later research revealed that even short-term periods (of two or three days) of high LCU scores resulted in minor aches, pains, colds, and other discomforts. What this means is that the everyday minor illnesses we take for granted, such as the common cold, appear more often when we are stressed for even just a couple of days. Headaches are more frequent when there is tension in our environment; stomachaches, hay fever, and other allergies are more likely to reappear in difficult times or when there are major changes in our physical or psychological state (Holmes & Holmes 1976).

Stress factors are the obvious problems that we encounter repeatedly in our present working and living situations. They include all the kinds of adjustment difficulties in new situations, such as moving to another city, taking a new job, and going to college. They also may be family problems, unhappy work relationships, high-pressure jobs, continued worry about one's family and relatives—any and all of these can be the kind of *profound* stress that causes equally pronounced changes in the psychophysiological balance of the body.

HELPLESSENESS AND LOSS: RECENT FINDINGS

When the Pressure Is On . . .

ULCERS: IN THE LABORATORY AND OFFICE. Psychologists accept clinical data and assessment research for their heuristic value and observation of "real life," but they are never happy until they can confirm these kinds of data with laboratory evidence. Selye had produced diseases of the vital organs which seemed remarkably like those in human beings. But these stressors were physiological: starvation, electrical shock, and toxic substances. Wolfe, Rahe, and Holmes had correlated illness and emotional problems. Was it possible to produce these kinds of diseases in laboratory animals as the result of psychological stress? Joseph Brady, an American psychologist, decided to try (Brady, Porter, Conrad, & Mason 1958). He chose chimpanzees as his subjects, which he estimated to be about as close as he could get to humans.

Clinically, ulcer patients seem to be hard-working, over-time "worriers," and business executives seem to be particularly prone to this kind of psychosomatic reaction. They have to make decisions quickly under pressure, and if they make the wrong ones, they may lose their jobs.

Brady yoked two monkeys to an apparatus that generated electrical shocks. Both monkeys were subjected to the shocks (which were not physiologically damaging) at twenty-second intervals, but one monkey, whom Brady called the executive monkey had a lever that would, when the monkey learned to use it, prevent the shocks. The other monkey (the control monkey) had no such lever. Brady reasoned that the monkey that could prevent the shock was in the same psychological position as the high-powered executive; that is, it was in a position of constant pressure and vigilance. In one experimental situation after another, the control monkey, who had nothing to do but receive the shocks, survived with apparently no lasting effects. But the "executive monkeys," the ones under continual psychological pressure as well, all developed severe ulcers and eventually died.

When We Experience Loss and Loneliness, and When We Are Frightened to Death

CANCER: REACTION TO LOSS. Another pioneering psychosomatic researcher, Harold G. Wolff, compared the records of survivors of prisoner-of-war camps and concentration camps six years after liberation with a similar population in terms of sex, age, and general socioeconomic level. He was not surprised to find that the ex-prisoners' physical resistance to diseases such as tuberculosis and intestinal disorders was lower than that of the nonprisoner population, that even after liberation they fell prey to these diseases; nor was he surprised that the liberated prisoners continued to commit suicide at a higher rate than normal. (The ex-prisoners had been psychologically "burned out" by their experiences.) What he had not expected to find was *twice the normal incidence of death from cancer* in the ex-prisoners (Wolff 1962). A past president of the American Cancer Society has stated that successfully treated cancer patients suddenly seem to develop cancer again after a serious emotional situation, such as the loss of a loved one or protracted unemployment (Berenblum 1967).

LONELINESS AND THE HEART DISEASES. The various illnesses collectively known as heart disease have been attributed to many factors in our society: cigarettes, high-cholesterol diets, and sedentary life. No doubt, all of these have some relationship to the incidence of heart disease.

UNDER PRESSURE: THE CASE OF AIR-TRAFFIC CONTROLLERS

One of the significant observations from the Brady experiment was the observation that the monkey that had to do the "worrying" was significantly more emotionally pressured than the control monkey was. One of the most stressful jobs in this country is that of the air-traffic controller. The air-traffic controller is the person who uses radar, weather instruments, and communications equipment to guide airline landings and take-offs.

Sidney Cobb of the University of Michigan and Robert Rose of Boston University compared the health records of 8,435 pilots and 5,199 controllers. Both groups of subjects work in life-death situations, but air-traffic controllers are under greater psychological stress since they (like the "executive monkeys") must make the decisions. The air-traffic controllers were found to have a far greater frequency of high blood pressure, diabetes, peptic ulcers, and so on (Cobb & Rose 1973).

But clinicians have long observed that persons suffering from the heart diseases seem to have common characteristics, and the picture we so often get is that of hard-driving, aggressive executives committed to completing a job, no matter what the pressure. They are committed (whether they want to admit it or not) to working long hours on a job with fewer and fewer vacations and with less and less recreational time and, in the end, without even the ability to relax off the job. Heart disease patients are the truly committed persons who put their hearts into their jobs until the pressure begins to kill them. Their calm exteriors belie the internal stress and pressure that they experience; yet they can continue to overwork and suppress their anger and anxiety until that moment when the internal stress "blows up" in the coronary artery. By then, the pressure is not so much a psychological difficulty as a medical emergency!

Type A: Potential victims of heart disease. In 1974 a book entitled *Type A Behavior and Your Heart* was published by two researchers. They admitted that although some of the factors contributing to heart disease in their patients could be linked to nonpsychological factors (diet, lack of exercise, smoking), in at least half of the cases, these factors were absent. After more than thirty years of studying coronary disease in the hospital, laboratory, and consulting rooms, they concluded that a certain type of personality, which they labeled the Type A personality, had certain behavioral characteristics. These characteristics include an excessively high competitive drive, whether in business or on the golf links, and a sense of continual pressure and not enough time to do everything they want to do so that they are always trying to do two or more things at once. They also are extremely aggressive, with a quiet rage that seems to seethe just below the surface. They generally have few hobbies or diversions outside their work and feel guilty when they relax, considering most recreations a waste of time and putting their driving energies into work. They also tend to abuse their bodies by eating too rich foods, and drinking more than average. They resemble what an early psychosomatic social scientist described as the typical heart patient: "They would rather die than fail." (Friedman & Rosenman 1974.)

If you know someone who hates to wait in line, strives to do too many things at once, often seems to be in a hurry, eats too much salt, is a fast talker who jumps on somebody else's sentence, and cannot bear to dawdle or "just plain play," you may know a person racing to a heart attack.

Loneliness as a factor in heart disease. But personality is only part of the story. There may be another factor in heart disease. In a word: loneliness. A heart specialist, James Lynch, points out that the case histories of heart victims reveals a high incidence of emotional isolation (Lynch 1977 [b]). For example, he quotes the well-known Fuchs study done on the residents of Nevada and a neighboring state, Utah (Fuchs 1974). Nevada has the second highest mortality rate in the nation, while Utah has one of the lowest. Both states have approximately the same average income (Nevada's is $1,000 more a year); both states have a high socioeducational level; and both states have the same proportion of urban-rural residents. What then is the difference? Nevada has one of the highest single, divorced, or separated populations, while Utah, with its strong family-based population, has one of the lowest. Furthermore, more than nine out of ten residents of Nevada were born out of state; fewer than four out of ten residents of Utah were born out of state (at the time of the study). There are simply more lonely people in Nevada than there are in Utah.

Lynch brings together other studies that link the heart diseases to the lack of warm, close personal relationships in one's life. Some of these factors appear in the patient's case history as death of a parent in early childhood, absence of sibling relationships, nonparticipation in sports or other social activities in college (Paffenbarger et al. 1966(a), 1966(b), 1968, 1969; Paffenberger & Asnes 1966).

THE EFFECTS OF HUMAN LOVE ON THE HEART

Does common sense recognize something that scientists and physicians cannot see? Why do we continue to use phrases such as *broken heart, heartbroken, heartsick, heartless, sweetheart?* Why do people persist in the notion that their fellow men die of broken hearts when no such diagnoses ever appear on twentieth-century death certificates?

Even though the effects of human love on the heart are still largely ignored by most scientists, times are changing. The larger question of the effects of human emotions on the development of cardiac disease is now being seriously considered by many scientists. (Friedman & Rosenman 1974; Lynch et al. 1977). Growing numbers of physicians now recognize that the health of the human heart depends not only on such factors as genetics, diet, and exercise, but also to a large extent on the social and emotional health of the individual (Lynch 1977).

But Lynch wants us to examine our lives even more closely than that. It is not simply a matter of living with other persons. Many of us can be married to each other in name only. Whether because of excessive dedication to our jobs or because of our life styles, many of us, he insists, live in a state of "psychological divorce" from our mates. "Our lives are essentially devoid of love," he writes.

We know now, also, that grief is a cause of death. Physicians may not be able to write that as the "cause of death" on the coroner's reports. Yet researchers have pointed out the frequency with which widows and widowers die soon after the demise of their spouses (Parkes 1972; Young 1963; Rees & Lutkins 1967). The frequency with which the widowed spouse dies in the first six months is particularly high. It is all very well to say that the death of a spouse has a high emotional impact on one's sleeping, eating, and recreational activities, but to think simply in terms of life-crisis units (LCUs) may be another way of avoiding the real issue, that we can die of a broken heart, says Lynch, and he is courageous enough to entitle his book *The Broken Heart: The Medical Consequences of Loneliness.* We need to have love in our lives; to love and be loved. We need to belong to someone and to some place.

WE COULD EVEN BE "FRIGHTENED TO DEATH." As the mind-body interrelationship is being better understood, the concept of *mindbody* or *bodymind* seems ever more valid. "Mindbody" is exactly the meaning of the word *psychosomatic. Psyche* is the Greek word for mind or soul, and *soma* is the Latin word for body. It is becoming more and more obvious that a serious "psychological" trauma can have a profound effect on the body.

Voodoo death. Psychologists began asking themselves whether or not the case for the *mindbody* relationship was strong enough to justify the stories of "voodoo death." We have all read about stories in which a native of some Caribbean island has died as the result of being cursed by a witch doctor or by some other psychological terror. Such cases have been described frequently by travelers, and one such case was described by an anthropologist who witnessed just such an event among the Australian aborigines. This poor victim was "boned to death" by his enemy.

> The man who discovers that he is being boned by an enemy is, indeed, a pitiable sight. He stands aghast with his eyes staring at the treacherous pointer, and with his hands lifted to ward off the lethal medium, which he imagines is pouring into his body. His cheeks blanch, and his eyes become glassy, and the expression on his face becomes horribly distorted. He attempts to shriek but usually the sound chokes in his throat, and all that one might see is froth at his mouth. His body begins to tremble and his muscles twitch involuntarily. He sways backward and falls to the ground, and after a short time appears to be in a swoon. He finally composes himself, goes to his hut, and there frets to death. [Basedow 1977]

Can such a thing be possible?

Laboratory voodoo. In 1956 a trio of psychologists performed an experiment on rats that seemed to suggest it is possible.

Insulin is the hormone that controls the metabolism of blood sugar. Most of us are familiar with the fact that if the body's pancreas malfunctions (so that no insulin is produced), the effect is the disease called diabetes. Fortunately, insulin can now be synthesized, and with daily injections of synthetic insulin, diabetic patients can live a fairly full and a longer life. Too much insulin injected into the blood stream, however, is also extremely dangerous and, in fact, can be lethal. This severe physiological reaction is called insulin shock and is accompanied by unconsciousness and even death. The psychologists (Sawry, Conger, and Turrell) injected rats with overdoses of insulin, and the result was unconsciousness and, in a few cases, death. At the same time that the rats were given these overdoses of insulin, the experimenters flooded the rats with a bright light. After the animals recovered from their insulin shock, the experimenters again gave the rats insulin injections and the bright light several more times. Each time the experimental animals fell into shock, and so on. Then the experimenters subjected the rats to a different experimental situation. Again under bright lights, they gave the animals an injection, but this time the needle did not contain insulin but a harmless saline solution which produces no experimental effect at all. You can guess the results of this experiment. Even without the insulin, the rats fell into insulin shock, which for all intents and purposes, was indistinguishable from the reaction produced by the insulin. Evidently we can be conditioned or frightened to death (Sawrey & Telford 1971). (See box 5.6.) It may be that when we put an old person in a nursing home, we consign him to death (Butler, 1975).

APPLICATIONS AND COPING TECHNIQUES

It must be obvious now that extreme stress results not only in psychological breakdown but also in physical breakdown. It is good to remember that life itself, even when we are going about our everyday humdrum routines, is *stressful*. Selye called attention, time and again, to the fact that we cannot avoid stress. It is a part of our everyday lives. Stress is part of the excitement of living, and we actually seek stimulation and challenging situations to avoid monotony. In fact, boredom itself can become a source of stress. What we need to learn to do is develop strategies for coping with stress.

1. Strategy for Dealing With Our Ailments

Persons who are ill often feel a sense of despondency and shame. They hide their emotional and physical suffering and loneliness. But recent research has indicated a direct correlation between self-expressiveness and cancer remission (Bazar 1983). We can do only so much with a purely physical approach to disease. The person's spirit needs to be involved also: the feeling that he or she *can* get better and that others want them to, the patient's own attitude is a potent force in their healing process. If there is an ill person in our family, we can help them to heal by allowing them to express their fears and concerns so they do not have to hide them.

2. Remain Alert to the Stressors in Our Lives

It is good to remember that *any kind of change* is stressful and to take on too many things at once may have a serious physical outcome. We do not suggest that you turn down an advancement in your job, but we urge you to remember that even this fortunate event may arouse anxiety, the anxiety to do well and the urge to "overdo" the work situation. A third or fourth child may be very welcome, but the problems of larger families do not multiply arithmetically but geometrically. Not only will there be that many more mouths to feed but that many more children to catch contagious diseases; that many more possibilities for expensive orthodontic work, eyeglasses, special shoes to be fitted (if one of them happens to have weak ankles or arches); that many more conferences with the school; and that many more involvements with PTA or Little League. If the parents are anxious to give their children "every advantage," there will be that many more music lessons, dancing lessons, and so on. We ask you to remember that when you "moonlight" a job to become more financially secure, you may be overtaxing your body and spirit. Many of you who are now in school already are engaged in many kinds of activities including part- or full-time work, taking care of families, attempting to study outside your classes and doing, perhaps, many other things that are part of the educational scene.

3. Become Aware of the Small Signals in the Body That Tell Us Our Physiological Defenses are Beginning to Crumble

We also have our own physical symptoms that signal that our body is beginning to show signs of stress. *This* person begins to get headaches; *that* person's sinuses are beginning to act up. Another bodily symptom may be a joint that is beginning to flare up again with bursitis or arthritis, or one's "susceptibility" to hay fever or allergy may start to increase. These are the early warning signs that all is not well and that you ought to slow down.

Unfortunately, most of us tend to ignore these symptoms. Instead of calling in sick for a day or so, we "pop" a headache pill or an antihistamine, gird ourselves up, and go to work or to school or that business party we do not really want to attend. Sure enough, later that day, we discover that our symptoms have gone away or are such that we can manage our responsibilities and the symptoms of stress, too. And we probably can. But if the pressures of work, studies, or family conflicts continue to pile up, our symptoms (which have gone away or which we have "blotted out" through aspirin and willpower) may suddenly erupt again in something more serious.

Some persons say, "Yes, but I've never been sick a day in my life. I've got a lot of physical stamina, and I can do a lot of things." This is certainly more true of some people than of others. We caution you that your ability to drive yourselves, burn the candles at both ends, stay up late and get up early, and abuse your bodies cannot last forever, and as all of us get older our ability to tolerate stress decreases. Sooner or later, we must all "pay the piper."

4. Learn to Understand the Language of the Body

Our body sends distress signals that bespeak more than just that something is wrong; they often indicate *what* is wrong (if we are willing to listen). If we have a headache or a backache, the question to ask ourselves is, Who or what is giving me the headache? If it is a backache, Who or what is on my back? Is it the party we dread going to? Is it a task we have taken on? Is it one of the kids or a relative whose behaviors are causing continual upheaval in the family? Take these clues as ideas only. Your body language and body signals will be singularly yours. Only you can interpret your body language. One person's headache may be quite different from another person's. Your cool, intelligent, objective self-analysis will provide you with the clue to the stressor (or stressors) in your life.

Lump in your throat? What situation would you like to cry about, or scream about, or is it something you just cannot "swallow"?

Knot in your stomach? What situation has you so tensed up you cannot relax? Or what piece of news can you not digest?

Abdominal cramps? Is there something going on in your life that is "cramping your style?" Do you feel squeezed by someone? Of are you in the middle of a situation or between two persons?

Cold or swelling of the mucous membranes (hay fever, sinus, etc.)? Has there been something in the last day or so that was particularly hurtful, something about which you did not cry—perhaps even denied that it made a difference to you but looking back now, you realize that it hurt you more than you had thought?

Sensitive areas in the shoulders? This is one of the signals that we have taken on too much responsibility. We are beginning to feel "the weight of the world" on our shoulders.

Constipated? What are you holding on to "for dear life"? It could be that you are simply too busy to take time out for the calls of nature; on the other hand, you may be so tense and "tight" that you are unable to let the bowels function easily.

Diarrhea? We all have had attacks of diarrhea as the result of illness, but there is another kind that seems to come just before we take an exam or have to go for an important interview. Actors getting ready for a play frequently have to run to the bathroom just before curtain time.

5. Provide Yourself With an Occasional "Getaway"

It is surprising the number of professional and business people who never call in sick. Look at the attendance records of an organization, and you will notice that although many persons have used every possible sick leave, emergency leave, personal leave, there are others who have accumulated years of unused sick and other personal leave time. Despite the warning signals from their body that all is not well, these people are just unable to let go of their responsibilities. They worry that something might go wrong at the office if they are not there. They maintain their perfect record until, at length, they come down with something really serious like a heart attack, ulcers, or whatever. An occasional sick leave or "mental health day" will help prolong that eventuality, but only if you do not worry about what is going on if you are not there.

What you do with that day off is, of course, up to you. Some of you may just enjoy staying in bed with your favorite book. Others would feel better doing something constructive around the house, like fixing that leak in the plumbing or puttering in the garden. Just because you stay home does not mean you have to be really sick. You can just be sick and tired of the problems and the people in the office, and a day away will give you a new perspective on both the problems and the people.

6. Find Several Outlets for Your Creative Energy

Sometimes we get so involved in a project or a responsibility that we cannot separate ourselves from what we are doing. All our *emotional* energy is being put into *that* project or *that* responsibility. Our feelings of self-worth all are tied up in the *success* of *that* project or *that* responsibility. If something goes wrong, we have a sense of failure, not just in that project or that responsibility but in *ourselves* as persons of value. For example, one of the most stressful situations in marriage is the conflict over how to raise children or what to do when they are acting up or having school problems. At these times, parents begin to feel a sense of self-doubt, that familiar, gnawing worry that "we didn't do something right." If we have invested our total concept of ourselves in "perfect, successful" children, we find our own self-worth going down the drain when they do not live up to our expectations. If we have devoted most of our time and energy into our career and suddenly find it boring or meaningless or more than we can handle, we may begin to wonder if life is worth living at all, and it is not surprising then that we begin to feel physically and emotionally low.

People who lead relatively *healthy*, rewarding lives have developed several areas of their lives. They may have a side hobby, which challenges and gives them a sense of achievement. During the middle period of his life Winston Churchill experienced professional failure. All during the 1930s, he was considered a political pariah, even by his own party. He had to go into political retirement during those years, and very few people came to see him or to consult with him. He had many moments of depression and despair, but he kept himself busy, by painting, by writing *History of the English-Speaking Peoples*, and by many other kinds of activities. He knew himself to be a person of worth, and he refused to let a temporary setback in his career change that attitude. Ultimately, as we all know, he was called back into Great Britain's highest office at the beginning of World War II, when Britain needed him most, and achieved his "finest hour."

7. When Emotional Tension is Rising Dangerously High, Find Techniques to Blow Off the Steam in Harmless Ways

Sometimes there are situations in which one would like to "tell somebody off" or "punch them in the jaw." But social consequences and psychological shame prevent us. What then to do with that anger and desire to lash out? We may be able to count to ten and cool down, but sometimes the anger is too deep and the sense of injustice too strong, and the suppression of the action is turned inward on ourselves so that we may feel irritable or depressed all day long. We snap at others, take it out on someone else, or we may simply seethe with indignation. We become aware that our blood pressure is rising. These emotions have their consequence: the acids of our stomach will increase, the increased adrenalin will keep our muscles tight, and we will have difficulty maintaining calm breathing. In these situations, we need to find a way to express our anger but in a place where it will not hurt anybody else.

Sometimes we simply need to have a tantrum no matter how grown up or adult we think we are, but it helps if we can use the energy of our tantrum in a constructive way. A woman of our acquaintance takes her feelings of aggression out in scrubbing and cleaning. "I get so angry at my family, sometimes, I send them all out and then scrub the kitchen to within an inch of its life. The sheer exasperation I feel comes out in tremendous energy. I can scrub the oven in no time flat, mop up the kitchen floor in a few minutes, and even do some of the baseboards—all within an hour." She laughs at this point and says, "By that time, I am feeling so self-righteous that I tell my family to fend for themselves for a while, while I go out and indulge in some luxuries for myself, like getting my hair done or buying myself something I need. The family has learned to let me alone at these times. One can be conscientious and self-denying just so long, then I need to take care of ME!"

SUMMARY POINTS TO REMEMBER

1. We are coming to understand that the body and mind (bodymind/mindbody) comprise an ecological unit. When we suffer too much anxiety or stress, we become dis-eased (ill-at-ease).

2. Primitive peoples ascribed disease to the work of evil-spirits, revengeful gods, or as punishment for sin.

3. In the 16th century the Doctrine of Specific Etiology was formulated which states the basic germ theory.

4. Psychologically induced physical symptoms are called variously *hysterical symptoms*, *hysterical conversion*, or *psychogenic symptoms*. Examples are hysterical blindness, glove anesthesia, and most cases of amnesia.

5. All of us suffer from some psychological deafness or psychological blindness which is called *perceptual defense*.

6. The psychosomatic approach to disease recognizes that most of our diseases have a psychogenic component.

7. Flight-or-Fight Syndrome is a state of emergency reaction designed to deal with an impending threat. The body undergoes many changes which put it in a highly charged adrenalergic state.

8. The General Adaptation Syndrome describes the changes the body goes through when it undergoes prolonged stress.

9. In the sixties, it was discovered that the more change in a person's life (even beneficial or "happy" changes) the more liable a person was to suffer a change in health.

10. Other research studies have indicated a strong correlation between stress, cancer, loneliness and heart disease, and rejection and premature death of the elderly.

11. Certain diseases may be correlated with certain personality "types": worriers and ulcers; hard-driving "Type A" persons and heart disease; lonely persons and heart disease.

12. The reader is urged to recognize his or her personal stress syndrome and to develop mechanisms to cope with it.

SIGNIFICANT TERMS AND CONCEPTS

accident proneness
alarm reaction
consignment to death

Doctrine of Specific Etiology
Flight-or-Fight Syndrome
General Adaptation Syndrome

hypnosis
hysterical conversion
hysterical symptoms

intoxication by stress
LCUs
life crisis units
perceptual defense
psychosomatic disease

psychogenic symptoms
stage of exhaustion
stage of resistance
stress

supression (as repression)
Type A personality
voodoo death
"wear and tear"

FILL IN THE BLANKS WITH SIGNIFICANT TERMS AND CONCEPTS

1. When we view our mind and body as an ecological unit it is more understandable that when we suffer too much s_____ we become ill.
2. A beginning correlation of physical symptoms and psychological condition was established when the use of h_____ suggestion seemed to cure physical symptoms, at least temporarily.
3. P_____ defense is the phenomena of psychological deafness or blindness. We believe that we all experience some amount of this.
4. Diseases such as hay fever, tension head-

ache, ulcers, and heart disease have been identified as p_____ d_____.
5. When the body undergoes many changes which result in a highly charged state in order to deal with impending threat we call that the F_____ -or-F_____ S_____.
6. The more change in a person's life the more apt he is to become ill. This demonstrates the correlation of change and s_____ which has already been correlated to illness and disease.
7. Heart disease has been correlated with T_____ personality type.

RECOMMENDED BOOKS FOR FURTHER READING

Butler, Robert N., 1975. *Why Survive? Being Old in America*. New York: Harper & Row Publishers, Inc. For a rollicking, rip-roaring angry dissertation on how we consign our elderly population to death, read this diatribe by a man who has made a lifetime study.

Cannon, Walter B., 1963. *The Wisdom of the Body*, 2nd ed. New York: W. W. Norton & Company, Inc. Cannon gave the scientific world a profound understanding of how the body reacts to emergency situations. He wrote it for the benefit of nonscientists and it is particularly recommended for students of nursing and other health-related professions.

Friedman, Meyer and Rosenman, Ray H. 1981. *Type A Behavior and Your Heart*. New York: Fawcett Book Group. This book presents the research on the hard-driving, ambitious personality type and the tendency toward heart attack.

Lynch, James J. 1977. *The Broken Heart: The Medical Consequences of Loneliness*. New York: Basic Books, Inc. Lynch is a physician who is a heart specialist and brings together the major research studies in this area and has dared to suggest that we can and do die from loneliness and the pain of separation. In short, we can die of a broken heart.

Selye, Hans. 1956. *The Stress of Life*. New York: McGraw-Hill Book Company. Selye is one scientist who can talk and write simply while dealing with a complex subject. The reader gains an understanding not only of the stress syndrome, but of the personal drama of the scientific quest as well.

Toffler, Alvin. 1970. *Future Shock*. New York: Random House, Inc. Future shock is no longer a distant, potential danger, says Toffler; rather, it is here and now. Future shock is a disease of change. This former best-seller is a shocker in itself.

6

*The Physical
Approaches
to Personality
Integration*

CONTRIBUTING TO A SOUND BODYMIND/MINDBODY
THROUGH THE BODY

THE PHYSIOLOGICAL NEEDS: MASLOW'S HIERARCHY
The Basic Physiological (Bodily) Needs

BODY-ENERGIZING APPROACHES FOR BODYMIND/MINDBODY
INTEGRATION
Gurdjieff: Breaking Through Our Conditioned Responses
Wilhelm Reich: Breaking Through Our Bodily Armor
Alexander Lowen: The Bioenergetic Approach

BODY-RELAXING APPROACHES FOR BODYMIND/MINDBODY
INTEGRATION
Edmund Jacobson: Progressive Relaxation
Massage
Yoga

THE RELEVANCE OF ANY PHYSICAL ACTIVITY TO BODYMIND/
MINDBODY INTEGRATION
Wolpe: Deconditioning-Reconditioning Approach

MIND/SPIRIT APPROACHES FOR BODYMIND/MINDBODY INTEGRATION
Meditation
Biofeedback Techniques

APPLICATIONS AND COPING TECHNIQUES

CONTRIBUTING TO A SOUND BODYMIND/MINDBODY THROUGH THE BODY

Because it was Sigmund Freud who opened up for us the field of psychotherapy as a way of dealing with our neurotic anxieties and ailments, the first five to six decades of the twentieth century tended to focus solely on the dialogic approach to psychotherapeutics. We developed more and more techniques of psychoanalysis, counseling, group therapy, individual therapy, existential encounter, and a host of other therapeutic methods that relied on the interpersonal and dialogic methods of personality integration. No one denies the efficacy of the counseling and group method for personal growth, and we devote the next chapter to exactly that. But another approach for bodymind integration has become more and more prominent in the past twenty to thirty years, and we discuss it in this chapter. This method focuses on the *physical* approach to bodymind integration and involves many and diverse types of physical therapies, ranging all the way from relaxation and meditational methods to the more strenuous jogging-yoga-running methods to the fascinating methods of **biofeedback** training, **autohypnosis,** and the various approaches known as **bioenergetics.**

Although some of these methods were once labeled esoteric, cultic, mystical, or with other adjectives implying skepticism, there is now increasing scientific evidence to justify these approaches with supporting demonstrations that these methods, *when appropriately applied,* can and do enable us to withstand and cope with the stress of life. Furthermore, these physical methods have been shown to increase our vigor and to counteract the effects of aging and crippling, which come about simply through years of living on this earth or through the diseases that prematurely age us.

It is strange, in one way, that it has taken us so long to recognize the advantages of keeping our bodies in good shape and to use these physical methods to improve our bodymind soundness. We have long known that persons who remain physically active and keep their bodies lean and healthy *do* live better, age later, and have more zest for the good that life has to offer. Dancers, for example, seem to keep their youth for many years, with faces clear of blemishes and few wrinkles compared to the rest of us. Tennis players remain active and alert, able to play tennis even into their sixties and, yes, seventies. There is no doubt, at all, that keeping the body physically energetic results in increased circulation, lower blood pressure, increased lung capacity and respiration, and longer sexual vigor and generally makes for good skin and muscle tone. We know now, too, that some of these approaches, such as meditation and biofeedback training, have a positive effect on such chronic ailments and diseases as migraine headaches, arthritis, and hypertension. And we are finally coming to recognize that what we put into our bodies by way of food (and lethal food additives), alcohol, drugs, contaminated water, and even prescribed medicines, will have deleterious effects upon the *bodymind*.

Furthermore, we have become largely a sedentary nation. It is not our fault, perhaps, since so much of what our society does has to do with office work—record keeping, writing, computing, telephoning, report making, and general planning and committee meetings— which keeps our bureaucratic and industrialized nation intact. It is well, then, for us to learn how to become physically strong and able and to find methods that are congruent with our individual personality style and patterning.

Once again, we urge our readers to ever remember their own individual uniqueness: What may be right for one person would not do at all for another. As you read through this chapter, and as you become more acquainted with the various approaches that are being developed, become introspective about what would be the best for you. We have known persons who went all out for some physically strenuous activity (such as jogging or playing tennis) who came down with exhaustion, "jogger's knee," or other disabling conditions. As the ancient Greeks and Chinese were ever wont to admonish: Moderation in all things! Nevertheless, athletic and other physical activity was deemed so important to the Greeks that they included it as one of the *liberal arts*, along with mathematics, language (rhetoric), music, and philosophy (their form of science, ethics, political science all rolled into one).

THE PHYSIOLOGICAL NEEDS: MASLOW'S HIERARCHY

The reader will remember Maslow's hierarchy of needs (box 1.7) from chapter 1. Most texts discuss the top level of self-actualizing, but we need to remember that the most basic, most primary need is the fulfillment of the physiological needs: air, food, water, freedom from pain, shelter, and the general needs of sheer survival. When one or the other of these basic elements of life becomes dangerously depleted, all our carefully built structure of self-esteem and feelings of belongingness and love, may tumble precipitously. Even the most self-actualizing person will no longer be functioning at that level if his or her survival needs are critically threatened. It has been said so many times that it has become a cliché—if Americans took as good care of their bodies as they do their automobiles, they would live into their hundreds.

Well, perhaps it is not so important to live long as to live our lives *well*, and that means to get in touch with our basic bodily needs. So before we discuss the physical therapeutic approaches, let us consider just how easily we can overlook the basic essentials of the health-filled life.

The Basic Physiological (Bodily) Needs

It is good, then, to understand some of our basic bodily requirements so that we can keep ourselves in good working condition. To the Greek admonition of "A sound mind in a sound body" we might add, "The sounder the body, the sounder the mind," and vice versa.

THE NEED FOR AIR. Our most basic need as a living organism is for air (oxygen). This is a continuing need from conception to death. Without air, we die in short order. Without oxygen the cells of the body begin to die, even within a few minutes. If these cells are injured or die in the brain, there is a cerebral vascular attack (stroke), and there can be eventual paralysis and even sensory numbness to the body, coma, and death. Air is, therefore, a vital need of our well-being. Our need for air is absolute, constant, and intense.

We are probably less aware of our need for air than for any of our other basic needs. It seems incredible that we scarcely pay attention to our breathing when we are living during what is surely one of the most "breath-taking" times in human evolution. Too many of us who live in a complex civilization breathe too often in a shallow way and too quickly: We do not give ourselves enough breathing room! How is it that civilized people in our times have developed this kind of shallow breathing? Psychoanalysts attribute this breathing behavior to our desire to avoid pain. Alexander Lowen (1956), for example, noted that children seeking to avoid the pain of a spanking consciously hold their breath and tighten or "deaden" their bodies. Has our civiization, then, become so painful for us that we have adopted this shallow breathing pattern in order to survive? Maybe so, but there are consequences. Lack of oxygen itself is one of the primary reasons for people's anxiety.

Frederick Perls, the founder of **gestalt** therapy, worked continually to help his patients and friends realize that they were not breathing adequately and that they held their breath in artificially, particularly in moments of anxiety. In other words, at precisely those times when we most need an adequate supply of oxygen, we "forget" to breathe. Yet, the more stressful the moment is, the more people need to turn their attention to breathing (Perls et al. 1951).

The gestalt therapy approach is one method of personality development that stresses the influence of breathing, and yoga is another. In the yoga view—and this is only one aspect of its comprehensive approach—calm, slow breathing itself deepens psychological awareness. This type of breathing is called *pranayama*, but the practice is never advised without a competent teacher. When we deal with breathing, we deal with life itself, and the consequences of tampering with this most basic bodily process could be extremely dangerous. Nevertheless, the practice of taking a few calm breaths daily does enable people to continue breathing adequately when anxiety threatens to overwhelm them.

THE NEED FOR FOOD. How do we know when we are hungry? Most of us would answer that question by saying "because of hunger pangs!" Research however has indicated people may eat, not in response to hunger pangs but just because they are tired, upset, or bored—or even when they are thirsty or cold instead (Schachter 1959).

Changes in modern eating habits have had a lot to do with losing touch with hunger. For example, we consume *more* starch, *more* fat, and *more* protein than ever before. And we are getting fat on it all: fat from food intake and fat from our lack of exercise. Being overweight has become a nationwide problem in some industrialized societies, and dieting a national pastime. Being overweight, we know now with some assurance, not only adds to the likelihood of heart problems but is also associated with diseases of the liver, kidneys, and other vital organs. Moreover, when we are overweight and have more bulk to carry around, we have less energy available to us for other pursuits and become tired more easily.

It is somewhat heartening to note that we are *finally* becoming conscious of the nonnutritive and toxic substances that we are taking into our bodies. We are beginning to realize how we have actually removed the most nourishing parts of grain kernels. We are beginning to examine how much refined sugar we are eating, which has no nutritive value save calories and has harmful side effects. A century ago Americans ate less than a pound of sugar each a year; we now consume over one hundred pounds of sugar a year for every man, woman, and child in the country. We are beginning to be aware of the toxic substances that are used to preserve and spice up our food. We are beginning to be concerned about the poisons we spray on crops, which we take into our systems along with the food. We finally are beginning to understand food as life energy, one we must respect and appreciate if we are to be truly healthful people (Lappe 1971).

Fasting. Fasting (cutting down radically on the intake of fluids and solids) may well be a needed discipline for a person glutted with food and fat. Aside from a way of getting back in touch with the balance of bodily functions, fasting has been periodically recommended by religious communities as a means of searching for religious understanding and mystical communion. Fasting undoubtedly does sharpen the bodily senses, and it can trigger profound insights into the essence of oneself—that is, increase sensitivity to one's inner life and one's surroundings (Bro 1971). This method of inducing altered states of consciousness has been practiced in many societies other than our own and in all of the major religions. The Indians of North and South America learned to fast as part of their traditional rites of passage, as did natives of other "primitive" societies. Since childhood, Americans have been fed the myth that a hearty breakfast is imperative for everyone. For some, eating is necessary in the morning just to be able to wake up. Actually, many people feel uncomfortable when they eat a large breakfast; they prefer to break their night fast later on in the day, after they have been up and around for a few hours.

THE NEED FOR WATER. In some respects our need for water is more intense than our need for food. People can live for weeks, even months, without food, but a lack of water will cause them to lose consciousness within a few days and die soon after. Unlike hunger, whose symptoms tend to diminish after a time of fasting, thirst increases in intensity over time until the desire for water completely dominates a person's thinking, feeling, and perceptions: Thirst eventually can drive a person literally insane.

As with hunger, we know now that thirst depends on more than just the perception of dryness in the throat, mouth, and on the lips. Like hunger, thirst is triggered by an imbalance of chemical substances in the blood and by other hormonal-neuronal effectors. Our need for water is more easily appreciated when it is pointed out that more than 98 percent of our blood cells are composed of water. For example, our blood, our lymph system, and the interior of our cell bodies all function in fluid balance. In addition, we give back water to the environment through sweat, tears, and urine. The intake of salt increases our need for water, as does warmth. In one sense, we may be land creatures, but we float in a fluid bodily environment. Dehydration is one of the most serious symptoms of an illness, and physicians work hard to restore our fluid level. Babies, in fact, can die very quickly from dehydration, much more quickly than from lack of food.

THE SEXUAL NEEDS. Sigmund Freud's initial psychological discoveries were made largely in the area of sexual repression. The Viennese Victorian era, Freud pointed out, was marked by suppression of sexual understanding and sensory awareness. We know more today about the sexual nature of the human animal and therefore are freer in acknowledging the sexual side of our sensory reality. At least, we *seem* more enlightened than our Victorian predecessors were. Nevertheless, we are still incredibly naive about sex as an instinct and sex as a socially learned attitude.

Part of that naiveté resides in the belief that our sexual responses are as instinctive as our other bodily needs are. This is not the case at all. Much of our sexuality is conditioned by our upbringing *and* by our cultural background *and* by our general state of health *and* by our personality type *and* by our emotional mood swings *and* by anything else that happens to be going on at the time—such as involvements with our job, upsets with family, and our professional endeavors.

The sexual urge becomes distinctly pronounced in the late teens and early years of the young adult, particularly in the young male. Indeed, he may have erotic dreams, and nocturnal emissions are common among adolescents. The adolescent also may engage in masturbation, and it is fortunate that we are coming to understand that masturbation does not have terrible and dire consequences (as was once believed). With the elimination of this superstition, masturbation is becoming more frequent also among adolescent girls and women (McCary 1978). There seems, however, to be a difference in the sexual drives of men and women in terms of age. The male sexual drive is more intense than that of the female from adolescence to about twenty-five years of age, gradually diminishing thereafter; while a female's sexual drive starts more slowly and reaches a peak in the mid-thirties. This difference in age-related sexual drive may be a culturally determined factor, but it has been verified by much research. It would seem that, for real sexual compatibility, it would be better for older women to marry younger men than the other way around, as is the common practice in Western society.

Western civilization has generally stereotyped the male and female sexual responses as predominantly aggressive, dominant, and assertive on the part of the male and more passive, responsive, and unassertive on the part of the female. But we are coming to understand this, in part, as a cultural role rather than as sheerly instinctive. There seems to be some indication that when women have played a generally secondary and passive role in the social-cultural-political world of a society, the woman has been passive in her sexual responses; when the woman has had a more equal social status, she also has been more sexually free and expressive. Our sexual behaviors generally are a reflection of our societal and cultural attitudes. Furthermore, when we observe animal behavior, we discover that it is generally the female that initiates the courtship and mating interchange, that she engages the attention of the male, and it is she that allows penetration when she is ready. There seems to be no such thing as rape in the animal world (Beach 1965).

Another determinant of the sexual drive is the person's psychological *type*. Introverted persons, who generally require more solitude and privacy than extraverted persons do, may also have less need for sexual interaction. Extraverted persons, who are more able to relate spontaneously to others, also may be more able to relate spontaneously on a sexual level. Persons who are endomorphic or who require a lot of physical activity also may require more sexual activity than the mesomorphic type. We need not berate ourselves for the type that we are or for whether we are getting all the sex we need, nor should we worry if we are closet satyrs. Americans tend to compare themselves needlessly with each other. As one wit has said: "Ever since sex polls have been published, Americans think they must have sex twice a week—whether they want it or not!"

Our general state of health will influence our sexual drive, as well as our body's natural rhythms. When we are tired or emotionally or physically exhausted, or even if the weather is too hot, we are less inclined toward exertion in any area. The point to be remembered is that our sexual drives are a function of our personalities and a function also of the situational factors in our lives. Although the sexual drive is one of the basic physiological drives, it is mediated by our culture and by our cortex, that is to say, our individual sexual needs and wants are more psychologically dominated than instinctual, in contrast to other life forms.

Our understanding of homosexuality also has expanded as more and more sociologists and anthropologists report their research findings. The Kinsey report of sexual behavior in the United States revealed that although only 4 percent of the population was exclusively homosexual, a much higher percentage of persons had engaged in both heterosexual and homosexual activity (37 percent of the men and 13 percent of the women). (Kinsey et al. 1948.) Although we in the West generally have been intolerant, some less developed societies have been much more tolerant of homosexual behavior. A survey of nearly two hundred societies reported that homosexuality was prevalent among seventy-six of them and, that of these seventy-six societies, forty-nine considered homosexuality an acceptable and normal sexual experience (Ford & Beach 1951). We are now beginning to view homosexuality as a preference rather than a perversion.

OTHER KINDS OF NEEDS.   We have discussed only the most basic physiological needs. There are many more-subtle and more-individual needs. Some of these we share with other life forms; others are distinctly human. There is the need, for example, for contact, touching, and affection, which is distinctly different from sexual and other emotional needs. Some people are "touchers"; they like to make contact with others through handclasps and handshakes, by putting an arm on another's shoulder, and by more intimate embraces; others prefer to maintain distance, have a "hands off" *territorial space* around them, and allow touching only after the relationship has won through their natural reserve. We do not have to decide which is better to be, only to be aware that again there are vast individual differences among us and to respect those differences.

We differ also in the need for privacy and solitude, in the amount of physical activity we need. We differ in the amount of excitement, novelty, or challenge we need. Some persons prefer a quiet life of dignity and calm; others like a faster tempo, the excitement of competition, and problems to be solved. We differ significantly too in what gives us pleasure. For some, it is being outdoors. For others, it is creating beauty in whatever form their consciousness takes. In our everyday world of work and domestic affairs, we sometimes get so hassled that we neglect these higher human needs, but their fulfillment helps us to integrate our life process and stabilize our existence. What matters is that we understand and appreciate our individual needs and find the opportunities, whenever possible, to fulfill them.

BODY-ENERGIZING APPROACHES FOR BODYMIND/ MINDBODY INTEGRATION

Gurdjieff: Breaking Through Our Conditioned Responses

One of the first persons, historically, to use the body as a way of personality integration and growth was a middle-European, G. I. Gurdjieff, whose work in this field was done in the two decades before World War I. He was something of a mysterious figure, who spoke several languages, and it was never absolutely sure where he was born or what was his nationality. Some said he was Turkish, others said he was Serbian, and so on, and Gurdjieff rather enjoyed the mystery surrounding his origins. He was somewhat flamboyant in personality and had much personal charisma, and the legends he allowed to be built up about himself suggest a certain bit of charlatanism. Nevertheless, he created what appears to be the first "growth center" for lay persons who wished to become more dynamic and creative. Our chief first-hand knowledge of him comes to us by way of biographical sketches (DeHartman 1964; Peters 1964; Hulme 1966; Ouspensky 1971). What is of interest for us was his insight into the body/mind relationship.

His essential thesis (underneath the trappings of pseudo-mystical teachings) went something as follows. In the course of our lives each of us tends to adopt certain characteristic (conditioned) postures when we sit, stand, walk, sleep. We have, in a sense, a very limited repertoire of bodily poses. Now these bodily stances, poses, gestures become more and more rigidified the older we become, as can be seen in the characteristic limited gaits of older persons. These stereotyped bodily postures have a feedback effect upon our *mind sets*, so that we become more rigid also in our way of thinking, feeling, and expressing ourselves.

Gurdjieff's insight was this: If we *break out* of these stereotyped (and conditioned) postures, stances, and gestures and learn to express our bodily movements in totally different ways, we will experience totally different feelings, thoughts, and perceptions of the world. For example, he had some of the intellectuals, writers, and other well-known personalities of his time do things they had never done before. He insisted that a man who was an incessant talker be quiet. (Now that was a new experience for him!) A professor type, who spent much of his time behind a desk writing, was told to build a stone wall by hand—rock by rock, stone by stone. One of the group methods he employed was to have the persons who came to his center whirl, twist, and turn around in exaggerated and uncomfortable poses and then order them to "freeze" as they were. The students had to hold these uncomfortable positions for several minutes, which was sometimes quite painful. But what Gurdjieff wanted was for them to feel their bodies in positions that were *not* natural or normal for them.

Despite the bizarre trappings of his teachings and his flamboyant teaching style, Gurdjieff seems to have caught sight of the body/mind relationship and was developing a method to personality integration through bodily experience and awareness.

Wilhelm Reich: Breaking Through Our Bodily Armor

A more sophisticated scientific theory of body-mind integration was formulated by Wilhelm Reich, a German-born psychiatrist who practiced and taught at the New School for Social Research in New York City. His theories tended to be discounted by American psychologists until recently because of their rather radical nature. Furthermore, as Reich became older, he became somewhat emotionally unstrung, and his unpopular pro-German political beliefs put him into disfavor with American social scientists in the 1930s and 1940s. Now his work into the field of bodily dynamics is being taken more seriously of late, and as the father of the bioenergetic movement, he deserves our consideration. Reich had practiced with considerable success for many years the original Freudian methods of free-association therapy. He noticed, however, that there are certain patterns of personality that do not profit from classical psychoanalysis, patterns of behavior that seemed to him designed to keep the person from becoming *aware of himself or herself, by deadening his or her bodily awareness*. Further investigation seemed to Reich to indicate that this deadening of physical awareness is accomplished by habitual *tensing of the muscles*, in much the same way people tense their muscles when they know they are going to get an injection—stiffening to ward off the pain!

Reich's theory is that certain persons have experienced so much psychological pain that they have become accustomed to walking, eating, breathing, and working with tensed-up muscles—as if to ward off pain (or any kind of stimuli from their environment). Certain parts of their body become stiff and hard from muscular tension, as if to provide some sort of psychic armor. A person with such "character armor" has a "character neurosis," which, said Reich, is much harder to treat than an "anxiety neurosis" is. Because anxiety neuroses are characterized by uncomfortable symptoms—headaches, butterflies in the stomach, flushes, depresson, stuttering, and the like—the person who has these symptoms is glad to get rid of them. The symptoms of a character neurosis, however, are *not painful* to the person—in fact, they *prevent* pain (or any sensation, for that matter) from entering into one's consciousness. Such persons do not want to give up the defending operation; it fits them too well, prevents pain, and wards off awareness. But in deadening themselves to the experience of anxiety, they also deaden and diminish their capacity for many other kinds of experience: awareness, free movement, free expression. In other words, their character not only protects them from imagined threat but also effectively prevents further growth (Reich 1949).

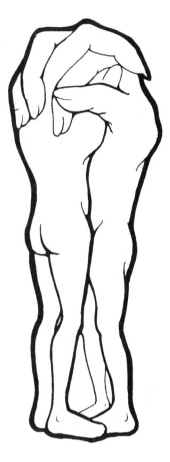

The many senses of the skin may be our most basic, most primitive, and deepest sensory modality.

SEGMENTAL ARRANGEMENT OF THE CHARACTER ARMOR. Since we inhibit and suppress our emotions by tensing particular muscles, it is relatively easy for the discerning eye to see where a person's blocks are, according to Reich. Whereas the person who is fully integrated expresses himself or herself in coordinated, graceful, and flowing movements, a person with a character neurosis exhibits a certain lack of coordination in his or her movements, a stiffness where the body has become armored.

According to Reich, the body from the top of the skull to the base of the spine may be divided into seven segmental "rings." If one of these rings becomes armored, there results a characteristic stiffness, a certain "deadness" to feelings in that area and also (and most important) certain organic dysfunctions. These seven rings are distributed at various points of the torso, from the pelvis to the head as follows:

The Ocular Ring. The ocular ring surrounds the head in the area of the eyes. If the ocular ring has become armored, the person sometimes will seem to have a rigid face mask; the eyes, said Reich, will be "cold" and staring. The rest of the face may smile, but the eyes will remain stiff and unsmiling. Deadening in the ocular ring also will result in a dysfunction of those areas. These persons may suffer eye strain, sties, and headaches centered on the eye area and on the sinuses.

The Ear, Nose, and Mouth Ring. Persons who have deadened this part of the face may be very unsmiling. Their jaws will be tight, and they may grit their teeth. Hard lines may form around the mouth. If there is a deadening of this part of the body, these persons may suffer from infected sinuses, hay fever, and painful infections of the middle ear. They may have occasional toothaches and gum decay and occasionally may be afflicted by cold sores on the lips or in the mouth.

The Neck and Throat Ring. An armoring of this part of the body may produce sore throats or hoarseness. Other possibilities are vocal cord nodules or a *globus hystericus* (lump in the throat). Persons with this kind of armoring may look as if they have stiff necks, and they find it difficult to turn their heads easily from side to side.

The Chest Ring. The chest ring covers the entire area from the neck to the diaphragm. Persons may have a caved-in chest, or, on the other hand, the chest may be pushed out, reminiscent of military bearing. At any rate, the chest is not flexible, and they may suffer from chest pains (real or imaginary), be vulnerable to pneumonia, tuberculosis, or emphysema. They may have asthmatic symptoms or general difficulty in breathing.

The Diaphragmatic Ring. The diaphragmatic ring covers the mid-torso. Persons who have armoring in this area may be subject to nausea or other stomach problems, including ulcers. They may have problems digesting food and need to vomit occasionally or suffer from "acid stomach."

The Intestinal Ring. Persons with an intestinal ring may suffer from cramps, from any of the diseases connected with the vital organs in that area, including diseases of the kidneys, liver, and pancreas. Reich said that although this area was one of the most vulnerable to affliction, it also is one of the easiest to "unlock." Problems associated with this area are diarrhea, constipation, flatulence, and cramps.

The Pelvic Ring. The pelvic ring is at the very bottom of the torso. People who have an armored pelvic ring will be vulnerable to the diseases of the sexual organs: menstrual cramps, problems with the uterus for women, and prostate gland cancer for men. Women may also be vulnerable to cancer of the uterus. Both men and woman may also be afflicted with sexual problems, such as frigidity, impotence, or satyriasis.

IS THERE ANY VALIDITY TO REICH'S ARMOR THEORY?   As yet, we simply cannot give a definite yes or no to that question. We are still in the area of speculation. But we can consider some of the evidence that suggests this kind of armoring is possible. You will recall, from chapter 5 that hysterical conversion entails a deadening of a part of the body, "psychological" in origin since no known neurological dysfunction can account for the sensory numbness or muscular paralysis. You will recall also that hysterical blindness and hysterical deafness already are clinically documented. We know also that if we remain tense (so that our muscles are in a continual state of contraction), we will block off our feelings. For example, if a child knows it is about to get a spanking, the child automatically tenses up its buttocks to defend against pain. If a physician is about to plunge a hypodermic needle into our arm, even the bravest and best of us will tighten up to defend against the anticipated pain.

UNLOCKING THE BODILY ARMOR. To unlock the ocular ring, Reich suggested that we use eye exercises: closing them tightly and opening them as wide as possible, frowning, looking around in all directions, as physicians frequently advise, to release tension, and finally, rolling the eyes. To unlock the lower half of the face, we can grimace and make faces (as children frequently do), stretch the mouth, stick out the tongue and curl it, and crinkle the nose. Unlocking the throat area involves more painful types of exercises, such as screaming, yelling, gagging, swallowing hard, stretching the neck, and turning the head from side to side. To unlock the chest, Reich suggested moving the shoulders around and up and down, as well as daily deep breathing. There are many exercises to aid the stomach and intestinal rings: forward and back bends, flipping the belly in and out (a yoga **asana**), and even belly dancing. Unlocking the pelvic area consists in imitating the bumps and grinds of the belly dancer.

Alexander Lowen: The Bioenergetic Approach

Although Alexander Lowen is the official founder of the field of bioenergetics, Lowen readily acknowledges Wilhelm Reich as his teacher and mentor. Lowen has practiced psychiatry and his form of bioenergetics all his life. His description of his first meeting and session is very illustrative of the Reichian approach. His definition of bioenergetics goes thusly: *a therapeutic technique to help a person get back together with his body and to help him enjoy to the fullest degree possible the life of the body* (Lowen 1975, p.43). While Lowen pays debt to his mentor, his development of bioenergetics eventually took slightly different dimensions. Reich often had a person lie down, crouch up, and become supine in the breathing-out exercises. Lowen reasons that we are upright bipedal bodies, as distinct from other life forms, and that bioenergetic exercises should be done primarily in an upright position, for that is how we meet the world for the most of our waking day. Keeping our backbone flexible is a key factor in remaining vital, sexual, and alive. He also quite frankly rests his bioenergetics on an integration not only of body and mind but of body, mind and spirit. When we describe a person as being "in good spirits" or having a "spritly energy," or if you feel yourself having a "rise in spirit," what is actually being described, says Lowen, is better physical contact with one's bodily self. What is happening is the increase of circulation, better and deeper breathing, and lessening of muscle tension. To be physically more expressive is (according to Reich) to feel psychologically more energized and spiritually more aware of one's emotions, one's perceptions, and one's feelings.

Why is the ability to stand with feet apart and arch one's back in all directions so important? Lowen explains it this way: A person who has a good "stance in life," who is able to keep his or her feet on the ground (in other words, is well grounded) but does not get knocked off balance easily is one who can bend but not break under the pushes and stresses that one meets in everyday living.

BODY-RELAXING APPROACHES FOR BODYMIND/MINDBODY INTEGRATION

Edmund Jacobson: Progressive Relaxation

In chapter 5 we discussed how anxiety can make us tense and produce physical symptoms. In fact, physicians have estimated that upward of 50 percent of all the symptoms of persons who come to their office are the result of emotional problems rather than because of some dysfunction of the body itself. Some decades ago, an American physician, Edmund Jacobson, proposed a method of relaxation for his patients that proved to be more effective than medicine was.

Jacobson hypothesized that since anxiety and stress increase muscular tensions, his patients could be relieved of many of their physical *conditioned tensions*. He called his approach *progressive relaxation*, a series of exercises that his patients could use to relax their tensions and anxieties (Jacobson 1938). Jacobson reported that correct application of his method, in which patients were taught to discover their tension patterns and then to exercise what he called self-operations control not only relieved their anxiety, but they were also healthier and had more energy for living.

Jacobson's instructions include procedures for gradually relaxing various parts of the body from the feet to the head. When we are tense, we then tighten our muscles and thereby interfere with the natural operations of our muscular and nervous systems. Tense muscles increase not only one's sense of fatigue but also the wear and tear on one's body (remember Selye's stress syndrome, discussed in chapter 5). Thus tension decreases our efficiency and our capacity to handle the current stressful situation. (It very likely also hastens the aging process.) When we begin to relax muscles, the nerves which are embedded in the muscles also begin to relax, and eventually the entire nervous system and brain relax, so that we can face the present conflict in a more relaxed manner. That is the basic thesis of Jacobson's theory. Jacobson called his method of relaxing *going negative*.

Going negative may be a difficult thing for the person to learn because we tend to live so tensed up most of the time. Furthermore, there is residual tension in our muscles even when they are normally relaxed. Therefore, going negative is a much more concerted effort of relaxing than normal relaxing. Why do we not learn to relax so completely if it is simply the process of allowing our residual tensions to dissipate from our muscles? Here is Jacobson's reply:

> To relax tension is the easiest thing in the world, for it requires just no work at all.
> If so, why does not the nervous person do this easy thing? The answer is clear. The nervous person does things the hard way! He piles up his own nervous

difficulties. The tense person has developed the habit of being tense. From habit, he fails to relax.

If you are a nervous person, it is time now for you to face the facts. It is easy to relax. You may be solving problems all day long and may be loath to give this up. [Jacobson 1938, 1976]

The relaxation program we have described is not the end of the method but the beginning. The next step is to take what you have learned into your everyday life. When you find yourself getting wrought up and tense, give yourself the instruction to "Go negative!" for a few minutes. With practice, you can do it anywhere with the result that the negative emotional problems will not affect you so severely. You ride over them in a state of calm bodymind integration.

Massage

One of the less active forms of awakening oneself to bodily consciousness is through massage, an age-old therapeutic method that decreases tension and engenders an experience of well-being and peacefulness. According to biblical tradition, the feet of a traveler were to be washed by the host or hostess, not only to cleanse his feet, but to encourage him to relax after his long and weary journey. In our own time, patients who are bedridden are given massages to increase circulation of the blood, and to prevent bedsores and the other symptoms that follow from lack of movement. Persons who have had a debilitating stroke or who suffer muscle paralysis or loss of sensation in the limbs are often given special kinds of body massage and exercise. All these techniques now have been gathered together to form a professional discipline called *physical therapy*. Athletes are often given massage to relax their bodies and to ease cramped muscles. We have long known that a skillful massage can ease tension headaches even more quickly than aspirin can.

Tension headaches are caused by the constriction of the muscles in the neck. When we get stressed or are resistant to doing something, we tighten our muscles, which has the effect of constricting our blood vessels. Now our brains are literally bathed in blood, for nervous tissue has a vital need for a constant supply of oxygen and nutrients. When the blood vessels to the brain are constricted, we begin to feel that pain known as headache. To ease the pain of headache, we need to ease the constriction of the arteries. Aspirin eases the pain. When the pain is eased, we relax and the headache may dissolve. But if we can simply learn to relax our cramped neck muscles, what is causing the head to ache may be eliminated. Therefore massaging the back of the head, the neck, the upper back, and down the spinal cord may permanently relieve the tension.

We have a lot more respect for this sense we call touch than we used to. The skin is our single largest organ, weighing about nine pounds and studded with sense receptors. The sense of touch is our most basic communication with the world. It is basic to our emotional stability from birth onward. Babies who receive a lot of skin stimulation through being held and loved and generally mothered are happier, better adapted to the world, more alert. Premature babies, who were once whisked away into isolation and therefore kept from being caressed and mothered, did not do as well as premature babies who were allowed to be held and stroked by the mother or by the nursing staff (Rice 1977). LeBoyer in his *gentle birth* does a great deal of stroking and massaging of the newborn, and it is wonderful to watch the baby respond to this basic and primitive method of touching, soothing, and smoothing the newborn (Leboyer 1976).

Those of you who have been witness to a birth of twin foals will know that the first foal to stand on its legs is the one the mare has licked first, thereby stimulating the sense receptors in the skin and ennervating the nervous system. We know, too, that if litters of dogs, cats, mice are not licked and stroked by the mother, they will die. And psychologist Harry Harlow demonstrated very clearly that if a baby monkey is prevented from being touched, licked, or pawed by the mother, its emotional-social growth may be so severely hampered as to render that little monkey unable to fend for itself in the gregarious monkey world. It may huddle in corners, unable to play and romp with the other monkey youngsters. Later it may be unable to perform the act of coitus. If a female reared in this way does produce young, it may not be able to care for them in a normal, comforting way (Harlow & Suomi, 1970). This need or drive we have to touch others of our kind even has a name attached now. It is called the **contact need**.

Any stimulation we can give our bodies, softening skin texture with harmless oils, or any stroking or massaging that we can do to stimulate sense reception, opens us to the world of feelings and experience. We are more able to take joy in the scent of a rose. We are more able to bask in the warmth of the sun. We are more sensitive to the touch of someone we love reaching out toward us in love and affection.

Yoga

Hatha yoga is a series of postures (we can call them stretching exercises) developed in India at a time when physical health and bodily ease were considered the first steps to personal growth and spiritual evolution. We have compared hatha yoga to the exercises of Western physical development, but there is a profound difference. The various positions in hatha yoga are not achieved as "violently" as in our Western forms of exercise but are done slowly, gently, rhythmically, and in a contemplative mood. The student of yoga first is taught to put the mind into a restful state of peace, and in that restful state of mind, the student moves from one yoga stretch to another. In actuality yoga is simply a very practical and systematic method of toning the muscles of the body to achieve that kind of balance between control and abandon that a dancer feels or that a skier experiences when skiing "perfectly." Not only are the muscles of the body toned, but the postures (called *asanas*) also pull and stretch the whole skeletal system, including the spinal cord. Part of the aging process is the encrustation of calcium deposits within the cartilage and ligaments along with a general rigidification of the spinal system and a loss of elasticity in the joints (Eisdorfer & Lawton 1971; Ingber 1982). The spinal

Pranayama, or breath control, is a yoga technique for psychological awareness.

stretching postures of yoga seem to be effective in reducing these calcium deposits, thus counteracting arthritis, bursitis, and other afflictions, of the skeletal and muscular systems. Improvement has been reported by practitioners of yoga who have been afflicted with these conditions. There have also been reports of laboratory and medical studies that indicate a general improvement of physical and emotional health (Naranjo & Ornstein 1971). Books on aging generally agree that daily gentle exercising, even walking, can reverse some of the problems associated with years of stress and sedentary inactivity.

It is easy to comprehend the more conventional asanas, the ones that correspond to some of our Western exercises such as bending at the waist or touching our hands to the floor, but what can we make of some of the more bizarre yoga postures such as standing on one's head or twisting one's body into unusual positions? The practitioners of yoga explain it this way: Our body is usually erect or lying down in a horizontal position. Our blood supply (which provides nutritive substances and oxygen to our bodily tissues and also drains away the wastes and poisons that have been built up) inevitably reaches certain parts of organs more easily than others. By reversing our center of gravity, we allow the blood to circulate more freely to our brains and to the undersides of our organs, which normally do not get this kind of blood revitalization.

We can only hope that there will be more adequate research on yoga itself. There has, of course, been much research on the benefits of physical exercise of any sort in slowing the aging process. Some of the beneficial results include toning the muscles, increasing the circulation of the blood, trimming excess adipose tissue, and reducing the calcium deposits in the tendons and cartilaginous tissues.

THE RELEVANCE OF ANY PHYSICAL ACTIVITY TO MINDBODY/BODYMIND INTEGRATION

We have been discussing rather esoteric types of physical methods toward bodymind personality integration. Since those early pioneers, the American public has become conscious of the need for physical exercise. We have engaged in many types of bodily improvement: jogging, running, jazzercise, isometrics, yoga, among others. It is not an uncommon sight (as we drive ourselves to work in city and suburb) to see the sprinters and joggers and runners working up a good sweat in their special suits and running shoes. We mentally cheer them on, for they are doing what they can to offset the deadly effects of our sedentary lives.

Furthermore, the medical field is now becoming aware of the age-retarding effects of physical activity. Research has confirmed the fact that even among our aged population, a certain amount of moderate physical exercise, be it no more than a good daily walk, will increase the general heart rate, circulation, and lung capacity for our senior citizens. Their health is better. Their psychology is better. Their sense of social adequacy is better. Whole programs for the aged are now being undertaken by wellness centers all across the United States.

There are other benefits that accrue from physical exercise. When we get out for a while and work up a good sweat in a tennis match, there is, along with the cleansing of the body (through a hard sweat), a kind of cleansing of the emotional tensions (from emotional upsets) that we carry around with us. In our daily interactions with others, we may find ourselves irritated, angered, or depressed by the events of everyday living. Running, handball, and any activity that allows our bodies to cleanse themselves with perspiration, also seem to eliminate (at least momentarily) the nagging and depressing thoughts we carry around. As the perspiration runs out of the skin, so too do anxiety and upset seem to run out of the pores of our mind. Our problems may still be there, way after the rest and shower and intake of liquid, but our psychology has changed. We are more relaxed, and we deal with these everyday problems and events in a calmer, more rational manner.

There is some evidence also that this feeling of well-being has a biological basis. Scientists are suggesting that runner's "high" may be associated with an increase in the endorphins of the brain. You will remember from a previous section

Obesity has become a national disease. A good dietary regime, together with physical exercise, can free us from this type of bodily armoring.

that the endorphins are a natural analgesic that the central nervous system emits. They not only lessen pain but seem to provide us with a general euphoria, a state of well-being (Prebish 1983).

Wolpe: Deconditioning-Reconditioning Approach

One of the first persons to appreciate what Jacobson had contributed to our understanding of bodymind integration was a physician, Joseph Wolpe. Furthermore, he seems to have discovered a remarkable way of integrating the work of Pavlov, the American learning theorists, and medical psychiatry into a method of dealing with one very specific phenomenon, namely overt fears and phobias (Wolpe 1958).

To understand Wolpe's work, let us illustrate it with a case of extreme fear (or phobia). Let us take a cat first, rather than a person, and assume that we condition the cat to be afraid of a certain cage in a certain room. In other words, we turn a neutral stimulus into a negative stimulus (or learning) which says *FEAR* to the cat every time the cat sees the cage. It is very easy to condition such a phobic response into a cat. All we need to do is put the cat in the cage a few times and shock it with electricity, and it will soon develop the pronounced stress response called *fear*: It fears the cage because that is where it experienced pain. If we place it in the cage again without shocking it, the cat still will show the same symptoms of stress: it will "freeze" and exhibit "escape behavior" and do this many times before the symptoms begin to diminish. In fact, they may never diminish!

If we take this conditioned cat and feed it in the same room, but first take away the cage, the cat will evenually begin to eat. When it is eating once again on a relatively fear-free schedule, we can quietly bring the cage back into the room and place it in the far corner. The cat may then eat cautiously, periodically stopping to check out its environment (to make sure it is safe). From then on it is only a matter of time, patience, and sensitivity to the cat's level of fear until the experimenter deconditions the cat's fear of the cage, so that all of the original fear responses are eliminated. While the cat is eating, the cage is brought closer and closer to the cat until it can eat right next to the cage! That is the reconditioning process. Wolpe put it this way *"If a response inhibitory of anxiety can be made to occur in the presence of the anxiety-evoking stimuli, it will weaken the bond between these stimuli and anxiety.* Wolpe has the patient work on his or her anxiety *situations* and *symptoms*, rather than spending time talking about the *causes* of this anxiety as is the more usual approach in the classic "talking therapies."

Wolpe has a three-step method for deconditioning the person's fear *in a particular situation.* Suppose, for example, a man was once in a severe automobile accident in which he was badly shaken up, so much so that he now has a phobia about riding in a car—the kind of queasy feeling some people get when they contemplate flying from New York to Chicago in an airplane. The person may even be all right until he gets into a car and then becomes so full of fear he has to get out of the car immediately. That is what a car phobia, or a plane phobia, or any other kind of phobia is: a "gut reaction" so unpleasant that the afflicted person has to flee from the situation. Wolpe's *systematic desensitization method* attempts to deal with just these kinds of catastrophic fear reactions. In the case of the car phobia, this three-step method would be approximately as follows:

1. The therapist would first have the person identify all the situations associated with automobiles that call forth his anxiety-fear response—for example, the picture of an automobile, the smell of gasoline. Wolpe believed the person needs to identify at least twelve to fifteen such situations; these fear responses are then ranked in order, from the response that calls forth the highest level of anxiety to the one that is least fearsome.
2. The therapist now gives the person training in progressive relaxation without mentioning the car phobia, and the training continues until the person can relax readily and easily on command. That completes the second step.[1]
3. The therapist now has the person examine the list of anxiety-evoking stimuli, and the actual desensitization method begins. Beginning with the least anxiety provoking stimulus (for example, a picture of a parked car), the person is instructed to concentrate on visualizing that stimulus until he begins to feel his anxiety level for a few seconds. After a brief rest, the therapist now repeats the relaxation instructions and then reintroduces the same car stimulus. This procedure is repeated over and over until the person can visualize the parked car and still remain relaxed and anxiety free.

    Once the person can visualize the parked car and remain emotionally detached from the stimulus, the therapist introduces the next, more anxiety evoking stimulus from the list compiled in step 1. The same process of relaxation and concentration is used until this stimulus also becomes anxiety free. This continues up the scale of the person's fears until he can finally visualize his most anxiety evoking fantasy (riding in the car in which he was hurt) and still remain calm, relaxed, and unattached to the stimulus. At that point, Wolpe said, he is free of his phobic symptom.

Obviously all the fantasizing in the world would be of little use if there were not some payoff, tangible results the person can use in his or her daily living. For example, can the car-phobic person who has gone through the visual desensitization procedure actually get into a car again and drive away anxiety free—that is, without anxiety overwhelming him or her? Wolpe reported just such successful results with his therapy. In fact, Wolpe claimed some extraordinary cures. One of these is helping young persons with homosexual leanings to overcome their aversion to heterosexual coitus and to participate in intimate relations with persons of the opposite sex. Whether or not Wolpe's patient-clients actually achieved this, his approach has proved an effective approach in many extremely phobic areas.

Incidentally, it may come as a relief to some of our readers who are timid drivers that one of the most prevalent problems Wolpe and his associates encounter in their clinic is a phobia about driving on the California freeways.

MIND/SPIRIT APPROACHES FOR BODYMIND/ MINDBODY INTEGRATION

Meditation

Various forms of meditation have swept the country. Yet there is still abysmal ignorance about what meditation is and is not. At its most profound level, meditation is a form of psychic experience, sometimes expressed as religious mysticism or as an "oceanic" oneness with the world. As a form of religious experience, it has been practiced by Catholic saints, Protestant mystics, Hassidic Jews, Islamic Sufis, Japanese Zen masters, Chinese Taoists and Buddhists, and Indian yogis, to mention but a few. At this level, it has been described as a method of experiencing the immediacy of the Godhead and of gaining the meaning of life (Underhill 1960). At its simpler levels it is a method by which a person can calm the everlasting hum of the body's hopped-up energies and the mind's restlessness and anxieties, achieving at last peaceful harmony of the mind-body-spirit. It has been compared to an altered state of consciousness, to prayer, to communion with the eternal forces of nature, to inner reflection, to deep introspection, to visions and clairvoyance, to "inner listening," and to oneness with the universe (Tart 1969).

The media have emphasized the dramatic and mysterious types of meditation. In photographs we are given a view of a transcendent being whose eyes are closed, sometimes in a trance. The person is sometimes seated in a "lotus position," with legs crossed and holding the fingers in a set position at the knees. Such photographs have frightened away many well-intentioned people who know full well the difficulty of assuming such a position without months of practice.

All that is really needed to practice meditation is the willingness to commit fifteen to twenty minutes a day to it, in a private place free from noise and intrusion. All one really needs is a comfortable chair to begin the kind of "letting go" devised by Edmund Jacobson to help his patient-students relax. There is nothing very mysterious about giving oneself a chance to withdraw for a small portion of the day and to rest one's weary *mind-body-spirit* away from the roar and tumult of the world.

SCIENTIFIC INVESTIGATION OF MEDITATION. Until recently, the practice of meditation has been described only through field observations of yogis in trance states. Reports of these deep trances describe incredible feats, such as the actual slowing of the heartbeat, reduction of oxygen intake, and the ability to blank out extremely painful situations. More recently these adepts have been studied in the laboratory and reported in scientific journals. One team of investigators, with the willing permission of a yogi "adept," monitored his vital bodily processes during an extended stay in an airtight box. The monitoring revealed that soon after his entrance into the box, the subject's heartbeat and breathing slowed and within the first half-hour dropped to one-fourth of its normal rate, far below the ordinary levels required for the maintenance of life itself. When the yogi was let out of his prison, he was discovered to be in excellent physical condition. This experiment has given more validity to the strange and extraordinary feats of the Indian yogis about which we have heard and read so much (Anand 1977).

Transcendental meditation is one of the best known and most widely publicized forms of meditation. We can be grateful to the practitioners of this meditation for their openness and their willingness to be studied under laboratory conditions and in long-term, follow-up studies. There have been many articles that vouch for the long-lasting effects of TM (as it is called). In general, physiological results obtained by transcendental meditation reveal the following among college students: increased blood flow and circulation, decreased oxygen consumption and a decrease in carbon dioxide production, increased skin resistance, an altered brain wave pattern, and a general "quiescence of the sympathetic nervous system" (Forem 1973; Benson, 1975).

Laboratory observations of persons engaged in deep meditation confirm that the body does, indeed, seem to slow down and become more rhythmic. The muscular system becomes less tense; the breathing becomes deeper, calmer, and slower; the heartbeat slows; the blood pressure can be reduced; and, in general, the whole body seems to function more easily (Denniston & McWilliams 1975; Goleman 1977; Kline 1980; Pine 1982). One may have many kinds of internal experiences. One may have a feeling of heaviness, of extreme lightness, or even of floating. One may suddenly see images as if projected on a screen. One certainly comes into direct contact with one's nonverbal inner dialogue with more heightened intensity. One may experience a strange sense of relief by not having to attend to all the usual daytime stimuli while in the waking state. One may have dreamlike experiences and not be asleep. One may receive subconscious material, which may border on artistic creativity, or experience some deeply anxiety provoking, repressed material. It is certainly one way to get to know oneself.

A recent review of a variety of meditational approaches does indicate that somatic arousal was reduced in a few of the studies (including electrodermal activity, blood pressure, and respiration rate). However, the reviewer believed these same effects can be found in persons who are able to give themselves to "simple resting" and relaxation. It is possible that meditation and deep relaxation are very similar ASCs (Holmes 1984).

Biofeedback Techniques

The single area of the bodily approach to personality integration that has received the most rigorous experimental research is biofeedback. Under conditions of training, college students and patients from the general population have been observed to lower their systolic blood pressure by using the biofeedback method. One biofeedback method is a technique by which people may become more in touch with their bodily reactions using feedback from an electronic monitoring device. The person closes his or her eyes and concentrates on deep relaxation. When our brain-wave pattern goes into a less active state (Alpha, Theta, or Delta) than our usual active waking state (Beta), the monitoring device produces a tone that feeds back the information. Sometimes the subject reports a wonderful feeling of deep calm; sometimes the subject describes the experience as being close to God, or some other mystical description (Tart 1972, 1975).

Another device for biofeedback is one that allows the subjects to observe their systolic blood pressure. By a learned technique they can watch their own blood pressure go down and thus realize that they can control their bodily reactions, a great hope for the hypertensive patient! Observations of this group, as compared to the control group, reveal that the average subject was able to lower his or her blood pressure by about 12 percent. They also report that sufferers of tension and migraine headaches were able to relax sufficiently so that their headaches were diminished partly or completely by biofeedback techniques that allowed them to monitor their own bodily muscle contraction.

William Greene and his associates at the Menninger Foundation have

---

Box 6.1

LEARNING TO CONTROL OUR BODY WITH BIOFEEDBACK

At New York City's Columbia-Presbyterian Center for Stress and Pain-Related Disorders, the various techniques used include relaxation, biofeedback, self-hypnosis, rhythmic breathing and exercise.

Certain disorders, such as migraines, are treated most successfully with biofeedback. "The patient is connected by sensor wires to a machine with a small screen that feeds back information on such physiological indexes of stress as blood pressure, tension in the facial muscles or, most frequently, the temperature of one's fingers—the colder, the tenser. By loosening their muscles, breathing deeply or letting their thoughts drift, patients learn that they can control their stress response; they can make their blood pressure drop or the temperature in their hands rise by as much as twelve to fourteen degrees." This information feedback makes us more aware of what is going on in our body—which gives us a greater amount of control over what we believe to be involuntary responses. Regaining our sense of control has been shown to be vital in healing and even in life-death crises.

Source: Claudia Wallis, with Ruth Mehrtens Galvin and Dick Thompson, reporters, in *Time*, June 6, 1983, pp. 50–54.

helped sufferers from migraine and other tension headaches by what they call *autogenic training*. Autogenic training is an interesting procedure and seems to be something that a group of persons could try out on their own. The persons sit in a darkened room in comfortable chairs and with their eyes closed. The trainer repeats in a soothing, quiet tone (some participants have called it a hypnotic monotone) instructions such as these:

> You are allowing yourself to relax . . . you feel yourself relaxing . . . you are allowing your head and neck to relax . . . you will allow the tiredness to drain from your body . . . soon you will be experiencing coolness in your head . . . you are allowing the warmth from your head to flow into your arms and hands . . . You feel the warmth leaving your head and neck . . . you feel the warmth flowing into your arms . . . (and so on).

The results of this training sometimes have been so surprisingly quick, report the trainers, that one woman got relief from a headache in only a few minutes (Moss 1972, 1979).

We are only beginning to understand how the bodymind works. But some hard scientific data are piling up showing that biofeedback methods are enabling hypertensive patients to lower their blood pressure and heart rate at will. Now some research suggests that even asthma and epileptic victims are being helped to gain some control over their maladies (Birbaumer & Kimmel 1979; Gatchel & Price 1979). A calmer mind evidently does promote a calmer (less-stressed) body.

APPLICATIONS AND COPING TECHNIQUES

This chapter is devoted to the physical self. So far we have seen how mental and emotional stress can create physical breakdown and disease. We also have noted how the continual stress in our lives can age our bodies prematurely. We have discussed the increasing attention of psychologists to the bodily approach to personality integration. And we have examined the need to remain sensorily aware of our internal and external physical environments.

It was not by chance that we placed this section toward the beginning of this book. We did so to emphasize that everything we do, feel, and experience and the ways in which we behave all have an effect on our bodily functioning. We need a body that is "at ease" so that we are able to deal more calmly and easily with daily events. A body at ease promotes a mind at ease. Accordingly, we suggest that the person who is seriously interested in maintaining quality of life always be aware of the following points.

1. Maintenance of Good Physical Health: Treat Your Body at Least as Well as you Treat Your Automobile

None of us would think of driving our cars for 50,000 miles without a checkup or a tune-up. Yet, we forget to take care of bodily needs, go without sleep, live on junk foods, and visit our physicians only when we have severe difficulties. We call the chronic diseases *silent* killers, and so they are. Their progressions are slow but inexorable. We can abuse ourselves with drugs and alcohol and cigarettes for just so long until suddenly we feel the first chest pains, or a sudden blurring of our vision tells the physician that our blood pressure is approaching the danger level.

The body is the physical vehicle in which we move and breathe and have our being. It is the structure through which we feel either joy or pain. It is by staying in touch with our physical selves that we remain rooted in reality. Emotions are bodily experiences. By remaining alert to what is going on within us, we are more alert to what is going on around us; that is, we are more "intelligent." When we eat too much, drink too much, deny ourselves the sleep we need, or burn our candles at both ends for long periods of time, we actually anesthetize ourselves to bodily signals. We get used to heartburn or to acid indigestion and cover the minor aches and pains with aspirins and other analgesics. We become so used to chronic fatigue and discomfort that we do not realize that we can feel better. We have become dull human beings.

2. Respect Your Individual Bodily Needs

We have devoted three chapters to your individual needs. We hope that you have come to respect your individual differences. All of us differ significantly. For example, some of us have less need for the usual eight hours of sleep, but some of us may need more, particularly when the stress in our lives is greater than usual. Our nutritional needs vary. Some persons seem to need a hearty breakfast while others may actually feel slightly nauseated by the idea of eating immediately upon arising. While some persons feel physically invigorated by spending a day in the blazing sun and surf of the beach, there are some persons to whom this experience may be harmful. Our reactions to climate differ significantly. Some feel exhilarated by cold weather and love nothing better than to ski, skate, or whatever, while others (who have poor circulation) may suffer during the coldest times of the year. Although most people enjoy a sunny day, some of us actually look forward to rainy days—our systems are made more buoyant by the increased negative ions of the atmosphere.

These are only a few of the ways in which we differ in bodily needs. There are many physical differences among us. Harmony with the self is to become aware of those differences and to allow ourselves a life style in accord with our individuality.

3. Devote Some Time Every Week to Physical Rejuvenation

Our civilization allows us little time and opportunity to be active. As children we ran and jumped, tumbled on the grass and rolled over, leaped into the air exuberantly and joyfully. We were natural "yogis," twisting, bending, and stretching our bodies. But as we grow older, more and more of our daily lives are spent behind desks, behind counters, behind the wheels of our automobiles. Sedentary activities take the place of active situations, with the result that our muscles, tendons, cartilages, vital organs, and glandular and nervous systems are slowly and insidiously aging prematurely. Our bodies are not getting the benefits of a healthy cardiovascular system, which provides oxygen and nutrition to the cells and tissues and which disposes of the waste substances and toxic elements. By incorporating some form of physical activity into our everyday life, we slow down or actually reverse the effects of stress in our lives.

As well, physical activity helps drain the emotional tensions built up in the body, cleanses the mind of its emotional concerns, and paves the way for a fresh viewpoint toward living and its associated complexities. Physical activity, then, can be said to be one of the significant approaches to mind-body health.

Unfortunately, it is too easy to slide into a lazy attitude toward physical integration. We rationalize and make excuses to avoid the effort it takes to keep our bodies in good shape. We say to ourselves that we cannot take the time, that we have too many things to do, or that the pressures of home or office prevent us from doing what we know we should do. What is really happening is that we have not yet understood the significance of taking care of the physical self. When we get a toothache or earache that is screaming for attention, we get to the dentist or physician as soon as we can get ourselves an appointment. Aging and chronic diseases (like hypertension) are "silent killers" because they creep up on us unnoticed. We often are unaware of their toll—until it is too late. Physical integration needs to be an ever-present awareness in our consciousness. Time must be given for it just as time is given to the other functions of our lives.

4. Choose Physical Activities That Accord With Your Individual Differences and With Your Life Style

When we discuss the need for physical activity with our students, we often hear the distressed response that they just cannot get out and jog every day, that they just are not the racquetball type, or that the idea of getting up each morning and doing the Canadian Royal Air Force exercises is not for them! With which we promptly agree.

Choose, therefore, physical activities that are in accord with your distinct preferences. For some that may be break dancing or ballet. For others swimming or golf may be more appropriate. It need not be an everyday event, but surely you deserve three or four times during the week to reenergize your body, for that is the real purpose of physical activity. Furthermore, a variety of activities will do you more good than the repetition of one type of exercise. Remember that what you are trying to do is to energize those parts of your body that are not usually used. Swimming develops the chest, arms, and legs, while disco or belly dancing invigorates the abdomen. You might very well have a weekly bowling date, go swimming on the weekend, and do yoga twice a week. A variety of activities exercises the different parts of the body and is a wholistic approach. The physical activity that you choose need not have the connotation of hard labor and exhaustion. Many professionals take time out on Wednesday afternoon or on Sunday for a game of golf. A good tour on the golf course is excellent, provided one does not use a golf cart but walks briskly from hole to hole.

5. In Moments of Emotional Stress: Try the Bioenergetic Approach to Dealing With Anxiety and Emotional Turmoil

There are times in our lives when the emotional pressure and stress become almost overwhelming. We sometimes experience so much anxiety that we are hard pressed to put one foot in front of the other to keep going about our normal routine. It sometimes seems as if we are just standing there and the whole sky is falling on our heads, and we don't know how to manage the moment-by-moment events that seem to be raining down all around us.

First, it may help to know that this is a common experience. Explosive events *do* seem to pile up over a period of a few days, a few weeks, maybe even a few months. Furthermore, at these times, because so much is happening that drains us emotionally, any little event that comes along seems more momentous than it is. Our bodyminds can become depressed and depleted—de-energized!

At these times, the bioenergetic approach does seem to drain the hurt and pain and to help us mobilize our physical energy. Now is the time to make that extra physical exertion through whatever bioenergetic approach that seems right for you: bioenergetics themselves, or running, jogging, exercise, jazzercise. Unless you experience it directly, you cannot imagine how efficacious working up a good physical sweat and reducing the tension in your muscles are in draining anxiety and heightening your ability to deal with the everyday world. If you are not used to it, you will feel "all done in," perspiring, grunting, moaning, aching. But at the same time, you won't have enough energy to feel anxious. Then in a few minutes or so, a sense of well-being will begin to build up all over your body. It begins slowly and then spreads throughout your physical being. Do not get up or do anything for a while. Just allow yourself to experience the increased blood flow, the more even heart rate, the calmer breathing that is happening to you. Notice how you are too busy to feel depressed, nervous, or anxious. As you become used to this kind of physical exercise, you should begin to experience a sense of euphoria, such a well-being of your bodymind that you will confront your problems with more strength of spirit and more physical vitality.

6. After Your Physical Activity, Try Some Meditation

For those who want to know what meditation is all about but find that they can't seem to quiet their minds, now is a good time to explore the matter. What you have done through your physical activity is empty your mind of the nagging and the anxiety and the upset. You are starting at a good place. You've cleaned out your mind, and now you can just let yourself stay calm and relaxed. You may want to try Jacobson's deep relaxation, if that has aroused your interest. Or you may want to go straight into one of the approaches to meditation. There are many good books on the subject. You may want to take this time to go into deep reflective prayer. You may simply imagine yourself at your favorite and most refreshing place, such as the beach or the mountains.

Some people will want to shower or bathe first, and that is also helpful for promoting bodymind or mindbody ease. But you may simply want to stay there and shower or bathe later, as the final step in being good to your bodymind or mindbody. As all our readers should know by now, a bodymind "at ease" will be far less likely to become "dis-eased."

7. A Tip for Teachers and Parents

Teaching school is especially trying. It is your job to keep thirty or more students interested in their schoolwork when most of them would rather be elsewhere. If you have been paying attention to this section, you know now how anxiety and stress can result in bodily and emotional fatigue. For many students, classroom work is *stressful* and *anxiety producing*. The symptoms of this stress and anxiety come out as class disturbance, acting up, or restlessness.

There are many and varied physical activities that promote mindbody integration and creative potential.

Physical activity will help reduce this emotional tension. You have seen it yourself after the children come back from recess. They may be a little overactive when they first come in, but in a few moments they settle down and seem to welcome a quiet period of desk work. Do not wait for recess to give them an emotional outlet. Every so often give the whole class a chance to take a physical break. Get them up on their feet doing things, walking around, or (for small children) playing "Simon Says." Give them a chance to use their voices (which is a type of motor activity) by singing or choral speaking. You may have encountered these suggestions in your educational methods courses, but now you can understand their special relevance to student well-being.

Parents, too, can profit by the calming effects of bioenergetic activity. When you have three or four youngsters in the house all day because the weather is inclement, and their noise and natural fun-making play is beginning to become a little more than you can manage, now is the time to get them into some kind of physical activity. The best thing, of course, is to get them out of doors, if only for a little time (even if the weather is inclement). They will be glad to come in out of the weather, take off their raincoats and boots, and settle down to a time of more reflective and introspective activity. If they have been bundled up against the weather, they will not come down "with their death," at all. They will be invigorated. But if you are anxious about their health, a hot bath or shower should allay these doubts.

Our physiological selves have a natural ebb-and-flow cycle. We enjoy moments of activity followed by moments of calm. The more we enable our children to get in touch with these natural rhythms, the better they will be able to develop an integration of bodymind as they grow and mature.

SUMMARY POINTS TO REMEMBER

1. One therapeutic approach to personality integration is psychotherapy. Another approach is through physical therapies.
2. Those who stay physically active also stay more youthful. We have become a sedentary nation.
3. Our most basic needs have to do with physiological survival.
4. Sigmund Freud pioneered in our modern understanding of our sexual needs. Our sexual needs are both biological and psychological. What we still do not appreciate is the individual difference of our sexual drive which varies according to our sex, age, health, personality type, and other life events.
5. We have many individual differences in our basic needs: the need for solitude, ex-

citement, or personal space are good examples.
6. One of the first "growth centers" was established in Europe under the direction of G. I. Gurdjieff who used physical activity as a way for intellectuals to experience ASCs.
7. Wilhelm Reich developed the concept of the character neurosis. He conceptualized our bodies as defending against pain by the building up of body armor arranged in seven segmental rings. These rings are the areas where armor deadens bodily experience resulting in various bodily symptoms of illness such as stomach problems, difficulty breathing, or headaches. In other words, where we have built up bodily armor we usually ex-

perience disease or illness in that part of the body.

8. Another approach to bodymind integration is through relaxation. Edmund Jacobson, an American physician, developed a deep relaxation method which he believed relieved his patients' physical symptoms and problems.

9. Massage has been a physical integration method for many centuries. Massage of the body awakens, excites, and soothes our most basic sense and organ: the touch senses of our skin.

10. Harry Harlow's experiments with animals support the primacy of the *contact* need—our need for touch.

11. Another approach to bodymind integration is yoga which is a series of stretching postures or asanas designed to keep the body supple and flexible.

12. In the last analysis, however, any physical activity from walking to swimming to mountain climbing will increase the body's vigor. Perspiration eliminates the body's toxins and cleanses the system.

13. Joseph Wolpe used Jacobson's progressive relaxation as a *base* for his conditioning therapy. This method has been particularly effective with phobias.

14. Meditation is a mind/spirit therapy that has been practiced for many centuries in all major religious and philosophic systems. Prayer is a form of meditation. Other meditations involve chanting, the use of a mantram silently within, and certain postures.

15. Biofeedback techniques enable the person to monitor his physical responses so as to relieve headache, induce calm, or experience a mystical euphoria.

SIGNIFICANT TERMS AND CONCEPTS

asc	going negative	physiological needs
asanas	growth center	pranayama
bioenergetics	isometric exercises	progressive relaxation
biofeedback	Kinsey Report	segmental rings
biofeedback techniques	letting go	sexual needs
body armor	mantram	systematic desensitization therapy
celibacy	massage	territorial space
character neurosis	masturbation	transcendental meditation
contact need	meditation	yoga
deconditioning therapy	nocturnal emissions	Zen Buddhism
gestalt therapy	phobia	

FILL IN THE BLANKS WITH SIGNIFICANT TERMS AND CONCEPTS

1. The need for air and food and water are considered to be p_____ n_____.

2. Our s_____ n_____ are both biological and psychological.

3. One of the pioneers in the use of physical activity as a way to experience an A_____ was Gurdjieff.

4. Wilhem Reich developed the concept of character neurosis and b_____ a_____. He even divided the body into seven rings of various resulting bodily illnesses.

5. Edmund Jacobson has contributed another approach to bodymind integration called p_____ r_____.

6. Another form of activity that satisfies the body's physiological needs that relies heavily on touch is m_____. This has been a method for body/mind mind/body integration for centuries.

7. Harlow's experiments with animals supports the concept of c_____ n_____. Without enough satisfaction of this need we don't even live as young babies.
8. B_____ t_____ give people information which is based on bodily response and enables the person to monitor this bodily response and relieve various physical ailments.
9. The physical approaches to personality integration also include the use of mantras, postures, chanting, etc.—various forms of m_____.

RECOMMENDED BOOKS FOR FURTHER READING

Hittleman, Richard. 1975. *Yoga: The Eight Steps to Health and Peace*. New York: Deerfield Communications. For an easy introduction to many aspects of yoga we heartily recommend this book—one of the best on the market and a very competent do-it-yourself manual.

Jacobson, Edmund. 1964. *Anxiety and Tension Control, A Physiologic Approach*. Philadelphia: J. B. Lippincott Company. Jacobson gives detailed yet easy to understand directions. Another book by the same author containing much of the same material is: *You Must Relax*, 5th rev. ed., 1976. (Wallingford, Ct: McGraw-Hill Book Company.)

Keller, Helen. 1961. *The Story of My Life*. New York: Dell Publishing Company. This autobiography gives us an insight into her "silent, dayless life" and into the worlds of meaning that came into existence for her when she learned to associate meanings with her perceptions of touching, tasting, and smelling.

Lowen, Alexander. 1975. *Bioenergetics*. New York: Penguin Books, Inc. For an in-depth understanding of the bioenergetic field this book is an excellent introduction and primer. Not only does Lowen describe his encounters with Reich but he is willing to self-reveal his own psychophysical therapy with Reich.

Montague, Ashley. 1971. *Touching: The Human Significance of the Skin*. New York: Columbia University Press. The skin, the largest sense organ of our body, is involved in the whole area of touching, feeling, pain, tickling, warmth, cold, sensuality, sexuality—even in the process of birth and physiological development of the newborn.

Ornstein, Robert E. 1977. *The Psychology of Consciousness*, 2nd ed. New York: Harcourt Brace Jovanovich, Inc. Ornstein, a research psychologist, attempts to fit Eastern and Western psychologies into some kind of organic correspondence. Some of the topics he discusses are yoga, meditation, breathing exercises, the *I Ching*, and other intuitive modes of consciousness. Of interest also is how he relates the significant differences in the functioning of the two sides of the brain (and therefore the two sides of our physical bodies).

Wolpe, Joseph. 1958. *Psychotherapy by Reciprocal Inhibition*. Stanford, CA: Stanford University Press. Wolpe describes how to treat neuroses and their corresponding fears and phobias using the desensitization methods he has developed. For the serious student of therapeutic techniques, this book is a must.

7

*Our One and Many
Selves: The Search
for Integration*

THE MORE DEBILITATING FORMS OF EMOTIONAL PATTERNING
    The Passive-Dependent Personality
    The Obsessive-Compulsive Personality
    Extreme Phobic Reactions
    The Severe Depressive Reaction
    Suicidal Depression
    The Hysteric Personality
    The Manic-Depressive Reaction
    The Schizophrenic Personality
    The Schizoid Personality
    Multiple Personality
    Psychopathic and Sociopathic Personalities

THE DEVELOPMENT OF THE DIALOGIC INSIGHT APPROACH TO
    GROWTH
    A Very Brief History of Therapeutic Treatment
    The Use of Hypnosis
    Freud: The Development of Psychoanalysis
    Sullivan: The Interpersonal Approach
    Rogers: The Client-Centered Approach
    Group Therapy
    Summary: A Shift in Paradigms
    Berne and Harris: Transactional Analysis
    Perls: Gestalt Therapy

THREE THERAPIES DIRECTED SPECIFICALLY TOWARD BEHAVIORAL
    CHANGE
    Stamfl: Implosive Therapy
    A Modified Implosive Approach
    Ellis: Rational-Emotive Therapy
    Glasser: Reality Therapy

OTHER THERAPIES

APPLICATIONS AND COPING TECHNIQUES

THE MORE DEBILITATING FORMS OF EMOTIONAL PATTERNING

In the previous chapters we looked at the commonalities and differences of fairly average human functioning. In this chapter, we shall consider some of the deviations of personality patterning. These extreme patternings occur if we have not had secure and constructive early experiences, or if the stress and change in our lives have become so severe that our usual functioning begins to break down. These breakdowns can happen to any of us from time to time, and we may find ourselves severely depressed, confused, disassociated, and even irrational. It may simply be that we have become so de-energized that we do not know how to integrate the events in our lives; it takes all we have to just keep going. In these situations, we may need dialogic therapies, either for a short time or for longer, until we can function better. We shall examine the different kinds of therapies and how they work.

The Passive-Dependent Personality

We already have discussed some of the fixations of personality patterning as described by Freud. One such personality patterning is that of the orally fixated person, who gratifies his or her libidinal drive through the primary erotic zone in and around the mouth, by excessive eating, drinking, smoking, and so on. Psychologically this person remains passively dependent on the environment to take care of his or her needs. For example, you may know someone who is always asking your opinion about even the most minor decisions of living: what to wear today, what movie to go to see, or what kind of a present to buy for a friend or relative you do not even know. These persons may not even seem capable of taking care of their bodily needs. Although they are adults (in the physical sense), they have not yet learned to pick up after themselves; they leave their clothes about and their dishes in the sink; and they are constantly borrowing things from you because they have not bothered to replenish their own household store. All in all, they seem to expect the world to take care of them.

The Obsessive-Compulsive Personality

If the person remains fixated at the second level of psychosexual development, Freud said, he or she develops into an *anal* personality and exhibits obsessive-compulsive habits. He or she is excessively concerned about dirt, small details,

Although psychoanalysis was brought to this country in the first part of the twentieth century, America's specific contribution has been the development of group psychotherapy.

and even the least bit of untidyness. As a result, he or she tends to be an overly tidy, excessively modest, compulsively exact person who "cannot see the forest for the trees." These persons may be obsessed with minor details and references to people you do not know, or they may go over the same subject time after time, driving you to boredom and confusion. Their offices are immaculate, their clothes creased and coordinated, and their work organized. All this is good, and sometimes these persons make excellent secretaries, treasurers, accountants, and computer operators, jobs in which exactness is desirable. But a hair out of place, a little dust on the furniture, a spot on their clothes, or papers slightly disarranged fills them with anxiety. Because they are concerned with the minutiae of daily living, they lack a larger perspective and often are passed over for positions of higher responsibility that require the ability to see the overall picture.

Still, people with these two personality patterns can and often do function fairly well in our society. We now come to those personalities that take a far more serious turn with the result either that the affected individuals are unable to cope adequately in our society or they become destructive to themselves or to the society in which they live.

Extreme Phobic Reactions

The obsessive-compulsive patterning (discussed above) can assume such an extreme form that it takes over a person's life. Whatever is disturbing the person becomes so obsessive that he or she cannot stop thinking the same thoughts over and over. In order to defend against these continual obsessive thoughts, the person develops counterphobic reactions and compulsive rituals to defend against them, over which he or she seems to have no control. A case history, reported by Davison and Neale, describes a woman whose anxiety about being attacked by germs was so overwhelming that she washed her hands no less than five hundred times a day. Not only did her hand washing occupy most of her waking existence, it also produced disfiguring and painful sores on her hands, wrists, and arms (Davison & Neale 1974). One is reminded of Lady Macbeth's compulsion to wash her hands as a way to rid herself of the guilt she felt for the murders committed by herself and her husband. While the others watch her strange ritual of hand washing, she is heard to murmur the fear of all such guilt-obsessed persons—the inability to cleanse themselves: "Here is the smell of blood still; all the perfumes of Arabia will not sweeten this little hand" (Shakespeare, *Macbeth*).

The Severe Depressive Reaction

We have all experienced occasional bouts of depression, those times when everything seems bleak and hopeless and when we can see no way out of whatever desperate situation in which we find ourselves. Any attempt to cheer us up only sends us further and further into despair. We are not talking about these occasional situations that we all encounter at some time but, rather, of those people whose constitutional psychic functioning prevents them from being able to cope with the normal stress of living. Whether from an inherited predisposition or from severe deprivation in early childhood, they have learned a kind of generalized (conditioned) hopelessness and helplessness. Whatever the cause of this severe depressive reaction, it has resulted in the abiding conviction that there is nothing they can do to change the events and sad course of their lives. One psychologist demonstrated a similar patterning in the laboratory. He conditioned dogs to shocks from which they could not escape. Later he placed the experimental dogs and a control group (which had not been given this kind of training) in a shock situation in which there *was* an easily discerned escape. The control dogs discovered the escape and used it at the first possible moment. In contrast, the experimental dogs did not even try to escape. Instead they remained passively tolerant of the shocks in a kind of dazed and helpless state. The psychologist reported also that the experimental dogs had a low level of norepinephrine, the hormone that helps to excite emergency arousal. He also noted that drugs that seem to mobilize the severely depressed persons to overcome their lethargic state are the very ones that stimulate the production of the emergency hormone, norepinephrine (Seligman 1975).

Suicidal Depression

Sometimes people have such severe depression that they choose the only escape from pain they can think of: suicide. One of the earliest studies of suicide was by Emile Durkheim. He first recognized the alienation factor in suicidal people's backgrounds and noted the frequency of the following situational factors: First, they were far from home and frequently had moved from a rural area to a large city with its more impersonal environment; second, they were out of contact with their families and old friends who had provided them with emotional support; and third, they were unable to establish new friendships despite all the people around them (Durkheim 1951). Although some of Durkheim's statistics have been criticized, it still is true that suicides are more prevalent among those who have moved away from home and who have not succeeded in establishing new relationships. A recent follow-up study of attempted suicides among a group of adolescents confirmed many of Durkheim's conclusions. Of forty-five adolescents, twenty-three had lost one or both parents through death, divorce, or separation (many fairly recently), and two-thirds had lost or anticipated the loss of a parent, boyfriend, or girlfriend (Grollman 1971).

But suicide is more than a situational occurrence. Many of us have had to confront the loneliness of living away from home and of feeling isolated and friendless. What, then, is the difference? Suicidal personalities often have suffered a crippling emotional deprivation in early childhood that prevents them from solving their situational problems. Anything may trigger the suicide attempt: academic problems in school, marital problems, and even conflict with parents. Paradoxically, suicidal students who blame their lack of academic achievement have done no more poorly than other college students. Another study described "typical" suicidal students as older, lonely, friendless, and isolated psychologically from others (Coleman 1976).

The Hysteric Personality

Another type of crippling reaction is called the *hysteric* personality. We already have discussed a few of the many manifestations of this disorder: physical symptoms by which the person converts free-flowing anxiety into disorders such as nonneurological paralysis or one disabling sickness after another. Psychologically, the "hysteric" exhibits a personality patterning in which the *feeling* function dominates almost to the exclusion of other traits. Hysterics literally are run by their emotions. They sometimes have been characterized as having a dramatic self-absorption, as if constantly "on stage." Their gestures are theatrical; their voices frequently have a considerably higher decibel level than the voices of those around them; and their conversation generally centers on themselves: *their* feelings, *their* emotions, *their* problems, *their* revelations, *their* families, and the injustices toward *them*. If we try to help these people, we soon enough discover that their difficulties are frequently of their own making and are exaggerated far out of proportion to reality. They are also ingenious at involving a vast number of persons in their emotional web: their families, their colleagues at work, their neighbors, their neighbors' children, even their minister, physician, attorney, and any person whose profession is to help such people.

They are also destructive to themselves. Psychologically any small incident, any chance remark can set them off on their emotional rockets. They hamper themselves in their vocational careers since their fellow workers soon learn to avoid them, and their employers bypass them for positions that deal with the public and for positions of authority that need "cool heads" and rational decision making. At a physical level they manage to incur organic problems that require surgery: removal of breasts, sexual organs, and other bodily tissues and structure because of cancer. One study, which compared persons labeled "hysteric personality" with a group of "nonhysteric" personalities, found the hysteric group to have had three times the mass weight of organs removed—a gruesome but extremely interesting measure of personality disintegration (Woodruff, Goodwin, & Guze 1974).

The Manic-Depressive Reaction

The manic-depressive reaction may actually be a type of hysteria in that these persons sometimes exhibit the type of functioning described as the "hysteric" pattern, with one important difference—in this personality complex, there are cyclic patterns. The first is the "high, euphoric" pattern in which these persons express great optimism about the present and the future, work out plans to improve their personal or professional life, talk and move with great energy, and concoct "fantastic" schemes to get rich, achieve fame, or gain power. They may undertake physical projects and actually accomplish them in record time. Their psychical energy is awesome. Then, suddenly, all the wind seems to go out of their sails, and they seem to go into reverse. They suddenly are "in the dumps," develop depression with its accompanying lethargy, and may even contemplate suicide.

The Schizophrenic Personality

In the so-called schizophrenic forms of deviancy, victims seem to be out of contact with the normal, commonly shared experience of what it is to be human. Schizophrenia is not, as commonly believed, a "split personality." When we become schizophrenic, our behaviors and thought patterns seem strange and at times bizarre to other persons (sometimes also to ourselves). Sometimes, in fact, our emotional response pattern undergoes such a "sea change" that we seem to be "turned inside out." Schizophrenics may giggle inanely when confronted with a frightening situation and can just as easily (and as unpredictably) become morose and withdrawn—"dead people" who refuse to allow further stimulation from their environment to get through to them. These persons may even become *catatonic*—they may sit for hours without moving or may not eat or walk for long periods of

Sometimes we can suffer a depression so severe that we feel helpless and hopeless. At such times our physical and psychological energy can seem to drain out of us.

time. They do not seem to be aware of things around them and may stand statue-like in an awkward position. Schizophrenics have other curious (to us) emotional responses: They can become morose when others seem happy—for example, at holiday celebrations—and can deviate in other directions thought "abnormal" by many in society.

The Schizoid Personality

"Schizoid" personalities appear to function as all the rest of us do. They work and support themselves and their families. They interact with others and carry on their daily round of activities with an apparent sense of direction.

The mark of schizoid personalities is that they *seem* to operate more effectively and completely than they really do. What distinguishes the schizoid life style is the "cool" and detached way of living with others. For example, they seldom seem to engage in spontaneous laughter, and many persons eventually come to see them as aloof, withdrawn, and emotionally disengaged. Such persons seem to prefer to work more with machines than with people and seldom have intimate relationships—the kind of relationships in which one feels free to share one's inner thoughts and feelings. They do not seem to feel at ease or derive joy from human relationships as most of us do. Schizoid personalities therefore can appear to be withdrawn in company, for they say little and show few emotional responses. They may seem on the surface, nonetheless, to have everything in hand.

Though such personalities can be highly developed on the intellectual level and do well (even brilliantly) in their careers, they do not seem to enjoy or encourage the company of other persons. According to one personality theorist, their posture and facial expressions are characteristically stiff, mechanical, even robotlike, and their smiles seem masklike (Lowen 1967).

Multiple Personality

Sometimes these persons are so fearful of the "dark" possibilities in their personalities that they attempt to repress all knowledge of their existence. These repressed emotions and feelings are still present even though they may be unaware of them consciously. When repression is complete and successful, these persons remain largely unaware of their dark impulses. But should these repressing defenses begin to fail, or even to break down, the dark impulses then can begin to emerge in an actual and distinct personality with a separate identity, not just as another aspect of personality.

There are many stories with the theme of multiple personality, such as Robert Louis Stevenson's novella *The Strange Case of Dr. Jekyll and Mr. Hyde* and Oscar Wilde's *Portrait of Dorian Gray*. But there have been actual cases of multiple personality recorded in medical history. One is discussed in a thoroughly absorbing book, *The Three Faces of Eve*, in which two psychiatrists describe their amazement and perplexity in discovering that a rather attractive but colorless housewife in her midtwenties is harboring a repressed personality quite different from her public personality. The public personality was completely unaware of her second personality, which emerged during periods of "headaches" and "blackouts." This second personality was cocky, brazen, aggressive, spontaneous, voluptuous—everything, in fact, that her public personality held to be unacceptable (Thigpen & Cleckley 1957).

Another, even more striking example of multiple personality was reported in the book *Sybil*. "Sybil" (a pseudonym) had been victimized by some of the most severe child abuse in the annals of child psychology. As a way of managing these childhood traumas, Sybil created for herself sixteen different personalities with distinctly different identities, interests, and even sexes. Although most of the sixteen identities were aware of the others and of Sybil, Sybil herself was unaware of their existence. The story of Sybil is at once the most fascinating and the most grisly of multiple-personality case histories (Schreiber, 1973).

Psychopathic and Sociopathic Personalities

There is another kind of pattern, which seems to be an *underdevelopment* of emotional behavior, called the *sociopathic* and *psychopathic* personality.

Psychopathics appear to value human life so little that they can snuff out another person's life much as we would slap down a mosquito—and with about as little sense of relationship with their victim! Interviews with psychopathic murderers seem to reveal just this curious lack of affect or feeling. They do not shoot or stab a victim in anger, rage, or fear. Nor do they kill while under the influence of alcohol, drugs, or "voices"—as the psychotic personality often does. Psychopaths simply shoot their victims, stab them, run them down with an automobile, or push them out of a window—in cold blood. The psychopath is the extreme deviant.

There are "milder" forms of sociopathy. Sociopaths may not murder their next-door neighbor, but they might "do him in" in other ways. They may sell him a car that is a "lemon" with full knowledge (and no remorse) that they have cheated the buyer. They may become an actual "carney" whose only object in life seems to be to fleece a "mark"—the general public. They may "borrow" money from a friend with no intention of paying it back, although they say they will. Or they may be professionals (physician, attorney, engineer) who are not living up to their codes of ethics.

We might call the sociopathic personality a moral moron. There is much truth in this term, for sociopathic personalities, when confronted with their lies or how they have hurt others, show little real concern or embarrassment. They may declare that they are going to reform, but it is an acting job, pure and simple, in order to keep people bound to them or to get out of the mess they have made. A psychiatrist, Hervey Cleckley, who made a lifelong study of sociopathic personalities, considered it a form of insanity. But since scoiopathic personalities hear no voices, have no obvious delusions, talk rationally, and are even rather charming, the psychiatric profession has not recognized the seeming rational exterior for what it is—simply, as Cleckley called it, *the mask of sanity* (Cleckley 1964).

Box 7.1 | **CHARACTERISTICS OF THE SOCIOPATHIC PERSONALITY**

1. Superficial charm and "intelligence"
2. Delusions and other signs of irrational thinking
3. Absence of "nervousness" or psychoneurotic manifestations
4. Unreliability
5. Untruthfulness and insincerity
6. Lack of remorse or shame
7. Inadequately motivated, antisocial behavior
8. Poor judgment and failure to learn by experience
9. Pathologic egocentricity and incapacity for love
10. General poverty in major affective (emotional) reactions
11. Specific loss of insight
12. Unresponsiveness in general interpersonal relations
13. Fantastic and uninviting behavior with drink and also without
14. Suicide rarely carried out
15. Sex life impersonal, trivial, and poorly integrated
16. Failure to follow any life plan

Source: Adapted from Hervey Cleckley, *The Mask of Sanity,* 4th ed. (St. Louis: C. V. Mosby Co., 1964).

THE DEVELOPMENT OF THE DIALOGIC INSIGHT
APPROACH TO GROWTH

We have named only a few of the devastating and destructive twists of personality patterning. What may be done for these personalities? What may be done for any of us, when we succumb to depression, near hysteria, a desire to run away from our problems, or any of the lesser forms of panic with which we are all familiar? To answer this, we shall study the development of another approach to personality integration—namely—dialogic (insight) therapy. The assumption basic to this kind of therapy is that by talking about one's life and problems, one develops not only insight but the ability to change one's life in constructive ways.

Therapy and *theapeutic* come from the Greek, meaning "to heal," and our *psychotherapy* today is (in that sense) the art and science of healing ills and suffering on the *psychological* plane. Much of that healing attention now focuses on enabling persons to cope with the pressures and tensions of our industrialized civilization.

For example, there can come a time for any of us when the difficulties in our lives have become so burdensome or when we find ourselves so prone to anxiety, that we feel emotionally crippled and unable to cope. Dialogic therapy may be private (between the person and a therapist or counselor) or it may be in a group (with others who also are trying to break through limitations, conditionings, and stereotypic patternings).

A Very Brief History of Therapeutic Treatment

It must not be thought that what we call madness, insanity, schizophrenia, or bouts of depression are modern phenomena. They have been described in literature since recorded history. Saul, King of Judah, is known to have suffered from severe depressions and to have become violent and even homicidal at times (I Samuel 16: 14–23).

In some cultures—for example, among the American Indians—"mad" people were treated with respect, since they were thought to be touched by the gods. In Europe in the Middle Ages, "insane" persons were thought to have lost their reason and sometimes even were thought to be possessed by demons. Since the devil was the personification of evil, "insane" persons were sometimes whipped, starved, or branded with hot irons in the belief that punishing the devil (who had taken over the personality) would persuade the evil spirit to leave.

Many of the mentally ill roamed the streets and byways in the latter years of the Middle Ages and just starved to death or became victims of ridicule and cruel treatment. Some women were even burned as witches.

There was a small step forward in the treatment of severe personality problems when insane persons were placed in asylums. Unfortunately, these places were often not much better than prisons, and the inmates were frequently chained to the walls as criminals were. The word *bedlam*—which has come to mean "a place of wild confusion and noise"—is actually a contraction of the name of a former insane asylum in Southwark, London: the Hospital of St. Mary of Bethlehem (Bedlam). The screaming of the patients could be heard clearly by passers-by, and the patients were sometimes exhibited like zoo animals (for a fee) to the curious and the thrill seekers.

Many kinds of treatments once used to heal the personality disintegration of persons now seem to us almost barbaric if not outright inhuman. In the snake-pit treatment, for example, the unfortunate patients were lowered by ropes into a pit full of snakes in the belief that the fright of the experience would shock them back into sensibility.

Treatment of insane personalities improved in France after the Revolution. A remarkable physician, Philippe Pinel, was put in charge of La Bicètre, an insane asylum in Paris. To the astonishment of his colleagues and despite their ridicule, Pinel insisted on changing the environmental conditions of the inmates. He removed their chains, cleaned up the dung and filth, and let the sun shine into the dungeons where the inmates were housed. Pinel treated his disorganized personalities not as "witless" creatures but with the same kindness and consideration he showed to other persons. His approach resulted in the improvement and release of many patients who otherwise might have remained in the asylum for the rest of their lives.

The Use of Hypnosis

Jean Charcot, another French physician, made another step forward when in the late nineteenth century he demonstrated that the apparently bizarre symptoms of stuttering, trembling, or the inability to walk and talk could be relieved under hypnosis. Charcot's discoveries in hypnosis and his treatment of the mentally ill constitute one of the really big breakthroughs in psychiatric treatment. He demonstrated, for example, that many of the *physical* symptoms and disabilities of the insane can have an underlying *psychological* cause and that if the cause is psychological, then the condition may be treated psychologically (Zilboorg & Henry 1941).

Among Charcot's students was a young Viennese physician named Sigmund Freud. Freud was already deeply interested in the problems of treating severe neurotic conditions and had come to Paris specifically to study under Charcot and learn his hypnotherapy. Upon his return to Vienna, Freud began to work with a colleague's patient, Anna O., a young woman suffering from "hysteria." This patient was a virtual cripple. Anna not only had trouble eating and sleeping, but she also had been suffering from frightening dreams at night and equally frightening delusions during the day. Using Charcot's hypnotic method, Freud enabled Anna to remember certain traumatic events in her earlier life, and as she began to remember those "lost" experiences in her life, her symptoms began to decrease in intensity.

Hypnosis is now beginning to be used in many areas not anticipated by early hypnotists. We will discuss hypnosis and its more modern uses more fully in chapter 11: "Altered States of Consciousness."

Freud: The Development of Psychoanalysis

One day Freud was unable to put Anna into a hypnotic trance. To enable her to work out a dream she had had the previous night, Freud suggested that instead of being hypnotized she speak consciously of everything she was thinking and feeling about her dream. That was the beginning of Freud's method of free association.[1] What Freud had discovered was a "talking cure" for the neuroses of his day.

Eventually Freud enlarged the "talking cure" into the theory and approach of *psychoanalysis*. In the classical form of psychoanalytic treatment, developed by Freud, patients came to the the therapist's office three to five times a week for an hour. Generally they lay down on a couch so they could be comfortable and relaxed and better able to free associate, discuss dreams, and reconstruct daily problems. The analyst sat behind the patient. The dark brown leather couch came to be a classic symbol of the psychoanalytic method.

Sullivan: The Interpersonal Approach

Psychoanalysis, transplanted to the United States in the twenties and thirties, was essentially more suited to the European aristocrat with plenty of time and money. Moreover, the American psychoanalyst Harry Stack Sullivan advanced the idea that a person who enters psychoanalytic psychotherapy is not necessarily ill or sick but is, more simply, experiencing difficulties in interpersonal relationships (Sullivan 1953).

With Sullivan, American psychoanalysis became analytic psychotherapy, or

In psychoanalysis, the patient lies back in a comfortable and relaxed manner so that he or she may "free associate" thoughts that come to mind. The patient is instructed not to censor but to allow any repressed thoughts to surface.

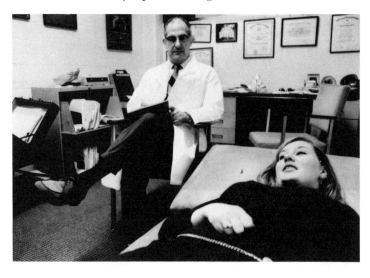

depth psychotherapy, and a more practical, weekly event in which two persons—the therapist (not "doctor") and the patient (or person)—sat together for an hour speaking to each other. The person no longer lay down on a couch, and the therapist was in full view rather than, as in psychoanalysis, seated behind the patient. Since the person was not required to come to the therapy several times a week, this approach also placed the therapy within the financial reach of many who could not otherwise afford psychoanalysis.

Rogers: The Client-Centered Approach

Carl Rogers took this idea even further. He even eliminated the word *patient* and replaced it with the word *client*. Carl Rogers said that all persons have a "healthy" aspect that influences them to find their own directions and conclusions. The therapist's role, in Rogers's approach, is to act not as a *doctor* but as a *sounding board*, to reflect the clients' feelings, thoughts, and concerns so that they can see for themselves what they actually are saying, feeling, and doing. An advantage of Rogers's **client-centered approach** to therapy has been that it encourages persons to grow toward self-direction: to find out for themselves what they want to do and be rather than depending solely on the judgments of their therapist. Rogers believed that when people come to trust their *own* perceptions, *own* feelings, *own* thoughts, they come also to *value* themselves as a reliable center of consciousness capable of deciding what to do with their lives (Rogers 1951). (See box 7.2.)

Group Therapy

In group psychotherapy a therapist (or a number of therapists) meets with a number of persons once a week for one to several hours at a time. In group therapy, group members interact not only with the therapist but with each other; in fact, part of the therapist's function is to enable the group members to observe their own and others' behaviors and to encourage them to try out behaviors with each other that are more satisfactory to them personally. The group itself may vary from as few as five to as many as ten or twelve or even twenty persons. The group members develop close relationships, similar to those in a family. But unlike family relationships, the group members are not forced to live with each other day in and day out, so the conflicts within the therapy group have time to heal between sessions. A young man suffering from resentment of his parents is thus enabled to work on those resentments in the group as he interacts with his peers and older members of the group. Likewise, an older person is able to appreciate the young man's difficulties without having to be the object of his resentment. Through many kinds of interchanges (discussion, questioning, listening, nonverbal communication, even violent disagreement), the group members gradually develop insight into their own difficulties. They also come to appreciate the problems of other group members, and it often is a relief just to know that other persons have problems—that we are not alone! Members not only learn to share the group's

Box 7.2

CARL ROGERS: CHARACTERISTICS OF PERSONS WHO UNDERGO THERAPY

FROM	TOWARD
1. Talks about problems *or* cannot define problems; aware of symptoms but unable to see any connection between symptoms and headaches: "I don't know why I have headaches—they just happen."	1. Insight into how behavior creates problems: "My headaches occur when I have to go to my husband's social functions."
2. Highly self-critical; critical of environment and others: "I'm no good!" "They're impossible to work for."	2. More positive about self and others; accepts self "as is": "He has his problems like everyone else."
3. Fixated on past unhappiness and history: "I had an unhappy childhood."	3. More focused on present, the here and now: "I'm trying to work myself out of the knot I've got myself into."
4. Behavior is defensive and reactive to others' opinions and desires: "But my family wouldn't like it."	4. More willing to act on own feelings and desires. Acts more independently: "My decision may distress my family but I think they'll see the reasonableness of it."
5. Large perceived difference between "real" self and "ideal" self. "People see me as happy go lucky. I hide my true feelings."	5. Sees self as more integrated, less distance between what one really is and what one would like to be: "I am me and if what I am satisfies others, that's fine, if not, that's too bad."
6. More either-or, black-white thinking: "My mother is a bitch."	6. More differentiated perceptions, can see "grays": "Sometimes she is irritable."
7. Sees self and world as fixed, unalterable; problems are permanent: "There's no use even trying. The cards are stacked against me."	7. Sees self, world, others as more loose, fluid. The world does not lock one in; there are possibilities for change: "I'm beginning to see possibilities for future advancement."

SOURCE: Adapted from Carl Rogers, *Client-Centered Therapy* (Boston: Houghton-Mifflin Co., 1951).

attention with their peers but also can share vicariously in the work each group member does on his or her particular difficulties. For that reason a person may come to a group for many weeks, even months, sit quietly, and not seem to do any therapeutic work on his or her own difficulties, yet *still improve markedly*.

There finally is the matter of cost: An hour of group therapy costs about one-fourth the fee for an hour of individual therapy, which means that many persons can afford the group experience who would not be able to consider individual psychotherapy. When we add up all these advantages and then consider also the advances in the techniques of group interaction in the last thirty-five years, it is easy to see why group therapy is so popular and why the demand for it continues to grow.

Summary: A Shift in Paradigms

From the foregoing discussion, the reader may have become aware of the change that has come about in the last several decades. We have made a paradigm shift. Formerly the therapeutic situation was limited to those who were considered sick and could not function in society. Now we understand the therapeutic situation as beneficial for any person wishing to explore his present involvements and work toward more creative ways of living in the world.

The medical model with its "model of psychiatrists-physicians" who have "a patient" with "symptoms" and "sickness" has evolved into a nonmedical model in which both the therapist and the person seeking further self-understanding work together in mutual respect. In the medical model the physician is the authority and diagnoses, treats, and pronounces the person as "cured" or "able to function"—"The doctor knows best." The nonmedical model emphasizes two persons working together with mutual respect and regard for each others' strengths and limitations. The therapist does *not* know what is best for the person—only the person wishing to increase his or her awareness and understanding can make the decision. (See box 7.3.)

What, then, is the benefit gained from the nonmedical model and the therapist who refrains from giving interpretations or telling the person what to do? Namely this: The therapist is "tuned in" to the person at a very deep level in a way that everyday friends or families are unable to be. The therapist has no ax to grind, no "moral" to preach, no wanting the person to be this way or that way as families and friends so often do. The therapist has spent many years developing a nonjudgmental, empathetic responsiveness and the ability to refrain from those thousand moral indictments well-intentioned family and friends direct at us. The therapist has learned to walk gently and patiently with the person through moments of tension, fear, doubt, self-recrimination, anger, and depression until the person comes out of the "valley of the shadow" feeling more whole, more integrated, more self-trusting, and more open to the possibilities of living.

Berne and Harris: Transactional Analysis

Transactional Analysis was founded and formulated by a psychiatrist, Eric Berne (Berne 1961), and has been popularly translated by a psychologist, Thomas Harris (Harris 1969). Transactional Analysis takes its name from its therapeutic approach, namely, to analyze any verbal or nonverbal **transaction** that occurs between two

Box 7.3

TWO MODELS OF PSYCHOTHERAPY: A SHIFT AWAY FROM THE MEDICAL MODEL

	THE MEDICAL MODEL	THE COUNSELING (NON MEDICAL) MODEL
Person seeking help	Is a patient; presents a list of symptoms.	Is a person with problems who wants to deal with them more effectively.
Therapist	Is a physician so diagnoses the disorder or neurosis.	Not a physician so does not diagnose.
Assumption #1	Some people are "sick" and need therapeutic treatment; others are "well" and do not need treatment.	We all have problems: Life itself is problematic. Almost everyone can benefit from the self-exploration and insight.
Assumption #2	The "doctor" is the authority: the patient is "treated." "The doctor knows best."	The therapist and the person work together in a more facilitative interaction. The therapist does *not* know best.
Assumption #3	The "doctor" understands what is wrong: is in best position to diagnose and prescribe for patient.	The person must come to own understandings, make own decisions. The therapist works with the person as he/she gets in touch with his/her own center of growth.

persons from moment to moment. Within all of us, explained Berne, there is a complex of three psychic states, the *exteropsyche*, the *neopsyche*, and the *archaeopsyche*, which have been simplified to the *parent-ego* state, the *adult-ego* state, and the *child-ego* state. The three ego states develop separately and at different times. Moreover, they seem to operate distinctly within the human personality. (See box 7.4.)

THE CHILD-EGO STATE. The child-ego state is the primary psychic state and, according to TA theorists, begins at the moment life begins—at conception. This state encompasses all the drives, needs, and impulses of the internal biological organism. At the psychological level, it is the *feeling* aspect of the personality. The child-ego state, then, is a complex of everything we have ever felt, wanted, tasted, smelled, and experienced as children, both the positive and negative aspects of our sensory and emotional awareness. We retain the child-ego state all our lives, no matter how mature and "adult" we may become.

The child in us has both its constructive and destructive elements. As a constructive element in our psychic makeup, the child-ego state represents our creative spontaneity (a child is spontaneous), our drive to venture out into the world (a child is adventurous), and our ability to laugh with joy, delight, and enthusiasm (for that is the essence of childhood). The child in us also has its negative aspects:

Box 7.4

OUR THREE EGO STATES: TRANSACTIONAL ANALYSIS

CHILD-EGO STATE	PARENT-EGO STATE	ADULT-EGO STATE
PERMANENT DATA		

Internal events:
  Desires
  Bodily needs
  Curiosity: exploratory
    needs
  Feelings
  Discover: experimental
    from birth to five
    years
	External events:
	  Admonitions
	  Dos and don'ts: all the
	    how tos
	  All verbal and
	    nonverbal
	      messages from
	      adults (birth to five
	      years) recorded as
	      TRUTHS
		Internal/External events:
		  Information gathering
		  Thinking: evaluating
		  Open-ended judgments
		  Predicting
		  Recommending

WHEN OVERDOMINANT		
Always in the grip of *feelings*—anger, tears, sadness, irrational fears	Uncreative: unquestioning Inhibited: rigid Opinionated: narrow- minded	Too "studied" Lack of spontaneity
WHEN USED CONSTRUCTIVELY		

Motivation: creativity
Excitement: growth
	Productive habits
	Life saving: Time saving
		Is what I felt and thought
		  as a child still
		  applicable?

PHYSICAL CLUES		

Quivering lip: tears
Temper
High-pitched voice
Shrugging shoulders
Rolling eyes: downcast
  eyes
Teasing: nose thumbing
Delight: giggling
Raising hand for
  permission
	Furrowed brow
	Pursed lips
	Pointing index finger
	Foot tapping: wringing
	  hands
	Hands on hips
	Arms folded across chest
	Tongue clucking: clearing
	  throat
	Sighing
		Listening attitude
		Thoughtful
		Interested in what person
		  is saying
		Unperturbed

VERBAL CLUES		
I wish I guess I want I don't know I don't care	Always . . . Never . . . How many times . . . You make me mad . . . If it weren't for you . . .	Let me see if I understand this . . . Who? What? Where? When? Why?

Source: Adapted from Thomas Harris, *I'm O.K.—You're O.K.* (New York: Harper & Row Publishers, Inc., 1969).

our sulkiness (no one can be as sulky as a child), our temper tantrums (those "terrible two" years), and our resentments and frustrations (the child's reaction to the "nos" of society). In other words, they include all those negative emotions and feelings that we have as children.

THE PARENT-EGO STATE. The parent-ego state begins to develop, said Berne, at the moment of birth and consists of all the "tapes" of the parents' verbal and nonverbal interactions with the child. In addition, the child is constantly "recording" the interactions ("transactions") of all the significant adults with each other. Thus the child is a kind of tape recorder of the external world around him or her for the first five years of life.

Specifically, the parent-ego state, as it develops in the person, consists of all those spoken rules and regulations of the parents (and older siblings), all the "shoulds" and "should nots," and all the nonverbal gestures, facial expressions, vocal murmurings, and postures peculiar to each of us. The parental role is largely to "socialize" the child, consisting of warnings, prohibitions, proverbs and maxims, injunctions to do something or not to do something, the imperatives "never" and "always," and the everlasting "Let me show you how to do it *right!*" Consequently, the parent-ego state within us is that part of us that says "no," "it can't be done," "watch out," or "mark my words"—the fears, concerns, and guards we develop as we grow up. The child is naturally impulsive and head-strong. The parent-ego state is the accumulation of 5000 years of maxims and admonitions. Without them, a child might never survive childhood.

THE ADULT-EGO STATE. Berne believed that the adult-ego state begins at about ten months of age, for it is then that the child is becoming autonomous—learning to crawl and generally able to get around on its own. The ten-month-old child is beginning to manipulate objects deliberately, to feed itself, to begin to point to things it wants, and so on. The adult-ego state is different from the parent-ego state in that the latter is "borrowed" from others and is introjected whole and without question. The adult-ego state is the "data-processing computer" that integrates the several sources of information coming to us. The *feelings* within that are the child-ego state: the *rules* and *regulations* prescribed and recorded by the parent-ego state and the *understandings* we gain in our adult-ego state. If our adult-ego state is working well, then our distortions from childhood are "corrected" as we get older. Thus if we are carrying a memory of resentment of our parents as the result of a disciplining, our adult-ego state allows us to form a new understanding of the events of that "terrible injustice," and we come to forgive our parents for the deed.

Still all three ego states are present within us, since all the recordings are permanent. We cannot erase them. Furthermore, if two people are talking together, six ego states can be conversing with each other. To put it more simply, when two persons are having a verbal transaction, they may interact as if six different persons are talking with each other. As an oversimplified example, let us imagine a verbal interaction between a husband and a wife:

HUSBAND: (*operating in adult state*) What happened to my cuff links?
WIFE: (*operating defensively in child state*) How would I know where they are!
HUSBAND: (*operating reprovingly in parent state*) Because you borrowed them, and I knew you wouldn't put them back!
WIFE: (*operating in "bad news" parent state*) Just like all men, you always blame things on women!

HUSBAND: (*operating now in his child state*) Oh, so now you're on a women's lib kick!
WIFE: (*suddenly emerging in her adult state*) I'm being silly! I guess I meant to put them back and didn't. I must have put them in my jewelry box. I'll come upstairs and look.
HUSBAND: (*now returning to his adult state*) I guess I got my back up, too. Don't bother to come upstairs, I'm right here! Yeah, here they are.

Berne's group-therapy attempts to enable each member of the group to recognize when he or she is being child or parent or adult, and to use each ego state appropriately: the child-ego state for emotional spontaneity and creativity; the parent-ego state for caution at undue risk-taking; and the adult-ego state for rational decision-making.

Berne said that the advantage of Transactional Analysis is that other approaches can take a long time to effect change, while TA is something the person is able to utilize immediately, by learning quickly to tolerate the anxieties of the past and to control the acting-out-behaviors so characteristic of the child and which are self-destructive.

Perls: Gestalt Therapy

The essence of Transactional Analysis is freeing ourselves from our games and other ritualistic behaviors. Another therapy that seeks to do the same thing is gestalt therapy, formulated by Frederick (Fritz) Perls, a psychiatrist who trained many persons in this approach. It was Perls's contention that wo do not operate as an integrated whole; that we have splits in our personality. We act out these splits in a constant struggle between our "top dog" and our "underdog." These two roles represent our parents, who vied with each other for authority and dominance in the family unit, and which we have introjected within our personality. Do not be misled by the terms for these forces within ourselves, for while the top dog often is the louder and more aggressive aspect of our personality, the underdog has powerful manipulative devices to get its own way—devices such as *martyrdom, weakness*, and *coyness*, which topple the top dog fairly frequently.

Since we have these "splits" in our personalities, we tend to manipulate others into positions of top dog while we act as underdog (or vice versa). The aim of gestalt therapy is to enable the person to see the splits within the self and how they have been projected onto others. In that way the person is able to become more "whole," which is precisely the meaning of *gestalt*.

THE FIGURE-GROUND RELATIONSHIP. According to gestalt psychology, we need to become aware of our sensory-experiencing as it changes from moment to moment, so that the meaning of the *figure* (what is occurring in the foreground of our consciousness) can be understood in relation to the *background* (all the possible stimuli in the environment to which we are not paying attention). When we can see both the *figure* and the *ground*, we have accomplished a complete *gestalt;* that is, at that moment we understand ourselves in relation to the world. The theory behind gestalt therapy is difficult to comprehend by reading about it (as you are now doing). Perhaps the theory will be easier to grasp by giving you a taste of gestalt therapy. The following is an actual therapy session with Dr. Perls himself, as it took place early in his professional career in the United States, and of which we were a part.

A gestalt-therapy session. In this group was a pert and attractive young woman (let us call her Miss Y) who came into the group with a smile and a hello for each of the other members of the group, almost all of whom were men. The group had not "started" yet, for Perls frequently allowed the therapy to evolve out of the situational "happenings" (often much to the surprise and consternation of the group members, who felt "caught unawares"). Mr. X, one of the group members, made a seemingly joking remark to the young woman, Miss Y, that went something like: "I see you are being your usual flirtatious self." The attention of most of us was immediately riveted on Miss Y, but Perls turned his attention to Mr. X.

PERLS: What do you "see," Mr. X, when you look at Miss Y?
MR. X: (somewhat startled by Perls' attention) I was just making a joke!
PERLS: Let us examine your "joke." What do you "see" when you look at Miss Y?
MR. X: I really didn't mean anything by the remark—it was just a remark.
PERLS: Would you direct your attention to Miss Y now?
MR. X: Sure.
PERLS: What do you "see"?
MR. X: I see a pretty, kind of flirtatious girl, that's all.
PERLS: Would you direct your remarks to her? (Perls always asked the group members to talk *to* a person, not talk *about* the person—which he called gossiping.)
MR. X: She heard me.
PERLS: We don't allow "gossip"; please direct your remark to Miss Y.
MR. X: All right, if you say so. Miss Y, I see you as being a very flirtatious person.
PERLS: What are you experiencing now, Mr. X?
MR. X: I'm looking at Miss Y, that's all.
PERLS: By experiencing, we mean what is going on in your body.
MR. X: You mean inside me?
PERLS: Ja!
MR. X: Well, my heart is pounding. You've made me nervous.
PERLS: (after some silence) Go on . . . what else do you experience?
MR. X: I'm feeling angry.
PERLS: Could you act out your anger?
MR. X: What?
PERLS: Could you act our your anger? Could you say what is making you angry at Miss Y?
MR. X: I don't know.
PERLS: Would you be willing to try?
MR. X: I don't know . . . maybe.
PERLS: Let us "see" your "maybe."
MR. X: Maybe I will; maybe I won't . . . Yeah, I guess I will. (to Miss Y) You make me mad!
PERLS: Could you tell her more how mad you are?
MR. X: I don't know. (To Miss Y) I get mad at women who flirt around with men.
PERLS: Could you tell Miss Y that you would like her to flirt with you?
MR. X: (suddenly very loud and obviously angry) Why should I! I resent her flirtatiousness. It's manipulative.

PERLS: Would you play Miss Y being manipulative?

MR. X: You mean act like Miss Y?

PERLS: (nods)

MR. X: I don't know if I can . . . All right, I will. (He then takes on a "female" voice and smiles to various persons in the room, saying "Good morning, dear" to each person. Although he does not do a very good job of imitating Miss Y, there is something authentic about his female impersonation.)

PERLS: Could you tell us who says "Good morning, dear" like that?

MR. X: Why, Miss Y, whenever she comes in the room.

PERLS: You didn't hear me. Who says, "Good morning, dear" to you like that? (It has become obvious to the rest of us that we have never heard Miss Y use that particular phrase when she greets us.)

MR. X: I don't know what you mean.

PERLS: Could you exaggerate "Good morning, dear."

MR. X: Good morning dear. Good Morning, DEAR! GOOD MORNING, DEAR! (He is speaking very loudly now, almost screaming, and his face is red. He seems to all of us to be genuinely angry.) GOOD MORNING! GOOD MORNING! GOOD MORNING!
(The room is very quiet now after this—a few moments of intense silence.)

PERLS: What is going on now?

MR. X: (He is visibly shaken, and it takes a few moments for him to respond.) That was my mother talking. She always said that to us when she came into the room.

PERLS: Go on.

MR. X: I can just see her, the bitch! (There follows here a rather involved session in which Perls requests Mr. X to act out each member of the family on one of these occasions: his mother, his father, his brother, and himself. After almost twenty minutes of this "role playing," Perls has Mr. X return his attention to Miss Y.)

PERLS: Can you look at Miss Y now?

MR. X: Sure.

PERLS: What are you seeing?

MR. X: I see Miss Y (then after a few moments) I also still see my mother. It's like a double image.

PERLS: Ah! Can you put your mother into the corner of the room?

MR. X: You mean in my imagination? (Perls nods) . . . O.K., she's over there in the brown chair.

PERLS: Now regard, if you please, your mother in the brown chair. Can you see her clearly?

MR. X: Yeah.

PERLS: Now look at Miss Y, and see if you can see her clearly.

MR. X: Not very. She looks a little fuzzy.

PERLS: Ah. Now, try to shuttle between the brown chair to Miss Y and back again until you can see them both very clearly.

MR. X: O.K. (He spends a lot of time "shuttling" his gaze from the chair to Miss Y and back again).

MR. X: She's gone now.

PERLS: Who?

MR. X: My mother. She's faded out.

PERLS: Now look at Miss Y, please.

MR. X: Yeah, I can see her pretty good now. She's sitting there . . . (correcting himself) You're sitting there looking at me, Miss Y. (Miss Y nods.)

PERLS: What is your experience?

MR. X: I'm not angry anymore, at least not at Miss Y. My heart's still pounding a little, but I feel calmer. (To Miss Y) I guess you're not as flirtatious as I thought.

This particular dialogue illustrates many gestalt principles and techniques of which we can illustrate only a few. First, let us examine Mr. X's figure-ground relationship. The figure in this situation was Miss Y's appearance in the room and her greetings to the group members. The ground was Mr. X's background of his mother and his family interactions, of which he was unaware when he reacted to Miss Y's behavior as he did (his joking about her flirtatiousness, his acting out what he assumed to be her behavior, his first angry words to her). Because Mr. X was unaware of his ground, he also was unaware that his reactions to Miss Y were based on his own private history. He had *projected* on her his own unresolved difficulties with his mother and the sibling rivalry with his brother. Whether or not Miss Y was actually flirting with the group members was inconsequential. What was important was Mr. X's "double image," how he "saw" Miss Y even in his very first statement, and how he was able to "see" her more neutrally afterwards.

The shuttling technique, demonstrated here, was one of the ways in which Perls enabled the person to "see" both the figure and the ground in proper perspective and to separate one from the other. Another principle of gestalt therapy is to stay with the *phenomenology* of the person: what he or she is experiencing "within"—bodily processes such as Mr. X's awareness of his heart pounding and also his faculty of sight, which in this instance became an important part of the therapy. (At one point, his vision actually became fuzzy.) Another aspect of the gestalt approach is the acting-out of intrapersonal conflict—in this situation Mr. X's anger with his mother and sibling rivalry with his brother.

Finally, you will note that during the therapy session there is very little, if any, interpretation about what is going on. Perls declined to let Mr. X "intellectualize" his phenomenology; instead, he was encouraged to act it out, exaggerate it, and "be it." At the end of the therapeutic session, there was no discussion of his "problems" and no "interpretations." It was enough that Mr. X had become aware of his dualism, what he chose to do with that awareness was not Perls's concern.

Other transcripts of Perls's therapeutic sessions can be found in *Gestalt Therapy Verbatim* (1967[a]), and there are several books by students of Perls. Perls also wrote an unorthodox and fascinating autobiography, *In and Out of the Garbage Pail* (1967[b]), in which he reveals his own top dog and underdog in all their frank dimensions.

THREE THERAPIES DIRECTED SPECIFICALLY TOWARD BEHAVIORAL CHANGE

In the therapies we have discussed, the aim is *insight*, on the assumption that insight leads to change in behavior. The therapies we will discuss now have behavioral change *as a specific objective*. You have already encountered one such therapeutic approach in Wolpe's deconditioning therapy in chapter 6. The objective of that method is to enable the person to face the feared situation (or phobia) under relaxed fantasy conditions and then to face the feared event in the "real-life situation."

Implosive Therapy Stamfl:

Implosive therapy is similar to Wolpe's desensitization therapy in that it forces the person to confront his or her phobic objects and dreaded fantasies. Implosive therapy differs from Wolpe's therapy fantasies in one noticeable way. In the beginning of Wolpe's treatment, the person is asked to relax until he or she can imagine the feared situation in its *least anxiety-provoking* aspect. Then gradually the person builds up his or her ability to face the next level of anxiety-provoking stimuli until finally the *most-feared* stimulus can be confronted. Wolpe's therapy is not only a *deconditioning*, it is also a gradual *reconditioning* so that the person feels more and more confident of his or her ability to deal with the situation.

In contrast to the gradual process of Wolpe's approach, implosive therapy presents the anxiety-provoking stimulus right at the beginning *in its most intense form*. The therapist literally floods the person with anxiety-provoking stimuli. On first watching this kind of therapy, it may seem extremely cruel. The therapist bombards the person with a steady stream of talk about the terrible things the person fears most. The person may sob, cry, scream, and writhe in agony while the therapy is going on, which may take between thirty and forty-five minutes. Of course, if the person wants, he or she may choose to leave the room and never come back. But we must remember that the person has been informed of the therapeutic approach ahead of time so it has not been sprung unannounced. The proponents of implosive therapy add that if the person can endure the treatment, in spite of the terrible anxiety, there is often a sudden collapse of the whole feared phobia or anxiety syndrome (Storms 1976). Patients have frequently remarked that their whole defense system has suddenly collapsed, and along with it the fear or phobia. It is, of course, exhausting for both the therapist and the person and takes a particular kind of individual to utilize this approach.

Wolpe has criticized this approach, and we certainly do not recommend it for the faint-hearted! Nevertheless, it seems to have worked for persons who have tried several other approaches to no avail.

We do not want to imply that one exposure to implosive therapy is adequate for the collapse of the feared situation or fantasy—although implosive therapists say it often is just that fast! Sometimes the person may need two or three exposures, even several, before the fear completely dissolves. The person often is told to do some "homework" by imagining the feared situation on his or her own through the week.

A Modified Implosive Approach

Some therapists have adapted the implosive-therapy approach, which prompted T. G. Stamfl, its founder, to decry the "watering down" of his method (Stamfl & Lewis 1967). Despite Stamfl's protest, we have developed a more moderate (even "watered down") version of this approach to enable persons to overcome a particular problem. We now describe this adaptation.

Each of us has had certain "signal reactions" to something we have been called by others. The appellations may be racially and ethnically prejudicial, or they may be more personally insulting and call attention to a particular aspect of our physical being. Our family may have tried to prohibit or repress certain behaviors in us, and one of the methods used may have been to give us "tyrannical" names such as "fatso," "stupid," "bossy" (Chase 1966), making us feel inadequate, ashamed, guilty, whatever. The object of them was to get us off balance.

We ask the persons to sit in the center of the group and to tell us a little bit about how their particular tyrannical name affects them. They may describe their feelings of shame, guilt, embarrassment, confusion when the word is directed to them. Then we ask them to relax and to imagine that they are in an invisible, impregnable bubble. They can hear everything that is going on, but nothing can penetrate the bubble. Then we ask all the members of the group to call them by the feared stimulus word, whatever it may be. The group members take turns in the name calling. When the persons indicate that the name calling is arousing negative feelings, we stop the procedure and say something like this:

> In a few minutes, we are going to start the name calling again. But this time, we are going to ask you to visualize something quite obscene but which is going to take the power out of that word. What you need to do is to visualize, every time someone calls you (stimulus word), a giant turd coming out of that person's mouth. For that is all name calling is, somebody else's garbage—not yours. If you can remember to think of those words simply as giant turds, we are going to begin the name calling again! The louder the person shouts the word, the angrier he or she seems, the larger is the turd coming out of that person's mouth. Are you ready? All right, get back into your impregnable bubble again.

With that we begin the procedure all over again, and in a very short time, the persons are smiling, giggling, and laughing. They have achieved a new **gestalt,** and the word has lost its power to tyrannize them.

Ellis: Rational-Emotive Therapy

In a sense, we all use rational-emotive therapy when we are talking to people who are upset or discouraged about something. We try to explain the uselessness of being upset or "buck them up" when they insist there is no way out of their predicament. If they go on and on with their self-sabotage, we try to show them how irrational that kind of thinking is. The difference between this informal level of therapy and what Albert Ellis does is largely a matter of refinement and expertise and the inclusion of a self-management program (Ellis 1974).

Ellis explained that it is not the original situation that creates our feelings of hopelessness and despair. The belief system we attach to it is the real cause of these feelings. Suppose, for example, that a student is having difficulty in her academic and social environment. She complains that she is stupid, that she cannot study, is a worthless person and a "born loser." At this point, Ellis explained, the person has herself all tied up in linguistic knots. Ellis educates his clients in general semantics and explains how their statements are irrational and therefore self-destructive. He has them practice turning their irrational statements into rational ones that objectify the problem. He tells them to stop generalizing by calling themselves names or categorizing themselves. (We have just discussed how *others* try to tyrannize us with words. What Ellis pointed out is how *we* tyrannize ourselves with labels.) He might ask our hypothetical student what she means by "stupid" and would it not be more rational to say simply that she has not yet learned how to study? What does she mean by "worthless?" Would it not be better to say that sometimes she feels discouraged, as we all do? In other words, he encourages the student to apply semantics to her self-reference system.

Ellis also starts the person on a program of self-management. If the student is failing math, Ellis may advise her to go out and find a tutor. He may give her some lessons on how to study and a study schedule that would start her studying thirty minutes a day with a gradual increase in the allotted time up to an hour or more a day. Ellis incorporates any technique into his method that will enable the client to manage his life more efficiently. The keynote in Ellis's rational-emotive therapy is DO IT. All the self-understanding and insight in the world will not get us to our goal without ACTION. People are instructed to go out and practice what they have discussed. Not only that, they must come back the following week and report on their activities!

If the first week's session has dealt with the student's tyrannical self-labeling as "stupid," the second week might be devoted to her calling herself a "born loser." Ellis insists on asking, what does that mean? The student answers that she does not have any friends, that she does not know how to make friends, and nobody wants her for a friend. Ellis may glance sternly at the young woman and ask her quite bluntly to describe how she has gone out and tried to make friends! Somewhat perplexed, the student may say that she does not go out much, in fact, she spends most of the time in her room watching television. "Well," demands Ellis, "How can you make friends when you spend your time watching television? You are not even trying!" Some RET therapists may order the person to take the television out of her room and use the time she normally spends watching it in some kind of social activity. Ellis said that the therapist may have to act as a kind of mother hen, social counselor, teacher, anything to direct the person's energies toward the kind of competence the client is lacking. In this situation, Ellis might ask the student what she likes to do. Our hypothetical student responds that she used to like to bowl, and she likes to go to the movies. Whom does she go with? questions Ellis. Actually, the student replies, she does not bowl anymore, and she generally goes to the movies alone.

Having this kind of information, Ellis and the student make a plan of social change and activity. The student will approach a person with whom she would like to make friends and suggest going to the movies. What if the person turns her down? asks the student. Go on to the next possible candidate for friendship. Also on the week's agenda the student is to investigate bowling alleys and bowling tournaments and report back.

All of this may sound very pragmatic and like nothing that anyone of us could not do. To a certain degree that is so, but most of us offer advice and leave the person to his or her own devices for better or worse. The RET therapist is willing to use any action, technique, theoretical approach, or whatever to enable the person to effect change.

Glasser: Reality Therapy

Reality therapy was formulated some thirty to forty years ago with the objective of enabling the person to overcome *failure*. Like RET, reality therapy stresses *doing*. The psychologist who developed reality therapy, William Glasser, did so to enable persons to overcome their feelings of failure (Glasser 1967). As a psychiatric resident at a veterans' hospital, he was struck by the number of people who were (in their own eyes and in the eyes of others) "losers" and "failures," such as the alcoholic, the mentally disturbed, the delinquent, and the chronically unemployed. Glasser noticed that one of the characteristics of "failures" is that they tend to bemoan their fate but to avoid the responsibility for it. Glasser's specific complaint was that although there was a lot of therapy, it was simply talk and not much action. Glasser is a man of action.

The questions directd to the person in therapy are as follows: *What are you doing about your problem? What did you do last week? What do you plan to do today when you leave here? What do you think you could do before you come back to see me next week?* These kinds of questions are a constant refrain in reality therapy.

If the client in reality therapy insists that he or she has no choices the therapy then may be to suggest alternative paths of action. Glasser emphasizes that much reality therapy is done by planning responsible behavior. This planning must not be overly ambitious, for that will simply invite more failure, which is just the pattern of behavior that needs to be avoided. If one plan does not work, another is tried.

Sometimes contracts are drawn up between the therapist and the person to motivate the person to work at his or her commitment. One of Glasser's convictions is that many problems are caused by people not living up to their contracts: Thus friendships are broken; employees are fired; parents and children find themselves at loggerheads—because people break their interpersonal contracts. A typical contract in reality therapy for an adolescent and parent might be something like this: If the adolescent cleans her room once a week, the parent will not nag about room cleaning for the rest of the week. Or it might be: If the youngster agrees to go to school (not skip for one week), the parent will agree to give him one late night out on the weekend. It is an exchange of fair play.

No excuses are accepted for breaking the contract, but there also are no judgments or punishments. Rather, there is a redetermination of a plan of action, a new contract, and a new commitment. Glasser does not believe in punishment, since that is precisely what the delinquent, alcoholic, or "born loser" is seeking. If the adolescent does not live up to the contract, he has broken the contract so that the parent also does not have to allow him one night out late or use of the car. Thus, Glasser believes, the adolescent begins to realize that his behavior has consequences.

Reality therapy has been quite effective with delinquents, but Glasser is most concerned with the use of reality therapy as preventive education. He would like to see it incorporated in the school system from elementary school to high school and believes that when young people begin to understand that successful adult living is to set goals (first small goals and then larger ones), and then to accomplish those goals, they then may avoid failure altogether.

OTHER THERAPIES

There are other types of therapies. Some may raise eyebrows simply by being mentioned, such as George Bach's "fight therapy" (Bach & Wyden 1969).

There is a therapy called *est*, founded and headed by a man who calls himself Gerhard Werner. The training consists of a grueling four-day marathon in which the participants go through a kind of endurance test. They are insulted, ordered about, verbally humiliated, and so forth, until their whole defensive gestalt system collapses, and they have nowhere else to go but up. The description of *est* sounds similar to implosive therapy except that it uses the group situation rather than the individual situation, and the treatment is not personal but includes all the group members.

In addition to these more forceful therapies are the intradynamic therapies such as art therapy, Ira Progoff's diary therapy (Progoff 1975), and Assagioli's psychosynthesis approach (Assagioli 1976). Progoff developed some interesting ways for people to analyze their current situation by writing about their life history and their present process. It is essentially the novelist's process but no less valid because of it. Assagioli's approach is, admittedly, a desire to integrate the emotional-intellectual-spiritual point of view. Art therapy is another way to delve into one's psychic symbolism and is very close to dream therapy as a path toward self-understanding (Kramer 1977).

APPLICATIONS AND COPING TECHNIQUES

We have tried to be objective in our discussions of various therapeutic approaches. The reader, however, will want to know how to assess the therapies and how they can be used for his or her personal benefit and professional career. To answer these questions, we offer the following considerations.

1. For the Person Who Experiences Occasional Bouts of Anxiety or Depression

If you have experienced the kinds of feelings described in the earlier part of this chapter, you may be wondering if you are a "closet" manic-depressive or a catatonic personality. Many students do have these kinds of thoughts when they begin to study some of the emotional patternings we described early in the chapter. It is a kind of "intern's disease" (in which the young medical student believes that he or she has several of the esoteric diseases studied in pathology courses). Only this time it refers to psychological symptomology.

In all probability, you are experiencing the usual everyday difficulties of coping with life. Being a student is not easy. You are doing your best to study. Many of you are working. You all are concerned about your finances. And you are interacting with many persons at an intimate social level. Many of you also are trying to take care of a family. College is stressful. Besides coming out as physical symptoms, the stress will come out in bouts of alienation and depression. That does not mean you are seriously emotionally disturbed. It does mean that you may need to slack off a little, rethink what you are doing and congratulate yourself on your accomplishments thus far, and get some needed rest and relaxation.

The truth is that all of us, no matter how integrated we may believe ourselves to be, from time to time have days when life seems more than we can handle. We even may fall into despair and lie on our beds for hours rather than get up and face the day. At these times, it is best to adopt the Taoist philosophy that all things are always changing—always in process. This problem will pass, so too will our lethargy and anxiety. All is ebb and flow. As we look back at our lives, we see that this is so; most of the things we worried about never happened and most of the problems we encountered were solved, and we were better persons for having gone through them. Just remember that we do not have to be adjusted all the time. We do not *always* have to cope successfully.

2. But Suppose That You Think It Is More Serious than an Occasional Inability to Cope!

Suppose you do think you have a long-standing problem, what can you do? Well, most cities usually have a counseling center where you can go, no matter what your finances are. Your own college or university probably has counselors who can help you sort out some of your difficulties. Very frequently it takes only a few sessions to "sort out your head" and for things to become more manageable. It is one of the blessings of these days, that no one thinks you "have to be crazy to see a shrink!" Those days are long past. It is better to process some of the unresolved problems that bother you than to suffer them needlessly. Just being able to talk about the things that are troubling you is helpful. The problems may still be there, but having someone with whom you can discuss them gives you the strength and support you need to see them from a more objective point of view.

3. Choosing Your First Group Therapy: Let Your Head Be Your Guide

The reader may very well be feeling rather bewildered at the vast array of therapeutic approaches. How does one go about choosing an approach for oneself or to use in one's profession with patients or in educating adults and children? If you are looking for your first experience in the encounter groups, we can offer no better guide than Everett Shostrom's article entitled "Let the Buyer Beware."

First, never respond to a newspaper advertisement. The encounter group leader should be a qualified professional who probably would not resort to newspaper advertising, which is not considered professional.

Second, do not participate in a group with fewer than six participants. Too small a group will not give a person "breathing room." The interpersonal dynamics can become so strong as to be almost overwhelming at times.

Third, do not enter an encounter group on impulse. Your decision should be made after thoughtful consideration.

Fourth, be cautious about participating in a group with close associates. You need all the privacy you can get, and strangers will not interfere with your privacy when you go home. Of course, there are exceptions to this rule. If you and a spouse are having marital problems and want to enroll in a Masters and Johnson sex therapy clinic, you go together. But in other situations it is a lot easier to discuss problems with a group of strangers just as some of us have had the experience on a long train or plane ride of a deep encounter with a perfect stranger.

Fifth, do not be fooled by attractive surroundings. The experience of the encounter group is an inner one.

Sixth, never stay with a group that has a particular ax to grind or an ideology that seeks converts. You want a broadly based experience so that you can choose your own path.

Seventh, never participate in a group that is not allied with some sort of professional group. Professional qualifications are the safest bet that you will receive expert leadership. [Shostrom 1969]

4. Before You Commit Yourself to a Therapist, Have an Exploratory Session

No enlightened person would be operated on without knowing who the surgeon is or what is to be done. Nor would you ever turn your car over to any mechanic with a blank check to fix it. In both situations you want information about the person you are hiring to help you. You want to know how he or she approaches the diagnosis and treatment of the problem at hand. You have the same right to know in regard to a therapist. Consider your first visit an exploratory one. Find out the therapist's basic philosophy of the therapeutic situation. How does he or she work with people? Does he or she belong to one specific therapeutic school? Or is the therapist eclectic, using many approaches. We, ourselves, shy away from sticking too rigidly to any one approach, but there are certain problems that seem to be benefited more by one approach than another. As you talk with the therapist, ask yourself if you feel comfortable with him or her. Does he or she seem to have *respect* for you? Is the therapist intimidating? Does he or she listen carefully to what you are saying and seem to withhold hasty judgments? When you leave, do you feel as if you have a sense of relaxation—that *here* is a person you can talk to, without embarrassment, without fear, without being morally "judged"?

Of course, it may take a few weeks before you can reveal the deepest and most fearful thoughts or events of your life. Such self-revealing takes time. But certainly by the end of the first session you should have some feeling that here is someone you can trust sufficiently so that you can begin that process of unravelling the threads of your present situation.

If you come away without some lightening of your burden or some insight, then our suggestion is to find someone else. *The choice is always yours.*

5. For Those Seeking Advanced Professional Training: Enlarge Your Professional Horizon

There are many of you who will be going into highly interpersonal fields. Some may be thinking of clinical psychology or counseling; others may be going into a related field such as one of the health professions or education. Whatever your field, it is worth your while to add to your professional skills as you continue your education. Nurses and dental assistants may not think of themselves primarily as therapists, but they are involved in the therapeutic situation. Healing the body can be improved if we know how to help patients verbalize and deal with their anxieties. Furthermore, there are many so-called apprehensive patients in the dentist's chair. Knowledge and understanding of therapeutic techniques will benefit both the patient and the staff. Persons considering the rehabilitation areas may want to enroll in courses or workshops devoted to specialized approaches like reality therapy or rational-emotive therapy. If you will be working with nonverbal children or adults, you may want to investigate the therapeutic forms of art and music.

As you advance in your professional training, you may want to take advantage of training in gestalt therapy or transactional analysis. Professionals constantly seek to improve their professional qualifications and to enhance their techniques. Furthermore, your own integrity and creativity will expand.

6. Helping Another Person to Grow Requires Recognizing and Working with the Person's Strengths

Carl Rogers emphasized the need of the therapist to *like* the person with whom he or she is working. He called it "unconditional positive regard." But what if we are working with an adolescent or sociopathic personality who is doing everything possible to annoy us or to dodge the real issues? It is difficult to maintain that positive regard when it seems the person is doing everything he or she can to obstruct our attempts to help. First of all, forgive yourself for giving way to momentary fits of irritation or discouragement. Then, try to discover at least one strength or attribute on which you can build. Glasser advises us to relate to the positive aspects of the person's character. If we get too caught up in people's miseries, complaints, or problems, we may simply reinforce their inadequacies, excuses, or limitations. It is better, says Glasser, to deal with them as we would anyone.

A psychiatrist we know is a consultant to a psychiatric ward. An old man of about sixty was brought to the hospital because his depressions had become so severe he had hardly stirred from his small fishing shack and was on the verge of starvation. He was dirty and toothless, and he smelled! Our psychiatrist friend, on learning of the old man's occupation, brought in a large maritime map that included the man's own home territory, spread it out on the bed and asked him for advice on fishing spots in that area. The old man responded instantly, and the two spent several hours in the next two weeks discussing the best fishing areas and types of lures and bait to use, and things of interest to fishermen the world over. The old man responded more to that approach than he had to the medication and "professional" and conventional approaches that had been tried. He left in two weeks and went home considerably brighter in appearance and manner.

We do not want you to think that the old man was cured. He comes back every so often when the world seems a little confusing again. He and the psychiatrist talk about what seems to be bothering him, but both enjoy talking over fishing news as well. With a little medication and a visit every three or four months or so, the old man avoids being put in an institution and becoming a complete invalid.

7. Remember That You Cannot Become a Therapist to the Whole World

As you gain more understanding of psychology and therapy and as you mature and become more compassionate, remember to safeguard your own emotional health. As a matter of fact, if you have chosen one of the interpersonal fields as your future career, the chances are that you are naturally warm and empathetic and that people gravitate to you for sympathy, understanding, counsel, and advice. As you learn professional techniques to enable others to grow, you may find that friends, neighbors, relatives, colleagues, and even people you do not know are knocking on your door for help.

You can do only so much. You cannot become therapist to the whole world. Although you may be personally gratified and even receive a certain amount of ego satisfaction from the attention, the time will inevitably come when you will have to learn to safeguard your own well-being. How can you do this?

First, explain to people that, like all professionals, you have to be cautious about working with people you know. Physicians are counseled not to treat or operate on family and friends. So it is with the helping professions, but what you can do is to *refer* them to agencies and/or specialists in the particular problem area. You might keep your own card file of agencies in your locale or elsewhere. Also keep articles from journals and a list of books that might be helpful. People seeking help will be grateful for even this much direction. You do not have to be the ultimate resource but just the first step in their own search for resources available. You may want to help them more directly, but referring them to the proper agency may be the most helpful thing you can do.

SUMMARY POINTS TO REMEMBER

1. Freud began his psychotherapeutic work using many approaches including hypnosis. Ultimately he abandoned hypnosis for the technique of free association from which the principles of psychoanalysis were drawn.

2. Psychoanalysis has had a few adherents in the United States but was eventually superceded for the most part by the more pragmatic (and economical) task-oriented counseling. Later group counseling made the therapeutic situation even more affordable and within the reach of most Americans.

3. Carl Rogers fostered a non-medical approach with his client-centered therapy. Rogers' therapy rests on the assumption that every person has within him a Center of Growth. The counselor's job is to aid the person in getting back in touch with this Center of Growth.

4. In the sixties and seventies many theories and types of therapy were developed. Eric Berne formulated Transactional Analysis with its constructs of three ego-states within every person: child, parent, and adult. The aim of T. A. is to use each of these ego-states appropriately.

5. Frederick Perls, German refugee psychiatrist from the Nazi regime in the thirties developed Gestalt Therapy. His techniques were swift when dealing with unresolved conflicts from the past and integrating "splits" in our personalities.

6. Some therapies are specifically directed toward behavioral *change* rather than psychological insight. We have already encountered one behavioral therapy, Wolpe's desensitation therapy which was focused specifically on de-conditioning fear and phobia. Related to Wolpe's de-conditioning therapy is implosive therapy which consists of a very intense flooding of a person with the anxiety-provoking stimuli.

7. Albert Ellis' Rational-Emotive Therapy (RET) is a very active approach involving the therapist in a variety of roles; therapist, teacher, coach, role-model: whatever it takes to effect change in the client.

8. William Glasser's Reality Therapy also stresses the doing aspect of behavior change. Working with delinquents, juveniles, alcoholics, and other "born losers," Glasser believes in objectives, goals, contracts—in short, plans of action!

9. All in all, there are many types of therapy: dialogic; behavioral, meditative, art, physical, etc. The reader is urged to consider each therapeutic approach and his or her personality style and individual situation.

SIGNIFICANT TERMS AND CONCEPTS

anal personality
catatonic
client-centered therapy
compulsion
depressive reaction
empathy
free association
hallucinations
hysteria
hysteric personality
implosive therapy

manic-depressive
   personality
multiple personality
obsession
obsessive-compulsive
   personality
oral personality
passive-dependent
   personality
phobic reactions
psychoanalysis

psychopathic
   personality
rational-emotive
   therapy
reality therapy
schizoid personality
schizophrenia
sociopathic personality
suicidal depression
transactional analysis
tyrannical names

FILL IN THE BLANKS WITH SIGNIFICANT TERMS AND CONCEPTS

1. Freud drew his principles of psychoanalysis from his technique of f_____ a_____.
2. Carl Rogers has developed a client-centered therapy that assumes that everyone has a C_____ of G_____ within them.
3. Transactional Analysis was formulated by Eric Berne. He describes three e_____-s_____ within everyone. The three e_____-s_____ are p_____, a_____, and c_____.
4. Wolpe designed desensitization therapy in order to d_____ f_____ and p_____.
5. Active therapeutic approaches include Albert Ellis' R_____-E_____ Therapy and William Glasser's R_____ Therapy.
6. If you are having difficulty resolving conflicts from the past and you seek swift resolve you would benefit from examining Fritz Perls's G_____ Therapy.
7. Some therapies are directed toward b_____ c_____ rather than toward P_____ i_____.

RECOMMENDED BOOKS FOR FURTHER READING

Berne, Eric. 1978. *The Games People Play*. Westminister, MD: Ballantine Books. Inc. We recommend this book of Berne's for all those who want to transcend the deadly "games" people play with each other. Berne doesn't tell us how to transcend our petty and repetitious dramas but he does give us a very good "close-up" of them.

Glasser, William. 1967. *Reality Therapy*. New York: Harper & Row Publishers, Inc. Glasser's own earnestness and humanity is very evident as is Carl Rogers' (see below) as he works his way toward a more effective *change* therapeutically for the "losers" of our society: the delinquent, the alcoholic, the socially or vocationally incompetent. Glasser's more recent book is *Positive Addiction*. New York: Harper & Row Publishers, Inc., 1976.

Harris, Thomas A. 1969. *I'm O.K.—You're O.K.* New York: Harper & Row Publishers, Inc. In highly readable and simple language, Harris lays out the fundamentals of transactional analysis including the child-ego state, the parent-ego state, and the adult-ego state.

Perls, Frederick S. 1967[a]. *Gestalt Therapy Verbatim*. John A. Stevens, ed. Lafayette, CA: Real People Press. This book is a series of transcribed tapes of Perls's actual therapeutic sessions while he was at our most famous growth center, Esalon, in Big Sur, California. The principles are amply demonstrated and it is a very good primer of this approach, gestalt therapy.

Rogers, Carl R. 1951. *Client-Centered Therapy*. Boston: Houghton Mifflin Company. For those who are interested in the non-medical approach to therapy (i.e. the humanistic approach).

Schreiber, Flora Rheta. 1973. *Sybil*. Chicago: Henry Regnery Company. One of the most extreme examples of multiple personalities yet reported is to be found in this book. With a schizophrenic and sadistic mother who abused her to the point of amnesiac retreat, Sybil was able to manage the physical and psychological trauma she experienced only by fleeing into sixteen different personalities.

Thigpen, Corbett H. and Cleckley, Hervey M. 1957. *The Three Faces of Eve*. New York: McGraw-Hill Book Company. This book describes the case of a young married woman who had three different personalities. The surface, conscious personality was unaware of the existence of the other two.

8

People Living Together: Love, Sex, Marriage, and Parenting

WHY IS IT SO HARD TO LIVE WITH THE PEOPLE WE LOVE?
    An Historical Overview of Sexual Arrangements and Family
      Structures
    The Wide Variations of Living Together Today

SOME FALLACIES AND REALITIES OF THE LOVING RELATIONSHIP
    The Fallacies of the Loving Relationship
    The Realities of Mate Selection
    Styles of Parenting: Authoritarian, Permissive, Authoritative
    The Wide Variation of Living Arrangements: Types of Marriages
      and Alternative Life Styles
    Some Dimensions of the Loving Relationship

APPLICATIONS AND COPING TECHNIQUES

WHY IS IT SO HARD TO LIVE WITH THE PEOPLE WE LOVE?

The family environment offers our greatest opportunity to experience love and intimacy. And during times such as these, when the world is seen as heavy enough and stressful to such extreme, we need a harbor of humanness—a place to recuperate, refurbish, and most of all, let go of our confusion and stress. For this we need a place that is free of anxiety, at least a good deal of the time. We need both time and space to relax our body, quiet our mind, unwind our emotions, and nourish our lagging spirit.

But alas, the all-too-true fact of life is that our homes are often the very place where many of our most bitter and most perplexing experiences occur. In the very place that could (and perhaps, should) be the most secure, the most loving, the most comfortable and nourishing for us, we all too often experience anger, frustration, pain, sorrow, and disappointment—all of which leads to further individual and cultural confusion. As a consequence, most Americans are ambivalent about marriage. We have very high expectations (ideals), but we also have a very high level of dissatisfaction (reality), resulting in the dissolution of many marriages. Yet we continue to believe in marriage. Most of us who dissolve our marriages continue to remarry at an astonishing rate (Glick 1980; Goetting 1982; Chilman 1983).

An Historical Overview of Sexual Arrangements and Family Structure

We have said that we *expect* more from the family, we *expect* more from love, and we *expect* more from our sexual relationships. Love, sex, and marriage have been idealized and connected in our fantasies as if they were one and the same: *lovesexmarriage*. Such has not always been the case in either Western or Eastern history. Although Judaic-Christian tradition states that a husband and wife should "cleave together," forsaking all others and "be as one flesh," that tradition has not always prevailed.

HEBREW POLYGAMY. The Seventh Commandment in the Book of Genesis is "Thou shalt not commit adultery," that is, one must not engage in a sexual relationship with other than one's legal spouse. Before the advent of the Ten Commandments, Hebrew patriarchs might have had one principal wife but were allowed to have concubines or even other wives (as did Abraham, Isaac, and Jacob).

The Seventh Commandment, presumably, was to reinforce the one-man-one-woman bonding, a return to Adam and Eve.

Yet even after the Ten Commandments, Hebrew leaders continued to have more than one wife and many concubines, as in the stories of David (the shepherd king) and after him, Solomon, who seems to have engaged in the pre-Christian tradition of marrying princesses of other lands as a way of cementing relationships with foreign potentates. Furthermore, the Hebrews had a legal custom that in Christian times became a *taboo:* a dead man's next (in age) brother was expected to marry the widow of the deceased to perpetuate his "seed" and to provide security for her (Ruth 1 : 11). It was a kind of life insurance.

GREEK BISEXUALITY. Athens may be said (at least at its highest cultural point) to have been a bisexual society. We admire that remarkable fifth-century Greek spirit (as it flowered in Athens) for its achievements in philosophy, architecture, sculpture, poetry, theater, mathematics, and rhetoric, and for the concept of democracy, but when we take a closer look at the lives of famous Athenian men, we discover that their idea of a fully developed, loving relationship was not with women but with other men. Generally the most perfect relationship was between an older, wiser, more experienced man and a younger man more physically beautiful and still growing (Kitto 1950). The relationship between these two was also that of mentor and student. Later, when the relationship dissolved and the younger man became more mature, he took, in turn, a younger male lover whom he instructed in the aesthetic and political aspects of living. This relationship was similar to the relationship we see today between an older man and a much younger woman. He delights in "molding" her character, taking a personal pride in her personality development; she, in turn, enjoys the husband-father-lover relationship that is a blend of her fairy-tale fantasies. This older man-younger woman liaison ends sometimes with an ironic twist: If the relationship does help her to grow she may, as the years go on, discover that, although she still admires this man, she has outgrown him, while he in turn has simply grown older. At that point she may look elsewhere for her emotional and sexual satisfaction. So it often was with the Greek older-younger male relationship, the difference being that they recognized the relationship was limited. Greece also had a tradition of female homosexuality. The word *lesbian* comes from the Greek Island of Lesbos, on which female homosexuality was supposed to be predominant. One citizen of Lesbos was the famous Greek poet Sappho, whose poems suggest her own homosexual inclinations.

Why was Athens an essentially bisexual society? How did the Athenians continue their genetic line if it was a predominantly male-male bonding society? To begin, Athenian men were required to have at least one male heir before they were permitted to engage in such activities as going to war, so as to provide Athens with a second generation. If they did not have a legal heir, they were permitted to adopt one. But most Athenians did have wives and families, and many were not homosexually inclined at all but led totally heterosexual lives.

As for the homosexual element, we need to consider the status of women in Athenian society. By and large, women were illiterate and were kept at home taking care of house, servants, and children. They did not participate in political and philosophic life. Historians tell us that they must have been rather pathetic creatures, treated like chattel, not the kind of educated persons with whom the philosophers could converse on a high level. What could be more natural than for philosophers and others to turn for their "higher" emotional needs to others like themselves with whom they could share not only the pleasures of bed but the pleasures of philosophic and artistic discourse?

ROMAN INFIDELITY AND DIVORCE. In Rome aristocratic women had a high status, almost unparalleled in ancient civilizations. Although Roman women could not hold political office or vote, they could inherit land and wealth and were important behind the scenes of political life. Roman women were highly educated, and dinners and parties were not just orgies but occasions to share influence and power, at which both sexes discussed philosophy, politics, esthetics, and the like. Early Roman society was based on the family, but in later years sexuality became part of the general political intrigue for which Rome became so famous. Although a woman could be divorced by her husband, he had to provide for her security, household maintenance, and even luxury, but divorce was far less prevalent than extramarital relations were. Love affairs between married men and women were far more frequent and sometimes not particularly discreet. Many famous Roman women are known to have taken and cast off lovers at will, a practice that was accepted provided they did not embarrass their husbands (Tranquillus 1923).

MEDIEVAL COURTLY LOVE. In the Middle Ages there arose a rather interesting romantic tradition. Since women of noble or royal blood had become politically valuable (they were assets to be married off to foreign royalty and nobility in order to establish and cement diplomatic relations), there was little chance for them to have premarital romantic attachments. The young princess, duchess, or countess often was betrothed, even married, at an early age, anywhere from birth to adolescence, to the sons of foreign royalty and nobility. Most likely she would not even see her husband until her wedding day. Or she might, on the other hand, be sent off to a foreign kingdom (with a small retinue of ladies-in-waiting and other servants) to live there and learn its language, customs, and duties. It must have been very difficult for girls to leave their country at so early an age, cut off from family, friends, and everything familiar.

Although these alliances occasionally did produce warm attachments, the life of a royal female was never very joyful. Medieval castles were cold and damp and, frequently, filthy and smelly. They were dark, too, since windows with glass did not come until the early Renaissance. The "lady" of the house also had the burdensome responsibilities of maintaining order and providing food for her lord's retainers, army, and servants, and for visiting lords with their retinues of serving men, sometimes even a small army. Although she might be addressed as "M'Lady," she was, all too frequently, not much more than an unpaid chatelaine or housekeeper. In addition to his wife, the master had his mistresses, and a king often kept a mistress at court and elevated her to a higher political position than his own wife, to the latter's evident humiliation. The medieval lord of the fief was not a very glamorous person. Beneath his elegant robes, he often was rather unsavory (bathing was not in vogue), frequently illiterate (Charlemagne, who established a school of learning in Paris, around A.D. 800, himself could barely write even his own name), and spent much of his time away hunting, fighting, or settling some minor territorial dispute. He spent little time at home, except between battles. In this bleak world, the lady of the castle led a lonely and isolated existence.

Down through the ages and across cultures, humanity has devised many bonding styles.

She was expected to maintain sexual fidelity and medieval piety. Often she did. But sometimes, she had a romantic lengthy affair of the heart, which we now call *courtly love* (Hunt 1959). The young man (who might be a member of her lord's retinue, a courtier, or a noble of a neighboring state) would put her on a high and romantic pedestal, pursuing her with poetry, music, and pleas of despair if she did not favor him with her heart, mind, and body. Much of his passion was sheer fantasy, just as movie and rock stars may be our fantasies today. She, in turn, was supposed to resist him at least for a time. If she finally gave way to his despair out of pity and love for his youth, it had to remain secret at all costs. If their affair was discovered (and it is exceedingly hard for us to imagine that it could long remain secret, for castles were not very private places), then both were pronounced guilty and punished. The story of King Arthur, Queen Guinevere, and Sir Lancelot is an excellent example of courtly love. How much of this tradition was fact and how much was merely the myth of the medieval era is hard to say. In any event, courtly love did inspire some beautiful poetry.

VICTORIAN SEXUAL REPRESSION. The Victorian era began in the early nineteenth century with the ascendance of Queen Victoria to the British throne. Women of that era were supposed to remain "innocent" and "pure" even in their married life. It was a scandalous admission for Benjamin Disraeli, the prime minister, to say publicly that his wife was an "angel in church" and a "courtesan in bed." There were "illicit" relationships, particularly between noble men and prostitutes, serving maids, or the governesses of their households. There was a tradition, also, of the governess or serving maid indoctrinating the adolescent sons in the mysteries of sexual pleasure. The governess who submitted (that is, was seduced) had to bear the shame of being a "fallen woman" while the young man was said simply to have sown his "wild oats."

AND STILL OTHER BONDING ARRANGEMENTS. Our history of marriage relationships and sexual practices has been very brief. We could have mentioned, for example, the medieval attitude toward the "pleasures of the flesh." The Church elevated celibacy above the state of marriage, declaring virginity to be a superior way of life, a more likely one for the salvation of one's soul. Traditionally these monasteries and convents ordained celibacy as one of its tenets on the grounds that freedom from the pleasures of the flesh allowed the spirit to transcend earthly attachments. In fact, the situation sometimes deteriorated into illegal sexual bonding between the nuns and priests. Lest there be any misunderstanding, monastic celibacy did not always lead to this kind of sub rosa sexuality. We hasten to add that, for many centuries, the religious life was able to maintain denial of the flesh fairly well. Nor should we perpetuate the fallacy that celibacy, any more than masturbation, leads to emotional ill health.

Celibacy is still a tradition in Hinduism and Buddhism. Yogananda, the Indian mystic who came to this country, tells us in his autobiography that his parents engaged in sexual activity only once a year and then only for reproduction (Yogananda 1972). We also could have mentioned that homosexuality still prevails as an accepted fact in the predominantly Arabic nations (Ellis 1960). We did not discuss the rather public sexual practices in certain primitive societies. Most

Western persons would find it difficult to have sexual intercourse in the public conditions of these societies like, for example, the pygmies of Africa (Hallet 1973).

In the United States there have been any number of experimental designs in living together and providing for family and community. Members of the Mormon Church attempted to live polygamously, but they were hounded in state after state until finally, polygamy was outlawed even in their home state of Utah (Kephart 1976). In the nineteenth century a Protestant sect in upstate New York, which came to be known as the Oneida Community, practiced a kind of group marriage in which every member of the group was considered married to every other member (Haughley 1975). Although they had sexual intercourse, they managed to forestall pregnancy, evidently by means of a practice known as **coitus reservatus,** or **coitus interruptus,**[1] or by engaging in sexual relations only after the woman had completed menopause. This group remained active for over thirty-five years before it disintegrated through internal and external pressure (Kephart 1976).

The Wide Variations of Living Together Today

As a consequence of the breakdown of our traditional ideas about how people may live together, there re-emerged in the sixties and seventies new and experimental modes of being and living together: communal living, group marriage, multiple parenthood, "parents without partners," a new interest in "open marriage," more liberal laws regarding homosexuals, adoption of children by single persons, and changing sexual roles, with more equality for women—all based on a revived interest in experiencing the love of our human heritage, of "peoplemaking" (Satir et al. 1976). It is no wonder that young men and women are bewildered about their future—a future that no longer seems to hold out a fairy-tale promise that they will all live "happily ever after."

This is not to say that the family is finished. Looking at the worst may be just the kind of beginning we need to make as we become fully conscious of living, loving, and being together. Marriage is a long-term personal investment of energy, so it demands the understanding that of all the institutions of civilized life the family is a definition of our most personal, private living.

SOME FALLACIES AND REALITIES OF THE LOVING RELATIONSHIP

In chapter 2 we discussed the animistic world of children and primitive societies (Bettelheim 1967; Piaget 1976). It is a world of make-believe and fairy-tales, with the prince and princess getting married and everyone living happily ever after. Unfortunately we continue this fairy-tale fallacy in many of today's romantic novels, movies, and soap operas, in which the hero and heroine go through many misunderstandings, struggles, and torments before the reaffirming kiss and promise of a wedding. We thus miss the whole point—for this is just where the story should begin. It is *after* marriage, generally, that the real problems and the real drama begin. It is after the honeymoon is over and the traditional roles and expectations are taken on—the babies come, and the household bills mount, perhaps without the available cash to meet them—that romance may begin to fade, and suddenly we find ourselves living with someone who is no longer accommodating and easy to be around. Nor is our spouse necessarily loving anymore. As one wit has said, "If love is blind, marriage is an eyeopener."

The Fallacies of the Loving Relationship

Sometimes we even help to write the "script" that later we find intolerable (Berne 1978). That masculinity we thought so romantic may later turn out to be cruelty, an unreasonableness, and perhaps even an abusiveness that is not the romantic image we had in mind.

LOVE IS NOT JEALOUSY. There is perhaps no more dangerous misconception than the one that jealousy is "the other face of love." A woman may enjoy her husband's jealousy, considering that to be a demonstration of her husband's love. But jealousy pertains more to the person who is exhibiting jealousy than to the subject of that jealousy. Jealousy implies a lack of trust in the partner as well as a lack of confidence in oneself in being able to retain the partner's attachment. A jealous person is not only jealous in love; that person will tend to be jealous of friends, relatives, and associates for many other kinds of attributes: their jobs, their salaries, their seeming good fortune, their good looks, everything in which he or she feels deficient by comparison. A jealous person is extremely hard to endure. The jealous person may not always express the jealousy directly; in that case, it will come out in devious and subtle ways: martyrdom, "game-playing" tactics involving revenge, irritability (such as slamming of cabinet doors), and sulking. The point to remember is that the jealousy (if the charges are unfounded) can never be stopped or satisfied by protestation, or even by proof of innocence.

LOVE IS NOT POSSESSIVENESS. One of the most destructive aspects of romance is the desire to possess the other's focus, interest, and energies all the time. In the first blush of attraction, it is natural for two persons to want to be together as much as possible, to learn about each other, and to share their interests and recreations. Eventually, however, as the two persons come to know each other well and have shared many mutual interests, there comes a time when both will have less need to be together, to do everything together, and to find complete satisfaction only in the other. A loving relationship, once it has been established, allows for individual preferences. For example, a man may like to go fishing alone or with friends. The wife may not enjoy fishing, but she puts up a fuss every time he gets out his fishing gear. A woman may enjoy being politically active in the community, but her husband resents the time she spends away from home.

Sometimes this conflict of interests has a tragic outcome. The person may give up that pleasure, be it fishing or hunting, athletic or political endeavor. The person loses that joy or interest, and a part of the self atrophies. Sometimes giving up one's extracurricular enjoyment may be done with the best of intentions or with no seeming upset; yet, later in life, we find people admitting that they wished they had not done so. It comes as a relief for them to learn it is not too late, if they have the courage and conviction, to return to that pursuit that once meant so much to them.

LOVE IS NOT JUST SEXUAL COMPATIBILITY. We have come a long way in recognizing that sexual compatibility enhances the marital relationship. Yet despite our more sexually liberated society, we may be overemphasizing the sexual component of a relationship. Surprising research on marital satisfaction has revealed that marital happiness does not necessarily depend on absolute sexual compatibility. Although a large percentage of men and women equated sexual compatibility with marital happiness, a number of long-term marital partners who had judged theirs as a "happy marriage," admitted that their sexual life was not as compatible as it is "supposed to be." In this instance, the couples attributed their marital happiness to other factors: tenderness on the part of the other along with thoughtfulness, a desire to please the other, and a "happy family life." These now classic studies revealed that "emotional support" and "doing things together" were two of the main ingredients of marital fulfillment (Blood & Wolfe 1965). One social scientist recommended affection rather than romantic love. Romantic love may grow from affection, he noted, while too often romantic love is followed by disenchantment, even hostility when "the honeymoon is over" (Van Den Haag 1973).

LOVE IS NOT SELF-SACRIFICE AND MARTYRDOM. In their early eagerness to please the other, lovers occasionally become martyrs to the relationship. "I will be anything you want me to be; I will do anything you want if it will make you happy." In the beginning, the other person may delight in such devotion, but all too often, the readiness to subjugate one's individuality and interests has other unhappy consequences. The one for whom we are sacrificing ourselves begins to take us for granted, loses interest in such a submissive male or female, and may end by finding another partner who mystifies, excites, and provides constant challenge. If we invite such treatment, then, in all probability, we shall get it.

There is a continuing drama played out over and over again, which many teachers and students will recognize. It goes like this: The young couple marry when the man is part way through college (or even just beginning) and the woman agrees, is even delighted, to put him through school. He is getting his M.D. or Ph.D., and she is getting her P.H.T. (Putting Husband Through school). Perhaps one, two, even three children come along. Now she frantically races to the nursery school or the babysitter to drop the children off before she goes to work and picks them up when she comes home. Sometimes her husband has a night class and cannot be home with her in the evening; sometimes she is typing part-time (to earn extra money); sometimes he shuts himself in the extra room so he can study. She understands completely, and though she is sometimes lonely and feels a little lost, she is proud to be able to contribute all her energies to him and to their future. She neglects herself physically, her clothing gets a little dowdy (she is saving money for next term's tuition or for doctors' bills), but she does not mind that.

Sometimes she wishes she had a chance to go to the movies more often or go to a restaurant with her husband, but she "makes do" with her bag lunch at work. The end of the story? Many readers will have anticipated it. She manages the seemingly impossible; she gets him through school to get whatever degrees he needs. *She* feels a sense of pride and achievement. In the meantime, *he* discovers that he has "grown" but that she has not. While she is feeling noble and happy, he begins having small talks with her about his needs, their marriage, and so on, and the marriage ends in divorce. (Often there is another female in the background who steps into the role of the wife the minute the divorce is final.)

What can be done to prevent this gradual disinterest in an emotional relationship? Those who specialize in sex education have suggested many remedies. The woman can occasionally use seductive techniques, including clothing (or no clothing), "teasing," or "appearing suddenly in his den with two cocktails for them." The man may become a very aggressive, dominant lover (particularly if he tends to be passive in the relationship). Others warn against the "too much, too soon" approach, which eventually ends in the satiation of one or both partners. Others have gone so far as to recommend aphrodisiacs, using mirrors and vibrators and perusing sensuous literature and art. Still others advise vacations from each other, extramarital affairs, and so on. Frankly, much of this advice sounds rather mechanistic. Our approach would be to urge each partner to develop an internal sense of self-worth. By self-worth we mean to continue to grow and to develop individual, self-rewarding interests and competencies. There is nothing so enticing as a vivacious person with interests. Two people can bring to each other their outside interests and experiences and retain that original charm. But again, we urge that couples do what is most appropriate for them.

LOVE IS NOT THE "ALL IN ALL." "Falling in love" (whatever that may mean to you) is not the solution to all life's problems; it is not "the happy ending" of one's current existence; it certainly is not a magic pill that will bring eternal happiness for the rest of one's life. Falling in love (being romantically involved with a person whom we trust and admire) is certainly an exhilarating experience. Loving another human being is one of the richest and most rewarding emotions we can ever have. Life takes on a new dimension; we seem to move to another level of consciousness; and there is a special quality to everything we see, hear, or touch. We are transported from our everyday world to a place beyond anything we ever imagined. Time may seem to expand, and paradoxically, one has a sense of timelessness. Love is so difficult to describe that even poets can only point to it with metaphors.

All that is true. But marriage counselors warn us that the rose-colored glasses of lovers blind us to what the other person really is. We do not see the blemishes in the other person; he or she is perfect. But of course, no one is perfect. Even the best of friends never get along perfectly. If you are getting along "perfectly," it simply may mean that one or the other is going along passively, giving up some aspect of the self for the other—a potentially destructive element already in the relationship. Relationship is give-and-take, understanding-misunderstanding, expectation-disappointment, and mutuality-conflict. After the rose-colored glasses are shattered, after we see that the other does have blemishes, after we understand that the other person is not perfect but has faults (as we all do), we will discover that all the problems we thought had disappeared magically are still there. Love does not remake the world. Love does not inherently change character (except perhaps temporarily). Love does not pay the bills. One of the most comic-tragic things we hear people say is "Oh, I know he/she is stubborn/irritable/jealous/lazy/(whatever), but I'll change all that after we get married." No one is ever radically changed by love or by marriage.

The Realities of Mate Selection

FACTORS THAT INFLUENCE CHOICE OF MATE.   We hope that no one still believes that marriages are "made in heaven." Generally the persons we are attracted to, come to love, and eventually marry are not those who differ from us in background, personality, or status. The very reverse is more often true. We marry persons similar to ourselves, and we marry those who live near us.

The propinquity factor. The most basic factor in "falling in love" is close proximity to that person. Very simply, we tend to become attached to a person with whom we have frequent contact, who has lived near us. Social scientists call this the *propinquity* factor. We really *are* more apt to marry the boy or girl "next door" than some stranger from far away. Of course, the boy next door, these days, may not come from our home town but may be from the neighboring dorm on our campus or the fellow whose desk is next to ours at work (Walster, Berscheid, & Walster 1973).

The similarity factor. We are also attracted to persons who are like ourselves, who come from the same general social class and the same ethnic group, have the same religion and the same type of education, are about the same age, and are equal in physical attractiveness and intelligence (Eckland 1974; Walster & Walster 1978). And we marry them.

Why is this so? Some persons have opined that there is some sense of confirmation of oneself as an individual. Since lovers tend to resemble each other to a remarkable degree, even in their physical appearance and attractiveness, in their mental and physical health, in their intelligence and in social warmth and family background, some social scientists have reasoned that we feel affirmed to be loved by someone who is much like ourselves (Burgess & Wallin 1953; Walster & Walster 1978). Some call it a *self-love,* but we should rather prefer to call it a keen sense of identity with another person. We have found a person so similar to ourselves that we can "let go" and be just ourselves. We don't have to explain our thoughts and actions and preferences. We can better understand each other since our experiences are similar. We can remove the "masks" of personality that we feel obliged to wear in order to be polite, to be "friendly," to be cooperative. We can be what Carl Rogers has called "the real me," and which the client in the therapeutic situation finds so nourishing (Rogers 1970).

One of the strongest components of a staisfactory marriage is the similarity factor: the two persons are similar in race and ethnic background, religion, education, and socioeconomic status.

The mutuality factor. Recently two psychologists published the findings of their research on married, cohabiting, and homosexual couples (Blumstein & Schwartz 1983). In an extensive survey, 12,000 people completed a thirty-eight-page questionnaire. After that, 600 persons were selected who could be classified in terms of short-, medium- and long-term relationships. They were interviewed in order to get more detailed information about intimate aspects of their lives.

The essential conclusion was that *mutuality of values* is the primary bond between happily married couples. For example, financial security is a very strong variable, but money management (*who* spends *how much* on *what*) is even more important. However, they add, the conflict over money is not just money but a measure of their whole value system.

For example, if both spouses accepted the wife's working, marital satisfaction seemed stable. Or if the wife stayed home because she wanted to, that could be a stabilizing factor, when both approved. It was only when the wife wanted to work, and the husband didn't like it or downright refused to let her that there was marital discord and unhappiness. One man said, "I find it odd that she wants to go out and do somebody else's dirty work when she could stay at home and enjoy the life we worked so hard to put together."

Another area of mutuality seems to be absolutely essential: how to raise children and whether mothers should stay home and bring up the children. Even how much and what kinds of discipline should be used could be a matter for dissension. When the wife and husband agree on guiding principles and appropriate disciplinary actions, the mutual caretaking helps give both a sense of partnership not only in the marriage but in the parental caretaking.

Mutuality and similarity interlink with the double standard. Men are more willing to marry women who are less educated, who come from a lower stratum of

Box 8.1

SIMILARITIES IN SPOUSES PREDICT GREATER COMPATIBILITY

Some research indicates that compatibility relates to amounts of agreement and/or disagreement between the spouses:

Employment. Type, place, hours of employment of the husband and wife
Residence. Geographical area, specific community, character of neighborhood, type of housing
Money matters. Amount needed, how earned, how managed
Parents, families. Relationships with parents and in-laws
Social life. Extent, type, leisure-time activities
Friends. Selection, relationships with men and women friends
Religion. Ideas, beliefs, personal faith, church affiliations, participation in religious activities
Values, philosophy of life. Individual ethics, morals, life goals, what individual wants out of life
Sex, demonstration of affection. Type, amount, frequency
Matters of conventionality. Manners, mores, living habits (i.e., table manners, dress, drinking, smoking, attitudes toward drug use or abuse, cleanliness)
Children. Number wanted, disciplining, caring for and educating them
Roles. Of husband and wife in and outside home

Source: Adapted from Rice, Phillip F. 1979. *Marriage and Parenthood.* Boston: Allyn & Bacon, Inc., p. 129.

society, who are younger, and/or who are less intelligent (Elder 1959; Jaco & Shephard 1975). Women, evidently, prefer to marry men who are generally "above" them in all these factors. Does that mean that if a man marries upward in education or social class the marriage is doomed? Not necessarily. In fact, the research indicates that sometimes such marriages can work out quite well, but only if both the husband and wife understand that education and intelligence are not synonymous. If she has the better education but respects the special abilities that he has and she has not, such marriages can work out quite well because of their complementary qualities. Husband and wife are not in competition with each other but act as resources for each other (Bowman 1974).

There is a catch to this upward mobility of the husband. He must be similar in intelligence to his wife. Evidently what is vital for the woman is that she can have respect for how he approaches the problems that come up in the marriage and that he be reasonable and intelligent in dealing with them (Goode 1956).

There has been an interesting surge in the last ten years of marriages between younger men and older women—and for them to proclaim their age difference publicly. We do not have much follow-up research on the success of these marriages. The ones we do hear about are between famous people, and most of these celebrity alliances are influenced by the difficulties that these marriages sustain in any event. We can, however, cite one of the most famous younger-man-older-woman alliances of all time—that of Benjamin Disraeli and his wife. She was above his social station, was far more wealthy than he, and a good deal older. Yet their marriage was one of the most successful, according to most biographers, and her death, when he was Queen Victoria's prime minister, left him bereft and heartsick (Swartz & Swartz 1976; Butler 1980).

Most of our marriages involve bridegrooms who are either slightly or considerably older than their brides—an actual 72 percent. Our current social trends indicate an increase in age-dissimilar marriages through the combined impact of "a high divorce rate, a high remarriage rate, and a growing population of middle-aged and older poeople. An increasing proportion of these people will be attracted to May-December marriages as a viable alternative life-style." (Berardo, Vera, & Berardo 1983, p. 57.)

THE GROWTH OF COMPATIBILITY. One of the advantages of an extended dating and courtship period is the growth of couple compatibility. By being "in relationship" for a fairly long while, two people can come to know just how compatible they really are. They have time to find out if they like the same kinds of activities and if they share the same values (Murstein 1971). They discover how the other reacts in various social situations. They have a chance to participate in activities that are related to "real life" and not just the kinds of glamorous things dating couples do upon first being together. Movies and theater and football games and passionate moments of sexual exploration *are* romantic and exciting. But it is only after two people have a chance to experience a number of practical, everyday situations and critical events (the kind that are similar to both the daily events of marriage and the crises of living) that they can discover if they like each other's ways of handling problems or general life style.

MARRYING OUTSIDE ONE'S SOCIAL CLASS, RACE, ETHNIC SUBCULTURE. Although black-white marriages are increasing, the percentage of people involved in such marriages, by the early seventies, was still only a fraction over 1 percent of our entire population (Heer 1974). Furthermore, divorce statistics of such marriages indicate that interracial marriages have the lowest stability rate (Heer 1974). Interfaith marriages do somewhat better (Babchuck et al. 1967; Besanceney 1965), depending largely on the environment in which the couple find themselves. Generally interfaith marriages do not do nearly as well in a small town as in the large metropolitan centers, with their more homogeneous mixes (Burchinal & Chancellor 1962; Christensen & Barber 1967). Small towns may be more nostalgic for Americans, with our predilection for songs about the "old home town" and Christmas cards showing a small snow-covered midwestern farm scene. But the chances for covert hostility in small towns (small-towners thrive on gossip!) and overt hostility (cross burning by KKK groups) are much higher. Interracial marriages fare much better in Hawaii, for example, where there are more Caucasian-Oriental marriages than in any other of our fifty states (Monahan 1966, 1970).

The moral of these statistics is painfully clear: Too wide a discrepancy between race, faith, social class, ethnic grouping, or any other demographic variable endangers the marital relationship. The more compatible these factors, the more likelihood for a successful outcome.

BEFORE MARRIAGE AND AFTER: CHANGING EXPECTATIONS AND ROLE IDENTITY. But a high compatibility score still does not insure success in marriage. Even the most compatible relationships can go awry. It is *still* true that the most prevalent and remarkable phenomenon of modern marriage is the fact that *the relationship between two people before and after marriage seems to change dramatically* and quite often, traumatically, for both partners.

Our readers will recognize the two sides of the argument in box 8.2 only too well—if not for themselves, then from the reports of close friends and relatives. What is most surprising to the couple is that they *thought* they knew what to expect. They had talked it all out beforehand. They had prided themselves on their compatibility score. Friends and relatives agreed they were a "well-matched" couple. Their genuine love and regard for each other, their mutual support system, their careful preplanning of how to deal with problems and other life situations were carefully thought out. Yet somehow all of these good feelings seem to have dissolved into feelings of confusion, despair, and not just a little bitterness.

What has happened? If social scientists could answer this question simply, a lot of marriages that are now headed for the divorce courts might be saved. There is no simple answer. But there are a lot of reasonable theories. Perhaps it is our present-day demand for perpetual emotional satisfaction. We seem to want to enter some kind of romantic perfection for the rest of our lives. And of course there are ever-present cultural pressures such as our technological environment, which is so alien to a nuclear family setup. How? Well, in many ways. For example, the sheer numbers of roles we are now expected to play.

THE MULTIROLES OF MODERN MARRIAGE PARTNERS. A prevalent theory of modern nuclear marriage is that it requires each partner to play more roles than ever before. One writer has identified at least eight different roles that the married person plays in the contemporary American family (Nye 1976). (Refer to box 8.3.) Once upon a time (in the extended family of rural America) the adult members of the household may have included members of several generations— Grandmother, Grandfather, widowed Uncle Will, young, orphaned Cousin Edna, in addition to Mother and Father and children. There was a sense of community to the small familial grouping. The housekeeping tasks, the farm tasks, the tasks of child raising were shared among the several adult members of the extended family. We would not propose that the extended rural family was as compatible as a Norman Rockwell *Saturday Evening Post* cover would have us believe. There is always dissension among people living together at close range—the greater the number of people living together, the greater the number of issues that can be argued over. But at least there was a sharing of responsibility. If Mom fell ill, at least there was Grandmother to take over the cooking, and Cousin Edna, though young, was a built-in baby sitter. If Father broke a leg or an ankle, there were other male members who could take over the farm jobs, and even the women could help out.

Consider now the modern wife-mother. When she falls ill, she has very little help with the toddlers or school-aged children. Her husband can't afford to take off more than a day or two from his job to help out. Too often the grandparents live

Box 8.2   **CHANGES IN ROLE EXPECTATIONS: BEFORE AND AFTER MARRIAGE**

A dramatic example in point (her side of the story first):

"I can't understand it. He was so understanding and thoughtful and helpful before we were married. We talked a lot about equality of the sexes and shared responsibility. I thought we knew what to expect. We met in a marriage-and-family course in college. And we discussed very rationally our commitment to each other: How we wanted to raise children—the whole nine yards! Or so I thought. Here it is five years later. I'm saddled with two children, and he doesn't seem to feel that he has to do anything more than bring home the bacon. He flops his feet on the table in front of the television set, and that's it. He thinks that I'm home all day with nothing to do. What happened to the idea that he would help with dishes? I can't even get him to take me to the movies or out to eat. He says if I want to go, *go*. He's not stopping me. As for eating out, he says he has to eat out at lunch. And he doesn't want to eat his dinner meal out too. Besides, it costs too much to get a baby sitter. And that's true, I know. But I'm tired, too. He expects me to fall into his arms at night with enthusiasm, but he doesn't take the time and effort to be affectionate and warm with me. He's become so selfish in his love making, even that isn't how we had once hoped and planned to be with each other. And I'm bored talking babytalk. Sometimes I feel like my vocabulary level has been reduced to the level of a three-year-old. What happened to us?"

And his side of the story may go like this:

"Gee, as soon as we got married she changed. I mean from the word go! Before the wedding, there wasn't anything she wouldn't do for me: sew on buttons, iron a shirt. We were living together before we got married, and I thought we knew each other well. We enjoyed sex. We planned things together in advance. We had fun. She didn't mind if I left my shirts hanging on the back of a chair. She was always glad to see me. I couldn't wait to get home from school to our apartment. She was always there, warm and welcoming. I thought we had it altogether. Now I'm a slob because I don't hang my clothes up the way *she* wants. When I come home, she meets me with one complaint after another about the kids or something that has broken down like the washing machine. She's on my case all the time because I didn't do this or that which I said I would. I do them . . . but sometimes it takes me a while to get a part to fix the damn washing machine. Only she wants it done *now*. I know kids make a lot of wash. But hell! I'm human, too. I'd like time off to enjoy myself a little, too. Sometimes I come home so tired all I want to do is eat, have a beer, and watch the ball game. She isn't fun in bed anymore either. She says I'm a lousy lover. And our sex life is winding down like an unwound clock. I'm beginning to think marriage ruins a perfectly good relationship!"

EIGHT BASIC ROLES WITHIN THE AMERICAN FAMILY

HOUSEKEEPER: Cleaning house, washing clothes, doing dishes, shopping, keeping the household books, preparing the meals.

PROVIDER: Earning the money to support the family.

CHILD CARE: Feeding, washing, dressing, caring for the children.

SOCIALIZATION: Passing on cultural values, attitudes, skills, and appropriate behaviors.

SEXUALITY: Responding to each other's sexual needs.

KINSHIP: Maintaining family contacts with relatives; maintaining a support system.

RECREATION: Organizing family recreational events.

THERAPEUTIC: Listening to, sympathizing with, helping, caring for, and understanding all other family members.

Source: Adapted from Nye, F.I. 1976. *Role Structure and Analysis of the Family.* Beverly Hills, CA: Sage Publications, Inc.

too far to come and help out. Even when she is well and working at top efficiency, the mother finds herself a very poorly paid housekeeper, cook, chauffeur, nurse, coordinator between home and school, a part-time or full-time wage earner, and her husband's therapist when there are problems at the office.

Consider also the plight of the modern husband-father. He finds himself working a full-time job, and when he's not working, he has to make sure the car gets to the garage or work on it himself, attend to anything else that may go wrong in the house or apartment, run his kids to dance classes or Little League baseball. He is supposed to "help out with the kids" and share the responsibilities of housekeeping if his wife is also working and they are what has come to be known as a dual-career family. In the meantime, modern life is a cycle of bureaucratic procedures, applications, licenses, fees, insurance policies to keep up to date with and to pay for—by two people who are also expected by the local, state, and federal governments to be bookkeepers, accountants, file clerks, and even amateur attorneys.

THE WOMAN MAKES THE MOST ADJUSTMENTS. No matter how much preplanning and talking a couple have engaged in before marriage, it is impossible to envision the complexities of modern married life. Even if the couple lived together for a time before they were married and before they became parents, their premarital situation bore small resemblance, in most cases, to what they are confronted with a few years after marriage. Before marriage their contributions to the relationship were voluntary. After marriage their contributions are expected, even demanded, particularly for the woman! Before marriage, she had little responsibility for his parents and relatives. After marriage, she finds that not only must she attend to the birthday celebrations of their own immediate family and her own parents and sisters and brothers, she is now the official record keeper and present buyer for *his* parents, his brothers and sisters—even his boss and his boss's secretary. She was not expected to be a hostess to his colleagues or business associates before marriage—she is now! Before marriage she didn't have to deal with what to do with the kids if she and her guy were feeling romantic. There weren't any. Most theorists agree that while the American husband and father may feel like a displaced person at times, it is the woman who has the burden of adjustment (Goode 1956). That is not to say, however, that she is held responsible for this situation.

THE ABSENTEE HUSBAND-FATHER. One of the reasons for the wife-mother's overwork is the absentee husband-father. He has left the homestead and the farm and gone into the factory, into the bureaucratic office, into the hospital, into the law office and court, into the school, college, and university. Someone had to fill the vacuum of tending to the household and the children and the financial-record keeping and so on. The person who filled the vacuum turned out to be the wife-mother. A large factor in the "breakdown of the American family" turns out to be our twentieth-century technocracy with its demands for employees to be away from the home nine hours a day or more, and for professionals in all fields to go to this or that convention, business meeting, sales conference—to all parts of our own country and across skies and seas to other countries (Whyte 1952, Cuber & Haroff 1965, Packard 1972). One University of California study revealed that the average faculty member spent sixty hours a week teaching, research writing, meeting with others—eight-and-one-half-hour work days, seven days a week (Strong et al. 1983).

THE PROBLEMS OF FINANCIAL STRESS. The research data are plain: Financial security and adequate income are one of the basic indicators of marital satisfaction (Scanzoni 1968; Renne 1970; Feldman & Feldman 1975). When bills mount and the income is inadequate to meet them, the normal stresses and strains of married life are compounded by anxiety and despair. Small tensions become large. Quarrels about how to spend the income and accusations back and forth about the other's spending become a cold war threatening to turn into a hot war and continuing warfare. If the husband begins to lose confidence in his role as breadwinner, he experiences frustration and failure (Lopata 1971). Feelings of inadequacy and failure may result in drinking, or a night out to "have a little fun." Too often these times of crisis, with their accompanying feelings of frustration and anger, frequently increased by the use of alcohol or drugs, result in abuse of the wife and children—sometimes even of the husband (Gelles 1978, 1979; Riggs 1981).

Even when both spouses are contributing to the family income, money and the management of it often become weapons of attack in the dissolving emotional security. She may go on spending sprees to punish him for his physical aggression or his sexual inadequacy. In retaliation, he may decide to keep such tight control over the checkbook that she determines to keep *her* money for *herself* so as to have some sense of independence (Kieren et al. 1975). Thus hostilities continue.

THE WORKING WIFE AND SELF-ESTEEM. It might be easy to say that when such problems come up because of their jobs or careers, it would be wise for the wife to take steps to "save" their marriage—by quitting her job. But in addition to the financial bind that would result, there is an additional factor we must consider. The working wife feels better about herself. While there are still women who do not want to work and do find fulfillment in wife-mother-housekeeper as a career,

Box 8.4

HOUSEWORK VERSUS WAGE EARNING: SATISFACTIONS AND DISSATISFACTIONS

HOUSEWORK	WAGE EARNING
Socially isolating. Works alone. Loneliness is a chief complaint.	Socially interacting. Daily contact satisfies social-emotional needs.
Sense of dullness from repetition. "Forever at war, forever alert, I spend my life in struggle with dirt."	Sense of achievement from production. Even with repetitive work, there is social interaction and thus a sense of achievement.
Long, endless, unstructured hours. No days off: "From rising dawn to setting sun a woman's work is never done."	Regular, specified, structured hours. Days off: a sense of "free time" when working hours are over. Work is done, now it's time for play.
No paycheck. Not only does the work never end, the money never comes in. No tangible recognition of worth.	A regular paycheck. Not only does the work end, the money does come in. At least there is some tangible recognition of worth.
Autonomous scheduling, pacing. Special events may take short-term priority—times to be in your own space at your own time, with modifications, of course.	Interdependent scheduling, pacing. A controlled schedule for a large part of the day leaves less chance for doing your own thing at your own time, which is basically possible after work only.
Opportunity for maximum involvement as spouse and parent—major sources of satisfaction.	Opportunity for financial independence and self-esteem. More widespread involvement, including working role.

even the factory worker likes to know she has money that is *hers* (Rapoport & Rapoport 1971; Propper 1972; Hall & Gordon 1973). She feels a sense of worth that she has some skill that others value. If she is a secretary, she knows that when she comes in after a day's absence, the boss is glad to see her so he can answer letters or have her there to fend off the other employees when he needs a few hours of privacy. The respect she gets from her work, which she does not get as chief cook and bottle washer at home, gives her a sense of appreciation for herself as a person with skills and talents. When we consider that *esteem* is one of the higher levels of that hierarchy of needs toward what Abraham Maslow calls self-actualizing, we can understand why she is loathe to go back to what she considers a routine of drudgery and nonappreciation. The studies done on wife-mothers who work and those who do not reveal, time and again, that the working wife rates higher in self-confidence and even in marital happiness than her counterpart who is staying home trying to fulfill a nineteenth-century idealization of "lady of the house." The romantic idea of a "lady of the house," of course, did not apply to the immigrant wives who came in waves in the nineteenth century and who went to work in the sweat shops of the big cities and the mill towns of New England. No, the nineteenth-century "lady of the house" was a woman whose husband had enough financial security for her to have one or more household servants and perhaps a governess to help with the cooking, household chores, and care of the children (Sennett 1969; Neidle 1975; Demos 1976). All our labor-saving devices can't make up for the lack of hired help.

THE HARD TRANSITION TO PARENTHOOD. Perhaps nothing is so crisis generating for the couple as the transition to parenthood. The modern mode of wife and husband working until the first child comes has many ramifications. The couple have been enjoying the fruits of their double income. They have had time to enjoy each other as "equal partners" and to explore their emotional and sexual relationship. They have privacy if they choose. They can vacation if they choose. The first years can truly be an extended honeymoon.

With the advent of the first child, all that will change quite precipitously. The young couple who have had only themselves to think about . . . or at least, with not much more concern than who is going to start breakfast in the morning, take out the garbage before going to work, pick up that night's dinner at the grocery, now have a dramatically different situation. The baby rather than the husband will now become the focus of the wife-mother's concern. The husband may well feel as if he is on the back burner. Mother suddenly has to get up at two or four in the morning to take care of the baby's needs, and she has never been a "morning person." (In fact, until she has had her second cup of coffee, she is hardly focused.) The income has been sharply cut down, and to boot, there are the added expenses of baby food, baby clothes, baby doctor, baby photographs (and who does not want the photographic history of baby in these swiftly passing "growing years"?). While she delights in being mother to her beautiful and wanted child, the sudden shift from job or career to the confines of her home may give her a sense of social loss. Still she does find happiness in mothering and in sharing the exciting events as baby develops with other young mothers in the neighborhood (Feldman 1971; Feldman & Feldman 1977).

But with another baby and another baby, not only is the excitement of new motherhood gone and the sight of diapers discouraging, she may well begin to miss the sense of esteem she felt as a valued worker. Particularly is this true of the well-educated professional mom. The woman's transition to parenthood is difficult. She is the one who has to curtail her social life, her working life, and her aspirations for a "career" (Rossi 1982).

The research also reveals that the greater the number of children that come along in a family, the lower the level of marital satisfaction (Feldman 1971)—not in all cases, of course, but in the majority of cases. Social scientists used to be worried about the wife-mother at the climacteric (the menopause and mid-life crisis). With her adolescent children leaving home, they said, the woman in her forties and fifties has no identity until she finds one again as grandmother. That may have been true once but no longer. Modern children are more demanding than any children in history. Our concern for them is higher than any time in history. The expense of raising them and sending them on to college is higher than any time in history. The delinquencies and problems we have to deal with are more complex than ever in our mass society. Parenthood in our times is emotionally exhausting, financially draining, and socially complex.

Parents now look forward to the emptying of the nest, when they can have more time, more energy, more privacy, and more money to enjoy their lives again. Do we sound harsh? We only mean to present the full reality. No one is denying the joys of parenthood and the pride and love we can have with our children. But the problems in raising children today are such that many couples are actually opting for a childless marriage—or at least delaying the decision (Houseknecht 1982; Mosher & Bachrach 1982; Price 1982). If you do choose to become parents, you might be better prepared if you understand that the parental bed is not a bed of roses. Some social scientists have even suggested two types of marriages, only one of which involves the willingness to take on the responsibility of parenting (Mead 1971). Others have suggested that parenting should be a privilege, not a right, accorded to persons who have the proper training and credentials, in much the same way we allow a woman or man to be a physician after much training and the earning of proper credentials (Mead 1971).

The obvious alternative is nonparenthood. The problems of raising children and the high cost of their education and welfare have caused increasing numbers of young marrieds to not only postpone having children but to remain childless (Juhasz 1980). In 1978 11 percent of all women aged eighteen to thirty-four reported that they expected to remain childless (U.S. Bureau of Statistics 1980). Furthermore, these young women and men tend to be college graduates and professionals who do not view children as necessary for a full life. They express the opinion that they expect to derive professional satisfaction in their careers with their nurturance needs taken care of by their nieces, nephews, younger cousins, and children of friends (Houseknecht 1978).

Styles of Parenting: Authoritarian, Permissive, Authoritative

Parenting, of course, has its own special rewards, particularly when the parents have wanted the children very much, even when they must struggle to make ends meet and do not have financial security (Rollins & Galligan 1978). Many of us have picked up a newspaper and read with interest (and amazement) about a couple adopting a whole family of orphans or a child with Down's syndrome. We have admired their feeling for children, and observed the smiling faces of the group. And we recognize that parenthood can truly be a rewarding experience, despite the ups and downs of children's growing-up years and the catastrophes of adolescence. Fortunately we have come to recognize, at least in part, that the old saying "Spare the rod and spoil the child" may lead not to happy children who are growing healthfully but to the kind of violence that breeds more violence.

But we must remember, too, that we have come through a rather heady period when the "child-centered family," with its unleashed hellions, is not the answer either. In fact, in one study of parents and children, the child who had come from the "laissez-faire" parental style was quite the most confused and anxious child upon entering kindergarten and first grade (Baumrind & Black 1967; Baumrind 1971). The researchers in this case, viewed the permissive parent as hardly much better than the authoritarian parent. Their advice to parents was to be warm but *authoritative*.

What is it to be authoritative? The researchers defined it as firm but loving control, which gives children feedback on their behavior in a kind and gentle way; guiding children in their activities but also being respectful of their interests, opinions, and unique personalities. Ah! There we have it once again—the urging by so many social scientists to be mindful that we are all uniquely distinctive personalities. When we recognize those individualities in our children as well as in ourselves, we can more ably help them grow more confident in their individuality.

Notice that we said we need to honor *our* individualities as parents, too. The Group for the Advancement of Psychiatry (1973), advises us that parenthood should be, and *can* be, creative self-growth provided that parents continue to recognize themselves as persons who also have needs and desires. Those must be respected if we are to be adequate as parents and fostering of our own personality integration. This group advises parents to think of parenthood in four stages. (See box 8.5.) We can derive a great deal of satisfaction from our children's continuing development as persons, and we may feel a measure of self-esteem that we have indeed produced happy children, sensible adolescents, and mature adults. But we must not let ourselves become too discouraged, and self-blaming if our children do not develop as we had imagined.

PROBLEMS OF PARENTING IN A TIME OF CHANGING TRADITIONS, OF CONTRADICTORY STANDARDS, AND OF CONFUSING "FUTURE SHOCK." *What* is a parent to do? The advice of most persons engaged in the study of personality and, in particular, in the study of parenting is to maintain open communication and support of one's child even when he or she strays off into destructive paths. They advise us to remember that parent hating and parent blaming is a phase that children often regret as they get older (although they may not be able to verbalize that regret). They advise us, too, that when a family can do things together, observe rituals and celebrations, and in general, have good times, there are lasting memories that the

---

Box 8.5	**FOUR PHASES OF PARENTHOOD**

1. ANTICIPATION: We think about parenthood: What will it mean, how will we raise our children. We do and don't want this responsibility (ambivalence). We need to change our self-image from our parents' children to our children's parents.
2. HONEYMOON: Time to adjust and learn. Bonding occurs during the first months after the baby's birth—between child and family members. We learn new roles now.
3. PLATEAU: From infancy through adolescence we experience a middle period—adapting to each and every behavioral level of the child along the way.
4. DISENGAGEMENT: We begin ending our active parental roles—definitely with the marriage of the children, possibly with their beginning a career and living on their own. When we have our own needs to be needed we have difficulty disengaging.

Source: Adapted from Group for the Advancement of Psychiatry. 1973. *The Joys and Sorrows of Parenthood*. New York: Charles Scribner & Sons.

child can recall after occasional bouts of delinquency or truancy or whatever. There are a legion of experiences that we all went through and came out of on the other end—a bit scathed perhaps, but in most cases, wiser.

The Wide Variation of Living Arrangements: Types of Marriages and Alternative Life Styles

We have come down very severely on the responsibilities and problems of parenting. What about marriage itself? Is it possible, we have all wondered from time to time, for marriage to be the rewarding thing it is "supposed to be," not just after one or two years but after ten, fifteen, twenty—even forty?

Yes, it can be. And there are such marriages. So the research tells us, anyway. These successful marriages may not be plentiful, but they do exist. They have been identified; they have been studied; they have been described and categorized. Do these research studies provide us with any definite answers? Well, not exactly. What they do tell us is that these happy marriages come in a variety of assortments, depending on the needs and wants of the couple, as well as their willingness to work things through, no matter how painful this working through can be at times.

One set of researchers, for example, identified two basic types of marriage: what they called the *utilitarian* marriage and the *intrinsic* marriage.

MARRIAGE STYLES: UTILITARIAN VERSUS INTRINSIC. Just as there are many types of life styles, so also are there various types of marriage styles. Two investigators, John Cuber and Peggy Harroff, studied "fairly happily married," prominent couples: They were considered happily married both by themselves and by others who knew them (Sheehy 1976). The researchers were surprised that happily married couples did not necessarily resemble each other in marriage style. In fact, they concluded from their study that there were at least five basic marriage styles. By marriage style they meant how the couples lived together, raised their children, interacted with others in their social milieus, and related to each other sexually. These five styles could be grouped under two general headings: the **utilitarian** marriage and the **intrinsic** marriage.

The intrinsic marriage is what is thought of as a romantic relationship, with each partner finding the other "indispensible" to fulfilling emotional needs. They share as many activities as they can, and each values and needs the physical and psychological proximity of the other. The fulfillment of emotional needs is a source of strength for both partners as well as a source of creative energy. Within intrinsic marriage are two subcategories, the *vital* intrinsic marriage and the *total* intrinsic marriage. The difference is a matter of degree rather than of kind: the *total* couple attempts to interact as much as they can, while the *vital* couple shares fewer activities and less time together. Nevertheless, both types of couples just "click" with each other; their loving is profound, and conflicts while they may be heated, can be resolved.

The utilitarian marriage is less personal, and the couple spends much less time with each other and at home. They may sleep in separate bedrooms, spend considerably more time in outside activities and with others, and may have casual extramarital affairs, which may be known and accepted by the other spouse. Yet the couples have a fondness for one another and have worked out a fairly viable relationship. Within utilitarian marriages are three subcategories: the *passive-congenial*, the *devitalized*, and the *conflict-habituated*. The passive-congenial style of marriage is frequently found in middle-aged couples who have never experienced any real depth of emotion for each other but who entered marriage in a cool, nonromantic way: They shared interests and each had a "common-sense" attitude toward raising children, and managing careers, home, finances, and so forth. The devitalized utilitarian marriage probably began with a vital interest in each other (and originally may have been an intrinsic marriage), but common interests and activities ceased to be shared emotionally. There is little overt tension or conflict, but their emotional and sexual interaction has become devitalized and infrequent.

The third kind of utilitarian marriage is the conflict-habituated marriage, and in fact, this conflict tension becomes the mode of relating.

One may think that the only satisfactory marriage is the intrinsic marriage, for obviously it is what most of us hope for when we are young. Unfortunately, there is a "catch-22" in the intrinsic marriage: it is much more vulnerable to swift change and deterioration. Because the persons put so much emphasis on each other to supply their emotional needs, sexual gratification, and so on, the intrinsic marriage does not seem to be able to sustain the demands on it for too long and ultimately may end in divorce, mutual conflict, or the more benign state of utilitarianism. The passive-congenial marriage that was utilitarian from the start has much less strain and tension, and the couple seldom experiences the same disillusionment and subtle resentment that a vital or total intrinsic couple may feel when the romance has faded.

THE CRISES IN PREVAILING SEXUAL/MARRIAGE MORES.   There has been a great deal of change in our attitude toward sex in the twentieth century, ranging all the way from Victorian denial and repression of sexual needs on one end of the spectrum to open sexuality with others outside of the marriage relationship on the other end. In between those two ends of the continuum we have seen played out sexual dramas of many kinds: a testing of new attitudes and concepts of sexuality in relationship to other institutions of our society—the family, the state, the church, and so forth. One of the big forces, of course, has been the pill. For the first time in history sex can now be separated from the act of procreation. We are still in process of transition, and it is natural that we are yet experiencing conflict and contradiction in our society as a whole. One thing for sure, we have come to accept that sex *is* a vital part of a healthy person's loving relationship with his or her spouse. We have diminished somewhat the hypocrisy of the double standard— that what is right for a man is not right for a woman, but there is still a wide discrepancy between what we say and what we do. We acknowledge sex as a part of adult human functioning, but we still do not know how to be open with our children regarding our own sexuality. We have become more sane in our harassment of homosexuals (in that we do not do the barbaric things we once did to them), but we still hound them and stare at them in public. We have admitted that sex is maybe OK for "mature" adolescents and appropriate for young marrieds, but it still seems slightly suspect for middle-aged adults and obscene for the elderly. In that respect our generally prevailing attitudes are still inclined to be quite adolescent, and we have much growing up to do.

SOME GAINS IN PREVAILING ATTITUDES. Still we are making some gains as a people regarding marriage and sexual relationships. We are no longer willing to accept spouse abuse and child abuse as part of the marriage contract (Anderson 1983; Magnuson 1983). We are coming to recognize that living within the bonds of matrimony does not imply that a man can beat his wife when he is drunk or depressed (O'Reilly 1983). Nor can he do that to his children (Kempe 1962; Bourne 1978; Helberg 1983; Kempe & Helfer 1980). We no longer accept husbands raping their wives as a marital right (Russell 1982; Dowd 1983). And we are coming to recognize that there is a great deal of sub rosa enjoyment of illicit sex in our society just as there is tacit approval of violence.

Recent surveys continue to report increasing numbers of extramarital sexual involvements (Peterson 1983). We are, however, recognizing that simply because a man or woman has extramarital experiences he or she has not necessarily experienced steady, deeply involved relationships (Cuber 1969; Gagnon 1977). In fact, an extramarital relationship does not mean a marriage is ruined even though divorce is a very common recourse (O'Neill & O'Neill 1972). We may even need to take a look at the difference between infidelity and extramarital relations. The essence of being faithful is to put our partner first and foremost in our lives—thus many spouses may not have had extramarital relations but have been unfaithful in other ways: in complaining about him, in sexual joking with other women, or in abandoning her with the children and escaping for a "good time with the boys." It is betrayal of love and not sexuality that wounds us most. Quite frequently a man will engage in sexuality outside his marriage but still regard his commitment to his wife and children as sacrosanct (Gagnon 1977; Kinsey et al. 1948, 1953; Tavris & Sadd 1977; Peterson 1983).

A woman often becomes involved in an extramarital affair when she feels neglected by her husband. Feelings of neglect and loneliness make her vulnerable to the attentions of other men. Suddenly she begins to feel worthy again and attractive rather than like (as one woman told us) "an old slipper" that makes her husband feel comfortable at home. An interesting aspect is that women who have affairs are much more likely than men to become emotionally involved and to want to separate from their husbands. For women sex is much more an affair of the heart than of the pelvis (Peterson 1983).

Some Dimensions of the Loving Relationship

We are now in a position to replace our fallacies about love with more realistic guidelines for nourishing relationships. Let it be understood, however, that we are, in our time, still in a stage of experimentation and exploration of how we evolve more loving give and take. What we are about to suggest, then, are guidelines, to be thought about and cogitated, not prescriptions to be swallowed whole. Furthermore, these guidelines are ideals and not definitions of specific behavior.

A LOVING RELATIONSHIP INCLUDES MANY EMOTIONS. We do not always have to "love" the other. Sometimes we can get bound up in guilt or remorse because we get angry at the other, irritable, or downright nasty. When we are young, we either "love" our parents or "hate them": *either-or*. That is the child's one-dimensional world (Piaget 1970). If we are not fixated at this child's level, we come to understand that our love for a person has many dimensions: pain as well as joy and conflict as well as agreement. Carl Rogers noted that sometimes when persons come for counseling they are confused about their feelings toward another. During counseling the person may discover he or she is truly angry at the spouse and that it is all right to be angry (Rogers 1951). Sometimes the person feels many emotions: impatience, upset—even, at times, indifference. These experiences do not mean "love has gone out the window"; they mean, rather, that there is a crinkle in the relationship that needs attention. The first step in ironing out the crinkle is recognizing that, at that moment, we do not feel "loving," we feel impatient, upset, angry—even indifferent. We stop the "tragedy" and step out of the "personal" aspect—we become more "impersonal," less defensive, and more open to what is going on with ourselves and with the other person. It is a little like saying, "Oh, I see we have come to an impasse for the moment. Let's see if I can understand what is happening from my side and from your side." He/she thinks/believes/wants this, and I think/believe/want that. It doesn't mean we don't love each other; it simply means we have hit one of those chuckholes or bumps that occur in any relationship. The thing we have to do is to see if we can talk it out, not at the top of our lungs, not by hurling accusations at the other, not with defensiveness, but with a willingness to share our point of view and to grasp that of our partner. We do not always have to be together; we do not always have to agree; and we do not even always have to resolve the situation *right now*! We can at least agree that we need to back off from each other for a while and resolve our differences when we both are calmer and less defensive.

George Bach's "fight therapy" may work for the aggressive person (Bach & Wyden 1969). What we may really need to do is learn to fight fairly. Learning to fight fairly requires several ground rules and the cooperation of both persons. For example, fighting fairly means not accusing the other of crimes but pointing out what disturbs us. Fighting fairly means discussing current situations, not all the problems from "day one" of the relationship. Fighting fairly means allowing the other person to express his or her feelings, to get them all out and not to jump in with, "Oh, I see, sure, I'll do that," or "Oh, I'm sorry, I won't do that again." Fighting fairly means making sure both end up feeling that they have arrived at a reasonable solution.

A LOVING RELATIONSHIP ALLOWS FOR INDIVIDUAL DIFFERENCES. Although we may marry persons similar to ourselves, we are, at the same time, always different. A loving relationship recognizes those differences and allows for them. One of the aspects of the parent-child relationship, particularly in the adolescent years, is the "generation gap" that both experience. The father may want the son to "follow in his footsteps," and he is disappointed when the son's inclinations and interests seem to point in other directions. A mother may feel confused because her daughter does not value the same things she does. An example: A young woman we know has a mother who is a socialite in her community, a socialite in the very best sense of the word. She involves herself in charitable pursuits, is a fund raiser, and gives banquets or dinners for liberal causes. The mother dresses very well and is a vibrant and outgoing person. By contrast, the daughter is introverted and does not value the gracious life. While she has a distinct type of beauty, she prefers jeans and other casual clothes, shuns make-up, and is, of all things, a farrier; that is, she shoes horses. Learning to be a farrier required almost a year of training. Although she was the only woman in the class, she was deemed an outstanding student. She is now trying to get into a college of veterinary medicine—to the dismay and bewilderment of her mother, who was taught that a lady does not do those kinds of things.

We understand these differences in parent-child relationships a little better than we used to. But we are not nearly so understanding of them in our marriage relationships. Allowing the other person his or her individual differences allows that person to grow. Allowing yourself to "own" your individual differences allows you to grow. Each person in a dyadic relationship needs space for those differences—this is ultimate freedom.

A LOVING RELATIONSHIP INCLUDES EMOTIONAL AND SPIRITUAL RE-NEWAL. The commitment to allow each other to express individual differences also necessitates the commitment to plan moments *together* and not just through the children. Although the American ideal is to have a wonderful family vacation together with the children, children can interfere with the relaxed, private intimacy of two people. Part of the attraction of a premarital or extramarital affair is the fact that the two persons are sharing something together free from the constraints of a small tot pounding on the bedroom door at those precious few moments of intimacy; free from the nagging routine of dishes, mowing the lawn, gathering dirty clothes for the laundry, or fixing the plumbing leak. How can two persons have a loving relationship when one or both are too exhausted to do anything at the end of a weary day but collapse in bed? The two persons are just living in the same house as contrasted with being together in a private place with time to relax, talk, and have a drink or watch the sun set, walk, or whatever. Studies of sexual frequency in marriage reveal that as each child comes along, the frequency of sexual intimacy decreases (McCary 1978). Parents owe it to themselves to leave the children occasionally at home with relatives or babysitters and plan an escape from the endless routine of diapers. Children can be a source of joy, but they also are demanding. Parents need some time just to be together, to share mutual interests, to talk without interruption, and for emotional and spiritual renewal.

A LOVING RELATIONSHIP EVOLVES. There is a natural evolution in the loving relationship, just as there is a natural evolution in the process of our lives. Our needs change from one developmental cycle to the next, as Erikson put it. Our values are different from one era to the next, said Levinson. In the early days of knowing each other, the romance of the relationship dominates. There seems to be an ever-present need to be together, to talk, to touch, to caress, and to share physical intimacy. But given enough time and privacy, this terrible urgency begins to recede, and other needs begin to take over: the need to put down roots, establish a life structure, pursue career goals, begin a family, and generally establish one's position in the community. The loving relationship requires an understanding of these elements, and some of its libidinal drive is diverted into other experiences. In that sense, the passionate desire to be together evolves into the excitement of sharing the activities of communal living and of looking forward to and planning for the future. As the life cycle continues, and if the relationship has been constructive for both persons, there is another dimension: having shared years of emotional experience. Having lived so long together and becoming familiar with the other's moods and subtle nuances, you can begin to talk a kind of "shorthand." Meanings do not have to be spelled out. A situation may suddenly be the occasion for a humorous or nostalgic reminiscence. Having weathered emotional storms and temporary setbacks, each has a wealth of knowledge of the other, and when one of the partners has had a hard day or receives bad news, the other knows instinctively what to do to help.

A LOVING RELATIONSHIP STAYS IN THE HERE-AND-NOW. One of the problems in any relationship (friendship, parent-child, husband-wife, lovers) is the tendency to assume that people and relationships will remain the same. People's conceptions of us remain what they were when they last saw us. College students see that when they go home after being away at school. The college student will feel different and is different, to some degree. But family and friends will still consider the college student as he or she was before. So it is with the persons in the loving relationship. Presumably, over the years, we both have grown; presumably, we have been pursuing our own creative and individual needs; presumably, we have been evolving from one life cycle to another. Our own needs will change; so will the other's needs.

We need to remember not to assume that what was right for one or both partners remains right year after year. It may come as a surprise to us when we hear our partner begin to express hopes and dreams never before expressed, perhaps not even experienced. This is not the time to say, "But you said you never wanted . . . " or "If I had known that you would suddenly want to do this, I never would have married you in the first place." We may suddenly discover that our partner (who has seemed happy and satisfied with life in general) is expressing ideas and needs completely alien (seemingly) to his or her past life style. The person may be at the age thirty or age forty transitions, to use Levinson's formulations, or may be at the point of life that Jung called the "search for one's soul."

A LOVING RELATIONSHIP ULTIMATELY TRANSCENDS EVERYTHING WE KNOW ABOUT IT. No matter how much advice you may receive from us or any other authority, the loving relationship transcends everything we know. We may be able to list some of the factors contributing to long-term marriages; we may be able to provide some insight into what can destroy a relationship. But, ultimately, no one can provide you or any two human beings with a prescription for happiness, successful marriage, or love.

Nor can we really describe the loving relationship. It is more than sexual compatibility; it is more than the satisfaction of personal needs or the search for the "neglected function"; it is more than just having someone conveniently in the background. Love has less to do with the pelvis than with the heart. It is less what we can *receive* from it than what we can *give* to it. It is less *expectation* than *commitment*. Masters and Johnson, 1970, those masters of sexual intimacy, end their book *The Pleasure Bond* with a chapter titled "Commitment." All the sexual techniques in the world do not replace the truly caring affection and regard two people have for each other. Masters and Johnson:

> In contrast, there is the commitment of concern, a bond in which a man and a woman mutually meet their obligations not because they feel impelled to do so. They do so in response to impulses, desires and convictions that are deeply rooted within themselves, not all of which do they fully understand. When they act in each other's best interest, even though this may at the time be in conflict with their own immediate wishes, they are saying to each other, in effect: "I care very much about your feelings—because your feelings affect mine. Your happiness adds to mine, your unhappiness takes away from my happiness, and I want to be happy." [Masters & Johnson 1970]

Furthermore, the essence of the loving relationship will always be more than any authority can ever know about it. Any two persons bring to their loving relationship their individuality, backgrounds, interests, and creativity. The loving relationship between two persons is not, cannot be the same as that of any other couple. All of our dos and don'ts are merely suggestions for interpersonal harmony. They may not work out in practice. There are no absolute prescriptions for a loving relationship any more than there are absolute prescriptions for "mental health," "success," or even "life."

Psychologists and psychiatrists are not magicians. We are people very much like yourselves trying to comprehend what living is all about. We observe people; we try to make our observations objective, and we draw conclusions. But we are well aware (most of us, anyway) that there are no magic love potions. Each couple must work out their problems, their despairs, and their barriers no matter what kind of advice and suggestions we may give. In the next chapter we will discuss some verbal and nonverbal techniques for relating to each other, and these techniques should be helpful in communicating, one of the very important ingredients of emotional relationships. Finally, none of us knows what two people can experience together in a loving relationship. It is an unpredictable, continuing process.

COHABITATION AND SINGLEHOOD. In 1980 the U.S. Census Bureau recorded 1.6 million couples living together. These persons have become a large enough part of our population to merit a newly defined census category: "persons of the opposite sex sharing living quarters." The number of persons choosing this life style has risen enormously (approximately 300 percent since the 1970 census) and so have the reasons for making this choice.

Basically cohabitation is an alternative to singlehood or marriage. Some couples consider cohabitation an option of convenience; for others cohabitation is like a trial marriage; for still others this is a permanent alternative replacing any plans for marriage. Whatever the overall goal of cohabitation, the couple does experience more intimacy, emotional security, and companionship than they would with a choice of singlehood (Stein 1976). However, a cohabitating couple may find little if any social support from family, friends, acquaintances, employers, and in some instances, even the law.

Many persons believe that cohabitating before marriage will give the couple a chance to know each other on a day-to-day basis and thus improve their chances for marital success. Research shows that those who cohabitate are as likely to divorce as those who do not live together before marriage (Newcomb and Bentler 1980).

APPLICATIONS AND COPING TECHNIQUES

We have taken some of the "romance" out of marriage, and that is as it should be, for it is the romantic part of marriage that seems to fade. Romance is the flower, the bloom of the plant, that fades. Love is more than romance. The flower fades, but the plant, if tended and cultivated and cared for, will survive the droughts and torrents. Love is the putting down of stable roots, the shooting forth of many branches, and the eventual blooming again. But like all growing things, enduring relationships need cultivation.

Every marriage counselor will have his or her favorite techniques for long-lasting relationships. You eventually will have your own techniques. No list can include them all, but we offer the following basic ones.

1. Maintain Direct and Sane Communication with Each Other

Without communication there is no relationship. Sometimes the first sign of a breakdown in a relationship is a breakdown in communication. Both persons begin to retreat behind a wall of silence, punctuated only by hostile and terse questions and answers. Although silence may be less immediately painful than screaming battles, silence ultimately can become the *modus operandus* of the marriage. The end has already come.

Raging battles, on the other hand, may clear the air, but the wounds suffered may permanently injure one or the other so that the marriage itself becomes disabled.

The issue then, revolves around how to confront the issues at hand—even those painful to discuss—without causing permanent wounds and without retreating into hostile silence. We need to change the "rules of the game" so that instead of blaming other persons for our unhappiness, we develop a "no blame" attitude for problems that arise.

We do not mean we avoid conflict, only that we handle it differently from the traditional "dumping," screaming, and hostile silence. We work through conflict with improved communication, which leads to growth, which further improves our communication. We need to learn how to speak with greater clarity

Recreational even organizer

Church member

Nurse

Maintenance man

Yard man

Grocery shopper

Therapist to family

Wage earner

Teacher and consultant

Chauffuer

Housekeeper

Lover

Bookkeeper and tax consultant

Child caretaker

Hostess

The modern nuclear spouse must perform a multitude of roles that once were shared by other extended family members.

Box 8.6   THREE THEORIES OF FAMILY-LIFE STAGES

DUVALL (1971)	HILL (1965)	SPANIER (1979)
I Married couple	I Establishment (newly married—childless)	I Couples married less than 6 years, with no children
II Childbearing families	II New parents (infant–3 years)	II Oldest child less than 6
III Families with preschool children	III Preschool family (child 3–6 and possibly younger siblings)	III Oldest child between 6 and 12
IV Families with school children	IV School-age family (oldest child 6–12 and possibly younger siblings)	IV Oldest child between 13 and 20
V Families with teenagers	V Family with adolescent	V All others with at least 1 child present
VI Launching families	VI Family with young adult (oldest 20, until oldest leaves home)	VI All others with no child still present at home
VII Empty nest to retirement	VII Family as launching center (from departure of first to last child)	VII No children in home and husband 65 or over
VIII Retirement to death (aging families)	VIII Postparental family: the middle years (after children have left home until father retires)	
	IX Aging family (after retirement of father)	

Source: Newman, Barbara M. and Newman, Phillip R. *Understanding Adulthood.* 1983. New York: CBS College Publishing, Holt, Rinehart & Winston, Inc., p. 286.

and directness, to listen with greater attention and understanding, and to declare ourselves with earnest sincerity—calmly, quietly, openly, humanly communicating. As we move toward creating this kind of family environment, we move toward creating the harbor of humanness we all seem to want and even need so much. (Communication skills are discussed in chapter 9.)

2. Allow Your Relationship to Grow, to Change, and to Process

As a part of this process, some social scientists view family life as a series of stages in much the same way that the life cycle can be viewed as a series of stages. While different observers list different numbers of stages, (see box 8.6), there is remarkable accord that the quality of family life is distinctly different for each of these stages. There are times when the marital satisfaction and happiness are high—stage I of newly married couples and again when the children have left home and the couple have more time for each other (stage VIII). There are times when family stress is high, as for example, when the house is full of adolescents and resounding with adolescent turmoil. Although most of the emphasis of this change in family and marital satisfaction has been focused on the presence, needs, and demands of the children, some of these dynamics must surely involve the adults in the family as they are making their way through their own particular life stage. In his twenties and thirties, the husband-and-father is putting tremendous energy into his job and advancement. The wife-and-mother, on the other hand, may not put the greater part of her physical and intellectual energies into her job until after mid-life—at the very time, in other words, when her husband is beginning to take a more "laid back" attitude toward his work.

Remember, we all have our individual pattern of growth and our individual timing as well as our individual process patterning. We need to welcome the differences for ourselves and those we love.

3. Make Room for Each Other as Part of Your Basic Commitment

Many things interfere with marriage. Children come, financial burdens increase, and job demands take precedence. Sometimes we sacrifice ourselves for "the sake of the children," or we bury ourselves in our work, or we mediate our relationship through other persons. Little by little, we are like two persons simply living under the same roof. It was not anything we did to hurt each other; it just happened—by errors of omission.

We may begin to talk to each other through the children. When he asks her about the news of the day, she replies that Johnnie had to stay home from school because of a cold. Their talk revolves around others: invalided mother, so-and-so at work today, the neighbors.

We need time to be together, to renew ourselves with each other. We need privacy away from intrusions, even the children, so that we can become acquainted with each other once again and rediscover each others' concerns, feelings, hopes, aspirations, and even the changes that have come about since our last encounter.

4. Encourage Each Person to Pursue Emerging Interests, Ambitions, and Individualities

Marriage is not possession. Nor is it ownership. It is a matter of two persons who come together for mutual sharing. Each person has unique interests and abilities, which need to be encouraged.

Give each other space and room to grow. Give each other some privacy and time alone. You are separate entities with distinct and individual personalities. Your likes and dislikes do not have to coincide precisely. Marriage is a coming together, but there is an ebb and flow to relationships, and sometimes there must be a pulling apart before we can come together again in true remeeting.

Furthermore, as you grow and mature, you may discover that you now would like to venture into activities and pursuits that did not interest you earlier. Allow your partner to do the same. Love allows the other to grow. Love has respect for the other person's individuality. Both of you will become more exciting persons as a result and therefore more exciting to each other.

5. Surprises Are Fun, but It Is Planning Together That Makes a Relationship Enduring

A man we know became somewhat more affluent. He wanted to do something for his wife for their anniversary, so he bought her a new car and surprised his wife with the keys to it on the morning of their anniversary. Her reaction was hurt. His reaction was anger at her hurt. It was an event that cropped up many times in arguments over the next few years. He was angry that she did not appreciate his gift; she was hurt that she was left out of the decision.

Although we generally are more neutral, we have to agree this time with the wife. Such "surprises" can do irreparable damage, though he may have had good intentions.

All major decisions and many minor ones need to be made together. Marriage and living together is a partnership, and a marriage of minds does not happen when there is a silent partner. Working out the details of a project or the various aspects of problems as they come along brings people closer together.

6. Remember It Is Sometimes the Little Things You Do Not Do That Erode Your Marriage

Most persons in a marriage are aware of the big problems. These are the things you quarrel about or are the bones of contention. If the two of you are at all serious about making a marriage last, you continually work at these problems. In the background, however, are the many small omissions that may be causing serious (and silent) erosion, things that may seem too small and petty to be mentioned but that foster resentment, hurt, and feelings of neglect. For example, one partner may forget that the two of you agreed to go out to dinner and works late at the office. Or one partner forgot to mention an after-dinner meeting, no big thing, since neither of you had special plans for the evening. Nevertheless, it just "slipped the mind," and the other partner begins to feel that he or she is just not important enough to be kept informed.

There is a way out of this and an easy one. Keep a common calendar of events. List all dates, meetings, and invitations. Review it daily and weekly. Check in with each other before making other dates or commitments. In the morning, before one or the other of you leave, review what is supposed to be happening during the day and evening. We do this with our office colleagues; surely we can do it for each other.

7. Finally, Remember That No Two Marriages Are Alike and None Are Perfect

Live for yourselves and not for those around you. Work out the details of your life in a way that is viable for both of you, regardless of how others are living their married arrangements. There are, ultimately, no dos and don'ts except those that the two of you contract together.

We have tended to dichotomize our lives. At work we have our *work* to do. At play we have our *play* to do. At home just what is it that we have to do? If it is only the same round of washing floors, cooking meals, mowing grass, making love, sitting with friends . . . raising children, the home will be seen as a "prison of love" (Mousseau 1982) (or hate). There must be spaces and times for many events to happen—not just work but play; not just conflict but loving interaction; not just the same drab routine but new experiences (to the beach or the mountains or camping). Family must not be simply an event we endure but a process of sharing growth and excitement—not simply a place that has to take you in when you go there but a place you love to go to. It is not easy in this day and age. It takes thoughtful planning and continual caring.

Perhaps this (in our time and space) is where our greatest challenge lies for cooperative choice and change.

SUMMARY POINTS TO REMEMBER

1. Americans are ambivalent about marriage. We have high expectations (ideals) but also a high level of dissatisfaction (reality).
2. The historical tradition of Western civilization has supported the one-man-one-woman bonding of Genesis, but actual history has provided a wide range of love, sex, and family bonding. At present, we seem to prefer serial monogamy punctuated by divorce.
3. Love is often confused for other attributes and behaviors including jealousy, possessiveness, self-sacrifice, martyrdom

or exclusivity. Mature love is not destructive but growing.

4. We choose our mates by way of certain factors; among them are the propinquity, the neutrality, and the similarity factors.
5. An extended courtship allows the couple to know each other in a variety of situations and to work out ways of processing problematic situations.
6. Modern marriage is vulnerable in many ways. Modern wives and husbands must play many more roles than in previous eras. As well, children interfere with marital time and privacy.
7. Financial stress magnifies any concurrent problems the family is having resulting in alcoholism, spouse abuse, child abuse, child neglect, and divorce.
8. Modern families are also adjusting to the phenomenon of double-income and double-career families, which is causing a displacement of traditional man/woman roles.
9. Working wives often have more of a feeling of self-worth and self-esteem than women who stay at home.
10. There is a wide range of parenting styles ranging from authoritarian to permissive. There are five basic styles of marriage identified: total, vital, passive congenial, devitalized, and conflict-habituated.
11. The loving relationship involves a wide spectrum of emotions which are not to be denied but are to be processed as problems come up and worked through. A truly loving relationship allows both persons to grow and evolve emotionally, intellectually, and spiritually.
12. Ultimately, a loving relationship transcends everything we know about it.

SIGNIFICANT TERMS AND CONCEPTS

adultery
alternative life styles
ambivalent
authoritarian parenting
authoritative parenting
battered wives
bisexuality
celibacy
child abuse
cohabitation
coitus interruptus
coitus reservatus
compatibility
conflict-habituated
    marriage
courtly love
devitalized marriage
double-income family

double standard
dual-career family
empty nest syndrome
extended family
extramarital
group marriage
homosexuality
infidelity
intrinsic marriage
lady of the house
laissez-faire parenting
lesbian
macho
masturbation
monogamy
mores
mutuality factor
nuclear family

open marriage
passive congenial
    marriage
permissive parenting
premarital
propinquity factor
roles
self-esteem
self-worth
serial monogamy
sexual abuse
similarity factor
spouse abuse
total marriage
upward mobility
utilitarian marriage
virility
vital marriage

FILL IN THE BLANKS WITH SIGNIFICANT TERMS AND CONCEPTS

1. Americans have a high level of dissatisfaction with marriage yet a very high level of expectation. This shows that we are a_____ about marriage.

2. At this time we have as our institutionalized ideal monogamy while in practice we prefer s_____ m_____.

3. Love used to be considered the basis for jealousy. Now we consider jealousy to be learned and relative to the culture. Love is not seen as the basis of jealousy. Love is not d_____ rather g_____.
4. In marriage in this country today women marry a man of slightly higher status, thus women are u_____ m_____ through marriage.
5. Some of the most basic stressors on marriage today are that we demand more from marriage than ever before; we must play many more r_____ than before; and children interfere with privacy and mobility.
6. Working wives often have a greater feeling of s_____ -e_____ and s_____ -w_____ than the wives who stay home.
7. Four basic forms of parenting are: a_____, a_____, p_____, and l_____.
8. Even our laws today reflect a growing intolerance for s_____ abuse and c_____ abuse.
9. The various types of marriage include c_____-h_____, d_____, p_____, c_____, v_____, and t_____.

RECOMMENDED BOOKS FOR FURTHER READING

Fromm, Erich. 1956. *The Art of Loving: An Inquiry Into the Nature of Love.* New York: Harper & Row Publishers, Inc. It is a classic in its field and represents a melding of the ideal of romantic love with the practical aspects of living with another person.

Hunt, Morton and Hunt, Bernice. 1977. *The Divorce Experience.* New York: McGraw-Hill Book Company. The Hunts have made divorce their life study. We recommend this book to anyone who has had a divorce or is about to go through one.

Huxley, Laura Archera. 1963. *You Are Not the Target.* New York: Farrar, Strauss and Giroux. We highly recommend this book for some of the simple and effective "recipes" she offers for learning what we have called the "impersonal" attitude.

Kephart, William M. 1976. *Extraordinary Groups: The Sociology of Unconventional Life-Styles.* New York: St. Martin's Press, Inc. Kephart presents some of the unusual types of family bonding in the United States since our inception including the Mormons and the famous Oneida community. These groups demonstrate very clearly that experimental forms of male-female bonding did not begin in the late 1960s but have been a part of our history.

Laing, R. D. 1967. *The Politics of the Family and Other Essays.* Westminister, Md: Ballantine Books, Inc. The politics of the family can and does breed neurosis on the unfortunate member who does not realize how subtle the forms of defense mechanisms can be. A real shocker and eye-opener!

Mead, Margaret. 1978. *Culture & Commitment: the New Relationships between the Generations in the 70s,* rev. ed. New York: Columbia University Press. Married several times herself and unafraid to cross cultural norms in her own evolution, Mead proposed several types of family bondings. She is a delight to read since she is always honest, amazingly direct, and witty.

Putney, Snell and Putney, Gail J. 1972. *The Adjusted American: Normal Neuroses in the Individual and Society.* New York: Harper & Row Publishers, Inc. The Putneys write about neuroses which they call "normal" but which are peculiarly American. Some of the neurotic American personality types they describe are the Martyr, the Wolf, the "Dutiful" family member, the Little Tin God, and the Jealous Wife.

9

*People Working
Together:
Vocational Choice,
Career Development,
and Interpersonal
Processing*

WORK AND CAREER AS PERSONALITY DEVELOPMENT
Work as Basic to Self-Esteem
Work as Basic to Family Stability
Work as Basic to a Person's Emotional and Physical Health
Work as Basic to our Identity

THE SOCIAL STRATIFICATION OF WORK IN AMERICA
Blue-Collar Workers
White-Collar Workers
The Double-Income Couple: A Change in the Family Scene

FACTORS INVOLVED IN VOCATIONAL CHOICE
Our Environmental Background: Our Limited Social Mobility
Our Personality Type
The College Experience as Moratorium and Exploration

CAREER SUCCESS: ENJOYING WHAT ONE DOES
The Working Class: Working to Live
The Professional Class: Living to Work

COMMUNICATION SKILLS AS A REQUISITE FOR CAREER SUCCESS
AND INTERPERSONAL PROCESSING
The Scientific Study of Language: General Semantics
Learning to Listen
Understanding Our Paralanguage

APPLICATIONS AND COPING TECHNIQUES

WORK AND CAREER AS PERSONALITY DEVELOPMENT

We all recognize that we need love, affection, people to belong to, and a sense of family. Erik Erickson's model of the life span specifies one's need for home and family, in whatever form it may take, as vital to the development of the young adult—the major task of the twenties (Erikson 1950). Abraham Maslow placed the *belonging needs* as the third level of his hierarchy (see page 27). Stabilizing ourselves within a family grouping and having that sense of trust and companionship (with those we love and who love us) give us that sense of strength and confidence to go out into the world and to confront the many challenges that are a part of everyday life.

Work as Basic to Self-Esteem

But there is yet another level of the human enterprise vital to our continuing development of personality integration: our work and our career development. Indeed, Maslow saw it as being the next higher level of personality integration on the way to self-actualizing. In Maslow's formulation it is through our work that we achieve our *esteem needs*. Not only do we gain a feeling of self-worth because others value what we contribute to our working community, we also gain a sense of self-worth from the fact that we can and are contributing something unique and special to others. We need to feel appreciated for what we can do. We need to feel that in some small area of the working world we are making our special mark. We need to feel that others recognize our special skills, talents, gifts. Man truly lives by more than bread alone. The accomplishments of successful careers (specifically useful results) lend dignity and distinction to our lives.

Work as Basic to Family Stability

Work influences many areas of family life. Most fundamental, of course, is the area of financial security. As pointed out in the previous chapter, when financial security collapses, the family itself is endangered. Small tensions become major stresses. The bills that need to be paid (but cannot be paid) become occasions of bitter accusation and hostile rebuke: *Who* did *what* with *how much?* Spouse abuse and child abuse are more apt to occur as the breadwinner becomes more insecure, unsure, and guilty about his or her failure to provide for the family. When economic hardship hits our society, alcoholism increases, more suicides are reported, homicide statistics rise, and admissions to psychiatric institutions, prisons, and juvenile-delinquent centers increase sharply (Brenner 1976; Kasl 1979; Thurrow 1982). Unemployment and substandard subsistence are not just problems of economics but major factors in individual and social welfare. They attack the very structure of family life at its roots (Liem & Liem 1979; Riegle 1982).

Work as Basic to a Person's Emotional and Physical Health

Besides the increase of suicide and psychiatric admissions to hospitals, financial insecurity wreaks havoc with our physical and emotional well-being. On their continuing investigations into major emotional impacts on health, Holmes and Rahe and their associates found that not only unemployment had great impact on a person's health, so also did retirement, any decrease in money, or changes of any kind in the working situation or work responsibilities (Holmes and Rahe 1967). A study, for example, of fifty-four unemployed in Detroit's recent automobile recession, disclosed some statistics on their health.

After two years of unemployment more than half showed "serious deterioration in their physical and psychological health. Seven had died, and one had committed suicide . . . figures that are much higher than actual predictions for the same age group." What makes Holmes and Rahe's study even more significant are two facts of the auto-industry unemployed. The first is that they were laid off in a general, impersonal cutback; that is to say, they were not fired because of incompetency or irresponsibility. The layoff was a part of the national recession and not a personal failure of the unemployed workers. The second fact to be considered is that the auto unions provide their unemployed workers with a fairly high level of unemployment insurance. Why, then, did their unemployment affect these men so acutely? Well, for one thing, work has to do with our very sense of identity, and without work this sense of identity can collapse very easily.

Work as Basic to Our Identity

First of all, a person's social contacts become limited when there is no work place. Whether we realize it or not, we all gain a sense of belongingness with the group of people with whom we work, even if this belongingness is punctuated with momentary flares of temper or personality disagreements. When we are laid off, we may see these persons occasionally in the beginning. But after a time, friends from work begin to disappear because the context of the working relationship has also disappeared. There simply is not that much to talk about any more.

Even when the unemployed person finds work again, he or she may have suffered a severe trauma to his or her psychological well-being. In his famous book *Working*, Studs Terkel noted that persons who had experienced unemployment during the Great Depression of the thirties were left with emotional scars in their living space, in particular, a lack of confidence in the future and in their ability to continue to hold jobs. For some no amount of lately acquired necessities and luxury possessions could assuage their sense that, at any time, their economic rug could be pulled out from under them (Terkel 1970).

In our democratic framework there is still a thin crust, to be sure, of "moneyed aristocracy," but for the large percentage of Americans it is not *who we are* that gives us an identity so much as *what we do;* that is to say, our chosen profession or business or career. When we meet other persons, their way of showing interest in us is to inquire, politely what we *do*. We answer, as the case may be, that we are a college professor or a physicist or a physician, accountant, attorney, nurse, writer, actor, and so forth. Then, on further inquiry, we may be asked if we are married. Do we have children? Where do we live? But generally speaking, it is by way of the nature of our working capacity or profession that Americans introduce themselves. Our identities are deeply involved with our work and careers as well as our family (Derr 1980).

THE SOCIAL STRATIFICATION OF WORK IN AMERICA

The stratification of our society is presented very clearly in our demarcation of workers into blue-collar, white-collar, executive, and/or professional classifications of work roles. This stratification will significantly affect a worker's family life style, living environment, possibilities for economic and social advancement, attitude toward leisure and what is done with it—and even the children's educational achievement.

Blue-Collar Workers

The blue-collar worker is generally the first to be hit with unemployment, particularly if his or her vocational skills are limited (Thurow 1982). It is blue-collar workers who express the most job dissatisfaction (Rubin 1976). For some their working situation is like a prison, cooping them up for forty hours a week. They often have little sense of pride, since they do not feel any personal involvement with their work, and the assembly-line worker has become the prototype for the alienation of our industrialized and technologized society. It is the blue-collar worker who generally has the burden of swing shifts and graveyard shifts, which disrupt the daily schedule of family life (Kantor 1977; Hood & Golden 1979). Consider, for example, the husband or wife who needs to sleep when the children are getting up in the morning for school or who are coming home after school to play. The need for sleep and the noise of children in the kitchen and letting off steam can result in continuing screaming at the spouse, "For heaven's sake, can't you keep them quiet so I can get some rest!" Furthermore, an evening shift or a graveyard shift, plays havoc with marital sex life (Mott et al. 1975; Packard 1972; Hennon & Cole 1981). Most studies of blue-collar workers and even low-level white-collar workers reveal low self-esteem and bouts of depression, anxiety, and unhappiness (Tiffany et al. 1970); and the reader is already aware that those are the characteristics associated with alcoholism, spouse abuse, child abuse; and antisocial criminal activities (LeMasters 1975).

White-Collar Workers

In contrast to the blue-collar worker, white-collar workers have more flexible hours to take care of family responsibilities and emergencies. If the blue-collar worker needs to take time off, the time clock records the hours lost. If his wife is ill, the white-collar worker can drive his children to school simply by phoning the office and saying that he'll be half an hour late (or whatever).

At the top end of the white-collar stratification and at the professional level there is even more control of one's schedule. One can even stay out of the office, if there is a deadline coming up and paper work to do, and work in the home in the study or elsewhere, to avoid the interruptions of the telephone or talkative colleagues.

But not even the upper-level white-collar worker or the professional will have complete freedom of behavior or control of his or her private affairs. Corporations and megacorporations have a special (if covert) interest in the lives of their workers. There are demands, both verbal and implied, which the young male and female executive and professional climbing aboard the company ship had better pay attention to—if they want to climb the corporate ladder (Whyte 1952; Packard 1972; Walker 1982).

The Double-Income Couple: A Change in the Family Scene

While there are many economic advantages for the family when the wife is working, there are also definite disadvantages. The increased financial independence may result in divorce (Ross & Sawhill 1975). The wife who had no financial means of her own and with children to care for was much more willing to put up with a lonely or abusive home environment. (See box 8.4.) Economically independent women do not have to put up with unsatisfactory marriages, neglect, alcoholism, or a man who is willing to invest his sexual energies elsewhere (Ross & Sawhill 1975). There is also a dynamic change in the power equation of spouses. A woman who is bringing in an income expects to be listened to and to have more input into decisions. She is willing to speak her mind and to "level with him" rather than to look up to him and avoid expressing herself. She feels more self-confident and more her own person. But while her self-esteem and self-confidence is higher, his (by contrast) may fall. Her power increases while his decreases (Blood & Wolfe 1960; Pearlin 1975).

The married woman who gets a job may find that she is suffering from *role overload* (Frieze et al. 1978). While she enjoys her status as income producer and

competent worker, she may well find that she hasn't freed herself from the home-maker role at all but has simply added to it. While her husband believes that he helps out at home (in fact, many husbands complain that they are doing too much), the data reveals that he spends perhaps only eleven hours a week in household tasks while the working wife is contributing fifty-one hours a week, on the aver-age. Furthermore, his contributions tend to involve the more enjoyable tasks such as shopping, an occasional turn at cooking, and some diswashing. She is still the spouse who mops the floor, scrubs the oven, and cleans the toilet (Scanzoni & Fox 1980; Condran & Bode 1982; Nichols & Metzen 1982).

Although the working wife still has the major responsibilities for the house and the family, there is an area in which she does get some relief, namely, child rearing. With her time taken up by her job, the husband finds himself more in-volved with the responsibilities of child rearing. Whether he wants to or not, the husband of the working wife becomes more of a father to his children. Some men have even expressed satisfaction in their role as "mother-father." But this kind of reaction is much more apt to be found in the educated class. The working-class husband may feel resentment in his increased child-care responsibilities and in the lowered housekeeping standards and convenience food meals (Skinner 1980; Hiller & Philliber 1982).

But problems or not, the double-income family, with all its consequences on the family structure, is here to stay. We shall probably still have that woman who prefers the homemaker role as her chief occupation, but there is no doubt that the number of working wifemothers will increase, not decrease, in the coming decades.

FACTORS INVOLVED IN VOCATIONAL CHOICE

Our Environmental Background: Our Limited Social Mobility

Most of us choose our occupation because we have had contact with the field in some way. If we have a physician for a father or mother, we are more likely to choose a career in medicine. A parent who has musical talent but who has not made any professional use of it may foster that musical talent in the child either directly or simply because the child grows up in an atmosphere where music is appreciated and played. Most farmers have a long tradition of farming in their genealogy, so to speak. In a sense, the propinquity factor occurs as a natural phenomenon in vocational choice as it does in marital choice. It is also true that children of working-class parents will tend to become working-class people themselves. This is not to say that social mobility upward does not occur. It does, but it can generally happen only one socioeconomic rung at a time. The child of a coal miner may be able to make the transition from rural Appalachia to the big city, but rarely will he or she be able to become a lawyer or a physician, no matter how hard he or she may dream of it during adolescent years. His or her schooling will have been far too substandard for the child to compete for a college scholarship. Even for the very gifted there are very few medical and law scholarships that provide full tuition, room and board, and necessary spending money—which a student would need coming from the poverty level of his or her parents. Thus our vocational choices are limited by virtue of the environment in which we grow up (Boyle 1966; Wilson 1959).

What we do should be consistent with our basic personality type. It is obvious that politicians need to be fairly extraverted since they are dealing in the arena of human affairs, while research scientists need to be introverted since they spend much time in solitude.

 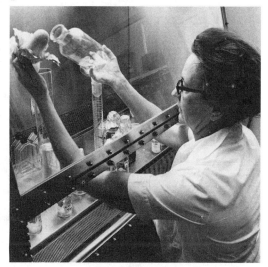

Our Personality Type

In the early development of psychology as a profession back in the thirties, forties, and fifties, psychologists developed many psychological tools for vocational choice and vocational placement. In point of fact, however, many of these tests tended to reveal very little in terms of surprising results for the young person who was trying to make a career choice. By and large, high school students will tend to choose vocations that seem to accord with how they see themselves. Girls who are considering vocations in science see themselves as analytic, curious, and precise. Boys who decide on business careers see themselves as aggressive, dominant, and energetic, and not artistic, idealistic, or scientific. Furthermore, young people will naturally gravitate toward what they are good at: Boys who are good athletes will choose a vocational goal as physical education coaches, and those who are competent in solving numerical problems will select a vocation dealing with numbers or numeric concepts, such as accounting or computer programming. Those who value warm human relationships will tend to choose areas where they can express such feelings, for instance, in the health services or teaching kindergarten or the primary grades (Dipboye & Anderson 1961). Generally speaking, then, we have a rough idea of what we like to do by the time we are into our adolescence, even if our ideas are idealistic and based on fantasy, not on reality or experience (Levinson 1978). But by the time we reach our late twenties, most of us will have found that we have deviated greatly from our adolescent fantasies and that our career development has taken many surprising twists and turns.

The College Experience as Moratorium and Exploration

Although, there are many students in high school who seem to know just what academic course and major they are going to follow when they get to college, most students are not at all confident about what they will major in. Perhaps their parents urged them to go because "education is something nobody can take away from you" or "it's a chance to improve yourself." Some young persons may go to college to avoid settling into work or simply to expand themselves as persons. There are a wide variety of reasons for going to college, and they are probably all valid to some degree. It is certainly true that one is more apt to find a college man to marry, if that is what a young woman wants. It is certainly an opportunity to experience a wider world view, if that is one's objective. And it certainly is a place to explore various vocational choices. There is no better place for young people to sort out their ideas, develop personally, and acquire a variety of social skills and vocational competencies. Even if college students do not immediately find their vocational goal in life, and even if they flounder around from one major to another, college does do one thing for them, says one social scientist. It gets them away from home, without their having to break violently with their parents and without their having to earn their own living, neither of which they are equipped for. It's not just getting away from home, of course. It is the fact that the relatively secure environment of college allows young people to consider new ideas, meet new persons, try out their fledgling wings in this or that arena (Rice 1979). Studies of college students on their entrance to college and their graduation from it reveal that college does have an effect on their thinking. They move from rigidity in their political and social ideas to flexibility; that is to say, they move from being black-white in their opinions—something is either this or that, right or wrong, good or evil—to recognizing that there exists a wide plurality of opinions and viewpoints. They had the opportunity to meet members of the faculty who take a personal interest in them and thus discover new role models. Finally, they overcome many of their earlier childlike world views and assumptions about the world (Madison 1969). They become more respectful of other cultures and other world views. In short, by the end of their college years they have moved from being narrow in their perspectives to being more relativistic in their approach to social problems (Perry 1970). They are, then, progressing up the Kohlbergian scale of universal and ethical/moral standards (p. 84). They may still truly believe that there is "an answer" to perplexing questions, and "a solution" to social ills, but at least their adolescent idealism has been tempered with deeper awareness that there is no *one* "cause" for this or that problem and that whatever problems we are confronted with are **multivariate in causation**.

THE FEMALE EXPERIENCE OF COLLEGE LIFE.   Although college-career women are now taken seriously, women are still less confident than men in their ability to go to the professional schools (Leland et al. 1979). They are still electing, in large majority, the lower level of professional education, leading to careers such as elementary and high school teacher and nurse rather than to professions such as college professor and physician. In comparison to Russia, more of whose physicians are women than men, we still have only a minority of women entering top levels of medicine. In our country women are still rarely to be found in engineering, political science, accounting, astronomy, economics, and architecture. Bright women still don't have as high aspirations vocationally as bright men (Leland et al. 1979).

Fear of success? What happens to women? We have known for a long time that girls show an earlier academic facility than boys from infancy up. Females are more verbal as children, have fewer academic problems, and make better grades than males right up until they reach high school. Then the rift noted above begins to appear in academic and vocational choice. This sudden reversal has puzzled many educators and psychologists. Perhaps it is **fear of success** (Horner 1970, 1972), namely, the feeling that there are many negative consequences for women who succeed in traditionally male areas. Because of our societal world view (with its consequent assumptions) women view successful competition with men as threatening men, as making themselves more unmarriageable and also less acceptable as wives and mothers (Horner 1970, 1972). Further research into this area has revealed that men do better than women in competitive tasks, while women do better than men in social tasks where cooperation, and not competition, is at stake (Horner 1972; Hoffman 1977)

The need for role models. Others have suggested that part of this difference in vocational aspiration comes from insufficient and inadequate role models for women. A team of researchers studied the behaviors of men and women students in college classes. In classes with men college professors, the male students were more likely than women to raise their hands to ask questions and to dissent from the instructor's point of view. But in those classes taught by women the female students showed less inhibition to raise questions or discuss the topics presented. In fact, their behavior was quantitatively and qualitatively similar to male students (Sternglanz & Lyberger-Ficek 1975).

There are other kinds of supportive evidence for the **role-modeling theory.** Research into the personality and background characteristics of women who have high-level career aspirations shows that they have come from families in which the mother worked herself or had considerable education. The women not only had role models in their mothers but also had support from both parents for their aspirations to high-level professional or business careers. In terms of personality structure, these women were more autonomous in their life style and did not feel that to be career successful meant a loss of their femininity or that they could not combine their vocational and familial aspirations (Parsons, Frieze, & Ruble 1975). Nevertheless, the woman who has high career aspirations in male-dominated areas knows she must maintain a delicate balance between her intellectual capabilities and her "feminine" abilities if she is to avoid covert and overt hostility from her male colleagues.

THE COLLEGE DROPOUT: SOMETIMES A POSITIVE STEP. Educators have long been concerned with the college dropout. The college dropout has been defined as that student who leaves his or her original college before the four years necessary for earning a B.A. or B.S. The dropout rates seem high when one takes a cursory look at the figures, up to 60 percent of the entering freshmen across the country in various universities and four-year and two-year colleges (Cope & Hannah 1975). But statistics are spuriously high in terms of ultimate college graduation, and the results are not nearly as drastic as they seem upon first reading. Many students drop out only temporarily and come back later—when they are more motivated after having earned a living "the hard way." Sometimes they have even married and produced a family, and now they want to pursue a higher-level vocational goal. Consequently, some educators have come to believe that the dropout decision is often a very positive step—they return to college not because they are satisfying their parents' aspirations but because they are now *themselves* motivated to earn a degree (Timmons 1978).

Furthermore, many men and women find themselves making a major job change even in their forties. As our life span continues to lengthen, we feel less time bound to remain in jobs we dislike and freer to make transitions in our vocational development as well, and by the very virtue that our technological society is burgeoning with new types of jobs every year, the possibilities for job transition and career advancement necessitates on-the-job training and postgraduate education. Our understanding of educational-vocational development has expanded from the idea of a two or four year commitment to a life-long process.

As more women become prominant in traditionally male arenas, young women students will have female models to counteract the fear-of-success syndrome.

CAREER SUCCESS: ENJOYING WHAT ONE DOES

The process concept of career choice and development gains some validity from research into job satisfaction. The workers who have the highest percentage of job dissatisfaction are younger people rather than older people. In several surveys carried out in the 1970s more persons over thirty claimed job satisfaction than those in their early twenties and teens (Quinn et al. 1974; Wilson & Wise 1975). Presumably by the time they had reached their thirties, they had found the areas they enjoyed and that seemed to suit their personality style and temperament.

Of course there are certain factors that make for job satisfaction, and it may come as a surprise to the younger of our readers that money is not at the top of the list. In fact, salary usually rates fourth or fifth on a specified list of factors. What comes ahead of money? Well, the environmental climate, so to speak. How pleasant a place is it to work? Are one's superiors understanding when problems come up? Can one talk to them in an easy manner? Are one's coworkers cooperative, or is there an under-the-surface tension that is ready to flare up in cross comments and departmental warfare? After all, when one spends the major part of one's waking day on the way to work, at work, or going home from work, it is important to have a job one enjoys. Other factors of job satisfaction are the opportunity to use one's talents and to have a certain flexibility and control over one's working schedules (Renwick et al. 1978; Quinn & Staines 1978). Another fact in job satisfaction is the possibility for advancement for those who are ambitious.

The Working Class: Working to Live

It can be easily deduced that professional people will be more content in their line of work than white-collar or blue-collar workers in that order. Professionals are often doing what they enjoy, and they have control of their schedule. Lowest on the scale of job satisfaction are the day workers, male and female, who have no control over their job and don't even know for sure if they will work at all. The cleaning woman will work in five or six different houses in a week, each employer expecting her to work at top efficiency and strength. She is exhausted at night, and there is little that makes her want to go back—except the money involved. The unskilled construction laborer may stand at the usual pick-up corner waiting for a sign that there is work today on the docks or on some construction site. Any satisfaction that these workers get comes mainly from being employed, from getting a daily or weekly paycheck, which gives them a sense of self-worth as a provider for the family.

There *are* some highly skilled blue-collar workers who enjoy their jobs: These are the men at the top of the labor career ladder—the tool-and-die man, the electrician, the auto mechanic specialist. They have a sense of self-esteem and self-worth because their highly valued technical skill keeps them in demand and because they have some control over their lives and work schedules. They are looked up to by other workers and considered a resource and an asset by their employers. They receive the highest wages, and they are the least affected by economic layoffs in times of recession and depression. They develop a sense of pride in their work and many times have higher incomes than the lower end of the white-collar worker. They are the princes, so to speak, of the blue-collar class, and they are in the minority.

The majority of blue-collar workers however, "clock in" their forty hours in order to pay bills, and enjoy their off time. Much of their off time, however, is spent "fixing up" around the house or trying to watch their favorite TV program in competition with their children. Sometimes, they are able to get away from the house to hunt or fish or go to a ball game. By and large, they work to live rather than living to work.

The Professional Class: Living to Work

By contrast, it is quite the other way around for the professionals: They may live to work. It is in working, in their careers, in their possibilities of job achievement that they fulfill those needs Maslow called *self-esteem* and *self-actualizing*. But the professionals are not without their problems as well. Basic to their success is their ability to deal with people and that means developing their communication skills.

COMMUNICATION SKILLS AS A REQUISITE FOR CAREER SUCCESS AND INTERPERSONAL PROCESSING

It may come as another surprise to the reader that incompetency in a job is one of the last reasons named for firing a worker. *The two top reasons employers do give for firing workers are absenteeism* (a worker who is frequently absent or late is simply holding up the company and everyone else) *and the inability to get along with coworkers* (Blum & Naylor 1968; Myers 1977; McCormic & Ilgan 1980).

Furthermore, almost all the surveys of successful leadership have shown that among the chief factors in successful career development and promotion to supervisory and management levels are the ability to communicate with others and the ability to bring out the best in one's employees. These are not the only factors, of course, but whether a man or a woman is promoted often rests on his or her ability to deal effectively with the people for whom they have responsibility. Textbooks on vocational development devote much of their content to just this subject, and professional courses in leadership devote a good deal of their allotted time to training in communication style. Earlier in this book we noted that certain personality types will have more natural ability in the arena of interpersonal affairs. Extraverted persons, for example, seem to possess the qualities that make them sensitive to the feelings and ideas of others. The *feeling* type will be able to put into words what a coworker may be wanting to say but does not know how to express. We do not mean to suggest that more introverted persons, or "thinking" types, are totally unsuitable for leadership. They can develop leadership skills and often do.

It is well, then, at this juncture, to lay out some of the principles involved in the area of interpersonal communication, for no matter whether we are a telephone-switchboard supervisor with only a half dozen people under us or manager of a large number of franchised businesses, we will need to develop our communication skills.

It should be noted by the reader that while this chapter is focused on organizational communication, the same principles can be applied to communication within our family grouping. It is a sad but true commentary that many of us will put our best foot forward with the persons we interact with in our world of work or in social situations of a more recreational type and then come home and deal quite otherwise with our spouse, our parents, our children, or our other relatives. We tend to *displace* the aggravation we may experience on the job or elsewhere on those who are nearest and dearest. We dump our garbage on them, so to speak, and which results in hurt feelings, angry retorts, all-out arguments, or stony silence. The ability to deal understandingly and gently with others is one of the keys to satisfaction in marriage as it is one of the keys to successful career development. We will, therefore, use examples from both arenas, inside our home environment as well as outside our home base.

The Scientific Study of Language: General Semantics

The study and scientific use of language has become a specialized science called linguistics. We shall turn our attention now to one area of linguistics, called general semantics. General semantics attempts to improve our communication so that language may be used not as a weapon but as a force for saner and more rational ways of interpersonal living. Alfred Korzybski, the founder of general semantics, went so far as to say that the way we use our language can make us scientific or irrational, sane or insane (Korzybski 1958). Consider, for example, the following: a man we know complains continually about his job: His supervisors are unreasonable; his colleagues are uncooperative; and his students are "dumb" and "trying to get away with things." Now all of these may have some measure of reality, and we do not want to imply otherwise. This man, however, never lets up on his pet topic. His working conditions are his constant subject matter to his friends, to his family, and to any of us who will listen to him. We suggested to him once that he discuss his contentions (in a rational and calm way) with his colleagues and supervisors. His retort silenced us for good: "No use trying to do that. Nobody will listen to me!" There is some truth to this, for many of us have become weary of his same old record, and we begin to edge away when he starts up. The point is that this man is "gossiping" continually. He may not call it gossip—he thinks that gossip is what women do with each other. He may call what he does griping or letting off the steam, or even voicing legitimate complaints. But the fact is that much of his creative energy is going into self-sabotage. He is giving himself a mind set that his working life is hell and that he is the target of his students and the scapegoat of his supervisors and colleagues. He is not trying to work out his personal upsets with others; he is actually promoting more and more disharmony within himself and with others. In short, he may be driving himself insane, and paranoia may be just around the corner.

IMPROVING OUR LISTENING SKILLS.   Listening is the basic form of communication. Ever since we were babies we have been listening: listening to our parents, listening to our teachers, listening to the radio or to television. We listen to our friends and to political speech makers. We listen to our employers or our colleagues. We spend innumerable hours listeining to everybody else at various meetings. Why, then, do we have to learn to listen? Sometimes we may feel that it would be nice to wear ear muffs to prevent ear pollution. The problem is that we do not listen well. Perhaps we do not listen well just because listening has been so much a part of our lives. Yet listening is undeniably the first step to effective communication.

Studies of listening reveal that we tend to hear what we want to hear and listen to what we want to listen to. We tend to "turn off" when we do not like what is being said, if we are bored, or if there is something about the person we do not like. Have you ever heard a student say, "I can't learn anything from him." If we listen further, we may hear the student say something like this: "I just don't like him. I don't like his personality." He or she has stopped listening. It is not so much that they cannot learn as they will not learn. One of the characteristics of successful students is their ability to learn from anyone, even those with irritating personalities, who are boring, or whatever. They have learned to get around their own resistance to listening; they are more interested in what the instructor is intending to convey than in how he or she says it.

The most important factor then in accurate listening is *our attitude:* whether we *want to* listen and whether we *want* to understand. *Our attitude* determines how attentive and open we are to what the speaker is saying. No other single factor of leadership is of such importance as how well we listen. By our attitude, we either open the doors of communication or we erect barriers to interpersonal relating.

Learning to Listen

If poor listening is a matter of bad habits, listening can be improved by developing good habits. It is not easy to learn how to listen, but it can be done. We know this because if there is one thing that psychologists, counselors, social workers, and psychiatrists are good at, it is listening. But it is not automatic. It is something we spend months and years developing in our professional training.

Good Listening is Objective (Nonjudgmental). Acquiring an objective attitude is the single hardest thing to do in real listening. Making judgments of what people are saying or doing or how they dress or where they come from is natural. We make assumptions about what lies behind the words and actions of others. We want to know what really makes them tick. We have learned over a time that people do not always reveal themselves when they talk; they sometimes camouflage their real feelings or motivations.

Nevertheless, no matter how much we know about the deviousness of human nature, real listening is accepting the person's words without making judgments. Carl Rogers, in teaching his students to be good therapists, advised them to adopt an attitude that has become a classic phrase of therapy. This attitude is *unconditional positive regard*—the ability to accept without negative judgment everything the person is saying and also what the person is trying to say (Rogers 1951).

Under conditions of complete acceptance, we help create a safe climate for the person to express his or her inner condition. The speaker can begin to drop his or her defenses. Almost all of us have one or two friends or relatives with whom we can be frank. We know that they are on our side, so to speak, and we can confess our frailties, mistakes, and pettiness, because they do not judge us—they love us.

Good Listening is Encouraging the Other to Speak. In daily life we cannot create that special climate of safety that is the mark of true therapy. Life is too busy and too fast. But we can make an attempt to try to understand the person. We can try to understand the speaker's frame of reference, even if it is not our own. We can listen to what the speaker has to say and encourage the speaker to express what is difficult to express. We do this by listening and nodding and asking pertinent questions and not by jumping in and giving our own opinions. We listen, despite how the person is speaking (angrily or sorrowfully or boringly).

If at work we are a supervisor, an employee coming in late for the third, fourth, or fifth time may really anger us. But if we challenge him or her while we are angry or irritable, we are only going to make that person more defensive than he or she already is, and that will only create further disharmony between us and the employee. As an employer or supervisor, we need to understand the difficulty the person has in getting to work on time. Perhaps that person has no car or a car that is more often *in* the repair shop than *out* of it. If this is the case, then we might be able to help the person find a solution. If the employee is one of those who has difficulty getting up in the morning (and there are many of us like that), perhaps the person would be willing to work a later shift. There are many solutions to a problem—but first we need to discover what the problem is. Discovering the real problem requires a receptive attitude on our part, a willingness to *listen* without boredom, anger, or irritation.

Learning Not to Accuse and Blame. Unfortunately, some persons adopt this attitude as part of their life style. As long as they blame others for their misfortune, they will never achieve the kind of self-understanding that leads to more harmonious, rewarding, and creative living. It is a kind of psychological trap.

Whatever situation we find ourselves in must to some extent be partly of our own making. *Conflicts with other persons*, crisis situations at work or at home, *involve us as well as other people*. We need to start then, as we attempt to iron out wrinkles in our relationships with others, to be aware, and wary, of accusing or blaming others for our unhappiness. This tendency has many names, such as *projection, scapegoating, or rationalization*.

Furthermore, accusing others of this and that puts them immediately into a defensive position. They may have no alternative at that point but to deny or to retaliate. What may have started out to be an attempt at peace suddenly becomes another battle in the interpersonal war. Eric Berne calls this situation "courtroom," with one spouse playing plaintiff and prosecuting attorney and the other spouse playing victim and defense attorney (Berne 1964). Sometimes another person or persons may be called in to act as corroborative witnesses, judge, or jury. As with most deadly games, nothing is achieved in the end but confusion. Getting something off our chest may be cathartic, but while we are getting it off our chest and feeling better, we may be making the other person so miserable and alienated that the last thing he or she wants to do at that point is hear another word. We may have so alienated that person that we have closed off any further communication, for a while anyway.

Instead of Accusation and Blaming: Self-Revealment. There is an alternative to starting out with accusations and blaming the other person, and that is self-revelation or "self-revealment."

Carl Jung called the outer personality the *persona*, or mask, we wear to hide our real selves. This mask is our public personality (Jung 1959c). Later Carl Rogers noted that people who have been engaged in therapy for some time begin to drop this mask and allow themselves to be what they really are or, as many of Rogers's clients put it, the "real me." What these persons discovered was the *real me* who comes out of hiding is not unlikeable at all. Since the *real me* is so often more authentic than the mask we ordinarily wear, other people seem to like us more and be more willing to listen and get to know us. Revealing the *real me* encourages others to be themselves as well, so they in turn are willing to take off their masks.

We adopt the mask (the persona) early in life. Young boys are taught not to cry; young girls are taught there are certain ways they can behave and cannot behave. It starts wihin the family group and continues through school. The culmination of masking probably comes as the result of interaction with our peers in high school. Adolescents strive desperately to be accepted by their peers. Individuality is not appreciated at this age as much as conformity to the ideal personality of the prevailing group. The adolescent who is not part of the inner circle feels somehow unacceptable. It is an unusual adolescent who can dare to be different, and that brave youngster pays the price. Thus the mask may very well be cemented at the high school level. One of the liberating aspects of college life is that one is now in an environment in which one can relate to others more candidly and more openly. We have come into contact with others like ourselves and with whom we can share more interests. A young man in high school who is not a "jock" may suffer problems of self-esteem. In college, however, he finds that his abilities in math, science, art, or literature are valued not only by his instructors but by other students who have similar interests. He can now be more himself.

Make requests, not demands. Suppose, for example, you live with someone who is not as tidy as you are, be it a spouse, a child, or a roommate. You come home to clothes strewn all over, dishes in the sink, and ashtrays full. Instead of screaming, "Damn it, clean up your mess," you can state your needs much more directly and with a lot less hostility. "Look, I get nervous when there is too much

SUGGESTIONS ON HOW TO BEGIN SELF-REVEALMENT

If self-revealment is new to you, we suggest that you begin gradually. One might begin with a statement such as:

> It isn't easy for me to say this, so I would appreciate it if you would just let me get this out before I lose my courage.
> Look, I'd like to straighten out this difficulty between us, and I don't know exactly how to go about it.
> I know we are having some conflict here, but we are both reasonable people. I'd like to see if we could arrange a time to do it when we are both relaxed and with no one else around.
> I'm feeling very upset about this, and I'm sure you must be too. I would like to explore our feelings with each other if you would like to as well.

These kinds of statements "test the water." If the other person responds at all positively, one can go on to the next level of self-revealment such as:

> "Part of the difficulty is that I feel very inadequate about this situation. I got defensive and said some things that weren't as accurate as they could have been."
> "I'd like you to know that I have a tendency to get steamed up about things. You know, I fly off the handle. I'm always sorry about it later. Of course that doesn't help the situation now. But I'm calmer and I think I am in a better position to work it out with you."

These are a few of the beginnings one can make. You will be able to say things in a way no one else can that is relevant to your situation, yourself, and the other person. You never need to be a doormat and invite being walked on. If the other chooses "to take advantage" of your willingness to be open, leave it at that and go about your business. If the other person makes concessions on his or her part, despite the awkwardness he or she may feel, take it in stages. Remember that the other person is probably feeling just as nervous as you are. But from this encounter may come an openness and a friendliness that you could not have imagined.

untidiness. I would like to come home to a neat place. Could you put your clothes away, do your dishes, and empty your ashtrays?" You have stated your needs clearly. You have put it as a request instead of a demand. And you have been polite. Unfortunately, a really untidy person cannot change overnight. But if the person has simply gotten careless lately but appreciates tidiness, too, this small request may be just the thing he or she needs in order to respond.

At this point the other person may say, "Sure, but I'd like you to do something for me. I have a thing about stockings in the bathroom. Will you dry them in your room instead of hanging them on the shower rod?" or "O.K., but do me a favor, too. Please turn the stereo down after eleven o'clock at night. I'm not a night owl and I need my sleep."

Self-assertiveness: stating clearly what you would like or need or want. We have urged you not to accuse or blame. We have suggested that you reveal yourself. Now we encourage you to state as clearly as possible what you want or need. We tend to assume, in this life, that other people are just like us. We want them to read our minds, as if we all are psychic. When a despairing spouse says to an aggravated partner, "Well, what do you want?" the partner may respond, "If you don't know, I won't tell you." Now what good does that do? We may be fearful of coming out and saying what we want. We may have learned that it is not right to be assertive. Yet effective communication needs clear communication.

Learning to be assertive is learning to enunciate your needs clearly. It is being frank about yourself rather than being aggressive toward the other person. When waiting with three or four others at a counter, and the salesperson turns to the customer who came in after you, you can assert yourself calmly and politely instead of aggressively and accusingly. An accusing statement goes like this, "Wait a minute, this isn't fair. I was here first." How is this accusing? You are implying that either the salesperson or the customer was unfair to you. An assertive statement makes reference to yourself, not another. "Pardon me, but I believe I'm next," is *assertive*, not hostile or aggressive. You will notice most people will give way to this kind of assertive but nonaccusing statement. It takes time to develop an assertive but nonhostile attitude. Learn to analyze your statements and the statements of others. Speaking is an art that can be learned. Speaking well gets you to where you want to go. Not speaking out or speaking with hostility gets you nowhere or gets you into a place you do not want to be.

Understanding Our Paralanguage

Underlying cultural determinants of our communication with each other has been called the *silent language* by psychologist E. T. Hall (1959). The nonverbal aspects of our face-to-face message sending are estimated by Harrison (1965) to be 65 percent. That means no more than 35 percent of the communication is verbal!

In addition, there are some nonsilent yet nonverbal determinants such as the sounds we make—*hmmm, uh-huh,* or even that sound, *unh,*—which indicate to the listener that we are listening, interested, and perhaps even groping to find the right words. Our tone of voice further communicates what we are saying and how open we are to our listener's responses.

Tone of voice: softly! softly! One of the barriers to effective communication often is not *what* the person says but *how* the person says it. Without realizing it, the speaker may say something which arouses resentment, hostility, and downright anger in the listener. A gentle reminder may sound like an outright rebuke, with the result that the listener may suffer indignation or humiliation. One often hears a person say, "It wasn't *what* he said that made me upset/angry/disgusted/insulted, it was *the way* he said it. By and large, if a supervisor or a foreman or a business manager speaks softly and slowly, the employee will be more willing and able to listen without getting defensive. If the speaker's message comes out loudly, quickly, and with a note of irritation in it, the listener is more apt to listen to the emotional quality than to the word being spoken.

As an experiment, say the following statement as if you were talking to an employee in two different ways: first, as if you were understanding and sympathetic to the employee's plight, and then as if you were very impatient with the employee's "stupidity." To make the experiment even more dramatic, ask several of your friends to do the experiment with you. Divide these willing subjects into two groups and deliver the messages one way to one group and the other way to the other group. Ask each volunteer to tell you what you were saying, thinking, and feeling. The statements are:

Will you please suspend all phone calls for a few minutes?
Miss Jones, step into my office for a minute. I would like to talk to you.
Mr. Jones, just what do you think is the cause of this particular production breakdown?

If you have carried out this experiment with any zest, you will discover that when you give the message "kindly," the subjects will have a totally different comprehension of the statement than when it was delivered "angrily," "loudly," or "impatiently." *How* we communicate actually may be at odds with what we are trying to convey. "A soft answer turneth away wrath" the saying goes, and so it does, most of the time. Our tone of voice, the pitch and volume of our speech register, and the rate and intensity of our communication all influence the listener's comprehension.

Communication is also a visual experience: body language. The ways people sit, hold their arms, cross their legs, and watch or do not watch the speaker influence us. Even such subtle clues as the flickering of an eyelid, a raised eyebrow, a certain tenseness and alertness of the body indicate how the listener is receiving the message, whether he or she agrees or disagrees and is interested or bored. The speaker, aware of the reaction or not, picks up these clues and will shift the line of argument, hesitate, speed up, or slow down the communication and make more or less of an effort to clarify what he or she is saying (Knapp 1972).

For example, psychologists are particularly observant of general body posture. The person may be exhibiting an openness in bodily expression: relaxed, leaning back easily and receptively, or even sitting with a forward thrust as if wanting to catch every word. Or the person may be exhibiting a closed system; that is, the person sits back, not forward, appears tight and tense, arms and legs crossed, brows furrowed, mouth pursed, and perhaps with the face turned slightly away so that the person is not looking straight at us but out of the corner of the eyes (Scheflen 1973).

Incongruent body-speech communication. Sometimes what a person says belies what his or her body is saying. For example, a person may be saying, "I see," "go on," or "that's very interesting," when his or her body posture is conveying the very opposite message. While the speaker is mouthing interest, comprehension, and agreement, the speaker's body language may be saying something else. The speaker's face may be slightly turned away, arms may be crossed, and he or she may be in state of tight muscular tension; in other words, exhibiting a closed system, (Fisher 1973). Which should one trust? If it has to be one or the other, we would sooner trust body language than words. We learn to dissemble early in life, that is, to be kind rather than brutally truthful, to be cautious about what we say rather than being open, and to be diplomatic rather than precise. Thus, our words frequently *camouflage* our real feelings and thoughts instead of expressing them. If we must choose between verbal language and body language, we choose the latter. Our bodies do not lie. If we are tired, it shows in our slumped shoulders; if we are angry, it appears in a certain set of the mouth, a flash of the eye, or a flare of the nostril.

In fact, many therapists take body language into account when dealing with their clients or patients. We become very sensitive to small bodily movements, sudden tensing of the muscles, or tapping of the fingers. Some psychologists believe that in our society, at least, there are certain physical signs that suggest that if the person is not downright lying, he or she is at least not telling everything. According to these psychologists, these gestures include nose touching, nose rubbing, and pursing the lips (Wolff 1943). We suggest that these not be taken at face value, however. Each person develops, in the course of a lifetime, certain idiosyncratic movements, and to read a person requires either knowing that person very well or years of experience in the art and psychology of interpersonal communication.

Territorial space. Scientists who have studied animal behavior have described what they call territorial space. In animals that tend to herd or breed together the breeding animals demarcate their nesting areas. Say they are penguins, should another penguin stray into that magic circle, the nesting penguins scream, flap their wings, and exhibit altogether aggressive movements until the invading penguin retreats. Those of you who have owned dogs will have noticed similar kinds of behavior. One's pet dog establishes a certain territory, and if a neighboring dog enters that space, your dog becomes heroically aggressive until the neighboring dog slinks off. The farther your own dog goes beyond its territorial space, however, the less courageous it becomes. Suddenly the two dogs are on the neighboring dog's territory, and now our aggressive watchdog suddenly becomes timorous and is chased back. The same has been noticed in sticklebacks (a type of fish); in fact, it is a common animal behavior (Ardrey 1966).

Humans, too, establish territorial space. We tend to have certain "favorite spots," an armchair or a special place on the couch. When that space is taken by another person in the family, we feel a little outraged. Children frequently fight over "I was there first"; that is, "That is now my territorial space." Children delight in establishing territorial space (Robertson 1963). Given a room to share, two children will divide the room very carefully into "mine" and "yours." This is part of creating a personal universe for oneself.

It is not remarkable that this kind of behavior appears in the work and social situation. Committee members at weekly meetings tend to return to the chairs that they first sat in (Argyle 1969). If a committee member comes late and finds someone in his or her chair, the latecomer appears a little confounded as if the other person has taken something from him or her. We speak of our home as "our castle" and we would be offended if we found someone had entered our house without our knowledge. People "own" their offices in the same way or their particular bench in the workshop. We speak of a person being "insensitive," "naive," "unsophisticated," or even "young" if that person is unaware of our territorial space and "invades" our domain without permission. Part of becoming experienced in the ways of the world is learning to be sensitive to another's space. We learn to approach a lunch table and ask others if it is "taken." This question is a "testing of the atmosphere." If the persons at the lunch table do not want strangers, they will indicate that they are having a private conversation, and we know to move on. If they laugh and pull a chair out, we know we are not invading a territorial place this time and that they are open to newcomers. Even when we enter a library, there are certain unwritten rules about sitting at a library table. If the library is occupied by only a few persons, we tend to sit at a table not already occupied. If the library is rather crowded, then we know we can sit at a table where there is another person, without undue invasion of territorial space.

PERSONAL DISTANCE. Even if we are not within our own home territorial space, we tend to carry around with us a zone of space that is ours, and we do not welcome people intruding on that space unless we have given them a signal that they may do so. E. T. Hall even established a correlation in terms of inches. A close space of three to twenty inches between two persons indicates intimacy, a distance of two to five feet is impersonal distance, and over six feet is public distance (Hall 1966). Woe to the young student who walks up to the stuffy college administrator as if he were approaching his best friend! One may observe a certain discomfort in the administrator's bearing; indeed, the administrator may well be offended.

In our culture close space between persons seems to be allied to sexual intimacy, in contrast to Arab cultures. Strangers in the Mideast will approach each other very closely while bartering. We Americans do not like a total stranger walking right up to us, within our "personal" zone. Certain persons are so threatened by this invasion of their personal space that they may even get angry and resentful. Persons who have difficulty in ego-strength or in self-control (such as schizophrenic patients and those with histories of violence) are much less able to tolerate invasion of their personal space and tend to lash out if their personal space is violated (Kinzel 1969).

Becoming sensitive to communication with others, then, is also becoming sensitive to their need for space and privacy and aware of the signals that go back and forth indicating that the distance can be changed. When persons are at odds, they need a larger space between them; as they come to agreement, the space can be narrowed and often is. It has been noted that in meetings we tend to look at those who agree with us and eventually end up sitting closer to our allies (Argyle 1969). After a series of meetings, committee members will begin to "polarize," that is, the conservative members will tend to congregate on one side of the table, and the radical or liberal members will tend to congregate on the other side. In order to offset this polarization, committee chairpersons sometimes will ask the members to take different seats. Even this mechanical tampering with the geography of a committee room may affect the psychology of its members.

The use of silence. Silence also is communication. It may mean, on the one hand, thoughtful listening, self-examination, and introspection; on the other, it may mean resentment, anger, or disagreement: it depends on the other nonverbal messages being sent.

Some persons are so uncomfortable with silence that they jump in to stave off the embarrassment that may be generating. A group of people who have been talking excitedly together become anxious when the conversation dies down and there seems nothing else to say. When there is silence in a work situation, one can simply leave, since the need for communication has apparently ended, but in a social situation, when one does not feel free to leave, silence is very difficult. Each member of the group gropes lamely for a new subject to provoke the interest of the group. Probably one of the real "acid" tests of easy and profound friendship is when two persons can allow silence to fall and be comfortable and easy in that silence. It is in silence that we walk together on a country lane watching the fall leaves; it is in silence that small murmurings become the most intimate of communications; it is in silence that we know that we have achieved a depth and profundity in our being with each other.

It seems appropriate that we start with the need to listen and that we end with the silence that comes between two friends or two colleagues at times of deep communication.

APPLICATIONS AND COPING TECHNIQUES

1. Remember That Vocational Development is a Process That Extends Over Many Years

Students who despair that they don't seem to know what they want to do vocationally can take heart that career choice and development is part of the process of human becoming. We grow into it, from our early adolescent years, with our fantasies and dreams that point toward our basic interests, to more and more reality-based decisions in college and early adulthood. Then after we select our areas of vocational choice, the process continues on, not only in our twenties, but even after that. Many successful persons make major career turnings in their "catch-30" time segment and may even make major personal and vocational changes during the midlife crisis (Levinson 1978; Sheehy 1976). Nor should we be overly concerned that we will come to these crossroads and choice-points. While crossroads decisions are never easy, we can bear in mind that these choice-points are part of our own personality integration. It is part of what Carl Jung called our **individuation** as persons.

2. Encouragement for Women Who Want to go Back to a Career After Years of Being Mother and Homemaker

Many women want to return to work after their child-bearing and child-rearing years are over, but they wonder about their skills and their ability to have a career later in life. We are very glad to be able to say that the research indicates that women can make excellent vocational adjustment even if they feel they are starting from scratch. One research study showed that those who were beset with low self-esteem and depression in their thirties because of "housewife stress," to coin an expression, and who went back to work in their forties and fifties, regained their self-confidence and self-esteem (Lopata 1971). (But there is a catch here, and that is that they must be willing to acquire new skills and up-to-date training.) It is our own experience that when women come back to school after many years, they do so with a motivation and intensity that puts the usual just-out-of-high-school student to shame. They know now what they want, and they want an education, a degree and work they can throw their energies into. They frequently make the best grades in class and skew the curve considerably. Furthermore, their experience with the real world enables them to appreciate what they read in their textbooks (such as this one), and they make valuable contributions to class discussion. For our own part (and we are not alone), we are always glad to see the older woman student (and older men, as well) coming back to class since their presence and their willingness to respond verbally to important social issues make their contributions to class discussions relevant and exciting. We caution the reader, however, that we know some male college professors who take an opposite point of view, and their intimidation of older women students amounts to sexual harassment of a different color.

3. Coping With Work, Career, and Family Life

Some women may wonder what effect working will have on their children and family life. The studies seem to indicate, in fact, that when mothers are feeling fulfilled and happier by working, their children are likely to be the happy beneficiaries of their generally positive attitude (Nye & Berardo 1973; Rapoport and Rapoport 1971; Yarrow et al. 1962). Nonworking mothers have more conflicts with their children and may take out some of their housewife-stress and unhappiness on their children. Employed mothers seem to derive more satisfaction from their children and look forward to spending *quality* time with their children. This increased family harmony is not achieved ipso facto. It is the result of more open discussion among family members about the organization and structure of family life and family routine. It requires family time so that all members can be candid about their dissatisfactions as well as about their wants and needs. It requires the willingness to make time for family activities and family outings. These kinds of family occasions become a storehouse of memories that the occasionally confused husband, the harried wife, the latchkey child, and the demanding adolescent can hold on to at times of work-schedule stress. But research shows the working wives and mothers do spend more undivided time with their children, particularly mothers of the educated class (Yorburg 1973; Rogers 1973; Propper 1972).

4. Solutions to Problems Require Time

When we try to straighten out an interpersonal difficulty, we sometimes make the mistake of thinking that we can iron out the wrinkles of a situation in one grand, open discussion. That may happen, particularly in a misunderstanding of one specific difficulty. More often than not, however, most communication difficulties are more long standing. A let's-settle-this-problem-once-and-for-all approach may lead to disappointment and discouragement. A more realistic approach is to realize that the communication process takes time. One session is not enough; one discussion is not enough; one solution may not be enough. In fact, one discussion may indicate the need for many others, since any interpersonal difficulty has many ramifications. Furthermore, seeing what needs to be done is not the same as doing what needs to be done. It is easier to talk about something than it is to put it into practice.

Since two of the most frequent arguments between married people are about the use and distribution of money and expectations for, and discipline of, children, let us take one of these as an example: the distribution of financial resources. The partners have grown up in families with different ideas about spending and saving money. Generally what happens is that one partner is apt to spend freely, while the other tends to be frugal. In order to achieve more balance, finance policy needs to be discussed. But we want to avoid accusations and blame. We accomplish this only when we refrain from interpreting the other person and interpret ourselves instead.

For example, we may start the discussion of the money situation by saying, "I feel as if I don't get a chance to buy the things I need" rather than "You spend so much money, there isn't any left over for me, so I have to scrimp." The other person may then say, "Well, I didn't know there was something you needed. Why didn't you say so?" At that point you might reveal a deeper concern, "Well, I'm a more saving type than you are, too—it's just part of my character, but I really have been wanting such and such," instead of saying. "Well, you never ask me if there is something I would like to have."

The two of you might then come to an agreement that a list of priorities will be drawn up. You may then decide on both a mutual budget and an individual budget.

5. Avoid Discussion, if at all Possible, When One or the Other of You is Tired or Under Pressure

All discussions of problems need to be approached as calmly as possible.

Even if both persons are fairly calm and rational people, environmental stress may be such that one or both of you will tend to snap or become irritated unnecessarily. Be open and frank about it. If one of you starts to discuss a sensitive area, tell the other that right now would not be a a good time for you to get into it since you feel harried and pressured, and you want to approach the problem as objectively as you can. There are few things so terribly urgent that a few more days of delay will hurt.

Remain aware of your nonverbal responses. Particularly watch your tone of voice. If you raise your voice unnaturally loud or hear yourself speaking stridently, you are putting the other person on the defensive, and your discussion may end up as another verbal battle. In fact, you can even say, "I feel myself getting an angry tone of voice, which I don't want to do, so I think I'd like to just have a few moments to collect myself, and try again a little more calmly." The other person will take that kind of a cue with admiration and will attempt to emulate it.

If the other person's paralanguage seems to indicate that the discussion is becoming more than he or she can handle (by moving away or by retreating into hostile silence or by beginning to shout), you might want to verbalize it in a very gentle way, "Are you getting irritated now? Because I don't want to cause that. Perhaps we should postpone any further discussion. But if it is true that you are upset, I'd like to hear just what exactly it is that is bothering you."

Give yourselves enough space and distance to move around in and breathe freely. When handling a sensitive situation with another person, do not get into a small cramped room in which your intrapersonal-interpersonal dynamics are going to bounce off the walls. You need room to breathe. So it is in any discussion situation. A person who is agitated can drain some of the emotional tension by getting up and moving about. A walk is a fine way of discussing something emotional since it allows both persons to talk or not talk, to stop and talk and then to walk on, perhaps silently for a while, each thinking out what has just been said. Or perhaps you are working together on a joint task, painting a house or raking the lawn. There may be no finer time to discuss the ins and outs of a situation since both of you are involved in a task together. You can speak intermittently and return to the task. There is a lot of breathing room here, and the dynamics are much less pent-up than when both of you are in a face-to-face, claustrophobic situation.

6. Avoid Accusation and Blame: Adopt a No-Fault Attitude

Discussions of this sort are not a matter of somebody's being right and somebody's being wrong. Do not keep a scorecard to tally points made by who was right. Go beyond judgment, adopt a no-fault attitude, and get on with the business of clearing out the underbrush and cutting a clear swath through the forest of miscommunication. There is no need to apologize for yourself, and do not insist on apologies from the other person. Apologies set up a "right-wrong" dimension, and that is a polarity you wish to avoid. Remember that what is needed is for both to see where the communication has broken down and to find ways to make needs and desires more explicit in the future.

Avoiding accusations and blame involves self-revealment and self-assertion, which we achieve only when we refrain from interpreting the other person and interpret ourselves instead.

7. For Parents: A Tip in Teaching Children How to Communicate

Children learn much more from example than from instruction. They will adopt their communication style from you. In families in which parents have learned to communicate well with each other and to work out individual differences, children will be more able to do that later on in life. As you and your spouse become more comfortable with, and adept in, working out interpersonal problems, let your children in on your process. We tend to think that we should never argue or confront each other in front of our children. That is certainly true if we cannot manage our hostile or angry feelings. But if you have worked out ways to "process" your misunderstandings and situational conflicts, your children will gain much from being able to observe how you do it. Later, in their adolescent years, you and they will have a much easier time managing conflicts and crises.

8. Learning to Deal with Working Wives and Working Husbands

The double-income family is here to stay, and it is obvious that we need ways to manage the work-home responsibilities for both the man and woman who spend eight or more hours at their place of work and have more responsibilities when they return home at night. Social researchers have been busily gathering some coping techniques for the dual-worker family, and their suggestions are manifold (Poloma 1972; Richardson 1979). We present a synopsis of them below, with two warnings. The first is that what will work for one couple may not work for another, and that all approaches to dealing with problems should be viewed as experimental. The second is that no matter how egalitarian we may seem to be at the verbal and written level, it will be many, many years before our society revises its basic assumption that homemaking, housework and child care is the responsibility of the woman (Holmstrom 1977; Boken and Viveros-Long 1981).

1. *Establish Career Priorities.*
2. *Establish Time Priorities.*
3. *Establish Household Job Duties and Priorities.*
4. *Lighten Expectations of Household Standards.*
5. *Use Outside Help If Your Finances Warrant It.*

SUMMARY POINTS TO REMEMBER

1. Satisfying work fulfills what Abraham Maslow called our esteem needs. But work is so basic to our identity in our soci- ety, that the unemployed are bereft of not only their belonging needs but their whole sense of safety and security is un-

dermined. Social ills and social problems increase dramatically.

2. Our working situation clearly stratifies us into blue-collar, white-collar, and executive and/or professional classes.

3. Blue-collar workers have numerous problems. They are the first to be laid off during recessions and depressions. They often experience alienation and lack of pride in their job. They are not in control of their schedules. Visits to physicians and other necessities mean time off from work. Revolving shifts and grave-yard shifts wreak havoc with their marital and parenting relationships.

4. White-collar workers have more control of their work, their time, and their lives. Even so, the corporation and megacorporation does exert influence and control over the lives of their executives.

5. A modern aspect of our working society is the entrance of women into the job market. Women at work no longer are considered as neglectful of their families so much as meeting an economic necessity as American parents strive to provide "everything" that money can buy for their children.

6. The double-income family does afford the middle-age couple economic and personal satisfactions, but the working wife may also experience role-overload.

7. Choice of work and final work selection or profession is a process situation extending over a period of years from adolescence into the late twenties and even beyond.

8. Women may still be "afraid of success" because it runs counter to our image of "femininity." Women who have made inroads into such areas have been those who have had strong role models in their own family.

9. Career success and job satisfaction is not related solely to money. More important factors of satisfaction are environmental climate and potentiality for advancement.

10. One of the chief skills necessary in all areas of management and professional work is the ability to communicate with superiors, colleagues, subordinates, and the general public. Two of the chief reasons for being fired are absenteeism and the inability to get along with others.

11. General semantics is the sane and scientific study of language.

SIGNIFICANT TERMS AND CONCEPTS

absenteeism
accusing
assertiveness
blaming
blue-collar worker
body language
career development
college drop-out
education (as a life long
   process)
empathy
empty-nest syndrome
environmental climate
esteem needs
fear of success

feminist
general semantics
grave-yard shift
intrinsic motivation
moratorium (college as)
nonverbal communication
on-the-job training
paralanguage
Persona (or mask)
personal distance
professional class
role-modeling theory
role overload
self-assertion

self-revealment
silent language
skilled labor
social mobility
social stratification
social status
swing shifts
sympathy
territorial space
unskilled labor
vocational choice
white-collar worker
work (as an American
   identity)

FILL IN THE BLANKS WITH SIGNIFICANT TERMS AND CONCEPTS

1. When our more basic needs are satisfied, our e_____ n_____ are satisfied with fulfilling work, according to Abraham Maslow.
2. The basic problems of grave-yard shifts, no paid time off from work and lay offs during economic recessions are characteristic of b_____ -c_____ w_____.
3. Those who have a good amount of control of their work, their time, and their lives are the w_____-c_____ w_____. However these people are controlled in various ways by the megacorporations' expectations of their behavior, both professionally and personally.
4. Older women are returning to the work arena and many are no longer experiencing the e_____ n_____ s_____ due to their children leaving home and no longer requiring mothering.
5. Two of the most important factors of job satisfaction are e_____ c_____ and potentiality for advancement. Money is not the only reason for job satisfaction.
6. Employment often requires good communication skills. Two of the main reasons people are fired are a _____ and the inability to get along with others.
7. Communication includes silence, listening, n_____ c_____, verbal paralanguage and personal and territorial space.

RECOMMENDED BOOKS FOR FURTHER READING

Bach, George and Wyden, Peter. 1969. *Intimate Enemy: How to Fight Fair in Love and Marriage*. New York: William Morrow & Company. For those who believe that confrontation "clears the air" and shakes the cobwebs out of a stale and stagnating relationship, these two psychologists suggest some very practical ways to "fight fair." Worth reading.

Chase, Stuart. 1966. *Tyranny of Words*. New York: Harcourt Brace Jovanovich, Inc. There is probably no better "turn on" for students who are interested in psycholinguistics. Chase is particularly interested in helping us divorce ourselves from words like "wop," "nigger," "spik," or any term that is emotionally laden.

Ginott, Haim G. 1965. *Between Parent and Child*. New York: Hearst Corporation, Avon Books. It provided parents new ways of interacting with their children without manipulating them and also without being manipulated. Another best-seller by the same author was *Between Parent and Teenager*. New York: Macmillan Publishing Company, Inc. 1973.

McGregor, Douglas. 1960. *The Human Side of Enterprise*. Wallingford, CT: McGraw-Hill Book Company. About a decade after Maslow proposed his hierarchy of needs, McGregor applied them to the world of work with his now famous Theory X-Theory Y, with the intention of making the work climate more fulfilling for more workers. A must for career and professional persons.

Nesbitt, John. 1982. *Megatrends: Ten New Directions Transforming Our Lives*. New York: Warner Books, Inc. This best-selling non-fiction book traces the current trends in our "high-tech" society and predicts changes that will affect us all.

Terkel, Studs. 1975. *Working*. New York: Avon Books. Simply a classic in the area of how people feel about their jobs, about themselves and their world views. Parts of this book are grim—but they are eye-openers.

10

Centering Ourselves: Transcending Personal Crisis

THE LIGHT AND THE DARK
    Jung and the Great Archetypal Themes
    Are We a Death-Denying Society?

THE ACCEPTANCE OF DEATH: ELISABETH KÜBLER-ROSS

FOR THE CRITICALLY ILL PATIENT AND THE FAMILY: SOME PRACTICAL
    SUGGESTIONS

UNEXPECTED DEATH: SUICIDE

LEARNING TO PROCESS CRISES: DEATH AND DIVORCE
    The Stages of Grief and Recovery
    Divorce as a Kind of Dying
    Reintegrating Oneself into Society after Death and Divorce
    Differences in Status Between the Formerly Married Woman and the
        Formerly Married Man
    Divorce and Children
    Chances for a Successful Remarriage

APPLICATIONS AND COPING TECHNIQUES

THE LIGHT AND THE DARK

Life is a matter of sun and shadow, times of even, easy living followed by times of intense crisis. No matter how earnestly we have coped with everyday existence, no matter that we have become highly integrated and self-sustaining personalities, to all of us shall come the darker moments of living.

When we are young, we do not concern ourselves with the shadow side of life. But, eventually, into all our lives will come those moments of pain and anguish that seem to darken our whole existence, that make us wonder what life is all about, and that call into question everything we have worked and struggled so hard to achieve and to acquire. We may contemplate giving up, running away from it all, or we may even toy with the idea of suicide. Even the strongest and most successful of us will have moments of disillusionment and "astonishment of heart."

As a people, we seem to do well as long as we are working hard at living; that is, pursuing our goals, organizing our lives, balancing our endless tasks, and relating to others in a variety of social contexts at home and in our offices. Our psychological mode works best when our occupation is busy-ness, when our tempo is activity, and when all signals are "go!" As a people, we seem to be able to surmount the small problems and obstacles encountered on our way to achievement and acquisition. We do not do as well in the "darker" moments.

We must not be hard on ourselves for this lag in our development as a people. As a nation, we were born only two hundred years ago; we do not yet have a sense of history. But we are arriving at a more mature consciousness, and we now are ready to deal with the shadow side of life. We are beginning to find ways of coping with shock and trauma. Eventually we may even come to understand times of crisis as part of the process.

Jung and the Great Archetypal Themes

Carl Jung insisted time and again that how we live our lives is how we confront the great **archetypal themes** of human existence (Jung 1953[b]). Archetypal themes deal with conception and birth, existence and nonexistence, joy and suffering, love and hate, crisis and resolution, dying and sorrow, and (finally) transcendence and rebirth.

Archetypal themes are not simply the domain of philosophers and psychologists but are reflected in every aspect of human society. They are the sum and substance of our literature, art, achitecture, and religions. They are reflected in our laws, customs, etiquette, mores, taboos, value systems and ideologies. How

we deal with these themes forms the basis of our culture and civilization. And of all these archetypal themes, the most significant may be the theme of death.

Are We A Death-Denying Society?

Some writers have said that Americans are unable to deal with death; that in some ways, the concepts of old age, sickness, poverty, and dying are taboo subjects in our society (Borkenau 1965). These writers have said that we hide these aspects of human existence from our awareness by herding the old, the sick, and the infirm into hospitals or convalescent homes, and nowhere is this more true than in how we deal with the dying. These writers have contrasted our "American way of death" (Mitford 1963) with how other cultures have integrated this aspect of human existence.

Elisabeth Kübler-Ross described the death of a farmer in her country of birth, Switzerland, as she remembered it (Kübler-Ross 1970). The old man had had a fall, and when it became evident that he would not survive, he finished his life in a most beautiful and graceful manner. He took care of the financial legalities of his small estate. He had long talks with various members of the family about the affairs of the farm and the house. His neighbors and friends visited him during his fairly long illness and made their farewells toward the end. His family were with him during his last moments. He received the last rites and died in dignity and peace. The funeral and burial were moving tributes to the man's life and achievements. In contrast, said Robert Neale, we isolate the old and dying. (Robert Neale is a psychologist who has worked in pastoral counseling.) Often we send them away to hospitals or rest homes literally to die. We try to hide the facts of the illness from the person and sometimes from the rest of the family and friends. We "protect" our children from having to witness the reality of growing old and dying. We send letters and cards for a "speedy recovery" even when there is no such possibility. When the person eventually dies, funeral attendance is small and attendance at the burial is even smaller. Such events as "laying out" the corpse or gathering at communal meals are passing out of popular custom. At the funeral we endeavor to "prettify" the corpse and make remarks about "how natural" the deceased appears. At the burial, or afterwards in our visits to the family, we shy away from dealing with the essential grief and loss the family members must be feeling and, instead, talk about mundane and inconsequential things like the weather and the political situation (Neale 1971).

Yet despite our denial of death, said Geoffrey Gorer, we are preoccupied with it. We buy murder mysteries as light, escapist literature; we crowd the movie houses that show murder and violence; we turn on our televisions to similar programs; and we buy newspapers in order to read about crime and death. Our lust and fascination, Gorer asserted, is pornographic. Sexual pornography, he explained, is a way of fulfilling a sexual need without actually being involved in the act. Likewise, our pornographic attitudes toward death are the result of consciously denying death and of viewing it vicariously and furtively through literature and the public media (Gorer 1967).

THE ACCEPTANCE OF DEATH: ELISABETH KÜBLER-ROSS

Our willingness to deal at all openly with death is a recent phenomenon, only within the last two decades. The person who has led this significant breakthrough is a psychiatrist, Elisabeth Kübler-Ross, who has done more to help us face the issues of death and dying than any other one person today. She has achieved this breakthrough not only by her books and articles but also by traveling throughout the country lecturing to colleges and universities, running workshops for the medical profession and for professionals and paraprofessionals in psychology, counseling, education, sociology, and so on. She has made films to use as teaching aids and has helped create courses for graduates and undergraduates all over the United States.

Her most famous book, *On Death and Dying*, (Kübler-Ross 1970), describes vividly how long and arduously she had to work before hosptials would allow her even to talk with patients with terminal illnesses. Her efforts to achieve acceptance of death as a proper study for research and for therapy were often sabotaged by hospital staffs. Physicians and nurses felt a need to "protect" their patients and tended to cling to the belief that, by and large, it was better not to deal directly with the patients concerning their illness. In a hospital full of patients, she would often be told there currently was no one "dying." Even if there were dying patients the medical staff often were obstinate in their opinion that the patients would not be able or not want to talk about it.

But Kübler-Ross found that the patients did welcome the opportunity to talk. It came, for many of them, as a relief to have someone to listen to them, willing to discuss their wants, needs, and wishes. It was therapeutic to have an end to the make-believe that frequently surrounds the terminally ill patient (Glaser & Strauss 1965). Kübler-Ross was willing to come and see them and help them work through their feelings, their fears, and their concerns when everyone else seemed to want to avoid any mention of the significant issue—their impending death.

Let it not be thought that Kübler-Ross rushed in and told the person that he or she was going to die. On the contrary, she was there not to inform the person about anything but rather to discover what the person needed—needed to know, needed to understand, needed to have confirmed, or needed to have answered. Kübler-Ross simply asked the patient, "How sick are you?" In that way, the patient was able to tell Kübler-Ross exactly what he or she knew, suspected, or wanted to know. Sometimes the patient turned out to be very sure that he or she was mortally ill, and it came as a blessed relief for that person to know one person, at least, who was willing to talk about death. Kübler-Ross learned to wait patiently, interview after interview, until the person was able to come to a calm acceptance (and understanding) of his or her own death. Our approach to death, like our approach to life, is individual, but as the result of her clinical observations, Kübler-Ross came to believe that most of us go through definite stages in coping with death. Specifically, she named the five stages: (1) denial and isolation, (2) anger, (3) bargaining, (4) depression, and finally, (5) acceptance. The reader is asked to remember (even as we describe these five stages) that the person or therapist working with the dying patient keeps alert to the patient's individual qualities, strengths, limitations, background, and circumstances, which will differ, many times significantly.

DENIAL AND ISOLATION. When a person is genuinely unaware of the seriousness of his or her condition and confronts the possibility of death for the first time, the typical reaction is *shock and denial*. "No, not me!" "I can't have cancer!" "Couldn't there be a mistake?" "Are you sure you have *my* x-rays?" "I just can't believe it. I just can't believe it."

Denial, or at least partial denial, is experienced by almost all patients in the beginning of their awareness or at some point in their illness. Anyone of us can deal with pain and threat just so long, and then we need to have moments of protection against that pain and shock: that is exactly what the stage of denial accomplishes. It acts as a buffer against the pain of realization until such time as the person can accept it more honestly.

Denial may also be present within the family, and sometimes, even the physician denies the eventuality of death. It has been suggested that the physician's desire to extend life is a part of his or her own denial system. After all, the job of the physician is to get people well; death may appear as a failure rather than as a natural part of the life-and-death process.

ANGER. Eventually, however, the patient begins to confront directly the reality of the illness, and when that happens, the most common reaction is anger. "Why me?" "Why does it have to happen to me now before . . .?" "If there really is a God, why does he let this happen?" The person may lash out at the spouse, at the physician and at nurses attending him or her. The rage may be direct, or it may be indirect: irritation and complaints at not being treated well, dislike of hospital food, or endless demands on the family members.

Actually rage is one of the better symptoms in the patient's process. Anger is energy. The patient is mobilizing his or her available resources to fight against the helplessness of the situation. The challenge now is to enable the patient to utilize and direct that angry energy in a useful and constructive manner. There is no magic formula for how that may be done. Kübler-Ross gave one example that seemed to fit the characteristics of one of her patients. Her patient was a businessman who was used to being in charge. Now he found himself at the mercy of others who told him when to eat and when to take his medicine, and woke him up in the middle of the night to check his vital signs. After some discussions with Kübler-Ross, the wife no longer just popped in to see her husband but, instead, would telephone him in the morning and ask when it would be convenient for her to come by. Her husband, who had been used to arranging his own appointment schedule at work, consulted his own schedule for the day (lab examinations, physical therapy appointment, etc), and together they decided when would be the best time for her to visit. After a while, the wife would take notes over the phone on what he needed, what office or home management papers he wanted her to bring, and her visits became something like those of a secretary. This particular man had a great need to adjust his affairs, both at home and in the office. Such an arrangement would not work for everybody, but there is certainly much that can be learned from this anecdote. Patients can be encouraged to take an active role and encouraged to say what they would like to do or whom they would like to see.

BARGAINING.   Eventually, the patient realizes that all the anger in the world will not extend life. At this point the stage of bargaining may begin. As children, we frequently bargain with our parents, with Santa Claus, or with God. "If I am good and do my schoolwork and dishes every night, perhaps I can . . ." So too does the patient begin to bargain unconsciously with God, the universe, the physicians, or whomever, as death becomes imminent. It is as if the person is reasoning: "If God has decided to take me from this earth and does not respond to my angry demands, perhaps he will react more favorably if I ask nicely."

One woman wanted "just enough time" to see her son get married, which was scheduled a few months away. The hospital staff and the family saw to it that the woman sustained her strength for the next few weeks, took her to the wedding, and remained with her through the ceremony. She looked radiant, and the wedding ceremony was a happy event for everyone. The hospital staff thought they had enabled the woman to become more realistic about her illness, but the first words the woman uttered when she got back to the hospital were "Don't forget I have another son."

DEPRESSION.   There comes a time, however, when the patient begins to realize that bargaining is not going to work forever. Energies begin to wane; operations exhaust emotional and physical strength. It is natural for depression to occur.

Unfortunately, the depression often carries with it indifference to physical appearance and a lack of desire to sustain relationships with those nearest and dearest. Patients may become withdrawn and listless and seem uninterested in maintaining contact with those who have come to visit. This stage makes it difficult for family members who are trying to support them emotionally and physically.

Kübler-Ross warned specifically against trying to cheer the patient up at this time. Cheering the person up, remarking on how good he or she looks, is *our* desire, not the patient's. The patient has come to realize that the end of life is coming. It is better to let the patient express the sorrow and the sense of ultimate loss. It is his or her way of "working through" or "processing" what is happening. Despite the pain and suffering of this stage, it also has its benefits. The patient is beginning to accept death more realistically than ever before. Allowing expression of the natural sorrow and grief of one's death will enable that realization to come more easily. One of the helpful things we can do for the patient is to say how much the patient has meant to us, how loved he or she has been, and what we will always treasure in our shared experiences. On first reading this suggestion, you may feel that you could never do that. We hasten to assure you that, at times of crisis, we frequently are able to express those things we might never otherwise. The nearness of death seems to allow us to put aside our natural reserve and to open our hearts to those we care for deeply.

ACCEPTANCE. Despite the suffering, the pain, the anger, and the depression of the previous stages, there comes a time when almost all patients enter a calm and almost luminous stage of acceptance. It does not come easily nor does it come to all dying persons. It comes to those who are willing to work through their feelings and who have the support of the hospital staff and their family and friends. If we do not leave patients isolated and alone so that they feel rejected, they will begin to contemplate their approaching end with a certain degree of expectation and peace. The patient's sleep becomes easier, as Kübler-Ross described it, like that of a newborn child. The patient seems to be withdrawing from the world, but it is a withdrawal different from that associated with the stage of depression: in Kübler-Ross's words, it is more like "the final rest before the long journey." The patient needs time for solitude. The time of activity and crisis are over, and the patient is preparing for the end in a contemplative manner. There are very few personal concerns or wasted emotions. Frivolous emotions (such as irritation, resentment, or anger) seem to belong to a world the patient is now leaving. The patient's communications seem to take on a nobility never before evidenced. At the great existential moment, the universal archetypal themes come to the fore: we are willing to speak more openly of the meaning of life and death. The patient may no longer see death as a cruel fate or as the Great Avenger but as a welcome friend or as "going home." We others must be willing to step onto this level of communication if we wish to remain in touch with the patient toward the end.

FOR THE CRITICALLY ILL PATIENT AND THE FAMILY: SOME PRACTICAL SUGGESTIONS

Even when a critically ill person may not be terminally ill, an extended illness or disability can bring much emotional and physcial stress to both the patient and the family. We may feel a sense of helplessness, not sure what we can do to help the patient and the rest of the family get through the time of stress. We, like the patient, may experience the five stages noted above, even when the patient may recover. "All of us are victims in a crisis!" said Anne Kliman, who worked with families in crisis situations. All the members of a family go through depression, isolation, and desperation. She added that we frequently become so "locked up" in our own thoughts that we stop sharing our grief and anxiety just when we need more than ever to communicate (Kliman 1978). Our own work with persons in critical situations, as well as with their families, has led us to offer the following coping techniques for families with a critically ill or disabled member. But remember, again, that these ideas are generalizations *only*. All must be evaluated in terms of your particular circumstances and your knowledge of the patient.

DEVELOP A LOVING BUT IMPERSONAL AWARENESS OF THE PATIENT'S NEEDS. Be prepared for outbursts of sorrow, anger, bargaining, and misery or periods of great courage and fortitude. Furthermore, this pendulum of reactions may swing violently back and forth. There is nothing neat and orderly about our emotional life in times of crisis. But do not, yourself, get caught up in the patient's depression or physical symptoms. Whatever the patient is experiencing, *you do not have* *to take on his or her symptoms,* a natural tendency in all of us if we love the person. Sometimes, he or she may even feel better seeing that we have picked up their depression or that we are upset. Nor do we have to become martyrs. We need our own strength and energies. We need not take offense or be hurt by the patient's demands. A hospital is, at best, a depressing environment. The hospital patient is given better care than ever before but is also more physically and psychologically assaulted than ever before. Patients are jabbed with needles, awakened for a check of vital signs, given intravenous injections, and sometimes intravenous feedings. They are rolled or pushed hither and yon for x-rays and other laboratory tests. And no matter how beneficial surgery is, it is a physically traumatic shock to the body. It is natural, then, for the patient to experience confusion, helplessness, and anger, and you may receive the backlash of all of this. By maintaining equilibrium, you can respond to the patient calmly and empathetically, without picking up the patient's emotions. You are not the person who is "to blame" for the situation. Lend the patient emotional and physical support, of course, but do not be the patient's scapegoat.

BE PREPARED FOR SURPRISING EMOTIONAL REACTIONS IN YOURSELF AND IN OTHER FAMILY MEMBERS.　One of the most difficult aspects of critical illness is the welter of emotions you may experience or that you may witness in other family members. You, too, can experience grief,, of course, but you may be surprised and dismayed to discern other less "socially acceptable" emotions in yourself and others. After the first shock of diagnosis and the consequent grief and concern, other kinds of emotions may erupt, particularly as the weeks and months drag on. You may spot elements of anger and irritation that the patient is consuming so much time and energy. Or you may yourself bargain and plead with the universe to "put the patient out of misery." You may find yourself bitter at the mounting expenses of the hospitalization, tests, and medical fees. Then, immediately, you may plunge into despair and guilt for such "unnatural thoughts."

But these are not unnatural thoughts and emotions. They are common, even if most families would be loath to admit their existence. If these feelings can be verbalized, much of this depression and guilt can be released, and the emotional and physical energies of the patient's family can be directed into more constructive channels.

ENCOURAGE THE PATIENT'S PHYSICAL RECOVERY.　For the critically ill person who has a good chance of recovery, the best medicine often is allowing the patient to come home and begin the process of physical self-support and autonomy. The patient may not be able to do much more than go to the bathroom and back, but that is the beginning of recovery. The patient needs to be encouraged to do more, which means we must learn not to overprotect and do too much for the patient. Persons who suffer disabling or crippling diseases can do much more for themselves than is frequently assumed. Part of the patient's recovery is psychological recovery, and that entails encouraging the patient *to get up, to get out,* and *to do something.* Even the family member who is going to have to use a wheelchair for the rest of his or her life can do certain household chores: small but significant preparation of meals, answering the telephone and conveying messages, managing the household accounts, babysitting with the older children, or whatever. Many agencies now work with disabled persons toward financial self-support. Family members need to work together for the person's recovery rather than to extend the person's helplessness.

PROVIDE EMOTIONAL SUPPORT.   Research indicates that instead of providing more emotional support for the critically terminally ill patient, we tend to isolate them from others and to withdraw from them. They soon realize what is happening. (Glaser & Strauss 1965). It is as though we are beginning to mourn them before they are gone. Or pehaps we fear that what they have is catching. One person who has been suffering from cancer for a number of years told us that one man she knows refused to accept a glass of water from her out of the absolute conviction that cancer is communicable.

This woman has had eleven years of battling melanoma cancer. She has been in and out of several different hospitals, has had sixteen operations, and has had many of her tissues and muscles cut out and replaced with prosthetic devices. Still, she remains, at fifty years of age, an extraordinarily beautiful and exuberant person. Her plea to the families of persons stricken with illness is to continue *to touch them, to hold them, to caress them, and to hug them*. She points out that there is more to touching than physical contact. A touch transmits emotional strength and spiritual nourishment. When her disease first was diagnosed, she told us, her husband adamantly "refused" to let her go; he fought for her life. So did many of the other family members. They surrounded her with love and emo-

The love and support we can provide for an ill person may have exceptional healing value: this is the holistic approach to sickness and health.

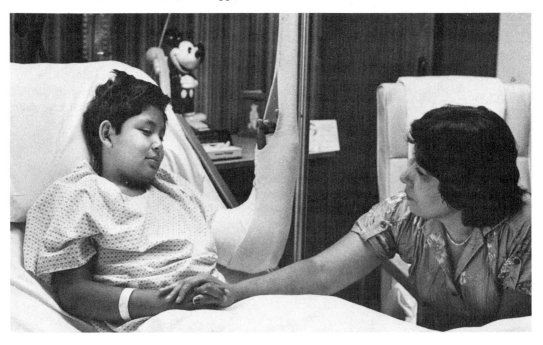

tional support, which in turn gave her the strength and will to live. She is a little critical of Kübler-Ross's five stages of death, "If I had 'accepted' death," she says, "I would not be alive today." We asked her if life was worth all the operations, the pain, and the necessity for prosthetic devices. "Oh, yes, to live a little longer with my husband and six children is worth every minute of it."

"Touching" or demonstrative affection is important, but many of us are *not* touchers—that is just not our way. If that is so, there is no sense in trying to become so. But if we have had a touching relationship with the person, we can continue to do so.

For those who are not naturally openly affectionate, there are many other ways "to touch." We can help the patient walk after an operation or when he or she is on the recovery list. Most medical advice urges patients to get back on their feet as soon as possible. When we visit them in the hospital or at home, we can help them to take small walks around the hospital ward or around the house. Physical therapy rooms are crowded, and there are few physical therapists. This small service is of inestimable help in the recovery of the patient, but of course, always check first with the patient's physician.

Another type of touching is massage, which is particularly therapeutic for those patients who have suffered a stroke or other physically numbing or paralyzing disease. Sometimes the very persons who are least affectionate are those who are able to give the patient a massage. Massage and rubdowns of this sort do many things: They increase the blood flow and circulation to that part of the body; retard atrophy of the muscles and nerves in the afflicted area; prevent development of bedsores, and at a psychic level, enable the person to stay "in touch" with that part of the body and so to reintegrate body and mind. Another odd effect of rubdowns and massages is the relief from pain that follows.

RELATE CREATIVELY TO THE CRITICALLY ILL OR DISABLED PERSON. Sometimes our attitudes toward critically ill or long-term-recovery patients are reflected in how we visit them in the hospital or at home. We may wear subdued clothing and long faces and talk in sepulchral tones. Without suggesting that visitors to the hospital room be dressed as if going out "on the town," we do urge you to have a cheerful countenance and wear clothes you would normally wear on a normal visit. Instead of bringing flowers (which tends to turn the sick person's room into something akin to a funeral parlor), we can bring items that relate to the person's family, interests, business, or hobbies: news from home, pictures, photographs, or appropriate reading material. We can bring things that the person can use for his or her stay in the hospital: a pair of comfortable slippers or bed socks, or a bed jacket or shawl.

One of the chief concerns that people express about the seriously ill or disabled patient is what to talk about with the patient. "I never know what to say," said one lady, "and then I ask inane things like 'how is the hospital food?' which is really silly since most institutional food tends to be dreary." Another person admitted that he once said to a patient who had had several operations that he was "looking just fine." He added, ruefully, "I wanted to bite my tongue off when I realized how hollow that sentence was." These kinds of statements reflect our inadequacy in relating to the hospitalized or disabled person. It may reflect also our uneasiness in unintentionally bringing up subjects that might be "hurtful" to the patient. What we need to do is to call on our own creative talents, skills, and competencies and bring them to the patient's bedside or wheelchair. What that will be depends on you and the situation (what the patient can and cannot do) and, of course, on the patient's own personality and interests.

If the patient enjoys reading but is unable to do so, and you are good at reading aloud, you and the patient may consider what book you could read aloud at your visits. A professor in our institution suffered a detachment of the retina first in one eye and then in the other. He underwent surgery in both eyes and for a considerable time was virtually blind. The other teachers at the school organized reading sessions; the hospital room became a gathering place for his friends and associates, and lively discussions and forums followed the reading sessions. We need to caution the reader to make sure not only that the reading material is of interest to the patient but also to keep alert to signs of fatigue or boredom by the patient. There are times when patients need to rest and be alone after the excitement of visitors.

ENCOURAGE AND PROMOTE THE PERSON'S STRENGTHS AND CAPABILITIES. When we treat an invalid as an invalid, he or she becomes more invalided. That is one of the many aspects of the self-fulfilling prophecy. When we do too much for the invalided or aged person, we actually are hastening the aging process. Sometimes we make decisions for a person who is quite capable of lucid and rational thought. We treat invalids sometimes, as if their minds are gone. Sometimes, this may very well be so, particulary when there has been some brain damage. Being hospitalized virtually reduces the person to infancy when even the vital life processes must be taken care of (with use of bedpan, spoon feeding, and so forth). But we tend to regard the patient as more helpless than he or she really is.

We need to think of the patient as having many strengths which we need to encourage, particularly in making decisions. Patients who must rest at home much of the day or who are confined to a bed or wheelchair will feel much more a part of the family if we assign some jobs to them that they can do. We should not be too concerned if a task may exhaust their energies. There is nothing as psychologically satisfying as knowing that you have put your best effort into something. Some of the jobs that even seriously invalided persons can perform are: telephone answering; repair service appointment-keeping; table-setting and clearing; turning on of stove; taking out of garbage; making shopping lists, etc.

UNEXPECTED DEATH: SUICIDE

When an aged person dies, there seems something natural about it. We take solace in knowing that the person has led a long and useful life. It seems in the natural order of things for a person to die after the biblical "three score years and ten." We may also be somewhat heartened if a person manages to reach the eighties with all faculties intact. We harbor a secret hope that we may do the same. If an

Hara-kiri beneath the Cherry Trees, after a Romance illustrated by Toyokuni.

Not all cultures have considered suicide to be a crime. Rather it has been viewed as an honorable alternative to disgrace, humiliation, capture, and other falls from grace.

adult is "cut down" in middle adulthood, we may grieve a little more, but (even so) we will be comforted if we know that the person's children are well into their adult years and are self-sufficient, if the widow has financial security, or that the surviving spouse may find someone else with whom to share the remaining years. If dying has been a long, painful, and sorrowful process, we may see the end as merciful. There are other kinds of deaths, however, which are not as easily understood and accepted, and which are difficult to work through. These deaths include the person who takes his or her own life, the person who dies as the result of an accident, and the untimely death of a young child.

In these situations it is *we* who are the victims and who need the healing. it is we who need to learn how to pick up the pieces of life and reconstruct our life process.

THE CRIME OF SUICIDE.   Death by suicide is, even today, one of our deep cultural taboos. Even our language suggests that a crime has been committed. We say that a person "took his own life" or that she "committed suicide." In the Judeo-Christian tradition, suicide carries a stigma that it is somehow an act against God and nature. The medieval church considered suicide as the unforgivable sin since no repentance was possible between the act and the death of the person. For centuries the bodies of suicides were desecrated by being pulled through the streets by horses and buried at crossroads where traffic would trample on their graves, and sometimes a stake was put through their hearts (as a final insult) so that their ghosts would not return to haunt the countryside. Until 1882 the bodies of suicides could not be buried by day but had to be taken to their final resting place in the dead of night.

SUICIDE IN SOCIETIES.   Suicide has not been as dishonorable and odious in other societies as it still is in ours. In many societies suicide has been an honorable resolution to a difficult and/or shameful situation. Zeno, the Greek Stoic, recommended suicide if one's physical condition prevented one from functioning as an effective human being. Better to die an honorable death than to live in misery and be helplessly dependent on others. Seneca, a Roman philosopher, admitted that although he would relish old age if he were functioning in body and mind, he would rather leave this world than live on blind, crippled, and of no use to anyone. The Japanese and Chinese both have had a long tradition of an honorable death by suicide. The Japanese *kamikaze* pilots of World War II were considered heroes and martyrs for their country. Even the early Christians had to be warned against voluntary martyrdom in the early Roman circuses (Faberow 1977).

AN ATTEMPT TO BEGIN AGAIN.　　Suicide by its very nature seems to strike terror and anguish into our innermost being. We are haunted for months and years afterwards and ask ourselves such questions as, "Why did he do it?" or "What was so terrible in her life that she had to end it?" We like to have reasons and answers and not one is sufficient. Even when there is a suicide note, we know that what is written on the suicide note does not sufficiently explain a person's wanting to put an end to life, the very thing that most of us hold dearer than all else. We suspect that even the suicide did not know all the reasons for this ultimate act. We know only that the person must have been plunged into such depths of despair that death seemed preferable to life. The survivors go over and over in their minds all the details of their interactions with the person: "Could it have been prevented?" "Did he seem all right when we last saw him?" "Did anyone ever hear her talk of committing suicide?" We may think to ourselves: If only we had listened more or paid more attention; if only we had answered that last letter; if only we had returned the telephone call . . . if only . . .

Why is death by suicide so haunting? Robert Neale has written cogently on the underlying reasons for our reactions and trauma (Neale 1971). Suicide, he explained, is an affront to what we consider to be good and viable. It is a rejection of our values. The suicide has passed judgment on us and found us wanting. He or she has cast off all that is prized by us. It is as though he or she has said, "What you find delightful, I find intolerable." Is that person wrong? Or are we? Neale asserted that even psychiatrists and psychologists do not understand the phenomenon of suicide, that labeling the person "neurotic" or "insane" is not an explanation, but a nonexplanation.

Neale suggested that suicide is an attack, yes, but an attack to right what is wrong. The suicide is trying to make an end of a bad start and to begin again. The suicide recognizes that life is a matter of birth, life, death, and rebirth (the great archetypal themes) and is trying to speed up the process. The suicide is unwilling to continue a living death, so he or she is choosing another existence. It is an attempt at affirmation. It is an act of radical transformation of the body, mind, and spirit. It may even be an act of faith.

What then is *wrong* with suicide? What is wrong, said Neale, is that it is too literal an act. All of us are transforming ourselves throughout our lives. Sometimes our personality transformation is a radical one as the result of personal crisis, but this transformation is part of the process of living. The suicide has mistaken radical transformation of the *personality* for a transformation of the *body*. The suicide does not understand that the process cannot be hurried. The suicide has recognized the need to begin again, but at the ultimate moment of despair, he or she saw only one way to begin again, and that was to come to an end. This was not an attack on God, as much as an end of a life mediated by Satan. We need to understand the suicide as wanting to start again. And the need to begin again is occurring within more and more people in our society.

STATISTICS ON SUICIDE.   We do not know how many people take their own lives. A very conservative estimate is that there are 28,000 suicides in our country every year. If we accept this figure, then at least 75 persons are dying by their own hand every day. But these figures are far from accurate, for suicide is frequently covered up by ministers, magistrates, and coroners. When Ernest Hemingway shot himself with a rifle, his wife originally reported the death as a "hunting accident." Many of the reported "hunting accidents" may actually be suicides of persons who did not want their families to suffer the guilt and opprobrium that follow. Besides the number of actual suicides that go unreported are the large number of *attempted* suicides that go unreported. Friends, physicians, and family engage in a conspiracy of silence to protect the person and to protect the family.

In consideration of all these facts, 28,000 suicides a year is an extremely deceiving figure. A more realistic figure may be upwards of 60,000 every year, and some have said that the figure may be closer to 100,000. If that is so, then suicide is tenth on the scale of killers in the United States alone. We now can begin to get a realistic view of suicide. It is not a rare and occasional offense against God and humankind but one of the more common paths to death. It is time we take suicide out of "the closet" and learn to understand it for what it is—one of the "separate paths" (Pearson 1977) to nonexistence, as one team of writers put it.

WORKING THROUGH OUR FEELINGS AFTER SUICIDE.   How do the survivors of suicide heal their agony and ease their burden of guilt and self-recrimination? They do it, first, by remembering the huge number of suicides and attempted suicides and realizing that it is far more common than we have been led to believe. That being so, the survivors need not berate themselves personally. Suicide is a societal problem! We can recognize that the burden of living became so great for the person that he or she believed it was impossible to manage one more moment of pain. For that, the suicide need not be condemned. At least that person chose to take his or her own life and not the life of another. We can cherish the brighter moments we shared with the person and not condemn ourselves mercilessly for the darker moments of conflict. We can forgive the person that act of suicide, for it is in that forgiveness that we can forgive ourselves. If we are unable to resolve our grief by ourselves, we can seek therapy to help us resolve the unfinished work of mourning and grief. (See box 10.1.)

LEARNING TO PROCESS CRISES: DEATH AND DIVORCE

When a person dies, and we bury him or her, only part of the task of the bereaved has been accomplished. The funeral and the burial are helpful in that they are the last remnants of the ancient "rites of passage" (vanGennep 1960) that allow the family and the community to recognize the person's transition from the state of life to the state of afterlife. But our funeral and burial rites are pitifully inadequate to catharize the grief we feel. Even the Catholic viaticum (which contains the ele-

Box 10.1

A THERAPEUTIC SESSION: WORKING THROUGH OUR FEELINGS AFTER SUICIDE (AN ACTUAL TRANSCRIPTION)

This young man was a student and had come to us to get over his depression and inability to do his school work. He was very intelligent and recognized that his personal situation had become critical. During therapy he referred to the death of his father, which had left him so bereft. (His father had committed suicide many years before.) The transcription follows:

DAVE: I was just thinking about my father, for a minute.

O'CONNELL: What about your father?

DAVE: Nothing much. He died when I was young. I didn't know him very well. It seems strange to be thinking of him right now. I hardly ever do.

O'CONNELL: Are you aware of what you are doing with your hands?

DAVE: *(Looking at his hands)* Oh, this? This is just a habit I have.

O'CONNELL: Your hands are speaking.

DAVE: You know, now that I come to think of it, my father used to do that. It's one of the memories that I have of him. He was away a lot of the time on business so I didn't get to know him very well. But I remember sometimes sitting next to him when he was home and watching him turn this ring around . . . Hmmmm!

O'CONNELL: What's going on now?

DAVE: It just occurred to me that I wear this ring on the same hand he did. I used to wish that ring was mine and now I've got one like it. Not exactly like it, but close enough. *(Silence)*. . . .

O'CONNELL: What's going on now?

DAVE: I was thinking about my mother. How dumb she always was. She used to think I didn't care whether my father died or not. She used to tell me that all the time.   .

O'CONNELL: Do you know how come she thought that?

DAVE: Sure I do! You see, my father didn't just die—he killed himself. . . . When it happened, there were a lot of people. I mean afterward. I had just come home from school, and there was my mother crying and the neighbors and the police and even some photographers shooting pictures. I don't remember exactly, but anyway my uncle called me over and told me what had happened. I couldn't believe it, I just couldn't believe it and then I started to cry. But he said I shouldn't cry because that would upset Mom. What a goddamn bastard! Anyway, he said I was to be a big man and all that, and I'd have to be the man in the family now and not to let my Mom see me crying because that would upset her even more. So I didn't cry. Not once. Not then. Not at the funeral. Not ever. So Mom came to the conclusion that I didn't have any feelings about my father.

O'CONNELL: But you did have feelings.

DAVE: You bet I did. *(He is suddenly holding his head and the tears are coming down quietly.)* I feel pretty stupid crying after all these years.

O'CONNELL: You have a right to cry. Everyone has the right to cry.

DAVE:	Yeah. You know I really did miss my Dad. I guess I never realized how much. *(He cries now still quietly)* Why does a person commit suicide? How does he do it, I mean? I can't imagine it. I can't even imagine it. *(He cries some more)* I feel a little better now.
O'CONNELL:	You look a little better. But what are your hands saying now?
DAVE:	Oh, I'm twisting the ring again.
O'CONNELL:	Something is still unfinished, evidently.
DAVE:	Isn't it just a habit?
O'CONNELL:	Nothing is ever "just." Would you be willing to take another step?
DAVE:	What?
O'CONNELL:	You've finally cried for your father. Are you willing to bury him now?
DAVE:	I have to get used to that idea . . . Yeah, I guess so. What do I have to do?
O'CONNELL:	Put your father over there. Do you want him alive or dead?
DAVE:	Alive. O.K. He's on the chair.*
O'CONNELL:	All right, what do you want to say to him now?
DAVE:	I guess I gotta say goodbye to you, Dad. I never really knew you to begin with. You never got to know me either. *(Turns to therapist)* Is that all?
O' CONNELL:	Are you ready to say goodbye? Have you said everything you've wanted to say?
DAVE:	I guess I want to tell him it wasn't right to do what he did.
O'CONNELL:	Tell him, now.
DAVE:	You know, it wasn't right to do that, Dad. It was just not right. Mom needed you. I needed you. And Tina and Betta needed you. God, I needed you so much. *(Breaks down now into real weeping and sobbing)* Every kid needs a dad. *(Weeps some more)* I guess I've said it all.
O'CONNELL:	How does your father seem to you now?
DAVE:	He's not there anymore. He's really gone.
O'CONNELL:	Can you say farewell?
DAVE:	Sure I can. Goodbye, Dad. I don't have to keep you alive anymore.

*It should be noted that this young man was used to the visualizing methods of gestalt therapy.

ment of blessing the person on his or her way to the other side) does not have its former solemnity and grandeur. After the funeral and after the condolences have been expressed, those who have been nearest and dearest to the person are left to manage their grief alone just at the time they need emotional support. It is only *after* the crisis is past that the real grief and suffering and mourning begin (Schneidman 1973). Moreover, in our society, we are supposed to be strong, courageous, and industrious. The mourner is supposed to grieve silently, keep up appearances, and get back into the swing of things as soon as possible.

In earlier days the widow, widower, and family wore black clothes or a black arm band for an extended period of time (a year was minimal) and were expected to lead quiet lives during this period of mourning. We regard this practice as unduly harsh on the family, but there was an advantage to it that our socially liberated society may have overlooked. The grieving family may have welcomed that time to withdraw from the world. Not to have to keep up appearances or to continue the social game while heart was heavy and spirit still oppressed was a help. It was a method of healing for the survivors. We seem to lack a method for that kind of healing at the present time. Yet it is a situation all of us will encounter in our lifetime. In the following sections we will discuss some of the ways of coping with grief and of learning how to survive the death of a loved one and also separation and divorce.

The process of saying goodbye sometimes requires anger. More frequently, it requires the necessary tears that were at first held back, the final words that were not then spoken. When people allow themselves to live these events through, there comes the finality of understanding that the lost one, the one who left, no longer has to be mourned—all that was unspoken or unsaid, undone and unfinished is now resolved . . . *consumata est*. And with this understanding the person knows relief: the slow filling up of expressive energy, which revitalizes the organism and his or her present life forces.

The Stages of Grief and Recovery

In a small book entitled *Up from Grief*, Bernadine Kreis, who lost her mother, father, and husband in quick succession, described her own experience of grief and recovery, along with the experiences of over five hundred persons who also went through the process of grief and recovery (Kreis 1969). As the result of her investigations, she concluded that grief and recovery have three stages, which if understood can be helpful when going through the mourning process. Like the stages of dying, these three stages must be thought of not as a series of discrete steps but as overlapping trends in the process toward recovery.

1. THE STAGE OF SHOCK.   Kreis explained that the state of shock is a protective device to enable us to manage the grim events that must be endured at the time of death. Shock numbs the pain and postpones the suffering so that we can get through what has to be done: notifying various friends and members of the family, arranging for funeral and burial, the endless bills, and sometimes feeding and caring for relatives who have come a long distance to attend the funeral.

In the state of shock, the persons who have been closest to the deceased may find themselves perplexed by confused and ambiguous feelings: wanting company but wanting also to be alone, feelings of being half dead and half alive, wanting (perhaps) to be buried with the person who died but experiencing also anger at the person for dying. In our state of shock we may distort reality, blame ourselves for not having done more, and regret the unkind things we said or the things we meant to do but did not. We may act out our shock by rebelling against society. Kreis described a widow who wore a red hat to the funeral. When her family expressed surprise, she insisted that her husband loved to see her in red. She told Kreis that later she realized that the red hat had been a symbol of defiance and anger, anger toward the fate that had made her a widow. Another example of such rebellion is beautifully described by Caitlin Thomas (widow of the poet Dylan Thomas) in her autobiography, *Leftover Life to Kill* (Thomas 1957), when she threw herself at the husbands of her friends in defiance of the social mores of the small Welsh village that had been their home.

During the stage of shock, not only will the survivors go through psychological changes, but frequently their appearance will undergo a change. Since they may eat little and lose weight, they may look haggard. If the stage of shock is severe, the person may not attend to external appearances as before, and the person's countenance may take on a somewhat "wild" or "vacant" look. Shock alienates us from ourselves, from our feelings, and from our thoughts. It follows then that we may even feel somewhat deranged but, fortunately, this stage generally does not last long.

2. THE STAGE OF SUFFERING. It may take some weeks for the shock to wear off. The signal that this is happening is, surprisingly enough, an *increase* in the amount of pain and grief. For that reason, Kreis called the next phase the stage of suffering. Kreis drew the analogy from medicine: When our bodies have received a deep physical wound and enter a state of shock, it is not until after the shock wears off that we begin to feel the pain. Likewise, said Kreis, the real suffering and pain of grief do not begin until the state of psychological shock begins to lift.

The stage of suffering is a significant part of the road to recovery, but it is a long and lonely part of the journey. It is at this time that the house seems empty, and life seems to have lost its meaning and purpose. The most difficult hours, said Kreis, are those we spent with our loved one, twilight and evening. Weekends may seem desperately long. In the stage of shock, one had a protective barrier for the pain and grief. One's actions were mechanical and automatic. In the stage of suffering one no longer has a buffer against pain and loneliness. The funeral and burial are long past; the thank-you notes have been written; and the legal details have been taken care of. Now our life is our own, but we are not sure what to do with it. We still are mourning, but we know that others do not want to be bothered with our suffering, so we put on that "face to meet the faces that we meet." We pretend a cheerful exterior to hide our vulnerability.

3. THE STAGE OF RECOVERY. The first sign that the stage of suffering is ending and that the stage of recovery is beginning is that we begin to worry about our future, what we can do with our lives, and Kreis warns us specifically to be careful about acting on our first impulses. They may turn out to have been destructive or dangerous choices. One such example is from the author's experience. A woman we know who was going through the stage of recovery took her old photograph albums and souvenirs and burned them. Although such an action may shock most of us, her explanation was that she was trying to confront the fact that her past life was dead. As a part of this desire, she decided to burn the things that would hold her to her past. It was a method of radical transformation for her. Would she do it again? she was asked. Probably not, was her answer.

Another aspect of recovery to keep in mind is that moments of pain, loneliness, and suffering will return time and again just when we think we have gotten through the worst of it. The road to recovery, even at this stage, is a forward-and-back affair, sometimes two steps forward and one back. We may, for example, find ourselves reliving memories of happier times. We may have dialogues with the loved one who still lives in our memory. We may be seduced into imagining the past was happier than it was, since we tend to remember happy times and forget the more painful ones.

But eventually there will come that moment of truth, that what has been can never be again. We must go on with the process of living.

Divorce as a Kind of Dying

No matter how terrible and unhappy a marriage has been, divorce can be experienced as a kind of "dying." Certainly one part of our existence is over. No matter how much stress there may have been in the marriage, separating ourselves from our spouse has the same characteristics (in kind if not degree) as separation by death. In this instance, we may grieve for our life that was but is no more, for our spoiled hopes and dreams, for the end of our illusions of a happy ending, or perhaps, even, our loss of innocence and childhood faith. Although the divorce may have ended the most painful relationship we ever had, it also ended the most intimate relationship we ever had.

The divorced person experiences the same kinds of readjustments as a widow or widower. Both widows and divorced women have the same kinds of vulnerabilities and problems so that the coping methods discussed below can be applied to both. The widower and the divorced man also have similar problems and will be discussed together. Let us call these persons the formerly married.

Reintegrating Oneself Into Society After Death and Divorce

Divorce occurs at all stages of marriage: marriages of only a few months or not quite a year, marriages of a few years, marriages of nine, ten, or twelve years, and even marriages of twenty or thirty years. The facts are that more and more people are getting divorced at all ages so that there are many persons returning to the social and business scene who formerly were married and now are single again. Reintegrating oneself back into society is difficult for both the divorced and the widowed person. The older the person is, the more difficult it tends to be. Nevertheless, there are some coping methods that can help the formerly married person construct a new life.

Differences in Status Between the Formerly Married Woman and the Formerly Married Man

In our society, divorced and widowed women have a more ambiguous social status than divorced or widowed men do. Although the formerly married woman may be interested in male companionship rather than in sexual engagement, the men who approach her may be looking for a primarily sexual, casual, emotional relationship. As one recently divorced woman in her early thirties expressed it, "I'm good enough to go to bed with, but I'm not good enough to marry." If the formerly married woman is content to have only a sexual relationship, she has less of a problem than does the woman who hopes to create another home-family relationship. Sometimes the formerly married woman discovers that invitations to social affairs are few, since her friends do not know how to invite her to parties or do not know any eligible men. The formerly married woman discovers that she is a kind of fifth wheel in an essentially man-woman social scene.

Formerly married men also have problems, although of a different kind. They are besieged with invitations to fill in at a party or to be introduced to another woman. Mel Krantzler, author of *Creative Divorce* (Krantzler 1973) and now a divorce counselor, admitted that the formerly married man may enjoy the sexual freedom that is now confronting him and may even "play the field" as he never did when he was young. But, said Krantzler, for a man in his thirties, forties, or fifties, womanizing can get boring, and the formerly married man begins to realize, soon enough, the emptiness of chasing sexual partners, which also requires a lot of creative energy. After a while, the formerly married man longs to settle down, but he too needs a time for healing. If the formerly married woman sees herself as a convenient sexual object for the exploitive male, the formerly married man, said Krantzler, seems to be expected to play the part of a sexually aggressive and exploitive male.

Divorce and Children

If the couple has had children, the woman and man have distinctive problems in relating to them and caring for them. The formerly married woman now may have the burden of caring for all the children's needs, which were once somewhat shared by her husband. Although the woman may be able to act as a parental guide for her daughters, it becomes increasingly difficult for her to relate to her sons as they get older, and frequently they become unmanageable, particularly if she has gone back to work. The formerly married woman may resent the differences in the relationship her children have with her as compared to that of her husband. She has the odious tasks, it seems to her, to see to their physical needs such as taking them to the dentist and doctor, to meet with school counselor, and to be the disciplinarian, which they increasingly resent as they get older. It seems to her that when the children are with their father, his associations with them are on the order of a holiday and entertainment, since the children frequently come back talking about going to the movies, the zoo or to a restaurant. She wishes she could relate to them similarly, but her job as a parent seems to boil down to supervising their homework, telling them to clean their rooms and to do their chores, or nagging them about coming in at night and checking their whereabouts.

Although the divorced woman may see the father's role as enviable, he too has problems relating to his children, although they are much different. The divorced father may be concerned that his interactions with his children are some-what artificial. In the beginning, it was fun to take them to the movies, to have a hamburger, or to the park for a picnic. After a while, however, he begins to run out of things that they can do together and the "holidays" take on a more enforced gaity than actual "fun." He worries also that perhaps his value to his children has less to do with any real affection they have for him than with what they can get out of him. Although they may relate casually to a woman that he brings into the pic-ture, their acceptance of her is usually not much more than tolerance of a person they view as a necessary intruder in their relationship with their father. They may not openly resist her presence, but they do not relate to her as "one of them" as their father had hoped.

If the father remarries, his relationship to his children may actually worsen, particularly if the woman he has married has children of her own. No matter how hard the woman may work to establish rapport with her husband's children, she will inevitably fall into the trap of "stepmother" since children love to dramatize this archetypal role. No matter how fair she tries to be with them, the first minute she must side with her own children in any squabble, she will hear the inevitable accusations that she always "sticks up" for her own children. Children are natural fairy-tale writers, story tellers, and actors, and it will salve their bruised feelings to cast her in the "wicked stepmother" role.

Chances for a Successful Remarriage

We have painted a rather dismal picture for the social and family scene of the for-merly married. Nevertheless, there is a brighter side. Second marriages usually tend to be happier overall than first marriages. Many reasons have been given for this. First, the remarried persons have a sense of acquiring back what they have lost: love, sex, home, stability, and status. Also, much has been added that puts more excitement into one's life: the relationship to the new spouse's friends, the spouse's own interests to be learned and shared, and companionship on holidays. The burdens of living alone have been eased by sharing the various tasks of main-taining a household (Hunt & Hunt 1977). There is another reason for the more enduring quality of second marriages. Some of the romantic illusions about mar-riage have dissolved, allowing both partners to approach marriage on a much more realistic basis. Both partners are more adult in that they realize that marriage is not perfect but a relationship of give and take. Both partners are more willing to resolve conflicts and know better how to compromise opposing points of view. A third reason is that both have more experience in self-management as the result of their first marriage. Both are more aware how money can become a major prob-lem, and both have had experience with budgeting or the lack of it. Finally, both want the marriage to work, and that implies less temptation to engage in extramarital affairs that might endanger their new marriage. Despite the frictions of stepchildren, they are wiser parents.

APPLICATIONS AND COPING TECHNIQUES

We have been able to discuss only a few of the negative crises that occur in human existence; namely, death, critical illness and disability, suicide, and divorce. There are many other kinds of crises that, though they occur more infrequently, can happen from time to time to any of us. Our house may burn down with all our possessions. We may incur problems with the law, and although we pay the price, we find that society has stigmatized us so that we cannot easily find lawful employment. We may be vulnerable to alcoholism and, as a consequence, lose our personal possessions and alienate our loved ones. We may have been orphaned at an early age. We may become disabled with a chronic disease, blindness, or deafness. What generally will enable us to survive these traumas and to process these events in our ongoing integration of personality?

1. Remember That All of Us Will Suffer Trauma of One Sort or Another

Frequently persons who have suffered a traumatic event tend to express openly or to themselves the questions, "Why did it happen to me?" "Why did God choose to make me suffer?" "Why did Fate single me out?" These thoughts and feelings have an animistic quality about them, as if vengeful spirits have lain in wait to hurt or destroy us. That is not the case. We all will die. The fact that our parents or our spouse or our child died earlier than we expected does not mean that a vengeful deity has thrown a lightning bolt at us in particular. The fact that one or the other of us has been crippled, has succumbed to a disabling disease, or has lost all our possessions does not mean that we have been singled out in some way for this dreadful fate. There is not a man or woman in the world who has not experienced at least one tragic event. The Old Testament states: "It rains on the just and unjust alike." You are not the only one upon whom tragedy and trauma have been visited. It is part of the human condition.

2. "Process" the Suffering: Recovery and Rehabilitation Requires Letting Go of the Suffering Itself

To deny the pain and suffering that tragedy and trauma incur is to bring on worse consequences. Denying our suffering may only "psychosomaticize" the pain, and the result may be physical sickness, a need for surgery, or an emotional breakdown. Allow yourself to feel the pain and to work through the suffering. It is better to express it than to repress it only to have it emerge as a crippling physical or emotional disease. Allow your friends to help you, at least those who genuinely desire to do so. Use your community agencies and resources. There are many types of crisis and rehabilitation centers. To name only a few: centers for disaster victims, alcohol and drug abuse, vocational rehabilitation, unmarried pregnant women and girls, rape, and child and spouse abuse. Rehabilitation and recovery will not come about without your determined attitude to work it through. There is no "magic pill" we can take that will transform our lives. It is a matter of will power and self-determination. Eventually there must come an end to tears and private pain. Suffering something through is cathartic, but there comes a point at which suffering can become destructive. We may hold on to grief and mourning as a kind of escape or excuse to resign from active life. Somewhere along the line, we need to draw up a plan for our lives, as Levinson would put it, to create a new life structure for ourselves. Tears may catharize emotion; they do not rebuild. For that, we need to adopt a realistic, practical attitude.

3. Learning to Say Goodbye and Hello

The process of redesigning our life and creating a new life structure requires saying goodbye: goodbye to our past, goodbye to our previous life structure, and goodbye to previous hopes and aspirations. Life itself is a constant process of beginnings and endings. We say goodbye to our childhood when we enter adulthood. We say goodbye to our old home when we move away to a new city for advancement. We process these small endings (even "dyings" if you will) so that we can make ready for what is to come.

Tragedy and trauma can be likened to leave-taking, but a leave-taking that was unexpected, violent, and overwhelming. Yet without the leave taking, we cannot prepare for the future. It may be a grim leave-taking, to be sure, but not until we have said goodbye can we say a genuine hello to what is to come.

4. For the Formerly Married Person: Some Suggestions

Kreis advised the unmarried person to face up honestly to his or her situation after widowhood or divorce. The going will be rough, but the road to recovery requires adventuring into the unknown. Even if some of the advice given here results in a negative experience, all your experiences, good or bad, are information and data for you to understand and analyze. They will all influence your new life.

1. Encourage new friendships.
2. Organize groups of people for social events.
3. As it seems indicated, renew your old friendships.
4. Confide in only one or (at the outside) two persons.
5. To all other persons, maintain a strong external appearance.
6. Do constructive work.

5. Learn to Use Your Personal Experiences for Your Own Growth and Creativity

It is not enough simply to survive and work through the critical events of life. Every experience we have, joyous or sorrowful, has a lesson to teach. Wisdom is not a given; it is the end process of all our experiences, if we are willing to learn from them. It may even be that we can learn more from painful experiences than we can from more positive ones. Great writers often were unhappy as children but used their unhappiness toward creation of their literature. Many famous people have been orphaned early in life, and it seems to have given them the understanding that they had only themselves on whom to rely.

Not only can we use personal misfortune for our further integration, we can also use it to help others. If we have suffered the devastation of divorce, we will be more equipped to help others who are suffering the pangs of divorce. Alcoholics Anonymous understands this principle very well. They know that it is *not* a person who never had a drinking problem who can help another alcoholic but rather those who have gone through the process of rehabilitation themselves.

6. Take a Nonjudgmental Attitude When You Know of Someone Who Has Suicided or Attempted to Do So

It is time to recognize that the forces on the individual in our society are reaching pressure-cooker intensity. It is simply requiring more and more expenditure of energy to survive the emotional, financial, and interpersonal blows that are avalanching in our technocracy. Some people just do not have the ego strength to keep going. Let us not look for blame: not in others, not in ourselves. Let us rather understand that this person is not able as are we to withstand the stresses of daily living. Instead of judging or "looking to blame" we can utilize our time and energy to better effect, to help the "fall-out victims" to survive what for them may be a real trauma.

7. Take Joy in Small Events

There is no way that we can avoid pain and suffering. Nor can we avoid death. These are the givens of life. But we can utilize our awareness of these givens and their counterparts, and we can take joy in even the small events of everyday life. (See box 10.2.) Pain and suffering and the "Shadow of Death" can be for us an ever-present reminder to *live* our lives, not to endure them. We do this by searching out opportunities to share loving moments with each other, by celebrating the *process of life,* that is to say, by being grateful for the privilege of seeing the dawn once more or watching the return of spring or biting into good and nourishing food. The *I Ching* calls it "the Power of the Small," and these small events can give our everday routine lives a joyous luminosity. And that transforms a life of dull boredom into a series of illuminated moments.

MASLOW REMINDS US TO COUNT OUR BLESSINGS

I have also become convinced that getting used to our blessings is one of the most important nonevil generators of human evil, tragedy and suffering. What we take for granted we undervalue and we are therefore too apt to sell a valuable birthright for a mess of potage, leaving behind regret, remorse, and a lowering of self-esteem. Wives, husbands, children, friends are unfortunately more apt to be loved and appreciated after they have died than while they are still available. Something similar is true for psychological health, for political freedoms, for economic wellbeing; we learn their true value after we have lost them . . . .

. . . My studies of low grumbles, high grumbles, and meta-grumbles all show that life could be vastly improved if we would count our blessings as self-actualizing people can and do and if they could retain their constant sense of good fortune and gratitutde for it.

Source: Abraham Maslow, *Motivation and Personality,* (New York: Harper & Row, 1954, pp. 163–64).

SUMMARY POINTS TO REMEMBER

1. Archetypal themes have to do with the basic issues of existence itself: birth, life, joy, pain, love, good-and-evil, and finally, death, rebirth and transcendence. These themes are reflected throughout the art and artifacts of each culture. Of all these themes, the most significant is death, for how we view death and how we deal with it determines (in large measure) how we live our lives.

2. We seem to be a death-denying society. In fact, many elements of death and dying are still taboo subjects in our culture. It was Elisabeth Kübler-Ross who opened our doors of communication with the dying.

3. We need to develop ways in which to stay in communication with chronically ill persons to enable them to take part in family life rather than insist they rest and do nothing.

4. More creative ways of relating to the hospitalized person are suggested.

5. One of the most difficult deaths to accept is the unexpected death. Of special significance in this category are the death of a young person and death by suicide.

6. Since suicide is on the rise and may be more related to the stresses of our society we need a more sane attitude and approach to suicidal-vulnerable persons.

7. Processing the experience of death of someone we love requires our willingness to grieve, to mourn, and to say goodbye to that person. The road to recovery may have very definite stages, consisting of shock, suffering, and recovery.

8. Divorce can also be experienced as a kind

of dying, particularly in the case of a long-standing marriage. The divorced person must be willing to suffer through the stages that lead to recovery and reintegration of self into society.

9. Reintegration into society of formerly married men and women is not easy. There is a difference in status between men and women. Formerly married women have a much more difficult time in finding themselves accepted into the social network and in finding another partner or mate.

10. Children and step-children complicate and often sabotage their parents' and step-parents' romantic involvements and ultimate remarriage. Step-children frequently exploit their mythical roles and cast their step-parents as the "wicked step-mother" or "wicked step-father."

11. Despite the difficulties experienced by the formerly married as they reintegrate their lives, second marriages do prove themselves more successful and happy. Apparently we learn much from our first marriages about how to live with another person or at least we develop a more realistic view of what living with another person involves.

SIGNIFICANT TERMS AND CONCEPTS

acceptance
American way of death
anger
Archetypal themes
bargaining
chronically ill
death-denying society
denial
depression
dying (psychologically)

formerly married persons
letting go (emotionally)
ideology
isolation
mythical themes
reintegration
recovery
shock
step-father role
step-mother role

suffering
suicide
taboo
terminally-ill
touch
transcendence
transformation
unexpected death
unforgiveable sin

FILL IN THE BLANKS WITH SIGNIFICANT TERMS AND CONCEPTS

1. Due to the facts that we don't even like to talk about death, that we place our dying people in hospitals or nursing homes, indicates that we are a d_____ d_____ s_____.

2. The five stages of death and dying identified by Kübler-Ross are: d_____, a_____, b_____, d_____ and a_____.

3. The death of a young person and death by suicide are usually u_____ d_____ and are especially difficult to accept.

4. The recovery process involved in the experience of the death of someone we love involves s_____, s_____, and then r_____.

5. Due to the fact that we view married people and not-married people differently in this society the formerly married person finds r_____ into the society difficult and in one sense this is experienced psychologically as d_____.

6. We have mythical themes that depict s_____-m_____ roles and s_____-f_____ roles as evil and wicked. Thus children and step-children are able to use these mythical roles to sabotage their parents' and step-parents' involvements with others.

7. Many people still consider suicide to be unacceptable and the u_____ s_____.
8. The basic process of existence itself seems to include birth, life, death, rebirth, and t_____. Death seems especially significant since how we view death greatly influences how we live our lives.

RECOMMENDED BOOKS FOR FURTHER READING

Kliman, Anne. 1978. *Psychological First Aid for Recovery and Growth.* New York: Holt Rinehart & Winston, Inc. The author presents some no-nonsense and practical suggestions for recovery from grief and reintegration into society.

Krantzler, Mel. 1973. *Creative Divorce.* Philadelphia: J. B. Lippincott Company. This book is valuable not only because it is frank and sometimes humorously self-revealing, but also because it comes from the man's perspective.

Kreis, Bernadine. 1969. *Up From Grief.* New York: The Seabury Press. For such a small book, this little treatise has been of invaluable aid for those who have experienced the death of a loved one.

Kübler-Ross, Elisabeth. 1970. *On Death and Dying.* Riverside, NJ: Macmillan Publishing Company. This book has become a classic in the field. Her warmth and humanity are evident as is her overwhelming courage and stamina. Practical examples of communicating with the dying person.

Neale, Robert E. 1971. *The Art of Dying.* New York: Harper & Row Publishers, Inc. This book is a plea to remove the stigma from suicidal death. He writes from the position of being a theologian and a humanitarian.

11

Altered States of Consciousness

DEFINING ALTERED STATES OF CONSCIOUSNESS
    Perceptual Defense
    Cognitive Dissonance

ASC-PRODUCING DRUGS: THEIR EFFECTS ON OUR NEUROBIOLOGY
    Input: Sensory Neurons
    Output: Motor Neurons
    Central Processing Neurons: The Brain and Spinal Cord
    Stimulants
    Depressors
    Pain-killers: Anesthetics and Analgesics
    Hallucinogens
    Marijuana
    Alcohol

THE ALTERED STATES OF MEDITATION
    What Is Meditation?

THE ALTERED STATE OF CONSCIOUSNESS WE CALL HYPNOSIS
    Some Theories About Hypnosis
    Uses of Hypnotism

THE ALTERED STATE OF CONSCIOUSNESS WE CALL DREAMS
    A Brief History of Dream Interpretation
    Freud's Contribution to the Study of Dreaming: The Royal Road
    to the Unconscious
    Basic Elements of Freud's Theory of Dreams
    Jung and the Discovery of the Symbolic Self in Dreams
    Our Need for Restful Sleep and Cathartic Dreaming: Scientific
    Advances

APPLICATIONS AND COPING TECHNIQUES: "TO SLEEP! PERCHANCE
    TO DREAM!"

DEFINING ALTERED STATES OF CONSCIOUSNESS

In this chapter we are entering an area that has come to hold a truly significant place in psychological exploration and research—what is called **altered states of consciousness (ASC)**. Now this concept is a truly significant advance in psychology because thirty, forty, and fifty years ago, psychologists were skeptical about terms such as altered states of consciousness. Although altered states of consciousness were discussed in the popular literature, ASCs seemed very mysterious. They did not seem to lend themselves very easily to research methods. Since that time, however, many types of ASCs have been investigated in the laboratory as well as in the field, and we are beginning to find research methods for studying these special states of existence and to understand a little about them.

But before we go any further with our discussion of ASCs, we need to have some kind of working definition. So let us find one.

Consider our everyday perceptions of the world—our "usual state of consciousness." This usual (unaltered) state of consciousness is the result of our physiology, our past conditionings, and our anticipation of future events. It is our total "bodymind set"—how we construct the world, the way we expect it to be. By and large we are creatures of habit, who operate in more or less the same way, day in and day out, relatively consistently unless something comes along to change our basic patterns of thinking, feeling, and acting. It is difficult for most of us to "see with our eyes and hear with our ears" since so many of our perceptions are based not on what is going on in the here and now but on what has happened to us in the past. We carry our usual state of consciousness around with us, and we think that what we experience *is* reality, when it is really what Joseph Chilton Pearce called our "cosmic egg" (Pearce 1971).

Perceptual Defense

We are also very good at defending ourselves against new perceptions and guarding against changes in our vision, hearing, thinking, feelings. We do that in a variety of ways, as for example, by defending ourselves (with our defense mechanisms) against too frightening or painful stimuli. A good example of this can be verified by almost any of our readers. How often have you known a mother who believes she has a very honest and cooperative son or daughter and refuses to believe reports from teachers or neighbors or relatives that, in fact, her child is far from honest or cooperative and has cheated, lied, or stolen or is a drug abuser. She *knows* that her child could not do that, and she stubbornly refuses (consciously or unconsciously) to change her perception of him or her. *That* is what we are talking about when we say that we humans are very good at *maintaining our usual* state of consciousness and preventing it from altering in any way.

Cognitive Dissonance

Another example of such defense has been called **cognitive dissonance** by psychologist Leon Festinger (1957). Cognitive dissonance is the state of conflict in which we are confronted with something that is diametrically opposed to everything we *wish* to think and believe about ourselves and our universe. Suppose, for example, that we are very prejudiced about homosexuality. We admire the macho style of the great athletes of tennis, football, and other sports. Suppose, then, that suddenly someone tells us that our favorite, masculine-looking athletic star is homosexual! What will be our reaction? Well, most likely, if we fear homosexuality we will (a) disbelieve the story to maintain our hero worship, or (b) "forget" all about it (repression), or (c) change our mind about our hero and decide he really is gay and no longer admire him. What is very unlikely is that we will change (alter) our attitudes that all homosexuals are really threatening to our sense of well-being. In other words, we will change the dissonant information so that we can go right on with our same mental set and behavioral set.

Every so often, however, something happens that manages to penetrate our normal perceptions despite our habitual blocking out of these stimuli, and the

---

Box 11.1	**ON COGNITIVE DISSONANCE**

An anecdote that has been traveling around the psychological circles for a number of years is wonderfully illustrative of cognitive dissonance.

A patient in a mental hospital was convinced that he was not alive, that in fact he was dead. The psychiatrist in charge had tried all the therapeutic techniques of his stock and trade to convince him otherwise. Still he persisted in his belief that he was dead.

In desperation, one day, the psychiatrist demanded of the patient if he knew whether dead men bleed or not.

The patient (who was very intelligent despite his delusion) replied haughtily, "Of course dead men don't bleed." Whereupon the psychiatrist grabbed the man's hand and punctured his finger tip with a needle. Immediately the finger oozed blood. The patient looked at his finger in astonishment, then at the psychiatrist.

"Well," queried the psychiatrist, "is your finger bleeding or isn't it?"

"Yes, it's bleeding. It sure is bleeding," said the patient uneasily.

"Have you had a change of mind?"

"Oh, yes," replied the patient, "I have indeed! I have just realized something I never realized before."

"And what is that?" asked the psychiatrist.

"That . . . that . . . " said the patient triumphantly, "that . . . dead men DO BLEED!"

"doors of perception" (Huxley 1970) are suddenly opened. Our "cosmic egg" has been cracked, and we glimpse more of what is here than we have allowed ourselves to know or believe before. In other words, we have experienced for that moment (which can be a brief second or hours or days) an altered state of consciousness. Altered states of consciousness can come through any number of situations: drugs, illness with high fever, running (a "runner's high"), semistarvation, cultural or physical isolation, dangerous or emotionally traumatic experiences, intense sexual experience, alcohol, meditation and prayer, hypnosis, therapeutic insight, art, music, intense scholarly work, and scientific breakthrough. In other words, altered states of consciousness occur when we allow an experience to take us "out of ourselves," so to speak. An altered state of consciousness can occur to us even by willing it, as those who have had "peak experiences" have testified (Maslow 1976).

ASC-PRODUCING DRUGS: THEIR EFFECTS ON OUR NEUROBIOLOGY

We begin our study of altered states of consciousness by discussing the effects of alcohol, tobacco, and other drugs. Not only are these substances capable of producing states of consciousness not usually experienced by most of us, their biological effects have actually been measured in the laboratory. These studies give us some insight as to what altered states of consciousness are. But to obtain these insights, we need to understand a little about how our neurological system operates.

Input: Sensory Neurons

Most of our readers will know that the basis for all our sensations and all our perceptions and all our movements (voluntary and involuntary) are the result of individual nerves called **neurons.** The neurons that allow us to see, hear, smell, and so on, are called **sensory neurons.** These sensory neurons have special receptor cells in our eyes, our inner ear, our nose, our mouth, and all over our skin and are fired by various kinds of physical energies. Light energy activates the visual receptors of our eyes. Molecules of air pressing on various structures of our ears eventually activate the auditory nerve receptors of our ears. Molecules of air in our nose activate the smell receptors of our nose. And so on! These receptors are the *input* aspect of biological life.

Output: Motor Neurons

There is also an output to biological life. The output neurons are called **motor neurons.** Motor neurons move our muscles and organs so that we can breathe, walk, digest food, urinate, talk, and so on. Every neuron of our body is activated by one physical energy and one only.

Central Processing Neurons: The Brain and Spinal Cord

When the receptor neurons are "fired," they fire other neurons by various routes throughout our body, and many of these neural pathways eventually reach the extraordinary complex of neurons we call our brain. The brain weighs only about three pounds; yet it transmits and processes so many incoming and outgoing nerve impulses that even at the high-technology state of our present society, the brain does the work of a computer that would occupy the space of three city blocks. It is at the level of the brain that all the sensory input we are receiving is filtered in or out, sorted, computed, and understood and from which all messages to all our voluntary (and many of our involuntary) muscles are sent out. We do not see or hear solely with our eyes or our ears. What we see and what we hear is really the neuronal activity that is being constantly processed and interpreted at the "visual" and "hearing" lobes of our cerebral cortex. Any damage to either of those areas (called a lesion) can result in not being able to make sense of incoming visual images or auditory messages, even if our eyes and ears are "normal." Such dysfunctionings have many kinds of names: agnosia, aphasia, specific learning disabilities, to name a few.

Now in certain respects, the neuronal cell is very like other biological cells in our body. Like other cell bodies, neurons have a nucleous, a soma (cell body) and a cell membrane. But in other respects, the neuron is quite different from other body cells, and one of the most significant differences is that *no neuron touches another neuron*. All neurons have a space or gap between them called a *synapse*. The fact that neurons do not touch at all means they can function in a way different from all other cells in our body. For example, they can communicate with thousands of other neurons just because they are not locked into each other.

But if all neurons do not physically touch each other, the question is, How do the neurons fire each other? Well, they do so by way of what is called *neurochemical transmitters*. These neurochemical transmitters are released by the **axonal endings** of one neuron, which then jump across the synaptic space and fire the **dendrite receptors** of other neurons. We have said that these neuronal chemical transmitters fire adjoining neurons. That is not always the case. Sometimes the neurochemical transmitter does just the opposite. It may inhibit the adjoining neurons and prevent them from firing. Or the chemical transmitters may inhibit some neurons and excite others. In short, the determining factors are the *type, amount, and frequency of chemical transmitters operating through the area of the synapse*. Usually these neurological operations follow a certain pattern during the course of our day/night cycles. But with any significant change in the operation of these neurochemical transmitters we will experience an altered state of consciousness.

What can alter these transmitters? Well, any substance we take into our bodies affects our neurochemical transmitters in one way or another by making them *fire* or fire faster or not fire at all. One group of substances is called **drugs.** Drugs then by definition, are any substances that alter the structure or functioning of the body in a significant way. Some drugs speed up the firing, and we call them **stimulants.** Some drugs slow down the firing, and we call them **depressants.** Some drugs inhibit firing altogether, and we call them **analgesics** or anesthetics. Other drugs can alter the firing in such a way that whole groups of neurons in the brain are fired or not fired in greatly altered patterns from the normal, causing highly unusual hallucinatory experiences. We call these drugs **hallucinogenics.** Whether we are depressed or stimulated or anesthetized or hallucinating, our bodyminds are experiencing a state of consciousness that is altered from our usual one.

Stimulants

Stimulants are those drugs that increase the rate of synaptic firing. The popular term for these kinds of drugs is *uppers*. They stimulate the body's neurological processes and for this reason they are also called pep pills. Stimulating drugs include the **amphetamines** called speed. Trade names for amphetamines include Benzadrine, Dexedrine, and Methedrine. The neurons that are affected are part of the autonomic nervous system. But in general they seem to give us additional "pep," or energy. As a result, these drugs are often used by persons who want to get through a day or night with more available energy. They have been used by truck drivers over long cross-country hauls. They have been used by students crash studying before exams. They have been used for the sheer euphoric "rush" they provide for persons intent on getting "high."

Many events alter our everyday consciousness resulting in Altered States of Consciousness (ASCs).

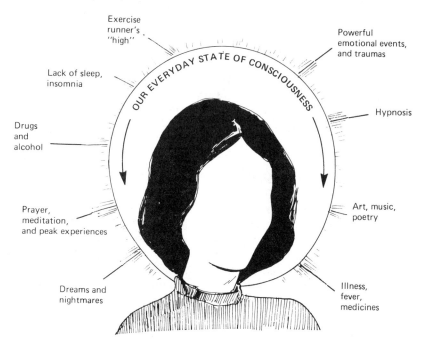

One of the most common of stimulants is *caffeine*. That means that those people who drink a lot of coffee are actually using a drug to stimulate their energy system. But caffeine is not only found in coffee, it is also found in large amounts in tea, cocoa, and in cola drinks. If cola is "It," the "It" is a lot of caffeine. Of course, we need to add that the energizing effects of "uppers" may result in a severe "crash," since eventually the souped-up condition of the body exhausts itself. (Keep in mind Selye's general adaptation stage of exhaustion.) A person who is "crashing" may have an excess need for sleep. When awake, he or she may exhibit extreme thirst, irritability, and disorders of the autonomic processes of digestion, excretion, urination, and respiration. Persons who use stimulants such as speed may also become easily aroused sexually and very sexually active, but at the same time it may be difficult to focus on any one thing, and powers of concentration are sorely diminished. Concentrated doses of amphetamine can produce symptoms that are similar to paranoid schizophrenia (Pickens & Heston 1979).

Depressors

The group of drugs that slow down or inhibit neural activity are popularly called downers. The strongest and most common downers on the market are the **barbiturates,** which some people call sleeping pills. What sleeping pills actually do is depress so much neural activity that the person relapses into a non-REM sleep state.[1] **Tranquilizers,** another type of depressor, are medically prescribed for people suffering from anxiety or the effects of stress: high blood pressure, insomnia, heart "palpitations." In general, tranquilizers and stimulants have opposite reactions. Women in our society are much more apt to be tranquilizer and barbiturate abusers, which must give us pause! We have made much, in our time, of the fact that men do not live as long, are more apt to come down with heart disease, and seem to suffer the more overt consequences of stress. Yet we know that women are experiencing stress as wives, as mothers, and as double-role working wives or single mothers. What they seem to be doing to cope with these stressors is to use depressors so that they do not feel their anxiety or stress, and popping sleeping pills at night to get ready for yet another stressful morrow (Hartmann 1973, 1978).

Painkillers: Anesthetics and Analgesics

Another group of drugs block the transmission of our sensory-pain neurons. Sometimes they are called painkillers, and we have a host of them. Since pain is a sensory activity that occurs in the *brain*, these drugs act by blocking out the neural messages before they reach the brain and are perceived as pain. Some painkillers are the mild local **anesthetics** that we apply on our skin to relieve bites and burns. What the medicine is doing is blocking the transmission of all the receptors on that area of our skin so that it is completely numb. When anesthetics are taken into our systems in large quantities, we become unconscious or can even lapse into coma or death.

But there is another group of painkilling drugs that affect only our *pain* receptors and leave all other sense receptors in operation (hot, cold, touch, taste, smell, and so on). These drugs are the analgesics and allow a person to function normally while obtaining relief from pain. The most common of these analgesic painkillers is aspirin. Next is probably novacaine (or derivatives). Most of us have had our mouths temporarily numbed and paralyzed when having our teeth worked on. Novacaine, then, is an anesthetic that acts on all our sense receptors, while aspirin is an analgesic that acts only on our pain receptors. An aspirin or two will probably relieve your headache pain, but you will not lose the sensation of touch in your forehead or scalp, and you will still have the feeling your head is in place and not lolling around like your benumbed tongue full of novacaine.

Aspirin is a mild painkiller. There are much more potent—and dangerous—painkillers, which are called the **opiates,** which are illegal to obtain except for medical purposes. Opiates are derived from opium, a sticky resin that oozes out of crushed poppy seeds. Opium has been used for centuries as a way of altering consciousness, particularly in the Far East. Opium and drugs that have been derived from opium have had some popularity as medical painkillers. Morphine is one such derivative. Heroin is another. The problem with all of the opiates is that they are not only dangerous in large doses but addicting even in small doses. Opiate abusers may experience euphoria for a while, but the ultimate consequences are very nasty: starvation (the user loses normal appetite), lethargy, and dullness, and when the effects of the opiates wear off, extreme sensitivity to stimuli that we all ordinarily do not "feel." For instance, a bright, sunny day may result in painful eyes or headache, or being touched on the skin may feel excruciatingly heavy. When a user attempts to quit "cold turkey," the next few weeks or months may be a living "hell on earth." It's as if the duration of sensory numbness is now being replaced with sensory super sensitivity, the kind that Edgar Allan Poe often described in his stories and poems. (Most biographers of Poe agree that he was addicted to one or several kinds of opiate drugs.)

This supersensitivity has been attributed to the cessation of the natural painkillers produced in our brains, which are called the **endorphins.** It takes many weeks after cold-turkey withdrawal for the brain to reach its optimum level of endorphin production (Barchas et al. 1978; Barker & Smith 1980; Willer et al. 1981).

Hallucinogens

The **hallucinogens** are a group of drugs that affect our neural firing at the level of the *brain*. Since the brain is where we "make sense" of the thousands of stimuli that are attempting to reach our consciousness, dramatic alteration of neuronal firing at this level will produce some unusual changes in our perceptions. These experiences do not correspond to our usual waking reality (the physical laws of time and space), so we call them **hallucinations,** and thus the name hallucinogens. The best-known drugs in this category, in our society, are **LSD, mescaline, psilocybin,** and **PCP.**

LSD was discovered in 1943, by Albert Hoffman, a Swiss scientist. He had synthesized the drug and accidentally licked some of it off his fingers. His subsequent experiences were so out of his ordinary state of consciousness, he was sure he had gone mad. Because LSD seemed to cause schizophrenic types of perception, Hoffman introduced it into mental institutions with the hope that it might prove useful in research on mental patients. For a while it was used in Europe and the U.S. for both research and treatment but it was eventually discarded. In the meantime LSD got into the hands of the youth culture of the sixties and was used as a way of achieving altered states of consciousness (along with other techniques such as hard rock, acid-light displays, meditation, and pseudomeditation). There is no doubt that LSD does achieve a different awareness of reality, but what this altered awareness is, is still open to question.

Most LSD research was done some years ago and is not being continued. Users of LSD often reported tremendous insights about themselves and discoveries about the world. It is apparent that the alteration of their normal perception does provide them with "cracks in their cosmic eggs." Colors become more intense. Space and time seem to be redefined. They sometimes seem to have suspended their ordinary conditioned responses to the world and to break through rigidly held stereotypic behaviors to new ones. Is it a genuine consciousness raising? In some respects, it did seem so. The problem is that users did not bring these insights and discoveries back with them in any sort of permanent way. If they had had mind-expanding insights, they were unable to recall them after their "trip" or to apply their experiences in any concrete fashion, so far as we know.

Of course there are bad "trips," too, under LSD. Some users have been so terrified by their experience that they have foresworn all association with it. An even more startling effect is the recurring flashback that occurs to some users long after they have discontinued its use. Recent research on those who have undergone the flashback effect seems to suggest that they are persons who are more likely to fantasize in their ordinary reality and therefore are more willing to "give in" or "go with" the fantasy flashbacks than those who opt for more "realistic" expeiences in their daily living (Heaton & Victor 1976).

Mescaline and psilocybin differ from LSD in that LSD is a purely synthetic agent, not found in nature. Mescaline and psilocybin are not only natural substances, derived from cactus buttons and mushrooms, respectively, they were, and still are, considered religious pathways by certain Indians in the American West and Central and South America. These two drugs were also taken up by the youth generation of the sixties and seventies, but little research data is available on either of them. Anecdotal reports indicate that, as with LSD, the user experiences other kinds of relationships to the world than our usual ones, and the dimensions of time and space are not as rigid as in our waking, normal reality but seem to be more permeable and transmutable, as they are in our dreams (Huxley 1970).

We still have not explained much about the effects of the hallucinogens. The truth is we simply don't know very much about what those effects are and from whence they arise, other than that neural transmission has been so altered that the person is processing visual and auditory and tactile and other sensations in less sequential and more holistic (right brain?) ways. Are these experiences more truthful and more universal? We simply do not know. At the present time, we know only that these ACSs are a different way of knowing and perceiving "reality" (Gazzaniga & LeDous 1978; Ornstein 1978; Ludlow & Doran-Quine 1979).

We have not discussed, as yet, the drug called PCP, or "angel dust," as it is popularly known. The reason for our separation of it from the other hallucinogens is that PCP (phencyclidine) is an extremely dangerous drug to use. Not only does it produce more bad "trips" than the other hallucinogens, it is also apt to be mixed with lethal substances, if brought "on the street." PCP can not only alter one's consciousness, it can make a person vulnerable to paranoid delusion, bizarre mood changes, and permanent impairment of sensory reception and motor coordination (Pickens & Heston 1979). While we generally try not to moralize, our advice to the reader about PCP is unequivocal: avoid it! It may cost you your sanity and your life.

Marijuana

Perhaps our most used illegal drug is marijuana. This is produced from the *cannabis sativa* plant. It is a very common plant, which grows all over the world, given certain weather conditions. As with the other drugs we have described, "grass" smokers frequently report feelings of calmness, less anxiety, heightened perception, more feelings of affection toward, and humor with, the world at large, a desire to talk and communicate with others, but more difficulty in actually speaking and less desire to get involved in activities. According to users, it is a good feeling just to observe oneself, observe others, and observe the phenomena of nature. The ritualistic use of marijuana in many primitive societies was also accompanied by religious ceremonies or has been central to them (Rubin and Comitas 1975). It has probably been used by the majority of persons in the U.S. at one time or another despite the fact that it is one of the drugs proscribed by the drug-enforcement agencies. How serious is the use of marijuana?

Well, according to the 1982 report by the National Academy of Science, marijuana abuse can be cause for concern just as abuse of any drug is cause of concern. It does tend to disturb users' time sense when they are "tripping," for example, but the committee found no long-term effects whatsoever. That is to say, marijuana is not as addictive as some of our other, legal drugs. Since visual-motor coordination is impaired, marijuana smokers should not be allowed to drive any more than those who have one or two alcoholic drinks. There was not conclusive evidence, according to the committee, that marijuana had long-term effects, such as birth defects, the alteration of genetic material, or damage to the structure of the brain. In addition, there have been reported very beneficial effects of marijuana for the treatment of high blood pressure, severe menstrual bleeding, and glaucoma. But perhaps its most important medicinal use has been found in its antinausea help for persons undergoing cancer chemotherapy (Lipton et al. 1978).

The irony of this section is that the committee overwhelmingly agreed that the worst drug abuse in the United States is not marijuana but alcohol, followed by heroin, and then the legal use of depressants such as Miltown or Equanil. These latter drugs are subsumed under the designation of **meprobamates,** and like alcohol affect motor coordination. In fact, the committee considered marijuana as a relatively small problem in comparison with alcohol and the legal meprobamates.

Alcohol

Alcohol abuse is partially or wholly responsible for some 100,000 deaths each year. Half of these are automobile accidents. The other half results from accidental or intentional shooting of neighbors, family members, or lovers while under the influence. Furthermore, alcohol abuse is responsible for over 25 percent of the admissions to state mental institutions. Unlike the effects of marijuana, the effects of alcohol are long lasting. The long-lasting effects are awesome and tragic, since the alcohol abuser undergoes deterioration not only of personality patterning but also the very brain tissue of the dominant hemisphere. It is likely, therefore, that many of the symptoms of chronic alcoholism are due to the destruction of large masses of brain cells. Alcohol-related brain-damage symptoms include the inability to remember things, the inability to think rationally or make long-term plans, sluggish speech articulation, loss of physical coordination, and disturbances in thinking—even to the point of hallucinations (called the D.T.'s)—and delusions of a paranoid nature. Anyone who has seen a relative or friend slowly deteriorating under alcohol (and that must include at least 90 percent of the readers of this book), knows

Our number one drug problem is alcohol which is responsible for more than 100,000 deaths per year, half of which are auto accidents.

first-hand the tragic consequences that ensue when a person who seems to have everything going for him or her shuns it all for the slow and tortuous physical and psychological suicide we call alcoholism (Blum 1977; Golden et al. 1981).

There are now many therapeutic groups for alcoholics and their families, designed to aid not only alcohol abusers but those who are near and dear (family and friends). The most prominent group is **Alcoholics Anonymous,** founded in the 1930s as a self-help technique for alcoholics who want to stop drinking. Among A.A.'s techniques are education (about the effects of alcohol), shared experiences by former alcohol abusers, crisis intervention when the member is under threat or has succumbed again "to the influence," and social and community support by the other A.A. members. A.A. has demonstrated its effectiveness as a therapeutic treatment program for alcohol abusers. Other A.A. group spin-offs include **Alanon,** groups for family or friends of alcoholics, and **Alateen,** a special group for the adolescent children of alcoholic parents.

A special drug, **antibuse,** has been developed for alcoholic-prone individuals. It has the effect of causing extreme nausea when a person takes an alcoholic drink.

While we would never favor a legally enforced ban on alcohol, as happened in the late twenties (resulting in that era known as Prohibition), we stand firmly with other social scientists that at the present time alcohol is our most dangerous and most abused social drug and our greatest legal evil. Americans have been apathetic toward the enormity of the drinking problem with its resulting consequences of traffic deaths, accidental fatal shootings, spouse abuse, child abuse, parent abuse, spontaneous vandalism, and violent muggings on the street—and the depletion of family finances and resources (Kutash et al. 1978; Feschbach et al. 1979; Isaacs 1981). We have been apathetic, but we are now beginning to become aware that alcoholism may be America's number one mental illness and social danger.

THE ALTERED STATES OF MEDITATION

We have spoken of meditation and the meditative experience elsewhere in this book, but we turn to it once again—this time as one of the altered states of consciousness rather than as a mindbody therapy or as a type of personality orientation. Unfortunately, very little of a scientific nature has been undertaken on meditation and the effects thereof. Most of the research has been done on one particular type of meditation, **Transcendental Meditation,** or TM, as it is often called.

TM was introduced to this country in 1959 and has many adherents all over the United States. Participants in TM have reported many psychological results of their meditational practices, such as an expanding of consciousness, feelings of harmony with the universe, and an increase in psychic energy (known in Hindi as *Prana,* or life force). Social scientists cannot evaluate inner experience very easily except to correlate anecdotal self-reports on an impartial basis. But other attributes can be measured, such as the physiological processes of the body. So when a group of the TMers came to Dr. Herbert Benson of Harvard Medical School and asked that he verify that they were able to lower their blood pressure voluntarily, he was skeptical. Now skeptical does not mean disbelief. It means suspended judgment: That is to say, scientists attempt to be aware of any basic assumptions, seeking to verify or reject all apparent observations.

Benson was willing to measure the effects of meditation while it was going on and afterwards. What he found was that the experienced TMers were able to voluntarily alter what scientists have always considered to be involuntary activities of the body, namely, lowered heart and respiration rates, lowered blood pressure, and an overall *hypometabolism* (a generally lowered rate of metabolism).

Benson also found that persons who meditated twice daily tended to have a lowered amount of blood lactate, which is a bodily chemical that is associated with tension and anxiety (Pitts & McClure 1967). In addition to these effects, experienced TMers could produce more alpha-wave frequencies than is ordinarily found in persons in our society. Alpha waves are produced when we are relaxed and also just before we are dropping off to sleep. Alpha waves are slow brain waves (about 8–12 cycles per second) in comparison to the fast, busy beta waves most of us produce in our everyday world.

As a result of his findings, Benson became convinced that meditation, at least Transcendental Meditation, was a technique that had therapeutic effects on the body. Rather than focus on the mind-expanding effects of TM, which he could not of course directly observe, Benson chose to publish the results of his physiological findings, which he called the *relaxation response* (Benson 1975). Relaxation methods were exactly what Jacobson was dealing with when he developed his progressive relaxation method of mindbody healing (see chapter 6). In fact, Jacobson had long before discovered that his relaxation methods had produced lowered blood pressure in his hypertensive patients and had also stabilized heart rate in chronic heart patients. He presented this information in a book for the lay public, *You Must Relax* (Jacobson 1976).

A recently published review of the literature came to the conclusion that meditation is no more therapeutic than resting and relaxing in terms of therapeutic effects on somatic (bodily) responses (Holmes 1984). Perhaps meditation is simply a way for us to get out of our "uptight" muscular control and psychological tenseness. The problem is, of course, as Jacobson pointed out so many years ago, Americans simply don't know how to relax.

Biofeedback methods have also been found to lower blood pressure, stabilize heart rate at more acceptable levels, and lower forehead temperature. Biofeedback methods, (described in chapter 6) are techniques whereby people receive information about their bodily responses and strive consciously to change these responses.

What is Meditation?

Reporting the known physiological changes that can come about in meditation, at least in Transcendental Meditation, does not say very much about what it is. The person who has not yet experienced any form of meditation will still be quite nonplused about what it is. While we cannot do much justice to this subject in a few paragraphs, we can at least undo some of the mysterious trappings that perplex and scare off the uninitiated. We need to make one note of caution, however: No matter what we say about what meditation is, we cannot describe it anymore than a bewildered parent can describe what sex or love really is to a curious child. Like many of the phenomena of living, it simply needs to be experienced.

Meditation comes in many forms. Meditational techniques have been developed in all the major religions, including Judaism and Christianity as well as the religious-philosophic systems of the Far East and Mideast. It is, first of all, a temporary retreat from the busy activities of the day and from the constant interactions we have with our family, friends, and working colleagues. It is, therefore, a centering of oneself within oneself—a quieting of the mindbody and a getting-in-touch with that center of growth which Carl Rogers has so eloquently described (Rogers 1961, 1971). Withdrawing from the pressures and crises and cares of the day allows us to let go of the bodily tension that builds up in our muscles and to let go of the emotions that are besetting us. These two simple facets of meditation not only provide some relief from the cares of our day, they also provide us with a dimension of neutrality so that when we come out of the meditational state, we have a more objective and wider perspective. Thus we are more "centered" when dealing with our daily concerns.

Some meditations suggest concentrating on a visual or auditory **mantram.** The Hindi *OM* is a long drawn-out release of sound, which has the effect of studying one's breathing response. The classic Tibetan mantram is *OM MANI PADME HUM*. The ancient Judaic prayer, the *Shema*, can also be considered a mantram, and so it became for Viktor Frankl, the psychotherapist we shall meet in chapter 12 who experienced the ultimate of human degradation in the horrors of a Nazi concentration camp. Catholics have used the *Ave Maria*, or *Hail Mary's*, of the rosary in mantram fashion. Any word or phrase will do, provided it carries with it a designation of peace and harmony. At its most basic level, the simple monotonous repetition of such a word will have the effect of calming one's overemotional and keyed-up physiology. Other meditations have the person concentrate or focus on a visual symbol, such as a mandala (described on page 394), a candle, or a Chakra pattern. A Chakra pattern is one of the psychic energy centers in the Hindi meditational system. Christians often concentrate on the cross as a symbol. Catholics may use the stations of the cross as symbols for their deepening understanding of their religious transformation. Of recent date, the yin-yang symbol has become popular, as a symbol that developed over centuries from the Chinese Taoist "Middle Way."

Many meditational techniques suggest certain breathing exercises or yogic asanas as a preparation for the deep relaxed state of meditation. But a walk or jogging or running can also prepare the body for deep relaxation (Glasser 1976). It is certainly not wise to eat anything before meditation since eating centers the body's energy in the stomach and in one's digestive processes. One's environment can also be made to be conducive for meditation.

But probably the most important aspect of meditation is the regularity of its practice. Just as in anything else—it is the practice that counts. The simple setting apart of a period in one's day, a time to withdraw into oneself and rest one's overactive mindbody and bodymind, will counteract the fatigue of the day (if it is done at night) or prepare the person to meet the activities of the day (if done in the morning). But meditation does more. It removes us from our ordinary mind sets and conditioned responses and usual ways of perceiving the world and its events. Meditation, when well practiced, seems to take us out of the normal paradigms of our mindbody processes naturally, that is to say, without drugs of any sort, and provides us with more comprehensive perspectives for assessing what it is we are doing and what further it is we want to do.

THE ALTERED STATE OF CONSCIOUSNESS WE CALL HYPNOSIS

When a professor asks a class of students what they would truly like to know about what pertains to psychology, one of the most frequently mentioned responses is the subject of hypnosis. And small wonder! Despite the more than 150 years that have passed since hypnosis was "discovered" and experimented with, it still seems a realm that smacks of magic and mystery. The truth is that despite psychology's investigation into this area, we still know very little about it, or at least very little that we are willing to discuss with any certainty.

Hypnosis (as we know it) had its modern beginnings in the middle of the nineteenth century when a physician by the name of Anton Mesmer discovered that certain physical problems people were experiencing could be relieved through hypnotic suggestion. Mesmer believed that what was happening was that certain fluids of the body, called humors, were out of balance, and that these fluids could be restored through the "magnetic forces" of the stars and planets. He also noted that the more mysterious or suggestive the surroundings of the patient were, the more easily the patient could be hypnotized and the more completely the symptoms seemed to disappear. Accordingly, he took to setting the stage by wearing theatrical, magicianlike robes and waving a wand around the patient and the other props he placed "on stage."

Surprisingly the patient who could not otherwise walk or talk normally was often able to do these things during the hypnotic session. There were several problems, however. One was that not all Mesmer's patients could be hypnotized. Secondly, after the hypnotic trance, the problems (which had disappeared during the trance) came back—if not immediately, then sometime after. Thirdly, Mesmer often pushed his patients so hard that they sometimes fell into a convulsion similar to grand mal epilepsy. Eventually he was denounced on both medical and moral grounds. Mesmerism fell into disrepute despite some continuing interests in it by certain other psychiatrists.

One of these psychiatrists was Jean Charcot, a French physician. Charcot discerned that hypnotism seemed to fit a certain "type" of patient. This patient was one for whom no neurological or other condition could account for the symptoms he or she (it was generally a female) was experiencing. Today we call this kind of symptom a psychological or *hysteric* symptom. These symptoms can range from numbness or paralysis for which there is no neurological explanation to amnesia (which is more often psychological than physical) or to very distressful pain for which no medical reason can be discovered. Charcot did not get much further with hypnotism in terms of curing his patients permanently than did Mesmer, but he had taken hypnotism out of the theatrical drama of Mesmer's presentations and brought it under the light of scientific investigation. Many brilliant persons went to Paris to witness Charcot's experiments in hypnosis, including Alfred Binet, the originator of the first IQ test, and our own remarkable pioneering American psychologist, William James. There was also in the audience, sitting very quietly but very alert to what was taking place, a certain young physician from Vienna by the name of Sigmund Freud (Fancher 1979).

Sigmund Freud's observations of Charcot's hypnotized patients enabled him to understand that the physical problems often observed in neurotic patients were part of the person's whole "mental illness." Freud's early treatment of his patients had included various techniques, including warm baths and even running mild electric currents through the afflicted areas. Now he tried hypnotism. Hypnotism had an advantage in that the patient could report (or so it seemed) "unconscious" material. Since that time, it has been suggested that some of the material that was dredged up via hypnosis may have been fantasy material. Nevertheless, use of hypnosis did provide Freud and his beginning patients with insights into some early family experiences, which they had repressed. Eventually, however, Freud, too, discarded hypnotism as a therapeutic technique because he had discovered several other techniques that were more potent and reliable: free association, dream interpretation, and the insights provided by "slips of the tongue."

Some Theories About Hypnosis

Hypnosis as a respectable subject for scientific investigation and therapeutic use in the United States reemerged only after World War II. Now hypnosis is generally considered one of the altered states of consciousness. The question is, Just what kind of a "state" is it? Some people seem to be able to do things under hypnosis that they cannot do otherwise; for example, they can remain so stiff and motionless that another adult can walk on them even as their bodies are suspended between two chairs. Petite women can lift heavy weights under hypnotic trance. Persons seem to be immune to pain and can block off all sounds, even loud ones, and yet stay in communication with the trance inducer. Let's look at some of the theories about hypnosis.

1. HYPNOSIS AS NARROWLY FOCUSED ATTENTION Ordinarily we are constantly responding to many stimuli, thousands of stimuli at any moment. Under hypnosis, subjects are able to block out all other sounds, even loud ones, and yet attend to the voice of the trance inductor. Thus the hypnotized person can be made to focus on a very narrow range of stimuli. Actually we all do this very thing every day. Consider yourself studying a book very earnestly. You may be unaware of anything that is going on around you, even that someone is trying to get your attention (Hilgard 1978).

2. HYPNOSIS AS CREATIVE FANTASY. Persons who are easily hypnotized seem also to be able (even in nonhypnotic states) to imagine themselves in a variety of roles and situations. As children they use fantasy as an escape from an unhappy childhood, and they tended to have imaginary playmates and treated their dolls and animals as if they were real persons. Furthermore, one of the hallmarks of very brilliant persons is the ability to imagine situations and ideas that are completely novel. Einstein reported that he began his creative thinking about relativity at the age of sixteen when he asked himself what the universe would look like if he were riding a beam of light from the sun to the earth (Bronowski 1974). In fact, many people are able to induce self-autohypnosis, and many books on that subject are available on the popular market (Barber 1970; Hilgard 1978).

3. HYPNOSIS AS CONDITIONED SUGGESTIBILITY. The research noted above also states that very hypnotizable subjects may, as children, have been severely punished and responded by giving into authority automatically and without question rather than resisting. But in that respect we have all been conditioned all our lives to certain behaviors of which we are hardly aware: our prejudices and our cultural attitudes, even our tendencies to develop certain illnesses.

4. HYPNOSIS AS HIGHLY MOTIVATED ROLE PLAYING. Almost all the research indicates that easily hypnotized subjects have a very positive attitude toward hypnosis, want to be hypnotized, and have good expectations concerning it. They are willing to role play themselves in various situations, and they can even be induced to do things they would normally not do (like shoot a gun with blanks at an imaginary person), provided they are convinced that there are legitimate reasons for doing it (i.e., the person to shoot at is about to murder someone near and dear). But again, such role playing is not that far from "normal" creativity. Novelists, for example, are able to role play all their characters in order to reveal their emotions and provide us with true-to-life dialogue. Biographies of Charles Dickens and Leo Tolstoy, for example, both note that they often felt as if they were all the characters in their stories, and they had dialogues with themselves in each of these roles. Dickens was discovered acting out the various parts of his novels in his writing chambers. Actors can role play behaviors that in their ordinary lives they would not dream of doing. Some actors have confessed that at times they get into their role so much that they have difficulty debriefing themselves after the play or movie is over.

5. HYPNOSIS AS "SPLIT CONSCIOUSNESS". It is well known that persons under hypnosis do not experience pain if given the hypnotic suggestion not to. Because this kind of situation is more easily researched under laboratory conditions, we have more information about how this phenomenon works. When Ernest Hilgard (1965) made the hypnotic suggestion to his hypnotized patients that they would not feel pain when their hands were dipped into ice water, they did not. Later, however, they did report that they were aware of some pain, but not much. Apparently they were able to split off emotional awareness of pain at a surface level, but at a deeper level they were aware that pain was present. Yet this can hardly be said to be strictly an effect of hypnosis since Hilgard was able to ask other subjects to *will* (consciously to control) their experience of pain, and most of them were able to do so. We know too, from many anecdotal reports that a person can be seriously hurt but not experience the pain until well after the emergency situation is over. We are therefore able to accomplish this splitting of ourselves when we need to in order to survive (Hilgard 1978). Well, we've said a lot about what hypnosis may or may not be. The issue is still wide open and of more interest to us now is what use we can make of it.

Uses of Hypnotism

There are many uses for hypnosis now. It has been used for the control of addictions such as smoking or nail biting, to some extent successfully. It has been used for the reduction of pain for persons with chronic pain problems, in dentistry, and in surgical proceedings where it is important for the person to remain conscious.

It has been used in police detection by having trained forensic hypnotists guide someone in recalling a situation and describing the events. In such cases, because of the fact that the hypnotized subject has a narrowed and focused attention on the past event and can relive it, the witness is often able to come up with a detail that had been forgotten or repressed. But care has to be taken not to make a suggestion to the witness, for it is now known that such suggestions will be taken over by the hypnotic subject as his or her own ideas. For that reason forensic hypnotists have to be carefully trained, and often their trance inductions are monitored by tape recorder or video so that others can check whether details were actually suggested by the hypnotist instead of coming spontaneously from the witness. Hypnosis can also be used for therapeutic situations, since persons under hypnosis can often remember details not remembered or not understood until then. Research has shown that under trance induction subjects can be age-regressed. Answers under such circumstances have been checked with records and found to be accurate (Orne 1982). Finally, we are all probably conducting self-hypnosis when we talk to ourselves and tell ourselves we can or cannot do something, in the way that persons regularly carry on monologues with themselves in everyday life. We can make this self-hypnosis beneficial by conscious autohypnotic practice and suggestion. In fact, that may be the practice of very successful persons who, in one form or another, are carrying out a variation of the theme, "Every day in every way I am getting better and better." It may be the basis for holistic healing, "miracle cures," and the mind-over-matter treatment that Christian Science uses. Hypnosis should not be practiced or indulged in lightly, however, despite its fascination of most lay persons. Qualified hypnotists are usually professionals in such areas as psychiatry, psychology, and forensics, who have devoted many hours to training in hypnosis and who have been certified in its practice. If you are interested in the therapeutic benefit that can be gained through hypnosis, see box 11.2 for the description of an actual hypnotic session.

Box 11.2

A HYPNOSIS SESSION (AN ACTUAL TRANSCRIPTION)

The reason for the induction was the fact that the subject was going into the hospital for a possible cancer in her breast. She had worked through what a mastectomy would mean to her, but she was unable to deal with one aspect of the operation—which was being anesthetized. She had a phobic reaction to the thought of anesthesia, and this fear was paramount in her dread of going into the hospital. She knew that the phobia had to do with an appendix operation that she had undergone at eleven years of age, which had been so traumatic for her that she had avoided contact with physicians and hospitals ever since. She told the hypnotist the following story:

My parents died before I was eight years of age, and I was cared for by my aunt and uncle, as their ward, for which they were given a weekly sum of money out of insurance that was left at the death of my parents. There were many things wrong with this arrangement. My aunt and uncle had three children of their own, and they did not like me, since I was half Jewish, and they were very anti-Semitic. Nevertheless they kept me, so to speak, but it was a very horrible situation, and I was often the scapegoat of their anti-Semitism. When I was eleven, I had a severe attack of appendicitis. I lay on the couch in the livingroom for some time before the doctor arrived. Then I was taken in a taxi to the hospital and put under anesthesia. I remember being very scared and wanting to tell someone, but when I started to say something, they simply clamped the anesthetic mask on my face, and I remember feeling that I was choking to death. When I woke up, people came in and out of the room, but no one talked to me. Or very little. I was in a room by myself and never saw anyone else, except my aunt. For ten days I was visited by my aunt and one or two nurses and the doctor. I never had other visitors. I never even saw the other patients in the hospital. I was kept by myself. The only gift or toy that I received was, one day, a bunch of letters came written by my classmates, I suppose, under the direction of the teacher. Ever since then, I have had a deathly fear of doctors, hospitals, and particularly, any kind of anesthesia. I have hated the doctor, ever since, because he made such a big gash in my abdomen. I have had weak muscles there ever since and a terribly large scar. I have never understood why he made such a big incision when I see other persons who have had such little scars.

We have condensed the subject's story considerably, but the following transcription of the hypnotic session that followed is more complete, in order to illustrate how the details of a situation can be perceived from a different perspective, a perspective that has less fear, anxiety and emotional content. The "facts" can be reinterpreted and understood at a new level. We pick up the tape after the induction has been completed.

HYPNOTIST: You are now eleven years old and reliving the appendicitis attack and operation.
SUBJECT: Yes.
HYPNOTIST: Where are you?
SUBJECT: In the hospital room.
HYPNOTIST: How are you feeling?
SUBJECT: Sleepy. . . .

HYPNOTIST: Let yourself sleep until you want to wake up.
(No response from subject for several minutes. The hypnotist told us later that he wasn't sure what was happening at this point and was again surprised by what was coming up.)

SUBJECT: I'm awake now.

HYPNOTIST: How are you feeling?

SUBJECT: All right. No pain. Glad of that.

HYPNOTIST: No pain.

SUBJECT: Yes. . . .

HYPNOTIST: Can you see your hospital room?

SUBJECT: Yes.

HYPNOTIST: Can you describe the room?

SUBJECT: Yes.

HYPNOTIST: What color are the walls?

SUBJECT: Kind of brown. Light brown. More like . . . beige. Curtains. Kind of lacy. Arm chair brown. Brown furniture. Dresser is brown. Just brown wood. Everything brown wood.

HYPNOTIST: What is the bed like?

SUBJECT: Hospital bed. You know, white iron rails and can be raised and lowered. . . . I want to pee.

HYPNOTIST: How can you do that?

SUBJECT: I don't know. I can't get up. I've been calling for the nurse but they don't hear me.

HYPNOTIST: Can you hear them moving around?

SUBJECT: No. I can't hear anything. I'm supposed to call them but I don't know how. They don't seem to hear me.

HYPNOTIST: Can you hear anything?

SUBJECT: No. Everything is so quiet. I seem to be in the front end of this house, off by myself. I can see trees out the window. The tops of trees.

HYPNOTIST: You said "house."

SUBJECT: This seems like a house.

HYPNOTIST: It doesn't seem like a hospital?

SUBJECT: No. Just a house, and I'm far away by myself. I can't hear anything or anybody. Everything is so quiet. (The hypnotist told us later that he was being very careful now because of what this might mean and was making very sure he didn't lead the subject.)

HYPNOTIST: What is happening now?
(The subject turned her face to the left.)

SUBJECT: Someone came in the room. I am telling them I have to pee. They say they will bring a bedpan. . . .

HYPNOTIST: Male or female?

SUBJECT: Female.

HYPNOTIST: How is she dressed?

SUBJECT: Dress with flowers on it. Yellow flowers. Pink flowers. Different colors.

HYPNOTIST: She is not in a uniform?

SUBJECT: Uniform?

HYPNOTIST: A nurse's uniform.

SUBJECT: No. Just a dress.
(The hypnotist then had the subject move forward in time to when she was leaving the hospital. The Subject talked of leaving with her aunt and being helped out by her aunt and someone else, also not in uniform. We pick up the transcription again.)

HYPNOTIST: You are walking out of your room?
SUBJECT: Yes.
HYPNOTIST: What do you see as you are walking out?
SUBJECT: Seems like a big hall. Other rooms going off from hall.
HYPNOTIST: Can you see into them?
SUBJECT: No. Too busy.
HYPNOTIST: Too busy?
SUBJECT: Too busy . . . walking.
HYPNOTIST: Can you describe where you are?
SUBJECT: I am downstairs.
HYPNOTIST: What do you see now?
SUBJECT: Big door. Have to go through the door. They are opening it.
HYPNOTIST: Where are you?
SUBJECT: Holding on to stairs.
HYPNOTIST: Can you see anything else?
SUBJECT: People. People are sitting on chairs. Old people. . . .
HYPNOTIST: Old people.
SUBJECT: Yes, very old people, I think. Wait a minute . . . I think this is not a hospital.
HYPNOTIST: You think it is not a hospital?
SUBJECT: No. More like . . . more like . . . just a house with upstairs and downstairs . . .
(The hypnotist ended the trance and instructed the subject to come into the present and retain her consciousness of the event. The following is an interview held immediately afterwards.)
HYPNOTIST: How are you feeling?
SUBJECT: Strange. It's like I understand something I never understood before. It wasn't a hospital at all. It was just a house. I don't know how to fathom that. How could I have had an operation in a house? . . . It was more like an old folks' home.
HYPNOTIST: An old folks' home?
SUBJECT: My God! That would explain a lot, wouldn't it? . . . Why I never saw anybody or heard anything . . . like other children. It was always quiet. They had me tucked away from the other patients. The thing about having to urinate. They didn't tell me about the buzzer.
HYPNOTIST: Buzzer?
SUBJECT: Yeah. The bed had a buzzer to call, but they didn't tell me. I guess most adults would know about that. But they didn't tell me. I guess they didn't understand about children. And there weren't really nurses. More like attendants.
HYPNOTIST: How do you explain all this?
SUBJECT: I think my aunt was trying to save money. They were poor. I think now that explains why I was there. A hospital would have cost too much.
HYPNOTIST: But you said there was insurance money for your being there.
SUBJECT: Yes, but my aunt would not have counted on it. She was so stingy. I guess from being poor. That would account for why there was no ambulance either. I went in a taxi, I remember that. I went home in a taxi. We didn't even have a car. There was no hospital in our town . . . Oh my! I just remembered. There *was* an old folks' home there. There really was. That's where I was!

THE ALTERED STATE OF CONSCIOUSNESS WE CALL DREAMS

Our particular society has not encouraged altered states of consciousness, but in former eras and even now in certain primitive societies, altered states of consciousness have been much sought after. The American Indian isolated himself and fasted for days when he wanted such an experience. Members of the Whirling Dervish sect of Sufism dance their way to such experiences hour after hour. The Bible recounts the Hebrew tradition of making a retreat "unto the high places" for divine revelation. In our society, on the other hand, we have tended to regard these altered states of consciousness as dangerous, embarrassing, or indications of hallucinations and/or madness. The drug-induced altered states of consciousness of the late 1960s and early 1970s did not add to our acceptance of these experiences, even though there is one altered state of consciousness that we all have and do experience—that ASC we call dreaming.

A Brief History of Dream Interpretation

THE PHYSICALIST APPROACH TO DREAMS. Living as we do, near the end of the twentieth century, it is difficult for us to realize that dreams were considered so much "stuff-and-nonsense" by the literate and elite of the nineteenth century. For them dreams were simply a reaction to physical distress. For example, if someone dreamed of being guillotined, the dream was thought to be the result of something that had fallen on his head as he slept or because he was being choked by bedclothes. If someone dreamed he was in a boat and the boat was in danger of sinking, the explanation was that he needed to urinate. Scrooge, in Charles Dickens's story *A Christmas Carol*, probably summed up the physicalist theory of dreaming when he reacted to his "night visitor" as nothing more than "a bit of undigested food."

THE MEDIEVAL APPROACH TO DREAMS: DEMONS AND DEVILS. This approach to dreaming came as a relief to the educated people of the nineteenth century. Since the beginning of time, dreams had been haunting people with their sexual content and the other confusing elements that disturbed their peace of mind. Frightening dreams were, in fact, called nightmares in Old English because they were believed to be caused by monsters (*mares*). During the medieval witch hunts erotic dreams were seen as the work of devils (*incubi* and *succubi*) that invaded the souls of innocent men and women. There is probably not one of us who cannot sympathize with Job's desperate cry, "You frighten me with dreams and terrify me with visions." (*Book of Job.*)

It was comforting, then, for people in the nineteenth century to be able to rid themselves at last of the disturbing belief that there was something real or important going on in their dreams. After all (they could say), these events and experiences happened during the "sleep of reason"! Clearly there could be little correspondence between these strange aspects and happenings of the dream self and those everyday experiences of the sensible, mature, and virtuous person in the waking state! The explanations of rational science provided just enough impetus for them to dismiss their dreams as essentially unimportant. Then as if heralding the new Age of Psychology, there appeared in 1900 a small book entitled *The Interpretation of Dreams* by an obscure (until then) Viennese psychiatrist, Sigmund Freud.

Freud put forth a preposterous, even scandalous, idea that dreams were not meaningless and unimportant at all but were indicative of a very deep and essential part of our personality, one that lay hidden beneath our conscious mind. He maintained always that dreams were the "royal road" to this unconscious and that we would do well to treat them seriously and learn to understand them.

He said also that dreams reveal the savage, infantile, uncivilized aspects of the self that each dreamer would prefer to ignore. He said, as well, that the lusty, exhibitionistic, and aggressive dream-self is just as valid a self as the one each person attempts to construct in the waking state. He said, finally, that the denial of the existence of this lusty and aggressive self in Victorian society was one cause of the psychological conflicts in that society.

Freud's contributions to the theory of dreams, as original and monumental as they certainly were, nevertheless did not burst full grown and independently from Freud's intellect. Ever since people first differentiated between their waking and dreaming states, they have been fascinated by dreams. There was a considerable amount of literature on dreams by Freud's time, much of which Freud knew and which he quoted extensively in his book. We summarize that history briefly now to set the stage for Freud's original insights.

THE BIBLICAL APPROACH TO DREAMING: DIVINE GUIDANCE. First, the Old Testament is not only a source of accounts of dreams but is one of the first handbooks on dream interpretation. For example, Joseph's position as a dream interpreter was good enough not only to secure his release from prison but also to gain him the chancellorship of the pharoah's court. Joseph's dreams may also have prompted his being sold into slavery, for he dared to interpret two early dreams as a prediction that one day he would be a mighty lord before whom all his brothers would bow down (Gen. 40–41).

Solomon at the beginning of his reign illustrates very clearly that the Hebrews believed that God could use the medium of dreams to appear to men. One of the loveliest dialogues between the Hebrews and Jehovah appears in the Book of Kings. In fact, all the way through the Old Testament, dreams play a very important role in the history of the Hebrews. The story of Jacob's ladder from heaven to earth with angels ascending and descending occurs as a dream. The fall of Jerusalem to Gideon is predicted in a dream of one of the soldiers defending the city.

The New Testament also provides examples of divine guidance in dreams. The birth, life, and death of Jesus is highlged by dream revelations in the Book of Matthew. (See box 11.3.)

DREAMS AS PREDICTORS OF FUTURE EVENTS. Even prior to biblical times, ancient civilizations had given much attention to their dreams as both divine revela-

Box 11.3.

SOME EXAMPLES OF DREAMS IN THE BIBLE

From the Book of Kings:

Solomon was not the heir to King David's throne, for he was not the oldest son of King David. It must have come as a surprise to him, then, when he became successor to the throne after all. At any rate, God appeared "in a dream" to Solomon and said: "Ask what you would like me to give you." Solomon's dream-self displays an astonishing humility in his reply:

> My God, you have made your servant king in succession to David, my father. But I am a very young man, unskilled in leadership. Your servant finds himself in the midst of this people of yours that you have chosen, a people so many that its number cannot be counted or reckoned. Give your servant a heart to understand how to discern between good and evil, for who could govern this people of yours that is so great?

God was pleased by this response and answered:

> Since you have asked for this and not asked for long life for yourself or riches or the lives of your enemies, but have asked for a discerning judgment for yourself here and now, I do what you ask: I give you a heart wise and shrewd as none before you has had and none will have after you.

But God rewarded Solomon even further:

> What you have not asked I shall give you too: such riches and glory as no other king ever had. And I will give you a long life, if you follow my laws and commandments as your father David followed them.

And then to remind us, the writer repeats again the setting of this dialogue: "Then Solomon awoke; it was a dream" (Kings 1:3)

From the Book of Matthew:

When Joseph discovered his bride-to-be, Mary, was pregnant, he was sorely distressed. But being a man of honor, he did not want to expose her publicly. He decided to divorce her quietly. The Lord's angel, however, Matthew went on to say, appeared to him in a dream and told him not to be afraid to take Mary for his wife, for her conception was "by the Holy Spirit" (Matthew 1:20).

Later the Magi, after their visit to the child Jesus, failed to inform Herod of the child's whereabouts—as he had instructed them to do—for they had been "warned in a dream not to go back to Herod" and thus returned to their own country by another route (Matthew 2:12). The Angel of the Lord appeared twice more to Joseph in dreams: first to tell him to take his family and flee into Egypt (Matthew 2:13), and then again to tell him that it was safe to return to Israel (Matthew 2:19–20).

In the last hours of Jesus's trial, there also is that well-known moment when Pilate, ready to pass sentence on a man he realized was not a criminal, received a plea for mercy from his wife:

> Now as he was seated in the chair of judgment, his wife sent him a message, "Have nothing to do with that man; I have been upset all day by a dream I had about him." [Matthew 27:6]

tion and as predictors of future events. Joseph's role as an accurate interpreter of dreams and predictor of future events is just such an example. Dreams were considered as important as the utterances of prophets and oracles. So established was the use of dreams as valid prophecy that the ancient Egyptians even published a book of dream symbols, what they meant, and what portent they had for the future. In the British Museum is a set of carefully preserved papyrus scrolls (called the Chester Beatty papyrus after its donor), which records some two hundred dreams and what they mean and which dates back to the city of Thebes twelve centuries before Jesus Christ.

The Great Sphinx at Giza records a little known dream of the mighty pharoah Thutmose IV (MacKenzie 1965).

Mohammed, the prophet of Islam, made a practice of relating his dreams each morning to his disciples and having them relate their own dreams. The art of dream interpretation was dignified as a science by Mohammed and his followers, who considered it one of the high orders of natural philosophy (MacKenzie 1965).

It will perhaps be clear to the reader by now that Freud did not begin from scratch when he undertook his master work on dreams. But it was Freud's particular genius to pull together the many diverse insights and intuitions of these other ages and to integrate their intuitions and discoveries systematically into his own clinical work as a psychiatrist.

Freud's Contribution to the Study of Dreaming: The Royal Road to the Unconscious

To Freud dreams were neither divine revelation nor prophecy and for that matter, had nothing to do with future events. They *were* to be believed, however, and in that respect (he wrote) he took his stand with the Ancients! But how *were* they to be believed? In Freud's words, they were the "royal road" to the unconscious, for it is in our dreams, he explained, that repressed material breaks through what he called our conscious "censor." But they come through disguised in symbols. That is why, he explained further, that dreams are difficult to understand. Why are they disguised? In Freud's theoretical formulations, if the repressed material came up undisguised, it would be so terrifying or so shameful to us that we would wake in horror to realize that we had such violent or erotic or embarrassing thoughts and feelings. All of us have experienced nightmares in which we have dreamt the most terrible of events and awaked with heart beating wildly, bathed in sweat, and once the terror has passed, grateful that it was "only a dream" after all. Dreams, he wrote, are the "guardians of sleep" (at least, ordinarily), and the fact that we dream in disguised symbols allows us to catharsize this repressed material without being unduly disturbed and so to continue resting peacefully.

Freud's understanding of dream symbols came from his study of neurotic patients, yes, but they came also from sources closer at hand. At part of his investigations into the unconscious, Freud reported and interpreted twenty-eight of his own dreams for his readers. From them and also from the dreams he gathered from his colleagues and family, Freud formulated his theory of the psychology of dreaming. All great philosophers, scientists and writers have drawn from their own experiences. So it was with Freud.

But it was not an easy task. His own self-revelations, he told us, necessitated considerable risk to himself as a person and as a professional. It entailed speaking of subject matter taboo in his society, namely, sexuality. We also need to remember that Freud himself was a very proper gentleman from the upper middle class, a scholar and scientist who by nature and training would have been naturally loathe to reveal himself so candidly. He actually confessed to this feeling several times in the eighth edition of *The Interpretation of Dreams*.

Although we know now that Freud's theory of dreaming was incomplete and that other investigations would extend his theory and develop still other approaches to dream theory, Freud still stands out as the father of contemporary dream theory, the benchmark against which any contribution to this new science must be measured, examined, and understood in time.

Basic Elements of Freud's Theory of Dreams

Freud believed, then, that dreams were what we ordinarily did not want to admit to ourselves in our waking existence. The way to understand our dreams, he wrote, was to note what went on during the twenty-four to forty-eight hours prior to the dream, for dreams use the "leftover refuse" of the day (by which he meant the ordinary, common activities and events of the day) to symbolize the libidinal strivings and incestuous wishes and the powerful and (often) violent emotions of our unconscious. Unravelling the real meanings behind the seeming innocuous dreams he called the *dream work*.

Let's discover, now, what is involved in dream work. Or in other words, let's understand how dreams, according to Freud, are meant to be interpreted and understood.

LATENT VERSUS MANIFEST DREAM CONTENT. Basic to the psychoanalytic theory of dreams is Freud's assertion that every dream has two levels. The first is the *manifest*, or surface, dream, the actual pictorial-auditory dream we remember upon awakening. The second level of the dream (which Freud called the *latent* content) is the real meaning of the dream. In other words, we disguise the real latent meanings of our dreams in the symbols of the storylike manifest dream.

The wish to kill one's father, for example, may be repressed consciously and transformed in a dream of seeing one's father melt away like a snowman. The wish to expose oneself may appear in a dream as having one's clothing blown off by the wind. The wish to have intercourse with one's mother may be expressed as making love to a woman who has no face and is therefore unrecognizable. If such desires were expressed literally in one's dreams, however, the censor would become immediately operative; the dreamer would then wake up.

CONDENSATION. According to Freud, a dream is always economical in expression, even laconic in its manner of conveying its message. A dream expresses ideas and feelings always in the briefest way possible. For that reason one dream symbol can stand for many things simultaneously. For example, a giant may stand for all the authority figures we have ever known: one's father, a policeman, or a school-teacher. Or a soldier may stand for an army, or a book may represent knowledge in general. These are called *collective objects* or *collective persons*.

A good way to know whether a semifamiliar figure or object is a product of condensation is to analyze the various elements. It may "look like A perhaps but may be dressed like B, may do something we remember C doing, and at the same time we may know that it is really D" (Freud 1961[a]). The next thing is to decide is what these four persons (A, B, C, and D) have in common—and *there* is the significant meaning.

DISPLACEMENT. Sometimes we dream a seemingly senseless dream, very neutral in tone, one that seems to have no emotional quality or purpose. Freud was particularly specific about such a dream. These kinds of "neutral" dreams, he said, very often disguise extremely violent, narcissistic, or primitive impulses and desires. Freud called this type of symbolism *displacement*. For example, a man dreams that he was throwing a wheel to his father. The latent interpretation of this dream reveals a deep-seated hatred by the man for his father whom he considers tyrannical; in fact, he wishes the old man were dead and out of his life. He might have dreamed that he had shot the man with a "revolver," but instead the manifest dream leads away from that taboo wish and instead disguises the wish by having the man throw something to his father that "revolves." In fact, the dream continues with the revolving instrument being thrown back and forth between the father and the man, further displacing the taboo wish by turning it into something as innocuous as a game of "catch."

VISUAL REPRESENTATION OF ABSTRACT IDEAS. A third explanation for the use of dream symbols, said Freud, is that often dreams attempt to describe abstract ideas that are difficult to express. The unconscious part of ourselves is concrete, rooted to things that can be expressed visually. For example, Freud noted two dreams that translated abstract ideas into concrete visual representations. The first was of a man who dreamed he was planing a piece of wood. At the time of the dream the man was in the process of revising and refining an essay he was writing, and the dream translated the idea as smoothing out and refining a piece of wood. A second dream, also by the same man, involved the visual image of a printed page falling away. In this instance, Freud said, the man was concerned about losing his train of thought as he was revising the article (Freud 1961[b]).

SEXUAL SYMBOLS. Freud's society was one of the most repressive eras in history, particularly in regard to human sexuality. Many of the dream symbols that appeared in Victorian dreams represented the sexual aspects of life. If Freud tended to oversexualize dream symbols, we can forgive him now since he was

The Old and New Testaments indicate that the Hebrews and early Christians relied on their dreams for divine guidance.

battling the hypocritical double standards of those days. He viewed elongated objects such as neckties, knives, sticks, spears, and even bananas as symbolizing the penis, and boxes, chests, cupboards, and even ovens as representing the vagina. Rooms, in dreams, also could represent women, and so could boats, cars, and other kinds of "boxes" that carry people around. A train going through a tunnel would be an excellent symbol for intercourse, as would also such physical activities as rocking in a chair, climbing, and swimming.

In a dream, a child is often symbolic of the genitals; so playing with one's child could be symbolic of masturbation, according to Freud. He noted that the penis is sometimes called by a male name. In English, for example, the words *dick* and *peter* are used to denote the penis. Similarly, fear of castration may be represented in a dream by having a finger or a leg cut off or even by a tooth falling out. The snake is then obviously a representation of the penis, particularly if the dreamer is a woman who is afraid of sexual intercourse.

Freud was one of the giants of the twentieth century, who reshaped our understanding of the nature of people. Perhaps no one said it better than Carl Jung, one of Freud's most brilliant students:

Freud's greatest achievement probably consisted in taking neurotic patients seriously and entering into their peculiar individual psychology. He had the courage to let the case material speak for itself . . . . He saw with the patients' eyes . . . . He was free of bias, courageous, and succeeded in overcoming a host of prejudices . . . . By evaluating dreams as the most important source of information concerning the unconscious processes, he gave back to mankind a tool that had seemed irretrievably lost. [Jung 1963]

Jung and the Discovery of the Symbolic Self In Dreams

By the time Freud published the final edition of his *Interpretation of Dreams* in 1916, a devoted group of psychoanalysts had gathered around him in Vienna. Many of these analysts were eventually to make original contributions to psycho-analytic theory and achieve public renown in their own right, for example, Wilhelm Reich, Alfred Adler, Otto Rank, Karen Horney, Ernest Jones, Wilhelm Steckel, and Carl Gustav Jung—to mention a few. We have chosen to speak of Jung and his theories because Jung's works, in particular his work on dreams, led psychology to a wider understanding of dream symbols.

JUNG'S APPROACH TO DREAMS AND DREAMING: THE CREATIVE UNCONSCIOUS. We must remember that Freud was, essentially, a *materialist;* that is to say, anything that smacked to Freud of "superstition" was "unscientific," and Jung's interest in mysticism, psychic events, and suprahuman forces made him very agitated (as Jung tells us in his autobiography [Jung 1963]). Eventually this disagreement between the two men was to force Jung to go his own way. Jung had come from a long line of Calvinist ministers, and while he had repudiated the narrowness of the established church, he believed there are forces beyond human comprehension of which humanity can only obtain the merest intuitions. He was convinced, however, that we *do* get these intuitions in our dreams, in our fantasies, in our poetic yearnings, in our art expressions, in our religious symbols, and even in our transient moments of unreality (Jung 1955; Jung et al. 1964). What was for Freud strictly the evidence of our primitive unconscious was for Jung evidence of universal consciousness. A dream was not, for Jung, simply the product of a neurosis, but sometimes represented the fragments of the "innumerable things beyond the range of human understanding" that we can never completely "define or comprehend" (Jung 1964).

SYNCHRONICITY One of the reasons Jung came to this conclusion was because he was immensely struck by the similarities of such symbols in very disparate sources. For example, he noted the appearance of the **mandala** (a circle or a quadrilateral or other geometric figure), which appeared over and over again in his patients who were breaking through to new levels of health and integration. The mandala has long been a symbol for harmony and wholeness in the Eastern philosophic and religious traditions. Such correlations could not, he believed, be simply "coincidental." In fact, he did not believe in coincidence at all—that is, what we call coincidental, meaning that there was no meaning to, or explanation for, an event.

He called such parallelisms events of **synchronicity.** He believed that while some persons may explain these parallel events as "just coincidence," we would do better to admit their existence even though we cannot explain their connection. He accepted the validity of the "irrational" aspects of our phenomenology just as Freud had earlier accepted the validity of our "nonsensical dreams." For Jung, then, dreams were more than the repository of our repressed libidinal drives. For Jung dreams were messages from our collective and creative **unconsciousness.** It is through our collective or racial unconscious that we are linked not only to all other human beings that have ever lived but also to all other beings presently living on this earth. Such ideas tended to make other scientists gasp, but our present understanding of our biological processes may make Jung's ideas more palatable. If it is true, as the biologists tell us, that the basic element of life is the simple protein we call DNA (deoxyribonucleic acid), and if (as they say) our genetic code is contained within this simple protein DNA, and if it is further true (as they point out to us) that all physical life forms are biologically related to each other, then Jung's idea of the relatedness of all human psychology is simply the "mental" side of this same relatedness. (Remember when Darwin proposed this relatedness of all life forms, he too shocked the scientific community and lay people. Now we accept his once-shocking relatedness of all life forms without too much question.)

PREDICTIVE DREAMS. For Jung, then, dreams were the tangible evidence of psychic processes within us that we do not ordinarily contact in our busy everyday activities. Like the biblical prophets of old and other ancient religious scribes, he believed that dreams could not only be revelations of universal forces but could be predictive of future events—for good or ill!

Jung provided several such predictive dreams. One of these concerns one of his patients whom Jung described as involved in a number of shady affairs and who was taking many risks as a result of these nefarious dealings. He then developed what Jung called "an almost morbid passion" for dangerous mountain climbing, illustrating the synchronicity of his vocational and avocational interests. One day this man dreamed that he was stepping off the summit of a high mountain into empty space. Jung believed that this dream was a message from the man's unconscious that he would do just that if he did not pay attention to his life. Jung warned him, but the man did not take heed, and six months later he fell to his death. A mountain guide who was witness to the accident described him as letting go of the rope "as if he were jumping into the air" (Jung 1964).

But dreams could also predict beneficial events. To illustrate this, we need to understand that Jung believed that what Freud might call simply erotic dreams were for Jung far more significant. He agreed with Freud that our dreams could be expressions of our libidinal natures but that these libidinal expressions could also be symbolic of psychic events.

Suppose, for example, a man dreams he is pregnant. A Freudian analyst might interpret this dream at the sexual level of content and then might say that the dream represents a wish fulfillment of the person to have a child and possibly also conveys homosexual overtones in the man's personality. A Jungian analyst might suggest a different interpretation of the dream. Knowing the man to be a writer or a scientist, for example, he might suggest that the dream is a symbolic representation of the person's intuition that he is on the verge of "giving birth" to a literary work or to a scientific discovery.

To comprehend more fully Jung's approach to dream interpretation, we need to consider more elements of his psychological system. We have already encountered his consideration of the polarities of our human nature with his "type" psychology, in chapter 2, and his archetypal themes of human existence in chapter 10. Here we elaborate more fully the wider dimensions of his theoretical framework.

THE PERSONAL VERSUS THE COLLECTIVE UNCONSCIOUS. Remember that whereas Freud had posited only a personal unconscious, Jung posited two types of human unconscious. Besides the personal consciousness, which marks the beginning of our individual existence from birth on, Jung asserted that we are heir to another aspect of memory, that collective or racial unconscious discussed earlier and which we share with all other humans and through which we are linked psychically to each other. Taking the human fetus as an analogy, Jung pointed out that in the mother's womb the developing embryo-fetus undergoes the phylogenetic history of the human race; that is, it goes through the stages of evolution leading up to a human, progressing from a one-celled organism, through a "fish" stage (complete with gill-like structures), until eventually the fetus becomes recognizable as a higher-order primate and finally resembles a human infant. Just as our *bodies* have evolved over millions of years so, too, according to Jung, our human pesonality has evolved psychologically—and we carry this psychological evolution in our collective unconscious. This archaic heritage, said Jung, explains some of the primitive, more savage sides of human personality, that aspect that emerges in violent interpersonal and international conflict. But within this racial unconscious, said Jung, there also is both the intuitional and rational dawn of human consciousness, as it has emerged and developed through countless centuries and eons. If we are able to recognize these primordial forces within our nature, not only will we be able to harness our destructive urges, we will also be able to tap into our deepest and most creative functioning and wisdom. By allowing ourselves all aspects of our nature we broaden the spectrum of our conscious personality processing. One way to get in touch with our hidden wisdom is, according to Jung, to come to terms with the archetypes of our personality.

THE ARCHETYPES OF HUMAN PERSONALITY Jung's definition of the archetype is a bit too elusive for many rational scientists, and there have been many interpretations of what Jung meant by *archetype*. The word itself has the same root as *archeology* and *archaic*, indicating something very old and deeply rooted in the development of humankind. More specifically, archetypes are prototypes of the first emotional-intellectual understandings and experiences of early humankind. Our earliest forebears were not rational (as we know it) in their thought processes: They explained natural occurences with emotional interpretations. Let us give one of Jung's examples. Early humankind was, no doubt, awed by the daily return of the sun as it rose each day in the east to lighten the night. Since they were unable to understand this natural event in a rational way, they gave an arational explanation for the rising of and setting of the sun. They personified the rise of the sun in the myth of a sun god who not only lightens the darkness of the night but who also enlightens human consciousness. Said Jung, "The archetype is a kind of readiness to produce over and over again the same or similar mythical ideas. Hence it seems as though what is impressed upon the unconscious were exclusively the subjective fantasy-ideas aroused by the physical process" (Jung 1959[a]).

What is important for us to understand is that Jung believed humankind still has the tendency to process our intellectual experiences in much the same symbolic ways. These emotional "predispositions" or "potentialities" still shape and influence our perceptions, no matter how modern, rational, scientific, or liberated we may believe ourselves to be (Jung 1959[b]).[2] In order to clarify what Jung meant, let us look briefly at two of the archetype polarities that Jungians believe to be the strongest forces in our personalities and which still emerge in our mythologies, our personal fantasies, and particlarly in our dream symbols.

OUR SEXUAL POLARITY: ANIMA AND ANIMUS Freud shocked many of his readers when he wrote that we are all biologically and psychologically double-sexed. Even though children are generally born masculine or feminine (with either male or female sexual organs), we retain much of the biology of the opposite sex, which he believed accounted for homosexuality. In fact, Freud believed that most of us have a certain latent homosexuality, even if we are predominantly and satisfactorily heterosexual in our adjustment. Such a statement no longer is so shocking to our more open sexual society and with our more liberal views toward homosexuality. We more or less accept that we do have both elements within our nature, even though we are predominantly one sex or the other.

Jung extended this thesis even further. In cultures that insist that certain behaviors are "masculine" and certain behaviors are "feminine," there develops a deeply significant polarity in our personalities, which he called the **Anima** and the **Animus**. If a young boy is taught to feel ashamed of his crying, told to be a "man," frowned on when he exhibits his softness and tenderness, and is made to think that such emotions are "feminine," he will come to resent or repress this side of himself and become lopsidedly "masculine." The modern slang for this type of personality is "macho" or the "machismo" personality style. He will emphasize the physically aggressive aspects or his intellectual self and repress his emotional and intuitional aspects. But we can only repress this side of ourselves; we cannot destroy it. Those denied, repressed aspects of the male will coalesce (to use Jung's word) in his unconscious and influence his behaviors in ways of which he is unaware. Sometimes, even, Anima breaks through and takes over his personality, and he finds himself bewildered by his own actions. Let us consider an example.

Suppose a man prides himself on being a "real man," as being "tough" or unemotional, capable of handling himself cooly in every situation, and suppose that this is generally true of most of his behaviors. Let us then suppose that he suddenly has an experience that makes a tremendous emotional impact on him. This experience may be so moving to him that its impact cuts through his "tough skin," and he finds himself out of control, crying perhaps, or at least overwhelmed by passions he has never even dreamed were possible. His own emotions may so confuse him that he finds himself not only bewildered but wondering if he is "losing his mind," so strange does he seem to himself. In one sense he has "lost his mind," at least that part of his mind with which he is most familiar, but he is in touch, perhaps for the first time in his life, with a deeper aspect of himself, a "mind" that he has long denied. He is probably not going crazy; he may be, in fact, more in touch with himself that he ever has been before; he is in touch with his Anima.

Some men are more in touch with their Anima. Usually these men are those we call artists, romantics, or idealists. Shakespeare said that "the poet, the lover, and the madman" are alike, and it may be because they allow their Anima more dominance over their personalities. The poets speak of their muse, the lovely goddess of inspiration; the lover speaks unceasingly of his beloved; and the madman flees from his demons, who more often than not are pictured as hags, witches, or she-devils. All of these are aspects of the soul—for that is what *Anima* means. Jung explained that the muse who inspires the poet, the beloved who seems to the lover the embodiment of all beauty and goodness, and the hag or witch who frightens the madman are all really the man's search and discovery of the denied feminine aspects of himself.

The Anima may be a frequent visitor of a man's dreams. It is that part of himself trying to break through the constraints of his unconscious mind so that he can take the next step in his psychological evolution. Jung said that the Anima could appear also in daydreams and fantasies, but that this experience could be so overwhelming that the mind could feel "shattered" by the experience. In a man's dreams the Anima is less overwhelming, except when she appears as a hag or a witch and awakens him as in a nightmare. More often she is gentler and appears as a strangely beautiful or exotic creature, a divine goddess, or a vague presence of soft femininity who cannot be seen or heard but of whom one is aware. How can a man know when a woman in his dreams is the embodiment of his own Anima and not a "real" woman? He instinctively knows that he has experienced something he has never experienced before. There is something magical, "numinous," unearthly (if you will) about her. He awakens with a sense of awe, filled emotionally and spiritually. (Jung was never afraid to use the word *spiritual*.) Perhaps the men who are reading this will have a dim or even a vivd recollection of such a dream. If so, perhaps they will realize that such a dream came at a particular time of their life, a time when they were on the verge of something "new" within themselves, or when they were filled with more energy and creative spirit. Do not be misled because the dream was erotic. Such biological symbolism simply means that there is a true blending of both sides of one's personality and infusion, even for a moment, of the dual aspects of one's nature.

The Animus is the denied "masculine" aspects of the female personality. The Animus, like its counterpart, the Anima, is the coalesced and opposite-sexed component of the female. In cultures in which the woman has been taught to repress her intellectual and assertive self, in which intelligence and aggressiveness is considered to be a threat to a man's status or disliked and rejected by both sexes as "unfeminine," these aspects of her personality will go underground and remain hidden or latent in her personality.

If a woman does not accept this so-called masculine aspect of herself, said Jung, she can evolve into that rather pathetic creature: the colorless, uninteresting mother/housewife with no identity as a person in her own right. Her conversation centers on her children, her house, her husband, her surgeries—there is nothing else of herself she can put forward. When her children are grown up and gone, her husband deeply involved in his work, she feels incomplete for the rest of her life since so much of her identity went with her departed children, and her husband no longer has the same kinds of need for her that he once had.

On the other hand, said Jung, she may take another route: Instead of subjugating herself to the men of her family, she can become an opponent, combating men and trying to conquer them. This opposition may be forthright and open, or it may assume more subtle forms of manipulation such as acting helpless, or by mothering her husband, or fawning on him until he feels trapped by his relationship to her.

THE PERSONA AND THE SHADOW   The **Persona** is the more recognizable of this pair of achetypes. In a way, it can be correlated with the word *personality*. The Persona is that part of ourselves of which we are conscious and that which we see when we look into a mirror, but it is only the outer husk of what also lies within. The word *Persona* means *"mask,"* the kind of mask that the ancient Greek and Roman actors used on stage. Most people cannot see beneath the masks we wear, and sometimes we ourselves are not aware that our public personalities are just that: the masks that disguise other aspects of ourselves. The poet T. S. Eliot expressed it well when he spoke of putting on "the face to meet the faces that we meet." The Persona can also be thought of as the role we take on, the stereotypical image we adopt as we become lawyers, physicians, or even psychologists, wise and omniscient. It also can be thought of as the way we portray ourselves as "sexy," "pure," "noble," or whatever.

There is something behind our Persona or mask, said Jung, and that is our **Shadow**. If the Persona is everything we like about ourselves, then the Shadow is everything we dislike about ourselves, the darker side that we deny and shun. But we can never turn away from it, for our psychic Shadow, like our real shadow, clings to us even when we turn our backs on it. Then, of course, there is a large part of ourselves that we do not know. We project our Shadows onto others, in scapegoat fashion.

In the history of humankind we have tended to externalize the conflicts within us, said Jung. What is "evil" in ourselves we project onto others. Thus we find scapegoats upon which to unleash our fury, our fear, our rejection, and so on. Some of the classic scapegoats have been the "Jew," the "nigger," the "Indian," the "gypsy"—anyone who seems different from ourselves. In our dreams, the Shadow is that fearsome person or thing that can frighten us. For a man, it may be an evil magician, the devil, or even a gorilla who is chasing him. For a female, it may be a witch or another same-sexed female monster or animal.

An interesting aspect of the Shadow is that it may not be necessarily evil to others—in fact, the Shadow often can represent some aspect of us about which we are simply embarrassed, even though others may admire that characteristic. For example, a businessman who prides himself on being penny-wise and not given to spontaneous acts of charity, may dream of a foolish man giving money to a beggar—his own dislike of impulsive acts of spontaneous generosity.

How may we recognize our Shadow-self in our dreams? The most obvious answer is that the Shadow-self is, in contrast to the Anima or Animus, the same sex as ourselves. The second way we can recognize the Shadow is that there is something quite familiar about the person, but again, it is not like anyone we know in our waking life. Generally, if we keep analyzing the dream, we begin to recognize that there is something about the Shadow that is similar to some part of ourselves, some part we dislike or some aspect of ourselves that bewilders us. For example, one man's Shadow turned out to be the fun-loving, spontaneous, maybe even irresponsible side of himself. The dreamer, himself, was a cautious person, very responsible, perhaps even overresponsible and conscientious. The Shadow person of himself was the side that wanted to break through his tendency to take on so much responsibility and to have a little fun. He saw his Shadow as irresponsible but that may have been simply his own overcautious self. He was probably not the type who would ever do anything foolish, even if he did loosen up quite a bit.

There is another clue to who the Shadow might be. Frequently in a dream we often start off with another person by our side who seems to be doing everything we are. That other person may be a little indistinct and may even suddenly drop out of the dream and reappear later. Sometimes that person even seems to be a shadowy twin self. Then we should ask ourselves, "If I were to divide myself into two different persons, how would I characterize my two selves?" The dreamer mentioned above said that he was highly responsible but that there was a self that resented how much work he took on, and he called it his irresponsible self.

INTERPRETING OUR DREAMS.   Learning to interpret one's dreams is not as difficult as one may think. In fact, our experience has been that, with only a little encouragement, most persons are able to get in touch with their dream symbols very quickly. Our method of dream interpretation is somewhat eclectic, since it draws from Freud, Jung, Perls, and many others. Mainly we ask persons to relate their dreams in the present tense and then with gentle questioning encourage them to make their own associations from the dream symbols. Sometimes we may get a flash of intuition about a certain dream symbol, and then we ask them if our flash fits. The dreamers are always encouraged to correct our impression or to validate it. *The key is to stay with their actual words.*

Many of our students have become very accomplished in recognizing their dream symbols.

There are many good books for those who wish to pursue their personal study of dreams, and we encourage you to peruse them, remembering always that a particular symbol interpretation may be relevant to one dream but not to another. You always are the final arbiter of your dream symbols—let no one tell you otherwise.

AN EXAMPLE OF DREAM THERAPY

Brooke's Dream: A Jungian Dream

This dream session was with an older woman who has had many tragic experiences, including the suicide of her husband seven years before. She has had to raise her children by herself and to continue to manage a 170-acre farm, virtually alone, which took all her available energy and spirit. The dream she related was as follows:

> In my dream, I am in a plowed field, which seems to be very fertile, but nothing is growing on it. As I am looking at the plowed fields, I am suddenly aware that I am leaving the ground, am looking around and rising into the air. I see the blue sky around me like a dome and as I look down, the furrowed fields are no longer earth but water, ocean, only with the same texture and quality of the plowed fields.

When she finished relating her dream, she added that she thought that she understood most of the dream.

O'CONNELL: Relate what you understand.

BROOKE: Well, I'm like the furrowed fields. I have a lot of richness in me, fertile like the land, but I haven't produced anything for a long time . . . since my husband died.

O'CONNELL: Go on.

BROOKE: The rising in the air seems to mean that I am beginning to leave off being so rooted to the earth and allowing myself to expand like the air.

O'CONNELL: New ideas, new goals. What about the water?

BROOKE: The water represents the nourishment of the earth so things can grow. The only thing is that the water-land is still brown— nothing is growing yet. But the potential is there. I am at a place where I want to do something for myself.

O'CONNELL: (After a pause) Brooke, do you notice that your dream contains three of the four universal elements? Do you recognize them?

BROOKE: Earth, air, and water.

O'CONNELL: What's missing?

BROOKE: Fire!

O'CONNELL: What does fire represent?

BROOKE: I have to put a fire under myself!

O'CONNELL: The fire of creation.

BROOKE: Yes. That fits very well. I better get "fired up."

Our Need for Restful Sleep and Cathartic Dreaming: Scientific Advances

Since Freud's and Jung's pioneering work on the meaning of dreams, psychologists have been investigating sleep and dreams in the research laboratory, and their findings are of considerable interest to us in the area of personal adjustment.

We know now, for example, that while we may dream at any time during our average eight hours of sleeping, our dream activity tends to be most prominent in what has been called REM sleep, or that sleep which shows rapid eye movement (Kleitman 1963). Not only do our eye muscles move, so do the other muscles in the body. Males may get an actual erection of the penis. Females may undergo a hardening of the nipples. It is presumed that these particular muscular contractions occur during erotic dreams, but that has not been firmly established as yet. These physiological observances are not so much visually observed as recorded on the electroencephalograph (commonly called the EEG machine). Yet at the same time most of the voluntary muscles of the body seem to become paralyzed. Even though our dreaming brain may send orders to our legs and arms to move (as if acting out the dream), REM sleep produces muscular inhibition so that we cannot move about (Arkin et al, 1978). At this juncture some have speculated that perhaps Freud was accurate; that dreams normally act as "guardians of our sleep."

We know, also, that not only is restful sleep necessary to our psychological health, so too is dreaming. Persons who are deprived of sleep for more than a hundred hours will begin to demonstrate considerable agitation, show suspiciousness and hostility toward others (as in paranoid schizophrenia), and even undergo hallucinations. Persons who have insomnia have been found to have more anxiety and muscular tension than persons who have no trouble getting to sleep (Johns et al. 1971; Marks & Monroe 1976; Monroe & Marks 1977).

Insomnia as an American symptom of stress seems to be very high, with anywhere from 10 to 30 percent of the population complaining about it (Raybin and Detre 1969), although women seem to have more trouble with sleep than men do (Raybin and Detre 1969). Certainly our propensity for taking sleeping pills seems to indicate that Americans have trouble getting a "good night's rest." Over twenty million Americans report their regular use (Luce and Segal 1969).

LONG- AND SHORT-SLEEPER TYPES. An interesting study has been done on sleep "types" (Baekeland & Hartmann 1982). The researchers divided their subjects into "long-sleepers" and "short-sleepers." Short-sleepers dozed off almost immediately and averaged about 5½ hours of sleep per night. Long-sleepers had trouble getting off to sleep, but once they did so, they averaged about 8½ hours of sleep. Not only were there differences in their sleep patterns, but the two kinds of sleepers had different personality patternings. The short-sleepers had been average sleepers until their teens, when they began to view their sleep as interruptions of their day activities. They often began to voluntarily cut down on their sleep as they got older. They were characterized by the researchers as the ambitious, energetic, and "on-the-go" type of person with strong ambitions for themselves. They were the type who may have had part-time jobs in school or engaged in many extracurricular activities. They tended to be conformists in their views and behaviors, and wanted to be seen as "normal," acceptable to others. They were also generally cheerful and optimistic about themselves and their future—all in all, fairly healthy extraverts. Despite the fact that their REM sleep averaged the same as the long-sleepers, they did not recall their dreams, and they reported that they had no apparent undue psychological problems.

Long-sleepers, on the other hand, not only looked forward to their "long winter's naps," they actually protected their sleep and nourished it. If they did not get their usual amount of sleep, they were generally anxious about it. As a group they were able to recall their dreams, and they were much more introverted than the short-sleepers, being rather shy, anxious, inhibited, and unsure of themselves in social situations. They seemed to use their dreams as a way of working out their personal problems, and some stated that sleep was a welcome escape for them, just as fantasy is a welcome escape for some—or TV watching! Do these results mean that the long-sleepers were "unhealthier" than the short-sleepers? Not necessarily. The short-sleepers were more like the type A personality we discussed in chapter 5 and may be (according to other researchers) more prone to heart attack later in life (Hicks 1979). Persons who sleep *much* longer than average, however—in the range of ten hours or more—or *much* shorter than average—in the range of four hours or less—may be showing severe signs of stress. Such persons, it was found, are more likely than others to die within six years, generally of heart attack, stroke, or even suicide.

It becomes obvious that the altered states of consciousness we call sleeping and dreaming are essential to our continued good mental, emotional, and physical well-being. Freud was probably right that dreaming is a fundamental and necessary process of catharsis in which we work out our daytime conflicts and anxieties. And this process of catharsis is going on all the time in our sleep whether we recall our dreams or not. Why then bother to try to remember more of our dreams and interpret them? Well, for several reasons. First, even though we are working through our problems and catharizing our anxieties (whether we remember the dreams or not), learning to remember our dreams and interpret them brings to our waking consciousness more self-awareness in our daily living. Second, interpreting our dreams speeds up the process of personality integration—by lightyears. Third, our dream life can be a source of great inspiration and insight simply because it is bringing to consciousness material not available to us previously. Many scientific insights and ideas have come to the great philosopher-scientists in their dreams (MacKenzie 1965). And dreams really may foreshadow future events.

We are not saying that dreams are predictive in a mysterious sense. But it may very well be true that when we ignore certain subliminal warnings in our waking existence, or are too busy to attend to them in the preoccupation of our busy lives, these warnings may very well re-emerge at night in our nighttime dreams—as with Jung's patient who saw himself jumping off a cliff but wouldn't heed the warnings of his deeper self. One researcher has collected evidence that we do tend to dream about each other at about the same time. His explanation is that when parents and children or spouses and/or lovers are experiencing conflict during the day, they will tend to dream about each other and the emotional anxieties they are having with each other (Hall 1966). Jung's assertions about dreams as predictive may not meet with prevailing scientific corroboration. But there is one assertion that Jung made that is getting substantial corroboration, and that is in the area of right-brain/left-brain activity.

DREAMS AND LEFT-BRAIN/RIGHT-BRAIN ACTIVITY. Jung had noted time and again that our dreams are representations of a different reality. Far from considering them symbolically disguised, as Freud thought, Jung believed dreams represented a more direct and uncensored perception of events as they are. Our knowledge of left-brain/right-brain hemispheres now indicates that emotions, dreaming, art, fantasy, and intuition may all be right-brain activity. Jung had said that while our dreams present more fragmentary knowledge, it is more precise because it is *not* dominated by our spoken language meanings. We know now that our language is primarily a left-brain activity, and it may be that dreams are less subject to our conditioned and stereotyped mind sets and defenses than are the perceptions of our dream activity because they are a right-brain activity. Our right-brain dreaming state may actually allow us to perceive what our ordinary and conditioned, left-brain, daytime consciousness will not.

APPLICATIONS AND COPING TECHNIQUES: "TO SLEEP! PERCHANCE TO DREAM!"

1. Tell Yourself Before You Go to Sleep That You Want to Remember Your Dreams

This is a crucial first step for people who have difficulty remembering their dreams. It is a kind of autosuggestion technique that seems to work. Some persons report instant success, but if you are a "non-dreamer" (that is, a nonrememberer), it may take many suggestions before this technique pays off. Remember that you have spent most of your life not remembering, so do not be discouraged if it takes several weeks to overcome many years of resistance. Remembering dreams is not easy for most of us; it takes practice.

2. Try to Wake Up Quickly and Earlier Than Usual

Dreams are forgotten very quickly, so quickly in fact, that within a few seconds of waking up, we can have forgotten them. If you wonder why this is so, let us give an analogy that you may understand. Once in a while when we are discussing something during the day, we lose the thread of what we were trying to say. If that is true even in our waking existence, it is that much more true of our nighttime thoughts. As soon as we begin waking up, our daytime thoughts push our previous ones (our dreams) away. We now know that the dream we remember is the last one we had before waking up. Also, if we are the type that wakes up slowly, we will have difficulty remembering what we have just been dreaming. So it is important to try to wake up quickly. One of the reasons nightmares are so well remembered is that we wake up very quickly, and we have no interfering thoughts that allow us to forget them.

If you are one of those persons who wake up slowly, find an alarm clock that will startle you awake. Set the alarm for a little earlier than usual so that you can "catch" yourself in the middle of a dream. As the time approaches for us to wake up, sleep researchers report, our sleep stages gradually become lighter, and our dreams begin to merge with our early morning thoughts. So the technique of waking earlier than your normal time sometimes produces results.

3. Keep a Notebook by Your Bed and Write Down Everything You Can Remember

People frequently insist they can remember their dreams, but the truth is that even if we have a very vivid dream, we may very well forget it by the end of the day. Our waking life is filled with so many of the urgencies of living that we simply forget what seemed so vivid on first waking up. Psychoanalysts, writers, and other introspective persons keep a special notebook by their bedside so they can record their dreams or whatever they can remember about them. Please accept that everything we dream is significant. Freud insisted on it, and so did Jung, and so has everyone who has made a serious study of dreams. We may not always understand the significance immediately, but pursuit of our dream symbols will eventually reveal it.

4. Do Not Run Away from Nightmares

When we have a bad dream, our tendency is to try to put it out of our minds as quickly as possible. It may come as a great surprise that most of our nightmares, once interpreted, usually turn out to be amazingly benign.

For example, a student of the authors once had the following dream. She was in her kitchen preparing a meal when she saw a horde of Chinese soldiers marching down toward her house and about to descend on her. She awoke trembling with the feeling that if she had not waked up, the soldiers would have marched over her house, her, and all her existence. Her only initial clue as to the meaning of the dream was the color of the uniforms of the soldiers: red and green. When asked what red and green symbolized, she answered rather puzzled, "Christmas . . . but I don't see what . . ." and then she stopped and a look of astonishment came over her face. She then told us that she knew exactly what the dream meant. Every Christmas, her husband's family, two adults and four children, came for a visit. The six of them together with her own family of five (her husband, three children, and herself) made eleven people she had to take care of, entertain, feed, clean up after, and so on. Although she enjoyed their visit, she also was overwhelmed by what seemed to her, at times, to be an army of people to take care of: Everyone had a grand time at Christmas but her. We can certainly sympathize with her anxiety and irritation, but her dream was certainly not as frightening as it had been when she did not understand it.

Likewise, death dreams do not need to be interpreted literally as signs of impending physical death—at least not in the authors' experience. For a very elderly person or someone clearly on a self-destructive course, a death dream may have some such related significance. But in general, if you dream that a friend is

| Box 11.5 | **INSOMNIA: SUGGESTIONS FOR TREATMENT** |

Insomnia comes in at least three forms: difficulty in falling asleep; awakening at night; and awakening too early to have gotten a good night's rest. Some 10 to 30 percent of Americans report one or the other of these kinds of insomnias. Persons who report insomnia also report higher levels of anxiety and more physical ailments generally, and they are shy, tense, and retiring in their social contacts. Furthermore, many persons who do not ordinarily suffer from insomnia may very well report insomnia at those times in their lives when they are experiencing greater stress. In other words, anxiety will tend to keep us from resting at the very time we most need to rest and sleep, further compounding our stress level. Thus the anxiety-insomnia-anxiety syndrome is cyclical. Anxiety reduces our sleep, and the lack of sleep creates more anxiety and stress, which then creates more insomnia. Americans with insomnia lean heavily on the use of sleeping pills, which compounds the problem still further since sleeping pills tend to rob us of REM sleep so necessary to emotional health (Johns et al. 1971; Marks & Monroe 1976; Monroe & Marks 1977).

There are several methods for dealing with anxiety about sleep that seem to have had some beneficial results in research studies. We pass on to you the results of these studies, with the caution that you need to try these methods out for yourself and discover which of them is most beneficial for you. Remember, always, that we are all different types of persons, and what may work for one may not work as well for someone else.

One characteristic of persons who suffer from insomnia is that they show more muscle tension than persons who sleep more normally. This muscle tension seems to have the effect of not permitting us to relax enough to let go in sleep (Haynes 1974). One suggested technique for falling asleep is to *let go* of the muscle tension in your body. In chapter 6 we discussed Jacobson's deep-relaxation method for letting go of muscle tension. Jacobson himself reported that this method seemed to have dramatically beneficial results in his insomniac patients, and sleep researchers since then have confirmed his findings (Weil & Godfried 1973; Lick & Heffler 1977). The person is instructed to get into bed and begin to relax muscle by muscle and, by so doing, falls asleep. There is another effect of such a practice: By concentrating on the progressive relaxation technique, the person avoids focusing on whatever fear or anxiety he or she is holding on to as the result of the day's occupation and thus prevents the build-up of more anxiety-caused muscle contraction. Instead of counting sheep jumping over a wall, one by one, one concentrates on relaxing muscles, one by one.

Another method for letting go to sleep is to write down in a journal or diary the things that have happened to you during the day and to write down those things you have to do on the morrow. In fact, journal or diary writing is not only a good technique for catharsizing the day's events and for cataloging the activities of the following day, it is also an excellent method of achieving personality integration. Many of the world's great thinkers, writers, and scientists, have used the diary/journal technique for their daily problems or for their inspired ideas. One of the reasons we cannot fall asleep at night is that we cannot seem to let go of the events of the day. We play them over and over like a tape in our heads. By writing them down in journal or diary fashion, we get them out of the recurring loop of our computer-brain, and having drained them in this way, we often can let go of the loop. If we find it hard to get to sleep because of the pressure of the things we have to do the next day (the people we have to see and the problems we have to solve), writing them down on our calendar of activities allows us to let go of the need to remember them since we have just committed them to paper—an externalized memory. And so to sleep. This is one of the techniques we ourselves have used at those times when the pressure of life threatens to interfere with our normal sleeping habits.

Allow yourself to daydream. Jerome Singer is a psychologist who has investigated daydreams in the same exploratory way that Sigmund Freud explored nightdreams. He suggests that if you suffer from insomnia at the onset of sleep, you should allow yourself to daydream pleasant images, such as being at your favorite beach spot or walking through meadows on a warm spring day (Singer 1975). Since daydreams are almost universal, and since they tend to occur naturally just before we go to sleep, Singer advocates the constructive use of them to turn off the mind tapes of the day. Singer has shared his personal daydreams with us in an open and candid way, as Freud and Jung have shared their nightdreams with us. We can learn to use our daydreams as well as our nightdreams for our constructive and creative use.

dying, it is more likely that he or she is "dying to you," that your relationship has become "dead," that what you once had together is now over. A dream of one's own death (again, in the authors' experience) generally refers to the end of some aspect of one's personality, the loss of innocence, perhaps, or the end of one's tendency to be impatient, or the destruction of some part of the ego.

If your dream deals with death, figure out what part of your personality is "dying" or what person is "dying to you." Then look for a rebirth symbol in your next dreams: an egg, a baby, or a flower blooming. Our dreams are marvellously biological in these symbols.

Calvin Hall, who has studied the relationship of dreams, has noticed that dreams may have a continuous thread (Hall 1966). One of our students had a series of four dreams over a period of time, which she was able to relate to her own development as a person.

In the first, she was studying for a test. In the next dream, she awoke in horror because she had been found cheating on a test. In a later dream, some four weeks later, she dreamed she was being tried and convicted for a crime. Some months later she dreamed of caging a tiger. She interpreted these dreams as her struggle to control her own fierce temper.

The dreams were reflecting something I have been trying to learn for a long time [studying for a test], which is not to lose my temper. The next dream reflected a moment in which I backslid [cheated]. Then I really determined to do something about my bad temper [the trial]. I think locking up the tiger means I am successfully controlling my temper.

5. Consider Your Dreams as Potential Sources of Wisdom, Solutions to Problems, Inspirations, and So On

There are many anecdotes about scientists, artists, and writers who in their dreams received creative inspiration and discovered solutions to complex problems or received guidance on what path to take regarding a life situation. A well-known example is August Kekule's suggestion in 1858 of the structural formula for benzene. Kekule had been working to discover the arrangements of the atoms in the benzene molecule for some time, and then in a dream he saw the atoms fitted together in a certain pattern, which subsequently proved to be correct. This led to the development of the many compounds containing carbon.

Research on highly creative individuals by human behavior scientists has confirmed that truly gifted individuals, whether scientists or artists, are very much in touch with their creative unconscious. We shall discuss this further in chapter 12. Suffice it to say here that dreams are a truly creative expression of every person. In actuality, you are the writer, the director, the scene designer, and the actors of your own dream plays. In fact, we know a humanities and art professor who encourages his students to paint their dreams as a form of creative expression. Using his idea, we encourage our readers to draw, color, or paint their dreams. Sometimes this becomes the simplest route to one's own dream symbols and interpretation. Jung frequently painted his own dreams, and you might want to look at his paintings.

6. When Searching for the Meaning of Your Dream Symbols, Be Open to Symbolic Art and Literature Wherever You May Find It

When asked how to know what kind of studies are necessary to be a psychoanalyst, Freud replied: a study of the humanities—literature, mythology, religion, art, archeology, and anthropology. We advise the same for understanding dream symbols. As Jung pointed out, symbols tend to be universal to all cultures. Writers and painters use symbols consciously and from the depths of their creative unconscious. One of the interesting facets of dream symbolism is that it seems to agree with symbolism in art, literature, religion, mythology, and the like. Freud pointed this out and so did Jung. Blue has always been the color of love and devotion in religious art: In medieval art the madonna is usually dressed in a white robe (standing for purity) but cloaked with a blue mantle (for her love of humanity). Blue also often represents love, lovingness, compassion, tenderness, and/or devotion in dreams, depending on the shade and hue. In fact, love is often red (passion) as in Valentine cards; tenderness and affection sometimes appear as pink; deep blue is a deep and devoted love. But we repeat that these are general symbols; you yourself may have a different association with a color, and only you can make that judgment. For example, blue for you may mean "having the blues," being depressed, or as in the case of one young Britisher, it may represent loyalty: "true blue."

Numbers are often significant—particularly since we are a very number-conscious culture. We identify ourselves by our age, our birthdate, and our social security number. We live in terms of number of minutes, hours, days, months, and years. We celebrate birthdays, holidays, and anniversaries. We deal in money, and even how much mileage we get to a gallon of gasoline. We need not go on. The essential thing is to get in touch with the significant numbers in your dream and discover the meanings to them. Three rabbits in one lady's dream stood for her three little helpless, sweet, and very un-toilet-trained children. One man dreamed of three doors, representing three possible alternative courses of action among which he was then trying to choose.

Those familiar with the symbolism of numbers may recognize their significance in dreams. Of particular interest, we think, is the number forty. We often say that "life begins at forty." Jung said that at forty, a person begins to take an interest in his or her transcendent-spiritual life. Students of the Bible will recognize the significance of the number forty, so often does it appear in both the Old and New Testaments. When Noah escaped the flooding of the earth, the rain continued for forty days and forty nights. When Moses led his people into the wilderness, it was for forty years. Catholics traditionally practice a forty-hour vigil during Lent in commemoration of Jesus' *withdrawal from the world* before his crucifixion. Putting all these together, what may we discern about the number forty? Let us suggest that forty denotes the radical transformation of a person or a people. God transformed the world of Noah through forty days of rain. Moses kept his people for forty years in the wilderness to weed out those who had grown soft and weak in Egypt and to produce a new generation of strong desert people. The "forty-hour vigil" represents the internal preparation of Jesus in Gethsemane for his final journey into Jerusalem and his ultimate illumination. Jung said that it is true that a new understanding of life is possible around forty, and thus we begin again. Can such symbolism be accidental? The longer we study this, the more we think not.

7. When You Run into Difficulty Interpreting Dream Symbols, Act Out the Symbol

The psychologist Frederick Perls had the dreamer play out every aspect of the dream—whether it was a person, an animal or an inanimate object. Perls's thesis was that every detail of the dream was some part of us or of our projection of the world. Whereas Freud called dream interpretation a royal road to the unconscious, Perls called dreams the royal road to personality integration. Perls's contention was that it was not necessary to have a cognitive understanding of our dream symbols. It is only necessary to be willing to admit to every aspect of our dreams. By "playing" each dream symbol, the person is able to "process" the dream material without cognitive understanding.

SUMMARY POINTS TO REMEMBER

1. ASC stands for the psychologically popular term, Altered States of Consciousness. ASCs are simply perceptual states that differ from our everyday consciousness (perceptions of the world). They may arise any number of ways: dreams, fever, drugs, alcohol, meditation and prayer, art and music, and so on.

2. We normally resist changing our perceptions and we blind our eyes and deafen our ears against contradictory information, a process psychologists call *perceptual defense*. Another term to know is *cognitive dissonance*, a condition in which there is a contradiction between what we want to believe and the facts.

3. Sometimes ASCs are produced through the ingestion of agents that change our neurological patterning; as for example, drugs and alcohol. As a matter of fact, the technical definition of a drug is any element which significantly alters the body's functioning.

4. There are several classifications of drugs depending on how they affect the body. They are called *depressants, stimulants, hallucinogens*, and pain-killers (anesthetics and analgesics).

5. It is generally agreed that of all the drugs on the legal and illegal markets, the most abused drug is alcohol. Alcohol is responsible for over 100,000 deaths per year, including drunken driving, shooting "accidents," alcoholic arguments, and alcohol-related crimes. The next most serious drug problem is the "over-the-counter" medicines of all types including the tranquilizers and meprobates.

6. Another method for inducing ASC is meditation which may actually alter the physiological processes of the body. Other methods designed to promote beneficial effects on the physiology of the body are biofeed-

back, hypnosis, autohypnosis, fantasy and daydreaming, and breathing exercises.

7. Hypnosis as an ASC inducer is still a hotly-debated issue as to exactly what is occurring. We may not know what is involved in hypnotism and hypnotic trance but we do know a number of ways to use hypnosis therapeutically: in chronic-pain reduction such as in dentistry, the alleviation of unwanted habits such as smoking, and for personal therapeutic insight of repressed material.

8. Another ASC-producing event is the phenomenon of dreaming. Throughout history (until the nineteenth century), great importance was given to dreams. Sigmund Freud returned dreams to the "proper study of mankind," insisting they are the "royal road" to the unconscious. Among other elements of dream interpretation are the manifest versus latent dream, dream symbols, and the discharge of repressed material.

9. Carl Jung also placed great importance on dreams but his approach to dreaming differed significantly in several respects. Jung believed dreams could be predictive. His term for simultaneous events was not coincidence but synchronicity. Jung believed, like Freud, that we have a personal unconscious, but he believed also in a collective unconscious through which we are interconnected not only to all our previous predecessors but also to all humans that now exist. Within our collective and racial unconscious, Jung believed were buried certain Archetypes of human personality which are ways of symbolically processing our human experiences. Some of these Archetypes were described: the *Anima* and *Animus*, the *Persona* and *Shadow*. The symbolic significance of the mandala was also discussed.

SIGNIFICANT TERMS AND CONCEPTS

Alanon
Alateen
alcohol
Alcoholics Anonymous
altered states of consciousness (ASCs)
amphetamines
analgesics
anesthetics
Anima
Animus
Archetypes
axonal endings
barbituates
biofeedback
chakra
cocaine
cognitive dissonance
collective unconscious
cosmic egg
D.T.'s

dendrite receptors
depressants
drugs
endorphens
enkephalins
flashback
hallucinogens
heroin
hypnotism
LSD
latent dream
mandala
manifest dream
mantram
marijuana
meditation
meprobates
mescalin
morphine
motor neurons

neural chemical transmitters
neurons
novacaine
opiates
PCP
peak experiences
perceptual defense
Persona
prana
pranayama
predictive
psilocybin
sensory neurons
Shadow
stimulants
synapse
synchronicity
TM meditation
tranquilizers
yin-yang

FILL IN THE BLANKS WITH SIGNIFICANT TERMS AND CONCEPTS

1. When we alter our state of perception to be different than our daily (usual) perception we are experiencing an a_____ s_____ of c_____.

2. We have certain ways of resisting reality by blinding our eyes and deafening our ears. When we do this we call this p_____ d_____. Sometimes we resist conflicting information which is mutually exclusive (i.e. both realities cannot exist together), and this contradiction between what we want to believe and the facts is called c_____ d_____.

3. Elements which alter the body's functioning significantly are d_____.

4. The various classifications of drugs include d_____, h_____, and s_____. Each group affects the body differently.

5. Of all the drugs used for which we have statistics a_____ is the drug most abused. What this means is that the greatest number of deaths that are drug related are a_____ related.

6. Some of the various inducers of ASCs include m_____, h_____, and b_____, and d_____.

7. Carl Jung believed that dreams could be p_____, that we have a c_____ unconscious, and that events are not coincidental rather s_____.

8. Jung believed that within our collective unconscious are certain A_____ of human personality—ways of symbolically processing human experience.

RECOMMENDED BOOKS FOR FURTHER READING

Assagioli, Roberto. 1976. *Psychosynthesis*. New York: Penguin Books, Inc. Assagioli broke away from Freud's group because he (Assagioli) insisted that the integration of personality must include spiritual as well as bio- logical aspects. He developed some of the approaches now used in psychology: encounter, meditation, directed imagery, and music therapy.

Faraday, Ann. 1981. *Dream Power*. New York: Berkley

Publishing Corporation. This book became an instant best-seller (1963) which means that Faraday's approach to dreaming was easy to read and had much to say. A more recent book by her in the same genre is *The Dream Game*. New York: Harper & Row Publishers Inc., 1974.

Freud, Sigmund. 1962[a]. *The Interpretation of Dreams, 1900*, Vol. V. London: Hogarth Press. Freud was a masterful writer and his knowledge extended over many disciplines: history, the humanities, philosophy, religion, mythology, and anthropology. He interwove this knowledge with his patients' case histories and dreams which makes his *major opus* an extraordinary and fascinating work.

Jung, Carl G. 1963. *Memories, Dreams, Reflections*, rev ed. Aniela Jaffe, ed. New York: Pantheon Books, Inc. For a truly remarkable autobiography, there is none superior to Jung's, in which he discusses his interior life, including his visions and dreams.

Metzner, Ralph. 1971. *Maps of Consciousness*. New York: Macmillan Publishing Inc. Metzner has followed closely the trial blazed by Jung. A clinical psychologist, Metzner investigates the mythological significance of the *I Ching*, Tantric philosophy and art, the *Tarot*, alchemy, astrology, and actualism. He explores these areas in terms of their correspondence to Western psychology.

Perls, Frederick S. 1967[a]. *Gestal Therapy Verbatim*. John A. Stevens, ed. Lafayette, CA: Real People Press. This book is a must for understanding and fully appreciating Perls's noninterpretive approach to dreams. Actual dream sessions are reproduced in this book, along with commentary by Perls himself.

Tart, Charles C. 1969. *Altered States of Consciousness: A Book of Readings*. New York: John Wiley & Sons, Inc. Charles Tart is the social scientist who has tried to bring together the various fields of research into ASC research and scholarship. It is an excellent basic book for those who are interested in the characteristics of various ASC.

12

The Choice is Always Ours: Toward Higher Levels of Personality Integration

THE MEMORABLE ORIGINALS: PERSONS "EVER IN PROCESS"

INSIGHTS OF THE PERSONALITY THEORISTS
    The Continual Development of One's Intellectual or Cognitive
        Function: The Rational Use of Reason
    The Steady Unfolding and Enriching of One's Emotional Repertory:
        The Self and the Interpersonal Dimension
    The Striving to Direct One's Destiny: Self-Fulfillment and
        Self-Realization
    Transcending Self: The Spiritual Dimension

INTEGRATION TECHNIQUES

THE MEMORABLE ORIGINALS: PERSONS "EVER IN PROCESS"

The memorable persons in history always have been originals. Think of some of the names that excite us: Albert Einstein, Marie Curie, Pablo Picasso, Georgia O'Keefe, George Sand, Joan of Arc, Abelard and Héloise, Shakespeare, Emily Dickinson, Gandhi, Theresa of Avila, Michelangelo, Freud, Florence Nightingale, Socrates, Darwin, Abraham Lincoln, Bach, Beethoven, Golda Meir, Albert Schweitzer, the Bronte sisters—the list is long. Such individuals light up the history of humankind like stars in the sky. We are always struck by the originality of their thinking, the depth of their feelings and their unique way of being. As artists, they perceived the world in ways that led the rest of us to rediscover its archetypal images and forms. As philosophers, they formulated new ideas. As musicians, they made us aware of sound and of silence and brought together harmonies that stir the soul. As social scientists and reformers, they risked their lives and reputations for their visions of humankind and of how men and women can live together. As scientists, they were ruthless in their fight against superstition, dogma, and ignorance.

They were men and women of spirit and passion. They dedicated their lives to self-awareness and to the greater awareness of us all. In Carl Rogers's phrase, they were "persons in process"—humankind evolving—and by their example and works, we too evolved with them.

We do not expect you to become a Socrates, a Gandhi, or a Marie Curie. They are among the giants of civilization. Each of us, however, can evolve in our own existence and further our personality integration to higher levels of awareness and creativity. We too, can be "persons in process." The *raison d'être* of humanistic psychology is to enhance that process. The humanist asserts that we do not have to lock ourselves into patterns of adjustment that are uncreative for us or destructive to society. Never before in history have we had the freedom to become ourselves. But freedom *to be* and freedom *to become* require a commitment to personality integration that is not for the faint-hearted. It requires courage and strength, not the external kind of courage and strength found on the battlefield but an internal kind that enables us to look into ourselves and to take responsibility for our lives. To know ourselves (as the Greeks said three thousand years ago) is to understand humankind.

In this final chapter we shall examine the most creative, integrated, fully functioning, and self-actualizing persons in society. We shall try to understand the processes that enabled them to achieve their goals and to become unique personalities. Finally, we shall attempt to discover some ways in which we can become more integrated and more creative within ourselves and in relation to the larger community.

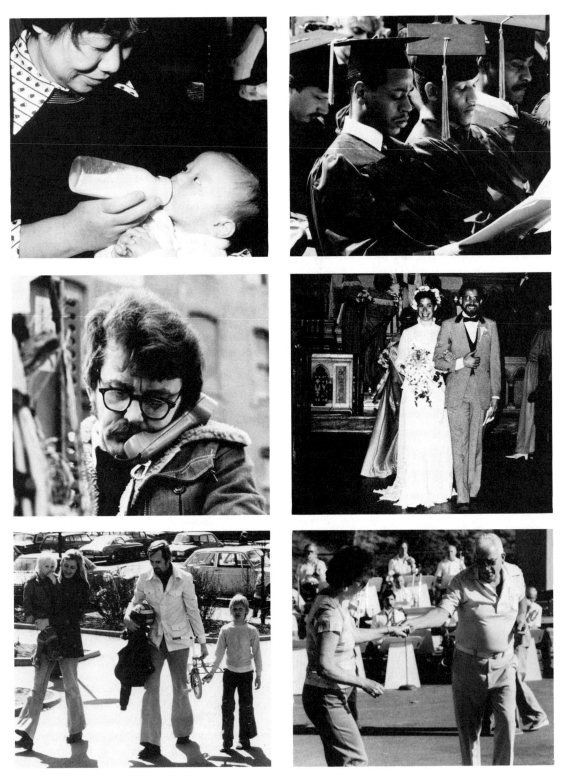

As persons ever in process we are constantly becoming: we are always being asked to let go of old ways of being and to welcome new ways of being.

It is good to hold up these memorable originals as models of personality integration, but in one respect these men and women are idealized concepts: There is something of the folk hero in each of them. We know the heights they attained, and we are awed by their courage to be what they could be. But folk heroes are one-dimensional personalities: It is the grand and transcendent qualities in them that are emphasized; we lose those other aspects of them that are forgotten in the course of time, the human frailties that are characteristic of us all. Beethoven and Michelangelo achieved heights of grandeur in music and art, but their tempers and depressions also were monumental. Albert Einstein has become something of the archetypal Wise Old Man, but in everyday life he was a shy and retiring individual who seemed somehow lost in the everyday world of human affairs. Albert Schweitzer seemed to many to be a living saint, but, as we mentioned earlier, visitors who traveled to Lambaréné, Africa, sometimes reported that he was one of the most uncompromising and authoritarian personalities they had ever come across. What we are saying is that even the great originals had their weaknesses and limitations. What lifted them beyond the average, however, what thrust them beyond their limitations was their *dynamic process*, and it is that process that we shall study.

An understanding of the process of personality integration must come not from legends of folk heroes but from the scientific observation of successful persons in their human totality. It must come by observing these persons in a variety of circumstances, noting not only what they have said about themselves and what they did when they were at the peak of their achievements but also what they did under stress and when they had setbacks and obstacles.

THE STUDY OF "PERSONS IN PROCESS."   A big step in understanding of the evolution of personality came when the American psychologist Carl Rogers began to study persons who were attempting to discover more viable and creative ways to live and work (Rogers 1951). Carl Rogers, as a psychotherapist, believed that we all have within us a "center of growth." He believed that if we can get in touch with this "center," we will discover what is truly right, energizing, rewarding, and consonant with our individual personality patternings. Rogers observed his own clients and listened to what they discovered as they moved forward in their own growth process. Later he observed and listened to persons in group therapy and in encounter groups as they reported their experiences with each other. His contributions helped us understand how people change in the course of therapy: how they experience themselves, and how they interact with others when they seem to be only "partly functioning," and then when they are "more fully functioning" persons.

Rogers's method was a kind of "before" and "after" photograph of human personality. He helped us to understand that personality is a matter of *process*. He emphasized that no one, not even the person in therapy, can predict the limits of human potential.

THE STUDY OF THE HIGHLY INTEGRATED AND CREATIVE PERSONALITY.   In the fifties American psychology took another step forward when it began to study human functioning at its "highest" level. The most famous of these studies is that by

Abraham Maslow (Maslow 1954). Maslow, another American psychologist who seems to us to have been one of the true originals, studied what he called highly "self-actualizing" persons: those who apparently can live according to their beliefs throughout most of their lives and can achieve their life goals and ambitions despite the exigencies of fate and fortune. Maslow considered his subjects to be among the healthiest types of personality in our society. He chose them from among friends and acquaintances as well as public personalities. Maslow's findings helped to affirm Rogers's belief that truly integrated and creative persons do not "just happen" but are the result of their own endeavors to become all that they can be. Their highly self-actualizing process came as a result of self-study, insight, uncompromising discipline, and self-development.

Maslow's research was not the only such study, nor was it the first of its kind. Others have studied the human personality at its highest level and have reported their findings on highly successful executives, the intellectually gifted, the highly creative artist or physicist, and the like. These studies have enabled us to understand how human personality can transcend limitations and obstacles. The research findings in these areas of personality development are many, but we shall try to summarize the observations and conclusions from these diverse sources and methodologies (see box 12.1).

Box 12.1	**SELF–ACTUALIZING PERSONS/INTEGRATED PERSONS**	
	PERSONALITY THEORISTS/ INVESTIGATORS	**SUBJECTS REFERRED TO AS:**
	Alfred Adler	Highly developed social feeling
	T. W. Adorno	Low-authoritarian persons
	Gordon Allport	Mature persons
	Frank Barron	Creative persons
	Viktor Frankl	Transcendental persons
	Sigmund Freud	Functioning persons
	Erich Fromm	Productive persons
	J. P. Guilford	Creative artists and engineers
	Karen Horney	Self-realized persons
	Carl Jung	Individuated persons
	Laurence Kubie	Creative persons
	Donald MacKinnon	Creative persons
	Abraham Maslow	Self-actualizing persons
	David McClelland	Successful executives
	Sidney Pressey	Geniuses
	Anne Roe	Artists
	Carl Rogers	Fully functioning persons
	Milton Rokeach	Open-minded persons
	Lewis Terman	Gifted persons
	C. W. Taylor	Creative scientists and artists

INSIGHTS OF THE PERSONALITY THEORISTS

Throughout all these studies four areas of competence appear in the subjects, four processes basic to all of us but which seem to be particularly well developed and articulated in the highly integrated person. These processes are components of that larger process, described in chapter 1, that we identify with human existence itself. The four processes are *psychological* (as distinct from physiological) and include:

1. The continual development of one's *intellectual* or *cognitive* function
2. The steady unfolding and enriching of one's *emotional* repertory
3. The continuing motivation to direct one's own destiny
4. The transcending quest to relate oneself to one's world

In substance, these four areas comprise the processes of the highly integrated, highly self-actualizing, transcending personality: *intellectual curiosity, emotional openness, energetic motivation* and *spiritual compassion* for others.

The Continual Development of One's Intellectual or Cognitive Function: The Rational Use of Reason

The first process of personality integration is the continuing and perhaps innate tendency of human beings to perceive their own world, to understand the physical properties of everything they see and hear, and to make some kind of sense out of their experiences. This human urge to make sense out of experience expresses itself in six-week-old infants as they learn to follow with interest the objects and the persons in their visual field. When the child grows to a point of self-locomotion, this urge takes the form of exploring its environment, even to biting and tasting the things it encounters. Feeling, tasting, and touching with fingers and mouth are the baby's primitive methods for learning about things. The child is discovering if things are hard, soft, or good to eat, or if something can be dropped, thrown, kicked, or sat on, or whether something is light or heavy or hot or cold. All of these events are the beginnings of its knowledge of the world (Piaget 1973, 1976).

It is because of their total absorption in wanting to know and classify the phenomena of their world that four-year-olds ask their "why," "where," and "how" questions: Why is the fire hot? Why does Daddy go to the office? Why do I have to go to sleep? Where does the sun go at night? How did I get to be born? Growing children are bombarded with events that they want to understand, and they spend many years in school learning about their world.

This basic process has been identified by many names. It has been called the "intellectual function" and the "thinking process." It has been seen as a "curiosity trait," a "sensoriperceptual modal function," "problem solving," "decision making," "creativity," and the "ability to analyze and synthesize." Individual success in developing this process is what is supposedly measured in tests of intellectual functioning (IQ tests).

This same *need to know* is manifested in the scientist's urge to investigate the universe, in the newspaper reporter's determination "to uncover the facts," in the scholar's research into ancient civilizations, and in the philosopher's continuing search into the nature of goodness, truth, and beauty. It is the same underlying process behind your own search for answers to such questions as, "Who am I?" "What is life?" and "What shall I do with my life?" It is also the impulse behind the student's quest for knowledge, and it is society's attempts to help us answer these questions for ourselves that are, at least ideally, the sum and substance of education (Kohlberg 1964).

HIGHLY INTEGRATED PERSONS ARE WILLING TO STRIVE ALL THEIR LIVES TO-WARD MORE PROFOUND INSIGHTS AND WIDER PERSPECTIVES. Many young persons, and even those in their twenties and thirties, have a spontaneous interest in life around them, but as we grow older and age, most of us seem to settle down into routine living. Our sense of interest in those issues that do not touch our immediate everyday world seems to fade. Reading books becomes a thing of the past and is replaced by the hypnotism of television, for example, or the quick scanning of newspaper headlines. In contrast, said Maslow, highly integrated persons never seem to lose their drive for learning about new things or their desire to delve more deeply into those things already familiar to them.

Not only do integrated persons retain their intellectual curiosity, they remain open to many kinds of new and novel situations. Because of this open attitude, and because they are constantly scanning their own thoughts and past experiences, they discover how events relate to each other. Consequently, we think of them as "highly creative" (MacKinnon 1965). Nor do they accept the "as is-ness" of things; that is to say, they do not accept simple and oversimplified answers for why things are as they are. They are persons who are willing to topple the accepted assumptions about the world—the "social" explanations people have given for such and such—and to discover more comprehensive explanations (Barron 1963). In short, their thinking is radical.

It is not easy to make a radical breakthrough in thought. It requires the willingness to let go of one's deeply felt values and to go against the current of one's early environment and conditioning. And that was precisely René Descartes's grand achievement: his declaration that he must be free to think for himself, even if that meant rejecting the authority of his teachers, his parents, his friends, even his church (Descartes 1960). He tells us that to find that freedom, he had to leave Paris and his native France and to live as a foreigner in other countries. It is interesting to note that these foreign countries were Protestant Germany and Protestant Sweden, where freedom of thinking was more possible than in Catholic France still under the hammer of the Inquisition. Descartes realized that it is very difficult to keep from sliding into an easy acceptance of traditional thought, attitudes, and beliefs. Every scientific and artistic breakthrough and every new social reform has been achieved by men and women who were willing to question long-held assumptions and break with unquestioned traditions: Charles Darwin, Sigmund Freud, Pablo Picasso, Margaret Sanger, Martin Luther King, to name a few. It is easy to get stuck in a rigid perceptual set, even for promising scholars, scientists, and artists. Lawrence S. Kubie, who studied the creative process for many years, wrote:

> There are scientists and engineers who produce brilliantly as students, and even through their graduate years of study, but then collapse. There are gifted investigators who turn out one or two creative achievements early in their careers, but thereafter are never productive again.

Kubie related this "freezing" of one's intellectual capacities to an "inflexibility of spirit and psychology." Creativity demands the willingness to hold open one's perception of reality, the continual willingness to look at a thing in many ways and from more than one point of view, the constant contemplation of a thing or event to gain new perspectives. Kubie concluded that flexibility is synonymous with health since it allows us the freedom to learn through experience and the freedom to make changes within and without. The noncreative person and the neurotic person, said Kubie, has frozen his or her behavior into "unaltering, repetitive and insatiable patterns." He went on to say:

> We see examples of such frozen behavior in all creative fields. In painting, we see it in men of worldwide reputations, men who after passing through some inner convulsion of the spirit start on a new "period," dominated perhaps by a new color or by a new subject matter, or a new way of applying the paint, or a new way of stressing outlines, or a new way of distorting proportions, each such innovation becoming as rigid as the work of the earlier periods. . . . [Kubie 1967]

Remaining flexible in one's thinking and behavior requires a certain humility of spirit; that is, integrated persons understand that there are no permanent answers, that no matter how diligently they may have pursued an idea, a question, or a task, they have only scratched the surface of what there is to know. Abraham Maslow discovered this sense of humility among his "self-actualizing" subjects. Despite their profound learning, they knew that their knowledge was only a little of what there was to be known. They knew that their achievements were only a small step in the process of human understanding of the world. They saw themselves as lifelong students and still were (even those in their sixties and seventies) concerned with the same basic issues and eternal questions that interested them as students. Maslow regarded them as philosophers, still willing and eager to learn from anyone, if they sensed that person had something to teach them. They also were more involved in the process of intellectual learning and insight than in the discoveries and achievements of that process. It is the search that delights the highly integrated person—the chase, the quest, the *process* (Maslow 1954).

HIGHLY INTEGRATED PERSONS ARE MORE WILLING TO PERCEIVE THE WORLD ACCURATELY: WITHOUT EITHER-OR THINKING, WITHOUT STEREOTYPIC PREJUDICE. Over and over we have emphasized that we do not see the world as it really is. What we experience as "reality" or "truth" is a combination of many factors: our sensory awareness (or blindness), sensitivity (or insensitivity) to others, prejudices (prejudgments), past experiences, fears and angers, and hopes and fantasies. All of these conspire to prevent us from perceiving accurately. Our understanding of events, things, and persons are seen "as through a glass darkly," a mirror that is fogged by our emotions and our defensive attitudes. The more "neurotic" we are, the less able we are to assess a situation clearly, while the "psychotic" lives in a world clearly removed from reality.

When we say that our world view is distorted by our prejudicial attitudes, we are speaking not just of prejudice toward persons different from us in race, creed, or color. These are the obvious prejudices. Rather, we are speaking of all those small, subtle attitudes to which we have been conditioned or that we have acquired without realizing it. Poor children overestimate the size of common coins, and hungry persons will see candy, cake, and ice cream in clouds and other amorphous shapes. Juries will tend to believe an attractive, well-dressed witness over a grubby witness. None of us, then, perceives the world with absolute accuracy.

The studies of highly creative persons, however, indicate that they are more able to see the world "as it really is" than the rest of us are. Maslow's healthy subjects could, in fact, describe the personalities of other persons with remarkable insight. Furthermore, they could see behind the masks and facades of personalities and were especially good at detecting the spurious and the phony.

What enables highly integrated persons to be as perceptive as they are? First, they are far less judgmental about what they observe in others and in the world. Since they do not have to judge what they observe, they are more detached and "scientific" in their conclusions. When we make extreme value judgments that something is good *or* bad, right *or* wrong, ugly *or* beautiful, based on our observations, we already are so emotionally involved that we cannot be good observers and reporters. Second, highly integrated persons are not as blinded by external appearances or stereotypic thinking as the rest of us are. They can accept the opinions of the fat person as being potentially as valid as those of the well-proportioned individual.

Third, highly integrated persons are more able to disattach themselves from past preconceptions and habits and conditionings so as to assess the current situation. Many of us, as we go about our daily work, are faced with the same situations over and over. The fact that we have dealt with these situations *in the past* tends to cause us to deal with the same situations in the future in the same way. We may keep treating our twelve-year-old son (now on the brink of adolescence) just as we treated him when he was, say, four years old, which infuriates him. What we need to do is to realize the changes in the growth and competence of our children from year to year, which is very difficult when we see them every day. But integrated persons are able to do just that. How we learn to do that, said Maslow, is by our willingness to break with past habits of stereotypic thinking, no matter how well those habits have served us in the past. This process of "emptying the mind," as it is called by Zen masters, is helpful in overcoming obstacles (Suzuki 1956).

Finally, being highly integrated is a matter of dissolving (insofar as we are able) our ego defenses so that we can hear what others are saying to us and can heed the facts at our disposal. Again, it is humility that reminds us that we do not know everything there is to know, no matter how learned or respected we have become in our professional or social milieu. We recognize that no matter what our standing, experience, or reputation is, others may have "a piece of the truth." This lack of ego is what distinguishes the wise person from the egotist about whom others say: "It's no use trying to tell him anything. He thinks he knows it all."

HIGHLY INTEGRATED PERSONS ARE MORE WILLING TO PERCEIVE THEMSELVES ACCURATELY. Hand in hand with the ability to perceive others more accurately is the ability to perceive oneself with a high degree of accuracy—that is, more objectively. Maslow's subjects did not deny their own shortcomings, even as they sought to overcome their limitations. Although they did not dwell on their imperfections, they were not impressed by their achievements. MacKinnon and his associates, studying the highly creative person, reported that their subjects were extremely candid about themselves and exhibited an extraordinary lack of defensiveness. They could speak with equal frankness about their abilities and their problems. Not only were they willing to reveal thoughts and feelings of the sort that others might prefer to keep to themselves, but they also showed no need for false modesty when discussing their strengths and abilities.

Most of us seem to wear a mask, a public face, or a public personality quite different from what we think ourselves to be. This public image is what we would like to be, it is our best self-concept. As we discussed in chapter 11, Carl Jung called this mask our *Persona*, which he contrasted with our *Shadow*. The latter is what we dislike about ourselves and keep hidden from others. But, said Jung, when we split ourselves off from this other side of ourselves, we deny ourselves one-half of our personal energy and creativity. It is not easy to stay in touch with the Shadow aspect, said Jung, but social scientists who have investigated the extremely creative individual are convinced that these persons are far more in touch with that side of themselves than the average person is. Creative writers, scientists, and artists, are more willing to look at the darker aspects of self and to delve into their creative unconscious. They do not deny their fantasies as much; they are more apt to remember their dreams; and they see themselves more completely for what they are. They are persons willing to see in themselves what others are afraid to see or are embarrassed by or are ashamed to admit. Because highly integrated people are willing to do that, they have less "split" in their personalities and thus are more "integrated" (Jung et al. 1964). It is just because highly integrated persons are willing to see themselves accurately that they are better able to see the world and others more accurately. Because they know themselves and their own human frailties, they do not project their negative feelings and negative thoughts onto others. Their insights into themselves then provide them with more complete insights into others. They have self-knowledge, and thus they have knowledge of others.

The Steady Unfolding and Enriching of One's Emotional Repertory: The Self and the Interpersonal Dimension

Perhaps nothing is as basic to human beings as their emotional response patterns. Even before babies can distinguish the shapes and sounds of their environment, they can express fear, frustration, or anger. Little by little, they are able to express delight, joy, and pleasure. But in babies, these are very primitive emotions and do

not have the same degree of subtlety as they have in adult human beings. Adults are capable of richer and more complex emotional experiences. Children are capable of self-love and love of a parent who treats them kindly, but they are largely incapable of empathy for another individual. They also are incapable of altruistic love until they reach a certain age. Adults, on the other hand, can be so intensely loving of parents, spouse, and children that their own happiness lies in taking care of their loved ones. Children can enjoy a pretty flower or a sunset for a few moments; it is the adult who is capable of awe, ecstasy, and thanksgiving.

Our emotional repertory increases with age until we can respond to the complexities of the composer's harmonies, a Gothic cathedral, poetry and song, and the immensity of the physical universe. Our ability to experience the numerous qualities of love is a manifestation of our growth as individuals. We may be more able to express our emotions spontaneously as children, but it is not until we reach adulthood that we can experience the deepest and richest emotions: human compassion and universal loving-kindness. But not all of us reach that level, perhaps only one out of every ten of us (Maslow 1954; Kohlberg 1964).

Furthermore, as we age some of us seem to close off to emotional experiences. Perhaps we have experienced too many disappointments, shocks, or sorrows. Or maybe we have become jaded with sophistication and overstimulation. Perhaps we have developed such a low threshold for pain that we block out emotions of all kinds to avoid being hurt or being disappointed yet again. Whatever the reason, it is true that some of us prefer to live within a narrow range of emotional existence. These people seem to say: "Life may be drab, but it is at least safer this way. I may not experience as many of the depths and heights that life can offer, but at least I have less bother and chaos, and fewer unwelcome surprises."

HIGHLY INTEGRATED PERSONS ALLOW THEMSELVES TO STAY OPEN TO EMOTIONAL EXPERIENCES. Being willing to allow oneself to experience one's own feelings entails also the willingness to experience many complex—even conflicting—emotions. We are taught as children, for example, that we should love our parents, and as parents that we should love our children—no matter what. Yet it seems obvious that when children are spanked or otherwise disciplined by their parents, they can momentarily have feelings of anger or resentment, even hatred. Likewise, when parents face for the hundredth time yet another instance of a child's tricks and manipulations, it is a relief for them to realize it is occasionally appropriate for them not to love their child, especially since they are in fact now furious with him or her.

After counseling, Rogers's subjects discovered that it is natural to feel love, anger, frustration, or confusion, all at the same time, toward another human being. With this discovery they felt much less confused since they were not repressing or denying their emotions. Rogers also discovered that his clients became more "fluid and changeable," less in need of arriving at fixed conclusions or retreating into static emotional states. This loosening and broadening of their emotional personality structure may be compared with findings in studies of the authoritarian personality in which a high degree of rigidity in thinking and behavior is exhibited and the person tends to experience a narrow spectrum of emotions.

For such persons the world remains dichotomized into good or bad, right or wrong, evil or virtue, or masculine or feminine (Adorno 1973; Rokeach 1973, 1979). This type of thinking is called *either-or thinking* and is the cause of much emotional heartache and cognitive "traps" or snarls that prevents clear thinking.

A person may say to himself or herself, "Either I am right and he is wrong or he is right and I am wrong." Such either-or thinking leads to feelings of failure, feelings of superiority, hard feelings, inaccurate perceptions, and the like. Rogers's subjects, in comparison, show a "middle ground" in their personalities and less of a need to come to fixed conclusions of right or wrong or good or bad.

Allowing ourselves to express emotions does not mean giving way to them, remarked Gordon Allport. When neurotics get depressed or have feelings of rejection or moments of discouragement, they give in to their feelings, which is to say they do not do anything to resist those feelings of discouragement or rejection or depression. They may even wallow in them. In contrast, said Allport, mature persons can tolerate moments of discouragement, loneliness, or rejection because mature people recognize them as transient states. Nor do they bewail these transient states because they realize that those states may become the yeast for the development of more universal empathy, love, and compassion (Allport 1955, 1975, 1981). Highly integrated persons are willing to accept and deal with all the experiences life presents to them. They are willing to process (work through) those moments of fear, grief, disappointment, shock, and sorrow because they know that life is a constant processing of the entire emotional spectrum. "When you pick up a stick," says a Zen proverb, "you pick up both ends of it." Even when it seems that the painful moments come more frequently than the moments of extreme contentment, highly integrated persons seem able to accept that fact expressed so well in the title of one of Robert Frost's poems: "Happiness Makes Up in Height for What It Lacks in Length."

HIGHLY INTEGRATED PERSONS PURSUE THEIR INNER LIVES WITH DILIGENCE. In the preface to his autobiography, *Memories, Dreams, and Reflections* (1963), Carl Jung warned the reader that the book would be a revelation of his *inner* life (his memories, dreams, and reflections) because, he explained, it was only his internal life that had meaning for him. Although he had known many great statesmen, writers, scientists, and artists and had treated them for their crisis transitions, these encounters were not the essential aspect of his life, nor did he consider the honors that had come to him important. What was important was his *interior life*, and it was precisely his inner life that he chose to reveal.

This statement reflects precisely the attitude of the highly integrated person, for it is *his* or *her* inner life that is valued: one's thoughts, meditations, ideas, projects, inspirations, and aspirations. Highly integrated persons observe the external world to learn more about it but always to further the growth and expansion of their internal understanding and awareness. They are in touch with their "center of growth" and are not as likely to get caught up in the distractions of the sensate life. They are inner oriented.

Studies of male creative artists, engineers, and scientists revealed that they were able to allow themselves a range of interests and emotions still thought, in the American culture at the time of the studies, to be "feminine." They could allow themselves to express the feminine or emotional side of their nature more readily than less creative individuals. Studies of creative women, on the other hand, revealed them to have more "masculine" interests and to be unafraid of expressing themselves in serious ways (Barron 1968; MacKinnon 1978).

Being willing to attend to one's inner life means being willing to get in touch with one's dreams and to learn to understand them. It also means the willingness to spend some time each day in meditation or reflection and the desire to become more self-analytic and self-knowledgeable.

HIGHLY INTEGRATED PERSONS ROOT THEMSELVES IN THE HERE-AND-NOW. The ability to enjoy the moment (to let go of the past and avoid preoccupation with the future) is called being in the here-and-now. Being in the here-and-now includes enjoyment of the senses. Frederick Perls, aware that many persons in our society had closed off much of their sensory awareness, advised his clients to pay attention to what was going on in their bodily responses *at the moment*—not to *think* it but to *experience* it. Perls's intuition of the sensory deficit in the "adjusted" person of our time is reflected also in Maslow's research findings with his self-actualizing subjects. Maslow called his self-actualizing subjects "good animals"—that is, they allowed themselves full enjoyment of their physical senses: They ate well, slept well, played well, were able to derive strong satisfaction from loving, sexual contact, and generally were able to "count their blessings."

Being in the here-and-now, being "good physical animals," and being "in touch with our bodies" are aids to creative inspiration. It is at this level that we receive the data and information we need to operate physically, emotionally, and intellectually. We receive continual bombardment of unconscious, preconscious, and conscious signals from our bones, muscles, joints, tendons, skin, apertures, and all the internal organs of our body pertaining to ingestion, digestion, egestion, respiration, and metabolism. The more we are in touch with these signals, the better we operate at the many levels of human functioning. Yet we know that some people have eliminated many of these data from their ongoing experience of themselves. They operate at a reduced level of sensory awareness; they have "deadened" themselves, so to speak, to their bodily feelings.

Most of us are aware that artists, poets, and sculptors allow themselves to experience their living, breathing, and sensing selves to an extraordinary degree. Musicians also seem to get in touch with their internal rhythms and harmonies, and athletes have a sense of their bodily coordinates to a remarkable degree. In fact, studies of creative persons in all areas, including physicists and mathematicians, reveal that they remain in touch with their bodily selves. This bodily self may even be the inspiration for people's technological achievements, said Herbert Gutman, who studied the creative process itself (Gutman 1967).

Consider, said Gutman, the basic tools of our society. How was it that humankind invented the lever, the hammer, or the chisel? It may be, he answered, that these tools are simply analogues of bodily dexterity. In early times, "scientists" observed their bodily capabilities and extended them. The hammer is an extended, heavier, and harder arm and fist. Nails and teeth probably were the forerunners of saws, chisels, screwdrivers, and awls. In the last analysis, tools are extensions of ourselves and perform essentially those actions that our bodies perform: pushing, pulling, sliding, rotating. Even the action of springs is exemplified by us when we jump. Stethoscopes and radar are really the extension of our ears; microscopes and telescopes extend our near and far vision. The computer resembles the "on-off" firing of neurons in our nervous system.

What may be applied to tools also can be applied to machines. Machines are simply hands and legs duplicated several times over. We have only two hands but a machine can have many. We have two legs; a machine can have two wheels (as in a bicycle) constantly in revolution, three wheels (as in a wheel barrow), four wheels (as in a car), many more (as in a truck), or simply one continuous wheel (as in a tractor). The creative scientist and inventor have improved on their bodies because they are in touch with their bodies.

Our bodies are our physical vehicles for autonomy, but they also are our inspiration for psychological and intellectual invention and progress. To be in touch with our physical selves is one of the ways to be in touch with our creative wellsprings.

The Striving to Direct One's Destiny: Self-Fulfillment and Self-Realization

We can never be completely in control of our environment or our destiny. We are born into a society not of our choosing, and we shall assuredly die when the Fates will it. There are powers and events over which we have little or no influence: the death of loved ones, natural catastrophes, accidents, and all the chance events of the natural world. No matter how hard we work to achieve position, esteem, security, family ties, prestige, and honor, no matter how carefully we work to make a success of our careers and interpersonal environment, there always is the possibility that our dreams and plans may go awry. What we thought we built as strongly as a castle may be toppled like a house of cards. What we thought was secure and firm as a rock may turn out to have been built on sand. No matter how we pursue our dreams of glory and romance, they may turn out to be always a mirage that retreats farther and farther into the distance. There is, then, a reality in the Greek allusion to the capriciousness of fortune.

The Fates notwithstanding, there has been a remarkable agreement among the studies of highly creative or highly integrated persons that they are determined, insofar as they are able, to direct their own destinies and to achieve their designated ends. Whether they are called "mature," "fully functioning," "self-actualizing," "individuated," "healthy," or whatever, on this one point all the researchers and theorists agree: these persons seek to control their lives, pursue their dreams, and master their environments. The integrated person, like the crippled poet, John Philip Henley, is determined to be "the master of his Fate and the captain of his Soul," no matter what Fate has ordained is his lot in life.

Allport noted that mature persons do not give up in the face of setbacks. They devise other ways to pursue their goals. You will remember from chapter 1 that Allport's mature persons acknowledged goals propriate to themselves and pursued these goals with diligence. But it does not matter to the mature person, said Allport, if he has succeeded in accomplishing *all* his or her goals. It is the quest that matters. We must have a place to direct our energies, he explained, for it is in having a goal to pursue that we remain vital, healthy, and alive. Goals and our pursuit of them, Allport continued, keep us "stretching, seeking, always going on." And if we do not attain all our goals? "Oh," replied Allport, "the loveliest of symphonies are often those that are unfinished."

Maslow called his self-actualizing subjects self-starters. They do not wait for "Santa Claus" to reward them; they are not "waiting for Godot" to tell them what to do. They decide what they want to do and chart their life course toward those goals. In short, they take responsibility for their own lives.

Studies of highly self-actualizing persons reveal that they were not docile schoolchildren or college students. Indeed, the indications are that they were sometimes so independent that they may have seemed rebellious or somewhat aggressive in their behavior. As adults, they may still make us slightly uncomfortable because they are not satisfied with the status quo. They may rock the boat a little and bring to our attention the facts of life that we really do not wish to see. They sometimes may seem to be rude or abrupt in their interpersonal relationships, not because they want to be impolite or inconsiderate, but because they are more absorbed in the task to be done than in being liked. Furthermore, their originality and unconventional apperceptions of the world may make them seem eccentric and restless, driven by inner forces, and so less attentive to social amenities. Although they may exude a magnetic charisma or be well liked, they are not overly concerned with public opinion, and they do not court popularity. Consequently, they may appear to be overly domineering and brusque.

HIGHLY INTEGRATED PERSONS ARE MORE WILLING TO BE THEMSELVES. Carl Rogers called this the willingness "to be that self which one truly is." As Rogers's subjects progressed through therapy, they began to lose their fear of showing themselves as they felt themselves to be. They allowed the "real me" to show outside, even if that "real me" should prove to be less acceptable to others than their Persona. Interestingly enough, the very reverse was true: Rogers's subjects discovered that their real personalities were as acceptable, if not more acceptable, to others. Why is the real self generally more acceptable to others? Because it is just that—real. It is the authentic side of a person, and no matter how attractive or charming the *Persona* may be, nothing wins our respect and admiration as much as authenticity and openness.

To become oneself, Rogers explained, requires giving up earlier notions of what others want us to be. Furthermore, it requires giving up one's own unrealistic or overidealized image of oneself—what psychologists call the self-concept. Rogers's subjects began to feel free of their own list of "shoulds" and "oughts": what they *should* do and *should* be like.

HIGHLY INTEGRATED PERSONS ARE MORE WILLING TO MAKE DECISIONS AND TO TAKE RESPONSIBILITY FOR THEIR LIVES. Another great universal theme of many of the personality theorists is the need, the willingness, and the ability *to work*.

When asked, finally, what was an "un-neurotic" person, Freud answered, someone who loves and who works. And Erich Fromm agreed, "To have a *work* to do!" Not just working for working—just to keep busy—but a work one can believe in, to be proud of, to *give* oneself to, so that in some way we are contributing to the community of humankind. Erich Fromm called this expressing the *productive* orientation, and he distinguishes it from other (neurotic) orientations: the submissive orientation and the power-dominated orientation. We may either create or destroy. We have no other alternative. It is in creation that we gain the fullest utilization of our human potential. In creating, Fromm wrote, we form our identity.

Working for something means also taking responsibility for something. Personality theorists agree overwhelmingly that being willing to assume responsibility for one's life, one's actions, one's work is a sign of the highly integrated person. The neurotic seeks to blame others for his or her inadequacies and mistakes. The highly integrated person does not.

One of the principal obstacles in the way of many persons' progress is the fixation on past misfortunes. This particular difficulty frequently comes up in therapy. In seeking to blame some event or person in their childhood (one parent or both, one's teachers, or "society") for the mess in their lives, such persons fail to see that the "blaming game" is a dead end, a vicious circle that leads nowhere except to more of the same. More important, it prevents persons from taking responsibility for their present actions and direction—until they see that they are thinking in a (vicious) circle.

As Carl Rogers's subjects gradually moved away from the endless demands of others and of themselves, they moved toward following their own desires. In doing so, they became more like Maslow's subjects again, for Maslow's subjects were self-structured and self-determining. In fact, Maslow's subjects exhibited decidedly unconventional thinking and action in private life, although they could assume the cloak of convention when it suited them. They were not wild-eyed bohemians and rebels. On the contrary, they realized their unconventionality might be confusing to others and preferred to dress in conventional garb, speak in a conventional manner, and work in a conventional way. Thus they could go about the routine, day-to-day tasks of working with others in slow, quiet, undramatic ways without calling attention to themselves and as a result achieve real progress.

When Rogers's clients moved away from pleasing others and toward pleasing themselves, they did not in any way turn into hedonists or thrill seekers. On the contrary, they were more willing to be self-governing and to take responsibility for their own lives and their own mistakes.

Great men and women, as Maslow pointed out, seem to be no less vulnerable to bad breaks and injustices than are the rest of us. What matters is how they transcend such difficulties; it is this quality that distinguishes them. Maslow's subjects knew how to remain stable in the face of life's contingencies. They, too, experienced anxiety, guilt, shame, sorrow, and grief, but they did not allow themselves to get trapped in self-pity and self-blame or in blaming others. They could be foolish, even stupid at times, but their willingness to admit their foolishness and their stupidity (and to learn from the experience) was one of the marks of their creativity and wisdom. They did not suffer any longer than necessary from their mistakes and follies, nor did they indulge themselves in endless remorse, shame, or guilt. They were willing to see their shortcomings realistically, but they attempted to learn from their mistakes and stupidities and to go on from there.

Transcending Self: The Spiritual Dimension

At the end of chapter 1 we discussed the possible trap of the growth model. You will recall that the trap in the adjustment model was conforming to other people's standards. The possible trap in the growth model, we said, was unbridled hedonism—self-interest to the extent of exploiting, manipulating, or even hurting others. Actually, we added, the trap is possible only if self-growth is misunderstood as "me *first, last,* and *always* and if *liberty* is misinterpreted to mean *license*. The highly integrated person does not fall into this trap.

HIGHLY INTEGRATED PERSONS ARE SELF-GOVERNING.   Rogers was well aware that self-interest and trusting one's own perceptions can become a handy excuse for unbridled egotism. He therefore raised an essential point when he asked: Does such self-direction lead to cruelty or exploitation of others? Rogers's reply: When the person becomes more self-functioning, he also becomes more socialized; at that point he does not need to have someone else control him or inhibit his aggressive impulses—*he is in control* of his impulses, and therefore of himself. Moreover, he does not become less sensitive to others in his environment, he becomes *more* sensitive, *more* accepting of others in the world—and of himself as well.

HIGHLY INTEGRATED PERSONS HAVE A COMMITMENT TO THE GROWTH OF OTHERS.   Maslow's research findings are similar. His subjects had a deep and abiding feeling of identification with others, a general feeling of loving-kindness, a genuine desire to help the human race. (In other walks of life, in other times, Maslow said, they may have been called people of God.) He found them to be highly ethical, and they often had a sense of mission—what might be described as a call or a vocation to serve others.

.This kind of steady love of mankind (even when we recognize that individual persons may disappoint us) the Romans called *caritas*, which may be loosely translated as "charity." *Caritas* is said to be the dominant quality of personality in the great saints and reformers of the world. John the Evangelist's last teaching, it is said, was, "Love one another!" Jesus of Nazareth's teaching to "Love your neighbor as yourself" is still remembered. It may well be that *caritas*—"charity," what we today call love and compassion—is a powerful force in transcending the personal difficulties and suffering of our individual lives and of attaining peace and certainty. It does seem at any rate to be the mark of certain *originals*—namely, those persons who are remembered for their "love of humankind." Today we might describe these people as loving persons.

Relating to one's world and becoming involved with it can be expressed in many vocations. It may be as a prophet or a priest, or it may be a diplomat. It may be as a reformer whose life is dedicated to sounding out the facts of life that people need to hear and few want to hear. It may be that tired diplomat who wearily boards yet another jetliner to fly to yet another far-off place in the world to stave off yet another territorial dispute threatening to become yet another world war. Or it may be a judge in a court attempting to do his or her best to mete out not only justice but mercy within the confines of culture-bound and obsolete laws.

A GROWING CONSCIOUSNESS OF HUMAN ECOLOGY.   Our twentieth century is a remarkable time, even as it has been a time of turbulence, stress, and change. To borrow from Charles Dickens: We live in the best of times and the worst of times. This we know, assuredly, from the demands that are being placed upon each of us, seemingly with ever-increasing frequency. But whatever else it is, life in the late twentieth century is an adventure, and a great part of this adventure is the great change taking place in the consciousness of people. We are beginning to understand ourselves as perhaps no other generations have ever done. Though we may struggle at times and sometimes stumble with our new awareness, there seems to be a growing understanding that we must begin to live together and work together—if we are to survive into the twenty-first century.

We also are accepting the knowledge (and the responsibility) that we ourselves are the creators and the destroyers of our own persons and, to an even greater extent, of our species and our total planetary environment. We are beginning to rid ourselves of the fallacies and dangers of looking to higher authorities for our salvation, and we also are beginning to give up the belief that "outer" authorities can tell us what to do and how to live our lives. We are beginning to get in touch with what it means to be free, to become aware of our choices, and to think of making changes in our society and ourselves that we want to make. Most important of all, we are beginning to acknowledge and understand that change in the world, our shared world, begins with change in ourselves; that, for example, violence in oneself breeds violence in one's children and, in turn, violence in the world at large. We are beginning to understand that all life on earth is related. We are living in a world of millions of persons on this planet—and we are beginning to develop a consciousness of human ecology. In the extended world of plants, trees, air, and water that kind of consciousness is called *ecological* thinking. It is a commitment to transcend to a greater level of consciousness—one sometimes referred to as the consciousness of the Transpersonal Self (Assagioli 1976).

ESTABLISHING SPIRITUAL MEANING FOR OURSELVES.   In 1942 a thirty-seven-year-old neurologist from Vienna was taken from his home and with fifteen hundred other prisoners was taken to one of the infamous Nazi concentration camps, the death camp known as Auschwitz. His name was Viktor Frankl, and he recorded his experiences for us in a small autobiography, *Man's Search for Meaning* (Frankl 1962). Every member of his family was destroyed in the Holocaust. He was stripped of all his possessions, and when he sought to save just one, a manuscript that would have been his first book, the reaction of a fellow prisoner made Frankl realize that he had arrived at the depths of all possible existence and that his former life was unalterably eradicated; that, in fact, his continued existence had no meaning to anyone but himself. For some time Frankl was not sure that his life had meaning even for himself, such was the suffering, filth, and horror that he saw all about him.

What saved him, wrote Frankl, what gave him the will to survive was the discovery of a piece of paper in the clothing of a dead Jew, which contained the one prayer fundamental to Judaism, the *Shema*: " . . . love your God with all your heart, with all your soul, and with all your means." It is difficult to put into words the multitude of meanings that are contained in this small prayer with all its harmonics, its undertones and overtones. It is not just a prayer, but a call to life. It contains the message that no matter what circumstances we find ourselves in, no matter what trials and tribulations we encounter, no matter how bitter the cup we drink from, life is sacred. Let us then go through these experiences courageously—and *not* lose heart, *not* lose faith, *not* give up. Life is sacred because it is not just for ourselves that we live but for our children and our children's children and for the children of all who follow after us.

Frankl returned from Auschwitz, convinced that there is something more to the process of living than pursuing personal happiness, something that inspires the human psyche in even the darkest moments and gives it the will and purpose to go on. He developed a therapy called *logotherapy*, which is based on the importance of meaning to human existence. Indeed, without meaning, the pursuit of happiness may not even be possible.

Frankl believed that without transcendent values and meaning in our life, we develop what he called *noogenic* neurosis, a state of apathy, aimlessness, and boredom. Frankl considered this state a condition of our times. We have lost traditional conventions, values, and meanings, he said, which accounts for our widespread pursuit of pleasure for its own sake and which must ultimately leave us unsatisfied and empty. Like Jung, Frankl believed that life without purpose and meaning is a nonlife. Like Jung, Frankl affirmed the need for spiritual values, a concept difficult to define because it implies the transcendence of human egotism. Given the freedom that we have, Frankl stressed the responsibility of each human being to choose a life with meaning outside the self. It is not a matter so much of *how* we live but *why* we live that leads to a creative life. We can suffer any ordeal, if there is a self-transcending purpose to our living, if we can give ourselves to something more than self. No person may choose that meaning for us. Meaning is derived by each of us according to what we learn from our experiences, the wisdom we garner from our suffering, and the creations we give to the world. Frankl believed that those who find meaning in life reach the state of self-transcendence, the ultimate state of being for the truly healthy, creative person.

There are three ways to establish meaning for ourselves, said Frankl. These three ways are three fundamental systems of value: experiential values, attitudinal values, and creative values.

Experiential values encompass our surrender to the beauty of nature or art. We may not have experiential fulfillment very often, since it is apt to occur only in "peak moments" of human existence. But when it comes, we must be ready to perceive it and absorb it.

Our **attitudinal values** are reflected in how we respond to and use the darker moments of existence. We are not inundated by suffering, but rather we allow pain and suffering to ennoble the spirit and psyche, to make us aware, even as we experience pain, loneliness, and death, that it is by loving others that we receive love. In this facet of his philosophy, a Jewish psychiatrist echoed the prayer of Francis of Assisi: "Let me not so much seek to be loved as to love."

With our **creative values** we realize ourselves through creative and productive work, a work we know gives something to other human beings as well as to ourselves. Work that helps us to forget our small self and relates us to the larger dimension of all life (thus all of humankind) gives joy to our life.

We, who face the ecological crises of the last decades of the twentieth century, have before us the opportunity to find meaning in our lives as never before. There is much work for us to do toward the preservation of peace on this earth and the survival of the planet for those who come after us. It is the continuing struggle, said Frankl, that gives excitement and purpose to our lives. There are many ways to work for that ecological peace. What changes that each of us works for must be our individual choice.

Creative values are the positive result of the other two values. In our determination to survive, in our affirmation of the will to live, in our discovery of a meaning to life itself, even in our most awful pain, we are given the inspiration and motivation to *create*. Why? Because we lose our preoccupation with our small self. Because we find something more noble to work for than a level of pleasure. Frankl warns us not to mistake pleasure for true happiness. Happiness is not achieved by seeking it. Happiness is rather the by-product of giving ourselves to other persons and transcendent purposes.

Frankl began to live for others at Auschwitz, to minister to their physical needs, to provide comfort and hope to them, to give them a sense that although many might lose their lives, perhaps some few could survive. It was this community of *spirit* that he sought to provide for his fellow prisoners. It is only in losing the self, Frankl agreed, that we find the self. Love, for Frankl, became the ultimate human experience—not just sexual and passionate love of man and woman (but also that) but love in the larger sense in our compassionate response to everyone whose paths we cross and in all the activities of our lives. If we have work that has meaning for us, we will love our work. We will work with love. We will create love-ly things.

Frankl's existential encounter with life and death and his transcendence to spiritual meaning are dramatic and awesome. But in a larger sense, all of us must deal, in one way or another, with spiritual values, says Carl Jung. It is to Carl Jung's work on this theme that we now turn.

CARL JUNG AND THE UNIVERSAL PERSONALITY. Carl Jung viewed human nature as consisting of polarities: We may be male but we are also female. We may be extraverted, but we have an introverted side. We may be essentially a thinking person, but we have reservoirs of feeling. We may be *conscious* beings but we have within us cauldrons of unconscious raw material seeking outward expression. We live on a physical/material plane, but we also have a spiritual self.

We may deny this spiritual aspect for many years. In fact, said Jung, in our materialistic Western orientation, we may go on denying our spiritual needs for the first half of our adult life. But eventually there comes a point (usually at mid-life) at which we discover that physical things (material objects) do not bring us happiness. We recognize that all the objects we have acquired and all the worldly goals we have achieved (of wealth and fame or power and prestige) are in and of themselves empty and worthless. He called this point the mid-life crisis (chapter 2). It is at this point (in and around age forty) that we come to recognize our spiritual bankruptcy.

We need not be devastated by this sudden recognition, for with it comes the opportunity to reach deep within ourselves in order to resolve and integrate the polarities of our nature. Within our creative and collective unconscious we may discover a richness and a strength and a wisdom that we have not utilized before. In fact, we cannot utilize it until that moment, Jung believed, for until that time we have lived more in accord with our parental identification and model than with our own truly individuated patterns of existence. As the result of our encounter with, and successful resolution of, the mid-life crisis, we can become what Jung called the individuated person—that man or woman who has truly become his or her "own person" (and continues becoming his or her "own person").

At the same time, and not paradoxically, we have become less narrow, less dogmatic in our consciousness and have achieved a more universal consciousness. We accept who we are as different and unique from others (individuals), but at the same time we accept ourselves as part of all humankind (universal). Where before we played a role (Jung called it wearing a Persona or mask), we now feel free to be *ourselves*. If we have been reticent to express tender emotions, we now find it easier to be affectionate and loving to others. If we have been intolerant of others, we now become accepting and compassionate.

Perhaps Jung was pointing toward that same level of functioning that Lawrence Kohlberg has called the highest level of moral-ethical valuing: the *universal-ethical-principle-orientation* (Kohlberg 1964). Such an orientation arises from the person's own inner universality, explains Kohlberg, and gives the Golden Rule as example: Do to others as you would want them to do to you. The Ten Commandments are concrete; they tell us, by and large, what *not* to do: lie, steal, kill, envy, and so on. The Golden Rule is abstract—and makes us think deeply about what we *could* do to live peacefully and lovingly with others. The Golden Rule does not demand the Old Testament justice of an eye for an eye and a tooth for a tooth. It bespeaks not of justice but of mercy. It is that deep insight that Shakespeare puts into the mouth of young Portia, masquerading as a male advocate. Shylock has demanded his literal pound of flesh out of Antonio's hide. When she presents her arguments to the court in legal terms, Portia is confounded time after time by legal rules: a contract is a contract and must be upheld. At length, she steps beyond manmade legality and appeals to a higher system of values: The Jew must be merciful! When Shylock sneers, "By what compunction must I?" she replies with that most eloquent of speeches, which begins, "The quality of mercy is not strained" and attributes mercy not just to the mightiest of kings but to God Himself. For she says, knowingly and well, "In the course of justice, none of us should see salvation!"

ABRAHAM MASLOW: "PEAK EXPERIENCES." In his study of self-actualizing persons, Maslow said that many of his subjects, in the pursuit of their inner reality, had reported deep mystical experiences—what Maslow preferred to call peak experiences:

> . . . feelings of limitless horizons opening up to the vision, the feeling of being simultaneously more powerful and also more helpless than one ever was before, the feeling of great ecstasy and wonder and awe, the loss of placing in time and space with, finally, the conviction that something extremely important and valuable had happened, so that the subject is to some extent transformed and strengthened even in his daily life by such experiences. [Maslow 1954].

These peak experiences, Maslow wrote, have very definite consequences and very important ones. They break us out of our fixated behaviors that have become clichés and prevent us from growth. They shake us loose of unnecessary anxieties. But also they develop in us a new kind of courage with which to face each day because they have given us a larger, more Olympian perspective—a perspective from which we derived a divine humor (Maslow 1976).

How does one know when one has a peak experience? As Maslow says, it is "unmistakable." We know when it happens. But others have spoken of this experience in more explicit terms. (See box 1.7.) We have a sense of our bodies, and at the same time, we feel limitless.

There is a sense of losing one's identity and, yet, also of gaining it for the first time in our life. There is a sense of joyousness: yet also great tranquility. We are, in that moment, aware of great illumination. We are aware also that we sense the ever-evolving, ever-in-process continuity of existence and the relatedness of all life.

THE SPIRITUAL DIMENSION IN ACTION. Whether it is called a peak experience or enlightenment or mystic understanding or spiritual awareness, the spiritual dimension not only gives one a sense of meaning to life, it brings with it a sense of purpose. Whether we find that purpose in helping the members of our immediate family grouping to grow and become more aware or whether we extend ourselves to those beyond our immediate kin, it is through loving and compassion for others that we fulfill the spiritual dimension of ourselves.

INTEGRATION TECHNIQUES

1. Consider Yourself a Lifelong Learner: Remain Cognitively Inquiring

Continuing to see themselves as "students of life" was one of the hallmarks of Maslow's self-actualizing persons. There is a great secret to this attribute, and that is the avoidance of the great sin of pride. Pride closes us off to further learning. It prevents us from learning what others have to offer and can teach us if we are open. The lack of pride implies humility of spirit, but we must not confuse humility with humbleness. Humbleness (as Charles Dickens knew so well and portrayed in his glaring character of Uriah Heep in *David Copperfield*) is the mask

Box 12.2	**ON THE SPIRITUAL DIMENSION**

The religious spirit is in us. It preceded the religions, and their task as well as that of the prophets, of the initiated, consists of releasing, directing, and developing it. The mystical aspiration is an essentially human trait. It slumbers at the bottom of our souls awaiting the event, or the man capable, in the manner of an enzyme, of transforming it into true mysticism, into faith. (Lecomte de Noüy, 1883–1947. French biophysicist. *Human Destiny.*)

Except for those rare spirits that are born without sin, there is a cavern of darkness to be traversed before that temple can be entered. The gate of the cavern is despair, and its floor is paved with the gravestones of abandoned hopes. There Self must die; there the eagerness, the greed of untamed desire must be slain, for only so can the soul be freed from the empire of Fate. But out of the cavern the Gate of Renunciation leads again to the daylight of wisdom, by whose radiance a new insight, a new joy, a new tenderness, shine forth to gladden the pilgrim's heart. (Bertrand Russell, 1872–1970. English mathematician, philosopher. *Mysticism and Logic.*)

It is only to be expected that for many people who have false ideas about themselves the (process of psychotherapy) is a veritable torture. For, in accordance with the old mystical saying, "Give up what thou hast, then shalt thou receive!" they are called upon to abandon all their cherished illusions in order that something deeper, fairer, and more embracing may arise within them. (Carl G. Jung, M.D., 1875–1961. Swiss psychiatrist. *Two Essays on Analytical Psychology.*)

The more the individual becomes sensitive and receptive to his inner image, the more he becomes whole and "healed." The fact that language has one root for the words "whole," "holy" and to "heal" conceals a deep truth; he who is whole is also healed; to be healed is to be made whole. And it is just because this predestined, unique "wholeness," which is called personality, is the real meaning and purpose of each life, that consciousness of this wholeness produces healing. It is "holy" in so far as it represents a profound experience of a luminous character; the idea of wholeness is, in other words, an archetype of deep significance. . . . Thus individuation implies a "coming to oneself." That is why the recognition of one's true self obliterates the cleavage and its accompanying fear. . . .

At the same time the integrated personality does not merely express the *individual* totality, for in the actualization of his own *a priori* wholeness the individual also discovers his relatedness to a super-individual centre. This centre is the self which is "paradoxically the quintessence of the individuum and at the same time of the collectivum." (Jung *Paracelsica*, p. 167) In other words: the experience of wholeness coincides with the experience of a centre of the personality and a meaning of life which transcends the individual. This is expressed for instance in the words of Nicolaus of Cusa who makes God say to man: "By thou thyself, and I shall be thine." (Gerhard Adler, b. 1904. English Jungian analyst. *Studies in Analytical Psychology.*)

of arrogance. Humility is the understanding that no matter what each of us learns, there is so much more to the world than we can possibly know. Humility means that we respect the special knowledge and skills of those with whom we live, with whom we work—even with whom we are diametrically opposed in political, economic, or philosophic beliefs. This humility makes it possible for others to approach us with their ideas, for they know that we are open to other points of view. Approachability is what makes the manager or executive a competent leader of persons. It is what allows parents to be understanding of their children and adolescents and fortifies the bonds of emotional communication between them. It is what allows persons of opposite persuasion to work coherently together in committee work and assigned tasks. It aids the teacher in fostering honest inquiry from students and promoting class discussion.

One of the problems that students in college often verbalize is their disinterest in one or the other of the subjects that they are taking since they do not see any need for it in their chosen profession. "What's the use of my taking art or music appreciation if I'm never going to use it?" asks engineering students in disgust. It seems to them that such a tedious rerquirement is taking them away from their purpose—to become an engineer. But Maslow himself urged young science students to become humanists as well. We have become too technologically oriented. We cannot look to science for solutions to ethical problems. Scientific discoveries can provide means for dealing with the social ills and ecological crises, but the ability to recognize these problems and these ills in the first place is a matter of *humanistic* sensitivity and ethical concern.

The proper educational base for the person who seeks higher levels of consciousness, then, is a broad grounding in the liberal arts, past and present. This kind of broad background prepares us well for independent thinking and con-

The integrated person is more willing to show the "real me" behind the Persona (mask).

certed action. We will be able to pursue the great social-political-economic debates in the public media and to read the books addressed to those issues. Highly integrated persons know that to be a vital leader today we must consider ourselves not only to be citizens of our own nation but citizens of the world, for world nations are now linked indissolubly in matters of agriculture, commerce, ecology, technology, industry, economic stabilty, political alliance or hostility, as in all areas of human concern. We can no longer afford to be either ignorant or innocent as a people if we are to retain our freedoms and if we are to survive on earth—much less, if we are to enjoy life on earth.

2. Choose a Meaning to Your Life: Then Give Yourself to That Purpose

Happiness is not a goal. It is what happens when we work for transpersonal goals. It matters less that we accomplish our objectives than that we have objectives to accomplish. It is the quest that matters and that brings to our lives a sense of joy and zest. A life with meaning gives us excitement because what we are doing makes our lives worthy. Call it self-esteem—that fourth level of Maslow's hierarchy of needs if you wish. Call it social consciousness, as Adler did, being a characteristic of the integrated person. Call it the propriate striving that Allport considered a mark of the mature person. Whatever it is called, having worthy goals not only prevents us from falling into boredom and ennui or being overcome by the suffering and trials of life, the goals motivate us to keep learning, to keep trying despite obstacles, and to energize ourselves toward achievement.

What shall be the meaning of your life? You and only you can make that choice if you are to live according to your unique process. As a parent, you may find that it is something as near to home as the raising of your own children to be conscious, creative beings. Or it may be taking care of children who have no parents of their own, as Mother Theresa has done in India. Or you may join the scientific search for a high-protein crop to aid our starving world populations. Or you may be one of the many members of your community willing to grow organically pure vegetables in a society that is heading for a "silent spring." There is not an area of business or politics or science that does not need the dedication of men and women willing to thrust their physical and psychological energies into making our world a better place to live. From this dedication to meaningful work and from the giving of ourselves to it, we have a chance for happiness, that elusive goal sought for by so many and achieved by so few.

3. In Problem Situations Develop Several Alternatives: Be Aware of, and Open to, a Number of Choices and Make the Best Possible Choice Available

Piaget described the infantile psychology as a compulsive organization of schemas. The infant must act on whatever sensory object draws its attention. Jangle a set of keys in front of a baby, and it must reach-grab-put-in-mouth (if it can) those keys. It cannot do otherwise. As the infant grows into child and adolescent, it becomes capable of choice. In fact, said Piaget, choice may be equated with intelligence. The more the number of choices we see as available to us, the more intelligent we are.

Consider the number of times you have heard a person say (or perhaps have said yourself), "I must do this, I don't have any choice in the matter." Once a person makes that statement and accepts its assumption, the person is effectively cutting off alternatives.

> I must stay with my husband/wife/boyfriend/girlfriend even if we are desperately unhappy. I have no choice because I don't want to hurt him/her. [The truth is they are hurting each other unbearably in the present.]
>
> I would like to quit my job and find one that is more satisfying and less stressful. But I have too many bills to pay, and I need the security of my present job. I can't quit. I have no choice but to stay at it. When I retire, maybe then I can do what I want to do. [The truth is that the stress of his life may not allow him to live that long.]
>
> I have to major in medicine. My parents want me to, and they have set their hearts on it. I need their financial support to go to school, and I don't have any choice but to continue in premedicine. [The truth may be that one's parents may not want their son or daughter to pursue a vocation he or she does not like.]

When we find ourselves in a situation that seems to be a no-choice situation, then we are at the point where we need to step back and recognize the box we have put ourselves into. No-choice assumptions make us a prisoner of our own thinking. We are no further along than the animistic thinking of primitive peoples or preoperational children. If we cannot ourselves discover other alternatives in our life making and develop strategies for exploring these alternatives, then we would do well to seek the help and counsel of others: our intimate friends or those who are professionally involved with helping people untangle the tangles and snares of the mental/emotional traps of their own making.

4. Develop Autonomy in Thought, Word, and Deed: Allow Individualation of Personality

Another mark of highly integrated persons is the ability to think for themselves. They do not follow the dictates of authority, any authority, with blind obedience as do preoperative children. They may stick to tried-and-true tradition and obey the laws of their nation, but they see themselves as choosing their own values and ethical principles and acting upon them. They do not allow themselves to be taken over, unquestioningly, by an ideology. They do not follow any leader, no matter how charismatic, without question or criticism. The Jonestown tragedy occurred because of the willingness of almost a thousand persons to be taken over body and mind by a person who promised paradise on earth provided he was given complete and undisputed allegience. The Jonestown tragedy shocked us as a nation because we had come to believe that only in Germany could a Hitler arise, and only in Italy would a Mussolini arise, and only in Russia could a Stalin arise. Highly integrated persons recognize that when an ideology allows no room for debate, our freedom to make independent choices has been lost. They may obey an unjust law, but they will seek to change it. They may follow an arbitrary ordinance, but they will protest its existence publicly and courageously. They may note that a Gallup poll finds "most persons" of a certain persuasion, but they are willing to be a minority of one if need be. They are unwilling to submit to a mass consciousness. They are willing to be the "individuated" people, who make their own decisions and develop life styles in accordance with their personality types. They are willing to demand equal rights, when need be, and they are careful to respect the rights of others. Highly integrated persons are willing to listen to the dissents of the minority—for that, ultimately, is the essence of a free people.

5. Stay Open to Emotional Experience: Pursue Your Interior Life and Develop a "Creative Conscience"

The person who acts from what has been called the *creative conscience* (May 1973[a]; 1973[b]) acts with courage and strength. This creative conscience has been identified by other terms: the still small voice within; the dictates of reason; the higher self; the universal perspective; mystical awareness; the Grace of God. In contrast to the person who follows others blindly, the person with a creative conscience dares to be himself or herself because he or she is acting from an inner conviction and not out of submission to others.

We can develop this creative conscience in many ways: through open discussion and debate with others, through prayer and meditation, through the study of great books, through our active participation in community and national programs that seek to alleviate our social evils. It comes in other ways as well; through the diligent study of our dream experiences, through the processing of the emotional hurt that we all experience at one time or another in our lives, through the empathetic sharing of another's suffering and heartache, through the willingness to stay open to life's experiences even if that means staying open to pain as well as joy.

6. Recognize That Wisdom Comes With Living Through Experience

Children may be smarter than we adults are at times (and indeed they can often outtalk us, outrun, outthink, outwit us), but they are not wiser than we. Wisdom comes only with years of experiencing life on earth. The more experiences we have, the more situations and events we process, the more profound becomes our understanding of what it means to be alive and aware. We develop patience, tolerance, generosity, and a larger world view as the result of living with courage, conviction, and purpose. Courage to live means that when tragedy strikes, or we become victim to injustice or calamity, we surrender to that event, not in abject submission, but in recognition that this is what is happening now. We do not deny it. We go through it. We accept what is and mourn what we must—and go on from there. Always we *learn* from experience. We are not given the choice to have or not have a life free from sorrow and pain. We do have the choice to use that experience for our further integration or to retreat from life as much as possible.

7. Be Open and Ready for Peak Experiences: Give Yourself to the Moment

Staying open to emotional experiencing prepares us for the moments that Maslow called peak experiences. Peak experiences come via many avenues—all of which require our total attention for total experiencing. These many avenues may be prayer or contemplation, giving birth or seeing your child born, listening to a symphony, pursuit of a scientific task, or the act of love. But peak experiences come only when we are wholly involved with the process of experiencing. Our attention is focused, our attitude receptive, our bodies relaxed and open to feelings and sensations: Our total mindbody being is present and attuned to that moment, that place, that experience.

Giving up mental and emotional control is difficult for many of us, for we tend to hang on to what we know—we fear the unknown. Sometimes we fear the unknown so much that we hold on to a difficult present in order to avoid the unfamiliar. We may find ourselves overwhelmed by feelings, fear that we are losing our sense of present reality, even that we may be dying. But it is only in the experience of the yet unknown that new perceptions are possible and that new ("higher") levels of consciousness are possible. The unknown is always feared. But if we are able to break with our conditioning, our fears, our habitual mental sets to these new levels of being, what follows are new levels of personality integration. We are more able to live and work with others. We are also more centered within our own being. We are that we are.

SUMMARY POINTS TO REMEMBER

1. The humanistic movement in psychology has focused on the creative and highest levels of personality integration under a variety of categories: the creative person, the mature person, the fully functioning person, the self-actualizing person, the self-realizing person, and so on.

2. Although these studies have used different

methodologies and different populations, they indicate four highly developed areas of personality functioning: intellectual curiosity, emotional openness, energetic motivation, and spiritual compassion.

3. Intellectually these persons are always in search of more comprehensive understandings of themselves and the world they live in. They seek factual truths and ever broader theoretical parameters of the universe. They do not freeze their creative talents into rigid thought forms but remain flexible in their thinking and response to new and experimental ideas. They are less stereotypic in their thinking and are more able to break their conditioned response patterns.

4. Emotionally they are more open to a wide range of experiences. They do not back away from emotional situations but welcome them as learning experiences. They recognize that our most painful experiences may be the opportunities for the most growth. They are good animals in the sense that they eat well, sleep well, enjoy their senses and other bodily feelings. They use all their emotional experiences as the grist for the creative processing.

5. Motivationally they are self-starters and determined to be masters of their fate and captains of their souls. They do not blame others and they learn by their mistakes. They enjoy the quest!

6. Spiritually they are continually transcending their present consciousness in search of more universal awareness. They are committed not only to their own growth but also to the growth of others. They recognize that we are all a part of the family of humankind. As they progress in their own evolutionary transcendence of consciousness they enable the rest of us to evolve with them. They enjoy the heights of human experiencing, what Maslow called the peak experience and others have called the mystic experience. They recognize that happiness is not a goal to be achieved but a by-product of putting our energies into a life of work and meaning.

SIGNIFICANT TERMS AND CONCEPTS

a priori
assumptions
attitudinal values
authoritarian
caste-and-class
center of growth
conditioning
consciousness
creative person
creativity
dynamic process
  (dynamics)
ecological thinking
either-or-thinking
emotional openness
emptying the mind
energetic motivation
freezing

fully functioning
good animals
here-and-now
human ecology
individuated persons
intellectual curiosity
intellectual functioning
logo therapy
mask
mid-life crisis
mystic experience
neurotic person
peak experiences
perceptual set
Persona
personality functioning
personality integration
process approach

persons-in-process
phenomenology
"real me"
spiritual bankruptcy
self
self-actualizing
self-realizing person
spiritual compassion
stereotypic thinking
surrendering
transcendence of
  consciousness
universal awareness
universal consciousness
universal-ethical orientation
Zen Buddhism

FILL IN THE BLANKS WITH SIGNIFICANT TERMS AND CONCEPTS

1. Persons who are demonstrating high levels of personality integration are described by various theorists as: the f_____ f_____ person, the s_____-a_____ person and the s_____-r_____ person.

2. Persons who are functioning at high levels of personality integration are less s_____ in their t_____ and they are more capable of breaking conditioned response patterns.

3. Those persons who are highly integrated are more willing to expose the "r_____ m_____" and put down their m_____ or P_____.

4. Having peak experiences is also a characteristic of having a high level of p_____ i_____.

5. Those persons who have highly integrated personalities enjoy the intensities of human experiencing. Maslow called these experiences peak experiences and others call them m_____ e_____.

6. The fully functioning person is continually transcending her present consciousness in a search for more u_____ a_____.

7. As persons with a highly integrated personality progress on their own evolutionary paths, they enable others to evolve with them. Thus we all move toward the t_____ of c_____.

RECOMMENDED BOOKS FOR FURTHER READING

Fromm, Erich. 1978. *Man for Himself*. New York: Fawcett Book Group. We could have chosen any Fromm book for he has continually dealt with the basic issues of human existence: freedom and choice, hate and love, fascism and democracy.

Jourard, Sidney M. 1971. *The Transparent Self: Self-Disclosure and Well-Being*, 2nd ed. New York: Van Nostrand Reinhold. As Jourard describes it, because we are afraid of rejection, hurt, or criticism, we hide behind various masks which prevent us from knowing one another.

Jung, Carl G. 1955. *Modern Man In Search of a Soul*. New York: Harcourt Brace Jovanovich. He came to the conclusion that one of the principal neuroses of persons living today is their rejection of the spiritual aspect of themselves. While the first half of one's life may indeed be occupied with advancement in the outer world, the second half of human existence is bankrupt unless the individual finds meaning to his existence.

Krishnamurti, J. 1972. *You Are the World*. New York: Harper & Row Publishers. Not an easy book to read and therefore recommended here primarily for students with a background of reading in psychology and philosophy. This volume is a collection of conversations between Krishnamurti and students at various universities.

Maslow, Abraham H. 1976. *The Farther Reaches of Human Nature*. New York: Penguin Books. Published posthumously, this book represents Maslow's conceptualizations of where human personality could go. He discusses the peak experience and what he called the transcending experience. He focuses on the creative person, blocks to creativity and the need for creative people.

May, Rollo. 1973[b]. *Love and Will*. New York: Dell. He is always concerned with how we may live with each other in loving and self-determining ways. He writes simply but profoundly.

Rogers, Carl R. 1961. *On Becoming a Person*. Boston: Houghton Mifflin. Along with Maslow, Rogers is responsible for the "third force" or humanistic movement's early growth. Rogers, too, studies the highly evolved and integrated person and describes him as *fully functioning*.

Notes

CHAPTER 1

1. Traditionally, we have generally stated that Wilhelm Wundt established psychology as a science in 1879 in Leipzig, Germany, but there is some evidence of late that psychology as a discipline was established at Harvard University around 1875 by the American psychologist, William James. James is reputed to have remarked that the first lecture on psychology he ever heard was the first lecture he gave (Fancher 1979).
2. Physics can be traced back to the Greeks; astronomy to the Persians, Egyptians, and Chaldeans; chemistry was begun in the laboratories of the alchemists of the Middle Ages; and medicine has its roots so far back in the history of most civilizations, its origins are lost in prehistory.
3. One of the debts we owe to an early father of modern science, René Descartes, is that he was the first to state his objection to accepting assumptions, any assumption, without some kind of evidence. It was a courageous statement for a French Catholic who lived at a time when the Inquisition was always on the hunt for "heretical" thinking.
4. We will do well to remember that these generalizations are no longer empirical data but are beliefs founded on data that we have done our best to abstract accurately. If our past is any indication of our future, there is much more fine-tuning of each and every scientific generalization forthcoming.
5. Jonathan Swift (1667–1745); an Anglo-Irish satirist, wrote a novel about one Gulliver, who sets out to see the world. Gulliver comes to the Kingdom of Lilliput, whose inhabitants are miniscule. They spend much time swarming over the huge Gulliver, to examine him in detail. But since they are so small and Gulliver so large, they have difficulty in recognizing his humanoid qualities—that he is the same species as they are.
6. An allusion to Martin Luther, the religious reformer who nailed a series of indictments on the door of a medieval church.
7. Homeostasis is a biological term that applies to an optimal and narrow level of physiological functioning. When our bodies vary too far and too long from this optimal functioning area we are in danger of illness or even death.
8. Integration, *n.* 1: the act or process or an instance of integrating . . . . integrate, *vb.* 1: to form into a whole; unite; *2a* to unite with something else . . . (*Webster's Collegiate Dictionary*).
9. A phrase formulated by the German existential philosophers Ludwig Binswanger and Martin Heidegger.

CHAPTER 2

1. Erik Erikson was not his given name; he adopted it as a part of his own identification process.
2. Pronounced pee-ah-jay, with the soft *j* sound like the *su* sound in mea*su*re or trea*su*re.
3. Consider also the alcoholic who lives in possession of "Demon Run" or the cocaine addict who has "a monkey on his back," i.e., they believe they are not responsible for their actions.

CHAPTER 3

1. Incidentally, Adler was of the opinion that this life style developed so early in life is not genetically determined but determined soley by one's early environment. Like Freud, he was convinced that the child's experience in his family constellation was the determining force in the child's personality development.
2. Being-in-the-world is not a Jungian concept but belongs to Martin Heidegger. Nevertheless, we use it here, since it seems to be very appropriate to the introversion-extraversion typology of Carl Jung.
3. Our leading statesmen, stateswomen, and diplomats, for example, need to be somewhat extraverted if we are to establish good communication with our allies and promote more cooperative attitudes with the "other side." It has been said that one of the chief liabilities of Richard Nixon was his basic introversion, that while in office he admitted fewer and fewer persons into the "oval" office. Obviously the great interpersonal responsibilities of public office necessitate great ability to deal easily and well in the extraverted world of state, national, and international politics.

CHAPTER 4

1. Paul Tillich is considered one of the great theological leaders of the twentieth century.

CHAPTER 5

1. A sensory modality is a sense category such as vision or hearing.
2. These findings are not so surprising when we consider what is involved in a change—any change—in our situation. Consider, for example, a vacation traveling by car to a distant place for a couple and their two young children. Almost any parent will admit that many hours of driving are a lot easier on the nerves if the children are not along. We are reminded of their wanting to stop for frequent rest periods and complaints that they are hungry. Then think of the mother's attempts to keep the children from getting bored and from fighting, and we immediately understand how vacation trips sometimes can be less happy and more tiring than was originally hoped and fantasized.

CHAPTER 6

1. Wolpe said that the deep relaxation he has been able to engender with his approach is the experience of tingling, numbness, and warmth (personal communication, 1973). He said that these sensations arise when the person is relaxing that particular portion of the body he has so far kept under tension. This correlates with the sensory phenomena reported by persons in the beginning stages of what has been called *meditation*, or in the beginning state in yoga therapy.

CHAPTER 7

1. In Freud's method of free association persons are supposed to be relaxed enough to speak of everything that comes into their "minds," their present awareness. This kind of honesty is bound to provoke change and growth, as Freud demonstrated in his treatment of many persons.

CHAPTER 8

1. *Coitus reservatus*, or *coitus interruptus*, is the practice in which the man withdraws from the woman's vagina before ejaculation, or orgasm.

CHAPTER 11

1. REM sleep is that period of sleeping when we dream very heavily. REM stands for Rapid Eye Movement which is characteristic of intense dreaming.
2. We draw our readers attention to the similarity of our functioning to Piaget's pre-operative stage of Animism, functionalism, and paralogic.

Bibliography

ADAMS, W. D. 1882. *Curiosities of Superstition*. London: J. Masters & Co.

ADDAMS, JANE et al. 1982. *Philanthropy and Social Progress: Seven Essays*. Delivered before the School of Applied Ethics at Plymouth, Mass. 1982 session. New York: Arno Press.

ADLER, ALFRED 1929. *Practices & Theory of Individual Psychology*. Atlantic Highlands, N. J.: Humanities Press.

———. 1930. Individual psychology. In C. A. Murchison, ed., *Psychologies of 1930*. Worcester, Mass.: Clark University Press, pp. 394–405.

———. 1931. *What Life Should Mean to You*. New York: G. P. Putnam's Sons.

———. 1959. *The Practice and Theory of Individual Psychology*. Totowa, N.J.: Littlefield, Adams & Co.

———. 1969[a]. *Education of the Individual*. Rpt. of 1958 ed. Westport, Ct: Greenwood Press.

———. 1969[b]. *The Diagnosis of a Life Style*, 2nd ed. Bernard Shulman, ed. Chicago: Alfred Adler Institute of Chicago, Inc.

———. 1970. *Education of Children*. Southbend In.: Regnery-Gateway, Inc.

———. 1971. *Practice and Theory of Individual Psychology*. Trans. P. Radin. 1929. Reprint. Atlantic Highlands, N.J.: Humanities Press.

ADLER, GERHARD. 1968. *Studies in Analytical Psychology*. 1948. Reprint. Westport, Conn.: Greenwood Press.

ADORNO, THEODORE W. 1973. *The Jargon of Authenticity*. Trans. Kurt Tarnowski and Frederic Will. Evanston, Ill.: Northwestern University Press.

AINSWORTH, MARY D. 1982. The development of infant-mother attachment. In Jay Belsky, *In the Beginning: Readings in Infancy*. New York: Columbia University Press, pp. 135–143.

ALEXANDER, FRANZ. 1963. *Psychosomatic Medicine*. New York: W. W. Norton & Co.

ALLPORT, GORDON W. 1955. *Becoming: Basic Considerations for a Psychology of Personality*. New Haven, Conn.: Yale University Press.

———. 1975. *The Nature of Personality: Selected Papers*. Reprint of 1950 ed. Westport, Conn.: Greenwood Press.

———. 1981. *Personality and Social Encounter: Selected Essays*. Chicago: University of Chicago Press.

ALLPORT, GORDON W.; VERNON, PHILLIP E.; AND LINDZEY, GARDNER. 1951. *Study of Values*, 3rd ed. Boston: Riverside Press.

ANAND, B. K.; CHHINA, G. S.; AND SINGH, B. 1977. Some aspects of electroencephalographic studies of yogis. In Philip G. Zimbardo and Floyd L. Ruch, eds., *Psychology and Life*. Glenview, Ill.: Scott, Foresman & Co., p. 304.

ANASTASI, ANNE. 1961. *Psychological Testing*. 2nd ed. New York: Macmillan Co.

———. 1965. *Individual Differences*. New York: John Wiley & Sons.

ANDERSON, KURT. 1983. Private violence. *Time*, September 5, pp. 18–19.

ANGST. 1961. *Time*, March 31, p. 46.

ANSBACHER, H. L. 1956. The individual psychology of Alfred Adler: A systematic presentation. In H. L. Ansbacher and R. R. Ansbacher, eds., *Selections from His Writings*. New York: Harper & Row, Publishers.

———. 1980. *Alfred Adler Revisited*. New York: Praeger Publishers.

ARDREY, ROBERT. 1966. *The Territorial Imperative*. New York: Atheneum Publishers.

ARENDT, HANNAH. 1970. *The Human Condition*. Chicago: Unviersity of Chicago Press.

ARIES, PHILIPPE. 1965. *Centuries of Childhood: A Social History of the Family*. New York: Random House.

ARGYLE, MICHAEL. 1969. *Social Interaction*. New York: Atherton Press.

ARKIN, A. M.; ANTROBUS, J. S.; AND ELLMAN, S. J., eds. 1978. *The Mind in Sleep: Psychology and Psychophysiology*. Hillsdale, N. J.: Erlbaum.

ASSAGIOLI, ROBERTO. 1976. *Psychosynthesis*. New York: Penguin Books.

ASSOCIATED PRESS. 1981. Public hangings would cut crime. London, January 19, 1984.

AZRIN, NATHAN. 1967. Pain and aggression. In *Readings in Psychology Today*. Del Mar, Calif.: CRM Books, pp. 114–21.

BABCHUCK, N. et al. 1967. Changes in religious affiliation and marital stability. *Social Forces* 45:551–55.

BACH, GEORGE, AND WYDEN, PETER. 1969. *Intimate Enemy: How to Fight Fair in Love and Marriage*. New York: William Morrow & Co.

BACKMAN, J. C.; GREEN, S.; AND WETNANEN, J. D. 1971. *Youth in Transition*, vol. 3: *Dropping Out—Problem or Symptom*. Ann Arbor: University of Michigan, Institute for Social Research.

BAEKELAND, FREDERICK, AND HARTMANN, ERNEST. 1982. In James V. McConnell, *Understanding Human Behavior*, 4th ed. New York: Holt, Rinehart & Winston, pp. 58–59.

BANDURA, A. 1977. *Social Learning Theory*. Englewood Cliffs, N.J.: Prentice-Hall.

BARBER, T. X. 1970. *LSD, Marihuana, Yoga and Hypnosis*. Chicago: Aldine Publishing Co.

BARCHAS, J. D.; AKEL, H; ELLIOTT, G. R.; HOLMAN, R. B.; AND WATSON, S. J. 1978. Behavioral neurochemistry in neuroregulators and behavioral states. *Science* 200: 964–73.

BARKER, J. L., AND SMITH, T. G., JR., eds. 1980. *The Role of Peptides in Neuronal Function*. New York: Dekker, Marcel.

BARRON, FRANK. 1963. The needs for order and disorder as motives in creative activity. In Calvin W. Taylor and Frank Barron, eds., *Scientific Creativity: Its Recognition and Development*. New York: John Wiley & Sons, pp. 157–58.

BARRON, FRANK. 1968. *Creativity and Personal Freedom*. rev. ed. New York: Van Nostrand Reinhold Co.

BARTH, KARL. *Ethics*. 1965. New York: Macmillan.

BASEDOW, HERBERT. 1977. *The Australian Aboriginal*. New York: AMS Press.

BAUM, A.; SINGER, J. E., AND BAUM, C. S. 1981. Stress and the environment. *Journal of Social Issues* 37: 4–35.

BAUMRIND, D. 1971. Harmonious parents and their preschool children. *Developmental Psychology* 4:99–102.

BAUMRIND, D., AND BLACK, A. E. 1967. Socialization practices associated with dimensions of competence in preschool boys and girls. *Child Development* 38:291–327.

BAZAR, JOAN. 1983. Growing role for emotions in treating host of diseases. *APA Monitor* 11.

BEACH, FRANK A. ed. 1965. *Sex and Behavior*. New York: John Wiley & Sons.

BENSON, H. 1975. *Relaxation Response*. New York: William Morrow & Co.

BERARDO, FELIX M.; VERA, HERMAN; AND BERARDO, DONNA. 1983. Age-Discrepant Marriages. *Medical Aspects of Human Sexuality* 17 (January): 57.

BERENBLUM, ISAAC. 1967. *Cancer Research Today*. Elmsford, N.Y.: Pergamon Press.

BERNE, ERIC. 1961. *Transactional Analysis in Psychotherapy*. New York: Grove Press.

BERNE, ERIC. 1978. *The Games People Play*. Westminister, Md.: Ballantine Books.

BESANCENEY, P. H. 1965. Interfaith marriages of Catholics in the Detroit area. *Sociological Analysis* 36: 38–44.

BETTELHEIM, BRUNO. 1967. *The Empty Fortress: Infantile Autism and the Birth of the Self*. New York: Free Press.

———. 1971. *Love Is Not Enough*. New York: Avon Books.

———. 1976. *The Uses of Enchantment: The Meaning and Importance of Fairy Tales*. New York: Alfred A. Knopf.

BIRBAUMER, NIELS, AND KIMMEL, H. D., eds. 1979. *Biofeedback and Self-Realization*. New York: Halstead Press.

BLOOD, ROBERT O., AND WOLFE, DONALD M. 1965. *Husbands and Wives: Dynamics of Family Living*. New York: Free Press.

BLUM, KENNETH, ed. 1977. *Alcohol and Opiates: Neurochemical and Behavioral Mechanisms*. Campbell, Calif.: Academy Press.

BLUM, MILTON L., AND NAYLOR, JAMES C. 1968. *Industrial Psychology: Its Theoretical and Social Foundations*, 3rd ed. New York: Harper & Row, Publishers.

BLUMSTEIN, PHILIP, AND SCHWARTZ, PEPPER. 1983. What makes today's marriages last. *Family Weekly*, November 13.

BOHANNAN, PAUL. 1977. Stepfathers and the mental health of their children. Report to the National Institute of Mental Health, U.S. Department of Health, Education and Welfare, December 1975. In Morton Hunt and Bernice Hunt, *The Divorce Experience*. New York: McGraw-Hill Book Co.

BOKEN, HALCYONE, AND VIVEROS-LONG, ANAMARIE. 1981. *Balancing Jobs and Family Life: Do Flexible Work Schedules Work?* Philadelphia: Temple University Press.

BORING, EDWIN, G. 1950. *A History of Experimental Psychology*, 2nd ed. New York: Appleton-Century-Crofts.

BORKENAU, FRANZE. 1965. The concept of death. In Robert Fulton, ed., *Death and Identity*. New York: John Wiley & Sons, pp. 42–56.

BOURNE, LYLE E. AND EKSTRAND, BRUCE R. 1976. *Psychology: Its Meaning & Principles*, 2nd ed. New York: Holt, Rinehart & Winston.

BOURNE, RICHARD. 1979. Child abuse and neglect: An overview. In Richard Bourne and Eli Newberger, eds., *Critical Perspectives on Child Abuse*. Lexington, Mass.: Lexington Books.

BOURNE, RICHARD, AND NEWBERGER, ELI H., eds. 1979. *Critical Perspectives on Child Abuse*. Lexington, Mass.: Lexington Books.

BOWLBY, JOHN. 1957. Observations of older children who

were deprived in infancy. In Eugene L. Hartley and Ruth E. Hartley, eds., *Outside Readings in Psychology*. New York: Thomas Y. Crowell Co., pp. 378–91.

———. 1960. Separation anxiety. *International Journal of Psychoanalysis* 41: 69–113.

BOWMAN, HENRY A. 1974. *Marriage for Moderns*, 7th ed. New York: McGraw-Hill Book Co.

BOYLE, R. P. 1966. The effects of the high school on students' aspirations *American Journal of Sociology* 71:628–39.

BRADY, JOSEPH; PORTER, R.; CONRAD, D.; AND MASON, J. 1958. Avoidance behavior and the development of gastroduodenal ulcers. *Journal of the Experimental Analysis of Behavior* 1: 69–72.

BRAZELTON, T. BERRY. 1981. *On Becoming a Family: The Growth of Attachment*. New York: Delacorte Press.

———. 1978. *Doctor and Child*. New York: Dell Publishing Co.

BRENNER, HARVEY. 1973. *Menal Illness and the Economy*. Cambridge, Mass.: Harvard University Press.

———. 1979. Influence of the social environment on psychopathology: the historic perspective. In James Barrett et al., eds., *Stress and Mental Disorder*. New York: Raven Press.

BRIDGES, JAMES R. 1930. *Psychology, Normal and Abnormal*. New York: D. Appelton & Co.

BRO, HARMON. 1971. *High Play: Turning on Without Drugs*. New York: Coward, McCann & Geoghegan.

BRONOWSKI, JACOB. 1974. *The Ascent of Man*. Waltham, Mass.: Little, Brown & Co.

BUBAUMER, NIELS, AND KEMMER, H. D., eds. 1979. *Biofeedback and Self-Regulation*. Hillsdale, N.J: Erlbaum.

BUBER, MARTIN. 1957. *Pointing the Way*. New York: Arno Press.

———. 1958. *Paths in Utopia*. Boston: Beacon Press.

———. 1970. *I and Thou*. Trans. W. Kaufman. New York: Charles Scribner's Sons.

BURCHINAL, L. G., AND CHANCELLOR, L. E. 1962. Proportions of Catholics, urbanism and mixed-Catholic marriages rates among Iowa counties. *Social Problems 9* (spring): 359–65.

BURGESS, E. W., AND WALLIN, PAUL. 1953. *Engagement and Marriage*. Philadelphia: J. B. Lippincott Co.

BURGESS, ERNEST W. et al. 1971. *The Family: From Traditional to Companionship*, 4th ed. New York: Van Nostrand Reinhold Co.

BURKE, RICHARD M. 1961. *Cosmic Consciousness*. New York: University Books.

BUTLER, DAVID. 1980. *Disraeli: Portrait of a Romantic*. New York: Warner Books.

BUTLER, ROBERT N. 1975. *Why Survive? Being Old in America*. New York: Harper & Row, Publishers.

BUTLER, R. N., AND LEWIS, M. J. 1977. *Aging and Mental Health*, 2nd ed. St. Louis: C. V. Moshey Co.

CANNON, WALTER B. 1963. *The Wisdom of the Body*, 2nd ed. New York: W. W. Norton & Co.

CARTER, H., AND GLICK, P. C. 1970. *Marriage and Divorce: A Social and Economic Study*. Cambridge, Mass.: Harvard University Press.

CHASE, STUART. 1966. *Tyranny of Words*. New York: Harcourt Brace Jovanovich.

CHILMAN, C. S. 1983. Remarriage and stepfamilies. In Eleanor Macklin and Roger Rubin, eds., *Contemporary Families and Alternative Life Styles: Handbook on Research and Theory*. Beverly Hills, Calif.: Sage Publications.

CHRISTENSEN, H. T., AND BARBER, K. E. 1976. Interfaith vs. intrafaith marriage in Indiana. *Journal of Marriage and the Family* 29:416–69.

CLECKLEY, HERVEY M. 1964. *The Mask of Sanity*, 4th ed. St. Louis: C. V. Mosby Co.

COBB, SIDNEY, AND ROSE, ROBERT. 1973. Hypertension, peptic ulcers, and diabetes in air-traffic controllers. *Journal of the American Medical Association* 224 (April): 489–92.

COLEMAN, J. C. 1976. *Abnormal Psychology and Modern Life*, 5th ed. Glenview, Ill.: Scott, Foresman & Co.

COMBS, ARTHUR W., RICHARDS, ANN COHEN, AND RICHARDS, FRED. 1976. *Perceptual Psychology: A Humanistic Approach to the Study of Persons*. New York: Harper & Row Publishers, Inc.

CONDRON, JOHN, AND BODE, JERRY. 1982. Rashomon, working wives and family division of labor: Middletown, 1980. *Journal of Marriage and the Family* 44 (May): 421–26.

CORBALLIS, M. C., AND BEALE, I. L. 1976. *The Psychology of Left and Right*. Hillsdale, N.J.: Erlbaum.

COOMBS, R. H. 1966. Value consensus and partner satisfaction among dating couples. *Journal of Marriage and the Family* 28 (May):166–73.

COOPER, DAVID. 1970. *The Death of the Family*. New York: Vintage Books, Random House.

COPE, R. AND HANNAH, W. 1975. *Revolving College Doors: The Causes and Consequences of Dropping Out, Stopping Out, and Transferring*. New York: John Wiley & Sons.

COWAN, RUTH. 1976. Two washes in the morning and a bridge party at night. *Women's Studies* 3 (Fall): 147–72.

CUBER, JOHN. 1969. Adultery: Reality vs. stereotype. In Gerhard Neubeck, ed., *Extramarital Relations*. Englewood Cliffs, N.J.: Prentice-Hall.

CUBER, JOHN, AND HAROFF, PEGGY. 1965. *Sex and the Significant Americans*. Baltimore: Penguin Books.

DAVIS, ALLISON et al. 1941. *Deep South: A Social Anthropological Study of Caste and Class*. Chicago: Unviersity of Chicago Press.

DAVISON, G. C., AND NEALE, JOHN M. 1974. *Abnormal Psychology: An Experimental Clinical Approach*. New York: John Wiley & Sons.

DE BEAUVOIR, SIMONE. 1974. *The Second Sex*. New York: Random House.

DEGLER, CARL. 1980. *At Odds*. New York: Oxford University Press.

DEHARTMAN, THOMAS. 1964. *Our Life with Mister Gurdjieff*. Totowa: N.J.: Cooper Square Publishers.

DEMOS, JOHN. 1970. *A Little Commonwealth*. New York: Oxford University Press.

———. 1975–76. The American family in past time. In H. Grunebaum and J. Christ, eds., *Contemporary Marriage*. Waltham, Mass.: Little, Brown & Co.

DENNISTON, DENISE, AND MCWILLIAMS, PETER. 1975. *The TM Book*. Allan Park, Mich.: Veremonger Press.

DERR, C. BROOKLYN, ed. 1980. *Work, Family and the Career: New Frontiers in Theory and Research*. New York: Praeger Publishers.

DESCARTES, RENÉ. 1960. *Discourse on Method*. Trans. Lawrence J. Lafleur. Indianapolis: Bobbs-Merrill Co.

DE TOCQUEVILLE, ALEXIS. 1944. In Bradley and Phillips, eds., *Democracy In America*. New York: Alfred A. Knopf.

DICKENS, CHARLES. 1981. *A Christmas Carol*. Reprint. Cutchogue. N.Y.: Buccaneer Books.

DIPBOYE, W. J., AND ANDERSON, W. F. 1961. Occupational stereotypes and manifest needs of high school students. *Journal of Counseling Psychology* 8: 296–304.

Discover: The News Magazine of Science. June, 1984, p. 10.

DOBRIZHOFFER. 1822. *The Abipones*, E. tr.; London, vol. ii.

DOLLARD, JOHN. 1937. *Caste and Class in a Southern Town*. New Haven, Conn.: Yale University Press.

DOLLARD, J., AND MILLER, N. E. 1966. What is a neurosis? In R. L. Wrenn, ed., *Basic Contributions to Psychology Readings*. Belmont, Calif.: Wadsworth Publishing Co., pp. 206–11.

DOUVAN, ELIZABETH; WEINGARTEN, HELEN; AND SCHEIBER, JANE L., eds. 1980. *American Families*. Dubuque, Iowa: Kendall/Hunt Publishing Co.

DOWD, MAUREEN. 1983. Rape: the sexual weapon. *Time*, September 5, pp. 27–29.

DUNBAR, FLANDERS. 1955. *Mind and Body: Psychosomatic Medicine*, rev. ed. Westminister, Md.: Random House.

DUNNE, DESMOND. 1953. *Yoga*. New York: Funk & Wagnalls.

DUNOUY, LECOMTE. *Human Destiny*. (na).

DURKHEIM, EMILE. 1951. *Suicide*. Riverside, N.J.: Free Press.

ECCLES, J. C. 1970. *Facing Reality: Philosophical Adventures by a Brain Scientist*. New York: Springer-Verlag New York.

ECKLAND, B. K. 1974. Theories of mate selection. In M. D. Sussman, ed., *Sourcebook in Marriage and the Family*, 4th ed. Boston: Houghton Mifflin Co., pp. 313–23.

EDWARDS, BETTY. 1979. *Drawing From the Right Side of the Brain: A Course in Enhancing Creativity and Artistic Confidence*. Los Angeles: J. P. Tarcher.

EGBERT, L.; BATLIT, G.; WELCH, C.; AND BARTLETT, M. 1964. Reduction of post operative pain by encouragement and instruction of patients. *New England Journal of Medicine* 270:825–27.

EISDORFER, C., AND LAWTON, M. P., eds. 1971. *The Psychology of Adult Aging*. Washington, D.C.: American Psychological Association.

ELDER, G. H. 1969. Appearance and Education in Marriage Mobility. *American Sociological Review* 34 (August):520.

ELKIND, DAVID. 1967. Egocentrism in adolescence. *Child Development* 38:1025–1034.

———. 1981. *The Hurried Child: Growing Up Too Fast, Too Soon*. Reading, Mass.: Addison-Wesley Publishing Co.

ELLIS, ALBERT. 1960. *The Art and Science of Love*. Secaucus, N.J.: Lyle Stuart.

———. 1974. *Humanistic Psychotherapy: The Rational-Emotive Approach*. New York: McGraw-Hill Book Co.

ERIKSON, ERIK. 1950. *Childhood and Society*. New York: W. W. Norton & Co.

———. 1963 *Childhood and Society*, 2nd ed. New York: W. W. Norton & Co.

FABEROW, NORMAN L. 1977. The cultural history of suicide. In Linnea Pearson, *Separate Paths*. New York: Harper & Row, Publishers.

FANCHER, RAYMOND. 1979. *The Pioneers of Psychology*. New York: W. W. Norton & Co.

FARADAY, ANN. 1981. *Dream Power*. New York: Berkley Publishing Corporation.

FARBER, SUSAN L. 1980. *Identical Twins Reared Apart*. New York: Basic Books, Inc.

FELDMAN, H. 1971. The effects of children on the family. In A. Michel, ed., *Family Issues of Employed Women in Europe and America*. Lieden, The Netherlands: E. F. Brill.

FELDMAN, H. AND FELDMAN, M. 1975. The family life cycle: some suggestions for recycling. *Journal of Marriage and the Family* 37 (May):277–84.

———. 1976–77. Effect of parenthood at three points in marriage. Unpublished manuscript.

FERREE, MYRA. 1976. The confused American housewife. *Psychology Today*, September, pp. 76–80.

FESHBACK, SEYMOUR, AND FRACZEK, ADAM, eds. 1979. *Aggression and Behavior Change: Biological and Social Processes*. New York: Praeger Publishers.

FESTINGER, L. 1957. *A Theory of Cognitive Dissonance*. Evanston, Ill.: Row, Peterson & Co.

FISHER, SEYMOUR. 1973. *Body Consciousness*. Englewood Cliffs. N.J.: Prentice-Hall.

FLASTE, R. 1976. Career ambitions: keeping the options open. *New York Times*, February 27, p. 15.

FORD, CLELLAN S., AND BEACH, FRANK A. 1951. *Patterns of Sexual Behavior*. New York: Harper & Row, Publishers.

FOREM, JACK. 1973. *Transcendental Meditation*. New York: E. P. Dutton Co.

FOULKES, DAVID. 1966. *The Pyschology of Sleep*. New York: Charles Scribner's Sons.

FRANK, LAWRENCE K. 1938. *Mental Hygiene XXII*.

———. 1964. Society as the patient. In W. Edgar Vinacke et al., eds., *Dimensions of Social Psychology*. Glenview, Ill.: Scott, Foresman & Co. pp. 50–53.

FRANKL, VIKTOR. 1962. *Man's Search For Meaning: An Introduction to Logotherapy*. Boston: Beacon Press.

FREEDMAN, DANIEL G. 1974. *Human Infancy: An Evolutionary Perspective*. New York: Halstead Press.

FREIDMAN, MEYER, AND ROSENMAN, RAY H. 1974. *Type A Behavior and Your Heart*. New York: Alfred A. Knopf.

FREUD, SIGMUND. 1933. *New Introductory Lectures on Psychoanalysis*. Trans. W. J. H. Sprott. New York: W. W. Norton & Co.

———. 1935(*a*). *The Ego and the Id*. London: Hogarth Press.

———. 1935(*b*). *A General Introduction to Psychoanalysis*. New York: Liverwright Publishing Corp.

———. 1949. *An Outline of Psycho-Analysis*. New York: W. W. Norton & Co.

———. 1952. *The Psychopathology of Everyday Life*, Vol. 6. London: Hogarth Press, pp. 1–310.

———. 1961. *Introductory Lectures on Psychoanalysis*. London: Hogarth Press.

———. 1962(*a*). *The Interpretation of Dreams. vol. v.* 1900. Reprint. The standard edition. London: Hogarth Press.

———. 1962(*b*). *Civilization and Its Discontents*. New York: W. W. Norton & Co.

FRIEDAN, BETTY. 1963. *The Feminine Mystique*. New York: W. W. Norton & Co.

FREIDMAN, MEYER AND ROSENMAN, RAY H. 1981. *Type A Behavior and Your Heart*. New York: Fawcett Book Group.

FRIEZE, IRENE et al. 1978. *Women and Sex Roles: A Social Psychology Perspective*. New York: W. W. Norton & Co.

FROMM, ERICH. 1956. *The Art of Loving: An Inquiry into the Nature of Love*. New York: Harper & Row, Publishers.

———. 1978. *Man for Himself*. New York: Fawcett Book Group.

FUCHS, VICTOR R. 1974. *Who Shall Live? Health, Economics and Social Choice*. New York: Basic Books.

GAGNON, JOHN. 1977. *Human Sexualities*. Glenview, Ill.: Scott, Foresman & Co.

GATCHEL, R. J., AND PRICE, KENNETH P., eds. 1979. *Clinical Applications of Biofeedback: Appraisal and Status*. New York: Pergamon Press.

GATLIN, LILA L. 1972. *Information Theory and the Living System*. New York: Columbia University Press.

GAZZANIGA, M. S., AND LEDOUX, J. D. 1978. *The Integrated Mind*. New York: Plenum Press.

GELLES, RICHARD. 1978. Violence toward children in the United States. *American Journal of Orthopsychiatry* 8 (October): 580–92.

———. 1979. *Family Violence*. Sage Library of Social Research, vol. 84. Beverly Hills, Calif.: Sage Publications.

GINOTT, HAIM C. 1965. *Between Parent and Child*. New York: Hearst Corporation, Avon Books.

———. 1973. *Between Parent and Teenager*. New York: Macmillan Publishing Company, Inc.

GINTZLER, ALAN. 1980. Endorphin-mediated increases in pain threshold during pregnancy. *Science*, October 10, pp. 193–95.

GLASER, BARNEY, G. AND STRAUSS, ANSELM L. 1965. *Awareness of Dying*. Chicago: Aldine Publishing Co.

GLASSER, WILLIAM. 1967. *Reality Therapy*. New York: Harper & Row, Publishers.

———. 1976. *Positive Addiction*. New York: Harper & Row, Publishers.

GLICK, PAUL. 1980. Remarriage: Some recent changes and variations. *Journal of Family Issues*, 1(4): 455–78.

GOETTING, ANN. 1982. The Six Stages of Remarriage: Developmental Tasks of Remarriage After Divorce. *Family Relations* 31 (April): 213–22.

GOLDEN, C. J.; GRABER, B.; BLOSE, I.; BERG, R.; COFFMAN, J.; AND BLOCK, S. 1981. Difference in brain densities between chronic alcoholic and normal control patients. *Science*, January, pp. 508–10.

GOLDSTEIN, HARVEY. 1940. Reading and listening comprehension rates at various controlled rates. *Contributions to Education*, 821. New York: Bureau of Publications, Teachers College, Columbia University.

GOLEMAN, DANIEL. 1977. *The Varieties of the Meditative Experience*. New York: E. P. Dutton.

GOODE, W. J. 1956. *Women in Divorce*. New York: Free Press.

GORDON, A. L. 1964. *Intermarriage*. Boston: Beacon Press.

GORER, GEOFFREY. 1967. *Death, Grief and Mourning*. New York: Doubleday & Co.

GRAYSTYN, E. AND MOLNAR, P. 1981. Sensory Functions: Proceedings of the 28th International Congress, Budapest, 1980. Elmsford, NY: Pergamon Press.

GREELEY, A. M. 1970. Religious intermarriage in a denominational society. *American Journal of Sociology* 75 (May): 949.

GREEN, HANNAH. 1964. *I Never Promised You a Rose Garden*. New York: Holt, Rinehart & Winston.

GRIER, WILLIAM H., AND COBBS, PRICE M. 1961. *Black Rage*. New York: Basic Books.

GROLLMAN, EARLE A. 1971. *Suicide*. Boston: Beacon Press.

GROUP FOR THE ADVANCEMENT OF PSYCHIATRY. 1973. *The Joys and Sorrows of Parenthood*. New York: Charles Scribner's Sons.

GUNTHER, BERNARD. 1968. *Sense Relaxation Below Your Mind*. New York: Collier Books.

GUTMAN, HERBERT. 1967. The biological roots of creativity. In Ross L. Mooney and Taher A. Razik, eds., *Explorations in Creativity*. New York: Harper & Row, Publishers, pp. 3–32.

GUZE, S. B. 1976. *Criminality and Psychiatric Disorders*. New York: Oxford University Press.

HALL CALVIN S. 1966. *The Meaning of Dreams*. New York: McGraw-Hill Book Co.

HALL D. T., AND GORDON, F. E. 1973. Career choices of married women: effects on conflict, role behavior, and satisfaction. *Journal of Applied Psychology* 58: 42–48.

HALL, E. T. 1959. *The Silent Language*. Garden City, N.Y.: Doubleday & Co.

———. 1966. *The Hidden Dimension*. Garden City, N.Y.: Doubleday & Co.

HALLET, JEAN-PIERRE. *Pygmy Kitabu*. 1973. New York: Random House.

HARLOW, H. F. 1958. The nature of love. *American Psychologist* 13: 673–85.

HARLOW, H. F., AND SUOMI, S. J. 1970. Nature of love simplified. *American Psychologist* 25: 161–68.

HARRINGTON MICHAEL. 1963. *The Other America: Poverty in the United States*. New York: Macmillan Co.

HARRIS, THOMAS. 1969. *I'm O.K.—You're O.K.* New York: Harper & Row, Publishers.

HARRISON, RANDALL. 1965. Nonverbal communications: exploration into time, space, action and object. In J. H. Campbell and H. W. Hepler, eds., *Dimensions in Communication*. Belmont, Calif.: Wadsworth Publishing Co., p. 161.

HARTMANN, E. L. 1973. *The Functions of Sleep*. New Haven, Conn.: Yale University Press.

———. 1978. *The Sleeping Pill*. New Haven, Conn.: Yale University Press.

HARTSHORNE, H., AND MAY, M. A. 1928–30. *Studies in the Nature of Character*, vol. 1: *Studies in Deceit*; vol. 2: *Studies in Self-Control*; vol. 3: *Studies in the Organization of Character*. New York: Macmillan Co.

HASSETT, JAMES. 1981. Ethics Survey Report. *Psychology Today*, November, 46–50.

HAUG, MARIE R., AND DOFNY, JACQUES. 1977. *Work and Technology: Studies in International Sociology*, vol. 10. Beverly Hills, Calif.: Sage Publications.

HAUGHEY, J. C. 1975. The commune-child of the 1970's. In J. O. DeLora and J. R. DeLora, eds., *Intimate Life Styles: Marriage and Its Alternatives*, 2nd ed. Pacific Palisades, Calif.: Goodyear Publishing Co., pp. 328–32.

HAYNES, S. N.; FOLLINGSTAD, D. R.; AND McGOWAN, W. T. 1974. Insomnia: sleep patterns and anxiety level. *Journal of Psychosomatic Research* 18: 69–74.

HEATON, R. K., AND VICTOR, R. G. 1976. Personality characteristics associated with psychedelic flashbacks in natural and experimental settings. *Journal of Abnormal Psychology* 85: 83–90.

HEER, D. M. 1974. The prevalence of black-white marriage in the United States, 1960 and 1970. *Journal of Marriage and the Family* 36 (May): 246–58.

HEIDEGGER, MARTIN. 1969. *Discourse Thinking*. Trans. J. M. Anderson and E. H. Freund. New York: Harper & Row, Publishers.

HEIDEGGER, MARTIN et al. 1972. *What Is Called Thinking*. Trans. J. Glen Gray and Fred Wieck. New York: Harper & Row, Publishers.

HELBERG, JUNE. 1983. Documentation in child abuse. *American Journal of Nursing* 83 (February): 236–39.

HENNON, CHARLES, AND COLE, CHARLES. 1981. Role strain and stress in split-shift relationships. *Alternative Life Styles*, 4 (May): 142–45.

HERRIGAN, J., AND HERRIGAN, J. 1973. *Loving Free*. New York; Grosset & Dunlap.

HICKS, ROBERT A. et al. 1979. Test anxiety level of short and long sleeping college students. *Psychological Report* 44 (September): 712–14.

HILGARD, ERNEST. 1965. *Hypnotic Susceptibility*. New York: Harcourt Brace Jovanovich.

———.1978. Hypnosis and consciousness. *Human Nature* 1 (January): 42–49.

HILLER, DANA, AND PHILLIBER, WILLIAM. 1982. Predicting marital and career success among dual-worker families. *Journal of Marriage and the Family* 44 (February): 53–62.

HITTLEMAN, RICHARD. 1975. *Yoga: The 8 Steps to Health and Peace*. New York: Deerfield Communications.

HOFFER, ERIC.1966. *The True Believer*. New York: Harper & Row Publishers, Inc.

HOFFMAN, S. 1977. Marital instability and the economic status of women. *Demography* 14: 67–76.

HOLDEN, CONSTANCE. 1984. Twins: reunited. *Science 80*. In Michael G. Walraven and Hiram E. Fitzgerald, eds. *Annual Editions*. Guilford, Conn.: Dushkin Publishing Group.

HOLMES, DAVID S. 1984. Meditation and somatic arousal reduction. *American Psychologist* 39 (January): 1–9.

HOLMES, T. H., AND RAHE, R. H. 1967. The social readjustment rating scale. *Journal of Psychosomatic Research*. 11: 213–17.

HOLMES, THOMAS H., AND HOLMES, T. STEPHENSON. 1976. Short-term intrusions into the life style routine. *Journal of Psychosomatic Research* 14 (June): 121–32.

HOLMSTROM, LINDA. 1977. *The Two-Career Family*. Cambridge, Mass.: Harvard University Press.

HOOD, J., AND GOLDEN, S. 1979. Beating time/making time: the impact of work scheduling on men's family roles. *Family Coordinator* 28 (October): 572–82.

HORNER, M. 1970(a). The motive to avoid success and changing aspirations of college women, ed. *Change Magazine*. New Rochelle, N.Y.: Women on Campus, 1970. A symposium at Ann Arbor, Mich. Center for Continuing Education of Women.

———. 1970(b). Femininity and successful achievement: a basic inconsistency. In Judith Bardwick et al., eds., *Feminine Personality and Conflict*. Belmont, Calif.: Wadsworth Publishing Co.

———. 1972. Toward an understanding of achievment-related conflicts in women. *Journal of Social Issues* 28: 157–75.

HORNEY, KAREN. 1942. *The Collected Works of Karen Horney*, vol. 2. New York: W. W. Norton & Co.

HOUSEKNECHT, SHARON K. 1978. Voluntary childlessness: a social psychological model. *Alternative Life Styles* 1 (August): 379–402.

———. 1982. Voluntary childlessness: toward a theoretical integration. *Journal of Family Issues* 3 (December): 459–71.

HULL, CLARK L. 1933. *Hypnosis and Suggestibility: An Experimental Approach*. New York: Irvington Publishers.

HULME, KATHRYN. 1966. *Undiscovered Country: A Spiritual Adventure*. Boston: Little, Brown & Co.

HUNT, MORTON. 1959. *The Natural History of Love*. New York: Alfred A. Knopf.

HUNT, MORTON, AND HUNT, BERNICE. 1977. *The Divorce Experience*. New York: McGraw-Hill Book Co.

HUXLEY, ALDOUS. 1970. *Doors of Perception*. New York: Harper & Row, Publishers.

———. 1979(a). *Brave New World*. New York: Harper & Row, Publishers.

———. 1979(*b*). *The Devils of Loudon*. New York: Harper & Row, Publishers.

HUXLEY, LAURA ARCHERA. 1963. *You Are Not the Target*. New York: Farrar, Strauss and Giroux.

INGBER, D. 1982. Yoga and unconsious bodily processes. *Science Digest*, February, pp. 28–29.

ISAACS, CHRISTINE. 1981. A brief review of the characteristics of abuse-prone parents. *Behavior Therapist* 4: 5–7.

JACO, D. E., AND SHEPHERD, M. 1975. Demographic homogeneity and spousal consensus: a methodological perspective. *Journal of Marriage and the Family* 37 (February): 161–69.

JACOBSON, EDMUND. 1938. *Progressive Relaxation*, 2nd ed. Chicago: University of Chicago Press.

———. 1964. *Anxiety and Tension Control, A Physiologic Approach*. Philadelphia: J. B. Lippincott Company.

———. 1976. *You Must Relax*, 5th rev. ed. Wallingford, Conn.: McGraw-Hill Book Co.

JAMES, WILLIAM. 1950. *The Principles of Psychology*. New York: Dover Publications.

JAYNES, JULIAN. 1977. *The Origin of Consciousness in the Breakdown of the Bicameral Mind*. Boston: Houghton Mifflin Co.

JOHNS, M. W.; MASTERSON, J. P.; AND BRUCE, D. W. 1971. Relationship between sleep habits, adrenocortical activity and personality. *Psychosomatic Medicine* 33: 499–507.

JONES, E. E. 1961. *The Life and Works of Sigmund Freud*. New York: Basic Books.

JOURARD, SIDNEY M. 1971. *The Transparent Self: Self-Disclosure and Well-Being*, 2nd ed. New York: Van Nostrand Reinhold Company.

JUBASZ, ANNE M. CREARY. 1980. Adolescent attitudes toward child rearing and family size. *Family Relations* 29 (January): 29–34.

JUNG, CARL G. *Paracelsica*. (*n.a.*)

———. 1924. *Psychological Types or the Psychology of Individuation*. New York: Harcourt Brace Jovanovich, Inc.

———. 1953(*a*). *Collected Works*, vol. 7, *Two Essays on Analytical Psychology*. New York: Bollingen Series.

———. 1953(*b*). *Collected Works: Psychology and Alchemy*. vol. 12. New York: Bollingen Series.

———. 1955. *Modern Man in Search of a Soul*. New York: Harcourt Brace Jovanovich.

———. 1959(*a*). Two essays on analytical psychology. In *Collected Papers*, vol. 7. Princeton, N.J.: Princeton University Press.

———. 1959(*b*). The archetypes and the collective unconscious. In *Collected Works*, vol. 9. Princeton, N.J.: Princeton University Press.

———. 1959(*c*). *Collected Works: Archetypes and the Collective Unconscious*. New York: Bollingen Series.

———. 1963. In *Memories, Dreams, Reflections*, rev. ed. Aniela Jaffe, ed. New York: Pantheon Books.

———. 1964. Approaching the Unconscious. In Carl G. Jung et al., eds., *Man and His Symbols*. Garden City, N.Y.: Doubleday & Co.

———. 1976. *The Portable Jung*. Joseph Campbell, ed. New York: Penguin Books.

JUNG, CARL, G. et al. eds. 1964. *Man and His Symbols*. Garden City, N.Y.: Doubleday & Co.

KAGAN, JEROME. 1978. *The Growth of the Child: Reflections on Human Development*. New York: W. W. Norton & Co.

KANTER, R. 1977. *Work and Family in the United States: A Critical Review and Agenda for Research and Policy*. New York: Russell Sage Foundation.

KASL, STANISLAW, AND COBB, SIDNEY. 1979. Some mental health consequences of plant closing and job loss. In Louis Ferman and Jeanne Gories, eds., *Mental Health and the Economy*. Kalamazoo, Mich.: Upjohn Institute for Employment Research.

KEENE, ROLAND et al. 1976. *Work and the College Student*. Carbondale, Ill.: Southern Illinois University Press.

KELLER, HELEN. 1961. *The Story of My Life*. New York: Dell Publishing Company.

KELLY, GEORGE A. 1974. *The Psychology of Personal Constructs*. Rpt of 1955 ed. New York: W. W. Norton & Company, Inc.

KELSEY, MORTON. 1976. *Healing and Christianity*. New York: Harper & Row, Publishers.

KEMPE, C. HENRY et al. 1962. The battered child. *Journal of the American Medical Association*, July 7.

KEMPE, C. HENRY, AND HELFER, RAY E., eds. 1980. *The Battered Child*. Chicago: University of Chicago Press.

KEPHART, WILLIAM M. 1976. *Extraordinary Groups: The Sociology of Unconventional Life-Styles*. New York: St. Martin's Press.

KIEREN, D.; HENTON, J.; AND MAROLY, R. 1975. *Hers and His: A Problem Solving Approach to Marriage*. Hindsdale, Ill.: Dryden Press.

KINSEY, A. C.; POMEROY, W. B.; AND MARTIN, C. E. 1948. *Sexual Behavior in the Human Male*. Philadelphia: W. B. Saunders Co.

———. 1953. *Sexual Behavior in the Human Female*. Philadelphia: W. B. Saunders Co.

KINZEL, A. S. 1970. Body buffer zone in violent prisoners. *American Journal of Psychiatry* 127: 59–64.

KITTO, HUMPHREY D. 1950. *The Greeks*. New York: Penguin Books.

KLEITMAN, A. NATHANIEL. 1963. *Sleep and Wakefulness*, 2nd ed. Chicago: University of Chicago Press.

KLIMAN, ANNE. 1978. *Psychological First Aid for Recovery and Growth*. New York: Holt, Rinehart & Winston.

KLINE, RICH. 1980. Meditators lower their cholesterol. *Prevention*, April, pp. 111 ff.

KLUCKHOLM, CLYDE. 1949. *Mirror for Man: The Relation of Anthropology to Modern Life*. New York: McGraw-Hill Book Co.

KOHLBERG, LAWRENCE. 1964. *Development of Moral Character and Moral Ideology, Review of Child Development Research*. vol. I. R. S. Hoffman and L. W. Hoffman, eds. New York: Russell Sage Foundation.

———. 1976. In T. Lickona, ed., *Moral Development and Behavior*. New York: Holt, Rinehart & Winston.

———. 1981. *The Philosophy of Moral Development: Es-

says in Moral Development. New York: Harper & Row, Publishers.

KOHLER, WOLFGANG. 1970. *Gestalt Psychology*. New York: Liveright Publishing Corporation.

KOMAROVSKY, MIRRA. 1967. *Blue-Collar Marriage*. New York: Vintage College Books.

KNAPP, MARK L. 1972. *Nonverbal Communication in Human Interaction*. New York: Holt, Rinehart & Winston.

KORRZYBSKI, ALFRED. 1958. *Science and Sanity*, 4th ed. Lakeville, Conn.: Institute of General Semantics.

KRAMER, EDITH. 1977. *Art Therapy in a Children's Community*. New York: Schocken Books.

KRANTZLER, MEL. 1973. *Creative Divorce*. Philadelphia: J. B. Lippincott Co.

KREIS, BERNADINE. 1969. *Up From Grief*. New York: Seabury Press.

KRISHNAMURTI, J. 1972. *You Are the World*. New York: Harper & Row Publishers, Inc.

KUBIE, LAWRENCE S. 1967. Blocks to creativity. In Ross L. Mooney and Taher A. Razik, eds., *Explorations in Creativity*. New York: Harper & Row, Publishers, pp. 33–42.

KÜBLER-ROSS, ELISABETH. 1970. *On Death and Dying*. Riverside, N.J.: Macmillan Co.

KUTASH, I. L.; KUTASH, S. B.; SCHLESINGER, L. B.; & ASSOCIATES. 1978. *Violence: Perspectives on Murder and Aggression*. San Francisco: Jossey-Bass.

LAING, R. D. 1967. *The Politics of the Family and Other Essays*. Westminister, Md: Ballantine Books, Inc.

———. 1976. *The Facts of Life*. New York: Pantheon Books.

LAPPE, FRANCES M. 1971. *Diet for a Small Planet*. New York: Ballantine Books.

LEBOYER, FREDERICK. 1975. *Birth Without Violence*. New York: Alfred A. Knopf.

———. 1976. *Loving Hands: The Traditional Indian Art of Baby Massaging*. New York: Alfred A. Knopf.

———. 1978. *Inner Beauty, Inner Light*. New York: Alfred A. Knopf, Inc.

LEE, IRVING, AND LAURA, LEE. 1968. *Handling Barriers in Communication*. Lakeville, Conn.: Institute of General Semantics.

LELAND, C. et al. 1979. *Men and Women Learning Together: Co-education in the 1980's*. Findings presented at conference: Men/Women/College, The Educational Implications of Sex Roles in Transition, December 1–2, 1978, at Brown University. Report published by Ford, Rockefeller, and Carnegie Foundations.

LEMASTERS, E. E. 1975. *Blue-Collar Aristocrats: Life-Styles at a Working-Class Tavern*. Madison, Wis.: University of Wisconsin Press.

LEVINE, MICHAEL, AND SHEFNER, JEREMY. 1981. *Fundamentals of Sensation and Perception*. Reading, Mass.: Addison-Wesley Publishing Co.

LEVINE, SOL, AND SCOTCH, NORMAN A., eds. 1970. *Social Stress*. Chicago: Aldine Publishing Co.

LEVINSON, DANIEL J.; DARROW, CHARLOTTE N.; KLEIN, EDWARD B.; LEVINSON, MARIA H.; AND MCKEE, PRAXTON. 1978. *The Seasons of a Man's Life*. New York: Alfred A. Knopf.

LICK, J. R., AND HEFFLER, D. 1977. Relaxation training and attention placebo in the treatment of severe insomnia. *Journal of Consulting and Clinical Psychology* 45:153–61.

LIEM, RANSAY, AND LIEM, J. 1979. Social support and stress: some general issues and their application to the problem of unemployment. In L. Ferman and J. Gordus, eds., *Mental Health and the Economy*. Kalamazoo, Mich.: Upjohn Institute for Employment Research.

LIPTON, M. A.; MASCES, D.; AND KELLAN, R. F., eds. 1978. *Psychopharmacology: A Generation of Progress*. New York: Raven Press.

LOPATA, H. Z. 1971. *Occupation: Housewife*. London: Oxford University Press.

LOWEN, ALEXANDER. 1969. *Betrayal of the Body*. New York: Macmillan Co.

———. 1975. *Bioenergetics*. New York: Penguin Books.

LUCE, G. G., AND SEGAL, J. 1969. *Sleep*. New York: Coward, McCann & Geoghegan.

LUDLOW, C. L., AND DORAN-QUINE, M. E., eds. 1979. *The Neurological Basis of Language Disorders in Children: Methods and Directions for Research*. Washington, D.C.: NIH Publication 79 (August): 440.

LYNCH, JAMES J. 1977. *The Broken Heart: The Medical Consequence of Loneliness*. New York: Basic Books.

MCCAREY, JAMES L. 1978. *McCary's Human Sexuality*, 3rd ed. New York: Van Nostrand Reinhold Co.

MCCAULLEY, MARY. 1977. *Application of the Myers Briggs Type Indicator to Medicine and Other Health Professions*. 2 vols. Gainesville, Fla.: Center for Applications of Psychological Type.

———. 1978. *Application of the Myers-Briggs Type Indicator to Medicine and Other Health Professions*, 2 vols. Gainesville, Fla.: Center for Applications of Psychological Type.

MCCLELLAND, DAVID, C.; ATKINSON, J. W.; CLARK, R. A.; AND LOWELL, E. A. 1953. *The Achievement Motive*. New York: Appleton-Century-Crofts.

MCCORMIC, ERNEST J., AND ILGAN, DANIEL R. 1980. *Industrial Psychology*, 7th ed. Prentice-Hall.

MCGRATH, COLLEEN. 1979. The crisis of domestic order. *Socialist Review*. January/February, pp. 11–30.

MCGREGOR, DOUGLAS. 1960. *The Human Side of Enterprise*. Wallingford, Ct.: McGraw-Hill Book Company.

MACKENZIE, NORMAN. 1965. *Dreams and Dreaming*. New York: Vanguard Press.

MACKINNON, DONALD W. 1965. What makes a person creative? In Robert S. Daniel, ed., *Contemporary Readings in General Psychology*, 2nd ed. Boston: Houghton Mifflin Co., pp. 153–57.

———. 1978. *In Search of Human Effectiveness: Identifying and Developing Creativity*. Buffalo, N.Y.: Creative Education Foundation.

MACLEAN, PAULE D. 1973. *Concept of the Brain and Behavior: The Clarence M. Hincks Memorial Lectures*, D. Campbell, I. J. Boag, and A. Levine, eds. Buffalo: N.Y.: Unviersity of Toronto Press.

MADDI, S. R., ed. 1980. *Personality Theories: A Comparative Analysis*, 4th ed. Homewood, Il: Dorsey Press.

MADISON, P. 1969. *Personality Development in College*. Reading, Mass.: Addison-Wesley Publishing Co.

MAGNUSON, ED. 1983. Child Abuse: The Ultimate Betrayal. *Time*, September 5, pp. 20–22.

MAIER, N. R. F. 1949. *Frustrations: A Study of Behavior without a Goal*. New York: McGraw-Hill Book Co.

———. 1973. *Psychology in Industrial Organizations*, 4th ed. Boston: Houghton Mifflin Co.

MARCUSE, HERBERT. 1974. *Eros and Civilization*. Boston: Beacon Press.

MARKS, P. A., AND MONROE, L. J. 1976. *Correlates of adolescent poor sleepers*. *Journal of Abnormal Psychology* 85: 243–46.

MASLOW, ABRAHAM H. 1954. *Motivation and Personality*, 2nd ed. New York: Harper & Row, Publishers.

———. 1976. *The Farther Reaches of Human Nature*. New York: Penguin Books.

MASTERS, WILLIAM H., AND JOHNSON, VIRGINIA E. 1970. *The Pleasure Bond*. Boston: Little, Brown & Co.

MAY, ROLLO. 1953. *Man's Search for Himself*. New York: Dell Publishing Company, Inc.

———. 1973(*a*). *Man's Search for Himself*. New York: Dell Publishing Co.

———. 1973(*b*). *Love and Will*. New York: Dell Publishing Co.

MEAD, MARGARET. 1971. Marriage in two steps. In Herbert Otto, ed., *The Family in Search of a Future*. New York: Appleton-Century-Crofts, pp. 75–84.

———. 1978. *Culture and Commitment: The New Relationships between the Generations in the 70's*, rev. ed. New York: Columbia University Press.

MENNINGER, KARL. 1967. Man against himself. In Joseph F. Perez, ed., *General Psychology: Selected Readings*. New York: Van Nostrand Reinhold Co.

———. 1968. *The Crime of Punishment*. New York: Viking Press.

MITFORD, JESSICA. 1963. *The American Way of Death*. New York: Simon & Schuster.

MONAHAN, T. P. 1966. Interracial marriage and divorce in the state of Hawaii. *Eugenics Quarterly* 13 (March): 40–67.

———. 1970. Are interracial marriages really less stable? *Social Forces* 48 (June): 461–73.

MONROE, L. J., AND MARKS, P. A. 1977. MMPI differences between adolescent poor and good sleepers. *Journal of Consulting and Clinical Psychology* 45: 151–52.

MONTAGU, ASHLEY. 1971. *Touching: The Human Significance of the Skin*. New York: Columbia University Press.

MORRIS, DESMOND. 1967. *The Naked Ape*. New York: McGraw-Hill Book Co.

———. 1970. *The Human Zoo*. New York: Dell Publishing Co.

MOSHER, WILLIAM, AND BACHRACK, CHRISTINE. 1982. Childlessness in the United States: estimates from the national survey of family growth. *Journal of Family Issues* 3 (December): 517–44.

MOSS, THELMA. 1972. *Psychics, Saints and Scientists*. [film] Cos Cob, Conn.: Hartley Film Foundation.

———. 1979. *The Body Electric: A Personal Journey into the Mysteries of Parapsychological Research, Bioenergy and Kirlian Photography*. Los Angeles: J. P. Tarcher.

MOTT, P. E. et al. 1975. *Shift Work: The Social, Psycho-logical, and Physical Consequences*. Ann Arbor: University of Michigan Press.

MOUSSEAU, JACQUES. 1982. The family, prison of love. A conversation with Phillippe Aries. In Lawrence R. Allman and Dennis T. Jaffe, eds., *Readings in Adult Psychology: Contemporary Perspectives*. New York: Harper & Row, Publishing.

MURSTEIN, B. I. 1971. A theory of marital choice and its applicability to marriage adjustment. In B. I. Murstein, ed., *Theories of Attraction and Love*. New York: Springer Publishing Co.

MUSSEN, PAUL HENRY; CONGER, JOHN J. WADE; KAGAN, JEROME; AND GEIWITZ, JAMES. 1979. *Psychological Development: A Life-Span Approach*. New York: Harper & Row, Publishers.

———. 1980. *Essentials of Child Development and Personality*. New York: Harper & Row, Publishers.

MYERS, CHARLES S. 1977. *Industrial Psychology*. Leon Stein, ed., New York: Arno Press.

NARANJO, CLAUDIO, AND ORNSTEIN, ROBERT E. 1971. *On the Psychology of Meditation*. New York: Viking Press.

NEAL ROBERT E. 1971. *The Art of Dying*. New York: Harper & Row, Publishers.

NEIDLE, CECYLE S. 1975. *America's Immigrant Women*. Boston: Twayne Publishers.

NEILL, A. S. 1978. *Freedom Not License!* New York: PBI Books.

NESBITT, JOHN. 1982. *Megatrends: Ten New Directions Transforming Our Lives*. New York: Warner Books.

NEWCOMB, MICHAEL and BENTLER, PETER. 1980. Assessment of personality and demographic aspects of cohabitation and marital success. *Journal of Personality Development 4*. (1) 11–24.

NEWMAN, BARBARA M., AND NEWMAN, PHILIP R. 1983. *Understanding Adulthood*. New York: CBS College Publishing, Holt, Rinehart & Winson.

NEWMAN, HORATIO, et al. 1982. *Twins: Study of Heredity and Environment*. Chicago: University of Chicago Press.

NEWTON, NILES, AND MODIIL, CHARLOTTE. 1980. Pregnancy: the closest human relationship. In Paul Henry Mussen, John J. Wade Conger, and Jerome Kagan, eds. *Readings in Child and Adolescent Psychology: Contemporary Perspectives*. New York: Harper & Row, Publishers, pp. 3–12.

NICHOLS, SHARON, AND METZEN, EDWARD. 1982. Impact of wife's employment upon husband's housework. *Journal of Family Issues*. 3 (June): 199–216.

NYE, F. I. 1976. *Role Structure and Analysis of the Family*. Beverly Hills, Calif.: Sage Publications.

NYE, F. I., AND BERARDO, F. M. 1973. *The Family: Its Structure and Interaction*. New York: Macmillan Co.

OAKLEY, ANN. 1974. *Sociology of Housework*. New York: Pantheon Books.

O'NEILL, NENA, AND O'NEILL, GEORGE. 1972. *Open Marriage: A New Life Style for Couples*. New York: M. Evans & Co.

O'REILLY, JANE. 1983. Wife beating: the silent crime. *Time*, September 5, pp. 23–26.

ORNE, MARTIN. 1982. In James V. McConnell, *Under-*

standing Human Behavior, 4th ed. New York: Holt, Rinehart & Winston, pp. 397–98.

ORNE-JOHNSON, D. 1973. Automatic stability and transcendental meditation. *Psychosomatic Medicine*, 35: 341–49.

ORNSTEIN, ROBERT E. 1977. *The Psychology of Consciousness*, 2nd ed. New York: Harcourt Brace Jovanovich.

————. 1978. The split and whole brain. *Human Nature* 1: 76–83.

OUSPENSKY, P. D. 1971. *The Fourth Way: A Record of Talks and Answers to Questions Based on the Teaching of G. I. Gurdjieff*. New York: Vintage Books.

PACKARD, VANCE. 1972. *A Nation of Strangers*. New York: Pocket Books.

PAFFENBARGER, R. S., AND ASNES, D. P. 1966. Chronic disease in former college students. III: Precursors of suicide in early and middle life. *American Journal of Public Health* 56: 1036.

PAFFENBARGER, RALPH S. et al. 1966(*a*). Chronic disease in former college students. I: Early precursors of fatal coronary heart disease. *American Journal of Epidemiology* 83: 328.

————. 1966(*b*). Chronic disease in former college students. II: Methods of study and observations on mortality from coronary heart disease. *American Journal of Public Health* 56: 97.

PAFFENBARGER, R. S.; THOME, M. C.; AND WING, A. L. 1968. Chronic disease in former college students. IX: Characteristics in youth predisposing to hypertension in later years. *American Journal of Epidemiology* 88: 25.

PAFFENBARGER, R. S.; KING, S. H.; AND WING, A. L. 1969. Chronic disease in former college students. IV: Characteristics in youth that predispose to suicide and accidental death in later life. *American Journal of Public Health* 59: 900.

PARKES, COLIN. 1972. *Bereavement: Studies of Grief in Adult Life*. New York: International Universities Press.

PARSONS, JACQUELINE. 1982. Sexual socialization and gender roles in childhood. In Elizabeth Allgeier and Naomi McCormick, eds., *Gender Roles and Sexual Behavior*. Palo Alto, Calif.: Mayfield Publishing Co.

PARSONS, J. E.; FRIEZE, I. H.; AND RUBLE, D. N. 1983. Intrapsychic factors influencing career aspirations in college women. In Barbara M. Newman and Philip R. Newman. *Understanding Adulthood*. New York: CBS College Publishing, Holt, Rinehart & Winston.

PAVLOV, IVAN P. 1927. *Conditioned Reflexes*. London: Oxford University Press.

————. 1960. *Conditioned Reflexes*. New York: Dover Publications.

————. 1979. *Lectures on Conditioned Reflexes*. 1927. Reprint. New York: St. Martin's Press.

PEARCE, JOSEPH C. 1971. *Crack in The Cosmic Egg*. New York: Julian Press.

PEARLIN, L. I. 1975. Status inequality and stress in marriage. *American Socioloigcal Review* 40: 344–57.

PEARSON, LINNEA. 1977. *Separate Paths*. New York: Harper & Row, Publishers.

PERLS, FREDERICK S. 1967(*a*). *Gestalt Therapy Verbatim*.

John A. Stevens, ed. Lafayette, Calif.: Real People Press.

————. 1967(*b*). *In and Out of the Garbage Pail*. Lafayette, Calif.: Real People Press.

PERLS, FREDERICK S. et al. 1951. *Gestalt Therapy: Excitement and Growth in the Human Personality*. New York: Dell Publishing Co.

PERRY, W. G. 1970. *Forms of Intellectual and Ethical Development in the College Years*. New York: Holt, Rinehart & Winston.

PETERS, FRITZ. 1964. *Boyhood with Gurdjieff*. George Ivanovich, ed. New York: E. P. Dutton.

PETERSON. 1983. Survey on young married and extramarital sexuality, 2 parts. *Playboy*, January, p. 108; March, p. 90.

PFEIFFER, E. 1974. *Successful Aging*. Durham, N.C.: Duke University Center for the Study of Aging and Human Development.

PHILLIPS, DOROTHY BERKLEY; HOWES, ELIZABETH BOYDON; AND NIXON, LUCILLE M., eds. 1975. *The Choice Is Always Ours: An Anthology on the Religious Way*. New York: Harper & Row, Publishers.

PIAGET, JEAN. 1970. *Genetic Epistemology*. New York: Columbia University Press.

————. 1973. *The Child and Reality: Problems of Genetic Psychology*. Trans. A. Rosin. Brooklyn Heights, N.Y.: Beekman Publishers.

————.1976. *The Grasp of Consciousness: Action and Concept in the Young Child*. Cambridge, Mass.: Harvard Unviersity Press.

PICKENS, R. W., AND HESTON, L. L., eds. 1979. *Psychiatric Factors in Drug Abuse*. New York: Grune & Stratton.

PINE, D. 1982. Meditators' atypical response to norepinephrine. *Health* 14 (July): 16.

PITTS, F. N., AND McCLURE, J. N. 1967. Lactate metabolism in anxiety neurosis. *New England Journal of Medicine* 277: 1329–36.

PLATKIN, S. 1981. The give and take of a 2 paycheck marriage. In *Marriage and Family 81/82 Annual Edition*. Guilford, Conn.: Dushkin Publishing Group, pp. 80–82.

POLANYI, MICHAEL. 1969. *Knowing and Being*. Chicago: University of Chicago Press.

POLOMA, M. M. 1972. Role conflict in the married professional woman. In C. Safilios-Rothschild, ed., *Toward a Sociology of Women*. Lexington, Mass.: Xerox.

PRABHAVANANDA, SWAMI, AND ISHERWOOD, CHRISTOPHER. 1953. *How to Know God: The Yoga Aphorisms of Patanjali*. New York: Harper & Row, Publishers.

PREBISH, CHARLES S. 1983. Running can be a religious experience. *Runner's World*, May, p. 106.

PRICE, JANE. 1982. Who waits to have children? and why? In Jeffrey Rosenfeld, ed., *Relationships: The Marriage and Family Reader*. Glenview, Ill.: Scott, Foresman & Co.

PROGOFF, IRA. 1975. *At a Journal Workshop: The Basic Text and Guide for Using the Intensive Journal*. New York: Dialogue House Library.

PROPPER, A. M. 1972. The relationship of maternal employment to adolescent roles, activities, and parental relationships. *Journal of Marriage and the Family* 34 (August): 417–21.

PROVENCE, SALLY, AND LIPTON, ROSE C. 1963. *Infants in Institutions*. New York: International Universities Press.

PUTNEY, SNELL, AND PUTNEY, GAIL J. 1972. *The Adjusted American: Normal Neuroses in the Individual and Society*. New York: Harper & Row, Publishers.

QUINN, R. P., AND STAINES, G. L. 1978. *The 1977 Quality of Employment Survey*. Ann Arbor: Institute for Social Research, University of Michigan.

QUINN, R. P.; STAINES, G. L.; AND McCULLOUGH, M. 1974. *Job Satisfaction: Is There a Trend?* Washington, D.C.: U.S. Department of Labor, Manpower Research, monograph no. 30.

RAHE, RICHARD H. 1974. Life change and subsequent illness reports. In E. K. Gunderson and Richard H. Rahe, eds., *Life Stress and Illness*. Springfield, Ill.: Charles C Thomas, pp. 60–61.

RAPOPORT, R. AND RAPOPORT, R. N. 1971. *Dual-Career Families*. New York: Penguin Books.

————. 1974. The dual-career family: a variant pattern and social change. In Arlene Skolnick and Jerome Skolnick, eds., *Intimacy, Family and Society*.

RAYBIN, J. B., AND DETRE, T. P. 1969. Sleep disorder and symptomology among medical and nursing students. *Comprehensive Psychiatry* 10: 452–62.

REES, W. D., AND LUTKINS, S. G. 1967. Mortality of bereavement. *British Medical Journal* 4:13.

REICH, WILHELM. 1949. *Character Analysis*. New York: Farrar, Strauss & Giroux.

REISS, I. L. 1973. Toward a sociology of the heterosexual love relationship. In M. E. Lasswell and T. E. Lasswell, eds., *Love, Marriage, Family: A Developmental Approach*. Glenview, Ill.: Scott, Foresman & Co.

RENAULT, MARY. 1958. *The King Must Die*. New York: Pantheon Books.

RENNE, K. S. 1970. Correlates of dissatisfaction in marriage. *Journal of Marriage and the Family* 33 (February): 54–67.

RENWICH, P.; AND LAWLER, E. 1978. What you really want from your job. *Psychology Today*, December, pp. 53–65.

RICE, F. P. 1966. *Harmony in Marriage*, bulletin 531. Orono: University of Maine, Cooperative Extension Service.

RICE, PHILIP F. 1979. *Marriage and Parenthood*. Boston: Allyn & Bacon.

RICE, RUTH D. et al. 1977. *21st Century Obstetrics Now*. Chapel Hill, N.C.: Napocic Publications.

RICHARDSON, J. G. 1979. Wife occupational superiority and marital troubles: an examination of the hypothesis. *Journal of Marriage and the Family*, 41: 63–72.

RIEGLE, DONALD. 1982. The psychological and social effects of unemployment. *American Psychologist* 37 (October): 1113–15.

RIESMAN, DAVID. 1973. *Lonely Crowd: A Study of the Changing American Character*. Abrvd. by D. Riesman et al., eds. New Haven, Conn.: Yale University Press.

RIGGS, KATHRYN. 1983. The battered woman: what makes her tick? Women's Crisis Support and Shelter Services of Santa Cruz County. In Bryan Strong et al., *The Marriage and Family Experience*. New York: West Publishing Co.

ROBERTSON, SEONAID. 1963. *Rosegarden and Labyrinth: A Study in Art Education*. Boston: Routledge & Kegan Paul.

ROGERS, CARL R. 1951. *Client-Centered Therapy*. Boston: Houghton Mifflin Co.

————. 1961. *On Becoming a Person*. Boston: Houghton Mifflin Co.

————. 1969. *Freedom to Learn*. Columbus, Ohio: Charles E. Merrill Publishing Co.

————. 1971. Toward a modern approach to values: the valuing process in the mature person. In Carl Rogers and Barry Stevens, eds., *Person to Person: The Problem of Being Human*. New York: Pocket Books, pp. 19–20.

————. 1973. *Becoming Partners*. New York: Dell Publishing Co.

————. 1979. *Freedom to Learn*, rev. ed. Columbus, Ohio: Charles E. Merrill Publishing Co.

ROKEACH, MILTON. 1973. *The Nature of Human Values*. New York: Free Press.

————. 1979. *Understanding Human Values: Individual and Societal*. New York: Free Press.

ROLLINS, B., AND GALLIGAN, R. 1978. The developing child and marital satisfaction of parents. In R. Lerner and G. Spanier, eds., *Child Influences on Marital and Family Interaction: A Life-Span Perspective*. New York: Academic Press, pp. 71–105.

ROSNER, STANLEY, AND ABT, LAWRENCE E., eds. 1970. *The Creative Experience*. New York: Grossman Publishers.

ROSS, HEATHER, AND SAWHILL, ISABEL. 1975. *Time of Transition*. Washington: Washington, D.C. Urban Institute.

ROSSI, ALICE S. 1982. Transition to parenthood. In Lawrence R. Allman and Dennis T. Jaffe, eds., *Readings in Adult Psychology: Contemporary Perspectives*. New York: Harper & Row, Publishers, pp. 263–76.

RUBIN, V., AND COMITAS, L. 1975. *Ganja in Jamaica*. Hawthorne, N.Y.: Mouton Publishers.

RUBIN, LILLIAN. 1976. *Worlds of Pain*. New York: Basic Books.

RUSSELL, BERTRAND. 1981. *Mysticism and Logic and Other Essays*, 2nd ed. B & N.

RUSSELL, DIANA. 1982. *Rape In Marriage*. New York: Macmillan Co.

SATIR, VIRGINIA et al. 1976. Changing with families. *Science and Behavior*.

SAWREY, J. M., AND TELFORD, C. W. 1971. *Psychology of Adjustment*. Boston: Allyn & Bacon.

SCANZONI, J. H. 1968. A social system analysis of dissolved and existing marriages. *Journal of Marriage and Family* 30 (August): 451–61.

SCANZONI, JOHN, AND FOX, G. L. 1980. Sex roles, family and society: the seventies and beyond. *Journal of Marriage and the Family* 42 (November): 743–56.

Schachter, Stanley. 1959. *The Psychology of Affiliation*. Stanford, Calif.: Stanford University Press.

Scheeckit, Marc A. 1979. *Drug and Alcohol Abuse: A Clinical Guide to Diagnosis and Treatment*. New York: Plenum Medical Books.

Scheflen, Albert E. 1973. *Body Language and Social Order*. Englewood Cliffs, N.J.: Prentice-Hall.

Schneidman, Edwin S. 1973. *Death of a Man*. New York: New York Times.

Schneidman, Edwin et al. 1970. *The Psychology of Suicide*. New York: Jason Aronson.

Schreiber, Flora Rheta. 1973. *Sybil*. Chicago: Henry Regnery Co.

Schultz, J. H. and Luthe, W. O., eds. 1969. *Antogenic therapy. Vol. III: Applications in psychotherapy*. New York: Grune & Stratton, Inc.

Schweitzer, Albert. 1980. *Reverence for Life*. Trans. R. H. Foller. 1969. Reprint. New York: Irvington Publishers.

Sears, Robert R.; Maccoby, E. E.; and Levin, H. 1957. *Patterns of Child Rearing*. New York: Harper & Row, Publishers.

Seligman, Martin E. 1975. *Helplessness: On Depression, Development and Death*. San Francisco: W. H. Freeman & Co.

Selye, Hans. 1956. *The Stress of Life*. New York: McGraw-Hill Book Co.

Sennett, Richard. 1969. Genteel backlash? Chicago 1886. In S. Thernstorm and R. Sennett, eds., *Nineteenth Century Cities*. New Haven, Conn.: Yale University Press.

Shanas, Ethel. 1962. *The Health of Older People: A Social Survey*. Cambridge, Mass.: Harvard University Press.

Sheehy, Gail. 1976. *Passages*. New York: E. P. Dutton & Co.

Sheldon, William H.; Stevens, S. S.; and Tucker, W. B. 1940. *The Varieties of Human Physique*. New York: Harper & Row, Publishers.

Shostrom, Everett. 1968. *Man the Manipulator*. New York: Bantam Books.

———. 1969. Let the buyer beware. *Psychology Today*, May, pp. 38–40.

Singer, Jerome L. 1975. *The Inner World of Daydreaming*. New York: Harper & Row, Publishers.

Skinner, B. F. 1938. *The Behavior of Organisms*. Englewood, N.J.: Prentice-Hall, Inc.

———. 1971. *Beyond Freedom and Dignity*. New York: Bantam/Vintage Books.

Skinner, Denise. 1980. Dual-career family stress and coping: a literature review. *Family Relations* 29 (October).

Snyder, S. H. 1976. The dopamine hypothesis of schizophrenia. *American Journal of Psychiatry* 133: 197–202.

Snyder, S. H.; Banerfee, S. P.; Yamanura, H. I.; and Greenberg, D. 1974. Drugs, neurotransmitters, and schizophrenia. *Science* 184: 1243–53.

Southey. 1819. *History of Brazil*. London, vol. iii.

Sperry, R. W. 1974. Lateral specialization in the surgically separated hemispheres. In F. O. Schmidt and F. G. Worden, eds., *The Neuro-Sciences: Third Study Program*. Cambridge, Mass.: MIT Press.

———. 1975. Left-brain, right-brain. *Saturday Review*, 2, 30–33.

Spranger, Eduard. 1928. *Types of Men: The Psychology and Ethics of Personality*. Trans. 5th Ger. ed. New York: Johnson Reprint Corp.

Springer, Sally, P. and Deutsch, Georg. 1981. *Left Brain, Right Brain*. San Francisco: W. H. Freeman & Co.

Stamfl, Thomas G. and Lewis, Donald J. 1967. Essentials of implosive therapy. *Journal of Abnormal Psychology* 72 (December): 496–503.

Stein, Peter. 1976. *Single*. Englewood Cliffs, N.J.: Prentice-Hall, Inc.

Sternglanz, S., and Lyberger-Ficek, S. 1975. *An Analysis of Sex Differences in Academic Interactions in the College Classroom*. Denver: Paper presented to the biennial meeting of the Society for Research in Child Development.

Storms, Lowell H. 1976. Implosive therapy: an alternative to systematic desensitization. In Virginia Binder et al., eds., *Modern Therapies*. Englewood Cliffs, N.J.: Prentice-Hall.

Strauss, Murray et al. 1980. *Behind Closed Doors*. Garden City, N.Y.: Anchor Books.

Strong, Bryan; DeVault, Christine; Suid, Murray; and Reynolds, Rebecca. 1983. *The Marriage and Family Experience*, 2nd ed. New York: West Publishing Co.

Sullivan, Harry, S. 1953. *The Interpersonal Theory of Psychiatry*, S. Penry and M. S. Gowel, eds. New York: W. W. Norton & Co.

Super, C. M. 1980. Cognitive development: looking across at growing up. In C. M. Super and S. Harkness, eds., *New Directions for Child Development, No. 8. Anthropological Perspectives on Child Development*. San Francisco: Jossey-Bass.

Suzuki, D. T. 1956. *Zen Buddhism, Selected Writings of D. T. Suzuki*, William Barrett, ed. Garden City, N.Y.: Doubleday-Anchor Books.

Swartz, Helen M., and Swartz, Marvin. 1976. *Disraeli's Reminiscences*. Briarcliff Manor, N.Y.: Stein & Day.

Szasz, Thomas. 1974. *The Myth of Mental Illness: Foundations of a Theory of Personal Conduct*, rev. ed. New York: Harper & Row, Publishers.

Tart, Charles T. 1969. *Altered States of Consciousness: A Book of Readings*. New York: John Wiley & Sons.

———. 1972. *Altered States of Consciousness*. Garden City, N.Y.: Doubleday & Co.

———. 1975. *States of Consciousness*. Guilford, Conn.: E. P. Dutton Publishing Group.

Tavris, Carol, and Sadd, Susan. 1977. *The Redbook Report on Female Sexuality*. New York: Dell Publishing Co.

Taylor, Edward B. 1964. *Early History of Mankind*. Chicago: University of Chicago Press.

Terkel, Studs. 1970. *Hard Times*. New York: Pantheon Books.

———. 1974. *Working People Talk About What They Do All Day and How They Feel About What They Do*. New York: Pantheon Books.

———. 1975. *Working*. New York: Avon Books.

THIGPEN, CORBETT H., AND CLECKLEY, HERVEY M. 1957. *The Three Faces of Eve*. New York: McGraw-Hill Book Co.

THOMAS, A.; CHESS, S.; AND BIRCH, H. G. 1970. The origin of personality. *Scientific American*, August, 102–109.

THOMAS, CAITLIN. 1957. *Left-over Life to Kill*. Boston: Little, Brown & Co.

THURROW, LESTER. 1982., The cost of unemployment. *Newsweek*, October 4, p. 70.

TIFFANY, DONALD et al. 1970. *The Unemployed: A Social-Psychological Portrait*. Englewood Cliffs, N.J.: Prentice-Hall.

TIMMONS, F. 1978. Freshman withdrawal from college: a positive step toward identity formation? A follow-up study. *Journal of Youth and Adolescence*, 7: 159–73.

TOFFLER, ALVIN. 1970. *Future Shock*. New York: Random House.

TRANQUILLUS, SUETONIUS C. 1923. *Lives of the Twelve Caesars*. Trans. Philemon Holland. New York: E. P. Dutton.

TSANG, Y. C. 1938. Hunger motivation in gastrectomized rats. *Journal of Comparative Psychology* 26 (January): 1–17.

TURKINGTON, C. 1983. Drugs found to block dapamine receptors. *APA Monitor*, April, p. 11.

UNDERHILL, EVELYN. 1960. *Practical Mysticism*. New York: E. P. Dutton.

———. 1977. *The Spiritual Life*. New York: Harper & Row, Publishers.

U.S. BUREAU OF CENSUS. 1980. Marital status and living arrangements: March, 1979. In *Current Population Reports*, series P-20, p. 349. Washington, D.C.: Government Printing Office.

VANDENHAAG, E. 1973. Love and marriage? In M. E. Lasswell and T. E. Lasswell, eds., *Love, Marriage, Family: A Developmental Approach*. Glenview, Ill.: Scott, Foresman & Co.

VANGENNEP, ARNOLD. 1960. *The Rites of Passage*. Chicago: University of Chicago Press.

WALKER, KATHRYN. 1982. At home: organizing eases the load. *U.S. News and World Report*, January 25, pp. 52–53.

WALKER, LEONORE. 1979. *The Battered Woman*. New York: Harper & Row, Publishers.

———. 1981. Battered women: sex roles and clinical issues. *Professional Psychology* 12 (February): 81–91.

WALLIS, CLAUDIA. 1983. Reported by Ruth Mehrtens Galvin/Boston and Dick Thompson/San Francisco. Medicine. *Time*, June 6, pp. 50–54.

WALSTER, E.; BERSCHEID, E.; AND WALSTER, G. W. 1973. New directions in equity research. *Journal of Personality and Social Psychology* 25 (February): 151–76.

WALSTER, E., AND WALSTER, G. W. 1978. *A New Look at Love*. Cambridge, Mass.: Addison-Wesley Publishing Co.

WARNER, W. LLOYD et al. 1949. *Social Class in America*. Chicago: Science Research Institutes.

WATSON, J. B. 1970. *Behaviorism*. New York: W. W. Norton & Company.

WATSON, J. B., AND RAYNOR, J. 1920. Conditioned emotional reactions. *Journal of Experimental Psychology* 3: 1–4.

WATTS, ALAN. 1970. *Nature, Man and Woman*. New York: Random House.

WECHSLER, D. 1949. *Wechsler Intelligence Scale for Children (WISC)*. New York: Psychological Corporation.

WEIL, G., AND GOLDFRIED, M. R. 1973. Treatment of insomnia in an eleven-year-old child through self-relaxation. *Behavior Therapy* 4: 282–94.

WHITE, R. 1976. *The Enterprise of Living*, 2nd ed. New York: Holt, Rinehart & Winston.

WHYTE, L. L. 1979. *The Unconscious Before Freud*. New York: St. Martin Press, Inc.

WHYTE, WILLIAM. 1952. *The Organization Man*. New York: Simon & Schuster.

WILLER, J. C.; DEHEN, HENRI; AND CAMBIER, JEAN. 1981. Stress-induced analgesics in humans: endogenous opiords and naloxone-reversible depression of pain reflexes. *Science* 212: 689–90.

WILLIAMS, JUANITA. 1980. Sexuality in marriage. In Benjamin Wolman and John Money, eds., *Handbook of Human Sexuality*. Englewood Cliffs, N.J.: Prentice-Hall.

WILLIAMS, ROGER. 1969. *Biochemical Individuality: The Basis for the Genototrophic Concept*. Austin: University of Texas Press.

———. 1977. *Free and Unequal: The Biological Basis of Individual Liberty*. Indianapolis: Liberty Press-Liberty Classics.

WILSON, A. B. 1959. Residential segregation of social classes and aspirations of high school boys. *American Sociological Review* 24: 836–45.

WILSON, COLIN. 1967. Existential psychology: a novelist's approach. In J. F. T. Bugental, ed., *Challenges of Humanistic Psychology*. New York: McGraw-Hill Book Co.

WILSON, S. R., AND WISE, L. 1975. *The American Citizen: 11 Years After High School*. Palo Alto, Calif.: American Institute for Research.

WOLFF, HAROLD G. 1962. A concept of disease in man. *Psychosomatic Medicine* 24 (January/February): 25–30.

WOLFF, W. 1943. *The Expression of Personality*. New York: Harper & Row, Publishers.

WOLPE, J. 1958. *Psychotherapy by Reciprocal Inhibition*. Stanford, Calif.: Stanford Unviersity Press.

———. 1973. *The Practice of Behavior Therapy*. New York: Pergamon Press.

WOOD, ERNEST E. 1972. Practical Yoga. N. Hollywood, Calif.: Wilshire Book Co.

WOODRUFF, R. A., JR.; GOODWIN, D. N.; AND GUZE, S. B. 1974. *Psychiatric Diagnosis*. New York: Oxford University Press.

WYLIE, PHILIP. 1955. *A Generation of Vipers*. New York: Holt, Rinehart & Winston.

WYLIE, PHILIP. 1971. *Sons and Daughters of Mom*. Garden City, N.Y.: Doubleday & Co.

YARROW, M. et al. 1962. Child-rearing in families of working and non-working mothers. *Sociometry* 25: 122–40.

YOGANANDA, PARAMAHANSA. 1972. *Autobiography of a Yogi*. Los Angeles: Self-Realization Fellowship.

YORBURG, B. 1973. *The Changing Family: A Sociological Perspective*. New York: Columbia University Press.

YOUNG, MICHAEL; BENJAMIN, B.; AND WALLIS, C. 1963. Mortality of widowers. *Lancet* 2: 454.

ZILBOORG, G., AND HENRY, G. W. 1941. *A History of Medical Psychology*. New York: W. W. Norton & Co.

ZINSSER, HANS. 1935. *Rats, Lice and History*. Boston: Little, Brown & Co.

Glossary

Note: The following glossary defines words and terms as they are used in this book rather than as they would be defined by a standard dictionary. If the term you are seeking is not here or still unclear, you may also want to consult the index.

abnormal: Describes behavior that deviates from the standard or average: the negative extreme as in low intellectual functioning or schizophrenic behavior.

absenteeism: The incidence of workers who do not report to work for whatever reason, including sickness, death in the family, as a sign of protest, or for purposes of plant sabotage.

abstraction: A concept or idea developed in the mind that may or may not have a valid basis in reality.

acceptance: The final stage of the acceptance of death, according to Elizabeth Kübler-Ross. The person has disengaged from the world and calmly awaits death.

accident proneness: The tendency to have more than the average number of accidents.

accommodation: Piaget uses this term for one of the twin processes by which we learn ever larger adaptations (intelligent choices) to the universe. We take in or *assimilate* the experiences of the world; then we respond (accommodate) to these experiences by enlarging one or more of our present schemas so as to fully incorporate the new event or understanding.

accusing behavior: Instead of accepting a problem as a breakdown in communication or purpose, the person lashes out at the other with accusations or blame.

acute: Sudden, sharp, and critical, demanding immediate attention, as compared to *chronic*.

adaptation: According to Piaget, the number of elements in, and the complexity of, an organism's response repertory and use of the environment.

addiction: Reliance on anything to the point of dependence where one feels physically or psychologically depressed without it.

adjustment psychology: The psychological thrust of the first half of the twentieth century (roughly), in which the person was expected to adjust to problematic situations in contrast to the humanistic thrust. (See *humanistic psychology*.)

adolescence: In human beings the period from puberty to early adulthood, roughly from the early teens to the early twenties.

adolescent egocentrism: According to David Elkind, adolescence is frequently marked by the inability to see a situation from any viewpoint other than one's own. (See also *egocentric thinking*.)

adultery: The violation of monogamous commitment and expectations.

Aesop's fables: A series of short stories by a Greek named Aesop. In these stories, written down almost two thousand years ago, animals act like humans, and human foibles are revealed in much the same way as in the Uncle Remus stories or many nursery tales.

aesthetic orientation: According to Spranger, the personality type of the individual who is motivated by beauty. Examples: the artist, the rose-herder, the art collector.

affect: The emotional "tone"-state of the person as contrasted to the intellectual or cognitive function. Some persons have little affect and seem to have fewer *warm* emotions.

affective processes: Affective denotes any state that deals with emotions or feelings. It is most often used in contrast to *cognitive* or *thinking functions*.

agism or ageism: The tendency to isolate the elderly and maintain prejudicial and stereotypic attitudes toward them.

Alanon: A spinoff organization of Alcoholics Anonymous. Small groups of persons who are related to or are friends of alcoholics meet to share, discuss, and work through mutual alcohol-related problems.

alarm reaction: The first stage of Seylë's general adaptation syndrome. Experimental animals under stress act, look, and are sick or diseased.

Alateen: A support group for children of alcoholics, who come together to share, discuss, and work through the problems associated with having one or two alcoholic parents.

Alcoholics Anonymous (AA): A support group for persons who are alcoholic. Meetings are composed of persons who are or have been alcohol abusive. Group meetings are designed for educational, rehabilitative, therapeutic, and social purposes.

altered state of consciousness (ASC): A distinctive change in one's perception of the universe and/or one's self-awareness. An ASC can be induced in many ways: drugs, starvation, sensory deprivation, meditation, sensory stimulation, religious experiences, and the like.

ambivalence: The existence of contradictory feelings toward a given situation.

"American way of death": As described by Jessica Mitford, Americans deal with death as if it were an elaborate and expensive show, which denies the reality and finality of death.

amnesia: Memory loss, usually following severe physical or catastrophic emotional events.

amphetamines: Drugs that speed up the neural functioning of the central nervous system. They are sometimes used as stimulants in depression and as diet pills in obesity. Most drug abusers call them *speed*.

anal personality (anal character): A person with fairly consistent patterns of behavior associated with bowel training. Character traits that result can be conceit, suspicion, ambition, obstinacy, defiance, miserliness, avarice, orderliness, and compulsive behavior.

anal stage: The second stage of Freud's psychosocial development, in which the libido is fixated at the anus. If the person remains fixated at this level, he or she exhibits an anal personality. (See *anal personality*.)

analgesic: Any drug that blocks the pain receptors but does not interrupt the functioning of the touch receptors. Aspirin is our most popular analgesic.

anesthetic: Any drug or other agent that renders the organism insensitive to all stimulation. It is usually accompanied by loss of consciousness.

anger: The second stage of Kübler-Ross's stages of acceptance of death. The person feels that he or she has been the victim of an outrage and may vent his or her anger on the doctor, nurses, spouse, children, friends, etc.

Anima/Animus: According to Jung, the anima represents the feminine polarity in a man's personality and is his inspiration and creativity when he allows himself to get in touch with it. The animus is the unconscious male component in a woman's personality and represents her intellectual and creative aspect.

animism: Primitive cause-and-effect explanations of natural events. Common phenomena such as lightning, accidents, sickness, and famine are attributed to malicious spirits or angry gods, who must be placated.

antagonistic behaviors: Those behaviors that cannot normally occur at the same time. Wolpe uses antagonistic behaviors to decondition a person's fears. If a person can stay relaxed while visualizing a feared object or event, the phobia will extinguish, since fear cannot exist in a state of relaxation.

antibuse: A drug developed to help alcoholics "kick the habit." This drug induces nausea and vomiting when the person drinks alcohol.

anxiety: Generalized feelings of apprehension, dread, and uneasiness often having to do with future events and anticipation of disaster. Anxiety differs from fear in that the latter is associated with a specific object or event, while anxiety is a diffuse emotion seemingly unconnected to specific situations. (See also *global anxiety* and *social anxiety*.)

anxiety neurosis: An emotional state that results in physiological symptoms. Among many others, these symptoms can be "queasy" stomach, insomnia, headaches, tics, alcoholism and drug abuse, excessive smoking, and overeating. (See also *character neurosis*.)

apathy: Listlessness, indifference. One of the consequences of overwhelming frustration.

Archetypal themes: These are the great themes of "the human condition:" birth, life, suffering, death, rebirth, transcendence, and transfiguration. They are also the themes of art, religion, literature, philosophy, and existential psychology.

Archetype: A Jungian concept that refers to the autonomous forces in the collective or racial unconscious. These archetypes represent the psychological development of the human race and are frequently expressed in art, religious symbolism, literature, mythology, and dreams. (See also *wise old man, wise old woman, wise child, trickster, shadow,* and *mandala*.)

asanas: The stretching postures of Hatha Yoga.

asocial behaviors: Behaviors that are not in the normal repertory of a given society or culture.

assertiveness: The willingness to state one's desires or needs in a forthright way but not beligerently (nor aggressively).

assimilation: According to Piaget, one of the twin processes of adaptation. It is the way we "take in" sensory experiences. (See also *accommodation* and *adaptation*.)

assumptions: These are inferences about observed events and are usually taken as fact even though they are inferences that may or may not have been originally based on fact.

asthma: A condition characterized by wheezing, difficulty in breathing, and a feeling that one is about to suffocate.

attitude: One's feelings or ideas about certain events or persons.

authoritarian parenting: The style of parenting that insists on obedience and seeks to control the child's behavior.

authoritarian personality: According to Adorno, a person whose motivation and belief system rests on power. The highly authoritarian person likes blind submission by his or her followers and in turn obeys without question his or her superiors.

authoritative parenting: A style of parenting that allows the child to be a child (and not as wise as a parent) but still respects the child's needs, wants, and individuality.

autogenic training: Learning to control one's physiological responses through concentration or meditation.

autohypnosis: The induction of hypnotic suggestibility by oneself to oneself.

autonomy: Erikson's term for the second life stage, in which children learn to stand on their own two feet and perform the basic functions of eating, defecating, walking, and so on by themselves. The capacity for self-determination. The functioning as an independent self. The capacity of the person to make valid choices in light of his or her needs.

average: The statistical average is the composite figure based on all persons measured. Of course, no such statistical abstraction actually exists: It is simply a construct.

axonal ending: The terminal endings of the neurons; they release neural chemical transmitters across the synapse, which fire (or do not fire) the adjoining neurons.

barbituates: Sedatives that slow down bodily functions, resulting in certain decreases of perceptual and cognitive dysfunctioning, bodily and intellectual performance, loss of motor skills. Prolonged use can lead to dependence and addiction.

bargaining: The third stage of Kübler-Ross's five stages toward the acceptance of death, in which the person tries to bargain for more life time from God, from the physicians, from anyone.

basic needs: In Maslow's theory of personality, these are the physiological needs of water, food, air, and so on.

basic trust: The first stage of Erik Erikson's psychosocial development. The baby who is given adequate physical and emotional mothering develops basic trust that the world will welcome him or her and take care of his or her needs.

behavior: Any response made by a person or other organism that can be observed and measured.

behavior modification: Therapeutic change through an adaptation of operant conditioning. Desirable behaviors are reinforced until the adult or child is responding in a more constructive manner.

behavior therapies: Therapies that aim not just at insight but at change. Includes Wolpe's deconditioning therapy of phobia, rational-emotive therapy, reality therapy, and implosive therapy.

behavioral predispositions: Characteristics of neonates that seem to be innate or inborn.

belief system: The entire set of categorizations and classifications (concepts, percepts, ideas, values, attitudes, judgments) that the individual brings to his or her everyday interactions with other persons and the prevailing institutions of society.

belonging and love needs: According to Abraham Maslow, the third level of a human hierarchy of needs.

benign: A state of being nonmalignant; harmless; kindly.

Bhagavad-Gita: An ancient Hindu religious epic, which recounts the story of Arjuna and Krishna. It is an allegory of human struggle and personality development.

bias: A tendency to lean toward an opinion; sometimes synonymous with prejudicial thinking.

bioenergetics: Therapeutic treatment that focuses on body posture and body language. Bioenergetic therapists believe that our character is revealed in our body language and that change in our posture will have feedback on our character.

biofeedback: A technique in which biological signals, such as heart rate, electroencephalographic activity, or blood pressure, are converted to visual or auditory signals so that persons become aware of them; i.e., biological signals are "fed back" to the subject.

birth trauma: As explicated by Otto Rank, the physical and psychological shock the neonate goes through in the birth process. The trauma the newborn has received is seen as the basis of all later child and adult anxiety.

blaming game: The tendency to blame others for our misfortunes.

blue-collar worker: Any worker who wears a "blue-collar," i.e., a blue work shirt that marks him or her as a manual laborer as distinct from a "white-shirted" office worker.

bodily awareness: An acceptance and appreciation of one's body with all one's feelings and functions. Maslow noted that highly self-actualizing persons have good bodily awareness.

body armor: The term used by Wilhelm Reich to indicate the deadening of our body areas so that we become less sensitive to emotional or physical pain. Unfortunately, we also deaden ourselves to *all* feelings.

born loser: A term popularized since 1950 to indicate any person whose life style is self-destructive and may lead to alcoholism, unemployment, prison, and so on.

caste and class: A caste system in a society means that members are born into a certain stratum and must remain there. A class system in a society means that members may change status and may achieve higher or lower status.

catatonic: A reaction in which the person's energy level drops to minimal activity. The person tends to be negative, rigid, and withdrawn and sometimes remains in the same position for hours, even days.

catharsis: A psychoanalytic term indicating the release of repressed emotions and "forgotten" thoughts through dreams, drama, literature, and other creative expressions.

celibacy: The state of existence in which the person voluntarily or involuntarily foregoes sexual activity.

center of growth: According to Carl Rogers, a kind of inner wisdom and, when the person is able to stay in touch with it, enables him or her to make propriate and creative decisions. (See *propriate strivings*.)

chakras: Hindu philosophy postulates the existence of seven energy centers along the spinal cord corresponding roughly to the major ductless glands. Meditation is supposed to open these centers and, in so doing, raise the person to a higher level of consciousness.

channeling of emotions: When an individual is under excessive stress, he or she will tend to channel anxiety into those emotions or defense mechanisms that provide the most emotional support.

character: The consistent and enduring aspect of an individual's personality patterning. It may be distinguished from *personality* in that the latter is what is *evident* while character may also include those traits that are not so observable and may even be quite contradictory to the external *persona*. (See *persona* and *shadow*.)

character armor: A Reichian concept that postulates that defense mechanisms not only are psychologically evident but can also be seen on the physical body as hardening or "armoring" of areas of the torso and head. As a result, these "rings" are more vulnerable to dysfunctioning and disease.

character neurosis: As contrasted to the anxiety neurosis, the character neurosis (according to Reich) results not in uncomfortable or painful symptoms but rather in no symptoms at all; in fact, the person cuts himself or herself off from bodily awareness. (See *character armor* or *body armor*.)

chauvinism: An unexamined belief that one's country, ideology, sex, race, and beliefs, etc., are superior to others.

child abuse: Any purposeful act that results in physical, emotional, mental, or sexual injury that causes the child's well-being to be significantly impaired.

child-centered family: The style of parenting that

came into vogue in the sixties and seventies, which focused mainly upon the child's needs and less upon the needs of the adults in the family. (See also *authoritarian parenting* and *authoritative parenting*.)

chronic: Describes a condition that exists over a long period of time, as contrasted to *acute*. (See also *acute*.)

chronically ill: Describes a person whose physical or emotional condition is rather permanently hampered and is limited in his or her ability to take part in the vocational or avocational arenas.

classical conditioning: Another name for Pavlovian conditioning or stimulus substitution conditioning. This type of conditioning was formulated by Ivan Pavlov and based on a change of status of a neutral stimulus to a conditioned stimulus by several pairings with the unconditioned stimulus. Also called *respondent conditioning*.

client-centered therapy: A system of psychotherapy based on the belief that the client himself or herself can solve his or her own problems if a warm, safe climate of trust has been established.

cocaine: A local anesthetic, which if injected or ingested may act as a stimulant inducing excitation, talkativeness, and muscular tremors.

cognition (cognitive functions or cognitive processes):   Those processes commonly called *thinking*, reasoning, judging. Also referred to as the intellectual processes. (See *affective processes*.)

cognitive dissonance: The condition in which one has beliefs or knowledge that conflict with each other or with one's usual perceptions and behaviors. When this condition arises, the person is motivated to reduce the dissonance through changes in behavior or cognition.

coitus: Sexual intercourse.

coitus interruptus: Interruption of the act of sexual intercourse by withdrawal of the penis from the vagina before ejaculation, usually with the intention of preventing impregnation.

coitus reservatus: The delay of climax until the penis is no longer inserted in the vagina, generally used as a method of birth control.

collective objects: A Freudian concept that states that in dreams one object or person can stand for many objects or persons.

collective unconscious: According to Jung, the human race retains in its memory archetypes of previous generations and civilizations. (See also *archetype, shadow, anima-animus, wise old man, wise old child,* and *trickster*.)

commonalities (scientific principles):   The general principles of behavior that guide human affairs, sometimes called principles, laws, facts.

company image: The impression a corporation intends to make for the general public through the popular media, public relations, dress codes of its employees, and so on.

company man: An employee who generally adheres to the policies of his or her company, attempts to uphold the company image, and is generally considered a loyal and trusted "member of the team," sometimes at the expense (but not always) of his or her personal consciousness.

compensation: A fairly benign defense mechanism in which the person performs well in one area to make up for a deficiency in another.

compensatory function: Jung believed that the person seeks to be a balanced organism. If an individual is weak in one function, he or she will tend to become stronger by finding a person strong in that function with whom to bond in marriage and/or friendship. (See also *four functions: intuitive, sensing, thinking, feeling*.)

compulsion: An excessive discharge of psychic energy in repetitive behavior, which is often focused on trivial and unimportant events. (See also *anal personality*.).

compulsive personality: One that is excessively orderly, rigid, and pedantic.

concrete operations: The third stage of Piaget's theory of cognitive development from about 7½ years of age to about 11½ years of age and older, in which the child is able to deal with two abstract concepts at one time and has more available operations by which to deal with algebraic functions and more sophisticated verbal material.

condensation: As used by Freud to describe dream symbols, it is the fusing of two or more objects, words, or persons.

conditioned response (CR):   A response aroused by a conditioned stimulus. A learned behavior.

conditioned stimulus (CS):   A neutral stimulus that when paired with an unconditioned stimulus eventually arouses a conditioned response (**CR**) similar to the unconditioned response and thereby becomes a conditioned stimulus.

conditioning: The learning of certain responses to certain environmental stimuli (classical conditioning) or the shaping of new behaviors through reinforcement (operant conditioning).

conditioning therapies: Therapies that treat the symptoms and do not depend on causal factors.

conflict-ridden marriage: A marriage style that is dominated by verbal quarrels or hostile silences, which reflect the constant state of tension and conflict.

congenial marriage: A marriage style in which the two persons have regard for each other and some mutual interests and responsibilities but are not passionately or "totally" involved with each other.

conjunctive traits: Those traits considered by Alfred Adler to be those that move toward harmonic interactions with other persons. They include cheerfulness, generosity, and all the so-called cardinal virtues. Altogether, they make up the "social feeling" or *gemeinschaftsgefuhl;* the hallmark of the highly evolved personality.

conscience: According to Freud, our superego or all the voices of our society that we introject (internalize) when we are young.

consciousness: That state of awareness when we experience ourselves as "I."

consignment to death: The phenomenon involved in arbitrarily committing an aged or sick person to a permanent-care residence without the person's active and willing participation. The aged person experiences psychological rejection, and death ensues more swiftly than anticipated.

contact need: Harry Harlow's term for the need for baby monkeys to be able to touch, cling, and be held by others of their kind. Harlow considers these skin senses to be of primary importance in our ability to love others.

conversion hysteria: Psychological repression that takes the form of a physical symptom such as psychological deafness, psychological blindness, or psychological paralysis.

coping: The attempts of the individual to manage his or her life problems.

corpus callosum: The fibers of neurons that connect the two hemispheres of the brain and through which the left and right brains communicate and integrate neural information.

correlation: The relationship of two or more variables (or events).

cosmic egg: The term used by John Chilton Pearce to describe our usual state of consciousness. Each of us believes we see and understand reality when in fact we are perceiving only the "cosmic egg" of reality we have created and that we carry around with us like a bubble. Every so often an event occurs that cracks this cosmic egg and that may enlarge our world view.

courtly love: The particular style of sexual attraction and bonding that developed in twelfth-century Europe. The lady of the manor (noblewoman) was wooed ardently by a knight or nobleman with, perhaps, a consequent adulterous affair.

creative fantasy: The therapeutic technique to increase creativity by having the person imagine or visualize certain possibilities.

creativity: The ability to see new relationships and to express them in any academic, scientific, or artistic, field of endeavor. It is not exactly coincidental with intelligence, although there is a positive correlation between the variables as measured by IQ tests.

crisis: Particular stages of development are considered to be crisis periods during which the individual is susceptible to change (because of the need for, and the process of, rebalancing or reorganizing in a state of homeostasis).

cross-era transitions: Levinson's term to indicate the major passages and turning points of our lives.

cultural lag: The time difference between the introduction of a material product into the culture and the correlated changes in the nonmaterial products (such as attitudes, values, norms, and laws).

culture: All the material (concrete) and nonmaterial (abstract) elements of any common group of people (members of a society) that are learned and shared by these members.

D.T.'s: The "delirium tremens" of the deteriorated alcoholic, characterized by motor incoordination, flights of unreality, and hallucinations.

daydream: A dreamlike fantasy while awake.

death-denying society: The concept that Americans are not able to accept the eventuality and reality of death; thus we are "death denying" as a society.

defense mechanisms: The unconscious maneuvers by which we defend against the pain of anxiety by repression, denial, projection, and so on.

delusions: Unreal beliefs.

demographic variables: The human factors that correlate with other given variables. In social science the common demographic variables are age, sex, race, ethnic group, socioeconomic status (SES), and intelligence.

dendrite receptors: The neuronal endings that are triggered by various physical energies. To put it more simply, our sense receptors of sight, hearing, taste, touch, pain, pressure, and so on.

denial: (1) Defense mechanism in which the person rejects the reality of actual events. (2) According to Kübler-Ross, the first stage of the acceptance of death, in which the person refuses to accept the reality of the diagnosis of impending death.

depressant: Any drug that effectively slows down the neurophysiological processes of the body.

depression: (1) The feeling of being "down," helpless, and apathetic. The person experiences a low level of energy and may even cease much of the normal everday activity. (2) According to Kübler-Ross, the fourth stage of the acceptance of death. The person has finally accepted the death sentence and is in mourning for the life and persons he or she must leave.

depressive reaction: A quantitative increase in "normal" sadness, gloom, melancholia, and anxiety, characterized by loss of energy, loss of drive, and loss of motivation.

developmental task: Erikson's concept of the competencies individuals need to master in response to a *developmental crisis*. These tasks represent eight basic life stages; however, they are being refined constantly during a lifetime.

deviant behavior: Any behavior not shared by most of the persons in one's society or peer group.

dialogic approach: A therapeutic situation that has as its central focus verbal interactions. Examples include psychoanalysis, gestalt therapy, and transactional analysis.

difficult child: One of the four personality "types" of infants. The child is easily agitated and difficult to soothe and exhibits minor physical disturbances such as colic. The personality type seems to last into adulthood.

disassociation: Feelings of unreality, which are attributed to the splitting off of unacceptable emotions and thoughts.

displacement: As related to dreams, the transference of strong emotions to the relatively neutral symbols.

doctrine of specific etiology: The theory that states that for every specific communicable disease there is a specific causal germ (bacterium, virus). As a "germ theory," however, it does not account for all the facts of disease and immunity.

double-bind: A condition of not being able to "win," i.e., you are "damned if you do and damned if you don't." The communication involved contains two messages that are contradictory and result in feelings of confusion, impotence, or frustration for the receiver of that communication.

double-income family: Any family in which both husband and wife earn incomes. (See *dual-career family*.)

double standard: The attitude that suggests that what is appropriate for one sex is not appropriate for the other or is not valued. Sexual behaviors and age are the two most common examples.

dream work: Freud postulated that the dreamer translates unacceptable wishes and feelings into disguised dream symbols.

drive state: A physiological condition in which there is a lack (such as food deprivation) that tends to increase the subject's behavioral output.

dual-career family: A family in which both husband and wife have a career in which they express their special abilities and receive a sense of satisfaction. This is not the same as a *dual-working family*, in which husband and wife have noncareer jobs held basically for the purpose of income.

dynamics: Pertaining to the underlying motivations of behavior, particularly "unconscious" behavior.

dynamic process: As applied to psychology, the idea that a person's inner psychic life is always in a state of change or process because of conflicting needs, drives, motivations, and aspirations, particularly as these psychic factors come into opposition with environmental forces.

easy child: One of the four personality "types" of infants lasting into adulthood. These children are flexible, adapt easily to new situations, and are emotionally responsive.

economic orientation: According to Spranger, descriptive of that personality type that is motivated by money, financial security, and all the comforts of "the good life."

ectomorph: According to Sheldon's physical classifications, a person who is "all skin and bones" and prefers intellectual activities. (See *endomorph* and *mesomorph*.)

ego: Latin for *I*, or the conscious aspect of personality that mediates between the superego and the id, and the self and the society.

ego integrity: The life task, according to Erikson, of old age, where the person develops a sense of worthwhileness for what has been done.

ego strength: The amount of psychic energy a person has to cope with life problems. A person with minimal ego strength will tend to "break down" over problems that will not affect another person who has more ego strength.

egocentric thinking: According to Piaget, the inability of the preoperative child to consider any situation from a perspective other than his or her own.

either-or thinking: Thinking that tends to be categorical, judgmental, and stereotypic. Examples: good/bad, right/wrong, virtue/vice.

Electra complex: A Freudian concept indicating excessive or highly sexualized affections between a father and his daughter. Incest is possible but is not implied in this term.

empathy: The ability to understand and appreciate another person's feelings or plight without making judgments about that person.

empirical data: Facts (data) gathered through the senses of sight, hearing, touch, taste, or smell. Typical methods include observation, interview, and survey.

empty-nest syndrome: The resulting dissatisfaction of a mother when her children have left the household to establish independent lives of their own.

emptying the mind: The Zen Buddhist phrase for letting go of anxiety-provoking thoughts and conditioned responses.

enculturation: The process by which societies perpetuate the culture and develop personality. (See also *socialization*.)

endomorph: The Sheldon classification in which the person's muscular structure predominates the physique, resulting in someone who is physically active and "always on the go." (See also *ectomorph* and *mesomorph*.)

endorphins: The natural analgesics produced by the brain.

environmental climate: The general emotional and intellectual tenor of an organization. This tenor may vary from pleasant, friendly, and stimulating to hostile and conflict ridden.

epistemology: That branch of philosophy that studies *how* we know what we know.

era: Levinson's term for the four great ages of human existence: youth, early adulthood, middle adulthood, later adulthood.

esteem needs: According to Maslow, the fourth level of our hierarchy of needs. We need to feel that we make a contribution to our society for which we are or can be appreciated and valued.

etc.: The symbol used by general semanticists to indicate all the variables that may exist but are not accounted for.

ethnic group: A group of people who share a common racial and/or cultural heritage that sets them apart from others.

ethnocentrism: The tendency to judge another culture in terms of our own. Even though we may realize that behaviors are relative to the culture within which they occur, it is difficult to become aware of our cultural preferences and not be ethnocentric. (We view our ways as superior.) This attitude is related to prejudice, chauvinism, and stereotypic thinking.

existential psychology: The school of psychology that deals with the person's inner experiences as compared to behaviorism (which focuses on observable, overt behaviors), or psychodynamics (which focuses on unconscious motivations).

extended family: A constellation of parents and their children and other relatives such as grandparents, great-grandparents, aunts and uncles, and nieces and nephews living together.

extraversion: That polarity of personality in which we focus on external events and other human beings.

extravert: A term used by Jung to describe the person whose primary orientation is focused on the outside world and on interactions with others. (See also *introvert*.)

fallacy: An erroneous belief.

fantasy: (1) A daydream; (2) sometimes used as a therapeutic approach designed to stimulate creativity and conscious decision making (based on the theory that no act occurs until it is imaged).

favorable ratio: According to Erikson, a beneficial balance of a life task to its opposite possibility. All school children feel a certain amount of *inferiority*, for example, but if the child has achieved a reasonable level of a sense of *industry*, he or she can be said to have achieved a *favorable ratio*.

fear of success: The tendency of women to lower their level of aspiration so as not to threaten men with their intellectual, academic, or vocational achievement and therefore remain more "feminine."

feeling function: One of Jung's *four functions*, in which emotions predominate. (See also *thinking*, *intuitive*, and *sensing function*.)

feminist: A person who supports the emergence of women into equal status with men.

femme fatale: A woman whose self-esteem lies in being sexually attractive to men.

field theory: Any theory that attempts to unite and explain many facts in a generalized statement.

figure-ground relationship: Perls's term to indicate the influence of past experiences on "here-and-now" perceptions.

fixation: Stereotypic behaviors that indicate a neurotic adaptation to certain events. A person may be fixated in one or more areas but be very flexible and creative in others.

flashback: The spontaneous and sudden remembrance of previous events or reexperience of previous events.

flexibility: The character trait of very creative persons. They are able to maintain experimental and many-sided perceptions of reality.

flight into failure: The tendency of some persons with a destructive life style to end in a disastrous situation: bankruptcy, alcoholism, drug abuse, delinquency, and so on.

Flight-or-Fight Syndrome: According to W. B. Cannon, the emergency reaction of the body to meet a threatening situation.

folklore: Stories that have been handed down through generations.

formal operations: According to Jean Piaget, the fourth and highest (adult) level of thinking. The person is able to use hypothetical-deductive reasoning to abstract new principles and paradigms.

formerly married person: Any divorced person who has not remarried.

four functions: According to Jung, we have four ways of taking in and evaluating information. (See also *thinking function, feeling function, sensing function,* and *intuitive function*.)

fratricide: The killing of one's brother, as in the story of Cain and Abel. One of society's taboos.

free association: The so-called talking cure invented by Freud wherein a person relates his or her "stream of consciousness" thoughts and feelings without attempting to censor or edit them.

fully functioning: Carl Rogers's term for persons who are growing and evolving in every part of their personality functioning.

general adaptation syndrome: According to Selyë, the changes the body goes through as the result of extended stress. (See also *stress*.)

general semantics: A branch of linguistics that attempts to increase clear communication between persons.

generalized responses: Behaviors that are similar to conditioned responses and aroused by similar, but not the original, conditioned stimuli. Example: After Albert was conditioned to fear a white rat, he exhibited generalized responses of fear (but not as intensely) to other white, furry objects, such as a muff.

generalized stimulus: Once a stimulus has been established to elicit a given response, then other similar stimuli may also elicit this given response. Example: A Vietnam veteran who has learned to fear rifle shots may flinch at a car's backfire.

generativity: According to Erikson, the life task of the seventh life stage or middle adulthood. The person needs to foster (generate) the growth and creativity of the next generation and contribute to the overall well-being of the society.

genocide: The destruction of a whole tribe, nation, or race.

gentle birth: A term used in connection with Leboyer's nonviolent birthing technique. Leboyer seeks to make the passage from the womb to extrauterine existence as easy and nontraumatic as possible for the baby.

geriatrics: The study of the psychology and problems of old age and of ways to assist the elderly.

gestalt therapy: A therapy devised by Frederick Perls and is focused on the disruption that occurs when we do not get to experience completion (or coming to *closure*); i.e., we are driven by *unfinished situations* or *incomplete gestalts*.

global anxiety: Anxiety that has to do with the destruction of the planet and survival of the human race.

"going negative:" Jacobson's term for a state of extreme relaxation.

grand mal epilepsy: The form of epilepsy in which the person has convulsions and loses consciousness. It is a life-threatening form of the disease.

grave yard shift: The work shift that begins in the late evening (approximately 11 P.M. or midnight) and continues until morning (7 or 8 A.M.).

growth group: Any group which assembles for the purpose of increasing effective behavior and creativity.

hallucination: The acceptance of certain phenomena as "external reality" when, in fact, the phenomena are internal, private, and autistic.

hallucinogens: Any drug such as psilocybin, LSD, and alcohol which induces hallucinations.

hedonism: The philosophic point of view that one's life goals should be aimed at pleasurable sense experiences, epitomized as, "Eat, drink, and be merry for tomorrow you may die." In psychology, hedonism can be correlated with Freud's *pleasure-pain principle*.

here-and-now: Focus on the immediate situation. In Gestalt therapy the person is encouraged to focus on his or her present feelings and emotions rather than dredge up past material.

heredity: The transmission of physical and psychological characteristics through genetic material.

heroin: A morphine derivative used as an anesthetic or narcotic. It is psychologically and physiologically addictive.

heterosexuality: A preference for sexual and emotional bonding with members of the opposite sex.

hierarchy of needs: According to Maslow, the five levels of needs characteristic of the human species. The first two levels are the physiological and safety needs, which we share with all animals. The other three levels are peculiarly human (belonging and love needs, esteem needs, and needs for self-actualization).

homeostasis: Changes the body goes through in order to adapt to the environment and maintain its equilibrium. For example, in hot weather the organism sweats, which lowers body temperature.

homosexuality: A preference for sexual and emotional bonding with members of the same sex.

hormones: Substances produced by the endocrine glands and released into the blood stream, where they then act upon body organs or other glands.

human becoming: According to Allport, the human experience is a continual opportunity for growth and maturity. He suggests that one think of oneself not as a human being but as a human becoming (i.e., always in process).

"the human condition:" Hannah Arendt's term for the understanding that we are all of us, without exception and no matter what our status in life, subject to the limits and perplexities of existence: pain, injustice, sickness, grief, and death.

humanism: A philosophy that asserts the dignity and worth of men and women and their capacity for self-realization.

humanistic psychology: The philosophic thrust to emphasize the growth potential of men and women and their ability to make free choices about the goals of life. This approach studies the person as a *whole* and chooses to focus not just on ill or neurotic persons but also on persons we consider healthy, growing, and creative.

hypnosis: A temporary state of consciousness either self-induced or induced by another person in which the subject's phenomenology is considerably altered from the ordinary waking mode or perception. The alterations may include memory, suggestibility, anesthesia, paralysis, and hallucinations.

hypochondria: Excessive concern for one's health, often without evidence that there is anything really wrong. This term should be clearly distinguished from the term *malingering*, which implies that the person is pretending sickness but knows that he or she is not really sick.

hypothesis: A statement that seeks to relate two or more facts (variables) or predict phenomena; a proposition worthy of scientific investigation.

hysteria: A condition in which emotional conflicts are converted to physical symptoms such as hysterical paralysis, blindness, deafness, and amnesia.

hysterical conversion: See *hysteria*.

id: Formulated by Freud, it is a concept that describes the deepest, most unconscious aspect of human personality; the pleasure-oriented, lustful, sexual, and narcissistic being that is born into this world.

identity: The fourth life task of Erikson's psychosocial development of personality. In our era it is during adolescence that the young girl or boy rejects parental or familial identity to seek her or his own identity.

ideology: A belief system that legitimates the social stratification system of a society and is the basis of institutional attitudes, beliefs, values, and prescriptions (roles).

implosive therapy: A form of deconditioning therapy developed by Stampfl in which the person is flooded with the phobic or anxiety-provoking stimuli until (presumably) the neurotic, avoidance defense mechanisms collapse.

impotent: Pertaining to lack of ability, strength, or power. Commonly used as a term for the inability to perform sexually.

incest: Sexual relations between persons of close blood ties. Incest is a strong taboo in almost all civilizations, and the taboo is considered a cultural universal, although the exact restrictions vary from culture to culture.

individual differences: The specifically unique characteristics that distinguish one person from another.

individuation: Carl Jung's term for the process by which the person emerges psychologically from group, tribal, or mass consciousness to become a unique and wholly creative person.

inductive reasoning: The process of deriving the general from the specific. The abstracted generalizations are seen as likely possibilities rather than fact and are the basis of our scientific theories.

industry: The major life task of the school child, as formulated by Erik Erikson:—in our society, the ability to read, write, and compute.

inferiority-superiority complex: As defined by Alfred Adler, this is the tendency of human beings to cover up their feelings of inferiority by seeking ways to be or act superior to others.

initiative: As formulated by Erikson, the task of the preschooler, which includes the acquisition of the principles of time, space, planning, cooperation with others, and imagination and creativity.

innate: Unlearned; inborn.

insulation: The defense mechanism used by persons who prefer not to get involved or concerned with social ills or emergency situations threatening others. It is a form of *denial*.

intelligence as choice: Piaget's definition of intelligence, which is, quite simply, *the more choices available to an organism in any given situation, the more intelligent is the life form*. Similarly, the more choices each of us has in confronting a situation and making a decision, the more intelligence we are displaying.

interactionist theory: A theory that attempts to bridge the nature-nurture controversy focusing on the fact that human beings have experience and symbolize and interpret their experience, i.e., we have individual and shared *definitions of reality.*

intimacy: Erikson's term for the life task of early adulthood. We learn to share ourselves with others physically and psychologically. In our society our usual expression of this stage of development is in our intimate relationships with members of the opposite sex, the most formal of which is marriage.

intoxication by stress: The tendency to become overstimulated by one's own hormonal level; i.e., a person may actually become addicted to a high stress level and find it enjoyable.

intrinsic motivation: Motivation that rises out of inner desire rather than because one is punished, prodded, coaxed, or otherwise motivated from an external source (*extrinsic motivation*).

introjection: The adoption of attitudes and values that may not be consistent with one's personality type. Also referred to as the process of internalization, which is the taking in of the attitudes, values, and norms of the society and claiming them as our own.

introspection: The process of self-analysis and self-examination.

introversion: That polarity in our personality functioning that focuses on our *internal* percepts, thoughts, and feelings.

introvert: Jung's term for the person who focuses on inner thoughts and feelings rather than on the actions of others. (See also *extravert.*)

intuitive function: One of Jung's *four functions* by which we sense what is not presently self-evident; the ability to imagine future possibilities and to make lightning-swift solutions to problems.

irreversibility: According to Piaget, the inability of the preoperative child to reverse an operation he or she has just made.

isolation: According to Kübler-Ross, part of the fourth stage of acceptance of death, which is accompanined also by depression and mourning.

isometric exercises: Exercises that use the body's muscular systems against each other in order to produce effective body building in a short time.

Kinsey Reports: Published in the late 1940s on men and the early 1950s on women. The first valid survey studies done on adult males and females on American sexual attitudes, values, and behaviors.

Krishna: The Hindu god representing supreme consciousness.

LSD: Lysergic acid diethylamide is one of a group of hallucinogenic drugs.

laissez-faire parenting: A style of parenting in which the parents do not take an active role in their children's upbringing. *Laissez faire* means to let them do as they will with a minimum of interference. Sometimes called *permissive parenting.* (See also *authoritarian parenting* and *authoritative parenting.*)

latency period: According to Freud, the period from about six years to puberty when the sexual drive is relatively quiescent.

latent dreams: The disguised or hidden meaning of the symbols of the dream.

life-crises units (LCUs): The greater the number of changes (LCUs) in a person's life, the more liable the person is to undergo emotional or physical illness. Each unit measures the relative amount of emotional impact of any given event.

lesbianism: Female homosexuality. Named for the Island of Lesbos in ancient Greece where this sexual preference was presumably maintained.

letting go (physically): The term used by Edmund Jacobson for very deep relaxation.

letting go (emotionally): One of the therapeutic ways of healing someone's grief after the death of a loved one.

libido: The instinctual drive for sexual expression.

life script: The way we program our lives and manipulate others into acting out our life expectations, goals, and even disappointments.

life space: According to Lewin the totality of all possible events that influence the individual—from the past, from the present, and from the future as it is contemplated by the individual.

life span: From conception to death.

life structure: According to Levinson, the life style and space we create for ourselves. Since Levinson says no life structure is ever perfect or permanent, we are constantly *destructuring* and *restructuring* it.

life style: As defined by Alfred Adler, it is the underlying motif or life theme of our individual existence.

life tasks: The particular major skills and competencies we need to master at any given segment of the life span.

logotherapy: Viktor Frankl's form of therapy that places importance on the discovery and formulation of creative meaning and spiritual values.

low-authoritarian persons: These persons maintain an open-minded approach when dealing with issues and persons and do not fall into stereotypic and *either-or thinking*.

macho: Derived from the Spanish *machismo*. A personality style that emphasizes certain traits that have been traditionally associated with masculine superiority: aggressiveness, combativeness, and sexual dominance.

macro approach (to science): The search for general principles based on large-scale phenomena, perhaps of entire civilizations. (See also *micro approach*.)

magical thinking: Primitive cause-and-effect thinking typical of childhood and animistic religions.

malingering: The act of feigning sickness as, for example, the little girl who complains of feeling sick so she won't have to go to school.

mandala: Generally, a quadrilateral or circular figure used as a meditative guide in Tibetan (Tantric) and other religious and philosophic studies; a way of altering consciouness.

manic-depressive psychosis (or personality): A kind of personality patterning characterized by extreme mood swings from depression to elation and vice versa.

manifest dream: According to Freud, the story content of a dream.

mantram (mantra): Any symbol, visual or auditory, that serves as a focus of attention, concentration, or meditation.

marker events: Levinson's term for those events that accompany transitional phases of our lives. Examples: divorce, sickness, change of job, death.

mask: Rogers's term for the trait persons display when they hide their real feelings, emotions, and attitudes from others. (See also *real me*.)

masturbation: The manipulation of one's own sexual organs to achieve orgasm.

matricide: The killing of one's mother, which is a strong societal taboo in most civilizations and religions.

mechanistic approach to human understanding: The assumptive base of some psychological explanations and models of human behavior; i.e., human achievement can be explained by need-drive tension and reduction.

mediate: The central-nervous-system process involved in assimilating and responding to our sense-modality precepts. It is the process involved in what we call thinking, cognition, judgment, evaluation, and so on.

meditation: The calming of body and mind so as to achieve a higher, more centered level of consciousness.

meprobates: Tranquilizers such as Equanol and Miltown the effects of which are emotional and motor relaxation.

mescalin: An alkaloid of the Mexican cactus peyote and a derivative of phenylethylamine. It has been used for centuries as a narcotic and was used in various Aztec and other Indian religious practices.

mesomorph: Sheldon's term for the muscular person who is very active and always "on the go." (See also *ectomorph* and *endomorph*.)

metaphysics: That branch of philosophy that considers primal cause. The study involves the system of principles underlying a particular world view or belief system seeking to explain the nature of being, the origin and structure of the world or reality.

micro approach (to science): The search for general principles based on small-scale phenomena such as individual interactions and individual interpretations of reality. (See also *macro approach*.)

midlife crisis: The natural reevaluation, destructuring, and restructuring of one's life style and life space that comes about at the age-forty period.

monogamy: One-man–one-woman bonding in a marriage-type relationship as opposed to other relationships, such as polygamy or group marriage. Monogamy also implies a marriage-type relationship that lasts for an entire lifetime with sexual exclusivity.

moral realism: According to Piaget, the first stage of morality in children up to the age of ten, characterized by grim justice *without* mercy. The child is centered on effect rather than on cause or motivation. (See also *moral relativity*.)

moral relativity: According to Piaget, the second stage of moral development, reached at ten years or later. The child is more able to consider motivation, cause, and extenuating circumstances. (See also *moral realism*.)

moratorium (college as): One of the values of the college experience is the opportunity to postpone commiting oneself to a particular vocation or life style or to adult responsibilities.

mores: (pronounced "morays") Strong ideas of right and wrong; values of such significance that we consider them vital to our well-being.

morphine: An opium derivative, which acts as a narcotic analgesic. Can be addictive.

motor neurons: The nerves that innervate (fire) the muscles of the body.

multiple personality: The condition in which a person seems to have two or more subpersonalities, although some have had as many as two dozen. These subpersonalities may or may not know of each other's existence.

multivariate causation: The concept that any effect has not one but two or more determinants.

mutuality factor: In successful marriage, the tendency for the couples to hold the same values and life-style preferences.

mysticism: The religious or meditative approach of persons who seek a direct experience of God or the Godhead or who hope (through insights of divine revelation) to come to a fuller comprehension of the universe and its meaning.

myth: A story, tale, fable, or epic that attempts to explain natural phenomena and the human condition.

myth of mental health: According to the authors, the concept of mental health is a misleading and erroneous one and does not exist in our everyday reality. (See also the *myth of mental illness*.)

myth of mental illness: According to Szasz, the concept of mental illness is an erroneous and misleading one. Most of our prisons and mental institutions are filled with those persons who are too poor and too badly educated to defend themselves against a label of mental illness. (See *myth of mental health*.)

Napoleonic complex: Named for Napoleon (because of his small height). The tendency of small persons to feel that they must prove themselves to be powerful; an example of Adler's inferiority-superiority complex.

narcissism: The need to seek pleasure in oneself. The term is taken from the Greek myth in which the beautiful Narcissus fell in love with his own image reflected in a pool. Narcissistic persons are essentially self-absorbed and unaware of the needs of others.

natural childbirth: The approach to pregnancy and childbirth that emphasizes the fact that they are healthy processes and not sicknesses to be treated. Drugs and surgical procedures are used only when necessary rather than as a usual part of the process, since the intent is to keep the process natural.

nature/nurture controversy: Another term for the controversy over heredity as the major influence on our behaviors versus environment (learning) as the major influence. At this time we consider both to be determiners of significance.

needs: The basic requirements for survival and adequate living.

neonate: The infant from birth to four weeks.

neotany: The period from the infancy of a species until its sexual maturation and adulthood.

neuralchemical transmitters: Chemicals released by the neurons at the synaptic level that facilitate or inhibit the firing of adjoining neurons.

neurasthenia: A nineteenth-century term to describe a state of chronic physical and psychological lethargy.

neurons: Individual nerves.

neuroses: Fixations or fixated behaviors, which are the result of early childhood experiences and the socialization process.

neurotic: Refers to a distorted sense of reality.

neutral stimulus (NS): Any stimulus that does not arouse a conditioned response. After pairing with an unconditioned stimulus, the NS becomes a conditioned stimulus arousing a specific conditioned response.

noctural emission: Ejaculations of semen while sleeping, generally as the result of erotic dreams.

nomadism: A defense mechanism in which the person is unable to maintain a stable life situation. He or she may become a hobo, change jobs frequently, or even switch from one sexual partner to another in an attempt to find "happiness" or "peace of mind."

norm: Refers to behaviors typical of a specific group or population.

normal: In psychiatry or psychology it implies freedom from a debilitating disorder. Growth psychologists are becoming more wary of using this term. Normal is defined as what most people experience or do.

norms: Guidelines for behavior that give us expectations and limitations. Norms become laws when we believe we need the power of formal sanctions (rewards and/or punishments).

novacaine: An anesthetic.

nuclear family: The ideal family of mother, father, and their children. Many families today are modified nuclear families in that there is often a stepparent/stepchild, etc., involved as the result of multiple marriages within a lifetime (olygamy).

numinous: Indicates the presence of the supernatural, the mystical, the aesthetic, or the spiritual.

obsession: A thought that occurs over and over.

obsessive-compulsive reaction (obsessive-compulsive personality): A neurotic reaction in which the person is subject to recurring thoughts and seems compelled to repeat certain behaviors. Lady Macbeth's handwashing ritual is a classic example.

Oedipus (Oedipal) complex: The term Freud used to represent excessive attachment of a son to his mother. Incest is possible but is not implied by this term.

on-the-job training: Employees are given vocational education as part of their jobs and thus are learning while they are earning.

open marriage: A marriage based on open, honest communication. The marriage is seen as the primary relationship, with other relationships being important yet secondary.

operant conditioning: A type of learning (conditioning) that depends on the prior behaviors of the organism. These emitted responses are reinforced (or not reinforced), and that has the effect of increasing (or decreasing) the frequency of these behaviors.

opiates: Morphine-related drugs, which anesthetize and are therefore used as pain killers.

optic chiasma: Neural crossover of the optic nerves. Because of this crossover there is synchronization of both eyes.

oral personality: According to Freud, the person who is fixated at the oral stage. Persons of this type expect the world to take care of them. They leave their clothes around, like others to wait on them. They are also called passive-dependent personalities.

oral stage: According to Freud, the first psychosocial stage of development. The baby finds erotic pleasure in activities involving the mouth such as sucking and eating.

organ inferiority: Refers to bodily organ or group of organs that demonstrate psychological as well as physical attributes. Inferior performance in certain functions. (See *Napoleonic complex*.)

orgasm: The emotional and physical climax of the sexual act. The state of euphoria resulting from the physiological release.

overcompensation: The attempt to make up for an actual or perceived inferiority in one area by becoming outstanding in another.

overconformity: A term employed to describe a lack of originality and initiative.

oversimplification: An explanation that does not so much explain something as explain it away with either-or statements or by resting on unquestioned or unquestionable assumptions.

own (or **owning**): A term employed by Fritz Perls in regard to the person who is becoming aware of his or her own projections.

PCP: See *hallucinogens*.

pain-attack response: The response of animals to pain, in which they attack other animals or even inanimate objects in the vicinity.

paradigm: A framework of thought that explains certain aspects of reality (as we construe it from one era to another).

paradigm shift: A qualitative change in our world view that generally involves a principle that may

have been present all along but was not recognized as such. The old paradigm is included but is viewed in a new and larger perspective.

paralanguage: All the postures, expressions, gestures, and activities, that give nonverbal messages (even things like personal distance).

paralogical: Outside the parameters of logic.

paranoid: Pertaining to the tendency toward delusional thoughts, particularly the idea that certain people are out to harm one.

passive-dependent personality: A person who has not learned to make his or her own decisions and stand on his or her own two feet. According to Freud, he or she is at the oral stage of psychosexual development.

patricide: The killing of one's father, considered by most societies as taboo.

patterning: An arrangement of the parts that forms a characteristic and unified impression to the observer.

Pavlovian conditioning: See *classical conditioning*.

peak experiences: Maslow's term for the experience that has been variously labeled the mystic experience, satori, Zen, enlightenment, cosmic consciousness.

peer group: A group whose members share the same age-stage interests, values, and tasks.

perceptual defense: A defense mechanism by which a person screens out disagreeable perceptions. When a particular event is too anxiety provoking, the human tendency is to not *perceive* it, in other words, to be psychologically deaf or blind to the event.

permissive parenting: The style of parenting that allows children to find their own limits via their own explorations.

Persona (or Mask): The mask worn by the ancient Greek and Roman actor to indicate his role in the play. In Jungian psychology the Persona refers to the "public face" we put on in front of others and that we frequently believe ourselves to be. (See also *shadow*.)

personal anxiety: Concern about one's personal survival, such as worry about paying the bills or concern over one's children. (See also *social anxiety* and *global anxiety*.)

personal distance: The amount of space a person maintains around himself or herself while relating to one or more other persons.

personality: The stable patterns of thinking, feeling, and acting that characterize an individual. (See also *socialization*, and *enculturation*.)

personality integration: The process or processes by which a person coordinates his or her mental, emotional, physical, and sociological experiences toward a unified pattern of goal-striving behaviors.

personality theorists: Social scientists who construct models of the way human personality functions. Outstanding personality theorists in this text are Freud, Maslow, Erikson, and Jung.

persons in process: Rogers's term for those persons who are aware and in touch with their own dynamics and who are willing to stay open to emotional experiencing. They are always in a process of change, growth, and evolution.

phallic stage: Freud's term to indicate a phase of libidinal development in which the child's genital organs play a dominant role. (See also *Oedipus complex* and *Electra complex*.)

phenomenology: The study of the subjective process of a person's experience; his or her thoughts, feelings, and percepts.

phobia: An exaggerated fear of something that renders one helpless to deal with the event in an objective and rational manner.

phobic reactions: Irrational, fearful responses. (See also *phobia*.)

physiological needs: According to Maslow, the basic biological needs we share with all animate life: food, water, air, freedom from pain, and so on.

pleasure-pain principle: Freud's doctrine to indicate that the infant is governed by hedonistic instincts. Ordinarily the pleasure-pain principle is mediated by the superego, but the psychopathic or sociopathic personality is still largely dominated by the desire to please the self regardless of the rights or feelings of others.

polarities: Jung believed the human personality is made up of oppositional forces (male/female; material/spiritual; anima/animus). The task of *personality integration* is to reconcile and harmonize these polarities. (See also *personality integration*.)

political orientation: Refers to that personality type who is motivated by power, i.e., has the ability to change the events of the world.

polygamy: The marriage of, or marriage-type bonding of, one woman with more than one man or of one man with more than one woman.

polymorphous perversity: According to Freud, the stages of sexual behaviors that can be manifested in the human personality from infancy to adulthood. If the libidinal drive is under- or oversocialized, the individual can remain fixated at one of these primitive levels.

prana: According to Sanskrit literature, the life force of the individual which has its origins in what the psychics call the mindstuff or basic energy of the universe.

pranayama: According to the Hindu philosophic system, breathing patterns that increase the availability of pranic life force or energy within the individual. (See also *prana*.)

predisposition: The tendency of any individual toward some physical or emotional behavior as the result of innate (genetic) factors.

process: The way the bodymind or mindbody responds to the qualitative and quantitative changes in the external and/or internal environment. Each of us develops a characteristic method of assimilating physical and emotional events and accommodating them toward our survival or further growth. (See also *ego strength*.)

professional class: The category of persons who have been trained, educated, or identified within a highly skilled vocational arena. Generally, professional persons have had to attend a highly competitive institution of higher learning and have received a specialized degree such as engineering, medicine, law.

progressive relaxation: Jacobson's method of training his subjects to a state of deep relaxation by focusing on the release of tension of individual muscles throughout the body. (See also *letting go*.)

propinquity factor: As used by sociologists, the major factor of mate selection: geographical nearness. One tends to fall in love with someone in one's near physical or social environment.

propriate strivings: Allport's terms for those strivings that are peculiar to the human race and vary according to the individual. This construct is in opposition to the insistence of the mechanistic approach, which says that all human endeavors and human achievement are nothing but the offshoots of our biological need-drive states.

proprioceptors: Cell receptors in the muscles of the body which convey information to the central nervous system (CNS) about internal physiology.

psilocybin: A drug, derived from a mushroom, which acts as a hallucinogen. (See also *hallucinogens*.)

psychoanalysis: The therapy originated by Freud that sought to alleviate the person's suffering from neurosis by bringing unconscious (repressed) material into consciousness through free association and dream analysis.

Psychoanalytic Congress of Vienna, The: The organization that was established in the first decade of the twentieth century to investigate and foster Freud's insights into the personality dynamics of the individual and, as well, to continue to study psychoanalytic methods of therapy.

psychogenic symptoms: Any physical problem that has its origins in psychological stress.

psychopath: A person who has not developed the normative values and behaviors of his or her society and era.

psychosexual theory of development: Freud's theory of the qualitative personality changes in the individual that result from the socialization process and the consequent development or fixations of the libidinal drive. (See also *oral stage*, *anal stage*, and *genital stage*.)

psychosocial theory of development: Erikson's theory of personality development; through eight life age-stages from birth to death.

psychosomatic illness (disease): The changes the body goes through as the result of psychophysical stress cause acute illness or dysfunctioning of some part of the bodymind or mindbody.

Pygmalion effect: The manner in which our perceptions of a person will tend to influence that person's behavior.

qualitative changes: Changes that are not simply the result of an additive function but are organizationally and functionally different from a previous stage. (See also *quantitative changes*.)

quantitative changes: Any change that comes about by simple additive measures. Examples are weight, height, and age. (See also *qualitative changes*.)

racial unconscious: Jung's term to indicate another type of memory besides our personal memory. The racial or collective unconscious extends back to the progenitors of our species and unites us with the rest of humankind.

raison d'être: French for the "reason it exists."

rational-emotive therapy: Albert Ellis's psychotherapeutic methods, which emphasize not only insight but effective change in the individual's behavior. A key understanding is that we often make a rational statement and follow it with an irrational statement of extremes.

rationalization: A defense mechanism in which the individual denies the actual situation by constructing a plausible but erroneous alibi.

reaction formation: A defense mechanism in which the individual denies his or her own negative feelings toward something or someone by exhibiting excessive positive behaviors toward that object or person.

"real me": Rogers's term for the feeling clients express when they remove the "mask" they believe they must wear and begin to reveal their true feelings and emotions.

reality principle: Freud's term for the way the *id* (based on the pleasure-pain principle) and the *su-*perego (based on the morality principle) are mediated into a civilized being, which we recognize as the *ego* (based on the reality principle). (See also *id*, *ego*, and *superego*.)

reality therapy: Glasser's approach to enabling the "born loser" to deal more adequately with his or her environment (i.e., reality).

rebirthing: The psychotherapeutic technique of having persons reexperience their infantile helplessness and/or rejection by recreating and reexperiencing their birth. The object is to reintegrate their psychodynamic processing and thereby achieve more adequate and effective interpersonal growth.

receptors: Structures that are sensitive to certain kinds of energies and transmit these energies to the central nervous system.

reciprocal inhibition: Wolpe teaches phobic patients to extinguish anxiety responses. His method is to induce deep relaxation in a patient and then have him or her imagine the feared object or event.

reflex: An unlearned, involuntary response to a stimulus.

regression: A defense mechanism in which persons revert to earlier and more primitive behaviors in response to environmental threat.

religious orientation: Describes that personality type that is motivated by a desire to understand the meaning of life as we know it.

repression: According to Freud, the basic defense mechanism that humans use to avoid overwhelming anxiety, guilt, shame, or memory of trauma. Repression differs significantly from forgetting, in that forgetting is a passive decay of unimportant material while repression is an active submerging into the unconscious.

rites of passage: According to vanGennep, the public rites, rituals, and ceremonies (religious or secular) by which the larger society or the immediate community recognizes a transition of status of one or more individuals. Universal rites of passage include puberty rites, marriage rites, and funeral rites.

role modeling: A process involved in the development and functioning of personality. We learn our personality style (patterning) by conscious or unconscious modeling (imitation) of persons in our environment. Albert Bandura is one of the chief exponents of this theory.

role overload: The term applied to the husband and wife (in a nuclear family) who have been forced to take on the multiroles of the extended family and the consequent feelings of overwhelming pressure and exhaustion.

rules of the game: The focus of children in the stage of moral relativity in which the rules of their play seem to be more important than the game itself.

safety needs: According to Maslow, the second level of his hierarchy of needs, which has to do with our need for order, stability, and security.

scapegoating: The act of taking out one's unhappiness or frustration on another or others in destructive ways.

schizoid personality: The person who has difficulty dealing with interpersonal relationships and manifests a "cool" affective personality. (See also *affect*.)

schizophrenia: That emotional patterning in which there is an evident split between the person's cognitive and affective processes. The person may exhibit severe disturbances in thought, confused language communication, bizarre nonverbal behaviors, and hallucinations that are evidently not drug induced.

second half of life: Jung's term for the life span after the midlife (age forty) crisis. He regarded it as qualitatively different from the first half in terms of needs, values, and behaviors.

segmental rings: According to Reich, the seven zones of our head and body, which are biological energy units. These "rings" may become deadened to feelings as the result of a character neurosis, leading to dysfunctioning or disease. (See also *body armor* and *character neurosis*.)

self-actualizing needs: According to Maslow, the highest human level of needs and ever reaching their higher potential of creativity and expression.

self-esteem: One's perception of self as worthwhile.

self-revealment: Allowing one's inner thoughts and feelings to be known to others.

sensing function: Jung's term to indicate that part of self involved with physical reality; the dimensions of space and geography. A good sensor can describe and map his or her physical environment with a good deal of accuracy. (See also *thinking, intuitive*, and *feeling functions*.)

sensory awareness: The ability of the person to be in touch with his or her body and its physiological reactions to internal and external stimuli.

sensory-motor stage: According to Piaget, the first qualitative stage of human cognition, from birth to about two years of age, marked by an absence of mediation as in higher cognition.

sensory neurons: Those neurons that transmit information to the central nervous system. (Our senses of touch, pain, pressure, taste, smell, hearing, vision, and so on.)

serial monogamy: The modern Western tendency to bond with more than one person over the course of a lifetime (with one person at a time) through the process of marriage and divorce. The other terms used are *successive monogamy* and *olygamy*.

sexism: The prejudicial and stereotypic thinking and preferential responding to women and men on the basis of their sex rather than on the basis of what they can and could do.

shadow: The archetypal opposite of the *persona*. The shadow is that part of ourselves that we dislike, disown, and deny. (See also *persona*.)

shaping behavior: An application of operant conditioning in which the desired behavior is reinforced and the undesirable behavior is nonreinforced.

shock (stage of): According to Kübler-Ross, a characteristic of the first stage of a person's reaction to terminal illness. The first stage is *denial*.

sibling: Term used to indicate any brother or sister; any two or more children who have the same parents.

sibling rivalry: The competition of brothers and sisters for their parents' affection.

silent language: The aspects of our paralanguage that communicate information to others. Examples are gestures, postures, and personal space.

similarity factor: One of the main variables in mate selection, i.e., how similar the couple is in age, values, attitudes, socioeconomic status, intelligence, and so on.

simplistic explanations: Statements that reduce human nature to either-or statements and do not allow for the complexity of human behavior. Example: Man is evil.

situational factor: (1) Hartshorne and May studies revealed that a child's honesty depends on the situational aspects, for example, whether there is a chance of getting caught in a wrongdoing. (2) This text emphasizes the situational aspects of personality breakdown or deviant behavior.

skilled labor: Work done by those employees who have a special skill or competence that is valued and needed by industry. Examples: electricians, plumbers, tool-and-die makers.

slow-to-warm child: One of the several personality patternings of neonates and infants, characterized by slow adaptational responses to emotional situations and new environments.

social anxiety: Concern for the welfare of others and for living up to the expectations of others.

social feeling (gemeinschaftsgefuhl): Adler's

phrase for the development of positive character traits, which provide a cross-current to the neurotic traits resulting from the inferiority-superiority complex that every human being has.

social roles: The expectations and limitations prescribed for a given social status. In order to keep a role, the basic role requirements must be filled.

social status: The basic unit of social organization; for each status there is a role. Each social status is a hierarchical position within the social-stratification system of a society.

social stratification: The resulting levels of social structure based on unequal access to the social rewards, usually of money, power, and prestige. The stratification system of a society is legitimated by the basic ideology of the society.

socialization: The process by which the culture is perpetuated and personality is developed.

socialization process: Freud's term to describe the weaning and toilet training of the child along with the other prohibitions being taught.

sociopath: A person who has not developed the normative behavior or typical response patterns and values of the society.

somatotypes: Sheldon's term for biological and physical bodies that have a correlation with emotional and intellectual characteristics. (See also *ectomorph*, *endomorph*, and *mesomorph*.)

"sour-grapes" defense: A defense mechanism in which we rationalize the inability to obtain a desired objective. (See also *rationalization*.)

speech center: That area in our left (dominant) brain which organizes our language capabilities. Dysfunctioning of this area produces *aphasia*, the inability to speak.

spiritual bankruptcy: Jung's term for those persons who have succeeded in accomplishing their material goals but have become aware that they have neglected the transcendent aspects of human living. (See also *transcendence*.)

spontaneous recovery: The sudden reappearance of a supposedly extinguished conditioned behavior.

spouse abuse: The battering of the wife by the husband or the husband by the wife. Emotional and mental abuse are more difficult to define and recognize.

stage of exhaustion: According to Selyë, the third and last stage of the general adaptation syndrome. It is the reaction to prolonged and overwhelming stress that results in disease and/or death.

stage of resistance: The second stage of Selyë's general adaptation syndrome, in which the or-

ganism seems to have successfully adapted to stress and behaves in a manner similar to that in healthy animals.

stagnation: According to both Erikson and Levinson, the life crisis that comes after the age-forty transition. In Erikson's developmental tasks stagnation is the result of not resolving the task of generativity.

stepmother role: The fairy-tale "bad" mother role, which has become a prevalent factor in second marriages and blended (or modified nuclear) families.

stereotypic behavior: Any act that is repetitive and "fixated." (See also *fixation*.)

stimulants: Any drug (or food) that speeds up neural functioning. Common stimulants are caffeine, nicotine, and the amphetamines.

stratification: The result of dividing out individuals according to certain characteristics. (See also *social stratification*.)

stress: (1) Any event in the environment that produces "wear and tear" on the organism. Excessive stress produces psychosomatic illness. (2) Seylë's term for any pressure from the environment that produces physical changes in the organism. Stress is a natural part of the "wear and tear" of the body, but excessive stress can lead to dysfunctioning of some part of the mindbody or bodymind.

sublimation: Directing "lower" infantile and aggressive impulses into more socially acceptable outlets.

subliminal: Below conscious awareness.

suffering: According to Kreis, the second stage of recovery from loss by death. The shock stage is over, and the person now experiences the pain of grief, loneliness, and depression.

suicide: The killing of oneself, once considered the "unforgivable crime."

superego: That part of the human personality that functions as the "voice of our society." Freud's term for *conscience*.

superiority-inferiority complex: See *inferiority-superiority complex*.

suppression: Suppression is not repression in that the person is consciously aware of having a socially condemned desire or thought but does not express it. In repression the person denies both the desire *and* the thought.

"sweet-lemons" defense: A defense mechanism in which a person responds to a disappointment by constructing a beneficial result.

swing shift: A work schedule that alternates between a normal day schedule, an evening schedule, and the graveyard shift. The swing shift produces considerable stress on the employee and the empolyee's family.

symbol: An image, object, or activity that stands for something more than just the literal name, description, or use.

synapse: The space between neurons over which chemical transmitters jump from one neuron to fire (or not fire) neighboring neurons.

synchronicity: Jung's term for events that come together in space and time. Alternative to the phenomenology that assigns these simultaneous events as pure "coincidence."

syndrome: A set of symptoms that appear together.

systematic desensitization: Devised by Wolpe, the psychophysical therapy that is based on the deconditioning of patients—ridding them of their phobias—so that they no longer fear certain objects or events but have more constructive conditioned responses.

TM: Transcendental Meditation, upon which much research has been done in terms of physiological changes. This meditation technique uses prescribed mantras. (See also *mantram*.)

taboo: An act that is profoundly repugnant to a society as, for example, incest. A negative value. (See also *values* and *mores*.)

tactile: Pertaining to the sense of touch.

Tao: An eastern philosophy of life that stresses the ebb and flow of existence.

theoretical orientation: Describes that personality type whose motivation is the desire for knowledge: scientists, journalists, academic scholars.

theory: The formulation of a scientific statement or group of statements that seek(s) to explain several facts and phenomena in the most direct way possible. A good or useful theory leads to valid predictions and the discovery of other facts and phenomena. A theory is based on empirical data. (See also *hypothesis* and *empirical data*.)

therapy: Any form of treatment that can be considered healing.

thinking: The cognitive or rational decision-making part of our consciousness.

thinking function: According to Jung, one of the four functions by which individuals process the events in their lives. (See also *four functions*, and *sensing, intuitive,* and *feeling functions*.)

tranquilizer: Any drug (or food) that calms or slows the bodymind or mindbody. Common tranquilizing drugs include the meprobates, such as Equanol and Librium, but other agents can also produce tranquilizing effects, including meditation, yoga, and exercise.

transactional analysis: The psychotherapeutic approach of Eric Berne, which seeks to analyze any interaction (transaction) between two or more persons within the perspective of three ego-states: parent, adult, and child (PAC).

transcendence: Rising above one's present limits; to go beyond one's present world view to a more comprehensive state.

transformation: Any *qualitative* change in the person's phenomenology and/or personality processing.

transpersonal: Referring to the universal themes of human existence (life, death, rebirth, the unfolding of generations) and their meaning and significance.

trauma: An injurious event, whether physical or psychological.

trickster: An archetype that polarizes the mischievous and spontaneous aspects of human personality. (See also *wise child*.)

twin studies: The many research investigations on differences and similarities of identical twins who were separated at birth and raised in different environments.

Type A Personality: A personality type that has been correlated with sudden heart attack and heart failure. Characteristics include driving competitiveness, ambition, impatience, and a life style in which the person juggles many tasks and commitments.

Type psychology: Jung's approach to individual differences. Jung believed persons were basically different types, not because of environmental experiences but because of innate biological propensities.

"tyranny of the should": According to Horney, the typical American is obsessed with the idea that he or she should be the perfect spouse, parent, employee, host, citizen, lover, and so on—to the point of its being an American neurosis.

unconditioned response (UCR): Any unlearned, reflexive-type behavior.

unconditioned stimulus (US): Any physical event that arouses an unconditioned response (innate, reflexive-type behavior).

unconscious: That part of human functioning of which we are unaware.

unforgivable sin: During the Middle Ages a tradition grew up that the sole "unforgivable sin" was suicide, presumably because there was no time for the person to repent his or her act of self-murder.

unskilled labor: Any work that does not require even a modicum of education, skill, or training.

upward mobility: Movement within a society from one level of social status to a higher level. (See also *social stratification* and *social status*.)

utilitarian marriage: A marriage in which the partners have a respectful and cordial relationship but are missing total and passionate romantic involvement.

valid: Demonstrated over and over again until believed to be founded on fact; continually capable of being verified.

validity: (1) The accuracy or truthfulness of any statement. (2) The validity of a test (such as an IQ test) is determined by whether it does actually measure what it purports to measure. (3) Validity of the individual is societal recognition that consideration of a person's dignity and inalienable rights and needs comes before any institution of which he or she is a part.

variable: Any factor (or characteristic) that can be described and measured.

virility: Having the quality of a mature male; manliness.

voodoo death: The sickness and ultimate demise of a person (generally in a primitive tribe) as the psychophysical consequences of having been cursed by one or more others.

Waiting for Godot: Samuel Beckett's play in which he expresses the concept that human beings tend to wait for others to motivate them to action and to provide answers and meaning to life's problems.

wear and tear: According to Selyë, the normal stress all of us experience day by day in our personal and workaday lives.

white-collar worker: Any worker who wears a "white shirt" at his or her place of employment, which is to say, a person who is not performing manual (blue-collar) labor.

wisdom of the body: An instinctive sense that maintains the body's homeostasis and health.

wise child: The archetype that personifies the wisdom of innocence, idealism, and spontaneity. (See also *trickster*.)

wise old man: The archetype that represents the wisdom of the masculine personality, i.e., logic, reason, the experience of observing human nature. The wise old man is the counselor, the prophet, the medicine man, the shaman.

wise old woman: The archetype that represents feminine wisdom, i.e. intuition, hunches, foresight, clairvoyance. Examples: the gypsy, the sybil, the oracle, the high priestess.

withdrawal: A defense mechanism in which the person retreats from active participation in his or her environment. Examples: excessive fantasy, television watching, drug and alcohol abuse.

work ethic: The essentially Puritan tradition and legacy that hard work is a valid way to earthly success and heavenly salvation. The work ethic contrasts sharply with the more traditional European approach to work as a reality of life but not necessarily ennobling and uplifting.

world view: In a broad sense, one's philosophy of life, an all-inclusive, coherent way of looking at life and the cosmos. From the German *Weltanschauung*, a sort of unconscious total fabric into which one incorporates all one's experiences and through which one sees the world. (See also *assumptions*.)

yin-yang: A symbol representing the oppositional forces of the universe: dark-light, male-female, creative-destructive, all of which are in constant flux. (See also *Tao*.)

yoga: Any Eastern technique for personality integration, such as meditation, asanas, service to others. (See also *personality integration*.)

Zen Buddhism: The especial sect of Buddhism developed in Japan, characterized by sudden insight and understanding. The traditional devices associated with these insights include the *haiku* (a seventeen-syllable poem), no-mind meditations, and the koan or paradoxical puzzle to be solved.

Index

A

abnormal, 17
absenteeism, 337
abstractions, 22
acceptance of death, 362
accident proneness, 184
accusing, 340–41, 350–51
adaptation, 73, 86
adjustment approach, 20
  on not wanting to adjust you, 20
Adler, Alfred, 99
  and individual differences, 99–105, 148–49
adolescence, 341
adult ego-state, 252
adultery, 270
Aesthetic orientation, 112–13, 116
affect, as right brain in origin, 133–34
affective process, 68
Alanon, 395
alarm reaction, 188
Alateen, 395
Albert, conditioning fear in, 151
alcohol, 394–99
  as a defense mechanism, 158
  as a drug, 394
Alcoholics Anonymous, 395
alcoholism, 329
Allport, Gordon, 24, 28
  study of values: vocational interest test, 120
altered states of consciousness (ASCs)
  and our "cosmic egg," 135–36
  definition of, 385

dreams and dreaming, 405–29
drugs, 387–95
hypnosis, 398–404
meditation, 395–98
Pearce, John Chilton, 135–36
American way of death, 358
amnesia, 161
  as hysterical conversion, 182
amphetamines, 389–90
Amundsen, Roald, 121
anal personality, 43, 48
anal stage, 41–42
analgesics, 390
  enkephalins, 159–60
  use of, 158–59
anesthetics, 390
anger, and acceptance of death, 360–61
Anima and Animus, 415–16
animism (primitive world view), 7
animistic thinking, 74
anxiety
  global, 18–19
  origins of in childhood, 145–53
  personal, 18
  social, 18–19
  symptoms of, 170
Archetypal themes, 356–57
Archetypes, 414–18
art and artists
  and sublimation, 41, 167
  as left-brain in function, 133–34
  as right-brain difference, 134
asanas, 218–20, 397

assumptions, 9, 10
   American, 105
   listening, 331, 339
   vs. theories, 11, 15
asthma, 185
asylums, 20
authoritarian parenting, 289–90
autoerotic, 41
autohypnosis, 205
autonomy, 56
average, statistical, 21
axonal endings, 388

B

bargaining, as a stage of death, 361
basic trust, 56
Benson, Herbert, 396
Berne, Eric, 34, 163, 249–53
bioenergetics, 205
   and dealing with anxiety, 230–31
   relevance to education, 230–31
   Alexander Lowen, 215–17
   Reichian theory, 212–15
biofeedback, 205, 396
   techiques, 225
birth trauma, 147
"black rage," 157
blaming, 341, 350–51
blue collar workers, 328
body language, 198–99, 344
"born loser," 107, 158

C

cancer, as reaction to stress and loss, 192
Cannon, Walter B., 186–87
career success, 336
   communication skills, 337–52
catastrophic statements, 172
celibacy, 274
center of growth, 444–45
   (*See also* Rogers, Carl)
chakra, 397
change
   effects of, 189–91
   as a tenet of growth psychology, 15, 22–23
character
   Adler's definition of, 104–105
   Chinese character as innate, 130–31
character armor, 213–15
character neurosis, 212–15

   vs. anxiety neurosis, 212
Charcot, 245
child abuse, 329
child ego-state, 250
choices
   conscious choice, 105
   as intelligence, 72–73
   as another term for "mistake," 29
   as tenet of growth psychology, 15, 22–23
Christian Science, 181–82
Christianity (*See* New Testament)
chronically ill person, suggestions for caring for, 362–66
cognition, 14
   Jungian approach, 109
cognitive process, 68
   development, 68–78
   dissonance, 386–87
   function of self-actualizing persons, 437–41
   styles: differences in right-brain/left-brain, 149–53
cognitive styles
   and Jung, 152
   left-brain/right-brain, 149–52
cohabitation, 152
coitus interruptus, 275
coitus reservatus, 275
collective unconscious, 414–15
college dropout, 334
college experience
   college dropout, 334
   female experience, 333–34
   and vocational choice, 332–33
commonalities, 3
   vs. individual differences, 96
common cold, 186
communication
   in career success, 336
   in marriage, 298
   skills, 337–52
compatibility
   in marriage, 282, 297
   sexual, 277, 297
compensation, 167–68
concrete operations, 75–76
conditioned
   helplessness in dogs, 238
   response, 151–52
   stimulus, 150–51
   tension, 216–17
conditioning, 3, 13, 137–38
   examples of, 154–55
   and laboratory voodoo, 196
   makes us less intelligent, 153

makes us robot-like, 153
conflict-habituated marriage, 292
consciousness, the quest for conscious awareness, 5
conventional morality, 84–85
corpus callosum, 132
"cosmic egg," 135–36
courtly love, 272
culture, 14, 98
  and communication, 346–47

D

death
  American way of, 358
  death denying society, 358
  five stages of acceptance, 359–62
  Kübler-Ross, 358–59
  our interest is pornographic, 358
defense mechanisms, 18
  as barriers to growth, 153
  compensation-overcompensation, 101–102
  healthy defenses, 166–68
  how to know when to use them, 155–56
  the need for, 145–46
  origins of our, 147–53
  perceptual defense, 183
  superiority-inferiority complex, 100–101
  as survival mechanisms, 145–46
demographic variables, 14
denial and isolation (acceptance of death), 360
depression (acceptance of death), 360–61
depressive reaction, 238
de-structuring (See structuring)
developmental process, 14–15
developmental psychology
  Erikson's psychosocial stages, 52–61
  Freud's psychosexual stages, 40–46
  Jung's four developmental stages, 50–51
devitalized marriage, 292
"difficult child," 128
disease, 179–233
  primitive beliefs, 179–80
  psychosomatic approach, 181–233
disequilibration, 8
divorce
  and children, 375–76
  kind of dying, 369–74
  rates, 283
  reintegration into society, 374
  and the step-parent role, 376
Doctrine of Specific Etiology, 181
dominant hemisphere, 132–33

double-income family, 329–30
double standard, 280, 293
dream therapy, an example of, 419
dreaming, as right-brain function, 133–34
dreams and dreaming
  left-brain/right brain, 421–22
  Freud, 405–406, 408–12
  history of, 405–409
  how to remember, 422–24
  Jungian approach, 412–18
  royal road to unconscious, 408–409
  symbolism, 408–12
drive states, 23
Durkheim, Emile, 239
dynamic process, 435

E

"easy child," 125–27
ectomorph, 123–24
Eddy, Mary Baker, 181
Edison, Thomas, 174
ego, 47
ego integrity, 60–61
ego strength, 23
egocentric thinking, 73–74
either-or thinking, 439–40
Electra complex, 43–45
Ellis, Albert, 250–60
emotional openness, 443–44
empirical data, 11, 100–101
emptying the mind, 440
endomorph, 123–24
endorphins, 159–60, 220–21
enkephalin, 159–60
environmental climate, 336
environmentalist
  Adler as, 105
  Freud as, 105
  Pavlov as, 105
  theory, 71
epilepsy
  and split-brain surgery, 131–33
  and William Penfield's temporal lobe experiments, 161
Erikson, Erik, 52–61
  stages of psychosocial development, 52–61
esteem needs, 326
ethnocentrism, 130–31
executive monkey, 192
exercise, 205, 220–21
extramarital affairs, 278
extraversion, 106–107, 112

F

failure
    and Thomas Edison, 174 .
    replace with *learning*, 173
    misuse of word, 173
    and reality therapy, 260
fairytales and folklore, 80–84
    relevance to child's preoperative world, 74
fallacy, fallacies, 17
family-life stages, 300
fantasy, uses of, 168
fasting, 208
favorable ratio, 61
feeling function, hysteria as excessive, 239
figure-ground relationship, 253–54
fixation, fixated, 43, 47–48, 87–88
flight into failure, 158
flight-or-fight syndrome, 186–87
folklore and fairytales (*See* fairytales and folklore)
formal operations, stage of, 76–77
formerly married persons, 374–75
forty, significance of, 427
four functions, Jung's, 108–112
Frankl, Viktor, 450–52
free association, 46
Freedman, Daniel, and individual differences,
    130–31
Freud, Sigmund, 98
    birth trauma, 147
    dreams and dreaming, 405–406, 408–12
    as extravert, 111
    glove anesthesia, 182
    use of hypnosis, 245
    passive-dependent personality, 236
    psychoanalysis, 246
    psychosexual theory, 40–49, 79
    talking cure, 246
    wife, Anna O., 245
functional dimension of preoperational stage, 74
future shock, and parenthood, 290–91

G

games people play, 163, 341
gemeinschaftsgefuhl, 103
general adaptation syndrome, 187–89
general semantics, 338
generalized response, 15
generalized stimuli, 151–52
generativity, 59–60
genital stage, 43
gentle birth, 148
gestalt therapy, 207, 253–56

Glasser, William, 260
glove anesthesia, 182
going negative, 216–17
grave-yard shift, 328
Greece, bisexuality, 271–72
grief, stages of, 372–74
group marriage, the Oneida Community, 275
group therapy, 247–49
growth psychology, tenets, 15–23
Gurdjieff, G. I., 211–12

H

Hartshorne and May studies, 79
heart disease
    and loneliness, 192
    and Type-A personality, 212
here-and-now, 445–46
    and the loving relationship, 296–97
heterogeneity, 21
heroin addiction, 159–60
hierarchy of needs, 24–27
homeostasis, 23, 186
homosexuality, 210
    in the Arabic nations, 274
Horney, Karen, 30
human becoming, 24, 28
human behavior, complexity of, 11–15
human ecology, 450
humanistic psychology, 17–28
humankind, historical models of, 6–10
human potentiality, psychology of, 17
"hurried child," 78
hypnosis, 245
    as an ASC, 398–404
    and Freud, 398–99
    hypnotherapy, an example of, 402–404
    theories of, 399–401
    uses of, 401
hypnotism
    J. M. Charcot, 181
    Sigmund Freud, 181
    as mesmerism, 181–82
hysteric personality, 239
hysterical
    blindness, 182
    conversion, 182–183
    deafness, 182

I

id, 46
identity, 58

implosive therapy, 257
incongruent body language, 344–45
individual differences, 96–97
 Alfred Adler, 99–105
 and biological differences, 124
 and education, 138
 as innate, 124–34
 and loving relationships, 294–95
 neonatal, 130–31
 and physical activity, 228
 psychology of, 17, 21–22
 and twin studies, 128–130
 variables, 98
individualized instruction, 138
individuation, 25, 136–37
industry, 58
inferiority, beginnings of, 148
infidelity, Roman, 272
initiative, 57
innate, 71
insomnia, treatment of, 424–25
insulation, 162
intelligence as choice, 72–73
interactionist theory of human development, 71
intoxication by stress, 189
intrinsic marriage, 291–92
introjection, 79
introspection, 31–32
introversion/extraversion, 106–107, 112
 and sexual needs, 210
intuition, as right-brain in origin, 133–34
intuitional function, 108–109

J

Jacobson, Edmund, 396
 progressive relaxation, 216–17
James, William, 18
jealousy, 276
Jung, Carl, 96
 Anima and Animus, 415–16
 Archetypes, 356–57, 414–18
 autobiography, 444–45
 collective unconscious, 414–15
 four developmental stages, 50–51
 dreams and dreaming, 412–18
 as introvert, 444–45
 Persona and Shadow, 417–18
 predictive dreams, 413–14
 synchronicity, 412–13
 type psychology, 105–12
 and the universal personality, 452–53

K

Kinsey report, 210
Kohlberg, Lawrence, 84–86, 88
Korzykski, Alfred, 338
Kübler-Ross, Elizabeth, 358–59
 five stages of acceptance of death, 359–62

L

lady of the house, 287
Laing, Ronald, 147–48
laissez-faire parenting, 289–90
latency stage, 43
latent dream, 409
Leboyer, Frederick, 148
left-brain/right-brain
 and dreaming, 421–22
 individuals, 131–35
"letting go"
 psychological, 87–88
 of suffering, 377–78
Levinson, Daniel, 61–66, 96
liberty as license, 449
libido, 40–47, 98
life crisis, 52, 54–55
life crisis units (LCUs), 189–91
life-span approach, 39
life style
 Alfred Adler, 99–100
 constructive and destructive, 99–100
life tasks, 52, 54–55
listening, 339–40
loneliness, and heart disease, 192, 194–95
love as caritas, 449
loving relationship
 dimensions of, 293–97
 fallacies and realities of, 275–79
LSD, 392–93

M

macro approach, 3
manic-depressive reaction, 240
manifest dream, 409
marijuana, 393–94
marriage
 absentee husband-father, 286
 adjustment, 285
 argument, 349
 compatibility factors, 282
 and communication, 298
 fallacies of, 275–79

marriage (*cont.*)
  financial stress, 286, 349–50
  history of, 270–75
  interfaith, 282
  interracial, 282
  and remarriage, 376
  and role expectations, 283
  types of, 291–93
martyrdom, 277
Maslow, Abraham, 24–28, 326
  counting our blessings, 380
  hierarchy of needs, 25–27
  "peak experiences," 453–54
  study of self-actualizing persons, 435–36
massage, 217–218
  and the ill person, 365
Masters and Johnson, 297
masturbation, 209
mate selection, 279–82
mechanistic models, 23–24
medieval marriage, 272
meditation, 71–73, 223–24, 229–30, 395–98
memorable originals, 433
mental health, myth of, 17–18
mental illness, myth of, 17
mescaline, 392
mesmerism, 181–82, 398–99
mesomorph, 123–24
metaphysics, 113
micro approach, 3
mid-life crisis, 50–51, 63–66
minor hemisphere, 133
models of human nature, 6–10
  Greek (Athenian), 6–10
  mechanistic, 23–24
  medieval, 6–10
  as "naked ape," 23
  primitive, 6–10
  Puritan, 6–10
  Renaissance, 6–10
  somatypes and personality, 122–24
  transcending, 31
money and finance, stress in marriage, 286
moral development
  education for, 89–90
  Hartshorne and May studies, 79–80
  Lawrence Kohlberg, 84–86, 88–89
  Piaget, 78–90
moral realism, 80
moral relativity, 82–84
Morris, Desmond, 23
motivations, Spranger's orientations chart, 118–19
motor neurons, 387
multiple personality, 241
mutuality factor, in mate selection, 280

N

Napoleonic complex, 100–101
narcotics, as defense mechanism, 158–60
nature, studies of infants, 124–34
nature vs. nurture, 105
  controversy, 130–31
  Jungian psychology, 105
need-drive state, 2–3
needs
  for air, 207
  belonging and love, 26–27
  contact, 210–218
  esteem, 26–27, 326
  food, 207
  hierarchy of, 24–27
  physiological, 25–29
  safety, 26–27
  self-actualizing, 27
  sexual, 209–210
  territorial space, 210
  touching the ill person, 364–65
  water, 208
neotony, 14
neurochemical transmitters, 388
neurosis, 18, 47–48
  Jungian definition, 11
neurotic, 18, 47–48
  Adler's definition, 102
  life styles, 102–103
  non-neurotic (positive) life styles, 103–105
neutral stimulus, 150–51
New Testament and Christianity
  compassion vs. Old Testament justice, 82–83
  and dreams, 406–408
no-fault attitude, 350–51
non-verbal communication, 343–47
"normal," 15
normal personality, 15
novacaine, 391
nuclear family, 283

O

object permanence, 71
obsessive-compulsive personality, 236
Oedipal complex, 43–45
Old Testament
  attitude toward disease, 179–80
  and dreams, 406–408
  justice, 82–83
operant conditioning, 152–53
opiate peptides, 159–60
opiates, 391

optic chiasma, 132
oral personality, 48
oral stage, 41–42
overcompensation, 167–168
   (See also compensation)

P

pain-attack response, 156
paradigms, 21
   a shift in, 249
paralanguage, 343–47
paralogical, a child is (Piaget), 76
parent ego-state, 252
parenthood
   and children, 288–89
   empty-nest syndrome, 288–89
   and happiness factor in marriage, 288
   phases of, 290
   styles of, 289–90
   transition to, 288
passages
   Gail Sheehy, 61–62, 67
   (See also rites of passage)
passive-dependent personality, 236
Pavlov, Ivan, 71
   conditioning neurosis in dogs, 150
   as environmentalist, 105
PCP, 393
Pearce, John Chilton, 133–34
perceptual defense, 385–86
Perls, Frederick, 163–64, 253–56, 445
Persona, 417–18, 441
personal distance, 346
personality, 10, 15
personality integration, 22
personality theory, 15
personality "types," 105–110
   Type-A and heart disease, 212
   Jung's typology, 106–12
persons-in-process, 435
phallic stage, 43
phenomenology, 40, 75
   a child's, 75
phobic reactions, 238
Piaget, Jean, 8, 68–69
   four stages of cognitive development, 69–77
   stages of moral development, 78–90
pill popping, 158
pleasure-pain principle, 46
Political orientation, 114–15
polygamy
   and the Mormon church, 274
   in the Old Testament, 270–71

polymorphous perversity, 98
possessiveness, 276
post-conventional morality, 85–86
pranayama, 207
pre-conventional morality, 84–86
prejudice, as unconscious conditioning, 151–152
preoperational stage, 73–74
process, 18, 22–23, 28, 31–32, 89
   of "letting go," 87
   and the loving relationship, 295–96, 301
   memorable originals, 433–35
   of recovery and rehabilitation, 377–78
   and recovery from trauma, 369–75
professional class
   living to work, 337
   vs. working class, 337
progressive relaxation, 216
projection, 165, 340
propinquity factor, in mate selection, 279
propriate strivings, 24, 120–21
   Roald Amundsen as example, 121
   Albert Schweitzer as example, 121
psilocybin, 392
psychoanalysis, 246
Psychoanalytic Congress of Vienna, 98–99
psychological "types," Freud vs. Jung, 111
psychopathic personality, 242–43
psychosexual development, 40–49
psychosocial development, 52–61
psychosomatic approach to disease, 181–232
psychotherapy *(See* therapy)

Q

qualitative changes, 39–40
quantitative changes, 39–40

R

Rank, Otto, 147
rational-emotive therapy, 258–60
rationalization, 161–62
reaction formation, 166
"real me" and self-actualizing persons, 447
reality principle, 48
reality therapy, 260–61
rebirthing therapy, 147–48
recovery, stage of grief, 373–74
reintegration into society, 374
regression, 157
Reich, Wilhelm, 212–15
Religious orientation, 117–18
remarriage, 376

repression, 41, 160
  as amnesia, 161
  repressed material, 46
  vs. suppression, 183
  Victorian, 209
re-structuring (*See* structuring)
rites of passage, 51–53
  and death, 369–70
Rogers, Carl, 25, 264–65
  characteristics of persons undergoing therapy,
    248
  the client-centered therapy, 247
  fully functioning persons, 448
role-modeling theory, 334
role models, need for female, 334
roles
  blue collar, white collar, executive, etc., 328
  expectations in marriage, 284
  multi-roles of modern marriage, 283–85
  social, 14, 283
  of working husband and wife, 329–30
Roman marriage and divorce, 272
rules of the game, Piaget, 82–83
runner's high, 220–21

S

sarcasm, ridicule, and wit, 156
scapegoating, 165, 340
schizoid personality, 241
schizophrenic personality, 240
Schweitzer, Albert, 121–22
second half of life, 50
segmental rings, 212–14
self-actualizing, 23–27, 88–90
  studies of persons, 435–54
  and work, 337
self-assertiveness, 343
self-awareness, the quest for, 5
self-esteem, 328–29
  and the professional class, 337
  and the working class, 336–37
  and the working wife, 290
self-preservation, 24
self-revealment, 341–42
self-understanding, the quest for, 5
sensing function, 108
sensory-motor stage, 69–73
sensory neurons, 387
sex
  needs for, 209–10
  related to personality type, 210
sexual compatibility, 277
  and the graveyard shift, 328–29

Shadow, 417–18, 441
Sheldon, William, 122–24
shock, stage of, 372–73
Shostrum, Everett, 164
sick persons, relating to them, 362–66
silence, use of, 347
silent hemisphere, 132–34
similarity factor, in mate selection, 279
singlehood, 297
situational factors
  of human experiencing, 17
  moral development, the Hartshorne and May
    studies, 79–80
Skinner, B. F., 71, 152
  as environmentalist, 105
"slow-to-warm child," 128
social feeling, Adler's, 103–104
Social orientation, 115–16
social roles, 14
  (*See also* roles)
socialization, 41, 46, 136–37
sociopathic personality, 242–43
somatotypes, 122–24
soul, 68
"sour grapes," 162
speech center, 131–32
spiritual, 96
  Carl Jung's definition, 105
  renewal and a loving relationship, 295
  Spranger's Religious orientation, 117
spiritual dimension
  Erikson, 60–61
  Frankl's logotherapy, 450–52
  Jung, 50
  Jung and the universal personality, 452–53
  Maslow's "peak experiences," 453–54
  and self-actualizing persons, 449–51
split-brain surgery, 132–33
spouse abuse, 329
Spranger, Eduard, 112
  orientations, 112–20
stage of exhaustion, 188
stage of resistance, 188
step-parent role, 375–76
stimulants, 389–90
stratification, 14, 98, 328
stress, 17, 187–89, 286
  and air-traffic controllers, 193
structuring, 62–63
  destructuring and restructuring, 62–63
subculture, 14, 98
  marrying outside one's, 282
sublimation, 41, 167
substitution, 167
success, William James' definition of, 18

suffering, stage of, 373
suicidal depression, 239
suicide, 356, 366–69
  as a crime, 367
  historical view, 367–71
  statistics on, 369
  therapy for, 369–71
Sullivan, Harry Stack, 149–50, 246
superego, 47
superiority-inferiority complex, 100–101
"sweet lemons," 162
symbols, 72–73
synchronicity, 412–18
systematic desensitization method, 222
Szasz, Thomas, 17

T

taboo, 271
tension reduction, 23
territorial space, 228, 345–46
theoretical orientation, 113–14
theories vs. assumptions, 11
therapy
  criteria for selecting, 262–63
  definition of, 244
  group therapy, 247–49
  history of, 244–45
  medical vs. nonmedical model, 248
therapy, physical
  bioenergetics, 230–34
  biofeedback training, 225
  exercise, 205, 220–21
  massage, 217–18
  meditation, 223–24
  progressive relaxation, 216–17
  Wolpe's systematic desensitization, 222
therapy, psychotherapy
  death-and-dying therapy, 359–62
  dream therapy, 408–18
  group therapy, 247–49
  hypnotherapy, 402–404
  implosive therapy, 257
  non-directive counseling, 247–48
  psychoanalysis, 246
  rational-emotive therapy, 258–60
  reality therapy, 260–61
  rebirthing therapy, 147–48
  Rogerian therapy, 247–48
  systematic desensitization (Wolpe's
    deconditioning therapy), 222
  transactional analysis, 249–53
thinking function, 109

total marriage, 291–92
touching
  needs for, 210
  and the ill person, 364–65
  infants' need of, 150
transactional analysis, 249–53
transcendental meditation, 395–396
transcending models of human nature, 31
transcending self, 449–54
tranquilizers, 390
transpersonal, 60
twin studies, 128–30
tyranny of the should, 30–31

U

ulcers, 191–92
  executive monkey, 192
unconscious motivation, 100
unconscious prejudice, 151–52
unconscious processes, 31–32, 46–47
unconscious strivings (Allport), 120
unexpected death, 366
upward mobility, 280–82, 331
utilitarian marriage, 291–92

V

values
  attitudinal, 451–52
  creative, 451–52
  experiential, 451–52
  study of, 120
vandalism, 157
vanGennep, Arnold, 51–52
verbal aggression, 156
vocational choice
  Allport's study of values, 120
  and the college experience, 332
  development, 347
  factors of, 331–34
  fear of success, 333
  and personality type, 332
  as process, 334
  and socioeconomic limitations, 331
  and women in college, 333
  women and return to work, 348
voodoo death
  in the laboratory, 196
  in primitive societies, 195–96

W

Watson, John B., 151
"wear and tear" of life, 189
white collar workers, 329
wisdom, 29
    dreams as, 426–27
    "inner wisdom" of the body, 186
withdrawal, 157
women
    and the college experience, 333
    fear of success, 333
    need for role models, 334
    and return to work, 348
work
    basic to emotional health, 327
    basic to family stability, 326
    basic to identity, 327
    basic to physical health, 327
    basic to self-esteem, 326
work ethic, 10

work satisfaction, 336
working, wives and husbands, 351
working class
    vs. professional class, 336–37
    working to live, 336–37
working wife
    vs. housewife, 287
    and self-esteem, 286–87
    transition to parenthood, 288
world-views, historical, 7–10

Y

yoga, 205, 218–20
yogic life, the four stages of, 51

Z

Zen masters, 440